PLAYFAIR
CRICKET ANNUAL 2012

KT-496-329

65th edition
EDITED BY IAN MARSHALL
All statistics by the Editor unless otherwise stated

PREFACE

Cricket moves at a heck of a pace, and these changes mean that the ICC and the ECB have a number of important decisions to make. One of the major issues facing the international game is the use of technology, and in particular the umpires' Decision Review System (DRS). I am very much in favour of DRS – it isn't perfect, but it gets a higher proportion of decisions right than the naked eye, which has to be a good thing. In my mind, the question now is simply how can we use it best? I am against umpires being the ones to call for DRS, as they will then want to check their decisions frequently (as sometimes now happens with run outs), and we already have a problem with too many delays in the game. I am disappointed that India are yet to adopt it, and hope they will do so very soon.

DRS has had a surprising effect on the way the game is evolving, especially in the way that batsmen are dealing with spin bowlers. England's recent series against Pakistan saw spinners largely on top, as they bowled wicket to wicket at pace and picked up many LBW decisions. As recently as 2003, with the introduction of T20 cricket, the demise of spin bowling as a major part of cricket was predicted. Now the top five bowlers in the shortest format are all spinners.

The second decision I would like to see the ICC make is to take action against the deteriorating standards of behaviour towards umpires. In the past, there was camaraderie between umpires and players, but this has now gone. The amount of aggro we see directed at umpires filters its way down to the amateur game, where I hear increasing numbers of stories that people giving up the role. We need umpires to control the game at all levels and we are in danger of losing them. My solution is to introduce a system of yellow and red cards to clamp down on dissent. If rugby can have a zero-tolerance attitude towards dissent, there is no reason why we can't do the same. At its most basic, this is about cricket showing how to treat people properly.

For the ECB, there are also some important decisions to be taken about the structure of the domestic game. They are to be applauded for the way they have helped the England team to emerge as the top Test nation in the world. The players have embraced the support given by the backroom staff – the sports psychologists, batting and bowling coaches and all the rest of them. I am convinced that one of the reasons things have worked so well for England is that they are able to work on a cycle of rest, preparation, practice and perform – this ensures the player is bang-on for every game he plays.

We need this same understanding to be given to the county game. At the moment, it is a relentless treadmill, where players are regularly travelling all over the country going from one game to another without a break. The ECB have a problem in that the 18 counties (all individual businesses) want to maximise the number of games they play and therefore their revenue. However, I believe we have too many County Championship games for the spectators to get a chance to see the best possible product. I also think it is odd that we play no 50-over cricket, when that format applies everywhere else, and I would suggest that in future we block off a period of the season to concentrate purely on Twenty20 cricket.

Finally, I would like to add a brief word to congratulate my home county Lancashire on winning their first championship since 1934. It was a wonderful effort from Glen Chapple's side, and they are now the latest custodians of the game in that county, so they must remain aware of the traditions, too. But for now they should enjoy not only receiving the pennant, but also a large cheque for winning the title. I hope they can do it again.

DAVID LLOYD

FOREWORD

Welcome to the 65th edition of the *Playfair Cricket Annual*. It covers a period of which it might truly be said: 'It was the best of times, it was the worst of times.' The best, for England fans at least, because England's superb performances during the summer enabled them not only to defeat Sri Lanka in a weather-affected series, but also to destroy India with stunning conviction. England needed to win the series by two Tests to ascend to the top of the ICC rankings, but instead emerged with a 4-0 whitewash. Just in case there was any thought of complacency in the side, admirably led by coach Andy Flower and captain Andrew Strauss, England suffered a shock reversal of fortune against Pakistan in the UAE. The series that begins in Sri Lanka after this volume goes to press will show how well England have learned to cope with spin-friendly conditions.

A second reason for it being the 'best of times' is a more personal one, as Lancashire, the county of my birth, finally won the County Championship outright for the first time since 1934. Having learned to love the game, and indeed how to score, at Whalley CC (the venue for the first Roses match in 1867), I was delighted that this particular hoodoo was overcome. It seemed appropriate, therefore, that we asked a Lancastrian to provide this year's Preface – and who better than David Lloyd?

Sadly, it was also the 'worst of times'. The scandal of spot-fixing and match-fixing in cricket seems to be growing. Not only did this last year see three Pakistani Test cricketers imprisoned, but also former Essex player Mervyn Westfield. There had been a slightly naïve and (dare I say it?) smug perception that somehow this was something that happened only on the subcontinent. As I write, the *Sunday Times* has discovered more evidence that the problem is a worldwide one. The cricketing authorities must move swiftly to deal with it, before the whole game is tainted. Players also have a duty to report any suspicions they might have to ensure that their profession is seen to be clean.

This year's *Playfair* includes only one modification: I have dropped the records for women's Test cricket and replaced them with women's IT20 records. This is due solely to the fact that there have been no women's Test matches in the last year, so the 2011 edition is still fully up to date (these records can also be found on our website). I do hope that the longer format of the game is not entirely abandoned by women's cricket. The women's game is going from strength to strength, especially in this country, but even in Bangladesh, where their women played their maiden LOI in November in a World Cup qualifier.

Bill Frindall always worried about the 'Curse of *Playfair*' – the damage wrought on the careers of those featured on the front cover of the annual. This year's cover star, switch-hitting Kevin Pietersen, seemed in danger of succumbing to it, but bounced back very strongly in the short forms of the game against Pakistan, and I hope he will continue to show excellent form during the coming season. I have little doubt that he will be fully motivated by taking on the country of his birth. England v South Africa will be a battle between the two top Test nations in the world at the moment, and gives cricket fans something to look forward to during a summer when the Olympics may prove a considerable distraction.

Finally, I must once more give a plug to our website www.playfaircricket.co.uk which will again feature weekly updates (as much as possible) throughout the domestic season, and occasionally during the winter, delivering the latest news on recent statistical highlights and other points of interest. It is also possible to link through to it via Facebook, for those who prefer to go that way.

Enjoy the season ahead, and let us hope that it is brilliant cricket performances that have us talking, and not anything more sinister.

IAN MARSHALL
Eastbourne, March 2012

ACKNOWLEDGEMENTS AND THANKS

This book could not be written without the help of many people giving freely of their time and expertise, so I must thank the following for all they have done to help ensure this edition of *Playfair Cricket Annual* could be written:

At the counties, I would like to thank the following for their help over the last year: Derbyshire – Tom Holdcroft and John Brown; Durham – Brian Hunt; Essex – Ashley Neave and Tony Choat; Glamorgan – Andrew Hignell; Gloucestershire – Lizzie Allen and Adrian Bull; Hampshire – Tim Tremlett and Tony Weld; Kent – Alison Davies and Jack Foley; Lancashire – Diana Lloyd and Alan West; Leicestershire – Elaine Pickering, Graham York and Paul Rogers; Middlesex – Rebecca Hart and Don Shelley; Northamptonshire – Tony Kingston; Nottinghamshire – Helen Palmer, Brian Hewes and Roger Marshall; Somerset – Guy Wolfenden and Gerald Stickley; Surrey – Steve Howes and Keith Booth; Sussex – Siobhan Edgar and Mike Charman; Warwickshire – Keith Cook and David Wainwright; Worcestershire – Joan Grundy, Neil Smith and Dawn Pugh; Yorkshire – Janet Bairstow and John Potter.

At the universities, Cambridge – Tony Gibbs; Durham – Graeme Fowler; Loughborough – Margaret Folwell; Oxford – Neil Harris. For the international umpires, thank you to Brent Silva; and Chris Kelly for the domestic umpires. To Alan Fordham, thank you for the Principal and Second XI Fixtures, and Philip August for the Minor Counties. Philip Bailey once again provided the first-class and List A career records, and he continues to be a vital help in compiling the book.

At Headline, my thanks go to Jonathan Taylor for his support and encouragement; Louise Rothwell was again a huge help in ensuring that the book was produced as swiftly as possible – one of us has to keep an eye on the schedule; Sam Eades, for looking after the publicity; and Sam Habib, now freelance, for all his help on running the *Playfair* website. John Skermer again played a vital role in checking the proofs. At Letterpart, the *Playfair* typesetter since 1994, Chris Leggett, Caroline Leggett, Lorraine Byfield and the rest of the team did a superb job on the setting. Next year I promise to try to be not so close to our deadlines. A promise I made last year as well . . .

Finally, on a personal level, I would like to thank my young daughters, Kiri and Sophia, who have begun to wonder if I will ever leave my office; and of course to my wife, Sugra, for being so understanding and patient, especially when the final push is on.

GUIDE TO USING PLAYFAIR

As last year, *Playfair* is divided into five sections as follows: Test match cricket, county cricket, international limited-overs cricket (including Twenty20), other cricket (IPL, Champions League, women's limited-overs cricket, universities), and fixtures for the coming season. Each section, where appropriate, begins with a preview of forthcoming events, followed by a review of events during the previous season, then come the player records, and finally the records section.

ENGLAND v WEST INDIES
SERIES RECORDS
1928 to 2009

HIGHEST INNINGS TOTALS

England	in England	619-6d	Nottingham	1957
	in West Indies	849	Kingston	1929-30
West Indies	in England	692-8d	The Oval	1995
	in West Indies	751-5d	St John's	2003-04

LOWEST INNINGS TOTALS

England	in England	71	Manchester	1976
	in West Indies	46	Port-of-Spain	1993-94
West Indies	in England	54	Lord's	2000
	in West Indies	47	Kingston	2003-04

HIGHEST MATCH AGGREGATE   1815 for 34 wickets   Kingston   1929-30
LOWEST MATCH AGGREGATE   309 for 29 wickets   Bridgetown   1934-35

HIGHEST INDIVIDUAL INNINGS

England	in England	285*	P.B.H.May	Birmingham	1957
	in West Indies	325	A.Sandham	Kingston	1929-30
West Indies	in England	291	I.V.A.Richards	The Oval	1976
	in West Indies	400*	B.C.Lara	St John's	2003-04

HIGHEST AGGREGATE OF RUNS IN A SERIES

England	in England	506	(av 42.16)	G.P.Thorpe (6 Tests) 1995
	in West Indies	693	(av 115.50)	E.H.Hendren 1929-30
West Indies	in England	829	(av 118.42)	I.V.A.Richards 1976
	in West Indies	798	(av 99.75)	B.C.Lara 1993-94

RECORD WICKET PARTNERSHIPS – ENGLAND

1st	229	A.J.Strauss (142)/A.N.Cook (94)	Bridgetown	2008-09
2nd	291	A.J.Strauss (137)/R.W.T.Key (221)	Lord's	2004
3rd	303	M.A.Atherton (135)/R.A.Smith (175)	St John's	1993-94
4th	411	P.B.H.May (285*)/M.C.Cowdrey (154)	Birmingham	1957
5th	218	P.D.Collingwood (161)/M.J.Prior (131*)	Port-of-Spain	2008-09
6th	205	M.R.Ramprakash (154)/G.P.Thorpe (103)	Bridgetown	1997-98
7th	197	M.J.K.Smith (96)/J.M.Parks (101*)	Port-of-Spain	1959-60
8th	217	T.W.Graveney (165)/J.T.Murray (112)	The Oval	1966
9th	109	G.A.R.Lock (89)/P.I.Pocock (13)	Georgetown	1967-68
10th	128	K.Higgs (63)/J.A.Snow (59*)	The Oval	1966

RECORD WICKET PARTNERSHIPS – WEST INDIES

1st	298	C.G.Greenidge (149)/D.L.Haynes (167)	St John's	1989-90
2nd	287*	C.G.Greenidge (214*)/H.A.Gomes (92*)	Lord's	1984
3rd	338	E.de C.Weekes (206)/F.M.M.Worrell (167)	Port-of-Spain	1953-54
4th	399	G.St A.Sobers (226)/F.M.M.Worrell (197*)	Bridgetown	1959-60
5th	265	S.M.Nurse (137)/G.St A.Sobers (174)	Leeds	1966
6th	282*	B.C.Lara (400*)/R.D.Jacobs (107*)	St John's	2003-04
7th	155*	G.St A.Sobers (150*)/B.D.Julien (121)	Lord's	1973
8th	99	C.A.McWatt (54)/J.K.Holt (48*)	Georgetown	1953-54
9th	150	E.A.E.Baptiste (87*)/M.A.Holding (69)	Birmingham	1984
10th	70	I.R.Bishop (44*)/D.Ramnarine (19)	Georgetown	1997-98

BEST INNINGS BOWLING ANALYSIS

England	in England	8-103	I.T.Botham	Lord's	1984
	in West Indies	8- 53	A.R.C.Fraser	Port-of-Spain	1997-98
West Indies	in England	8- 92	M.A.Holding	The Oval	1976
	in West Indies	8- 45	C.E.L.Ambrose	Bridgetown	1989-90

BEST MATCH BOWLING ANALYSIS

England	in England	12-119	F.S.Trueman	Birmingham	1963
	in West Indies	13-156	A.W.Greig	Port-of-Spain	1973-74
West Indies	in England	14-149	M.A.Holding	The Oval	1976
	in West Indies	11- 84	C.E.L.Ambrose	Port-of-Spain	1993-94

HIGHEST AGGREGATE OF WICKETS IN A SERIES

England	in England	34	(av 17.47)	F.S.Trueman	1963
	in West Indies	27	(av 18.66)	J.A.Snow	1967-68
		27	(av 18.22)	A.R.C.Fraser	1997-98
West Indies	in England	35	(av 12.65)	M.D.Marshall	1988
	in West Indies	30	(av 14.26)	C.E.L.Ambrose	1997-98

RESULTS SUMMARY
ENGLAND v WEST INDIES – IN ENGLAND

		Series			Lord's			Manchester			The Oval			Nottingham			Birmingham			Leeds			Chester-le-St		
	Tests	E	WI	D	E	WI	D	E	WI	D	E	WI	D	E	WI	D	E	WI	D	E	WI	D	E	WI	D
1928	3	3	-	-	1	-	-	1	-	-	1	-	-												
1933	3	2	-	1	1	-	-	-	-	1	1	-	-												
1939	3	1	-	2	1	-	-	-	-	1	-	-	1												
1950	4	1	3	-	-	1	-	1	-	-	-	1	-	-	1	-									
1957	5	3	-	2	1	-	-				1	-	-	-	-	1	-	-	1	1	-	-			
1963	5	1	3	1	-	-	1	-	1	-	-	1	-				1	-	-	-	1	-			
1966	5	1	3	1	-	-	1	-	1	-	1	-	-	-	1	-				-	1	-			
1969	3	2	-	1	-	-	1	1	-	-										1	-	-			
1973	3	-	2	1	-	1	-				-	1	-				-	-	1						
1976	5	-	3	2	-	-	1	-	1	-	-	1	-	-	-	1				-	1	-			
1980	5	-	1	4	-	-	1	-	-	1	-	-	1	-	1	-				-	-	1			
1984	5	-	5	-	-	1	-	-	1	-	-	1	-				-	1	-	-	1	-			
1988	5	-	4	1	-	1	-	-	1	-	-	1	-	-	-	1				-	1	-			
1991	5	2	2	1	-	-	1				1	-	-	-	1	-	-	1	-	1	-	-			
1995	6	2	2	2	1	-	-	1	-	-	-	-	1	-	-	1	-	1	-	-	1	-			
2000	5	3	1	1	1	-	-	-	-	1	1	-	-				-	1	-	1	-	-			
2004	4	4	-	-	1	-	-	1	-	-	1	-	-				1	-	-						
2007	4	3	-	1	-	-	1	1	-	-										1	-	-	1	-	-
2009	2	2	-	-	1	-	-																1	-	-
	80	30	29	21	8	4	7	6	5	4	7	6	3	-	4	4	2	4	2	5	6	1	2	-	-

ENGLAND v WEST INDIES – IN WEST INDIES

		Series			Bridgetown			Port-of-Spain			Georgetown			Kingston			St John's			North Sound		
	Tests	E	WI	D	E	WI	D	E	WI	D	E	WI	D	E	WI	D	E	WI	D	E	WI	D
1929-30	4	1	1	2	-	-	1	1	-	-	-	1	-	-	-	1						
1934-35	4	1	2	1	1	-	-	-	1	-	-	-	1	-	1	-						
1947-48	4	-	2	2	-	-	1	-	-	1	-	1	-	-	1	-						
1953-54	5	2	2	1	-	1	-	-	-	1	1	-	-	1	1	-						
1959-60	5	1	-	4	-	-	1	1	-	1	-	-	1	-	-	1						
1967-68	5	1	-	4	-	-	1	1	-	1	-	-	1	-	-	1						
1973-74	5	1	1	3	-	-	1	1	1	-	-	-	1	-	-	1						
1980-81	4	-	2	2	-	1	-	-	1	-				-	-	1	-	-	1			
1985-86	5	-	5	-	-	1	-	-	2	-				-	1	-	-	1	-			
1989-90	4	1	2	1	-	1	-	-	-	1				1	-	-	-	1	-			
1993-94	5	1	3	1	1	-	-	-	1	-	-	1	-	-	1	-	-	-	1			
1997-98	6	1	3	2	-	-	1	1	1	-	-	1	-	-	-	1	-	1	-			
2003-04	4	3	-	1	1	-	-	1	-	-				1	-	-	-	-	1			
2008-09	5	-	1	4	-	-	1	-	-	1				-	1	-	-	-	1	-	-	1
	65	13	24	28	3	4	7	6	7	6	1	4	4	3	6	6	-	3	4	-	-	1
Totals	145	43	53	49																		

ENGLAND v SOUTH AFRICA
SERIES RECORDS

1928 to 2009-10

Key to grounds: Durban – [1]Lord's, [2]Kingsmead; Johannesburg – [1]Old Wanderers, [2]Ellis Park, [3]Wanderers.

HIGHEST INNINGS TOTALS

England	in England	604-9d	The Oval	2003
	in South Africa	654-5	Durban[2]	1938-39
South Africa	in England	682-6d	Lord's	2003
	in South Africa	572-7	Durban[2]	1999-00

LOWEST INNINGS TOTALS

England	in England	76	Leeds	1907
	in South Africa	92	Cape Town	1898-99
South Africa	in England	30	Birmingham	1924
	in South Africa	30	Port Elizabeth	1895-96

HIGHEST MATCH AGGREGATE 1981 for 35 wickets Durban[2] 1938-39
LOWEST MATCH AGGREGATE 378 for 30 wickets The Oval 1912

HIGHEST INDIVIDUAL INNINGS

England	in England	219	M.E.Trescothick	The Oval	2003
	in South Africa	243	E.Paynter	Durban[2]	1938-39
South Africa	in England	277	G.C.Smith	Birmingham	2003
	in South Africa	275	G.Kirsten	Durban[2]	1999-00

HIGHEST AGGREGATE OF RUNS IN A SERIES

England	in England	753	(av 94.12)	D.C.S.Compton	1947
	in South Africa	656	(av 72.88)	A.J.Strauss	2004-05
South Africa	in England	714	(av 79.33)	G.C.Smith	2003
	in South Africa	625	(av 69.44)	J.H.Kallis	2004-05

RECORD WICKET PARTNERSHIPS – ENGLAND

1st	359	L.Hutton (158)/C.Washbrook (195)	Johannesburg[2]	1948-49
2nd	280	P.A.Gibb (120)/W.J.Edrich (219)	Durban[2]	1938-39
3rd	370	W.J.Edrich (189)/D.C.S.Compton (208)	Lord's	1947
4th	286	K.P.Pietersen (152)/I.R.Bell (199)	Lord's	2008
5th	237	D.C.S.Compton (163)/N.W.D.Yardley (99)	Nottingham	1947
6th	206*	K.F.Barrington (148*)/J.M.Parks (108*)	Durban[2]	1964-65
7th	152	I.R.Bell (199)/S.C.J.Broad (76)	Lord's	2008
8th	154	C.W.Wright (71)/H.R.Bromley-Davenport (84)	Johannesburg[1]	1895-96
9th	99	A.Flintoff (95)/S.J.Harmison (6*)	The Oval	2003
10th	92	C.A.G.Russell (111)/A.E.R.Gilligan (39*)	Durban[2]	1922-23

RECORD WICKET PARTNERSHIPS – SOUTH AFRICA

1st	338	G.C.Smith (277)/H.H.Gibbs (179)	Birmingham	2003
2nd	257	G.C.Smith (259)/G.Kirsten (108)	Lord's	2003
3rd	319	A.Melville (189)/A.D.Nourse (149)	Nottingham	1947
4th	214	H.W.Taylor (121)/H.G.Deane (93)	The Oval	1929
5th	212	A.G.Prince (149)/A.B.de Villiers (174)	Leeds	2008
6th	171	J.H.B.Waite (113)/P.L.Winslow (108)	Manchester	1955
7th	123	H.G.Deane (73)/E.P.Nupen (69)	Durban[2]	1927-28
8th	150	G.Kirsten (130)/M.Zondeki (59)	Leeds	2003
9th	137	E.L.Dalton (117)/A.B.C.Langton (73*)	The Oval	1935
10th	103	H.G.Owen-Smith (129)/A.J.Bell (26*)	Leeds	1929

BEST INNINGS BOWLING ANALYSIS

England	in England	9- 57	D.E.Malcolm	The Oval	1994
	in South Africa	9- 28	G.A.Lohmann	Johannesburg[1]	1895-96
South Africa	in England	7- 65	S.J.Pegler	Lord's	1912
	in South Africa	9-113	H.J.Tayfield	Johannesburg[3]	1956-57

BEST MATCH BOWLING ANALYSIS

England	in England	15- 99	C.Blythe	Leeds	1907
	in South Africa	17-159	S.F.Barnes	Johannesburg[1]	1913-14
South Africa	in England	10- 87	P.M.Pollock	Nottingham	1965
	in South Africa	13-192	H.J.Tayfield	Johannesburg[3]	1956-57

HIGHEST AGGREGATE OF WICKETS IN A SERIES

England	in England	34	(av 8.29)	S.F.Barnes	1912
	in South Africa	49	(av 10.93)	S.F.Barnes	1913-14
South Africa	in England	33	(av 19.78)	A.A.Donald	1998
	in South Africa	37	(av 17.18)	H.J.Tayfield	1956-57

RESULTS SUMMARY
ENGLAND v SOUTH AFRICA – IN ENGLAND

	Tests	Series E	SA	D	Lord's E	SA	D	Leeds E	SA	D	The Oval E	SA	D	Birmingham E	SA	D	Manchester E	SA	D	Nottingham E	SA	D
1907	3	1	–	2	–	–	1	1	–	–	–	–	1									
1912	3	3	–	–	1	–	–	1	–	–	1	–	–									
1924	5	3	–	2	1	–	–	1	–	–	–	–	1	1	–	–	–	–	1			
1929	5	2	–	3	–	–	1	1	–	–	–	–	1				–	1	–			
1935	5	–	1	4	–	1	–	–	1	–	–	–	1				–	–	1	–	1	
1947	5	3	–	2	1	–	–	1	–	–	–	–	1				1	–	–			1
1951	5	3	1	1	1	–	–	–	1	1	–	–	1				1	–	–	1	–	
1955	5	3	2	–	1	–	–	1	–	1	–	–	1				–	1	–	1	–	
1960	5	3	–	2	1	–	–	–	–	1	1	–	–				–	1	–	1	1	
1965	3	–	1	2	–	–	1				–	1	–							–	1	
1994	3	1	1	1	1	–	–				–	1	–				1	–	–			
1998	5	2	1	2	–	1	–	1	–	–				–	1	–	–	–	1	1	–	–
2003	5	2	2	1	–	1	–	1	–	–	1	–	–	–	1	–				1	–	–
2008	4	1	2	1	–	–	1				–	1	–	1	–	–	–	1	–			
	61	27	11	23	6	4	4	6	3	3	6	–	7	2	1	3	3	4	4	4	2	2

ENGLAND v SOUTH AFRICA – IN SOUTH AFRICA

	Tests	Series E	SA	D	Port Elizabeth E	SA	D	Cape Town E	SA	D	Johannesburg E	SA	D	Durban E	SA	D	Pretoria E	SA	D
1888-89	2	2	–	–	1	–	–	1	–	–									
1891-92	1	1	–	–				1	–	–									
1895-96	3	3	–	–	1	–	–	1	–	–	1	–	–						
1898-99	2	2	–	–				1	–	–	1	–	–						
1905-06	5	1	4	–				1	1	–	–	3	–	1	–	–			
1909-10	5	2	3	–				1	1	–	1	1	–	–	1	–			
1913-14	5	4	–	1	1	–	–				–	2	–	1	–	1	1	–	–
1922-23	5	2	1	2				1	–	1	–	1	1	1	–	–			
1927-28	5	2	2	1				1	–	–	1	1	–	–	1	1			
1930-31	5	–	1	4				1	1	–	1	1	–	–	2	–			
1938-39	5	1	–	4				1	–	–	–	–	2	1	–	1	–	–	1
1948-49	5	2	–	3	1	–	–	–	–	1	–	–	2	1	–	–			
1956-57	5	2	2	1	–	1	–	1	–	–	–	1	1	1	–	–			
1964-65	5	1	–	4	–	–	1	1	–	–	–	2	1	–	–	1			
1995-96	5	–	1	4	–	–	1	–	–	1	–	1	–	–	–	1	–	–	1
1999-00	5	1	2	2	–	–	1	1	–	–	–	1	–	–	1	–	1	–	–
2004-05	5	2	1	2	1	–	–	–	1	–	1	–	–	–	–	1	–	–	1
2009-10	4	1	1	2	–	–	–	1	–	–	–	1	–	1	–	–	–	–	1
	77	29	18	30	5	1	3	9	5	5	8	10	9	6	2	10	1	–	3

	Tests	Series E	SA	D
Totals	138	56	29	53

TOURING TEAMS REGISTER 2012

Neither West Indies nor South Africa had selected their 2012 touring teams at the time of going to press. The following players who had represented those teams in Test matches since 1 October 2010 were still available for selection:

WEST INDIES

Full Names	Birthdate	Birthplace	Team	Type	F-C Debut
BARATH, Adrian Boris	14.04.90	Chaguanas, Tr	Trinidad	RHB/OB	2006-07
BAUGH, Carlton Seymour	23.06.82	Kingston	Jamaica	RHB/WK	2000-01
BENN, Sulieman Jamaal	22.07.81	St James	Barbados	LHB/SLA	1999-00
BISHOO, Devendra	06.11.85	New Amsterdam	Guyana	LHB/LB	2007-08
BRATHWAITE, Kraigg Clairmonte	02.12.92	St Michael	Barbados	RHB/OB	2008-09
BRAVO, Dwayne John	07.10.83	Santa Cruz	Trinidad	RHB/RFM	2001-02
BRAVO, Darren Michael	06.02.89	Trinidad	Trinidad	LHB/RMF	2006-07
CHANDERPAUL, Shivnarine	16.08.74	Unity Village	Guyana	LHB/LB	1991-92
EDWARDS, Fidel Henderson	06.02.82	St Peter	Barbados	RHB/RF	2001-02
EDWARDS, Kirk Anton	03.11.84	Barbados	Barbados	RHB/OB	2005-06
GAYLE, Christopher Henry	21.09.79	Kingston	Jamaica	LHB/OB	1998-99
NASH, Brendan Paul	14.12.77	Attadale, W Aus	Jamaica	LHB/LM	2000-01
PASCAL, Nelon Troy	25.04.87	St David's, Gren	Windward Is	RHB/RF	2007-08
POWELL, Kieran Omar Akeem	06.03.90	Nevis	Leeward Is	LHB/RM	2007-08
RAMPAUL, Ravindranath	15.10.84	Preysal	Trinidad	RHB/RFM	2001-02
ROACH, Kemar Andre Jamal	30.06.88	St Lucy	Barbados	RHB/RF	2007-08
RUSSELL, Andre Dwayne	29.04.88	Jamaica	Jamaica	RHB/RF	2006-07
SAMMY, Darren Julius Garvey	20.12.83	Micoud, St Lucia	Windward Is	RHB/RM	2002-03
SAMUELS, Marlon Nathaniel	05.01.81	Kingston	Jamaica	RHB/OB	1996-97
SHILLINGFORD, Shane	22.02.83	Dominica	Windward Is	RHB/OB	2000-01
SIMMONS, Lendl Mark Platter	25.01.85	Port-of-Spain	Trinidad	RHB/RMF	2001-02
SMITH, Devon Sheldon	21.10.81	Sauters, Grenada	Windward Is	LHB/OB	1998-99

SOUTH AFRICA

Full Names	Birthdate	Birthplace	Team	Type	F-C Debut
AMLA, Hashim Mahomed	31.03.83	Durban	Dolphins	RHB/RM	1999-00
BOTHA, Johan	02.05.82	Johannesburg	Warriors	RHB/OB	2000-01
BOUCHER, Mark Verdon	03.12.76	East London	Cape Cobras	RHB/WK	1995-96
DE LANGE, Marchant	13.10.90	Tzaneen	Titans	RHB/RF	2010-11
DE VILLIERS, Abraham Benjamin	17.02.84	Pretoria	Titans	RHB/WK	2003-04
HARRIS, Paul Lee	02.11.78	Salisbury, Rhodesia	Titans	RHB/SLA	1998-99
IMRAN TAHIR, Mohammad	27.03.79	Lahore	Dolphins	RHB/LBG	1996-97
KALLIS, Jacques Henry	16.10.75	Cape Town	Cape Cobras	RHB/RFM	1993-94
MORKEL, Morne	06.10.84	Vereeniging	Titans	LHB/RFM	2003-04
PETERSEN, Alviro Nathan	25.10.80	Port Elizabeth	Lions	RHB/OB	2000-01
PHILANDER, Vernon Darryl	24.06.85	Bellville	Cape Cobras	RHB/RFM	2004-04
PRINCE, Ashwell Gavin	28.05.77	Port Elizabeth	Warriors	LHB/OB	1995-96
RUDOLPH, Jacobus Andries	04.05.81	Springs	Titans	LHB/LBG	1997-98
SMITH, Graeme Craig	01.02.81	Johannesburg	Cape Cobras	LHB/OB	1999-00
STEYN, Dale Willem	27.06.83	Phalaborwa	Cape Cobras	RHB/RF	2003-04
TSOTSOBE, Lonwabo Lopsy	07.03.84	Port Elizabeth	Warriors	RHB/LFM	2004-05

When the final squads are announced, a complete version of the touring parties and tour previews will be posted on www.playfaircricket.co.uk

STATISTICAL HIGHLIGHTS IN 2011 TESTS

Including Tests from No. 1985 (Australia v England, 5th Test) and No. 1988 (South Africa v India, 3rd Test) to No. 2024 (South Africa v Sri Lanka, 2nd Test) and No. 2026 (Australia v India, 1st Test).

TEAM HIGHLIGHTS
HIGHEST INNINGS TOTALS

710-7d	England v India	Edgbaston
644	England v Australia	Sydney
631-7d	India v West Indies	Kolkata

LOWEST INNINGS TOTALS

47	Australia v South Africa	Cape Town
82	Sri Lanka v England	Cardiff
96	South Africa v Australia	Cape Town

HIGHEST MATCH AGGREGATE

1448-39	India (482 & 242-9) v West Indies (590 & 134)	Mumbai

LARGE MARGINS OF VICTORY

Inns & 242 runs	England (710-7d) beat India (224 & 244)	Birmingham
319 runs	England (221 & 544) beat India (288 & 158)	Nottingham

NARROW MARGINS OF VICTORY

Two wickets	Australia (296 & 310-8) beat South Africa (266 & 339)	Johannesburg
7 runs	New Zealand (150 & 226) beat Australia (136 & 233)	Hobart

CLOSE FINISH

Scores level	India (482 & 242-9) v West Indies (590 & 134)	Mumbai

This was the second time in all Tests (previously Zimbabwe v England, Test No. 1348) that a Test had been drawn with the scores level.

SIX FIFTIES IN AN INNINGS

West Indies (590) v India	Mumbai

60 EXTRAS IN AN INNINGS

	B	LB	W	NB		
63	11	34	3	15	England (710-7d) v India	Birmingham

BATTING HIGHLIGHTS
DOUBLE HUNDREDS

I.R.Bell	235	England v India	The Oval
A.N.Cook	294	England v India	Birmingham
K.P.Pietersen	202*	England v India	Lord's
K.C.Sangakkara	211	Sri Lanka v Pakistan	Abu Dhabi
Taufiq Umar	236	Pakistan v Sri Lanka	Abu Dhabi
I.J.L.Trott	203	England v Sri Lanka	Cardiff
Younus Khan	200*	Pakistan v Bangladesh	Chittagong

HUNDRED IN EACH INNINGS OF A MATCH

| J.H.Kallis | 161 | 109* | South Africa v India | Cape Town |

FASTEST HUNDRED

| M.J.Prior (126) | 107 balls | England v Sri Lanka | Lord's |

HUNDRED ON TEST DEBUT

| K.A.Edwards | 110 | West Indies v India | Roseau |
| S.E.Marsh | 141 | Australia v Sri Lanka | Pallekele |

CARRYING BAT THROUGH COMPLETED INNINGS

R.S.Dravid	146*	India v England	The Oval
T.M.K.Mawoyo	163*	Zimbabwe v Pakistan	Bulawayo
D.A.Warner	123*	Australia v New Zealand	Hobart

LONG INNINGS (Qualification: 600 mins and/or 400 balls)

Mins	Balls			
773	545	A.N.Cook (294)	England v India	Birmingham
645	453	T.M.K.Mawoyo (163*)	Zimbabwe v Pakistan	Bulawayo
644	431	K.C.Sangakkara (211)	Sri Lanka v Pakistan	Abu Dhabi
712	496	Taufiq Umar (236)	Pakistan v Sri Lanka	Abu Dhabi
517	409	I.J.L.Trott (203)	England v Sri Lanka	Cardiff

NOTABLE PARTNERSHIPS

Qualifications: 1st-4th wkts: 250 runs; 5th-6th: 225; 7th: 200; 8th: 175; 9th: 150; 10th: 100.

Third Wicket
| 350 | I.R.Bell/K.P.Pietersen | England v India | The Oval |
| 251 | A.N.Cook/I.J.L.Trott | England v Sri Lanka | Cardiff |

Fourth Wicket
| 258 | S.E.Marsh/M.E.K.Hussey | Australia v Sri Lanka | Pallekele |

Fifth Wicket
| 259 | Younus Khan/Asad Shafiq | Pakistan v Bangladesh | Chittagong |

Seventh Wicket
| 224 | V.V.S.Laxman/M.S.Dhoni | India v West Indies | Kolkata |

BOWLING HIGHLIGHTS

SEVEN WICKETS IN AN INNINGS

M.de Lange	7- 81	South Africa v Sri Lanka	Durban
Harbhajan Singh	7-120	India v South Africa	Cape Town
H.M.R.K.B.Herath	7-157	Sri Lanka v Australia	Colombo (SSC)

TEN WICKETS IN A MATCH

V.D.Philander	10-102	South Africa v Sri Lanka	Centurion
Saeed Ajmal	11-111	Pakistan v West Indies	Providence
I.Sharma	10-108	India v West Indies	Bridgetown

FIVE WICKETS IN AN INNINGS ON DEBUT

R.Ashwin	6- 47	India v West Indies	Delhi
D.A.J.Bracewell	5- 85	New Zealand v Zimbabwe	Bulawayo
P.J.Cummins	6- 79	Australia v South Africa	Johannesburg
M.de Lange	7- 81	South Africa v Sri Lanka	Durban
J.L.Pattinson	5- 27	Australia v New Zealand	Brisbane
V.D.Philander	5- 15	South Africa v Australia	Cape Town
Elias Sunny	6- 94	Bangladesh v West Indies	Chittagong
N.M.Lyon	5- 34	Australia v Sri Lanka	Galle

HAT-TRICKS

S.C.J.Broad	England v India	Nottingham

60 OVERS IN AN INNINGS

H.M.R.K.B.Herath 61.4-16-126-3	Sri Lanka v Pakistan	Abu Dhabi

ALL-ROUND ACHIEVEMENTS

A HUNDRED AND FIVE WICKETS IN AN INNINGS

R.Ashwin (103 and 5-156)	India v West Indies	Mumbai
Shakib Al Hasan (144 and 6-82)	Bangladesh v Pakistan	Mirpur

WICKET-KEEPING HIGHLIGHTS

SIX WICKET-KEEPING DISMISSALS IN AN INNINGS

Adnan Akmal	6ct	Pakistan v New Zealand	Wellington
M.V.Boucher	6ct	South Africa v Sri Lanka	Centurion

NO BYES CONCEDED IN AN INNINGS OF 550

594-5d	Mushfiqur Rahim	Bangladesh v Pakistan	Chittagong

FIELDING HIGHLIGHTS

FOUR CATCHES IN AN INNINGS IN THE FIELD

D.J.G.Sammy	4ct	West Indies v Bangladesh	Dhaka
Taufiq Umar	4ct	Pakistan v West Indies	Basseterre

LEADING TEST AGGREGATES IN 2011
1000 RUNS IN 2011

	M	I	NO	HS	Runs	Avge	100	50
R.S.Dravid (I)	12	23	3	146*	1145	57.25	5	4
K.C.Sangakkara (SL)	11	21	–	211	1034	49.23	4	4

RECORD CALENDAR YEAR RUNS AGGREGATE

	M	I	NO	HS	Runs	Avge	100	50
M.Yousuf Youhana (P) (2006)	11	19	1	202	1788	99.33	9	3

RECORD CALENDAR YEAR RUNS AVERAGE

	M	I	NO	HS	Runs	Avge	100	50
G.St A.Sobers (WI) (1958)	7	12	3	365*	1193	132.55	5	3

1000 RUNS IN DEBUT CALENDAR YEAR

	M	I	NO	HS	Runs	Avge	100	50
M.A.Taylor (A) (1989)	11	20	1	219	1219	64.15	4	5
A.N.Cook (E) (2006)	13	24	2	127	1013	46.04	4	3

50 WICKETS IN 2011

	M	O	R	W	Avge	Best	5wI	10wM
Saeed Ajmal (P)	8	487.0	1193	50	23.86	6-42	3	1

RECORD CALENDAR YEAR WICKETS AGGREGATE

	M	O	R	W	Avge	Best	5wI	10wM
M.Muralitharan (SL) (2006)	11	588.4	1521	90	16.90	8-70	9	5
S.K.Warne (A) (2005)	14	691.4	2043	90	22.70	6-46	6	2

50 WICKET-KEEPING DISMISSALS IN 2011

	M	Dis	Ct	St
M.S.Dhoni (I)	12	50	47	3

RECORD CALENDAR YEAR DISMISSALS AGGREGATE

	M	Dis	Ct	St
I.A.Healy (A) (1993)	16	67	58	9
M.V.Boucher (SA) (1998)	13	67	65	2

MOST CATCHES BY FIELDERS IN 2011

	M	Ct
D.J.G.Sammy (WI)	10	18

RECORD CALENDAR YEAR FIELDER'S AGGREGATE

	M	Ct
G.C.Smith (SA) (2008)	15	30

TEST MATCH SCORES
WEST INDIES v PAKISTAN (1st Test)

At Providence Stadium, Guyana, on 12, 13, 14, 15 May 2011.
Toss: West Indies. Result: **WEST INDIES** won by 40 runs.
Debuts: West Indies – D.Bishoo; Pakistan – Mohammad Salman.

WEST INDIES

D.S.Smith	b Hafeez	13	lbw b Hafeez		1
L.M.P.Simmons	lbw b Ajmal	49	c Ali b Riaz		21
D.M.Bravo	lbw b Riaz	25	lbw b Ajmal		8
R.R.Sarwan	c Salman b Rehman	23	(5) c Shafiq b Ajmal		11
S.Chanderpaul	b Ajmal	27	(6) not out		36
B.P.Nash	lbw b Ajmal	5	(7) run out		3
†C.S.Baugh	lbw b Ajmal	4	(8) c Akmal b Ajmal		7
*D.J.G.Sammy	c Akmal b Rehman	12	(9) lbw b Rehman		9
K.A.J.Roach	c Ali b Ajmal	24	(4) lbw b Ajmal		3
R.Rampaul	lbw b Hafeez	14	c Ali b Ajmal		2
D.Bishoo	not out	2	c Akmal b Ajmal		24
Extras	(B 5, LB 7, W 1, NB 2)	15	(B 7, LB 17, W 2, NB 1)		27
Total	**(98 overs; 380 mins)**	**226**	**(61.5 overs; 275 mins)**		**152**

PAKISTAN

Mohammad Hafeez	b Rampaul	4	lbw b Roach		2
Taufiq Umar	lbw b Sammy	19	lbw b Rampaul		0
Azhar Ali	b Sammy	34	c Baugh b Rampaul		0
*Misbah-ul-Haq	lbw b Bishoo	2	(5) lbw b Sammy		52
Asad Shafiq	lbw b Bishoo	2	(4) b Rampaul		42
Umar Akmal	c Baugh b Bishoo	33	lbw b Sammy		47
†Mohammad Salman	lbw b Bishoo	4	lbw b Sammy		0
Abdur Rehman	not out	40	c Smith b Rampaul		6
Umar Gul	c Baugh b Rampaul	5	lbw b Sammy		1
Saeed Ajmal	lbw b Rampaul	1	(11) b Sammy		3
Wahab Riaz	c Baugh b Roach	5	(10) not out		11
Extras	(B 6, LB 3, NB 2)	11	(B 2, LB 11, NB 1)		14
Total	**(64.4 overs; 264 mins)**	**160**	**(73 overs; 303 mins)**		**178**

PAKISTAN	O	M	R	W	O	M	R	W
Umar Gul	13	0	40	0	8	2	21	0
Mohammad Hafeez	13	5	22	2	9	1	15	1
Abdur Rehman	29	11	51	2	11	1	25	1
Saeed Ajmal	33	14	69	5	23.5	6	42	6
Wahab Riaz	10	1	32	1	10	1	25	1

WEST INDIES	O	M	R	W		O	M	R	W
Roach	10.4	2	40	1		13	1	30	1
Rampaul	17	5	27	3		21	6	48	4
Sammy	12	6	16	2	(4)	17	7	29	5
Bishoo	25	6	68	4	(3)	21	5	56	0
Nash						1	0	2	0

	FALL OF WICKETS			
	WI	P	WI	P
Wkt	1st	1st	2nd	2nd
1st	15	5	3	2
2nd	71	57	23	2
3rd	127	60	35	2
4th	136	62	47	83
5th	142	66	59	135
6th	159	80	74	135
7th	162	130	86	160
8th	175	135	99	163
9th	198	141	104	166
10th	226	160	152	178

Umpires: B.F.Bowden (*New Zealand*) (66) and A.L.Hill (*New Zealand*) (23).
Referee: A.G.Hurst (*Australia*) (43). **Test No. 1991/45 (WI469/P357)**
In the first innings, Simmons (41) retired at 81 and resumed at 159.

WEST INDIES v PAKISTAN (2nd Test)

At Warner Park, Basseterre, St Kitts, on 20, 21, 22, 23, 24 May 2011.
Toss: Pakistan. Result: **PAKISTAN** won by 196 runs.
Debuts: West Indies – K.C.Brathwaite.

PAKISTAN

Mohammad Hafeez	c Simmons b Rampaul	8	b Sammy		32
Taufiq Umar	c Baugh b Rampaul	11	run out		135
Azhar Ali	run out	67	c Sammy b Bishoo		53
Asad Shafiq	c Bishoo b Rampaul	0	c Baugh b Roach		4
*Misbah-ul-Haq	c Samuels b Bishoo	25	not out		102
Umar Akmal	c Rampaul b Sammy	56	b Bishoo		30
†Mohammad Salman	c Samuels b Bishoo	13	c Roach b Rampaul		8
Abdur Rehman	c Baugh b Sammy	3			
Tanvir Ahmed	lbw b Bishoo	57	(8) not out		4
Wahab Riaz	c Baugh b Roach	0			
Saeed Ajmal	not out	23			
Extras	(LB 3, W 4, NB 2)	9	(W 7, NB 2)		9
Total	(109.5 overs; 401 mins)	272	(6 wkts dec; 112.2 overs; 454 mins)		377

WEST INDIES

L.M.P.Simmons	c Umar b Ahmed	0	c Hafeez b Rehman		24
K.C.Brathwaite	c Umar b Riaz	15	b Ahmed		0
D.M.Bravo	c Shafiq b Hafeez	24	lbw b Riaz		50
R.R.Sarwan	st Salman b Ajmal	20	lbw b Rehman		0
M.N.Samuels	c Umar b Ajmal	57	c Salman b Rehman		6
B.P.Nash	c Misbah b Hafeez	6	c Umar b Ajmal		30
†C.S.Baugh	lbw b Rehman	6	lbw b Rehman		18
*D.J.G.Sammy	c Umar b Rehman	16	c Misbah b Ajmal		41
K.A.J.Roach	lbw b Hafeez	29	run out		12
R.Rampaul	not out	32	c Akmal b Ajmal		20
D.Bishoo	c Umar b Ajmal	1	not out		3
Extras	(B 4, LB 4, NB 9)	17	(B 8, LB 6, W 6, NB 6)		26
Total	(83.5 overs; 305 mins)	223	(80.3 overs; 307 mins)		230

WEST INDIES	O	M	R	W	O	M	R	W
Roach	23	9	51	1	21	6	58	1
Rampaul	26	4	68	3	24.2	6	87	1
Sammy	28	6	70	2	23	3	64	1
Bishoo	32.5	11	80	3	38	5	149	2
Nash					6	0	19	0

PAKISTAN	O	M	R	W	O	M	R	W
Tanvir Ahmed	7	1	22	1	5	0	10	1
Wahab Riaz	11	1	59	1	10	1	39	1
Abdur Rehman	29	10	55	2	24.3	10	65	4
Saeed Ajmal	28.5	10	56	3	31	7	79	3
Mohammad Hafeez	8	0	23	3	10	1	23	0

FALL OF WICKETS

	P	WI	P	WI
Wkt	1st	1st	2nd	2nd
1st	17	0	82	5
2nd	22	22	158	59
3rd	24	54	167	63
4th	74	94	296	77
5th	167	100	358	115
6th	176	107	367	135
7th	187	144	–	171
8th	187	158	–	193
9th	194	218	–	227
10th	272	223	–	230

Umpires: B.F.Bowden (*New Zealand*) (67) and E.A.R.de Silva (*Sri Lanka*) (49).
Referee: A.G.Hurst (*Australia*) (44). **Test No. 1992/46 (WI470/P358)**

ENGLAND v SRI LANKA (1st Test)

At Sophia Gardens, Cardiff, on 26, 27, 28, 29, 30 May 2011.
Toss: Sri Lanka. Result: **ENGLAND** won by an innings and 14 runs.
Debuts: Sri Lanka – N.L.T.C.Perera.

SRI LANKA

N.T.Paranavitana	b Tremlett	66	c Strauss b Tremlett		0
*T.M.Dilshan	b Swann	50	c and b Tremlett		10
K.C.Sangakkara	c Prior b Anderson	11	c Strauss b Swann		14
D.P.M.D.Jayawardena	c Strauss b Anderson	4	c Strauss b Tremlett		15
T.T.Samaraweera	c Swann b Anderson	58	b Swann		0
†H.A.P.W.Jayawardena	c Prior b Broad	112	c Prior b Tremlett		3
M.F.Maharoof	run out	16	c Prior b Swann		0
N.L.T.C.Perera	c Tremlett b Broad	25	c Bell b Broad		20
H.M.R.K.B.Herath	c Trott b Swann	25	lbw b Swann		3
B.A.W.Mendis	not out	1	not out		12
R.A.S.Lakmal	c Broad b Swann	2	c Cook b Broad		0
Extras	(B 9, LB 21)	30	(B 5)		5
Total	**(118.4 overs; 528 mins)**	**400**	**(24.4 overs; 117 mins)**		**82**

ENGLAND

*A.J.Strauss	c D.P.M.D.Jayawardena b Lakmal	20
A.N.Cook	c H.A.P.W.Jayawardena b Maharoof	133
J.M.Anderson	c D.P.M.D.Jayawardena b Mendis	1
I.J.L.Trott	b Dilshan	203
K.P.Pietersen	lbw b Herath	3
I.R.Bell	not out	103
E.J.G.Morgan	not out	14
†M.J.Prior		
S.C.J.Broad		
G.P.Swann		
C.T.Tremlett		
Extras	(B 10, LB 4, NB 5)	19
Total	**(5 wkts dec; 155 overs; 637 mins)**	**496**

ENGLAND	O	M	R	W	O	M	R	W
Anderson	28	8	66	3				
Broad	33	4	113	2	(1) 7.4	1	21	2
Tremlett	26	9	81	1	(2) 10	2	40	4
Swann	24.4	2	78	3	(3) 7	1	16	4
Trott	6	0	29	0				
Pietersen	1	0	3	0				
SRI LANKA								
Lakmal	22	4	68	1				
Perera	24	5	81	0				
Dilshan	16	1	60	1				
Maharoof	28	3	92	1				
Mendis	21	4	66	1				
Herath	44	7	115	1				

FALL OF WICKETS

	SL	E	SL
Wkt	1st	1st	2nd
1st	93	46	1
2nd	114	47	10
3rd	133	298	33
4th	159	305	36
5th	243	465	43
6th	278	–	43
7th	346	–	43
8th	397	–	52
9th	397	–	82
10th	400	–	82

Umpires: Alim Dar (*Pakistan*) (64) and B.R.Doctrove (*West Indies*) (32).
Referee: J.Srinath (*India*) (16). **Test No. 1993/22 (E909/SL199)**

ENGLAND v SRI LANKA (2nd Test)

At Lord's, London, on 3, 4, 5, 6, 7 June 2011.
Toss: Sri Lanka. Result: **MATCH DRAWN**.
Debuts: None.

ENGLAND

*A.J.Strauss	lbw b Welagedara	4	lbw b Welagedara		0
A.N.Cook	c Maharoof b Fernando	96	st H.A.P.W.Jayawardena b Herath		106
I.J.L.Trott	lbw b Lakmal	2	b Herath		58
K.P.Pietersen	c Dilshan b Lakmal	2	b Herath		72
I.R.Bell	c Paranavitana b Welagedara	52	not out		57
E.J.G.Morgan	lbw b Lakmal	79	c Lakmal b Fernando		4
†M.J.Prior	b Herath	126	run out		4
S.C.J.Broad	lbw b Welagedara	54	c H.A.P.W.Jayawardena b Fernando		3
G.P.Swann	c Paranavitana b Welagedara	4			
C.T.Tremlett	not out	24			
S.T.Finn	b Herath	19			
Extras	(B 3, LB 7, W 4, NB 10)	24	(LB 12, W 1, NB 18)		31
Total	**(112.5 overs; 509 mins)**	**486**	**(7 wkts dec; 78.1 overs; 361 mins)**		**335**

SRI LANKA

N.T.Paranavitana	c Strauss b Finn	65	lbw b Trott		44
*T.M.Dilshan	b Finn	193			
K.C.Sangakkara	c Prior b Tremlett	26	(2) c Morgan b Tremlett		12
D.P.M.D.Jayawardena	c Cook b Finn	49	(3) c Pietersen b Broad		25
T.T.Samaraweera	c Prior b Tremlett	9	(4) not out		17
†H.A.P.W.Jayawardena	c Swann b Finn	40	(5) not out		12
M.F.Maharoof	lbw b Broad	2			
H.M.R.K.B.Herath	st Prior b Swann	26			
C.R.D.Fernando	c Strauss b Swann	5			
R.A.S.Lakmal	not out	0			
U.W.M.B.C.A.Welagedara	c Broad b Swann	6			
Extras	(B 25, LB 23, W 8, NB 2)	58	(B 7, LB 3, W 6, NB 1)		17
Total	**(131.4 overs; 597 mins)**	**479**	**(3 wkts; 43 overs; 183 mins)**		**127**

SRI LANKA	O	M	R	W		O	M	R	W	FALL OF WICKETS				
											E	SL	E	SL
Welagedara	28	4	122	4		10	1	50	2	*Wkt*	*1st*	*1st*	*2nd*	*2nd*
Lakmal	25	2	126	3		17	0	70	0	1st	5	207	0	13
Maharoof	17	5	57	0		7	0	24	0	2nd	18	288	117	66
Fernando	17	2	77	1		20.1	2	92	2	3rd	22	370	244	96
Herath	18.5	1	64	2		24	2	87	3	4th	130	394	305	–
Dilshan	7	1	30	0						5th	201	394	312	–
										6th	302	409	319	–
ENGLAND										7th	410	466	335	–
Broad	32	5	125	1	(2)	9	2	29	1	8th	414	472	–	–
Tremlett	30	8	85	2	(1)	9	1	31	1	9th	452	472	–	–
Finn	33	8	108	4	(4)	8	2	31	0	10th	486	479	–	–
Swann	32.4	5	101	3	(3)	12	2	19	0					
Pietersen	4	0	12	0	(6)	1	0	2	0					
Trott					(5)	4	1	5	1					

Umpires: B.R.Doctrove (*West Indies*) (33) and R.J.Tucker (*Australia*) (9).
Referee: J.Srinath (*India*) (17).   **Test No. 1994/23 (E910/SL200)**

ENGLAND v SRI LANKA (3rd Test)

At The Rose Bowl, Southampton, on 16, 17, 18, 19, 20 June 2011.
Toss: England. Result: **MATCH DRAWN**.
Debuts: Sri Lanka – H.D.R.L.Thirimanne.

SRI LANKA

N.T.Paranavitana	lbw b Tremlett	11	c Swann b Anderson		10
H.D.R.L.Thirimanne	c Strauss b Anderson	10	c Strauss b Tremlett		38
*K.C.Sangakkara	c Prior b Anderson	2	c sub (A.P.Rouse) b Anderson		119
D.P.M.D.Jayawardena	c Prior b Tremlett	4	c Prior b Broad		6
T.T.Samaraweera	c Pietersen b Tremlett	31	(6) not out		87
†H.A.P.W.Jayawardena	c Morgan b Swann	43	(7) not out		6
N.L.T.C.Perera	c Prior b Tremlett	2			
H.M.R.K.B.Herath	c Anderson b Tremlett	12	(5) lbw b Swann		36
C.R.D.Fernando	not out	39			
R.A.S.Lakmal	c Prior b Tremlett	0			
U.W.M.B.C.A.Welagedara	c Morgan b Broad	7			
Extras	(B 2, LB 15, W 4, NB 2)	23	(B 16, LB 9, W 1, NB 6)		32
Total	**(64.2 overs; 295 mins)**	**184**	**(5 wkts; 104 overs; 434 mins)**		**334**

ENGLAND

*A.J.Strauss	c Paranavitana b Welagedara	3
A.N.Cook	c Samaraweera b Fernando	55
I.J.L.Trott	c H.A.P.W.Jayawardena b Lakmal	4
K.P.Pietersen	c H.A.P.W.Jayawardena b Perera	85
I.R.Bell	not out	119
J.M.Anderson	c H.A.P.W.Jayawardena b Welagedara	27
E.J.G.Morgan	c H.A.P.W.Jayawardena b Lakmal	71
†M.J.Prior	c D.P.M.D.Jayawardena b Perera	0
S.C.J.Broad	c sub (H.K.S.R.Kaluhalamulla) b Lakmal	0
G.P.Swann		
C.T.Tremlett		
Extras	(B 2, W 3, NB 8)	13
Total	**(8 wkts dec; 92.4 overs; 435 mins)**	**377**

ENGLAND	O	M	R	W		O	M	R	W
Anderson	23	7	56	2		30	9	81	2
Broad	19.2	3	51	1	(3)	18	4	51	1
Tremlett	20	5	48	6	(2)	21	5	66	1
Swann	2	0	12	1		25	6	57	1
Pietersen						7	1	30	0
Trott						3	0	24	0

SRI LANKA	O	M	R	W
Welagedara	24	3	90	2
Lakmal	24.2	2	99	3
Fernando	10.2	0	47	1
Perera	32.4	5	101	3
Herath	9	0	33	0
D.P.M.D.Jayawardena	10	0	5	0

FALL OF WICKETS

	SL	E	SL
Wkt	1st	1st	2nd
1st	23	4	25
2nd	23	14	38
3rd	29	120	110
4th	39	191	185
5th	89	236	326
6th	91	373	–
7th	117	374	–
8th	158	377	–
9th	166	–	–
10th	184	–	–

Umpires: Alim Dar (*Pakistan*) (65) and R.J.Tucker (*Australia*) (10).
Referee: A.G.Hurst (*Australia*) (45). **Test No. 1995/24 (E911/SL201)**

WEST INDIES v INDIA (1st Test)

At Sabina Park, Kingston, Jamaica, on 20, 21, 22, 23 June 2011.
Toss: India. Result: **INDIA** won by 63 runs.
Debuts: India – V.Kohli, P.Kumar, A.Mukund.

INDIA

A.Mukund	b Rampaul	11	c Baugh b Bishoo	25
M.Vijay	c Bishoo b Rampaul	8	lbw b Rampaul	0
R.S.Dravid	c Sammy b Bishoo	40	c Sarwan b Bishoo	112
V.V.S.Laxman	c Sammy b Bishoo	12	c and b Sammy	0
V.Kohli	c Baugh b Edwards	4	c Baugh b Edwards	15
S.K.Raina	c Bishoo b Rampaul	82	c Sammy b Bishoo	27
*†M.S.Dhoni	c Simmons b Bishoo	0	c Edwards b Bishoo	16
Harbhajan Singh	c Bishoo b Edwards	70	lbw b Sammy	5
P.Kumar	lbw b Edwards	4	b Sammy	0
A.Mishra	c Sarwan b Edwards	6	c Bravo b Sammy	28
I.Sharma	not out	0	not out	5
Extras	(B 1, LB 2, NB 6)	9	(B 8, LB 2, NB 9)	19
Total	**(61.2 overs)**	**246**	**(94.5 overs)**	**252**

WEST INDIES

A.B.Barath	c Dhoni b Kumar	64	c Raina b Kumar	38
L.M.P.Simmons	c Vijay b Sharma	3	b Sharma	27
R.R.Sarwan	lbw b Sharma	3	c Kohli b Sharma	0
D.M.Bravo	c Dhoni b Kumar	18	b Kumar	41
S.Chanderpaul	c Mukund b Harbhajan	23	c Raina b Kumar	30
B.P.Nash	c Raina b Kumar	1	lbw b Mishra	9
†C.S.Baugh	c Vijay b Harbhajan	27	c Kohli b Harbhajan	0
*D.J.G.Sammy	b Sharma	1	c Laxman b Mishra	25
R.Rampaul	not out	14	c Dhoni b Sharma	34
F.H.Edwards	c Dhoni b Mishra	7	not out	15
D.Bishoo	c Raina b Mishra	4	b Raina	26
Extras	(B 1, LB 3, NB 4)	8	(B 1, LB 13, W 2, NB 1)	17
Total	**(67.5 overs)**	**173**	**(68.2 overs)**	**262**

WEST INDIES	O	M	R	W	O	M	R	W
Edwards	16	1	56	4	20	1	70	1
Rampaul	18.2	2	59	3	22	3	49	1
Sammy	13	3	42	0	27	11	52	4
Bishoo	11	2	75	3	24.5	2	65	4
Simmons	2	0	8	0				
Nash	1	0	3	0	(5) 1	0	6	0
INDIA								
Kumar	18	5	38	3	16	3	42	3
Sharma	17	6	29	3	17	3	81	3
Mishra	13.5	1	51	2	13	1	62	2
Harbhajan Singh	19	5	51	2	16	3	54	1
Raina					6.2	1	9	1

FALL OF WICKETS

	I	WI	I	WI
Wkt	1st	1st	2nd	2nd
1st	15	18	0	62
2nd	30	35	56	63
3rd	64	91	57	80
4th	69	95	100	148
5th	83	102	148	149
6th	85	147	166	150
7th	231	148	183	181
8th	236	152	183	188
9th	246	169	239	223
10th	246	173	252	262

Umpires: I.J.Gould (*England*) (19) and D.J.Harper (*Australia*) (95).
Referee: J.J.Crowe (*New Zealand*) (46).　　Test No. 1996/83 (WI471/I449)

WEST INDIES v INDIA (2nd Test)

At Kensington Oval, Bridgetown, Barbados, on 28, 29, 30 June, 1, 2 July 2011.
Toss: West Indies. Result: **MATCH DRAWN**.
Debuts: None.

INDIA

A.Mukund	c Samuels b Rampaul	1	c Baugh b Edwards		48
M.Vijay	c Baugh b Rampaul	11	c Baugh b Rampaul		3
R.S.Dravid	c Baugh b Sammy	5	c Sarwan b Edwards		55
V.V.S.Laxman	c Barath b Bishoo	85	c Sammy b Edwards		87
V.Kohli	c Sammy b Rampaul	0	c Sammy b Edwards		27
S.K.Raina	c Barath b Bishoo	53	not out		12
*†M.S.Dhoni	c Chanderpaul b Edwards	2	c Chanderpaul b Edwards		5
Harbhajan Singh	c Barath b Edwards	5	not out		6
P.Kumar	st Baugh b Bishoo	12			
A.Mithun	b Edwards	0			
I.Sharma	not out	1			
Extras	(B 5, LB 4, W 11, NB 6)	26	(B 4, LB 9, W 5, NB 8)		26
Total	**(68 overs)**	**201**	**(6 wkts dec; 102 overs)**		**269**

WEST INDIES

A.B.Barath	c Kohli b Sharma	3	c Raina b Sharma		27
L.M.P.Simmons	c Dhoni b Kumar	2	c Dravid b Sharma		14
R.R.Sarwan	lbw b Sharma	18	c Raina b Kumar		8
D.M.Bravo	c Dhoni b Mithun	9	c Dhoni b Mithun		73
D.Bishoo	c Kohli b Sharma	13			
S.Chanderpaul	b Mithun	37	(5) lbw b Harbhajan		12
M.N.Samuels	not out	78	(6) lbw b Sharma		9
†C.S.Baugh	c Dravid b Harbhajan	2	(7) not out		46
*D.J.G.Sammy	lbw b Sharma	15	(8) lbw b Sharma		0
R.Rampaul	c Vijay b Sharma	0	(9) not out		0
F.H.Edwards	c Dhoni b Sharma	0			
Extras	(LB 3, W 5, NB 5)	13	(B 5, LB 6, NB 2)		13
Total	**(73.5 overs)**	**190**	**(7 wkts; 71.3 overs)**		**202**

WEST INDIES	O	M	R	W	O	M	R	W		FALL OF WICKETS			
Edwards	19	2	56	3	23	4	76	5			I	WI	I	WI
Rampaul	16	6	38	3	28	6	72	1		*Wkt*	*1st*	*1st*	*2nd*	*2nd*
Sammy	19	4	52	1	24	8	45	0		1st	1	3	26	18
Bishoo	14	1	46	3	27	4	63	0		2nd	8	5	89	27
										3rd	38	30	154	55
INDIA										4th	38	53	232	109
Kumar	23	3	67	1	16	6	41	1		5th	155	57	247	132
Sharma	21.5	7	55	6	19.3	4	53	4		6th	167	134	253	201
Mithun	15	6	34	2	13	3	50	1		7th	183	143	–	202
Harbhajan Singh	14	3	31	1	19	2	42	1		8th	187	186	–	–
Raina					4	1	5	0		9th	189	190	–	–
										10th	201	190	–	–

Umpires: Asad Rauf (*Pakistan*) (35) and I.J.Gould (*England*) (20).
Referee: B.C.Broad (*England*) (43).   Test No. 1997/84 (WI472/I450)

WEST INDIES v INDIA (3rd Test)

At Windsor Park, Roseau, Dominica, on 6, 7, 8, 9, 10 July 2011.
Toss: India. Result: **MATCH DRAWN**.
Debuts: West Indies – K.A.Edwards, K.O.A.Powell.

WEST INDIES

A.B.Barath	b Sharma	12	c Kohli b Kumar		6
K.O.A.Powell	c Laxman b Kumar	3	c Raina b Sharma		4
K.A.Edwards	c Dhoni b Sharma	6	c Dhoni b Harbhajan		110
D.M.Bravo	c Dhoni b Sharma	50	c Kumar b Harbhajan		14
S.Chanderpaul	c Dhoni b Patel	23	not out		116
M.N.Samuels	b Kumar	9	lbw b Harbhajan		0
†C.S.Baugh	b Harbhajan	60	c Mukund b Kumar		10
*D.J.G.Sammy	c Mukund b Harbhajan	20	c Mukund b Harbhajan		17
F.H.Edwards	b Sharma	3	c Kumar b Raina	(10)	30
R.Rampaul	not out	0	run out	(9)	1
D.Bishoo	b Sharma	0	c Dravid b Raina		1
Extras	(B 8, LB 10)	18	(B 8, LB 2, W 1, NB 2)		13
Total	**(76.3 overs)**	**204**	**(131.3 overs)**		**322**

INDIA

A.Mukund	c Barath b Bishoo	62	lbw b F.H.Edwards		0
M.Vijay	c Baugh b F.H.Edwards	5	c Bishoo b Rampaul		45
R.S.Dravid	b Sammy	5	not out		34
V.V.S.Laxman	st Baugh b Chanderpaul	56	not out	(5)	3
V.Kohli	c Baugh b Sammy	30			
S.K.Raina	lbw b F.H.Edwards	50	c and b Rampaul	(4)	8
*†M.S.Dhoni	c Bishoo b F.H.Edwards	74			
Harbhajan Singh	c Baugh b F.H.Edwards	12			
P.Kumar	c Samuels b Bishoo	23			
I.Sharma	c Barath b F.H.Edwards	2			
M.M.Patel	not out	4			
Extras	(B 8, LB 3, W 3, NB 10)	24	(LB 1, NB 3)		4
Total	**(108.2 overs)**	**347**	**(4 wkts; 32 overs)**		**94**

INDIA	O	M	R	W		O	M	R	W
Kumar	16	7	22	2		21	6	44	2
Sharma	21.3	4	77	5		27	5	76	1
Patel	20	7	48	1		24	5	71	0
Harbhajan Singh	15	7	26	2		42	14	75	4
Raina	4	1	13	0		15.3	2	32	2
Mukund						2	0	14	0

WEST INDIES	O	M	R	W		O	M	R	W
F.H.Edwards	28.2	3	103	5		8	1	19	1
Sammy	28	7	51	2	(3)	5	0	26	0
Bishoo	38	2	125	2	(4)	8	1	17	0
K.A.Edwards	4	0	19	0					
Chanderpaul	10	0	38	1					
Rampaul					(2)	11	2	31	2

FALL OF WICKETS				
	WI	I	WI	I
Wkt	1st	1st	2nd	2nd
1st	17	13	8	0
2nd	24	18	10	73
3rd	35	116	40	86
4th	84	168	201	–
5th	99	172	201	–
6th	158	275	223	–
7th	199	308	255	–
8th	200	339	256	–
9th	204	343	321	–
10th	204	347	322	–

Umpires: Asad Rauf (*Pakistan*) (36) and R.A.Kettleborough (*England*) (3).
Referee: B.C.Broad (*England*) (44).   **Test No. 1998/85 (WI473/I451)**

ENGLAND v INDIA (1st Test)

At Lord's, London, on 21, 22, 23, 24, 25 July 2011.
Toss: India. Result: **ENGLAND** won by 196 runs.
Debuts: None.

ENGLAND

*A.J.Strauss	c Sharma b Khan	22	lbw b Harbhajan		32
A.N.Cook	lbw b Khan	12	c Dhoni b Kumar		1
I.J.L.Trott	lbw b Kumar	70	b Sharma		22
K.P.Pietersen	not out	202	c Dhoni b Sharma		1
I.R.Bell	c Dhoni b Kumar	45	c Dhoni b Sharma		0
E.J.G.Morgan	c Dhoni b Kumar	0	c Gambhir b Sharma		19
†M.J.Prior	c Dhoni b Kumar	71	not out		103
S.C.J.Broad	lbw b Kumar	0	not out		74
G.P.Swann	b Raina	24			
C.T.Tremlett	not out	4			
J.M.Anderson					
Extras	(B 14, LB 8, W 1, NB 1)	24	(B 7, LB 8, W 2)		17
Total	(8 wkts dec; 131.4 overs; 603 mins)	474	(6 wkts dec; 71 overs; 312 mins)		269

INDIA

A.Mukund	b Broad	49	b Broad		12
G.Gambhir	b Broad	15	(4) lbw b Swann		22
R.S.Dravid	not out	103	(2) c Prior b Anderson		36
S.R.Tendulkar	c Swann b Broad	34	(5) lbw b Anderson		12
V.V.S.Laxman	c Trott b Tremlett	10	(3) c Bell b Anderson		56
S.K.Raina	lbw b Swann	0	c Prior b Anderson		78
*†M.S.Dhoni	c Swann b Tremlett	28	c Prior b Tremlett		16
Harbhajan Singh	c Prior b Tremlett	0	c Tremlett b Anderson		12
P.Kumar	c Strauss b Broad	17	b Broad		2
Z.Khan	b Anderson	0	not out		0
I.Sharma	c Prior b Anderson	0	lbw b Broad		1
Extras	(B 5, LB 12, W 1, NB 12)	30	(B 2, LB 6, NB 6)		14
Total	(95.5 overs; 420 mins)	286	(96.3 overs; 437 mins)		261

INDIA	O	M	R	W		O	M	R	W		FALL OF WICKETS			
												E	I	E	I
Khan	13.3	8	18	2							Wkt	1st	1st	2nd	2nd
Kumar	40.3	10	106	5	(1)	20	2	70	1		1st	19	63	23	19
Sharma	32	5	128	0	(2)	22	6	59	4		2nd	62	77	54	94
Harbhajan Singh	35	3	152	0	(3)	21	1	66	1		3rd	160	158	55	131
Dhoni	8	1	23	0		0	16	0			4th	270	182	55	135
Raina	2.4	1	25	1	(4)	6	1	43	0		5th	270	183	62	165
											6th	390	240	107	225
ENGLAND											7th	390	241	–	243
Anderson	23.5	6	87	2		28	7	65	5		8th	451	276	–	256
Tremlett	24	5	80	3		21	4	44	1		9th	–	284	–	260
Broad	22	8	37	4		20.3	4	57	3		10th	–	286	–	261
Trott	6	1	12	0	(5)	2	0	11	0						
Swann	19	3	50	1	(4)	22	3	64	1						
Pietersen	1	0	3	0		3	0	12	0						

Umpires: Asad Rauf (*Pakistan*) (37) and B.F.Bowden (*New Zealand*) (68).
Referee: R.S.Madugalle (*Sri Lanka*) (125).   **Test No. 1999/100 (E912/I452)**

ENGLAND v INDIA (2nd Test)

At Trent Bridge, Nottingham, on 29, 30, 31 July, 1 August 2011.
Toss: India. Result: **ENGLAND** won by 319 runs.
Debuts: None.

ENGLAND

*A.J.Strauss	c Raina b Kumar	32		c Dhoni b Sreesanth	16
A.N.Cook	lbw b Sharma	2		c Yuvraj b Sharma	5
I.J.L.Trott	c Laxman b Sreesanth	4	(7)	c Dravid b Kumar	2
K.P.Pietersen	c Raina b Sreesanth	29		c Dhoni b Sreesanth	63
I.R.Bell	c Dhoni b Sharma	31	(3)	c Laxman b Yuvraj	159
E.J.G.Morgan	lbw b Kumar	0	(5)	c Dhoni b Kumar	70
†M.J.Prior	c Dravid b Sreesanth	1	(6)	c Dhoni b Kumar	73
T.T.Bresnan	c Dravid b Sharma	11		c Dravid b Kumar	90
S.C.J.Broad	c Tendulkar b Harbhajan	64		run out	44
G.P.Swann	c Mukund b Kumar	28		c sub (W.P.Saha) b Sharma	3
J.M.Anderson	not out	6		not out	1
Extras	(B 2, LB 8, W 3)	13		(B 9, LB 5, W 2, NB 2)	18
Total	**(68.4 overs; 320 mins)**	**221**		**(120.2 overs; 527 mins)**	**544**

INDIA

A.Mukund	c Pietersen b Anderson	0		c Strauss b Bresnan	3
R.S.Dravid	c Cook b Bresnan	117		c Prior b Broad	6
V.V.S.Laxman	c Prior b Bresnan	54		b Anderson	4
S.R.Tendulkar	c Strauss b Broad	16		lbw b Anderson	56
S.K.Raina	c Morgan b Anderson	12		c sub (S.L.Elstone) b Bresnan	0
Yuvraj Singh	c Prior b Broad	62		c Cook b Bresnan	8
*†M.S.Dhoni	c Anderson b Broad	5		lbw b Bresnan	6
Harbhajan Singh	lbw b Broad	0		c sub (S.L.Elstone) b Bresnan	46
P.Kumar	b Broad	0		b Anderson	25
I.Sharma	c Bell b Broad	3		not out	8
S.Sreesanth	not out	7		b Broad	0
Extras	(B 4, LB 3, W 4, NB 1)	12		(B 1)	1
Total	**(91.1 overs; 386 mins)**	**288**		**(47.4 overs; 223 mins)**	**158**

INDIA	O	M	R	W		O	M	R	W	FALL OF WICKETS				
Kumar	22	8	45	3		36	5	124	4		E	I	E	I
Sharma	22	4	66	3		29.2	4	131	2	Wkt	1st	1st	2nd	2nd
Sreesanth	19	1	77	3		27	5	135	2	1st	7	0	6	6
Harbhajan Singh	4.4	0	22	1	(5)	9	1	47	0	2nd	23	93	57	13
Yuvraj Singh	1	0	1	0	(4)	11	0	51	1	3rd	73	119	219	31
Raina						8	0	42	0	4th	85	139	323	37
										5th	85	267	329	55
ENGLAND										6th	88	273	339	55
Anderson	26	8	80	2		17	3	51	3	7th	117	273	458	107
Broad	24.1	8	46	6		14.4	5	30	2	8th	124	273	540	129
Bresnan	21	6	48	2		12	2	48	5	9th	197	273	540	153
Trott	4	1	18	0						10th	221	288	544	158
Swann	12	0	76	0	(4)	3	0	21	0					
Pietersen	4	0	13	0	(5)	1	0	7	0					

Umpires: Asad Rauf (*Pakistan*) (38) and M.Erasmus (*South Africa*) (6).
Referee: R.S.Madugalle (*Sri Lanka*) (126).   **Test No. 2000/101 (E913/I453)**

ENGLAND v INDIA (3rd Test)

At Edgbaston, Birmingham, on 10, 11, 12, 13 August 2011.
Toss: England. Result: **ENGLAND** won by an innings and 242 runs.
Debuts: None.

INDIA

G.Gambhir	b Bresnan	38	c Swann b Anderson		14
V.Sehwag	c Prior b Broad	0	c Strauss b Anderson		0
R.S.Dravid	b Bresnan	22	c Prior b Anderson		18
S.R.Tendulkar	c Anderson b Broad	1	run out		40
V.V.S.Laxman	c Broad b Bresnan	30	c Prior b Anderson		2
S.K.Raina	b Anderson	4	lbw b Swann		10
*†M.S.Dhoni	c Strauss b Broad	77	not out		74
A.Mishra	c Prior b Broad	4	c Broad b Swann		22
P.Kumar	c Prior b Bresnan	26	c Bopara b Broad		40
I.Sharma	c Cook b Anderson	4	lbw b Broad		0
S.Sreesanth	not out	1	c Pietersen b Bresnan		5
Extras	(B 4, LB 14)	18	(B 6, LB 6, W 7)		19
Total	**(62.2 overs; 271 mins)**	**224**	**(55.3 overs; 259 mins)**		**244**

ENGLAND

*A.J.Strauss	b Mishra	87
A.N.Cook	c Raina b Sharma	294
I.R.Bell	b Kumar	34
K.P.Pietersen	lbw b Kumar	63
E.J.G.Morgan	c Sehwag b Raina	104
R.S.Bopara	lbw b Mishra	7
†M.J.Prior	c Tendulkar b Mishra	5
T.T.Bresnan	not out	53
S.C.J.Broad		
G.P.Swann		
J.M.Anderson		
Extras	(B 11, LB 34, W 3, NB 15)	63
Total	**(7 wkts dec; 188.1 overs; 773 mins)**	**710**

ENGLAND	O	M	R	W	O	M	R	W
Anderson	21.2	3	69	2	18	3	85	4
Broad	17	6	53	4	12	4	28	2
Bresnan	20	4	62	4	10.3	3	19	1
Swann	4	0	22	0	13	1	88	2
Pietersen					2	0	12	0

INDIA	O	M	R	W
Kumar	40	13	98	2
Sreesanth	36	4	158	0
Sharma	37.1	7	159	1
Mishra	43	2	150	3
Raina	28	1	83	1
Tendulkar	4	0	17	0

FALL OF WICKETS

	I	E	I
Wkt	1st	1st	2nd
1st	8	186	3
2nd	59	252	35
3rd	60	374	40
4th	75	596	56
5th	92	605	87
6th	100	613	89
7th	111	710	130
8th	195	–	205
9th	224	–	221
10th	224	–	244

Umpires: S.J.Davis (*Australia*) (32) and S.J.A.Taufel (*Australia*) (68).
Referee: R.S.Madugalle (*Sri Lanka*) (127).   Test No. 2001/102 (E914/I454)

ENGLAND v INDIA (4th Test)

At The Oval, London, on 18, 19, 20, 21, 22 August 2011.
Toss: England. Result: **ENGLAND** won by an innings and 8 runs.
Debuts: None.

ENGLAND

*A.J.Strauss	c Dhoni b Sreesanth	40
A.N.Cook	c Sehwag b Sharma	34
I.R.Bell	lbw b Raina	235
K.P.Pietersen	c and b Raina	175
J.M.Anderson	c Laxman b Sreesanth	13
E.J.G.Morgan	c Dhoni b Sreesanth	1
R.S.Bopara	not out	44
†M.J.Prior	not out	18
T.T.Bresnan		
S.C.J.Broad		
G.P.Swann		
Extras	(B 6, LB 8, W 7, NB 10)	31
Total	**(6 wkts dec; 153 overs; 662 mins)**	**591**

INDIA

V.Sehwag	lbw b Anderson	8		b Swann	33
R.S.Dravid	not out	146		c Cook b Swann	13
V.V.S.Laxman	c Prior b Broad	2		b Anderson	24
S.R.Tendulkar	c Anderson b Swann	23		lbw b Bresnan	91
S.K.Raina	st Prior b Swann	0	(6)	lbw b Swann	0
I.Sharma	c Cook b Swann	1	(10)	not out	7
*†M.S.Dhoni	c Prior b Anderson	17		c Swann b Broad	3
A.Mishra	c Bell b Bresnan	43	(5)	b Swann	84
G.Gambhir	c Pietersen b Broad	10	(8)	c Morgan b Swann	3
R.P.Singh	c Anderson b Bresnan	25	(9)	c Prior b Broad	0
S.Sreesanth	c Morgan b Bresnan	0		b Swann	6
Extras	(B 8, LB 9, W 7, NB 1)	25		(B 12, LB 7)	19
Total	**(94 overs; 378 mins)**	**300**		**(91 overs; 387 mins)**	**283**

INDIA	O	M	R	W		O	M	R	W
Singh	34	7	118	0					
Sharma	31	7	97	1					
Sreesanth	29	2	123	3					
Raina	19	2	58	2					
Mishra	38	3	170	0					
Tendulkar	2	0	11	0					

ENGLAND	O	M	R	W		O	M	R	W
Anderson	16	7	49	2		17	4	54	1
Broad	21	3	51	2		20	6	44	2
Bresnan	17	3	54	3	(4)	11	2	30	1
Swann	31	5	102	3	(3)	38	6	106	6
Pietersen	7	1	27	0	(6)	2	0	17	0
Bopara	2	2	0	0	(5)	3	0	13	0

FALL OF WICKETS

		E	I	I
Wkt	1st	1st	2nd	
1st	75	8	49	
2nd	97	13	64	
3rd	447	68	118	
4th	480	93	262	
5th	487	95	262	
6th	548	137	266	
7th	–	224	269	
8th	–	264	269	
9th	–	300	275	
10th	–	300	283	

Umpires: S.J.A.Taufel (*Australia*) (68) and R.J.Tucker (*Australia*) (11).
Referee: R.S.Madugalle (*Sri Lanka*) (128).   **Test No. 2002/103 (E915/I455)**

ZIMBABWE v BANGLADESH (Only Test)

At Harare Sports Club, on 4, 5, 6, 7, 8 August 2011.
Toss: Bangladesh. Result: **ZIMBABWE** won by 130 runs.
Debuts: Zimbabwe – C.R.Ervine, K.M.Jarvis, T.M.K.Mawoyo, B.V.Vitori.

ZIMBABWE

T.M.K.Mawoyo	c Mahmudullah b Rubel	43	b Robiul	35
V.Sibanda	c Mushfiqur b Rubel	78	c sub (Nasir Hossain) b Rubel	38
H.Masakadza	c Kayes b Robiul	104	c and b Shakib	5
*B.R.M.Taylor	c Mushfiqur b Robiul	71	not out	105
C.R.Ervine	lbw b Mahmudullah	6	(7) not out	35
†T.Taibu	c Nafees b Shakib	23	c Robiul b Shafiul	59
E.Chigumbura	c Shafiul b Shakib	5		
R.W.Price	lbw b Rubel	4	(5) lbw b Razzak	4
K.M.Jarvis	not out	4		
B.V.Vitori	c Robiul b Shakib	12		
C.B.Mpofu	st Mushfiqur b Razzak	2		
Extras	(B 4, LB 11, W 1, NB 2)	18	(LB 2, W 4, NB 4)	10
Total	**(131 overs; 538 mins)**	**370**	**(5 wkts dec; 92 overs; 392 mins)**	**291**

BANGLADESH

Tamim Iqbal	c Taylor b Vitori	15	b Mpofu	43
Imrul Kayes	c Price b Vitori	4	c Taibu b Jarvis	31
Shahriar Nafees	b Price	50	b Jarvis	9
Mohammad Ashraful	c Taibu b Chigumbura	73	b Vitori	39
Mahmudullah	c Mawoyo b Vitori	13	(6) c Taibu b Mpofu	11
*Shakib Al Hasan	c Taibu b Mpofu	68	(7) c Taylor b Chigumbura	6
†Mushfiqur Rahim	c Mawoyo b Vitori	27	(5) c Ervine b Mpofu	28
Abdur Razzak	lbw b Mpofu	11	b Chigumbura	43
Shafiul Islam	b Jarvis	5	b Jarvis	7
Rubel Hossain	not out	16	not out	8
Robiul Islam	b Price	0	lbw b Jarvis	12
Extras	(B 1, NB 4)	5	(B 4, LB 2, NB 1)	7
Total	**(96.2 overs; 422 mins)**	**287**	**(57.3 overs; 272 mins)**	**244**

BANGLADESH	O	M	R	W		O	M	R	W
Shafiul Islam	22	8	38	0		11	3	29	1
Robiul Islam	30	4	106	2		13	1	48	1
Rubel Hossain	29	3	84	3	(4)	17	2	75	1
Shakib Al Hasan	26	5	62	4	(6)	18	4	60	1
Abdur Razzak	22	2	57	1	(3)	20	5	49	1
Mahmudullah	2	0	8	1	(5)	12	3	27	0
Imrul Kayes						1	0	1	0

ZIMBABWE	O	M	R	W		O	M	R	W
Vitori	24	5	66	4		14	1	56	1
Jarvis	16	1	67	1		16.3	4	61	4
Mpofu	23	5	72	2	(4)	10	0	51	3
Chigumbura	19	4	47	1	(3)	15	3	50	2
Price	14.2	4	34	2		2	0	20	0

FALL OF WICKETS

Wkt	1st (Z)	1st (B)	2nd (Z)	2nd (B)
1st	102	13	69	65
2nd	162	36	79	87
3rd	304	102	83	102
4th	317	136	92	140
5th	317	190	205	167
6th	326	246	–	174
7th	344	258	–	174
8th	352	266	–	224
9th	368	275	–	228
10th	370	287	–	244

Umpires: H.D.P.K.Dharmasena (*Sri Lanka*) (3) and B.N.J.Oxenford (*Australia*) (2).
Referee: R.S.Mahanama (*Sri Lanka*) (32).   Test No. 2003/9 (Z84/B69)

SRI LANKA v AUSTRALIA (1st Test)

At Galle International Stadium, on 31 August, 1, 2, 3 September 2011.
Toss: Australia. Result: **AUSTRALIA** won by 125 runs.
Debuts: Australia – T.A.Copeland, N.M.Lyon.

AUSTRALIA

S.R.Watson	c H.A.P.W.Jayawardena b Herath	22	c Samaraweera b Welagedara		0
P.J.Hughes	c Paranavitana b Lakmal	12	lbw b Dilshan		28
R.T.Ponting	c Mathews b Herath	44	c Herath b Lakmal		4
*M.J.Clarke	lbw b Herath	23	c H.A.P.W.Jayawardena b Herath		60
M.E.K.Hussey	lbw b Dilshan	95	c Paranavitana b Herath		15
U.T.Khawaja	b Welagedara	21	lbw b Welagedara		26
†B.J.Haddin	c Mathews b Kaluhalamulla	24	c D.M.P.D.Jayawardena b Herath		0
M.G.Johnson	c H.A.P.W.Jayawardena b Lakmal	14	c H.A.P.W.Jayawardena b Herath		8
R.J.Harris	lbw b Lakmal	1	c and b Herath		23
T.A.Copeland	c Paranavitana b Kaluhalamulla	12	not out		23
N.M.Lyon	not out	0	c Samaraweera b Dilshan		13
Extras	(B 3, LB 2)	5	(B 4, LB 4, NB 2)		10
Total	**(86.4 overs; 347 mins)**	**273**	**(59.2 overs; 240 mins)**		**210**

SRI LANKA

N.T.Paranavitana	lbw b Watson	29	lbw b Harris		0
*T.M.Dilshan	c Ponting b Copeland	4	b Harris		12
K.C.Sangakkara	c Clarke b Lyon	10	c Hussey b Watson		17
D.P.M.D.Jayawardena	run out	11	b Harris		105
T.T.Samaraweera	lbw b Watson	26	c Haddin b Johnson		0
†H.A.P.W.Jayawardena	lbw b Watson	0	b Harris		0
A.D.Mathews	b Lyon	5	b Watson		95
H.K.S.R.Kaluhalamulla	c Ponting b Lyon	9	c Clarke b Johnson		0
H.M.R.K.B.Herath	c Johnson b Lyon	0	c Copeland b Harris		12
R.A.S.Lakmal	not out	2	c Johnson b Lyon		5
U.W.M.B.C.A.Welagedara	c and b Lyon	1	not out		4
Extras	(LB 4, W 1, NB 3)	8	(B 1, LB 1, W 1)		3
Total	**(50 overs; 216 mins)**	**105**	**(95.5 overs; 385 mins)**		**253**

SRI LANKA	O	M	R	W	O	M	R	W	FALL OF WICKETS			
										A	SL	A	SL
Welagedara	15	5	61	1	6	3	13	2	Wkt	1st	1st	2nd	2nd
Lakmal	17	2	55	3	8	3	23	1	1st	28	4	0	0
Herath	24	3	54	3	23	3	79	5	2nd	36	24	5	15
Kaluhalamulla	21	2	76	2	14	3	61	0	3rd	91	44	61	52
Dilshan	9.4	1	22	1	8.2	1	26	2	4th	112	87	110	63
									5th	157	87	110	68
AUSTRALIA									6th	205	88	112	210
Harris	8	5	6	0	20	5	62	5	7th	234	100	130	221
Copeland	12	3	24	1	16	6	20	0	8th	236	100	170	242
Johnson	9	1	26	0	19	6	56	2	9th	251	103	178	249
Lyon	15	3	34	5	19.5	2	73	1	10th	273	105	210	253
Watson	6	1	11	3	(6) 13	6	19	2					
Clarke					(5) 6	0	16	0					
Ponting					2	0	5	0					

Umpires: Alim Dar (*Pakistan*) (66) and R.A.Kettleborough (*England*) (4).
Referee: B.C.Broad (*England*) (45).   Test No. 2004/21 (SL202/A730)

SRI LANKA v AUSTRALIA (2nd Test)

At Pallekele International Cricket Stadium, on 8, 9, 10, 11, 12 September 2011.
Toss: Sri Lanka. Result: **MATCH DRAWN**.
Debuts: Sri Lanka – S.Prasanna; Australia – S.E.Marsh.

SRI LANKA

N.T.Paranavitana	c Haddin b Harris	0	c Haddin b Hussey		55
*T.M.Dilshan	b Copeland	4	c Watson b Harris		36
K.C.Sangakkara	c Hughes b Hussey	48	c Clarke b Harris		69
D.P.M.D.Jayawardena	c Hussey b Copeland	4	c Clarke b Copeland		51
T.T.Samaraweera	c Haddin b Harris	17	c Haddin b Watson		43
†H.A.P.W.Jayawardena	c Harris b Lyon	18	c Haddin b Harris		21
A.D.Mathews	c Haddin b Johnson	58	not out		11
H.K.S.R.Kaluhalamulla	c and b Lyon	4	not out		4
S.Prasanna	b Harris	5			
R.A.S.Lakmal	not out	7			
U.W.M.B.C.A.Welagedara	c Copeland b Johnson	2			
Extras	(B 2, LB 4, NB 1)	7	(B 6, LB 20, NB 1)		27
Total	**(64.1 overs; 267 mins)**	**174**	**(6 wkts; 114.3 overs; 471 mins)**		**317**

AUSTRALIA

S.R.Watson	b Lakmal	36
P.J.Hughes	c Paranavitana b Kaluhalamulla	36
S.E.Marsh	c Sangakkara b Lakmal	141
*M.J.Clarke	c D.P.M.D.Jayawardena b Welagedara	13
M.E.K.Hussey	c Sangakkara b Samaraweera	142
U.T.Khawaja	not out	13
†B.J.Haddin	c Sangakkara b Kaluhalamulla	1
M.G.Johnson	b Kaluhalamulla	0
R.J.Harris	not out	9
T.A.Copeland		
N.M.Lyon		
Extras	(LB 9, W 1, NB 10)	20
Total	**(7 wkts dec; 132 overs; 515 mins)**	**411**

AUSTRALIA	O	M	R	W		O	M	R	W	FALL OF WICKETS			
											SL	A	SL
Harris	16	7	38	3		22	8	54	3	Wkt	1st	1st	2nd
Copeland	12	5	24	2		27	10	63	1	1st	2	60	81
Watson	10	5	17	0	(4)	20	9	43	1	2nd	10	95	128
Johnson	15.1	1	48	2	(3)	23.3	4	61	0	3rd	14	116	229
Lyon	10	2	41	2		15	1	52	0	4th	57	374	270
Hussey	1	1	0	1		4	2	2	1	5th	76	391	301
Clarke						3	0	16	0	6th	128	392	307
										7th	133	392	
SRI LANKA										8th	150	–	–
Welagedara	23	3	74	1						9th	166	–	–
Lakmal	23	2	102	2						10th	174	–	–
Prasanna	23	3	80	0									
Dilshan	14	4	32	0									
Kaluhalamulla	43	7	103	3									
Sangakkara	2	0	4	0									
Samaraweera	4	0	7	1									

Umpires: A.L.Hill (*New Zealand*) (24) and R.A.Kettleborough (*England*) (5).
Referee: B.C.Broad (*England*) (46).   Test No. 2005/22 (SL203/A731)

SRI LANKA v AUSTRALIA (3rd Test)

At Sinhalese Sports Club, Colombo, on 16, 17, 18, 19, 20 September 2011.
Toss: Sir Lanka. Result: **MATCH DRAWN**.
Debuts: Sri Lanka – R.M.S.Eranga.

AUSTRALIA

S.R.Watson	c Dilshan b Eranga	8	lbw b Herath		21
P.J.Hughes	b Lakmal	0	c Thirimanne b Herath		126
S.E.Marsh	b Herath	81	c Thirimanne b Herath		18
R.T.Ponting	c H.A.P.W.Jayawardena b Lakmal	48	c D.M.P.D.Jayawardena b Herath		28
*M.J.Clarke	c H.A.P.W.Jayawardena b Eranga	6	c Paranavitana b Herath		112
M.E.K.Hussey	b Eranga	118	c Welagedara b Dilshan		93
†B.J.Haddin	c H.A.P.W.Jayawardena b Eranga	35	c Lakmal b Herath		30
M.G.Johnson	c Herath b Welagedara	8	c Eranga b Welagedara		4
P.M.Siddle	c Paranavitana b Welagedara	0	lbw b Herath		26
T.A.Copeland	c D.M.P.D.Jayawardena b Welagedara	1	c Paranavitana b Eranga		3
N.M.Lyon	not out	3	not out		1
Extras	(LB 4, W 1, NB 3)	8	(B 5, LB 11, W 6, NB 4)		26
Total	(104.3 overs; 445 mins)	316	(138.5 overs; 604 mins)		488

SRI LANKA

N.T.Paranavitana	c Ponting b Johnson	46	not out		2
H.D.R.L.Thirimanne	b Siddle	28	not out		4
K.C.Sangakkara	c Haddin b Siddle	79			
D.P.M.D.Jayawardena	c Haddin b Watson	51			
*T.M.Dilshan	c Haddin b Copeland	83			
A.D.Mathews	not out	105			
†H.A.P.W.Jayawardena	c Clarke b Copeland	47			
R.M.S.Eranga	b Siddle	12			
H.M.R.K.B.Herath	lbw b Siddle	3			
U.W.M.B.C.A.Welagedara	run out	1			
R.A.S.Lakmal	b Johnson	13			
Extras	(B 1, LB 2, NB 2)	5	(W 1)		1
Total	(174 overs; 739 mins)	473	(0 wkts; 2 overs; 7 mins)		7

SRI LANKA	O	M	R	W		O	M	R	W		FALL OF WICKETS			
												A	SL	A	SL
Welagedara	21	6	75	3	(3)	24	3	88	1					
Lakmal	21	3	60	2		22	2	86	0	Wkt	1st	1st	2nd	2nd
Eranga	23.3	6	65	4	(1)	18.5	2	62	1	1st	0	56	62	–
Herath	27	5	78	1		52	11	157	7	2nd	22	97	122	–
Dilshan	12	0	34	0		19	0	62	1	3rd	101	198	188	–
Thirimanne						1	0	7	0	4th	120	210	220	–
Paranavitana						2	0	10	0	5th	190	331	396	–
										6th	265	412	448	–
AUSTRALIA										7th	293	436	452	–
Copeland	40	10	93	2		1	0	3	0	8th	293	444	471	–
Siddle	35	8	91	4						9th	295	450	486	–
Johnson	35	6	122	2						10th	316	473	488	–
Watson	26	8	54	1										
Lyon	34	5	91	0	(2)	1	0	4	0					
Hussey	2	1	5	0										
Ponting	2	0	14	0										

Umpires: Alim Dar (*Pakistan*) (67) and A.L.Hill (*New Zealand*) (25).
Referee: B.C.Broad (*England*) (47).   **Test No. 2006/23 (SL204/A732)**

ZIMBABWE v PAKISTAN (Only Test)

At Queens Sports Club, Bulawayo, on 1, 2, 3, 4, 5 September 2011.
Toss: Pakistan. Result: **PAKISTAN** won by seven wickets.
Debuts: Zimbabwe – G.A.Lamb; Pakistan – Aizaz Cheema, Junaid Khan.

ZIMBABWE

T.M.K.Mawoyo	not out	163	b Ajmal		12
V.Sibanda	st Adnan Akmal b Ajmal	45	c Ajmal b Cheema		5
H.Masakadza	b Ajmal	11	b Cheema		8
*B.R.M.Taylor	lbw b Ajmal	10	b Ajmal		5
†T.Taibu	c Adnan Akmal b Sohail Khan	44	c Adnan Akmal b Cheema		58
C.R.Ervine	c and b Junaid Khan	49	lbw b Hafeez		6
G.A.Lamb	lbw b Ajmal	39	lbw b Hafeez		7
R.W.Price	c Ali b Cheema	6	b Hafeez		0
B.V.Vitori	c Younus Khan b Cheema	14	c Umar b Hafeez		7
K.M.Jarvis	b Cheema	0	not out		25
C.B.Mpofu	b Cheema	8	c Adnan Akmal b Cheema		0
Extras	(B 7, LB 13, W 1, NB 2)	23	(B 4, LB 1, W 2, NB 1)		8
Total	**(150.4 overs; 645 mins)**	**412**	**(56.3 overs)**		**141**

PAKISTAN

Mohammad Hafeez	c Lamb b Masakadza	119	b Price		38
Taufiq Umar	lbw b Jarvis	4	c Taibu b Jarvis		8
Azhar Ali	c Taibu b Lamb	75	c Lamb b Price		22
Younus Khan	c Taylor b Price	88	not out		14
*Misbah-ul-Haq	c Vitori b Lamb	66	not out		6
Umar Akmal	c Taylor b Lamb	15			
†Adnan Akmal	run out	36			
Saeed Ajmal	b Price	28			
Sohail Khan	c Ervine b Mpofu	11			
Junaid Khan	c Ervine b Mpofu	6			
Aizaz Cheema	not out	0			
Extras	(B 4, LB 14)	18			
Total	**(156.1 overs)**	**466**	**(3 wkts; 21.4 overs)**		**88**

PAKISTAN	O	M	R	W		O	M	R	W
Sohail Khan	24	8	62	1		6	1	19	0
Aizaz Cheema	28.4	11	79	4		11.3	5	24	4
Junaid Khan	29	14	55	1	(5)	2	0	9	0
Saeed Ajmal	54	13	143	4	(3)	22	4	53	2
Mohammad Hafeez	9	1	30	0	(4)	15	4	31	4
Azhar Ali	6	1	23	0					

ZIMBABWE	O	M	R	W		O	M	R	W
Vitori	25	3	103	0	(3)	2	0	15	0
Jarvis	24	4	79	1	(1)	5	0	17	1
Mpofu	22	5	64	2					
Price	50.1	24	69	2	(2)	10.4	2	35	2
Lamb	28	2	120	3	(4)	4	0	21	0
Masakadza	7	2	13	1					

FALL OF WICKETS

Wkt	1st Z	1st P	2nd Z	2nd P
1st	71	8	9	19
2nd	91	196	19	49
3rd	111	218	31	80
4th	176	318	31	–
5th	270	357	45	–
6th	365	415	61	–
7th	374	424	61	–
8th	394	455	69	–
9th	394	466	135	–
10th	412	466	141	–

Umpires: I.J.Gould (*England*) (21) and R.J.Tucker (*Australia*) (12).
Referee: D.C.Boon (*Australia*) (1).   **Test No. 2007/15 (Z85/P359)**

PAKISTAN v SRI LANKA (1st Test)

At Sheikh Zayed Stadium, Abu Dhabi, on 18, 19, 20, 21, 22 October 2011.
Toss: Pakistan. Result: **MATCH DRAWN**.
Debut: Sri Lanka – A.N.P.R.Fernando (also known as Nuwan Pradeep).

SRI LANKA

Batsman	1st innings		2nd innings	
N.T.Paranavitana	c Akmal b Gul	37	lbw b Gul	0
H.D.R.L.Thirimanne	c Younus Khan b Ajmal	20	run out	68
K.C.Sangakkara	c Akmal b Cheema	2	lbw b Ali	211
D.P.M.D.Jayawardena	c Hafeez b Junaid Khan	28	b Ajmal	4
*T.M.Dilshan	c Akmal b Ajmal	19	b Junaid Khan	9
A.D.Mathews	not out	52	lbw b Gul	22
†H.A.P.W.Jayawardena	b Junaid Khan	0	c Akmal b Cheema	120
H.M.R.K.B.Herath	lbw b Junaid Khan	0	not out	23
R.A.S.Lakmal	c Hafeez b Gul	18	(10) b Gul	0
U.W.M.B.C.A.Welagedara	c Umar b Junaid Khan	11	(9) c Akmal b Gul	8
A.N.P.R.Fernando	c Akmal b Junaid Khan	1	run out	0
Extras	(LB 3, W 1, NB 5)	9	(B 4, LB 11, NB 3)	18
Total	(74.1 overs; 334 mins)	197	(168 overs; 707 mins)	483

PAKISTAN

Batsman	1st innings		2nd innings	
Mohammad Hafeez	lbw b Herath	75	not out	12
Taufiq Umar	run out	236	lbw b Welagedara	2
Azhar Ali	b Welagedara	70	not out	4
Younus Khan	lbw b Welagedara	33		
*Misbah-ul-Haq	c H.A.P.W.Jayawardena b Herath	46		
Asad Shafiq	not out	26		
Umar Gul	c Mathews b Herath	0		
†Adnan Akmal				
Aizaz Cheema				
Saeed Ajmal				
Junaid Khan				
Extras	(B 3, LB 3, W 3, NB 16)	25	(NB 3)	3
Total	(6 wkts dec; 174.4 overs; 710 mins)	511	(1 wkt; 10 overs; 37 mins)	21

PAKISTAN	O	M	R	W		O	M	R	W
Umar Gul	11	1	37	2		25	3	64	4
Aizaz Cheema	15	5	51	1		32	1	108	1
Mohammad Hafeez	9	3	12	0	(5)	22	4	42	0
Junaid Khan	14.1	3	38	5		31	6	83	1
Saeed Ajmal	25	5	56	2	(3)	55	8	167	1
Azhar Ali						3	1	4	1
SRI LANKA									
Welagedara	30	5	80	2		5	2	9	1
Lakmal	24	3	108	0		2	1	1	0
Herath	61.4	16	126	3		2	0	8	0
Fernando	27	1	107	0		1	0	3	0
Dilshan	32	6	84	0					

FALL OF WICKETS

Wkt	1st SL	1st P	2nd SL	2nd P
1st	48	118	0	7
2nd	51	278	153	–
3rd	79	360	160	–
4th	112	436	191	–
5th	112	511	233	–
6th	112	511	434	–
7th	114	–	466	–
8th	168	–	477	–
9th	193	–	481	–
10th	197	–	483	–

Umpires: A.L.Hill (*New Zealand*) (26) and R.J.Tucker (*Australia*) (13).
Referee: D.C.Boon (*Australia*) (2).   **Test No. 2008/38 (P360/SL205)**

PAKISTAN v SRI LANKA (2nd Test)

At Dubai International Cricket Stadium, on 26, 27, 28, 29 October 2011.
Toss: Sri Lanka. Result: **PAKISTAN** won by nine wickets.
Debut: Sri Lanka – J.K.Silva.

SRI LANKA

N.T.Paranavitana	c Misbah-ul-Haq b Gul	6	c Younus Khan b Ajmal	72
H.D.R.L.Thirimanne	lbw b Gul	1	b Hafeez	8
K.C.Sangakkara	c Shafiq b Rehman	78	lbw b Rehman	30
D.P.M.D.Jayawardena	c Misbah-ul-Haq b Gul	6	b Ajmal	5
*T.M.Dilshan	c Misbah-ul-Haq b Junaid Khan	7	lbw b Junaid Khan	3
A.D.Mathews	c Akmal b Junaid Khan	19	not out	52
†J.K.Silva	lbw b Rehman	20	c Ajmal b Junaid Khan	8
K.T.G.D.Prasad	c Akmal b Ajmal	7	b Rehman	33
H.M.R.K.B.Herath	c Younus Khan b Ajmal	29	c Misbah-ul-Haq b Ajmal	15
U.W.M.B.C.A.Welagedara	st Akmal b Ajmal	48	lbw b Ajmal	4
R.A.S.Lakmal	not out	0	b Ajmal	8
Extras	(B 5, LB 7, NB 6)	18	(B 14, LB 3, NB 2)	19
Total	(79 overs; 327 mins)	239	(109.5 overs; 452 mins)	257

PAKISTAN

Mohammad Hafeez	lbw b Prasad	33	not out	59
Taufiq Umar	c Silva b Prasad	27	b Herath	1
Azhar Ali	lbw b Dilshan	100	not out	29
Younus Khan	b Dilshan	55		
*Misbah-ul-Haq	c Jayawardena b Welagedara	41		
Saeed Ajmal	c Mathews b Welagedara	20		
Asad Shafiq	c Jayawardena b Prasad	59		
†Adnan Akmal	c Silva b Dilshan	41		
Abdur Rehman	b Herath	0		
Umar Gul	lbw b Herath	2		
Junaid Khan	not out	0		
Extras	(B 10, LB 10, W 2, NB 3)	25	(B 4, LB 1)	5
Total	(141.1 overs; 593 mins)	403	(1 wkt; 24.1 overs; 83 mins)	94

PAKISTAN	O	M	R	W		O	M	R	W	FALL OF WICKETS				
Umar Gul	19	2	78	3		15	3	39	0		SL	P	SL	P
Junaid Khan	15	2	57	2		17	4	38	2	Wkt	1st	1st	2nd	2nd
Saeed Ajmal	26	9	45	3	(5)	30.5	9	68	5	1st	3	63	22	17
Abdur Rehman	17	5	40	2		33	7	65	2	2nd	24	64	95	–
Mohammad Hafeez	2	0	7	0	(3)	14	2	30	1	3rd	30	181	113	–
										4th	45	275	116	–
SRI LANKA										5th	73	283	141	–
Welagedara	29	7	79	2	(2)	2	1	1	0	6th	127	324	166	–
Prasad	32	2	104	3	(1)	3	0	23	0	7th	154	394	222	–
Herath	37	5	89	2		10.1	2	29	1	8th	154	397	243	–
Lakmal	24	8	54	0						9th	229	399	247	–
Dilshan	19.1	1	57	3	(4)	9	0	36	0	10th	239	403	257	–

Umpires: A.L.Hill (*New Zealand*) (27) and S.K.Tarapore (*India*) (1).
Referee: D.C.Boon (*Australia*) (3).   Test No. 2009/39 (P361/SL206)

PAKISTAN v SRI LANKA (3rd Test)

At Sharjah Cricket Stadium, on 3, 4, 5, 6, 7 November 2011.
Toss: Sri Lanka. Result: **MATCH DRAWN**.
Debut: Sri Lanka – C.K.B.Kulasekara. ‡ H.D.R.L.Thirimanne

SRI LANKA

N.T.Paranavitana	c Younus Khan b Gul	4	not out		76
*T.M.Dilshan	c Younus Khan b Ajmal	92	c Hafeez b Gul		4
K.C.Sangakkara	c Younus Khan b Ajmal	144	c Shafiq b Hafeez		51
D.P.M.D.Jayawardena	lbw b Junaid Khan	39	lbw b Gul		20
A.D.Mathews	c Akmal b Rehman	17	lbw b Ajmal		13
†J.K.Silva	c Ali b Ajmal	39	lbw b Ajmal		0
C.K.B.Kulasekara	lbw b Ajmal	15	b Ajmal		7
H.K.S.R.Kaluhalamulla	lbw b Gul	1			
K.T.G.D.Prasad	c Akmal b Junaid Khan	17			
H.M.R.K.B.Herath	not out	34	(8) not out		1
U.W.M.B.C.A.Welagedara	b Gul	0			
Extras	(LB 5, NB 6)	11	(LB 6, W 1, NB 2)		9
Total	**(153.3 overs)**	**413**	**(6 wkts dec; 58 overs; 259 mins)**		**181**

PAKISTAN

Mohammad Hafeez	c Jayawardena b Welagedara	6	run out		13
Taufiq Umar	st Silva b Herath	19	c Sangakkara b Kaluhalamulla		39
Azhar Ali	b Kulasekara	53	lbw b Herath		7
Younus Khan	b Welagedara	122	c sub‡ b Welagedara		11
*Misbah-ul-Haq	c Dilshan b Kaluhalamulla	89	not out		9
Asad Shafiq	c Silva b Welagedara	16	not out		7
†Adnan Akmal	lbw b Herath	7			
Abdur Rehman	c Paranavitana b Welagedara	3			
Umar Gul	c Mathews b Herath	5			
Saeed Ajmal	not out	12			
Junaid Khan	b Welagedara	0			
Extras	(LB 2, W 3, NB 3)	8	(LB 1)		1
Total	**(138.2 overs)**	**340**	**(4 wkts; 57 overs)**		**87**

PAKISTAN	O	M	R	W		O	M	R	W
Umar Gul	29.3	10	76	3		15	1	44	2
Junaid Khan	27	4	94	2		5	3	9	0
Saeed Ajmal	51	4	132	4	(5)	16	2	50	3
Abdur Rehman	45	14	103	1	(3)	12	1	38	0
Mohammad Hafeez	1	0	3	0	(4)	10	1	34	1
SRI LANKA									
Welagedara	35.2	10	87	5		9	3	19	1
Prasad	4	0	9	0					
Kulasekara	25	7	65	1	(2)	3	0	15	0
Herath	42	14	85	3	(3)	22	14	19	1
Kaluhalamulla	25	5	74	1	(4)	19	9	21	1
Dilshan	7	1	18	0	(5)	4	0	12	0

FALL OF WICKETS

	SL	P	SL	P
Wkt	1st	1st	2nd	2nd
1st	4	8	5	20
2nd	177	35	80	30
3rd	261	133	127	57
4th	300	233	155	77
5th	304	258	155	–
6th	330	277	178	–
7th	331	282	–	–
8th	359	289	–	–
9th	413	336	–	–
10th	413	340	–	–

Umpires: S.K.Tarapore (*India*) (2) and S.J.A.Taufel (*Australia*) (70).
Referee: D.C.Boon (*Australia*) (4).   **Test No. 2010/40 (P362/SL207)**

BANGLADESH v WEST INDIES (1st Test)

At Zahur Ahmed Chowdhury Stadium, Chittagong, on 21, 22‡, 23‡, 24, 25 October 2011.
Toss: Bangladesh. Result: **MATCH DRAWN**.
Debuts: Bangladesh – Elias Sunny, Nasir Hossain. ‡ no play

BANGLADESH

Tamim Iqbal	c Brathwaite b Samuels	52	c Baugh b Sammy	37
Imrul Kayes	c Baugh b Rampaul	10	c Baugh b Rampaul	13
Shahriar Nafees	c Baugh b F.H.Edwards	32	b Samuels	50
Raqibul Hasan	lbw b Sammy	41	not out	10
†*Mushfiqur Rahim	c Bishoo b F.H.Edwards	68	not out	2
Shakib Al Hasan	c Baugh b Samuels	40		
Naeem Islam	not out	36		
Nasir Hossain	c Baugh b Bishoo	34		
Elias Sunny	c Sammy b Bishoo	0		
Shahadat Hossain	st Baugh b Bishoo	9		
Rubel Hossain	not out	5		
Extras	(B 8, LB 5, W 5, NB 5)	23	(B 4, LB 2, NB 1)	7
Total	**(9 wkts dec; 122.4 overs)**	**350**	**(3 wkts dec; 42 overs)**	**119**

WEST INDIES

L.M.P.Simmons	c Raqibul b Shahadat	7	c Rubel b Shakib	44
K.C.Brathwaite	c Kayes b Sunny	33	lbw b Sunny	0
K.A.Edwards	lbw b Sunny	17	not out	28
D.M.Bravo	c Nafees b Sunny	2	not out	24
S.Chanderpaul	c Nafees b Sunny	49		
M.N.Samuels	c Raqibul b Sunny	24		
†C.S.Baugh	b Sunny	30		
*D.J.G.Sammy	b Shakib	58		
R.Rampaul	c Mushfiqur b Shakib	8		
F.H.Edwards	not out	0		
D.Bishoo	b Shakib	0		
Extras	(B 2, LB 2, NB 7, Pen 5)	16	(LB 2, NB 2)	4
Total	**(68 overs)**	**244**	**(2 wkts; 22 overs)**	**100**

WEST INDIES	O	M	R	W	O	M	R	W
F.H.Edwards	18.4	1	88	2	9	0	37	0
Rampaul	23	8	42	1	11	1	26	1
Sammy	26	8	53	1 (4)	6	1	9	1
Samuels	25	4	73	2 (3)	16	3	41	1
Bishoo	30	6	81	3				

BANGLADESH	O	M	R	W	O	M	R	W
Shahadat Hossain	5	1	19	1 (2)	4	0	21	0
Rubel Hossain	15	2	52	0 (4)	2	0	3	0
Shakib Al Hasan	18	2	53	3	6	1	34	1
Elias Sunny	23	0	94	6 (1)	6	0	34	1
Nasir Hossain	7	1	17	0	2	0	2	0
Naeem Islam					2	0	4	0

FALL OF WICKETS

	B	WI	B	WI
Wkt	1st	1st	2nd	2nd
1st	26	19	32	5
2nd	110	44	72	58
3rd	159	52	116	–
4th	238	114	–	–
5th	255	137	–	–
6th	274	152	–	–
7th	317	212	–	–
8th	317	229	–	–
9th	345	244	–	–
10th	–	244	–	–

Umpires: H.D.P.K.Dharmasena (*Sri Lanka*) (4) and N.J.Llong (*England*) (10).
Referee: A.J.Pycroft (*Zimbabwe*) (19).   **Test No. 2011/7 (B70/WI474)**
Shahriar Nafees (21*) retired at 58-1 and resumed his innings at 255-5.

BANGLADESH v WEST INDIES (2nd Test)

At Shere Bangla National Stadium, Mirpur, on 29, 30, 31 October, 1, 2 November 2011.
Toss: West Indies. Result: **WEST INDIES** won by 229 runs.
Debut: Bangladesh – Suhrawadi Shuvo.

WEST INDIES

K.C.Brathwaite	c Kayes b Rubel	50	run out		0
K.O.A.Powell	b Shuvo	72	c Nasir b Shakib		12
K.A.Edwards	lbw b Shakib	121	b Shuvo		86
D.M.Bravo	lbw b Nasir	12	c Mushfiqur b Shuvo		195
S.Chanderpaul	c Mushfiqur b Nasir	18	(6) not out		59
K.A.J.Roach	b Shakib	6	(5) c Islam b Shuvo		12
M.N.Samuels	c and b Nasir	48			
†C.S.Baugh	c Kayes b Shakib	6			
*D.J.G.Sammy	hit wkt b Shakib	1			
F.H.Edwards	lbw b Shakib	9			
D.Bishoo	not out	2			
Extras	(B 2, LB 4, W 3, NB 1)	10	(B 6, LB 4, W 5, NB 4)		19
Total	**(126.4 overs; 512 mins)**	**355**	**(5 wkts dec; 111.3 overs)**		**383**

BANGLADESH

Tamim Iqbal	c Bravo b F.H.Edwards	14	c Sammy b Bishoo		83
Imrul Kayes	c Brathwaite b F.H.Edwards	29	c K.A.Edwards b F.H.Edwards		9
Shahriar Nafees	c Bravo b F.H.Edwards	7	c and b Sammy		18
Raqibul Hasan	lbw b F.H.Edwards	0	c Sammy b Samuels		17
†*Mushfiqur Rahim	c Chanderpaul b F.H.Edwards	0	b Bishoo		69
Shakib Al Hasan	b Bishoo	73	c Chanderpaul b Sammy		55
Naeem Islam	run out	45	lbw b Bishoo		3
Nasir Hossain	c K.A.Edwards b Samuels	42	lbw b Bishoo		3
Suhrawadi Shuvo	c Brathwaite b Bishoo	15	c Sammy b Bishoo		0
Shahadat Hossain	b Bishoo	4	not out		1
Rubel Hossain	not out	2	b Roach		7
Extras		–	(B 6, LB 1, NB 6)		13
Total	**(68 overs)**	**231**	**(80.2 overs)**		**278**

BANGLADESH	O	M	R	W		O	M	R	W		FALL OF WICKETS				
Shahadat Hossain	16	1	76	0	(6)	11	0	57	0			WI	B	WI	B
Rubel Hossain	24	3	71	1	(1)	12	2	36	0		*Wkt*	*1st*	*1st*	*2nd*	*2nd*
Shakib Al Hasan	34.4	12	63	5		21	1	79	1		1st	100	14	0	26
Nasir Hossain	25	6	52	3	(2)	25	5	78	0		2nd	155	36	33	73
Suhrawadi Shuvo	23	3	73	1		26.3	3	73	3		3rd	180	46	184	124
Naeem Islam	4	0	14	0	(4)	12	2	38	0		4th	226	46	240	168
Raqibul Hasan						4	0	12	0		5th	232	59	383	256
											6th	319	143	–	260
WEST INDIES											7th	337	195	–	264
F.H.Edwards	13	0	63	5		14	0	56	1		8th	339	225	–	264
Roach	9	0	52	0		13.2	2	49	1		9th	348	225	–	271
Sammy	10	3	32	0		13	4	19	2		10th	355	231	–	278
Bishoo	23	4	62	3		25	6	90	5						
Samuels	13	2	22	1		15	2	57	1						

Umpires: H.D.P.K.Dharmasena (*Sri Lanka*) (5) and N.J.Llong (*England*) (11).
Referee: A.J.Pycroft (*Zimbabwe*) (20).　　　　　**Test No. 2012/8 (B71/WI475)**

ZIMBABWE v NEW ZEALAND (Only Test)

At Queens Sports Club, Bulawayo, on 1, 2, 3, 4, 5 November 2011.
Toss: New Zealand. Result: **NEW ZEALAND** won by 34 runs.
Debuts: Zimbabwe – R.W.Chakabva, N.Ncube, M.N.Waller;
New Zealand – D.A.J.Bracewell, D.G.Brownlie.

NEW ZEALAND

M.J.Guptill	c Taibu b Masakadza	109	(2) b Jarvis		0
B.B.McCullum	b Jarvis	14	(1) lbw b Price		11
K.S.Williamson	run out	49	lbw b Jarvis		68
*L.R.P.L.Taylor	c Chakabva b Ncube	76	(5) lbw b Jarvis		76
B.J.Watling	c Chakabva b Mpofu	39	(6) c Taylor b Price		3
D.G.Brownlie	c Taylor b Price	63	(8) b Jarvis		9
D.L.Vettori	c Taylor b Mpofu	40	c Ncube b Mpofu		31
†R.A.Young	not out	9	(9) not out		35
D.A.J.Bracewell	b Mpofu	0	(10) not out		1
J.S.Patel	c Mawoyo b Mpofu	12	(4) b Jarvis		9
C.S.Martin	b Price	0			
Extras	(B 7, LB 3, W 2, NB 3)	15	(B 3, LB 3, NB 3)		9
Total	(143.3 overs; 582 mins)	426	(8 wkts dec; 71 overs; 313 mins)		252

ZIMBABWE

T.M.K.Mawoyo	c Watling b Vettori	5	b Guptill		52
V.Sibanda	c Taylor b Brownlie	93	lbw b Bracewell		13
H.Masakadza	b Bracewell	22	c Brownlie b Bracewell		19
*B.R.M.Taylor	lbw b Vettori	50	c Watling b Martin		117
T.Taibu	c Patel b Vettori	20	c Guptill b Vettori		63
M.N.Waller	not out	72	lbw b Vettori		29
†R.W.Chakabva	run out	37	c Young b Bracewell		5
R.W.Price	lbw b Vettori	0	(9) c Young b Bracewell		4
K.M.Jarvis	c Taylor b Martin	6	(10) not out		2
C.B.Mpofu	c Williamson b Vettori	0	(11) lbw b Vettori		0
N.Ncube	b Martin	3	(8) b Bracewell		14
Extras	(LB 3, W 1, NB 1)	5	(B 5, LB 4, NB 4)		13
Total	(121.5 overs; 461 mins)	313	(108.1 overs; 453 mins)		331

ZIMBABWE	O	M	R	W		O	M	R	W
Jarvis	28	6	98	1		18	1	64	5
Ncube	25	4	80	1		10	0	41	0
Mpofu	34	10	92	4	(4)	14	1	54	1
Price	42.3	7	118	2	(3)	29	5	87	2
Masakadza	11	4	20	1					
Waller	3	0	8	0					

NEW ZEALAND	O	M	R	W		O	M	R	W
Martin	25.5	6	74	2		22	3	85	1
Bracewell	23	12	51	1		25	2	85	5
Vettori	43	13	70	5		38.1	14	71	3
Patel	23	1	91	0		13	1	51	0
Brownlie	4	0	13	1	(6)	1	0	2	0
Williamson	2	0	9	0					
Guptill	1	0	2	0	(5)	9	0	28	1

FALL OF WICKETS

	NZ	Z	NZ	Z
Wkt	1st	1st	2nd	2nd
1st	40	24	5	25
2nd	115	83	23	61
3rd	247	159	36	157
4th	275	193	155	265
5th	320	198	167	287
6th	401	284	179	303
7th	407	286	199	321
8th	407	299	236	329
9th	425	300	–	329
10th	426	313	–	331

Umpires: M.Erasmus (*South Africa*) (7) and B.N.J.Oxenford (*Australia*) (3).
Referee: B.C.Broad (*England*) (48).   Test No. 2013/14 (Z86/NZ365)

INDIA v WEST INDIES (1st Test)

At Feroz Shah Kotla, Delhi, on 6, 7, 8, 9 November 2011.
Toss: West Indies. Result: **INDIA** won by five wickets.
Debuts: India – R.Ashwin, U.Yadav.

WEST INDIES

K.C.Brathwaite	st Dhoni b Ojha	63		lbw b Ojha	2
K.O.A.Powell	lbw b Ojha	14		c Gambhir b Ashwin	0
K.A.Edwards	c and b Ojha	15		b Yadav	33
D.M.Bravo	b Ashwin	12	(5)	lbw b Ashwin	12
S.Chanderpaul	lbw b Sharma	118	(6)	lbw b Ashwin	47
M.N.Samuels	c Dhoni b Ashwin	15	(7)	b Ashwin	0
†C.S.Baugh	lbw b Ojha	27	(8)	c Dhoni b Yadav	7
*D.J.G.Sammy	lbw b Ojha	5	(9)	b Ashwin	42
R.Rampaul	lbw b Ashwin	12	(10)	c Ojha b Ashwin	18
F.H.Edwards	c Sehwag b Ojha	10	(4)	c Dhoni b Sharma	1
D.Bishoo	not out	0		not out	9
Extras	(B 4, LB 8, NB 1)	13		(B 1, LB 8)	9
Total	**(108.2 overs; 442 mins)**	**304**		**(57.3 overs; 235 mins)**	**180**

INDIA

G.Gambhir	run out	41		lbw b Samuels	22
V.Sehwag	st Baugh b Bishoo	55		b Sammy	55
R.S.Dravid	c Sammy b Rampaul	54		b F.H.Edwards	31
S.R.Tendulkar	lbw b F.H.Edwards	7		lbw b Bishoo	76
V.V.S.Laxman	c Baugh b Bishoo	1		not out	58
Yuvraj Singh	c K.A.Edwards b Sammy	23		b Sammy	18
*†M.S.Dhoni	b Sammy	0		not out	0
R.Ashwin	c Baugh b Sammy	0			
I.Sharma	c Baugh b Samuels	17			
P.P.Ojha	not out	3			
U.Yadav	b Rampaul	0			
Extras	(B 5, W 1, NB 2)	8		(B 1, LB 14, NB 1)	16
Total	**(52.5 overs; 247 mins)**	**209**		**(4 wkts; 80.4 overs; 339 mins)**	**276**

INDIA	O	M	R	W		O	M	R	W
Sharma	25	5	80	1	(4)	14	2	49	1
Yadav	19	5	52	0	(5)	7	0	36	2
Ojha	34.2	9	72	6	(1)	14	4	37	1
Ashwin	27	4	81	3	(2)	21.3	5	47	6
Sehwag	2	0	5	0					
Yuvraj Singh	1	0	2	0	(3)	1	0	2	0

WEST INDIES	O	M	R	W		O	M	R	W
F.H.Edwards	11	1	57	1		15	3	51	1
Rampaul	14.5	2	44	2		10	0	34	0
Sammy	8	1	35	3		16	0	56	2
Bishoo	14	0	55	2	(5)	22	2	56	1
Samuels	5	0	13	1	(4)	16	0	57	1
Brathwaite						1.4	0	7	0

FALL OF WICKETS

	WI	I	WI	I
Wkt	1st	1st	2nd	2nd
1st	25	89	0	51
2nd	45	100	17	95
3rd	72	113	26	162
4th	180	120	53	233
5th	200	152	63	275
6th	269	152	63	–
7th	281	154	84	–
8th	281	203	124	–
9th	304	209	157	–
10th	304	209	180	–

Umpires: H.D.P.K.Dharmasena (*Sri Lanka*) (6) and R.J.Tucker (*Australia*) (14).
Referee: J.J.Crowe (*New Zealand*) (47). **Test No. 2014/86 (1456/WI476)**

INDIA v WEST INDIES (2nd Test)

At Eden Gardens, Kolkata, on 14, 15, 16, 17 November 2011.
Toss: India. Result: **INDIA** won by an innings and 15 runs.
Debuts: None.

INDIA

G.Gambhir	c Barath b F.H.Edwards	65
V.Sehwag	c Barath b Sammy	38
R.S.Dravid	b Brathwaite	119
S.R.Tendulkar	c Samuels b Bishoo	38
V.V.S.Laxman	not out	176
I.Sharma	c Baugh b Roach	0
Yuvraj Singh	lbw b Sammy	25
*†M.S.Dhoni	c Baugh b Roach	144
R.Ashwin	not out	4
P.P.Ojha		
U.Yadav		
Extras	(B 6, LB 5, W 2, NB 9)	22
Total	**(7 wkts dec; 151.2 overs; 615 mins)**	**631**

WEST INDIES

A.B.Barath	c Sehwag b Yadav	1	c Laxman b Sharma	62
K.C.Brathwaite	c Gambhir b Ashwin	17	c Dhoni b Yadav	9
K.A.Edwards	lbw b Ojha	16	lbw b Sharma	60
D.M.Bravo	b Yadav	30	c Dravid b Ojha	136
S.Chanderpaul	lbw b Ashwin	4	b Yadav	47
M.N.Samuels	b Yadav	25	lbw b Ashwin	84
†C.S.Baugh	lbw b Ojha	13	c Dravid b Ojha	3
*D.J.G.Sammy	c Dhoni b Ojha	18	b Yadav	32
K.A.J.Roach	run out	2	b Ashwin	1
F.H.Edwards	lbw b Ojha	16	not out	15
D.Bishoo	not out	8	b Yadav	0
Extras	(LB 3)	3	(B 9, LB 4, W 1)	14
Total	**(48 overs; 179 mins)**	**153**	**(126.3 overs; 515 mins)**	**463**

WEST INDIES	O	M	R	W	O	M	R	W
F.H.Edwards	22.2	1	81	1				
Sammy	25	0	132	2				
Roach	26	1	106	2				
Samuels	27	0	104	0				
Bishoo	45	2	154	1				
Brathwaite	6	0	43	1				
INDIA								
Ojha	22	5	64	4	(3) 32	5	104	2
Yadav	7	1	23	3	(1) 17.3	1	80	4
Ashwin	14	3	49	2	(4) 40	4	137	2
Sharma	5	2	14	0	(2) 25	4	95	2
Yuvraj Singh					3	0	14	0
Sehwag					9	2	20	0

FALL OF WICKETS			
	I	WI	WI
Wkt	1st	1st	2nd
1st	66	3	23
2nd	149	30	117
3rd	205	42	161
4th	345	46	269
5th	346	92	401
6th	396	99	411
7th	620	120	417
8th	–	129	421
9th	–	129	463
10th	–	153	463

Umpires: B.N.J.Oxenford (*Australia*) (4) and R.J.Tucker (*Australia*) (15).
Referee: J.J.Crowe (*New Zealand*) (48). **Test No. 2015/87 (I457/WI477)**

INDIA v WEST INDIES (3rd Test)

At Wankhede Stadium, Mumbai, on 22, 23, 24, 25, 26 November 2011.
Toss: West Indies. Result: **MATCH DRAWN (SCORES LEVEL)**.
Debut: India – V.R.Aaron.

WEST INDIES

A.B.Barath	c Dhoni b Ashwin	62	c Laxman b Ojha		3
K.C.Brathwaite	c Kohli b Ashwin	68	c Tendulkar b Ojha		35
K.A.Edwards	c Dhoni b Sharma	86	st Dhoni b Ojha		17
D.M.Bravo	c Dhoni b Aaron	166	c and b Ojha		48
K.O.A.Powell	c Dhoni b Ojha	81	lbw b Ashwin		11
M.N.Samuels	c Dravid b Ashwin	61	st Dhoni b Ojha		0
†C.S.Baugh	b Aaron	4	b Ashwin		1
*D.J.G.Sammy	c Dhoni b Aaron	3	c Dhoni b Ashwin		10
R.Rampaul	c Kohli b Ashwin	10	c Tendulkar b Ojha		0
F.H.Edwards	not out	11	not out		2
D.Bishoo	b Ashwin	12	lbw b Ashwin		0
Extras	(B 8, LB 16, NB 2)	26	(B 3, LB 4)		7
Total	(184.1 overs; 736 mins)	590	(57.2 overs; 225 mins)		134

INDIA

G.Gambhir	c Baugh b Rampaul	55	c Sammy b F.H.Edwards		12
V.Sehwag	b Sammy	37	c Sammy b Bishoo		60
R.S.Dravid	b Samuels	82	c sub (D.Ramdin) b Samuels		33
S.R.Tendulkar	c Sammy b Rampaul	94	c K.A.Edwards b Samuels		3
V.V.S.Laxman	c Samuels b F.H.Edwards	32	c Barath b Rampaul		31
V.Kohli	c F.H.Edwards b Bishoo	52	c Sammy b Bishoo		63
*†M.S.Dhoni	b Sammy	8	c K.A.Edwards b Rampaul		13
R.Ashwin	c Barath b Rampaul	103	run out		14
I.Sharma	c Bravo b Samuels	5	b Rampaul		10
V.R.Aaron	b Samuels	4	not out		2
P.P.Ojha	not out	0			
Extras	(B 1, W 4, NB 5)	10	(NB 1)		1
Total	(135.4 overs; 596 mins)	482	(9 wkts; 64 overs; 278 mins)		242

INDIA	O	M	R	W		O	M	R	W		FALL OF WICKETS		
												WI	WI	I
Sharma	32	9	84	1	(2)	8	2	15	0		Wkt	1st	1st	2nd	2nd
Aaron	28	4	106	3	(3)	4	0	23	0		1st	137	67	6	19
Ojha	48	10	126	1	(1)	27	5	47	6		2nd	150	138	30	101
Ashwin	52.1	6	156	5		15.2	0	34	4		3rd	314	224	91	106
Sehwag	16	1	61	0		2	0	3	0		4th	474	287	112	113
Kohli	2	0	9	0							5th	518	322	112	165
Tendulkar	6	0	24	0	(6)	1	0	5	0		6th	524	331	117	189
											7th	540	428	120	224
WEST INDIES											8th	563	455	129	239
F.H.Edwards	28	4	116	1		7	0	28	1		9th	566	463	134	242
Rampaul	24.4	3	95	3		16	1	56	3		10th	590	482	134	–
Sammy	26	3	90	2										
Samuels	17	0	74	3	(3)	25	0	93	2					
Bishoo	40	6	106	1	(4)	16	0	65	2					

Umpires: A.L.Hill (*New Zealand*) (28) and B.N.J.Oxenford (*Australia*) (5).
Referee: D.C.Boon (*Australia*) (5). Test No. 2016/88 (I458/WI478)

SOUTH AFRICA v AUSTRALIA (1st Test)

At Newlands, Cape Town, on 9, 10, 11 November 2011.
Toss: South Africa. Result: **SOUTH AFRICA** won by eight wickets.
Debuts: South Africa – Imran Tahir, V.D.Philander.

AUSTRALIA

S.R.Watson	c Kallis b Steyn	3		lbw b Steyn		4
P.J.Hughes	c Boucher b Philander	9		c Rudolph b Morkel		9
S.E.Marsh	lbw b Watson	44	(10)	lbw b Philander		0
R.T.Ponting	lbw b Steyn	8	(3)	lbw b Philander		0
*M.J.Clarke	b Morkel	151	(4)	lbw b Philander		2
M.E.K.Hussey	c Boucher b Morkel	1	(5)	c Prince b Morkel		0
†B.J.Haddin	c Prince b Steyn	5	(6)	c Boucher b Philander		0
M.G.Johnson	c Morkel b Philander	20	(7)	c Amla b Philander		3
R.J.Harris	c Morkel b Philander	5	(8)	c Smith b Morkel		3
P.M.Siddle	c De Villiers b Morkel	20	(9)	not out		12
N.M.Lyon	not out	1		c De Villiers b Steyn		14
Extras	(B 5, LB 7, W 1, NB 4)	17				–
Total	**(75 overs; 349 mins)**	**284**		**(18 overs; 95 mins)**		**47**

SOUTH AFRICA

J.A.Rudolph	b Harris	18	(2)	c Haddin b Siddle	14
*G.C.Smith	b Watson	37	(1)	not out	101
H.M.Amla	lbw b Watson	3		c Clarke b Johnson	112
J.H.Kallis	c Ponting b Watson	0		not out	2
A.B.de Villiers	lbw b Harris	8			
A.G.Prince	lbw b Watson	0			
†M.V.Boucher	lbw b Watson	4			
V.D.Philander	c Ponting b Harris	4			
D.W.Steyn	not out	9			
M.Morkel	run out	1			
Imran Tahir	b Harris	5			
Extras	(LB 4, W 1, NB 2)	7		(LB 4, W 1, NB 2)	7
Total	**(24.3 overs; 130 mins)**	**96**		**(2 wkts; 50.2 overs; 232 mins)**	**236**

SOUTH AFRICA	O	M	R	W		O	M	R	W
Steyn	20	4	55	4		5	1	23	2
Philander	21	3	63	3		7	3	15	5
Morkel	18	2	82	3		6	1	9	3
Imran Tahir	10	1	35	0					
Kallis	6	0	37	0					

AUSTRALIA	O	M	R	W		O	M	R	W
Harris	10.3	3	33	4		14	2	67	0
Johnson	5	0	26	0	(4)	11	1	61	1
Siddle	4	1	16	0	(2)	12.2	0	49	1
Watson	5	2	17	5	(3)	10	0	44	0
Lyon						3	1	11	0

FALL OF WICKETS

	A	SA	A	SA
Wkt	1st	1st	2nd	2nd
1st	9	24	4	27
2nd	13	49	11	222
3rd	40	49	13	–
4th	143	73	13	–
5th	158	73	15	–
6th	163	77	18	–
7th	202	77	21	–
8th	214	81	21	–
9th	273	83	21	–
10th	284	96	47	–

Umpires: B.R.Doctrove (*West Indies*) (34) and I.J.Gould (*England*) (22).
Referee: R.S.Mahanama (*Sri Lanka*) (33). **Test No. 2017/84 (SA359/A733)**

SOUTH AFRICA v AUSTRALIA (2nd Test)

At New Wanderers Stadium, Johannesburg, on 17, 18, 19, 20, 21 November 2011.
Toss: South Africa. Result: **AUSTRALIA** won by two wickets.
Debut: Australia – P.J.Cummins.

SOUTH AFRICA

J.A.Rudolph	c Haddin b Watson	30	(2) c Haddin b Cummins		24
*G.C.Smith	c Clarke b Johnson	11	(1) c Hughes b Lyon		36
H.M.Amla	c Ponting b Cummins	19	c Haddin b Johnson		105
J.H.Kallis	c Khawaja b Siddle	54	c Clarke b Cummins		2
A.B.de Villiers	c Cummins b Siddle	64	c Clarke b Cummins		73
A.G.Prince	c Johnson b Lyon	50	run out		2
†M.V.Boucher	c Lyon b Siddle	3	c Watson b Lyon		13
V.D.Philander	lbw b Lyon	0	c Haddin b Cummins		23
D.W.Steyn	not out	15	c Haddin b Cummins		41
M.Morkel	c Watson b Clarke	6	b Cummins		0
Imran Tahir	c Hughes b Clarke	0	not out		4
Extras	(B 9, LB 2, W 2, NB 1)	14	(B 5, LB 2, W 7, NB 2)		16
Total	**(71 overs; 313 mins)**	**266**	**(110 overs; 480 mins)**		**339**

AUSTRALIA

S.R.Watson	c Tahir b Kallis	88	b Philander		0
P.J.Hughes	c De Villiers b Philander	88	c Kallis b Philander		11
U.T.Khawaja	lbw b Steyn	12	c Kallis b Tahir		65
R.T.Ponting	lbw b Steyn	0	c Rudolph b Morkel		62
*M.J.Clarke	c De Villiers b Morkel	11	b Philander		2
M.E.K.Hussey	b Steyn	20	lbw b Philander		39
†B.J.Haddin	lbw b Tahir	16	c Boucher b Philander		55
M.G.Johnson	not out	38	not out		40
P.M.Siddle	b Tahir	0	c Tahir b Steyn		4
P.J.Cummins	c Boucher b Steyn	2	not out		13
N.M.Lyon	lbw b Tahir	2			
Extras	(B 4, LB 8, W 3, NB 4)	19	(B 1, LB 7, W 4, NB 7)		19
Total	**(76.4 overs; 360 mins)**	**296**	**(8 wkts; 86.5 overs; 401 mins)**		**310**

AUSTRALIA	O	M	R	W		O	M	R	W
Johnson	16.1	4	67	1	(2)	30	4	101	1
Cummins	15	3	38	1		29	5	79	6
Siddle	15	4	69	3		27	10	71	0
Watson	3.5	1	13	1					
Lyon	13	2	52	2	(4)	16	4	57	2
Hussey	4	0	10	0	(5)	5	0	14	0
Clarke	4	1	6	2	(6)	2	1	2	0
Ponting					(7)	1	0	8	0

FALL OF WICKETS

	SA	A	SA	A
Wkt	1st	1st	2nd	2nd
1st	24	174	40	0
2nd	43	192	75	19
3rd	123	193	90	141
4th	129	212	237	145
5th	241	228	249	165
6th	243	233	260	215
7th	243	255	266	287
8th	245	255	314	292
9th	258	285	314	–
10th	266	296	339	–

SOUTH AFRICA	O	M	R	W		O	M	R	W
Steyn	18	3	64	4	(2)	23	1	98	1
Philander	15	4	47	1	(1)	20	3	70	5
Morkel	17	4	62	1		19	6	43	1
Kallis	13	2	56	1	(5)	9	1	28	0
Imran Tahir	13.4	2	55	3	(4)	15.5	0	63	1

Umpires: B.F.Bowden (*New Zealand*) (69) and I.J.Gould (*England*) (23).
Referee: R.S.Mahanama (*Sri Lanka*) (34).   Test No. 2018/85 (SA360/A734)

AUSTRALIA v NEW ZEALAND (1st Test)

At Woolloongabba, Brisbane, on 1, 2, 3, 4 December 2011.
Toss: New Zealand. Result: **AUSTRALIA** won by nine wickets.
Debuts: Australia – J.L.Pattinson, M.A.Starc, D.A.Warner.

NEW ZEALAND

B.B.McCullum	c Warner b Starc	34	(2) c Ponting b Pattinson		1
M.J.Guptill	c Haddin b Siddle	13	(1) c Khawaja b Pattinson		12
K.S.Williamson	c Khawaja b Lyon	19	(4) c Ponting b Pattinson		0
*L.R.P.L.Taylor	b Pattinson	14	(5) c Haddin b Pattinson		0
J.D.Ryder	c Warner b Starc	6	(6) c Hussey b Lyon		36
D.G.Brownlie	not out	77	(7) c Warner b Siddle		42
D.L.Vettori	run out	96	(8) c Clarke b Hussey		17
†R.A.Young	c Clarke b Siddle	2	(9) not out		11
D.A.J.Bracewell	c Clarke b Lyon	0	(3) c Haddin b Pattinson		2
T.G.Southee	c Hussey b Lyon	17	c Warner b Lyon		8
C.S.Martin	b Lyon	1	c Starc b Lyon		0
Extras	(B 9, LB 1, W 3, NB 3)	16	(LB 15, W 2, NB 4)		21
Total	**(365 mins; 82.5 overs)**	**295**	**(223 mins; 49.4 overs)**		**150**

AUSTRALIA

D.A.Warner	c Young b Southee	3	(2) not out		12
P.J.Hughes	c Guptill b Martin	10	(1) c Guptill b Martin		7
U.T.Khawaja	run out	38	not out		0
R.T.Ponting	lbw b Martin	78			
*M.J.Clarke	c Southee b Martin	139			
M.E.K.Hussey	c Ryder b Vettori	15			
†B.J.Haddin	c Martin b Guptill	80			
P.M.Siddle	c Taylor b Vettori	0			
J.L.Pattinson	c Taylor b Bracewell	12			
M.A.Starc	not out	32			
N.M.Lyon	c Brownlie b Southee	5			
Extras	(LB 6, W 3, NB 6)	15			
Total	**(603 mins; 129.2 overs)**	**427**	**(1 wkt; 12 mins; 2.2 overs)**		**19**

AUSTRALIA	O	M	R	W		O	M	R	W
Pattinson	15	1	64	4		11	5	27	5
Siddle	24	8	57	2		16	3	44	1
Starc	20	1	90	2		6	0	33	0
Lyon	21.5	1	69	4		11.4	2	19	3
Hussey	2	0	5	0		4	1	7	1
Warner						1	0	5	0

NEW ZEALAND	O	M	R	W		O	M	R	W
Vettori	37	13	88	2					
Southee	28.2	5	103	2	(1)	1	0	11	0
Martin	28	5	89	3	(2)	1	1	0	1
Bracewell	26	3	104	1	(3)	0.2	0	8	0
Guptill	3	0	18	1					
Brownlie	3	0	11	0					
Williamson	4	0	8	0					

FALL OF WICKETS

	NZ	A	NZ	A
Wkt	1st	1st	2nd	2nd
1st	44	3	10	11
2nd	56	25	17	–
3rd	78	91	17	–
4th	93	177	17	–
5th	96	237	28	–
6th	254	345	69	–
7th	256	345	121	–
8th	259	374	123	–
9th	290	418	141	–
10th	295	427	150	–

Umpires: Alim Dar (*Pakistan*) (68) and Asad Rauf (*Pakistan*) (39).
Referee: A.J.Pycroft (*Zimbabwe*) (21).   **Test No. 2019/51 (A735/NZ366)**

AUSTRALIA v NEW ZEALAND (2nd Test)

At Bellerive Oval, Hobart, on 9, 10, 11, 12 December 2011.
Toss: Australia. Result: **NEW ZEALAND** won by 7 runs.
Debut: New Zealand – T.A.Boult.

NEW ZEALAND

B.B.McCullum	c Haddin b Pattinson	16	(2)	c Hughes b Pattinson	12
M.J.Guptill	c Haddin b Siddle	3	(1)	c Haddin b Siddle	16
J.D.Ryder	lbw b Pattinson	0		st Haddin b Hussey	16
*L.R.P.L.Taylor	lbw b Siddle	6		c Clarke b Pattinson	56
K.S.Williamson	c Haddin b Starc	19		c Ponting b Siddle	34
D.G.Brownlie	b Pattinson	56		c Haddin b Pattinson	21
†R.A.Young	b Pattinson	0		lbw b Siddle	9
D.A.J.Bracewell	c Clarke b Siddle	12		b Lyon	4
T.G.Southee	b Starc	18		c Hussey b Lyon	13
T.A.Boult	not out	0		c Hussey b Lyon	21
C.S.Martin	b Pattinson	0		not out	2
Extras	(B 2, LB 12, W 1, NB 5)	20		(B 4, LB 11, W 5, NB 2)	22
Total	**(45.5 overs; 211 mins)**	**150**		**(78.3 overs; 349 mins)**	**226**

AUSTRALIA

D.A.Warner	c Taylor b Martin	15	(2)	not out	123
P.J.Hughes	c Guptill b Martin	4	(1)	c Guptill b Martin	20
U.T.Khawaja	c Young b Martin	7		c Taylor b Boult	23
R.T.Ponting	lbw b Southee	5		c Southee b Bracewell	16
*M.J.Clarke	b Bracewell	22		c Taylor b Bracewell	0
M.E.K.Hussey	c Young b Boult	8		lbw b Bracewell	0
†B.J.Haddin	c McCullum b Bracewell	5		c Taylor b Southee	15
P.M.Siddle	c Guptill b Bracewell	36		c Ryder b Southee	2
J.L.Pattinson	c Williamson b Boult	17		c Guptill b Bracewell	4
M.A.Starc	lbw b Boult	4		b Bracewell	0
N.M.Lyon	not out	1		b Bracewell	9
Extras	(B 1, LB 8, NB 3)	12		(B 3, LB 18)	21
Total	**(51 overs)**	**136**		**(63.4 overs; 317 mins)**	**233**

AUSTRALIA	O	M	R	W		O	M	R	W
Pattinson	13.5	3	51	5		21	7	54	3
Siddle	13	3	42	3		25	11	66	3
Starc	11	4	30	2		19	6	47	0
Lyon	8	4	13	0	(5)	7.3	1	25	3
Hussey					(4)	5	0	15	1
Ponting						1	0	4	0

NEW ZEALAND	O	M	R	W	O	M	R	W
Martin	16	1	46	3	16	4	44	1
Boult	13	4	29	3	12	1	51	1
Southee	12	2	32	1	19	3	77	2
Bracewell	10	3	20	3	16.4	4	40	6

FALL OF WICKETS

	NZ	A	NZ	A
Wkt	1st	1st	2nd	2nd
1st	10	7	36	72
2nd	11	24	36	122
3rd	25	31	73	159
4th	56	35	139	159
5th	60	58	171	159
6th	60	69	178	192
7th	105	75	190	194
8th	146	131	203	199
9th	150	131	203	199
10th	150	136	226	233

Umpires: Asad Rauf (*Pakistan*) (40) and N.J.Llong (*England*) (12).
Referee: A.J.Pycroft (*Zimbabwe*) (22).　　　　Test No. 2020/52 (A736/NZ367)

BANGLADESH v PAKISTAN (1st Test)

At Zahur Ahmed Chowdhury Stadium, Chittagong, on 9, 10, 11, 12 December 2011.
Toss: Pakistan. Result: **PAKISTAN** won by an innings and 184 runs.
Debut: Bangladesh – Nazimuddin.

BANGLADESH

Tamim Iqbal	c Akmal b Cheema	9	b Hafeez		15
Nazimuddin	c Hafeez b Gul	31	c Ajmal b Rehman		78
Shahriar Nafees	c Khan b Cheema	0	lbw b Ajmal		28
Mohammad Ashraful	c Akmal b Gul	1	c Hafeez b Rehman		0
†*Mushfiqur Rahim	lbw b Ajmal	4	(7) lbw b Rehman		49
Shakib Al Hasan	c Hafeez b Rehman	8	lbw b Rehman		51
Mahmudullah	lbw b Ajmal	18	b Ajmal		0
Nasir Hossain	c Ali b Rehman	41	(5) c Hafeez b Cheema		3
Elias Sunny	c Khan b Ajmal	2	not out		20
Shahadat Hossain	b Rehman	8	c Gul b Cheema		21
Rubel Hossain	not out	3	absent hurt		
Extras	(LB 9, NB 1)	10	(B 2, LB 5, NB 3)		10
Total	**(51.2 overs; 231 mins)**	**135**	**(82.3 overs; 344 mins)**		**275**

PAKISTAN

Mohammad Hafeez	lbw b Sunny	143
Taufeeq Umar	lbw b Mahmudullah	61
Azhar Ali	c Rahim b Shahadat	26
Younus Khan	not out	200
*Misbah-ul-Haq	lbw b Sunny	20
Asad Shafiq	c Nafees b Sunny	104
†Adnan Akmal	not out	6
Abdur Rehman		
Umar Gul		
Saeed Ajmal		
Aizaz Cheema		
Extras	(LB 21, W 1, NB 12)	34
Total	**(5 wkts dec; 176.5 overs; 707 mins)**	**594**

PAKISTAN	O	M	R	W		O	M	R	W	FALL OF WICKETS		
Mohammad Hafeez	3	1	9	0	(3)	7	2	21	1		B	P	B
Umar Gul	13	5	33	2	(1)	13	2	45	0	Wkt	1st	1st	2nd
Aizaz Cheema	11	4	35	2	(2)	7.3	1	40	2	1st	17	164	24
Saeed Ajmal	18	5	40	3		25	7	74	2	2nd	19	220	74
Abdur Rehman	6.2	2	9	3		30	7	88	4	3rd	20	265	75
										4th	28	311	80
BANGLADESH										5th	47	570	158
Shahadat Hossain	27	3	113	1						6th	71	–	205
Rubel Hossain	25	1	97	0						7th	81	–	210
Mahmudullah	30	7	94	1						8th	97	–	252
Shakib Al Hasan	41.5	7	121	1						9th	118	–	275
Elias Sunny	47	7	123	3						10th	135	–	–
Nasir Hossain	2	0	5	0									
Mohammad Ashraful	4	0	20	0									

Umpires: B.R.Doctrove (*West Indies*) (35) and S.K.Tarapore (*India*) (3).
Referee: J.Srinath (*India*) (18). **Test No. 2021/7 (B72/P363)**

BANGLADESH v PAKISTAN (2nd Test)

At Shere Bangla National Stadium, Mirpur, on 17, 18, 19, 20, 21 December 2011.
Toss: Pakistan. Result: **PAKISTAN** won by seven wickets.
Debuts: None.

BANGLADESH

Tamim Iqbal	c Cheema b Gul	14	c Misbah b Gul		21
Nazimuddin	lbw b Cheema	0	b Rehman		12
Shahriar Nafees	c Akmal b Gul	97	lbw b Gul		0
Mahmudullah	b Cheema	0	c Rehman b Cheema		32
Nasir Hossain	c Akmal b Cheema	7	b Rehman		79
Shakib Al Hasan	run out	144	c Ali b Cheema		6
†*Mushfiqur Rahim	c Akmal b Gul	40	c Ajmal b Rehman		53
Elias Sunny	lbw b Ajmal	12	b Ajmal		4
Shahadat Hossain	not out	21	c Khan b Rehman		1
Nazmul Hossain	run out	0	not out		8
Robiul Islam	lbw b Ajmal	0	st Akmal b Ajmal		0
Extras	(LB 3)	3	(B 9, LB 8, W 1)		18
Total	**(107.2 overs; 486 mins)**	**338**	**(82.1 overs; 325 mins)**		**234**

PAKISTAN

Mohammad Hafeez	c Rahim b Nazmul	14	c Shahadat b Shakib		47
Taufeeq Umar	c Nafees b Nazmul	130	c Nazimuddin b Nazmul		3
Azhar Ali	c Rahim b Shakib	57	b Sunny		34
Younus Khan	c Rahim b Sunny	49	not out		16
*Misbah-ul-Haq	c Mahmudullah b Shakib	70	not out		6
Asad Shafiq	lbw b Robiul	42			
†Adnan Akmal	st Rahim b Shakib	53			
Abdur Rehman	c Mahmudullah b Shakib	24			
Umar Gul	c Sunny b Shakib	11			
Saeed Ajmal	b Shakib	0			
Aizaz Cheema	not out	1			
Extras	(LB 3, NB 16)	19	(NB 1)		1
Total	**(154.5 overs; 655 mins)**	**470**	**(3 wkts; 20.5 overs; 94 mins)**		**107**

PAKISTAN	O	M	R	W		O	M	R	W		FALL OF WICKETS			
												B	P	B	P
Umar Gul	28	1	102	3		13	4	34	2		*Wkt*	*1st*	*1st*	*2nd*	*2nd*
Aizaz Cheema	26	4	73	3		15	2	61	2		1st	0	23	24	7
Mohammad Hafeez	9	3	27	0	(5)	3	0	8	0		2nd	16	150	24	70
Saeed Ajmal	24.2	3	64	2		23.1	6	55	2		3rd	21	245	54	101
Abdur Rehman	19	0	66	0	(3)	27	12	51	4		4th	43	293	76	
Younus Khan	1	0	3	0							5th	223	359	95	
Azhar Ali					(6)	1	0	8	0		6th	305	389	212	
											7th	305	430	221	
BANGLADESH											8th	331	464	226	
Shahadat Hossain	16	1	82	0	(3)	4	0	26	0		9th	332	465	228	
Robiul Islam	23	3	78	1	(4)	1	0	8	0		10th	338	470	234	
Nazmul Hossain	24	5	61	2	(1)	5	1	19	1						
Mahmudullah	15	2	45	0											
Shakib Al Hasan	40.5	7	82	6	(2)	10	1	47	1						
Elias Sunny	27	4	95	1	(5)	0.5	0	7	1						
Nasir Hossain	9	0	24	0											

Umpires: B.R.Doctrove (*West Indies*) (36) and S.K.Tarapore (*India*) (4).
Referee: D.C.Boon (*Australia*) (6).　　　　　　　　**Test No. 2022/8 (B73/P364)**

45

SOUTH AFRICA v SRI LANKA (1st Test)

At SuperSport Park, Centurion, on 15, 16, 17 December 2011.
Toss: South Africa. Result: **SOUTH AFRICA** won by an innings and 81 runs.
Debuts: None.   ‡ F.D.M.Karunaratne

SRI LANKA

N.T.Paranavitana	b Philander	32	c Boucher b Steyn		4
*T.M.Dilshan	c Philander b Steyn	6	c Boucher b Philander		6
K.C.Sangakkara	c Kallis b Philander	1	c Boucher b Philander		2
D.P.M.D.Jayawardena	c Smith b Steyn	30	run out		15
T.T.Samaraweera	c Boucher b Philander	36	c Boucher b Morkel		32
A.D.Mathews	c Kallis b Philander	38	c Boucher b Philander		5
†J.K.Silva	c Boucher b Philander	0	c Kallis b Tahir		17
N.L.T.C.Perera	c Kallis b Tahir	1	c Smith b Steyn		21
H.M.R.K.B.Herath	not out	14	c Boucher b Philander		23
U.W.M.B.C.A.Welagedara	b Steyn	4	c and b Philander		10
C.R.D.Fernando	b Steyn	0	not out		4
Extras	(B 1, LB 7, W 4, NB 6)	18	(LB 1, NB 10)		11
Total	(47.4 overs; 236 mins)	180	(39.1 overs; 201 mins)		150

SOUTH AFRICA

J.A.Rudolph	c Paranavitana b Perera	44
*G.C.Smith	lbw b Fernando	61
D.W.Steyn	run out	0
H.M.Amla	c Mathews b Perera	18
J.H.Kallis	c Mathews b Welagedara	31
A.B.de Villiers	c sub‡ b Perera	99
A.G.Prince	c Silva b Mathews	39
†M.V.Boucher	c Silva b Welagedara	65
V.D.Philander	c Jayawardena b Dilshan	4
M.Morkel	c Samaraweera b Welagedara	4
Imran Tahir	not out	29
Extras	(B 1, LB 1, W 3, NB 12)	17
Total	(122 overs; 561 mins)	411

SOUTH AFRICA	O	M	R	W		O	M	R	W
Steyn	10.4	3	18	4		10	2	36	2
Philander	13	2	53	5		11.1	1	49	5
Morkel	10	1	48	0	(4)	9	0	36	1
Kallis	8	2	31	0	(3)	5	3	13	0
Imran Tahir	6	0	22	1		4	1	15	1

SRI LANKA	O	M	R	W
Welagedara	31	4	96	3
Perera	24	1	114	3
Mathews	9	4	13	1
Fernando	28	2	128	1
Dilshan	7	1	17	1
Herath	23	4	41	0

FALL OF WICKETS			
	SL	SA	SL
Wkt	1st	1st	2nd
1st	11	88	11
2nd	12	90	11
3rd	66	125	19
4th	91	136	37
5th	156	173	66
6th	156	270	70
7th	157	303	104
8th	175	344	133
9th	180	350	145
10th	180	411	150

Umpires: S.J.Davis (*Australia*) (33) and R.J.Tucker (*Australia*) (16).
Referee: B.C.Broad (*England*) (49).   **Test No. 2023/18 (SA361/SL208)**

SOUTH AFRICA v SRI LANKA (2nd Test)

At Kingsmead, Durban, on 26, 27, 28, 29 December 2011.
Toss: Sri Lanka. Result: **SRI LANKA** won by 208 runs.
Debuts: South Africa – M.de Lange; Sri Lanka – L.D.Chandimal.

SRI LANKA

N.T.Paranavitana	c Boucher b De Lange	12	c Prince b Morkel		9
*T.M.Dilshan	c Morkel b Tahir	47	c Smith b Steyn		4
K.C.Sangakkara	c Boucher b De Lange	0	c Smith b Herath		108
D.P.M.D.Jayawardena	b Morkel	31	lbw b De Lange		14
T.T.Samaraweera	c Prince b De Lange	102	b Tahir		43
A.D.Mathews	c and b De Lange	30	c Boucher b Steyn		3
†L.D.Chandimal	c Boucher b Morkel	58	c Boucher b Steyn		54
N.L.T.C.Perera	c Amla b De Lange	12	c Kallis b Steyn		12
H.M.R.K.B.Herath	c Boucher b De Lange	30	not out		8
U.W.M.B.C.A.Welagedara	c Amla b De Lange	2	c Amla b Steyn		10
C.R.D.Fernando	not out	0	c Prince b Morkel		3
Extras	(LB 8, NB 6)	14	(B 5, LB 3, W 1, NB 2)		11
Total	**(108.2 overs)**	**338**	**(78.2 overs; 344 mins)**		**279**

SOUTH AFRICA

*G.C.Smith	c Chandimal b Welagedara	15	(2) c Jayawardena b Fernando		22
J.A.Rudolph	c Welagedara b Perera	7	(1) c Jayawardena b Perera		26
H.M.Amla	c Chandimal b Welagedara	54	run out		51
J.H.Kallis	c Jayawardena b Welagedara	0	c Paranavitana b Herath		0
A.B.de Villiers	c Jayawardena b Welagedara	25	(6) lbw b Herath		69
A.G.Prince	c Jayawardena b Herath	11	(5) c Paranavitana b Fernando		7
†M.V.Boucher	c Dilshan b Herath	3	lbw b Herath		7
D.W.Steyn	not out	29	lbw b Herath		43
M.Morkel	b Herath	0	lbw b Dilshan		5
Imran Tahir	st Chandimal b Herath	11	not out		0
M.de Lange	c Chandimal b Welagedara	9	b Herath		0
Extras	(W 1, NB 3)	4	(B 6, LB 1, W 3, NB 1)		11
Total	**(54.4 overs)**	**168**	**(87.3 overs)**		**241**

SOUTH AFRICA	O	M	R	W		O	M	R	W
Steyn	23	5	63	0	(2)	20	3	73	5
Morkel	21	3	61	2	(1)	18.2	4	46	2
de Lange	23.2	3	81	7		13	2	45	1
Imran Tahir	32	3	101	1	(5)	16	1	64	2
Kallis	9	1	24	0	(4)	11	1	43	0

SRI LANKA	O	M	R	W		O	M	R	W
Welagedara	16.4	3	52	5		16	5	33	0
Perera	9	3	27	1		13	0	48	1
Dilshan	1	1	0	0	(4)	11	2	35	1
Herath	20	7	49	4	(5)	30.3	7	79	5
Mathews	2	0	11	0	(6)	3	0	9	0
Fernando	6	0	29	0	(3)	13	3	29	2
Samaraweera						1	0	1	0

FALL OF WICKETS				
	SL	SA	SL	SA
Wkt	1st	1st	2nd	2nd
1st	35	22	4	37
2nd	47	27	20	88
3rd	84	27	44	97
4th	117	103	138	106
5th	162	106	161	116
6th	273	118	245	133
7th	289	119	245	232
8th	335	119	262	232
9th	337	145	276	241
10th	338	168	279	241

Umpires: S.J.Davis (*Australia*) (34) and R.A.Kettleborough (*England*) (6).
Referee: B.C.Broad (*England*) (50).　　　　　　　　**Test No. 2024/19 (SA362/SL209)**

SOUTH AFRICA v SRI LANKA (3rd Test)

At Newlands, Cape Town, on 3, 4, 5, 6 January 2012.
Toss: Sri Lanka. Result: **SOUTH AFRICA** won by ten wickets.
Debuts: None.

SOUTH AFRICA

*G.C.Smith	b Prasad	16	(2) not out	0
A.N.Petersen	c Dilshan b Welagedara	109	(1) not out	1
H.M.Amla	lbw b Prasad	16		
J.H.Kallis	c Mathews b Herath	224		
A.B.de Villiers	not out	160		
J.A.Rudolph	not out	51		
†M.V.Boucher				
D.W.Steyn				
M.Morkel				
Imran Tahir				
V.D.Philander				
Extras	(LB 1, W 1, NB 2)	4	(NB 1)	1
Total	(4 wkts dec; 139 overs; 576 mins)	580	(0 wkts; 0 overs; 1 min)	2

SRI LANKA

H.D.R.L.Thirimanne	b Morkel	23	c Amla b Kallis	30
*T.M.Dilshan	c Smith b Tahir	78	c Boucher b Philander	5
K.C.Sangakkara	c Amla b Steyn	35	c Kallis b Tahir	34
D.P.M.D.Jayawardena	c Kallis b Steyn	30	c Kallis b Morkel	12
T.T.Samaraweera	c Kallis b Philander	11	not out	115
A.D.Mathews	c Boucher b Steyn	1	lbw b Philander	63
†L.D.Chandimal	c Boucher b Morkel	35	c Kallis b Philander	1
N.L.T.C.Perera	b Tahir	5	c Morkel b Tahir	30
H.M.R.K.B.Herath	lbw b Philander	1	c and b Kallis	0
K.T.G.D.Prasad	c Petersen b Philander	9	st Boucher b Tahir	16
U.W.M.B.C.A.Welagedara	not out	0	b Kallis	14
Extras	(B 6, LB 3, NB 2)	11	(B 1, LB 15, W 6)	22
Total	(73.5 overs; 317 mins)	239	(107.5 overs; 466 mins)	342

SRI LANKA	O	M	R	W		O	M	R	W	FALL OF WICKETS				
											SA	SL	SL	SA
Welagedara	29	7	107	1						Wkt	1st	1st	2nd	2nd
Perera	22	1	131	0						1st	25	70	12	–
Prasad	30	2	154	2	(1)	0	0	2	0	2nd	56	126	79	–
Mathews	12	0	47	0						3rd	261	149	83	–
Herath	42	4	108	1						4th	453	184	98	–
Dilshan	4	0	32	0						5th	–	189	240	–
										6th	–	194	248	–
SOUTH AFRICA										7th	–	219	304	–
Steyn	20	5	56	3		20	3	56	0	8th	–	220	306	–
Philander	19	7	46	3		20	4	54	3	9th	–	236	327	–
Morkel	13.5	2	74	2		19	4	68	1	10th	–	239	342	–
Imran Tahir	21	1	54	2		32	7	106	3					
Kallis						14.5	2	35	3					
Smith						2	0	7	0					

Umpires: R.A.Kettleborough (*England*) (7) and R.J.Tucker (*Australia*) (17).
Referee: B.C.Broad (*England*) (51). **Test No. 2025/20 (SA363/SL210)**

AUSTRALIA v INDIA (1st Test)

At Melbourne Cricket Ground, on 26, 27, 28, 29 December 2011.
Toss: Australia. Result: **AUSTRALIA** won by 122 runs.
Debut: Australia – E.J.M.Cowan.

AUSTRALIA

E.J.M.Cowan	c Dhoni b Ashwin	68	(2) lbw b Yadav		8
D.A.Warner	c Dhoni b Yadav	37	(1) b Yadav		5
S.E.Marsh	c Kohli b Yadav	0	b Yadav		3
R.T.Ponting	c Laxman b Yadav	62	c Sehwag b Khan		60
*M.J.Clarke	b Khan	31	b Sharma		1
M.E.K.Hussey	c Dhoni b Khan	0	c Dhoni b Khan		89
†B.J.Haddin	c Sehwag b Khan	27	c Laxman b Khan		6
P.M.Siddle	c Dhoni b Khan	41	c Dhoni b Yadav		4
J.L.Pattinson	not out	18	(10) not out		37
B.W.Hilfenhaus	c Kohli b Ashwin	19	(11) c Laxman b Sharma		14
N.M.Lyon	b Ashwin	6	(9) lbw b Ashwin		0
Extras	(LB 21, W 2, NB 1)	24	(B 5, LB 2, W 1, NB 5)		13
Total	**(110 overs; 488 mins)**	**333**	**(76.3 overs; 335 mins)**		**240**

INDIA

G.Gambhir	c Haddin b Hilfenhaus	3	c Ponting b Siddle		13
V.Sehwag	b Pattinson	67	c Hussey b Hilfenhaus		7
R.S.Dravid	b Hilfenhaus	68	b Pattinson		10
S.R.Tendulkar	b Siddle	73	c Hussey b Siddle		32
I.Sharma	c Haddin b Hilfenhaus	11	(10) not out		6
V.V.S.Laxman	c Haddin b Siddle	2	(5) c Cowan b Pattinson		1
V.Kohli	c Haddin b Hilfenhaus	11	(6) lbw b Hilfenhaus		0
*†M.S.Dhoni	c Hussey b Hilfenhaus	6	(7) b Pattinson		23
R.Ashwin	c Haddin b Siddle	31	(8) c Cowan b Siddle		30
Z.Khan	b Pattinson	4	(9) c Cowan b Pattinson		13
U.Yadav	not out	2	c Warner b Lyon		21
Extras	(W 1, NB 3)	4	(LB 10, W 2, NB 1)		13
Total	**(94.1 overs; 417 mins)**	**282**	**(47.5 overs; 228 mins)**		**169**

INDIA	O	M	R	W	O	M	R	W
Khan	31	6	77	4	20	4	53	3
Sharma	24	7	48	0	(3) 12.3	0	43	2
Yadav	26	5	106	3	(2) 20	4	70	4
Ashwin	29	3	81	3	22	4	60	1
Sehwag					2	0	7	0

AUSTRALIA	O	M	R	W	O	M	R	W
Pattinson	23	6	55	2	15	2	53	4
Hilfenhaus	26	5	75	5	18	4	39	2
Siddle	21.1	2	63	3	9	1	42	3
Lyon	17	2	66	0	5.5	0	25	1
Hussey	5	0	15	0				
Warner	2	0	8	0				

FALL OF WICKETS

	A	I	A	I
Wkt	1st	1st	2nd	2nd
1st	46	22	13	17
2nd	46	97	16	39
3rd	159	214	24	58
4th	205	214	27	68
5th	205	221	142	69
6th	214	238	148	81
7th	286	245	163	117
8th	291	254	166	142
9th	318	259	197	142
10th	333	282	240	169

Umpires: M.Erasmus (*South Africa*) (8) and I.J.Gould (*England*) (24).
Referee: R.S.Madugalle (*Sri Lanka*) (129).   **Test No. 2026/79 (A737/I1459)**

AUSTRALIA v INDIA (2nd Test)

At Sydney Cricket Ground, on 3, 4, 5, 6 January 2012.
Toss: India. Result: **AUSTRALIA** won by an innings and 68 runs.
Debuts: None.

INDIA

G.Gambhir	c Clarke b Pattinson	0	c Warner b Siddle		83
V.Sehwag	c Haddin b Pattinson	30	c Warner b Hilfenhaus		4
R.S.Dravid	c Cowan b Siddle	5	b Hilfenhaus		29
S.R.Tendulkar	b Pattinson	41	c Hussey b Clarke		80
V.V.S.Laxman	c Marsh b Pattinson	2	b Hilfenhaus		66
V.Kohli	c Haddin b Siddle	23	lbw b Pattinson		9
*†M.S.Dhoni	not out	57	c and b Hilfenhaus		2
R.Ashwin	c Clarke b Hilfenhaus	20	c Lyon b Hilfenhaus		62
Z.Khan	c Cowan b Hilfenhaus	0	c Marsh b Siddle		35
I.Sharma	c Cowan b Hilfenhaus	0	lbw b Lyon		11
U.Yadav	c Haddin b Siddle	0	not out		0
Extras	(B 3, LB 6, W 2, NB 2)	13	(B 6, LB 3, W 2, NB 8)		19
Total	**(59.3 overs)**	**191**	**(110.5 overs)**		**400**

AUSTRALIA

D.A.Warner	c Tendulkar b Khan	8
E.J.M.Cowan	lbw b Khan	16
S.E.Marsh	c Laxman b Khan	0
R.T.Ponting	c Tendulkar b Sharma	134
*M.J.Clarke	not out	329
M.E.K.Hussey	not out	150
†B.J.Haddin		
P.M.Siddle		
J.L.Pattinson		
B.W.Hilfenhaus		
N.M.Lyon		
Extras	(B 2, LB 13, W 4, NB 3)	22
Total	**(4 wkts dec; 163 overs)**	**659**

AUSTRALIA	O	M	R	W		O	M	R	W
Pattinson	14	3	43	4		23	4	106	1
Hilfenhaus	22	9	51	3		32.5	8	106	5
Siddle	13.3	5	55	3		24	8	88	2
Hussey	2	0	8	0	(6)	2	0	5	0
Lyon	8	0	25	0	(4)	20	2	64	1
Clarke					(5)	9	0	22	1

INDIA	O	M	R	W
Khan	31	4	122	3
Yadav	24	2	123	0
Sharma	33	2	144	1
Ashwin	44	5	157	0
Sehwag	23	1	75	0
Kohli	8	0	23	0

FALL OF WICKETS			
	I	A	I
Wkt	1st	1st	2nd
1st	0	8	18
2nd	30	8	100
3rd	55	37	168
4th	59	325	271
5th	96	–	276
6th	124	–	286
7th	178	–	286
8th	178	–	342
9th	186	–	384
10th	191	–	400

Umpires: M.Erasmus (*South Africa*) (9) and I.J.Gould (*England*) (25).
Referee: R.S.Madugalle (*Sri Lanka*) (130).   **Test No. 2027/80 (A738/I460)**

AUSTRALIA v INDIA (3rd Test)

At W.A.C.A. Ground, Perth, on 13, 14, 15 January 2012.
Toss: Australia. Result: **AUSTRALIA** won by an innings and 37 runs.
Debut: India – R.Vinay Kumar.

INDIA

G.Gambhir	c Haddin b Hilfenhaus	31	c Hussey b Starc		14
V.Sehwag	c Ponting b Hilfenhaus	0	c Haddin b Siddle		10
R.S.Dravid	b Siddle	9	b Harris		47
S.R.Tendulkar	lbw b Harris	15	lbw b Starc		8
V.V.S.Laxman	c Clarke b Siddle	31	c Marsh b Hilfenhaus		0
V.Kohli	c Warner b Siddle	44	c Haddin b Siddle		75
*†M.S.Dhoni	c Ponting b Hilfenhaus	12	c Ponting b Siddle		2
R.Vinay Kumar	lbw b Starc	5	c Clarke b Hilfenhaus		6
Z.Khan	c Clarke b Hilfenhaus	3	c Clarke b Hilfenhaus		0
I.Sharma	c Haddin b Starc	2	c Cowan b Hilfenhaus		0
U.Yadav	not out	4	not out		0
Extras	(B 2, LB 2, W 1)	5	(B 1, LB 5, W 3)		9
Total	**(60.2 overs)**	**161**	**(63.2 overs)**		**171**

AUSTRALIA

E.J.M.Cowan	b Yadav	74
D.A.Warner	c Yadav b Sharma	180
S.E.Marsh	c Laxman b Yadav	11
R.T.Ponting	b Yadav	7
*M.J.Clarke	c Dhoni b Khan	18
M.E.K.Hussey	c Sehwag b Vinay Kumar	14
†B.J.Haddin	c Dhoni b Khan	0
P.M.Siddle	b Yadav	30
R.J.Harris	c Gambhir b Yadav	9
M.A.Starc	not out	15
B.W.Hilfenhaus	c Kohli b Sehwag	6
Extras	(LB 3, W 2)	5
Total	**(76.2 overs)**	**369**

AUSTRALIA	O	M	R	W	O	M	R	W
Harris	18	6	33	1	16	3	34	1
Hilfenhaus	18	5	43	4	18	6	54	4
Starc	12.2	3	39	2	12	4	31	2
Siddle	12	3	42	3	15.2	5	43	3
Hussey					2	0	3	0

INDIA	O	M	R	W
Khan	21	3	91	2
Yadav	17	2	93	5
Vinay Kumar	13	0	73	1
Sharma	18	0	89	1
Sehwag	7.2	0	20	1

FALL OF WICKETS			
	I	A	I
Wkt	1st	1st	2nd
1st	4	214	24
2nd	32	230	25
3rd	59	242	42
4th	63	290	51
5th	131	301	135
6th	138	303	148
7th	152	339	171
8th	152	343	171
9th	157	357	171
10th	161	369	171

Umpires: Alim Dar (*Pakistan*) (69) and H.D.P.K.Dharmasena (*Sri Lanka*) (7).
Referee: R.S.Madugalle (*Sri Lanka*) (131).   **Test No. 2028/81 (A739/I461)**

AUSTRALIA v INDIA (4th Test)

At Adelaide Oval, on 24, 25, 26, 27, 28 January 2012.
Toss: Australia. Result: **AUSTRALIA** won by 298 runs.
Debuts: None.

AUSTRALIA

E.J.M.Cowan	c Laxman b Ashwin	30	(2) lbw b Ashwin		10
D.A.Warner	lbw b Khan	8	(1) c and b Ashwin		28
S.E.Marsh	b Ashwin	3	lbw b Khan		0
R.T.Ponting	c Tendulkar b Khan	221	not out		60
*M.J.Clarke	b Yadav	210	c Saha b Yadav		37
M.E.K.Hussey	run out	25	lbw b Sharma		15
†B.J.Haddin	not out	42	not out		11
P.M.Siddle	c Saha b Ashwin	2			
R.J.Harris	not out	35			
B.W.Hilfenhaus					
N.M.Lyon					
Extras	(B 3, LB 17, W 8)	28	(LB 6)		6
Total	**(7 wkts dec; 157 overs; 636 mins)**	**604**	**(5 wkts dec; 46 overs; 191 mins)**		**167**

INDIA

G.Gambhir	c Hussey b Siddle	34	c Haddin b Harris		3
*V.Sehwag	c and b Siddle	18	c Ponting b Lyon		62
R.S.Dravid	b Hilfenhaus	1	c Hussey b Harris		25
S.R.Tendulkar	c Ponting b Siddle	25	c Cowan b Lyon		13
V.V.S.Laxman	c Haddin b Lyon	18	c Marsh b Lyon		35
V.Kohli	lbw b Hilfenhaus	116	run out		22
†W.P.Saha	b Harris	35	(8) c Haddin b Siddle		3
R.Ashwin	lbw b Siddle	5	(9) not out		15
Z.Khan	c Haddin b Siddle	0	(10) c Warner b Hilfenhaus		15
I.Sharma	b Hilfenhaus	16	(7) c Haddin b Harris		2
U.Yadav	not out	0	c Haddin b Lyon		1
Extras	(B 1, W 1, NB 2)	4	(LB 3, W 2)		5
Total	**(95.1 overs; 378 mins)**	**272**	**(69.4 overs)**		**201**

INDIA	O	M	R	W		O	M	R	W
Khan	31	4	96	2		13	1	38	1
Yadav	26	1	136	1	(4)	5	0	23	1
Ashwin	53	6	194	3	(2)	20	2	73	2
Sharma	30	6	100	0	(3)	8	0	27	1
Sehwag	16	0	55	0					
Kohli	1	0	3	0					

AUSTRALIA	O	M	R	W		O	M	R	W
Harris	25	7	71	1		19	5	41	3
Hilfenhaus	22.1	5	62	3		11	2	35	1
Siddle	15	2	49	5		14	5	47	1
Lyon	21	5	48	1		21.4	4	63	4
Clarke	6	1	23	0	(6)	2	0	9	0
Hussey	6	0	18	0	(5)	2	0	3	0

FALL OF WICKETS

	A	I	A	I
Wkt	1st	1st	2nd	2nd
1st	26	26	39	14
2nd	31	31	40	80
3rd	84	78	40	100
4th	470	87	111	110
5th	520	111	147	162
6th	530	225	–	166
7th	533	230	–	166
8th	–	230	–	170
9th	–	263	–	193
10th	–	272	–	201

Umpires: Alim Dar (*Pakistan*) (70) and H.D.P.K.Dharmasena (*Sri Lanka*) (8).
Referee: R.S.Madugalle (*Sri Lanka*) (132).　　　　**Test No. 2029/82 (A740/I462)**

PAKISTAN v ENGLAND (1st Test)

At Dubai International Cricket Stadium, on 17, 18, 19 January 2012.
Toss: England. Result: **PAKISTAN** won by ten wickets.
Debuts: None.

ENGLAND

*A.J.Strauss	b Ajmal	19	c Akmal b Gul		6
A.N.Cook	c Akmal b Hafeez	3	c Akmal b Gul		5
I.J.L.Trott	c Akmal b Cheema	17	c Akmal b Gul		49
K.P.Pietersen	lbw b Ajmal	2	c Rehman b Gul		0
I.R.Bell	c Akmal b Ajmal	0	lbw b Ajmal		4
E.J.G.Morgan	lbw b Ajmal	24	c Akmal b Rehman		14
†M.J.Prior	not out	70	lbw b Ajmal		4
S.C.J.Broad	lbw b Ajmal	8	c Shafiq b Rehman		17
G.P.Swann	b Rehman	34	c Shafiq b Rehman		39
C.T.Tremlett	lbw b Ajmal	1	c Hafeez b Rehman		0
J.M.Anderson	lbw b Ajmal	12	not out		15
Extras	(LB 2)	2	(B 4, LB 1, NB 2)		7
Total	**(72.3 overs; 309 mins)**	**192**	**(57.5 overs; 271 mins)**		**160**

PAKISTAN

Mohammad Hafeez	lbw b Swann	88	not out	15
Taufiq Umar	b Broad	58	not out	0
Azhar Ali	c Prior b Broad	1		
Younus Khan	lbw b Trott	37		
*Misbah-ul-Haq	lbw b Swann	52		
Asad Shafiq	c Prior b Anderson	16		
†Adnan Akmal	st Prior b Swann	61		
Abdur Rehman	b Anderson	4		
Umar Gul	c Morgan b Broad	0		
Saeed Ajmal	c Cook b Swann	12		
Aizaz Cheema	not out	0		
Extras	(B 2, LB 5, NB 2)	9		–
Total	**(119.5 overs; 507 mins)**	**338**	**(0 wkts; 3.4 overs; 14 mins)**	**15**

PAKISTAN	O	M	R	W		O	M	R	W
Umar Gul	12	4	35	0		19	5	63	4
Aizaz Cheema	12	0	43	1		7.2	1	9	0
Mohammad Hafeez	6	3	5	1		2	0	4	0
Abdur Rehman	18	5	52	1	(5)	12	2	37	3
Saeed Ajmal	24.3	7	55	7	(4)	17.3	4	42	3

ENGLAND	O	M	R	W		O	M	R	W
Anderson	30	7	71	2		2	1	7	0
Tremlett	21	6	53	0					
Broad	31	8	84	3	(2)	1.4	1	8	0
Swann	29.5	3	107	4					
Trott	8	2	16	1					

FALL OF WICKETS

	E	P	E	P
Wkt	1st	1st	2nd	2nd
1st	10	114	6	–
2nd	31	128	25	–
3rd	42	176	25	–
4th	42	202	35	–
5th	43	231	74	–
6th	82	283	87	–
7th	94	288	87	–
8th	151	289	135	–
9th	168	319	135	–
10th	192	338	160	–

Umpires: B.F.Bowden (*New Zealand*) (70) and B.N.J.Oxenford (*Australia*) (6).
Referee: J.Srinath (*India*) (19). **Test No. 2030/72 (P365/E916)**

PAKISTAN v ENGLAND (2nd Test)

At Sheikh Zayed Stadium, Abu Dhabi, on 25, 26, 27, 28 January 2012.
Toss: Pakistan. Result: **PAKISTAN** won by 72 runs.
Debuts: None.

PAKISTAN

Mohammad Hafeez	b Panesar	31	lbw b Panesar		22
Taufiq Umar	b Swann	16	b Swann		7
Azhar Ali	b Broad	24	c Prior b Anderson		68
Younus Khan	b Broad	24	b Panesar		1
*Misbah-ul-Haq	lbw b Broad	84	lbw b Panesar		12
Asad Shafiq	lbw b Swann	58	c Anderson b Panesar		43
†Adnan Akmal	lbw b Broad	9	c Strauss b Broad		13
Abdur Rehman	b Swann	0	lbw b Swann		10
Saeed Ajmal	lbw b Anderson	0	c Anderson b Panesar		17
Umar Gul	not out	0	not out		10
Junaid Khan	c Swann b Anderson	0	b Panesar		0
Extras	(B 8, LB 1, NB 2)	11	(B 5, LB 6)		11
Total	**(96.4 overs; 377 mins)**	**257**	**(99.2 overs; 371 mins)**		**214**

ENGLAND

*A.J.Strauss	c Shafiq b Hafeez	11		lbw b Rehman	32
A.N.Cook	lbw b Ajmal	94		c and b Hafeez	7
I.J.L.Trott	b Rehman	74	(7)	lbw b Rehman	1
K.P.Pietersen	c Hafeez b Ajmal	14		lbw b Rehman	1
I.R.Bell	lbw b Gul	29	(3)	b Ajmal	3
E.J.G.Morgan	c Hafeez b Ajmal	3	(5)	b Rehman	0
†M.J.Prior	lbw b Ajmal	3	(6)	c Shafiq b Ajmal	18
S.C.J.Broad	not out	58		b Rehman	0
G.P.Swann	lbw b Rehman	15		lbw b Ajmal	0
J.M.Anderson	b Hafeez	13		c Gul b Rehman	1
M.S.Panesar	lbw b Hafeez	0		not out	0
Extras	(B 5, LB 7, NB 1)	13		(LB 9)	9
Total	**(112 overs; 461 mins)**	**327**		**(36.1 overs; 143 mins)**	**72**

ENGLAND	O	M	R	W		O	M	R	W		FALL OF WICKETS			
Anderson	19.4	5	46	2		14	3	39	1			P	E	P	E
Broad	24	4	47	4		20	9	36	1		*Wkt*	*1st*	*1st*	*2nd*	*2nd*
Panesar	33	9	91	1		38.2	18	62	6		1st	51	27	29	21
Swann	18	2	52	3		27	5	66	2		2nd	61	166	29	26
Trott	2	0	12	0							3rd	98	198	36	33
											4th	103	203	54	37
PAKISTAN											5th	203	207	142	56
Umar Gul	13	1	53	1	(2)	3	0	5	0		6th	216	227	170	68
Junaid Khan	8	0	33	0							7th	243	268	172	68
Mohammad Hafeez	22	4	54	3	(1)	8	3	11	1		8th	257	291	198	71
Saeed Ajmal	40	6	108	4	(3)	15	7	22	3		9th	257	327	208	72
Abdur Rehman	29	9	67	2	(4)	10.1	4	25	6		10th	257	327	214	72

Umpires: S.J.Davis (*Australia*) (35) and B.N.J.Oxenford (*Australia*) (7).
Referee: J.Srinath (*India*) (20).   Test No. 2031/73 (P366/E917)

PAKISTAN v ENGLAND (3rd Test)

At Dubai International Cricket Stadium, on 3, 4, 5, 6 February 2012.
Toss: Pakistan. Result: **PAKISTAN** won by 71 runs.
Debuts: None.

PAKISTAN

Mohammad Hafeez	lbw b Broad	13	lbw b Panesar	21
Taufiq Umar	lbw b Anderson	0	c Strauss b Anderson	6
Azhar Ali	c Prior b Broad	1	c Cook b Swann	157
Younus Khan	c Prior b Broad	4	lbw b Broad	127
*Misbah-ul-Haq	lbw b Anderson	1	lbw b Panesar	31
Asad Shafiq	lbw b Panesar	45	lbw b Panesar	5
†Adnan Akmal	lbw b Broad	6	b Panesar	0
Abdur Rehman	c Pietersen b Swann	1	c Anderson b Swann	1
Saeed Ajmal	lbw b Panesar	12	c Anderson b Swann	1
Umar Gul	b Anderson	13	lbw b Panesar	4
Aizaz Cheema	not out	0	not out	0
Extras	(LB 3)	3	(B 10, LB 1, NB 1)	12
Total	**(44.1 overs; 191 mins)**	**99**	**(152.4 overs; 572 mins)**	**365**

ENGLAND

*A.J.Strauss	st Akmal b Rehman	56	lbw b Rehman	26
A.N.Cook	c Akmal b Gul	1	c Khan b Ajmal	49
I.J.L.Trott	lbw b Gul	2	c Rehman b Ajmal	18
K.P.Pietersen	lbw b Rehman	32	b Ajmal	18
I.R.Bell	st Akmal b Ajmal	5	c Shafiq b Gul	10
E.J.G.Morgan	lbw b Rehman	10	c Akmal b Gul	31
†M.J.Prior	b Rehman	6	not out	49
J.M.Anderson	b Rehman	4	(10) c Khan b Ajmal	9
S.C.J.Broad	lbw b Ajmal	4	(8) c Umar b Gul	18
G.P.Swann	c Rehman b Ajmal	16	(9) c Shafiq b Gul	1
M.S.Panesar	not out	0	lbw b Rehman	8
Extras	(B 1, LB 4)	5	(B 4, LB 8, NB 3)	15
Total	**(55 overs; 233 mins)**	**141**	**(97.3 overs; 410 mins)**	**252**

ENGLAND	O	M	R	W	O	M	R	W		FALL OF WICKETS			
Anderson	14.1	3	35	3	28	7	51	1			P	E	P	E
Broad	16	5	36	4	24	7	55	1		*Wkt*	*1st*	*1st*	*2nd*	*2nd*
Panesar	13	4	25	2	56.4	13	124	5		1st	1	5	16	48
Swann	1	1	0	1	39	6	101	3		2nd	8	7	28	85
Trott					2	0	14	0		3rd	18	64	244	116
Pietersen					3	0	9	0		4th	21	75	331	119
										5th	21	88	339	156
PAKISTAN										6th	39	98	345	159
Umar Gul	7	1	28	2	20	5	61	4		7th	44	106	346	196
Aizaz Cheema	4	0	9	0	4	0	9	0		8th	78	121	350	203
Saeed Ajmal	23	6	59	3	(5) 27	9	67	4		9th	85	133	363	237
Abdur Rehman	21	4	40	5	41.3	10	97	2		10th	99	141	365	252
Mohammad Hafeez					(3) 5	2	6	0						

Umpires: S.J.Davis (*Australia*) (36) and S.J.A.Taufel (*Australia*) (71).
Referee: J.J.Crowe (*New Zealand*) (49).   **Test No. 2032/74 (P367/E918)**

NEW ZEALAND v ZIMBABWE (Only Test)

At McLean Park, Napier, on 26, 27, 28 January 2012.
Toss: Zimbabwe. Result: **NEW ZEALAND** won by an innings and 301 runs.
Debuts: Zimbabwe – S.W.Masakadza, F.Mutizwa.

NEW ZEALAND

B.B.McCullum	lbw b Jarvis	83
M.J.Guptill	c Taibu b S.W.Masakadza	51
K.S.Williamson	run out	4
*L.R.P.L.Taylor	retired hurt	122
D.G.Brownlie	c Taibu b H.Masakadza	0
D.L.Vettori	st Taibu b Cremer	38
†B.J.Watling	not out	102
D.A.J.Bracewell	b Vitori	11
T.G.Southee	c Waller b Cremer	44
T.A.Boult	not out	5
C.S.Martin		
Extras	(B 1, LB 21, W 2, NB 11)	35
Total	(7 wkts dec; 123.4 overs; 535 mins)	**495**

ZIMBABWE

T.M.K.Mawoyo	b Martin	2	c Guptill b Martin		2
H.Masakadza	c Brownlie b Boult	0	c McCullum b Martin		0
F.Mutizwa	b Martin	6	c Watling b Bracewell		18
*B.R.M.Taylor	c Guptill b Bracewell	9	c Watling b Martin		2
†T.Taibu	c Brownlie b Boult	2	c Williamson b Bracewell		4
M.N.Waller	c Brownlie b Southee	23	lbw b Bracewell		0
R.W.Chakabva	lbw b Bracewell	3	c Brownlie b Martin		63
A.G.Cremer	lbw b Vettori	3	c Bracewell b Williamson		26
S.W.Masakadza	not out	3	c Watling b Martin		21
K.M.Jarvis	run out	0	not out		0
B.V.Vitori	c Brownlie b Southee	0	c Watling b Martin		0
Extras		–	(B 4, LB 3)		7
Total	(28.5 overs; 135 mins)	**51**	(48.3 overs; 208 mins)		**143**

ZIMBABWE	O	M	R	W		O	M	R	W
Jarvis	32.4	7	120	1					
Vitori	25	3	94	1					
S.W.Masakadza	23	2	102	1					
H.Masakadza	21	6	45	1					
Cremer	22	2	112	2					

NEW ZEALAND	O	M	R	W		O	M	R	W
Martin	6	2	5	2		8.3	3	26	6
Boult	9	3	24	2	(5)	9	4	15	0
Bracewell	6	2	12	2		10	4	26	3
Vettori	4	3	2	1		10	1	25	0
Southee	3.5	0	8	2	(2)	8	2	20	0
Guptill						1	0	12	0
Williamson						2	0	12	1

FALL OF WICKETS

	NZ	Z	Z
Wkt	1st	1st	2nd
1st	124	2	2
2nd	131	8	3
3rd	195	8	5
4th	196	19	12
5th	278	19	12
6th	392	24	37
7th	466	46	100
8th	–	50	134
9th	–	50	143
10th	–	51	143

Umpires: Enamul Haque (*Bangladesh*) (1) and R.J.Tucker (*Australia*) (18).
Referee: D.C.Boon (*Australia*) (7).   **Test No. 2033/15 (Z87/NZ368)**
L.R.P.L.Taylor retired hurt at 365-5.

ENGLAND TEST MATCH AVERAGES 2011

These averages cover the 10 Tests played by England included in this book, against Sri Lanka and India at home, and Pakistan in the UAE.

BATTING AND FIELDING

	M	I	NO	HS	Runs	Avge	100	50	Ct/St
T.T.Bresnan	3	3	1	90	154	77.00	–	2	–
I.R.Bell	10	16	3	235	886	68.15	4	2	4
A.N.Cook	10	16	–	294	897	56.06	3	3	9
K.P.Pietersen	10	16	1	202*	762	50.80	2	4	6
M.J.Prior	10	15	4	126	551	50.09	2	3	32/3
I.J.L.Trott	8	14	–	203	526	37.57	1	3	2
S.C.J.Broad	10	13	2	74*	344	31.27	–	4	4
E.J.G.Morgan	10	16	1	104	444	29.60	1	3	7
A.J.Strauss	10	16	–	87	406	25.37	–	2	15
G.P.Swann	10	10	–	39	164	16.40	–	–	8
C.T.Tremlett	5	4	2	24*	29	14.50	–	–	3
J.M.Anderson	9	11	3	27	102	12.75	–	–	9
M.S.Panesar	2	4	2	8	8	4.00	–	–	–

Also played: R.S.Bopara (2 Tests) 7, 44* (1ct); S.T.Finn (1) 19.

BOWLING

	O	M	R	W	Avge	Best	5wI	10wM
T.T.Bresnan	91.3	20	261	16	16.31	5- 48	1	–
M.S.Panesar	141	44	302	14	21.57	6- 62	2	–
S.C.J.Broad	387	97	1002	46	21.78	6- 46	1	–
J.M.Anderson	356	91	992	37	26.81	5- 65	1	–
C.T.Tremlett	182	45	528	19	27.78	6- 48	1	–
G.P.Swann	360.1	51	1138	38	29.94	6-106	1	–

Also bowled: R.S.Bopara 5-2-13-0; S.T.Finn 41-10-139-4; K.P.Pietersen 36-2-147-0; I.J.L.Trott 37-5-141-2.

ICC TEST RANKINGS*

	Team	Matches	Points	Rating
1	England	41	4830	118
2	South Africa	28	3277	117
3=	India	46	5111	111
3=	Australia	42	4655	111
5	Pakistan	35	3781	108
6	Sri Lanka	35	3426	98
7	West Indies	30	2654	88
8	New Zealand	24	1998	83
9	Bangladesh	18	76	4

Zimbabwe had not played sufficient games to secure a ranking.
* As of 6 March 2012.

INTERNATIONAL UMPIRES AND REFEREES 2012

ELITE PANEL OF UMPIRES 2012

The Elite Panel of ICC Umpires and Referees was introduced in April 2002 to raise standards and guarantee impartial adjudication. Two umpires from this panel stand in Test matches while one officiates with a home umpire from the Supplementary International Panel in limited-overs internationals.

Full Names	Birthdate	Birthplace	Tests	Debut	LOI	Debut
ALIM Sarwar DAR	06.06.68	Jhang, Pakistan	70	2003-04	149	1999-00
ASAD RAUF	12.05.56	Lahore, Pakistan	40	2004-05	95	1999-00
BOWDEN, Brent Fraser	11.04.63	Auckland, New Zealand	70	1999-00	170	1994-95
DAVIS, Stephen James	09.04.52	London, England	36	1997-98	106	1992-93
DHARMASENA, H.D.P.Kumar	24.04.71	Colombo, Sri Lanka	8	2010-11	32	2008-09
DOCTROVE, Billy Raymond	03.07.55	Marigot, Dominica	36	2000	112	1997-98
ERASMUS, Marais	27.02.64	George, South Africa	9	2009-10	41	2007-08
GOULD, Ian James	19.08.57	Taplow, England	25	2008-09	67	2006
HILL, Anthony Lloyd	26.06.51	Auckland, New Zealand	28	2001-02	93	1997-98
KETTLEBOROUGH, Richard Allan	15.03.73	Sheffield, England	7	2010-11	18	2009
TAUFEL, Simon James Arthur	21.01.71	Sydney, Australia	71	2000-01	172	1998-99
TUCKER, Rodney James	28.08.64	Sydney, Australia	18	2009-10	26	2008-09

ELITE PANEL OF REFEREES 2012

Full Names	Birthdate	Birthplace	Tests	Debut	LOI	Debut
BOON, David Clarence	29.12.60	Launceston, Australia	7	2011	11	2011
BROAD, Brian Christopher	29.09.57	Bristol, England	51	2003-04	202	2003-04
CROWE, Jeffrey John	14.09.58	Auckland, New Zealand	49	2004-05	165	2003-04
MADUGALLE, Ranjan Senerath	22.04.59	Kandy, Sri Lanka	132	1993-94	265	1993-94
MAHANAMA, Roshan Siriwardena	31.05.66	Colombo, Sri Lanka	34	2004	179	2004
PYCROFT, Andrew John	06.06.56	Harare, Zimbabwe	22	2009	48	2009
SRINATH, Javagal	31.08.69	Mysore, India	20	2006	111	2006-07

INTERNATIONAL UMPIRES PANEL 2012

Nominated by their respective cricket boards, members from this panel officiate in home LOIs and supplement the Elite panel for Test matches. Specialist third umpires have been selected to undertake adjudication involving television replays. The number of Test matches/LOI in which they have stood is shown in brackets.

			Third Umpire
Australia	B.N.J.Oxenford (7/34)	P.R.Reiffel (-/15)	S.D.Fry (-/3)
Bangladesh	Nadir Shah (-/40)	Enamal Haque (1/38)	Sharfuddoula (-/5)
England	N.J.Llong (12/55)	R.K.Illingworth (-/10)	R.J.Bailey (-/1)
India	S.K.Tarapore (4/23)	S.Asnani (-/7)	V.A.Kulkarni (-/-)
			P.R.Sundaram (-/-)
New Zealand	G.A.V.Baxter (-/35)	C.B.Gaffaney (-/9)	B.G.Frost (-/-)
Pakistan	Zamir Haider (-/14)	Ahsan Raza (-/6)	Shozab Raza (-/-)
South Africa	J.D.Cloete (-/18)	S.George (-/3)	A.T.Holdstock (-/-)
Sri Lanka	E.A.R.De Silva (49/121)	R.E.S.Martinesz (-/4)	R.Palliyaguru (-/-)
West Indies	P.J.Nero (-/6)	J.S.Wilson (-/1)	G.O.Brathwaite (-/2)
			N.Duguid (-/-)
Zimbabwe	R.B.Tiffin (44/126)	O.Chirombe (-/8)	T.J.Matibiri (-/-)

Test Match statistics to 6 March 2012; LOI statistics to 10 March 2012.

TEST MATCH CAREER RECORDS

These records, complete to 6 March 2012, contain all players registered for county cricket in 2011 at the time of going to press, plus those who have played Test cricket since 1 October 2010 (Test No. 1971). Records are for performances for the country shown, and do not include figures for multi-national teams.

ENGLAND – BATTING AND FIELDING

	M	I	NO	HS	Runs	Avge	100	50	Ct/St
K.Ali	1	2	–	9	10	5.00	–	–	–
T.R.Ambrose	11	16	1	102	447	29.80	1	3	31
J.M.Anderson	66	87	34	34	626	11.81	–	–	34
G.J.Batty	7	8	1	38	144	20.57	–	–	3
I.R.Bell	72	122	14	235	5078	47.01	16	28	57
I.D.Blackwell	1	1	–	4	4	4.00	–	–	–
R.S.Bopara	12	17	1	143	553	34.56	3	–	6
T.T.Bresnan	10	8	1	91	318	45.42	–	3	3
S.C.J.Broad	44	59	8	169	1440	28.23	1	9	13
M.A.Carberry	1	2	–	34	64	32.00	–	–	1
R.Clarke	2	3	–	55	96	32.00	–	1	1
P.D.Collingwood	68	115	10	206	4259	40.56	10	20	96
A.N.Cook	75	131	7	294	6027	48.60	19	27	66
R.D.B.Croft	21	34	8	37*	421	16.19	–	–	10
S.T.Finn	12	13	9	19	35	8.75	–	–	3
J.S.Foster	7	12	3	48	226	25.11	–	–	17/1
S.J.Harmison	62	84	23	49*	742	12.16	–	–	7
M.J.Hoggard	67	92	27	38	473	7.27	–	–	24
G.O.Jones	34	53	4	100	1172	23.91	1	6	128/5
S.P.Jones	18	18	5	44	205	15.76	–	–	4
R.W.T.Key	15	26	1	221	775	31.00	1	3	11
A.Khan	1								–
J.Lewis	1	2	–	20	27	13.50	–	–	–
A.McGrath	4	4	–	81	201	40.20	–	2	3
D.L.Maddy	3	4	–	24	46	11.50	–	–	4
S.I.Mahmood	8	11	1	34	81	8.10	–	–	–
E.J.G.Morgan	16	24	1	130	700	30.43	2	3	11
G.Onions	8	10	7	17*	30	10.00	–	–	–
M.S.Panesar	41	55	19	26	195	5.41	–	–	9
D.J.Pattinson	1	2	–	13	21	10.50	–	–	–
K.P.Pietersen	81	139	7	227	6428	48.69	19	25	50
L.E.Plunkett	9	13	2	44*	126	11.45	–	–	3
M.J.Prior	50	76	15	131*	2699	44.24	6	19	149/7
M.R.Ramprakash	52	92	6	154	2350	27.32	2	12	39
C.M.W.Read	15	23	4	55	360	18.94	–	1	48/6
O.A.Shah	6	10	–	88	269	26.90	–	2	2
A.Shahzad	1	1	–	5	5	5.00	–	–	2
R.J.Sidebottom	22	31	11	31	313	15.65	–	–	5
A.J.Strauss	92	163	6	177	6490	41.33	19	26	109
G.P.Swann	39	46	6	85	905	22.62	–	4	33
J.C.Tredwell	1	1	–	37	37	37.00	–	–	1
C.T.Tremlett	11	13	4	25*	98	10.88	–	–	4
M.E.Trescothick	76	143	10	219	5825	43.79	14	29	95
I.J.L.Trott	26	44	4	226	2126	53.15	6	8	11

ENGLAND – BOWLING

	O	M	R	W	Avge	Best	5wI	10wM
K.Ali	36	5	136	5	27.20	3- 80	–	–
J.M.Anderson	2365.2	539	7587	249	30.46	7- 43	11	1
G.J.Batty	232.2	34	733	11	66.63	3- 55	–	–
I.R.Bell	18	3	76	1	76.00	1- 33	–	–
I.D.Blackwell	19	2	71	0	–	–	–	–
R.S.Bopara	54.2	9	212	1	212.00	1- 39	–	–
T.T.Bresnan	338.3	92	968	41	23.60	5- 48	1	–
S.C.J.Broad	1502.3	332	4491	145	30.97	6- 46	4	–
R.Clarke	29	11	60	4	15.00	2- 7	–	–
P.D.Collingwood	317.3	51	1018	17	59.88	3- 23	–	–
A.N.Cook	1	0	1	0	–	–	–	–
R.D.B.Croft	769.5	195	1825	49	37.24	5- 95	1	–
S.T.Finn	345.4	74	1346	50	26.92	6-125	3	–
S.J.Harmison	2198.4	426	7091	222	31.94	7- 12	8	1
M.J.Hoggard	2318.1	493	7564	248	30.50	7- 61	7	1
S.P.Jones	470.1	78	1666	59	`28.23	6- 53	3	–
A.Khan	29	1	122	1	122.00	1-111	–	–
J.Lewis	41	9	122	3	40.66	3- 68	–	–
A.McGrath	17	1	56	4	14.00	3- 16	–	–
D.L.Maddy	14	1	40	0	–	–	–	–
S.I.Mahmood	188.2	25	762	20	38.10	4- 22	–	–
G.Onions	238.1	43	869	28	31.03	5- 38	1	–
M.S.Panesar	1648	352	4633	140	33.09	6- 37	10	1
D.J.Pattinson	30.1	2	96	2	48.00	2- 95	–	–
K.P.Pietersen	181.3	12	731	5	146.20	1- 0	–	–
L.E.Plunkett	256.2	40	916	23	39.82	3- 17	–	–
M.R.Ramprakash	149.1	16	477	4	119.25	1- 2	–	–
O.A.Shah	5	0	31	0	–	–	–	–
A.Shahzad	17	4	63	4	15.75	3- 45	–	–
R.J.Sidebottom	802	188	2231	79	28.24	7- 47	5	1
G.P.Swann	1598.4	311	4736	166	28.53	6- 65	11	1
J.C.Tredwell	65	13	181	6	30.16	4- 82	–	–
C.T.Tremlett	447.4	109	1311	49	26.75	6- 48	2	–
M.E.Trescothick	50	6	155	1	155.00	1- 34	–	–
I.J.L.Trott	56	5	227	3	75.66	1- 5	–	–

TEST　　　**AUSTRALIA – BATTING AND FIELDING**

	M	I	NO	HS	Runs	Avge	100	50	Ct/St
M.A.Beer	1	2	1	2*	4	4.00	–	–	1
D.E.Bollinger	12	14	7	21	54	7.71	–	–	2
M.J.Clarke	80	132	13	329*	5909	49.65	19	21	89
T.A.Copeland	3	4	1	23*	39	13.00	–	–	2
E.J.M.Cowan	4	6	–	74	206	34.33	–	2	8
P.J.Cummins	1	2	1	13*	15	15.00	–	–	1
X.J.Doherty	2	3	–	16	27	9.00	–	–	4
P.R.George	1	2	–	2	2	1.00	–	–	–
B.J.Haddin	43	71	8	169	2257	35.82	3	10	160/4
R.J.Harris	10	14	4	35*	127	12.70	–	–	2
N.M.Hauritz	17	24	7	75	426	25.05	–	2	3
B.W.Hilfenhaus	21	29	10	56*	281	14.78	–	1	6
P.J.Hughes	17	32	1	160	1072	34.58	3	3	7
M.E.K.Hussey	70	121	13	195	5489	50.82	16	27	70
P.A.Jaques	11	19	–	150	902	47.47	3	6	7
M.G.Johnson	47	69	10	123*	1287	21.81	1	6	13
S.M.Katich	56	99	6	157	4188	45.03	10	25	39
U.T.Khawaja	6	11	2	65	263	29.22	–	1	3
N.M.Lyon	10	12	5	14	55	7.85	–	–	4
S.E.Marsh	7	11	–	141	301	27.36	1	1	4
M.J.North	21	35	2	128	1171	35.48	5	4	17
T.D.Paine	4	8	–	92	287	35.87	–	2	16/1
J.L.Pattinson	4	5	2	37*	88	29.33	–	–	–
R.T.Ponting	162	276	29	257	13200	53.44	41	61	193
C.J.L.Rogers	1	2	–	15	19	9.50	–	–	1
P.M.Siddle	31	44	8	43	587	16.30	–	–	13
S.P.D.Smith	5	10	1	77	259	28.77	–	2	3
M.A.Starc	3	4	2	32*	51	25.50	–	–	1
D.A.Warner	6	10	2	180	419	52.37	2	–	9
S.R.Watson	32	58	2	126	2135	38.12	2	16	24

AUSTRALIA – BOWLING

	O	M	R	W	Avge	Best	5wI	10wM
M.A.Beer	38	3	112	1	112.00	1-112	–	–
D.E.Bollinger	400.1	78	1296	50	25.92	5- 28	2	–
M.J.Clarke	316	49	916	24	38.16	6- 9	1	–
T.A.Copeland	108	34	277	6	37.83	2- 24	–	–
P.J.Cummins	44	8	117	7	16.71	6- 79	1	–
X.J.Doherty	75.5	11	306	3	102.00	2- 41	–	–
P.R.George	28	3	77	2	38.50	2- 48	–	–
R.J.Harris	322.4	83	927	41	22.60	6- 47	2	–
N.M.Hauritz	700	143	2204	63	34.98	5- 53	2	–
B.W.Hilfenhaus	798.3	187	2371	82	28.91	5- 75	2	–
M.E.K.Hussey	77	9	215	6	35.83	1- 0	–	–
M.G.Johnson	1778.4	321	5946	190	31.29	8- 61	7	2
S.M.Katich	173.1	21	635	21	30.23	6- 65	1	–
N.M.Lyon	269.2	41	832	29	28.68	5- 34	1	–
M.J.North	209.4	37	591	14	42.21	6- 55	1	–
J.L.Pattinson	135.5	31	453	25	18.12	5- 27	2	–
R.T.Ponting	95.5	23	273	5	54.60	1- 0	–	–
P.M.Siddle	1069.4	268	3310	114	29.03	6- 54	5	–
S.P.D.Smith	62	10	220	3	73.33	3- 51	–	–
M.A.Starc	80.2	18	270	8	33.75	4- 70	–	–
D.A.Warner	3	0	13	0	–	–	–	–
S.R.Watson	527.2	117	1569	56	28.01	6- 33	3	–

TEST　　　　**SOUTH AFRICA – BATTING AND FIELDING**

	M	I	NO	HS	Runs	Avge	100	50	Ct/St
H.M.Amla	56	98	7	253*	4275	46.97	14	21	52
J.Botha	5	6	2	25	83	20.75	–	–	3
M.V.Boucher	143	200	23	125	5390	30.45	5	35	519/23
Z.de Bruyn	3	5	1	83	155	38.75	–	1	–
M.de Lange	1	2	–	9	9	4.50	–	–	1
A.B.de Villiers	71	120	14	278*	5239	49.42	13	27	97/1
H.H.Gibbs	90	154	7	228	6167	41.95	14	26	94
A.J.Hall	21	33	4	163	760	26.20	1	3	16
P.L.Harris	37	48	5	46	460	10.69	–	–	16
C.W.Henderson	7	7	–	30	65	9.28	–	–	2
Imran Tahir	5	6	3	29*	49	16.33	–	–	2
J.H.Kallis	149	252	38	224	12177	56.90	41	55	176
N.D.McKenzie	58	94	7	226	3253	37.39	5	16	54
J.A.Morkel	1	1	–	58	58	58.00	–	1	–
M.Morkel	36	43	4	40	497	12.74	–	–	11
A.N.Petersen	10	19	1	109	682	37.88	2	3	6
V.D.Philander	4	4	–	23	31	7.75	–	–	2
A.G.Prince	66	104	16	162*	3665	41.64	11	11	47
J.A.Rudolph	40	71	8	222*	2238	35.52	5	9	23
G.C.Smith	95	166	11	277	7748	49.98	23	30	122
D.W.Steyn	51	64	16	76	757	15.77	–	1	13
L.L.Tsotsobe	5	5	2	8*	19	6.33	–	–	1
C.M.Willoughby	2								

SOUTH AFRICA – BOWLING

	O	M	R	W	Avge	Best	5wI	10wM
H.M.Amla	7	0	28	0	–	–	–	–
J.Botha	169.3	29	573	17	33.70	4- 56	–	–
M.V.Boucher	1.2	0	6	1	6.00	1- 6	–	–
Z.de Bruyn	36	8	92	3	30.66	2- 32	–	–
M.de Lange	36.2	5	126	8	15.75	7- 81	1	–
A.B.de Villiers	33	6	99	2	49.50	2- 49	–	–
H.H.Gibbs	1	0	4	0	–	–	–	–
A.J.Hall	500.1	95	1617	45	35.93	3- 1	–	–
P.L.Harris	1468.1	336	3901	103	37.87	6-127	3	–
C.W.Henderson	327	79	928	22	42.18	4-116	–	–
Imran Tahir	150.3	16	515	14	36.78	3- 55	–	–
J.H.Kallis	3122	781	8872	273	32.49	6- 54	5	–
N.D.McKenzie	15	0	68	0	–	–	–	–
J.A.Morkel	32	4	132	1	132.00	1- 44	–	–
M.Morkel	1169.2	214	3944	119	30.57	5- 20	4	–
A.N.Petersen	12	1	36	1	36.00	1- 2	–	–
V.D.Philander	126.1	27	397	30	13.23	5- 15	4	1
A.G.Prince	16	1	47	1	47.00	1- 2	–	–
J.A.Rudolph	110.4	13	432	4	108.00	1- 1	–	–
G.C.Smith	226.2	28	839	8	104.87	2-145	–	–
D.W.Steyn	1755.3	333	6068	263	23.07	7- 51	17	4
L.L.Tsotsobe	145	35	448	9	49.77	3- 43	–	–
C.M.Willoughby	50	18	125	1	125.00	1- 47	–	–

TEST **WEST INDIES – BATTING AND FIELDING**

	M	I	NO	HS	Runs	Avge	100	50	Ct/St
A.B.Barath	9	17	–	104	478	28.11	1	4	11
C.S.Baugh	18	31	2	68	527	18.17	–	3	37/5
S.J.Benn	17	27	3	42	381	15.87	–	–	7
D.Bishoo	10	17	6	26	118	10.72	–	–	7
K.C.Brathwaite	6	12	–	68	292	24.33	–	3	3
D.J.Bravo	40	71	1	113	2200	31.42	3	13	41
D.M.Bravo	13	24	2	195	1155	52.50	3	6	5
G.R.Breese	1	2	–	5	5	2.50	–	–	1
S.Chanderpaul	137	234	37	203*	9709	49.28	24	56	56
C.D.Collymore	30	52	27	16*	197	7.88	–	–	6
F.H.Edwards	51	82	26	30	367	6.55	–	–	9
K.A.Edwards	6	12	1	121	595	54.09	2	3	5
C.H.Gayle	91	159	6	333	6373	41.65	13	33	85
B.P.Nash	21	33	–	114	1103	33.42	2	8	6
N.T.Pascal	2	2	–	10	12	6.00	–	–	1
K.O.A.Powell	4	8	–	81	197	24.62	–	2	–
R.Rampaul	13	24	7	40*	279	16.41	–	–	3
K.A.J.Roach	14	23	5	29	161	8.94	–	–	6
A.D.Russell	1	1	–	2	2	2.00	–	–	1
D.J.G.Sammy	21	36	–	58	626	17.38	–	1	29
M.N.Samuels	37	67	5	105	1824	29.41	2	13	19
R.R.Sarwan	87	154	8	291	5842	40.01	15	31	53
S.Shillingford	5	7	1	27	65	10.83	–	–	3
L.M.P.Simmons	8	16	–	49	278	17.37	–	–	5
D.S.Smith	33	58	2	108	1384	24.71	1	5	28

WEST INDIES – BOWLING

	O	M	R	W	Avge	Best	5wI	10wM
A.B.Barath	1	0	4	0	–	–	–	–
S.J.Benn	730.1	126	2112	51	41.41	6- 81	3	–
D.Bishoo	454.4	65	1413	39	36.23	5- 90	1	–
K.C.Brathwaite	7.4	0	50	1	50.00	1- 43	–	–
D.J.Bravo	1077.4	213	3426	86	39.83	6- 55	2	–
G.R.Breese	31.2	3	135	2	67.50	2-108	–	–
S.Chanderpaul	290	50	883	9	98.11	1- 2	–	–
C.D.Collymore	1056.1	245	3004	93	32.30	7- 57	4	1
F.H.Edwards	1462.1	163	5768	154	37.45	7- 87	11	–
K.A.Edwards	4	0	19	0	–	–	–	–
C.H.Gayle	1142.5	224	2995	72	41.59	5- 34	2	–
B.P.Nash	82	13	247	2	123.50	1- 21	–	–
N.T.Pascal	17	2	59	0	–	–	–	–
R.Rampaul	405.1	78	1215	35	34.71	4- 48	–	–
K.A.J.Roach	430.4	84	1403	43	32.62	6- 48	2	–
A.D.Russell	23	2	104	1	104.00	1- 73	–	–
D.J.G.Sammy	628.4	132	1773	59	30.05	7- 66	4	–
M.N.Samuels	425	47	1423	19	74.89	3- 74	–	–
R.R.Sarwan	337	33	1163	23	50.56	4- 37	–	–
S.Shillingford	241.2	24	795	14	56.78	4-123	–	–
L.M.P.Simmons	32	1	147	1	147.00	1- 60	–	–
D.S.Smith	1	0	3	0	–	–	–	–

TEST **NEW ZEALAND – BATTING AND FIELDING**

	M	I	NO	HS	Runs	Avge	100	50	Ct/St
A.R.Adams	1	2	–	11	18	9.00	–	–	1
B.J.Arnel	5	10	3	8*	34	4.85	–	–	3
H.K.Bennett	1	1	–	4	4	4.00	–	–	–
T.A.Boult	2	3	2	21	26	26.00	–	–	–
D.A.J.Bracewell	4	7	1	12	30	5.00	–	–	1
D.G.Brownlie	4	7	1	77*	268	44.66	–	3	7
J.E.C.Franklin	27	38	6	122*	683	21.34	1	2	11
M.J.Guptill	19	35	1	189	1148	33.76	2	7	20
G.J.Hopkins	4	7	1	15	71	11.83	–	–	9
B.B.McCullum	61	104	6	225	3560	36.32	6	20	169/11
T.G.McIntosh	17	33	2	136	854	27.54	2	4	10
A.J.McKay	1	2	1	20*	25	25.00	–	–	–
H.J.H.Marshall	13	19	2	160	652	38.35	2	2	1
C.S.Martin	65	94	47	12*	112	2.38	–	–	14
J.S.Patel	13	18	3	27*	188	12.53	–	–	8
J.D.Ryder	18	33	2	201	1269	40.93	3	6	12
T.G.Southee	16	27	4	77*	485	21.08	–	2	6
L.R.P.L.Taylor	34	62	2	154*	2571	42.85	6	15	60
D.L.Vettori	108	166	23	140	4389	30.69	6	23	57
B.J.Watling	7	13	3	102*	347	34.70	1	1	13
K.S.Williamson	9	16	–	131	492	30.75	1	3	4
R.A.Young	5	10	3	57	169	24.14	–	1	8

NEW ZEALAND – BOWLING

	O	M	R	W	Avge	Best	5wI	10wM
A.R.Adams	31.4	5	105	6	17.50	3- 44	–	–
B.J.Arnel	156	35	502	9	55.77	4- 95	–	–
H.K.Bennett	15	2	47	0	–	–	–	–
T.A.Boult	43	12	119	6	19.83	3- 29	–	–
D.A.J.Bracewell	117	30	346	21	16.47	6- 40	2	–
D.G.Brownlie	8	0	26	1	26.00	1- 13	–	–
J.E.C.Franklin	747.1	136	2648	80	33.10	6-119	3	–
M.J.Guptill	46.2	3	196	5	39.20	3- 37	–	–
B.B.McCullum	6	1	18	0	–	–	–	–
A.J.McKay	31	5	120	1	120.00	1-120	–	–
H.J.H.Marshall	1	0	4	0	–	–	–	–
C.S.Martin	2159.2	451	7268	218	33.33	6- 26	10	1
J.S.Patel	592	123	1936	40	48.40	5-110	1	–
J.D.Ryder	82	23	280	5	56.00	2- 7	–	–
T.G.Southee	505.2	98	1740	42	41.42	5- 55	1	–
L.R.P.L.Taylor	15	3	43	2	21.50	2- 4	–	–
D.L.Vettori	4608.5	1152	11980	356	33.65	7- 87	20	3
K.S.Williamson	48	0	205	3	68.33	1- 12	–	–

TEST

INDIA – BATTING AND FIELDING

	M	I	NO	HS	Runs	Avge	100	50	Ct/St
V.R.Aaron	1	2	1	4	6	6.00	–	–	–
R.Ashwin	6	10	2	103	284	35.50	1	1	1
M.S.Dhoni	67	106	12	148	3509	37.32	5	24	192/28
R.S.Dravid	163	284	32	270	13265	52.63	36	63	209
G.Gambhir	48	87	5	206	3712	45.26	9	19	33
Harbhajan Singh	98	138	22	115	2164	18.65	2	9	42
M.Kartik	8	10	1	43	88	9.77	–	–	2
Z.Khan	83	113	23	75	1114	12.37	–	3	18
V.Kohli	8	15	–	116	491	32.73	1	3	10
P.Kumar	6	10	–	40	149	14.90	–	–	2
V.V.S.Laxman	134	225	34	281	8781	45.97	17	56	135
A.Mishra	13	19	2	84	392	23.05	–	2	6
A.Mithun	4	5	–	46	120	24.00	–	–	1
A.Mukund	5	10	–	62	211	21.10	–	1	5
P.P.Ojha	14	15	11	18*	70	17.50	–	–	6
M.M.Patel	13	14	6	15*	60	7.50	–	–	6
C.A.Pujara	3	5	–	72	107	21.40	–	1	6
S.K.Raina	15	26	2	120	710	29.58	1	6	20
W.P.Saha	2	4	–	36	74	18.50	–	–	2
V.Sehwag	95	165	6	319	8095	50.91	22	31	73
I.Sharma	45	67	25	31*	432	10.28	–	–	11
R.P.Singh	14	19	3	30	116	7.25	–	–	6
S.Sreesanth	27	40	13	35	281	10.40	–	–	5
S.R.Tendulkar	188	311	32	248*	15470	55.44	51	65	113
J.D.Unadkat	1	2	1	1*	2	2.00	–	–	–
M.Vijay	12	20	–	139	609	30.45	1	2	10
R.Vinay Kumar	1	2	–	6	11	5.50	–	–	–
U.Yadav	6	9	5	21	28	7.00	–	–	1
Yuvraj Singh	37	57	6	169	1775	34.80	3	10	31

INDIA – BOWLING

	O	M	R	W	Avge	Best	5wI	10wM
V.R.Aaron	32	4	129	3	43.00	3-106	–	–
R.Ashwin	338	42	1069	31	34.48	6- 47	2	–
M.S.Dhoni	13	1	58	0	–	–	–	–
R.S.Dravid	20	4	39	1	39.00	1- 18	–	–
Harbhajan Singh	4608.3	848	13084	406	32.22	8- 84	25	5
M.Kartik	322	74	820	24	34.16	4- 44	–	–
Z.Khan	2786.3	558	9153	288	31.78	7- 87	10	1
P.Kumar	268.3	68	697	27	25.81	5-106	1	–
V.Kohli	11	0	35	0	–	–	–	–
V.V.S.Laxman	54	12	126	2	63.00	1- 2	–	–
A.Mishra	582.5	79	1862	43	43.30	5- 71	1	–
A.Mithun	120	21	456	9	50.66	4-105	–	–
A.Mukund	2	0	14	0	–	–	–	–
P.P.Ojha	767.1	162	2147	62	34.62	6- 47	2	–
M.M.Patel	443	95	1349	35	38.54	4- 25	–	–
S.K.Raina	148.3	17	524	13	40.30	2- 1	–	–
V.Sehwag	618.5	74	1889	40	47.22	5-104	1	–
I.Sharma	1472.3	267	5037	133	37.87	6- 55	3	1
R.P.Singh	422.2	59	1682	40	42.05	5- 59	1	–
S.Sreesanth	903.1	162	3271	87	37.59	5- 40	3	–
S.R.Tendulkar	695.4	82	2445	45	54.33	3- 10	–	–
J.D.Unadkat	26	4	101	0	–	–	–	–
R.Vinay Kumar	13	0	73	1	73.00	1- 73	–	–
U.Yadav	168.3	21	742	23	32.26	5- 93	1	–
Yuvraj Singh	142.1	13	501	9	55.66	2- 9	–	–

TEST **PAKISTAN – BATTING AND FIELDING**

	M	I	NO	HS	Runs	Avge	100	50	Ct/St
Abdul Razzaq	46	77	9	134	1946	28.61	3	7	15
Abdur Rehman	15	18	2	60	220	13.75	–	1	5
Adnan Akmal	13	15	2	61	327	25.15	–	2	43/6
Aizaz Cheema	6	5	5	1*	1	1.00	–	–	1
Asad Shafiq	13	19	2	104	637	40.34	1	4	11
Azhar Ali	21	39	4	157	1511	43.17	2	13	14
Azhar Mahmood	21	34	4	136	900	30.00	3	1	14
Junaid Khan	5	5	1	6	6	1.50	–	–	1
Misbah-ul-Haq	34	58	10	161*	2173	45.27	3	16	35
Mohammad Hafeez	26	50	5	143	1644	36.53	4	7	17
Mohammad Salman	2	4	–	13	25	6.25	–	–	2/1
Mohammad Sami	35	54	14	49	475	11.87	–	–	7
Naved-ul-Hasan	9	15	3	42*	239	19.91	–	–	3
Saeed Ajmal	20	28	9	50	227	11.94	–	1	6
Sohail Khan	2	1	–	11	11	11.00	–	–	–
Tanvir Ahmed	4	5	1	57	116	29.00	–	1	1
Taufiq Umar	40	75	4	236	2784	39.21	7	13	44
Umar Akmal	16	30	2	129	1003	35.82	1	6	12
Umar Gul	43	59	9	65*	541	10.82	–	1	9
Wahab Riaz	7	9	3	27	57	9.50	–	–	1
Younus Khan	76	133	11	313	6398	52.44	20	25	86

PAKISTAN – BOWLING

	O	M	R	W	Avge	Best	5wI	10wM
Abdul Razzaq	1168	219	3694	100	36.94	5- 35	1	–
Abdur Rehman	808.4	188	2053	75	27.37	6- 25	2	–
Aizaz Cheema	174	34	541	20	27.05	4- 24	–	–
Azhar Ali	11	2	44	1	44.00	1- 4	–	–
Azhar Mahmood	502.3	111	1402	39	35.94	4- 50	–	–
Junaid Khan	148.1	36	416	13	32.00	5- 38	1	–
Mohammad Hafeez	375	74	899	26	34.57	4- 31	–	–
Mohammad Sami	1224.5	192	4391	84	52.27	5- 36	2	–
Naved-ul-Hasan	260.5	36	1044	18	58.00	3- 30	–	–
Saeed Ajmal	1091.5	221	2857	107	26.70	7- 55	5	2
Sohail Khan	57	11	245	1	245.00	1- 62	–	–
Tanvir Ahmed	102.5	16	393	16	24.55	6-120	1	–
Taufiq Umar	13	2	44	0	–	–	–	–
Umar Gul	1476.5	234	5099	157	32.47	6-135	4	–
Wahab Riaz	164.2	27	580	17	34.11	5- 63	1	–
Younus Khan	111	16	410	7	58.57	2- 23	–	–

TEST **SRI LANKA – BATTING AND FIELDING**

	M	I	NO	HS	Runs	Avge	100	50	Ct/St
L.D.Chandimal	2	4	–	58	148	37.00	–	2	3/1
T.M.Dilshan	77	125	11	193	4662	40.89	12	20	78
R.M.S.Eranga	1	1	–	12	12	12.00	–	–	1
A.N.P.R.Fernando	1	2	–	1	1	0.50	–	–	–
C.R.D.Fernando	39	46	16	39*	249	8.30	–	–	10
H.M.R.K.B.Herath	35	49	11	80*	606	15.94	–	1	8
D.P.M.D.Jayawardena	128	213	13	374	10086	50.43	29	40	181
H.A.P.W.Jayawardena	43	58	8	154*	1594	31.88	4	3	81/26
H.K.S.R.Kaluhalamulla	6	8	1	12	44	6.28	–	–	–
C.K.B.Kulasekara	1	2	–	15	22	11.00	–	–	–
K.M.D.N.Kulasekara	12	17	1	64	262	16.37	–	1	4
R.A.S.Lakmal	10	12	4	18	55	6.87	–	–	2
M.F.Maharoof	22	34	4	72	556	18.53	–	3	7
A.D.Mathews	22	34	6	105*	1116	39.85	1	7	12
B.A.W.Mendis	16	17	6	78	164	14.90	–	1	2
M.T.T.Mirando	10	14	3	15*	94	8.54	–	–	3
M.Muralitharan	132	162	56	67	1259	11.87	–	1	72
N.T.Paranavitana	27	50	4	111	1543	33.54	2	10	21
N.L.T.C.Perera	5	9	–	30	128	14.22	–	–	–
K.T.G.D.Prasad	9	10	–	47	195	19.50	–	–	1
S.Prasanna	1	1	–	5	5	5.00	–	–	–
T.T.Samaraweera	71	114	20	231	5022	53.42	14	27	41
K.C.Sangakkara	106	179	12	287	9347	55.97	28	38	167/20
J.K.Silva	3	6	–	39	84	14.00	–	–	5/1
H.D.R.L.Thirimanne	5	10	1	68	230	25.55	–	1	2
W.P.J.U.C.Vaas	111	162	35	100*	3089	24.32	1	13	31
U.W.M.B.C.A.Welagedara	17	23	4	48	159	8.36	–	–	4

SRI LANKA – BOWLING

	O	M	R	W	Avge	Best	5wI	10wM
T.M.Dilshan	397.3	61	1190	29	41.03	4- 10	–	–
R.M.S.Eranga	42.2	8	127	5	25.40	4- 65	–	–
A.N.P.R.Fernando	28	1	110	0	–	–	–	–
C.R.D.Fernando	995.1	141	3662	97	37.75	5- 42	3	–
H.M.R.K.B.Herath	1456.2	273	4120	120	34.33	7-157	7	–
D.P.M.D.Jayawardena	92.1	18	297	6	49.50	2- 32	–	–
H.K.S.R.Kaluhalamulla	297.3	54	902	21	42.95	5- 82	1	–
C.K.B.Kulasekara	28	7	80	1	80.00	1- 65	–	–
K.M.D.N.Kulasekara	279.4	56	879	26	33.80	4- 21	–	–
R.A.S.Lakmal	264.5	38	984	18	54.66	3- 55	–	–
M.F.Maharoof	490	107	1631	25	65.24	4- 52	–	–
A.D.Mathews	157	28	501	7	71.57	1- 13	–	–
B.A.W.Mendis	665.3	102	2014	62	32.48	6-117	3	1
M.T.T.Mirando	278	35	1040	28	37.14	5- 83	1	–
M.Muralitharan	7285.5	1786	18023	795	22.67	9- 51	67	22
N.T.Paranavitana	17	0	86	1	86.00	1- 26	–	–
N.L.T.C.Perera	116	13	502	7	71.71	3-114	–	–
K.T.G.D.Prasad	243.2	16	1076	18	59.77	3- 82	–	–
S.Prasanna	23	3	80	0	–	–	–	–
T.T.Samaraweera	220.1	36	687	15	45.80	4- 49	–	–
K.C.Sangakkara	13	0	42	0	–	–	–	–
H.D.R.L.Thirimanne	1	0	7	0	–	–	–	–
W.P.U.C.J.Vaas	3906.2	895	10501	355	29.58	7- 71	12	2
U.W.M.B.C.A.Welagedara	519.3	94	1843	47	39.21	5- 52	2	–

TEST   **ZIMBABWE – BATTING AND FIELDING**

	M	I	NO	HS	Runs	Avge	100	50	Ct/St
R.W.Chakabva	2	4	–	63	108	27.00	–	1	2
E.Chigumbura	7	13	–	71	192	14.76	–	1	2
A.G.Cremer	7	14	1	26	58	4.46	–	–	3
C.R.Ervine	2	4	1	49	96	32.00	–	–	3
S.M.Ervine	5	8	–	86	261	32.62	–	3	7
M.W.Goodwin	19	37	4	166*	1414	42.84	3	8	10
K.M.Jarvis	4	7	4	25*	37	12.33	–	–	
G.A.Lamb	1	2	–	39	46	23.00	–	–	2
H.Masakadza	19	38	1	119	954	25.78	2	3	8
S.W.Masakadza	1	2	1	21	24	24.00	–	–	–
T.M.K.Mawoyo	4	8	1	163*	314	44.85	1	1	3
C.B.Mpofu	9	17	6	8	27	2.45	–	–	
F.Mutizwa	1	2	–	18	24	12.00	–	–	
N.Ncube	1	2	–	14	17	8.50	–	–	1
R.W.Price	21	36	7	36	242	8.34	–	–	4
V.Sibanda	6	12	–	93	320	26.66	–	2	4
T.Taibu	28	54	3	153	1546	30.31	1	2	57/5
B.R.M.Taylor	14	28	1	117	791	29.29	2	5	14
B.V.Vitori	3	5	–	14	33	6.60	–	–	1
M.N.Waller	2	4	1	72*	124	41.33	–	1	1

ZIMBABWE – BOWLING

	O	M	R	W	Avge	Best	5wI	10wM
E.Chigumbura	172.1	29	595	12	49.58	5- 54	1	–
A.G.Cremer	167	18	707	15	47.13	3- 86	–	–
S.M.Ervine	95	18	388	9	43.11	4-116	–	–
M.W.Goodwin	19.5	3	69	0	–	–	–	–
K.M.Jarvis	140.1	23	506	14	36.14	5- 64	1	–
G.A.Lamb	32	2	141	3	47.00	3-120	–	–
H.Masakadza	60	16	117	5	23.40	1- 9	–	–
S.W.Masakadza	23	2	102	1	102.00	1-102	–	–
C.B.Mpofu	241.2	43	889	20	44.45	4- 92	–	–
N.Ncube	35	4	121	1	121.00	1- 80	–	–
R.W.Price	1004.3	240	2838	79	35.92	6- 73	5	1
T.Taibu	8	1	27	1	27.00	1- 27	–	–
B.R.M.Taylor	7	0	38	0	–	–	–	–
B.V.Vitori	90	12	334	6	55.66	4- 66	–	–
M.N.Waller	3	0	8	0	–	–	–	–

TEST **BANGLADESH – BATTING AND FIELDING**

	M	I	NO	HS	Runs	Avge	100	50	Ct/St
Abdur Razzak	9	17	5	43	214	17.83	–	–	3
Elias Sunny	3	5	1	20*	38	9.50	–	–	1
Imrul Kayes	16	32	–	75	549	17.15	–	1	16
Mahmudullah	12	24	2	115	664	30.18	1	4	10
Mohammad Ashraful	57	111	4	158*	2419	22.60	5	8	24
Mushfiqur Rahim	28	55	4	101	1480	29.01	1	9	41/9
Naeem Islam	6	11	2	59*	264	29.33	–	1	2
Nasir Hossain	4	7	–	79	209	29.85	–	1	2
Nazimuddin	2	4	–	78	121	30.35	–	1	1
Nazmul Hossain	2	4	2	8*	16	8.00	–	–	–
Raqibul Hasan	9	18	1	65	336	19.76	–	1	9
Robiul Islam	3	6	2	12	21	5.25	–	–	2
Rubel Hossain	12	21	11	17·	84	8.40	–	–	5
Shafiul Islam	6	12	1	53	149	13.54	–	1	1
Shahadat Hossain	33	62	17	40	459	10.20	–	–	8
Shahriar Nafees	21	42	–	138	1126	26.80	1	7	17
Shakib Al Hasan	26	49	2	144	1630	34.68	2	9	9
Suhrawadi Shuvo	1	2	–	15	15	7.50	–	–	–
Tamim Iqbal	24	46	–	151	1748	38.00	4	10	8

BANGLADESH – BOWLING

	O	M	R	W	Avge	Best	5wI	10wM
Abdur Razzak	355.3	48	1185	18	65.83	3- 93	–	–
Elias Sunny	103.5	11	353	12	29.41	6- 94	1	–
Imrul Kayes	2	0	8	0	–	–	–	–
Mahmudullah	286.5	33	973	24	40.54	5- 51	1	–
Mohammad Ashraful	269.1	11	1208	20	60.40	2- 42	–	–
Naeem Islam	64	5	206	1	206.00	1- 11	–	–
Nasir Hossain	70	12	178	3	59.33	3- 52	–	–
Nazmul Hossain	54.5	10	194	5	38.80	2- 61	–	–
Raqibul Hasan	7	1	17	1	17.00	1- 0	–	–
Robiul Islam	90	10	359	4	89.75	2-106	–	–
Rubel Hossain	337	23	1415	17	83.23	5-166	1	–
Shafiul Islam	166	22	569	9	71.12	3- 86	–	–
Shahadat Hossain	805.2	80	3386	68	49.79	6- 27	4	–
Shakib Al Hasan	1063.3	212	3011	96	31.36	7- 36	9	–
Suhrawadi Shuvo	49.3	6	146	4	36.50	3- 73	–	–
Tamim Iqbal	4	0	10	0	–	–	–	–

INTERNATIONAL TEST MATCH RESULTS

Matches completed by 6 March 2012.

	Opponents	Tests	E	A	SA	WI	NZ	I	P	SL	Z	B	Tied	Drawn
							Won by						Tied	Drawn
England	Australia	326	102	133	–	–	–	–	–	–	–	–	–	91
	South Africa	138	56	–	29	–	–	–	–	–	–	–	–	53
	West Indies	145	43	–	–	53	–	–	–	–	–	–	–	49
	New Zealand	94	45	–	–	–	8	–	–	–	–	–	–	41
	India	103	38	–	–	–	–	19	–	–	–	–	–	46
	Pakistan	74	22	–	–	–	–	–	16	–	–	–	–	36
	Sri Lanka	24	9	–	–	–	–	–	–	6	–	–	–	9
	Zimbabwe	6	3	–	–	–	–	–	–	–	0	–	–	3
	Bangladesh	8	8	–	–	–	–	–	–	–	–	0	–	0
Australia	South Africa	85	–	48	19	–	–	–	–	–	–	–	–	18
	West Indies	108	–	52	–	32	–	–	–	–	–	–	1	23
	New Zealand	52	–	27	–	–	8	–	–	–	–	–	–	17
	India	82	–	38	–	–	–	20	–	–	–	–	1	23
	Pakistan	57	–	28	–	–	–	–	12	–	–	–	–	17
	Sri Lanka	23	–	14	–	–	–	–	–	1	–	–	–	8
	Zimbabwe	3	–	3	–	–	–	–	–	–	0	–	–	0
	Bangladesh	4	–	4	–	–	–	–	–	–	–	0	–	0
South Africa	West Indies	25	–	–	16	3	–	–	–	–	–	–	–	6
	New Zealand	35	–	–	20	–	4	–	–	–	–	–	–	11
	India	27	–	–	12	–	–	7	–	–	–	–	–	8
	Pakistan	18	–	–	8	–	–	–	3	–	–	–	–	7
	Sri Lanka	20	–	–	10	–	–	–	–	5	–	–	–	5
	Zimbabwe	7	–	–	6	–	–	–	–	–	0	–	–	1
	Bangladesh	8	–	–	8	–	–	–	–	–	–	0	–	0
West Indies	New Zealand	37	–	–	–	10	9	–	–	–	–	–	–	18
	India	88	–	–	–	30	–	14	–	–	–	–	–	44
	Pakistan	46	–	–	–	15	–	–	16	–	–	–	–	15
	Sri Lanka	15	–	–	–	3	–	–	–	6	–	–	–	6
	Zimbabwe	6	–	–	–	4	–	–	–	–	0	–	–	2
	Bangladesh	8	–	–	–	4	–	–	–	–	–	2	–	2
New Zealand	India	50	–	–	–	–	9	16	–	–	–	–	–	25
	Pakistan	50	–	–	–	–	7	–	23	–	–	–	–	20
	Sri Lanka	26	–	–	–	–	9	–	–	7	–	–	–	10
	Zimbabwe	15	–	–	–	–	9	–	–	–	0	–	–	6
	Bangladesh	9	–	–	–	–	8	–	–	–	–	0	–	1
India	Pakistan	59	–	–	–	–	–	9	12	–	–	–	–	38
	Sri Lanka	35	–	–	–	–	–	14	–	6	–	–	–	15
	Zimbabwe	11	–	–	–	–	–	7	–	–	2	–	–	2
	Bangladesh	7	–	–	–	–	–	6	–	–	–	0	–	1
Pakistan	Sri Lanka	40	–	–	–	–	–	–	16	9	–	–	–	15
	Zimbabwe	15	–	–	–	–	–	–	9	–	2	–	–	4
	Bangladesh	8	–	–	–	–	–	–	8	–	–	0	–	0
Sri Lanka	Zimbabwe	15	–	–	–	–	–	–	–	10	0	–	–	5
	Bangladesh	12	–	–	–	–	–	–	–	12	–	0	–	0
Zimbabwe	Bangladesh	9	–	–	–	–	–	–	–	–	5	1	–	3
		2033	326	347	128	154	71	112	115	62	9	3	2	704

	Tests	Won	Lost	Drawn	Tied	Toss Won
England	918	326	264	328	–	443
Australia	740	347	194	197	2	373
South Africa	363	128	126	109	–	175
West Indies	478	154	158	165	1	251
New Zealand	368	71	148	149	–	187
India	462	112	147	202	1	231
Pakistan	367	115	100	152	–	174
Sri Lanka	210	62	75	73	–	112
Zimbabwe	87	9	52	26	–	49
Bangladesh	73	3	63	7	–	38

INTERNATIONAL TEST CRICKET RECORDS

(To 6 March 2012)

TEAM RECORDS

HIGHEST INNINGS TOTALS

952-6d	Sri Lanka v India	Colombo (RPS)	1997-98
903-7d	England v Australia	The Oval	1938
849	England v West Indies	Kingston	1929-30
790-3d	West Indies v Pakistan	Kingston	1957-58
765-6d	Pakistan v Sri Lanka	Karachi	2008-09
760-7d	Sri Lanka v India	Ahmedabad	2009-10
758-8d	Australia v West Indies	Kingston	1954-55
756-5d	Sri Lanka v South Africa	Colombo (SSC)	2006
751-5d	West Indies v England	St John's	2003-04
749-9d	West Indies v England	Bridgetown	2008-09
747	West Indies v South Africa	St John's	2004-05
735-6d	Australia v Zimbabwe	Perth	2003-04
729-6d	Australia v England	Lord's	1930
726-9d	India v Sri Lanka	Mumbai	2009-10
713-3d	Sri Lanka v Zimbabwe	Bulawayo	2003-04
710-7d	England v India	Birmingham	2011
708	Pakistan v England	The Oval	1987
707	India v Sri Lanka	Colombo (SSC)	2010
705-7d	India v Australia	Sydney	2003-04
701	Australia v England	The Oval	1934
699-5	Pakistan v India	Lahore	1989-90
695	Australia v England	The Oval	1930
692-8d	West Indies v England	The Oval	1995
687-8d	West Indies v England	The Oval	1976
682-6d	South Africa v England	Lord's	2003
681-8d	West Indies v England	Port-of-Spain	1953-54
679-7d	Pakistan v India	Lahore	2005-06
676-7	India v Sri Lanka	Kanpur	1986-87
675-5d	India v Pakistan	Multan	2003-04
674-6	Pakistan v India	Faisalabad	1984-85
674-6d	Australia v England	Cardiff	2009
674	Australia v India	Adelaide	1947-48
671-4	New Zealand v Sri Lanka	Wellington	1990-91
668	Australia v West Indies	Bridgetown	1954-55
664	India v England	The Oval	2007

660-5d	West Indies v New Zealand	Wellington	1994-95
659-4d	Australia v India	Sydney	2011-12
659-8d	Australia v England	Sydney	1946-47
658-8d	England v Australia	Nottingham	1938
658-9d	South Africa v West Indies	Durban	2003-04
657-7d	India v Australia	Calcutta	2000-01
657-8d	Pakistan v West Indies	Bridgetown	1957-58
656-8d	Australia v England	Manchester	1964
654-5	England v South Africa	Durban	1938-39
653-4d	England v India	Lord's	1990
653-4d	Australia v England	Leeds	1993
652-7d	England v India	Madras	1984-85
652-7d	Australia v South Africa	Johannesburg	2001-02
652-8d	West Indies v England	Lord's	1973
652	Pakistan v India	Faisalabad	1982-83
651	South Africa v Australia	Cape Town	2008-09
650-6d	Australia v West Indies	Bridgetown	1964-65

The highest for Zimbabwe is 563-9d (v WI, Harare, 2001), and for Bangladesh 488 (v Z, Chittagong, 2004-05).

LOWEST INNINGS TOTALS
† One batsman absent

26	New Zealand v England	Auckland	1954-55
30	South Africa v England	Port Elizabeth	1895-96
30	South Africa v England	Birmingham	1924
35	South Africa v England	Cape Town	1898-99
36	Australia v England	Birmingham	1902
36	South Africa v Australia	Melbourne	1931-32
42	Australia v England	Sydney	1887-88
42	New Zealand v Australia	Wellington	1945-46
42†	India v England	Lord's	1974
43	South Africa v England	Cape Town	1888-89
44	Australia v England	The Oval	1896
45	England v Australia	Sydney	1886-87
45	South Africa v Australia	Melbourne	1931-32
46	England v West Indies	Port-of-Spain	1993-94
47	South Africa v England	Cape Town	1888-89
47	New Zealand v England	Lord's	1958
47	West Indies v England	Kingston	2003-04
47	Australia v South Africa	Cape Town	2011-12

The lowest for Pakistan is 53† (v A, Sharjah, 2002-03), for Sri Lanka 71 (v P, Kandy, 1994-95), for Zimbabwe 51 (v NZ, Napier, 2011-12), and for Bangladesh 62 (v SL, Colombo PPS, 2006-07).

BATTING RECORDS
5000 RUNS IN TESTS

Runs			M	I	NO	HS	Avge	100	50
15470	S.R.Tendulkar	I	188	311	32	248*	55.44	51	65
13288	R.S.Dravid	I/ICC	164	286	32	270	52.31	36	63
13200	R.T.Ponting	A	162	276	29	257	53.44	41	61
12260	J.H.Kallis	SA/ICC	150	254	39	224	57.02	41	55
11953	B.C.Lara	WI/ICC	131	232	6	400*	52.88	34	48
11174	A.R.Border	A	156	265	44	205	50.56	27	63
10927	S.R.Waugh	A	168	260	46	200	51.06	32	50
10122	S.M.Gavaskar	I	125	214	16	236*	51.12	34	45
10086	D.P.M.D.Jayawardena	SL	128	213	13	374	50.43	29	40
9709	S.Chanderpaul	WI	137	234	37	203*	49.28	24	56

72

Runs			M	I	NO	HS	Avge	100	50
9347	K.C.Sangakkara	SL	106	179	12	287	55.97	28	38
8900	G.A.Gooch	E	118	215	6	333	42.58	20	46
8832	Javed Miandad	P	124	189	21	280*	52.57	23	43
8830	Inzamam-ul-Haq	P/ICC	120	200	22	329	49.60	25	46
8781	V.V.S.Laxman	I	134	225	34	281	45.97	17	56
8625	M.L.Hayden	A	103	184	14	380	50.73	30	29
8540	I.V.A.Richards	WI	121	182	12	291	50.23	24	45
8463	A.J.Stewart	E	133	235	21	190	39.54	15	45
8231	D.I.Gower	E	117	204	18	215	44.25	18	39
8178	V.Sehwag	I/ICC	96	167	6	319	50.79	22	32
8114	G.Boycott	E	108	193	23	246*	47.72	22	42
8032	G.St A.Sobers	WI	93	160	21	365*	57.78	26	30
8029	M.E.Waugh	A	128	209	17	153*	41.81	20	47
7760	G.C.Smith	SA/ICC	96	168	11	277	49.42	23	30
7728	M.A.Atherton	E	115	212	7	185*	37.70	16	46
7696	J.L.Langer	A	105	182	12	250	45.27	23	30
7624	M.C.Cowdrey	E	114	188	15	182	44.06	22	38
7558	C.G.Greenidge	WI	108	185	16	226	44.72	19	34
7530	Mohammad Yousuf	P	90	156	12	223	52.29	24	33
7525	M.A.Taylor	A	104	186	13	334*	43.49	19	40
7515	C.H.Lloyd	WI	110	175	14	242*	46.67	19	39
7487	D.L.Haynes	WI	116	202	25	184	42.29	18	39
7422	D.C.Boon	A	107	190	20	200	43.65	21	32
7289	G.Kirsten	SA	101	176	15	275	45.27	21	34
7249	W.R.Hammond	E	85	140	16	336*	58.45	22	24
7212	S.C.Ganguly	I	113	188	17	239	42.17	16	35
7172	S.P.Fleming	NZ	111	189	10	274*	40.06	9	46
7110	G.S.Chappell	A	87	151	19	247*	53.86	24	31
6996	D.G.Bradman	A	52	80	10	334	99.94	29	13
6973	S.T.Jayasuriya	SL	110	188	14	340	40.07	14	31
6971	L.Hutton	E	79	138	15	364	56.67	19	33
6868	D.B.Vengsarkar	I	116	185	22	166	42.13	17	35
6806	K.F.Barrington	E	82	131	15	256	58.67	20	35
6744	G.P.Thorpe	E	100	179	28	200*	44.66	16	39
6490	A.J.Strauss	E	92	163	6	177	41.33	19	26
6428	K.P.Pietersen	E	81	139	7	227	48.69	19	25
6398	Younus Khan	P	76	133	11	313	52.44	20	25
6373	C.H.Gayle	WI	91	159	6	333	41.65	13	33
6361	P.A.de Silva	SL	93	159	11	267	42.97	20	22
6227	R.B.Kanhai	WI	79	137	6	256	47.53	15	28
6215	M.Azharuddin	I	99	147	9	199	45.03	22	21
6167	H.H.Gibbs	SA	90	154	7	228	41.95	14	26
6149	R.N.Harvey	A	79	137	10	205	48.41	21	24
6080	G.R.Viswanath	I	91	155	10	222	41.93	14	35
6027	A.N.Cook	E	75	131	7	294	48.60	19	27
5949	R.B.Richardson	WI	86	146	12	194	44.39	16	27
5909	M.J.Clarke	A	80	132	13	329*	49.65	19	21
5842	R.R.Sarwan	WI	87	154	8	291	40.01	15	31
5825	M.E.Trescothick	E	76	143	10	219	43.79	14	29
5807	D.C.S.Compton	E	78	131	15	278	50.06	17	28
5768	Salim Malik	P	103	154	22	237	43.69	15	29
5764	N.Hussain	E	96	171	16	207	37.19	14	33
5762	C.L.Hooper	WI	102	173	15	233	36.46	13	27
5719	M.P.Vaughan	E	82	147	9	197	41.44	18	18
5570	A.C.Gilchrist	A	96	137	20	204*	47.60	17	26
5502	M.S.Atapattu	SL	90	156	15	249	39.02	16	17

73

Runs			M	I	NO	HS	Avge	100	50
5489	M.E.K.Hussey	A	70	121	13	195	50.82	16	27
5444	M.D.Crowe	NZ	77	131	11	299	45.36	17	18
5410	J.B.Hobbs	E	61	102	7	211	56.94	15	28
5407	M.V.Boucher	SA/ICC	144	202	23	125	30.20	5	35
5357	K.D.Walters	A	74	125	14	250	48.26	15	33
5345	I.M.Chappell	A	75	136	10	196	42.42	14	26
5334	J.G.Wright	NZ	82	148	7	185	37.82	12	23
5312	M.J.Slater	A	74	131	7	219	42.84	14	21
5248	Kapil Dev	I	131	184	15	163	31.05	8	27
5239	A.B.de Villiers	SA	71	120	14	278*	49.42	13	27
5234	W.M.Lawry	A	67	123	12	210	47.15	13	27
5200	I.T.Botham	E	102	161	6	208	33.54	14	22
5138	J.H.Edrich	E	77	127	9	310*	43.54	12	24
5105	A.Ranatunga	SL	93	155	12	135*	35.69	4	38
5078	I.R.Bell	E	72	122	14	235	47.01	16	28
5062	Zaheer Abbas	P	78	124	11	274	44.79	12	20
5022	T.T.Samaraweera	SL	71	114	20	231	53.42	14	27

The most for Zimbabwe is 4794 (112 innings) by A.Flower, and for Bangladesh 3026 by Habibul Bashar (99 innings).

750 RUNS IN A SERIES

Runs			Series	M	I	NO	HS	Avge	100	50
974	D.G.Bradman	A v E	1930	5	7	–	334	139.14	4	–
905	W.R.Hammond	E v A	1928-29	5	9	1	251	113.12	4	–
839	M.A.Taylor	A v E	1989	6	11	1	219	83.90	2	5
834	R.N.Harvey	A v SA	1952-53	5	9	–	205	92.66	4	3
829	I.V.A.Richards	WI v E	1976	4	7	–	291	118.42	3	2
827	C.L.Walcott	WI v A	1954-55	5	10	–	155	82.70	5	2
824	G.St A.Sobers	WI v P	1957-58	5	8	2	365*	137.33	3	3
810	D.G.Bradman	A v E	1936-37	5	9	–	270	90.00	3	1
806	D.G.Bradman	A v SA	1931-32	5	5	1	299*	201.50	4	–
798	B.C.Lara	WI v E	1993-94	5	8	–	375	99.75	2	2
779	E.de C.Weekes	WI v I	1948-49	5	7	–	194	111.28	4	2
774	S.M.Gavaskar	I v WI	1970-71	4	8	3	220	154.80	4	3
766	A.N.Cook	E v A	2010-11	5	7	1	235*	127.66	3	2
765	B.C.Lara	WI v E	1995	6	10	1	179	85.00	3	3
761	Mudassar Nazar	P v I	1982-83	5	8	2	231	126.83	4	1
758	D.G.Bradman	A v E	1934	5	8	–	304	94.75	2	1
753	D.C.S.Compton	E v SA	1947	5	8	–	208	94.12	4	2
752	G.A.Gooch	E v I	1990	3	6	–	333	125.33	3	2

HIGHEST INDIVIDUAL INNINGS

400*	B.C.Lara	WI v E	St John's	2003-04
380	M.L.Hayden	A v Z	Perth	2003-04
375	B.C.Lara	WI v E	St John's	1993-94
374	D.P.M.D.Jayawardena	SL v SA	Colombo (SSC)	2006
365*	G.St A.Sobers	WI v P	Kingston	1957-58
364	L.Hutton	E v A	The Oval	1938
340	S.T.Jayasuriya	SL v I	Colombo (RPS)	1997-98
337	Hanif Mohammed	P v WI	Bridgetown	1957-58
336*	W.R.Hammond	E v NZ	Auckland	1932-33
334*	M.A.Taylor	A v P	Peshawar	1998-99
334	D.G.Bradman	A v E	Leeds	1930
333	G.A.Gooch	E v I	Lord's	1990
333	C.H.Gayle	WI v SL	Galle	2010-11
329*	M.J.Clarke	A v I	Sydney	2011-12

74

329	Inzamam-ul-Haq	P v NZ	Lahore	2001-02
325	A.Sandham	E v WI	Kingston	1929-30
319	V.Sehwag	I v SA	Chennai	2007-08
317	C.H.Gayle	WI v SA	St John's	2004-05
313	Younus Khan	P v SL	Karachi	2008-09
311	R.B.Simpson	A v E	Manchester	1964
310*	J.H.Edrich	E v NZ	Leeds	1965
309	V.Sehwag	I v P	Multan	2003-04
307	R.M.Cowper	A v E	Melbourne	1965-66
304	D.G.Bradman	A v E	Leeds	1934
302	L.G.Rowe	WI v E	Bridgetown	1973-74
299*	D.G.Bradman	A v SA	Adelaide	1931-32
299	M.D.Crowe	NZ v SL	Wellington	1990-91
294	A.N.Cook	E v I	Birmingham	2011
293	V.Sehwag	I v SL	Mumbai	2009-10
291	I.V.A.Richards	WI v E	The Oval	1976
291	R.R.Sarwan	WI v E	Bridgetown	2008-09
287	R.E.Foster	E v A	Sydney	1903-04
287	K.C.Sangakkara	SL v SA	Colombo (SSC)	2006
285*	P.B.H.May	E v WI	Birmingham	1957
281	V.V.S.Laxman	I v A	Calcutta	2000-01
280*	Javed Miandad	P v I	Hyderabad	1982-83
278*	A.B.de Villiers	SA v P	Abu Dhabi	2010-11
278	D.C.S.Compton	E v P	Nottingham	1954
277	B.C.Lara	WI v A	Sydney	1992-93
277	G.C.Smith	SA v E	Birmingham	2003
275*	D.J.Cullinan	SA v NZ	Auckland	1998-99
275	G.Kirsten	SA v E	Durban	1999-00
275	D.P.M.D.Jayawardena	SL v I	Ahmedabad	2009-10
274*	S.P.Fleming	NZ v SL	Colombo (SSC)	2002-03
274	R.G.Pollock	SA v A	Durban	1969-70
274	Zaheer Abbas	P v E	Birmingham	1971
271	Javed Miandad	P v NZ	Auckland	1988-89
270*	G.A.Headley	WI v E	Kingston	1934-35
270	D.G.Bradman	A v E	Melbourne	1936-37
270	R.S.Dravid	I v P	Rawalpindi	2003-04
270	K.C.Sangakkara	SL v Z	Bulawayo	2003-04
268	G.N.Yallop	A v P	Melbourne	1983-84
267*	B.A.Young	NZ v SL	Dunedin	1996-97
267	P.A.de Silva	SL v NZ	Wellington	1990-91
267	Younus Khan	P v I	Bangalore	2004-05
266	W.H.Ponsford	A v E	The Oval	1934
266	D.L.Houghton	Z v SL	Bulawayo	1994-95
262*	D.L.Amiss	E v WI	Kingston	1973-74
262	S.P.Fleming	NZ v SA	Cape Town	2005-06
261*	R.R.Sarwan	WI v B	Kingston	2004
261	F.M.M.Worrell	WI v E	Nottingham	1950
260	C.C.Hunte	WI v P	Kingston	1957-58
260	Javed Miandad	P v E	The Oval	1987
259	G.M.Turner	NZ v WI	Georgetown	1971-72
259	G.C.Smith	SA v E	Lord's	2003
258	T.W.Graveney	E v WI	Nottingham	1957
258	S.M.Nurse	WI v NZ	Christchurch	1968-69
257*	Wasim Akram	P v Z	Sheikhupura	1996-97
257	R.T.Ponting	A v I	Melbourne	2003-04
256	R.B.Kanhai	WI v I	Calcutta	1958-59
256	K.F.Barrington	E v A	Manchester	1964

255*	D.J.McGlew	SA v NZ	Wellington	1952-53
254	D.G.Bradman	A v E	Lord's	1930
254	V.Sehwag	I v P	Lahore	2005-06
253*	H.M.Amla	SA v I	Nagpur	2009-10
253	S.T.Jayasuriya	SL v P	Faisalabad	2004-05
251	W.R.Hammond	E v A	Sydney	1928-29
250	K.D.Walters	A v NZ	Christchurch	1976-77
250	S.F.A.F.Bacchus	WI v I	Kanpur	1978-79
250	J.L.Langer	A v E	Melbourne	2002-03

The highest for Bangladesh is 158* by Mohammad Ashraful (v I, Chittagong, 2004-05).

20 HUNDREDS

			200	Inn	E	A	SA	WI	NZ	I	P	SL	Z	B
51	S.R.Tendulkar	I	6	311	7	11	7	3	4	–	2	9	3	5
41	J.H.Kallis	SA	2	254	7	4	–	8	5	6	6	1	3	1
41	R.T.Ponting	A	6	276	8	–	8	7	2	8	5	1	1	1
36	R.S.Dravid	I	5	286	7	2	2	5	6	–	5	3	3	3
34	S.M.Gavaskar	I	4	214	4	8	–	13	2	–	5	2	–	–
34	B.C.Lara	WI	9	232	7	9	4	–	1	2	4	5	1	1
32	S.R.Waugh	A	1	260	10	–	2	7	2	2	3	3	1	2
30	M.L.Hayden †	A	2	184	5	–	6	5	1	6	1	3	2	–
29	D.G.Bradman	A	12	80	19	–	4	2	–	4	–	–	–	–
29	D.P.M.D.Jayawardena	SL	6	213	6	2	5	1	3	6	1	–	1	4
28	K.C.Sangakkara	SL	8	179	2	1	3	3	3	5	7	–	2	2
27	A.R.Border	A	2	265	8	–	3	5	4	6	1	–	–	–
26	G.St A.Sobers	WI	2	160	10	4	–	1	8	3	–	–	–	–
25	Inzamam-ul-Haq	P	2	200	5	1	–	4	3	3	–	5	2	2
24	G.S.Chappell	A	4	151	9	–	5	3	1	6	–	–	–	–
24	Mohammad Yousuf	P	4	156	6	1	–	7	1	4	–	1	2	2
24	I.V.A.Richards	WI	3	182	8	5	–	1	8	2	–	–	–	–
24	S.Chanderpaul	WI	1	234	5	4	5	–	1	7	1	–	–	1
23	G.C.Smith	SA	4	168	6	2	–	7	1	3	1	–	1	3
23	J.L.Langer	A	3	182	5	–	2	3	4	3	4	2	–	–
23	Javed Miandad	P	6	189	2	6	–	2	7	5	–	1	–	–
22	W.R.Hammond	E	7	140	–	9	6	1	4	2	–	–	–	–
22	M.Azharuddin	I	–	147	6	2	–	4	–	2	–	3	5	–
22	V.Sehwag	I	6	167	1	3	5	2	–	2	4	5	–	–
22	M.C.Cowdrey	E	–	188	–	5	3	6	2	3	3	–	–	–
21	G.Boycott	E	1	193	–	7	1	5	2	4	3	–	–	–
21	R.N.Harvey	A	2	137	6	–	8	3	–	4	–	–	–	–
21	G.Kirsten	SA	3	176	5	2	–	3	2	3	2	1	1	2
21	D.C.Boon	A	1	190	7	–	3	3	6	1	1	–	–	–
20	K.F.Barrington	E	1	131	–	5	2	3	3	3	4	–	–	–
20	Younus Khan	P	3	133	2	–	3	2	1	5	–	5	–	2
20	P.A.de Silva	SL	2	159	2	1	–	2	2	5	8	–	1	1
20	M.E.Waugh	A	–	209	6	–	4	4	1	1	3	1	–	–
20	G.A.Gooch	E	2	215	–	4	–	5	4	5	1	1	–	–

† Includes century scored for Australia v ICC in 2005-06.

The most for New Zealand is 17 by M.D.Crowe (131 innings), for Zimbabwe 12 by A.Flower (112), and for Bangladesh 5 by Mohammad Ashraful (107 innings).

The most double hundreds by batsmen not included above are 6 by M.S.Atapattu (16 hundreds for Sri Lanka), 4 by L.Hutton (19 for England), 4 by C.G.Greenidge (19 for West Indies), and 4 by Zaheer Abbas (12 for Pakistan).

HIGHEST PARTNERSHIP FOR EACH WICKET

1st	415	N.D.McKenzie/G.C.Smith	SA v B	Chittagong	2007-08
2nd	576	S.T.Jayasuriya/R.S.Mahanama	SL v I	Colombo (RPS)	1997-98
3rd	624	K.C.Sangakkara/D.P.M.D.Jayawardena	SL v SA	Colombo (SSC)	2006
4th	437	D.P.M.D.Jayawardena/T.T.Samaraweera	SL v P	Karachi	2008-09
5th	405	S.G.Barnes/D.G.Bradman	A v E	Sydney	1946-47
6th	351	D.P.M.D.Jayawardena/H.A.P.W.Jayawardena	SL v I	Ahmedabad	2009-10
7th	347	D.St E.Atkinson/C.C.Depeiza	WI v A	Bridgetown	1954-55
8th	332	I.J.L.Trott/S.C.J.Broad	E v P	Lord's	2010
9th	195	M.V.Boucher/P.L.Symcox	SA v P	Johannesburg	1997-98
10th	151	B.F.Hastings/R.O.Collinge	NZ v P	Auckland	1972-73
	151	Azhar Mahmood/Mushtaq Ahmed	P v SA	Rawalpindi	1997-98

BOWLING RECORDS
200 WICKETS IN TESTS

Wkts			M	Balls	Runs	Avge	5 wI	10 wM
800	M.Muralitharan	SL/ICC	133	44039	18180	22.72	67	22
708	S.K.Warne	A	145	40705	17995	25.41	37	10
619	A.Kumble	I	132	40850	18355	29.65	35	8
563	G.D.McGrath	A	124	29248	12186	21.64	29	3
519	C.A.Walsh	WI	132	30019	12688	24.44	22	3
434	Kapil Dev	I	131	27740	12867	29.64	23	2
431	R.J.Hadlee	NZ	86	21918	9612	22.30	36	9
421	S.M.Pollock	SA	108	24453	9733	23.11	16	1
414	Wasim Akram	P	104	22627	9779	23.62	25	5
406	Harbhajan Singh	I	98	27651	13084	32.22	25	5
405	C.E.L.Ambrose	WI	98	22104	8500	20.98	22	3
390	M.Ntini	SA	101	20834	11242	28.82	18	4
383	I.T.Botham	E	102	21815	10878	28.40	27	4
376	M.D.Marshall	WI	81	17584	7876	20.94	22	4
373	Waqar Younis	P	87	16224	8788	23.56	22	5
362	Imran Khan	P	88	19458	8258	22.81	23	6
356	D.L.Vettori	NZ/ICC	108	27653	11980	33.65	20	3
355	D.K.Lillee	A	70	18467	8493	23.92	23	7
355	W.P.J.U.C.Vaas	SL	111	23438	10501	29.58	12	2
330	A.A.Donald	SA	72	15519	7344	22.25	20	3
325	R.G.D.Willis	E	90	17357	8190	25.20	16	–
310	B.Lee	A	76	16531	9554	30.81	10	–
309	L.R.Gibbs	WI	79	27115	8989	29.09	18	2
307	F.S.Trueman	E	67	15178	6625	21.57	17	3
297	D.L.Underwood	E	86	21862	7674	25.83	17	6
291	C.J.McDermott	A	71	16586	8332	28.63	14	2
288	Z.Khan	I	83	16719	9153	31.78	10	1
274	J.H.Kallis	SA/ICC	150	18792	8910	32.51	5	–
266	B.S.Bedi	I	67	21364	7637	28.71	14	1
263	D.W.Steyn	SA	51	10533	6068	23.07	17	4
261	Danish Kaneria	P	61	17697	9082	34.79	15	2
259	J.Garner	WI	58	13169	5433	20.97	7	–
259	J.N.Gillespie	A	71	14234	6770	26.13	8	–
252	J.B.Statham	E	70	16056	6261	24.84	9	1
249	M.A.Holding	WI	60	12680	5898	23.68	13	2
249	J.M.Anderson	E	66	14192	7587	30.46	11	1
248	R.Benaud	A	63	19108	6704	27.03	16	1
248	M.J.Hoggard	E	67	13909	7564	30.50	7	1
246	G.D.McKenzie	A	60	17681	7328	29.78	16	3
242	B.S.Chandrasekhar	I	58	15963	7199	29.74	16	2
236	A.V.Bedser	E	51	15918	5876	24.89	15	5
236	J.Srinath	I	67	15104	7196	30.49	10	1
236	Abdul Qadir	P	67	17126	7742	32.80	15	5
235	G.St A.Sobers	WI	93	21599	7999	34.03	6	–

Wkts			M	Balls	Runs	Avge	5 wI	10 wM
234	A.R.Caddick	E	62	13558	6999	29.91	13	1
229	D.Gough	E	58	11821	6503	28.39	9	–
228	R.R.Lindwall	A	61	13650	5251	23.03	12	–
226	S.J.Harmison	E/ICC	63	13375	7192	31.82	8	1
226	A.Flintoff	E/ICC	79	14951	7410	32.78	3	–
218	C.L.Cairns	NZ	62	11698	6410	29.40	13	1
218	C.S.Martin	NZ	65	12956	7268	33.33	10	1
216	C.V.Grimmett	A	37	14513	5231	24.21	21	7
216	H.H.Streak	Z	65	13559	6079	28.14	7	–
212	M.G.Hughes	A	53	12285	6017	28.38	7	1
208	S.C.G.MacGill	A	44	11237	6038	29.02	12	2
208	Saqlain Mushtaq	P	49	14070	6206	29.83	13	3
202	A.M.E.Roberts	WI	47	11136	5174	25.61	11	2
202	J.A.Snow	E	49	12021	5387	26.66	8	1
200	J.R.Thomson	A	51	10535	5601	28.00	8	–

The most for Bangladesh is 100 in 33 Tests by Mohammad Rafique.

35 OR MORE WICKETS IN A SERIES

Wkts			Series	M	Balls	Runs	Avge	5 wI	10 wM
49	S.F.Barnes	E v SA	1913-14	4	1356	536	10.93	7	3
46	J.C.Laker	E v A	1956	5	1703	442	9.60	4	2
44	C.V.Grimmett	A v SA	1935-36	5	2077	642	14.59	5	3
42	T.M.Alderman	A v E	1981	6	1950	893	21.26	4	–
41	R.M.Hogg	A v E	1978-79	6	1740	527	12.85	5	2
41	T.M.Alderman	A v E	1989	6	1616	712	17.36	6	1
40	Imran Khan	P v I	1982-83	6	1339	558	13.95	4	2
40	S.K.Warne	A v E	2005	5	1517	797	19.92	3	2
39	A.V.Bedser	E v A	1953	5	1591	682	17.48	5	1
39	D.K.Lillee	A v E	1981	6	1870	870	22.30	2	1
38	M.W.Tate	E v A	1924-25	5	2528	881	23.18	5	1
37	W.J.Whitty	A v SA	1910-11	5	1395	632	17.08	2	–
37	H.J.Tayfield	SA v E	1956-57	5	2280	636	17.18	4	1
36	A.E.E.Vogler	SA v E	1909-10	5	1349	783	21.75	4	1
36	A.A.Mailey	A v E	1920-21	5	1465	946	26.27	4	2
36	G.D.McGrath	A v E	1997	6	1499	701	19.47	2	–
35	G.A.Lohmann	E v SA	1895-96	3	520	203	5.80	4	2
35	B.S.Chandrasekhar	I v E	1972-73	5	1747	662	18.91	4	–
35	M.D.Marshall	WI v E	1988	5	1219	443	12.65	3	1

The most for New Zealand is 33 by R.J.Hadlee (3 Tests v A, 1985-86), for Sri Lanka 30 by M.Muralitharan (3 Tests v Z, 2001-02), for Zimbabwe 22 by H.H.Streak (3 Tests v P, 1994-95), and for Bangladesh 18 by Enamul Haque[2] (2 Tests v Z, 2004-05).

15 OR MORE WICKETS IN A TEST († On debut)

19- 90	J.C.Laker	E v A	Manchester	1956
17-159	S.F.Barnes	E v SA	Johannesburg	1913-14
16-136†	N.D.Hirwani	I v WI	Madras	1987-88
16-137†	R.A.L.Massie	A v E	Lord's	1972
16-220	M.Muralitharan	SL v E	The Oval	1998
15- 28	J.Briggs	E v SA	Cape Town	1888-89
15- 45	G.A.Lohmann	E v SA	Port Elizabeth	1895-96
15- 99	C.Blythe	E v SA	Leeds	1907
15-104	H.Verity	E v A	Lord's	1934
15-123	R.J.Hadlee	NZ v A	Brisbane	1985-86
15-124	W.Rhodes	E v A	Melbourne	1903-04
15-217	Harbhajan Singh	I v A	Madras	2000-01

The best analysis for South Africa is 13-132 by M.Ntini (v WI, Port-of-Spain, 2004-05), for West Indies 14-149 by M.A.Holding (v E, The Oval, 1976), for Pakistan 14-116 by Imran Khan (v SL, Lahore, 1981-82), for Zimbabwe 11-257 by A.G.Huckle (v NZ, Bulawayo, 1997-98), and for Bangladesh 12-200 by Enamul Haque II (v Z, Dhaka, 2004-05).

NINE OR MORE WICKETS IN AN INNINGS

10- 53	J.C.Laker	E v A	Manchester	1956
10- 74	A.Kumble	I v P	Delhi	1998-99
9- 28	G.A.Lohmann	E v SA	Johannesburg	1895-96
9- 37	J.C.Laker	E v A	Manchester	1956
9- 51	M.Muralitharan	SL v Z	Kandy	2001-02
9- 52	R.J.Hadlee	NZ v A	Brisbane	1985-86
9- 56	Abdul Qadir	P v E	Lahore	1987-88
9- 57	D.E.Malcolm	E v SA	The Oval	1994
9- 65	M.Muralitharan	SL v E	The Oval	1998
9- 69	J.M.Patel	I v A	Kanpur	1959-60
9- 83	Kapil Dev	I v WI	Ahmedabad	1983-84
9- 86	Sarfraz Nawaz	P v A	Melbourne	1978-79
9- 95	J.M.Noreiga	WI v I	Port-of-Spain	1970-71
9-102	S.P.Gupte	I v WI	Kanpur	1958-59
9-103	S.F.Barnes	E v SA	Johannesburg	1913-14
9-113	H.J.Tayfield	SA v E	Johannesburg	1956-57
9-121	A.A.Mailey	A v E	Melbourne	1920-21

The best analysis for Zimbabwe is 8-109 by P.A.Strang (v NZ, Bulawayo, 2000-01), and for Bangladesh 7-36 by Shakib Al Hasan (v NZ, Chittagong, 2008-09).

HAT-TRICKS

F.R.Spofforth	Australia v England	Melbourne	1878-79
W.Bates[7]	England v Australia	Melbourne	1882-83
J.Briggs[7]	England v Australia	Sydney	1891-92
G.A.Lohmann	England v South Africa	Port Elizabeth	1895-96
J.T.Hearne	England v Australia	Leeds	1899
H.Trumble	Australia v England	Melbourne	1901-02
H.Trumble	Australia v England	Melbourne	1903-04
T.J.Matthews (2)[2]	Australia v South Africa	Manchester	1912
M.J.C.Allom[1]	England v New Zealand	Christchurch	1929-30
T.W.J.Goddard	England v South Africa	Johannesburg	1938-39
P.J.Loader	England v West Indies	Leeds	1957
L.F.Kline	Australia v South Africa	Cape Town	1957-58
W.W.Hall	West Indies v Pakistan	Lahore	1958-59
G.M.Griffin[7]	South Africa v England	Lord's	1960
L.R.Gibbs	West Indies v Australia	Adelaide	1960-61
P.J.Petherick[1/7]	New Zealand v Pakistan	Lahore	1976-77
C.A.Walsh[3]	West Indies v Australia	Brisbane	1988-89
M.G.Hughes[3/7]	Australia v West Indies	Perth	1988-89
D.W.Fleming[1]	Australia v Pakistan	Rawalpindi	1994-95
S.K.Warne	Australia v England	Melbourne	1994-95
D.G.Cork	England v West Indies	Manchester	1995
D.Gough[7]	England v Australia	Sydney	1998-99
Wasim Akram[4]	Pakistan v Sri Lanka	Lahore	1998-99
Wasim Akram[4]	Pakistan v Sri Lanka	Dhaka	1998-99
D.N.T.Zoysa[5]	Sri Lanka v Zimbabwe	Harare	1999-00
Abdul Razzaq	Pakistan v Sri Lanka	Galle	2000-01
G.D.McGrath	Australia v West Indies	Perth	2000-01
Harbhajan Singh	India v Australia	Calcutta	2000-01

Mohammad Sami[7]	Pakistan v Sri Lanka	Lahore	2001-02
J.J.C.Lawson[7]	West Indies v Australia	Bridgetown	2002-03
Alok Kapali[7]	Bangladesh v Pakistan	Peshawar	2003
A.M.Blignaut	Zimbabwe v Bangladesh	Harare	2003-04
M.J.Hoggard	England v West Indies	Bridgetown	2003-04
J.E.C.Franklin	New Zealand v Bangladesh	Dhaka	2004-05
I.K.Pathan[6/7]	India v Pakistan	Karachi	2005-06
R.J.Sidebottom[7]	England v New Zealand	Hamilton	2007-08
P.M.Siddle	Australia v England	Brisbane	2010-11
S.C.J.Broad	England v India	Nottingham	2011

[1] On debut. [2] Hat-trick in each innings. [3] Involving both innings. [4] In successive Tests.
[5] His first 3 balls (second over of the match). [6] The fourth, fifth and sixth balls of the match.
[7] On losing side.

WICKET-KEEPING RECORDS
100 DISMISSALS IN TESTS†

Total			Tests	Ct	St
544	M.V.Boucher	South Africa/ICC	144	521	23
416	A.C.Gilchrist	Australia	96	379	37
395	I.A.Healy	Australia	119	366	29
355	R.W.Marsh	Australia	96	343	12
270†	P.J.L.Dujon	West Indies	79	265	5
269	A.P.E.Knott	England	95	250	19
241†	A.J.Stewart	England	82	227	14
228	Wasim Bari	Pakistan	81	201	27
220	M.S.Dhoni	India	67	192	28
219	R.D.Jacobs	West Indies	65	207	12
219	T.G.Evans	England	91	173	46
206	Kamran Akmal	Pakistan	53	184	22
201†	A.C.Parore	New Zealand	67	194	7
198	S.M.H.Kirmani	India	88	160	38
189	D.L.Murray	West Indies	62	181	8
187	A.T.W.Grout	Australia	51	163	24
176	I.D.S.Smith	New Zealand	63	168	8
174	R.W.Taylor	England	57	167	7
172†	B.B.McCullum	New Zealand	51	161	11
165	R.C.Russell	England	54	153	12
164	B.J.Haddin	Australia	43	160	4
156	M.J.Prior	England	50	149	7
152	D.J.Richardson	South Africa	42	150	2
151†	K.C.Sangakkara	Sri Lanka	48	131	20
151†	A.Flower	Zimbabwe	55	142	9
147†	Moin Khan	Pakistan	66	127	20
141	J.H.B.Waite	South Africa	49	124	17
133	G.O.Jones	England	34	128	5
130	Rashid Latif	Pakistan	37	119	11
130	K.S.More	India	49	110	20
130	W.A.S.Oldfield	Australia	54	78	52
122	D.Ramdin	West Indies	42	119	3
119	R.S.Kaluwitharana	Sri Lanka	49	93	26
112†	J.M.Parks	England	43	101	11
107	H.A.P.W.Jayawardena	Sri Lanka	43	81	26
107	N.R.Mongia	India	44	99	8
104	Salim Yousuf	Pakistan	32	91	13
101†	J.R.Murray	West Indies	31	98	3

The most for Bangladesh is 87 (78 ct, 9 st) by Khaled Masud in 44 Tests.
  † Excluding catches taken in the field

25 OR MORE DISMISSALS IN A SERIES

28	R.W.Marsh	Australia v England	1982-83
27 (inc 2st)	R.C.Russell	England v South Africa	1995-96
27 (inc 2st)	I.A.Healy	Australia v England (6 Tests)	1997
26 (inc 3st)	J.H.B.Waite	South Africa v New Zealand	1961-62
26	R.W.Marsh	Australia v West Indies (6 Tests)	1975-76
26 (inc 5st)	I.A.Healy	Australia v England (6 Tests)	1993
26 (inc 1st)	M.V.Boucher	South Africa v England	1998
26 (inc 2st)	A.C.Gilchrist	Australia v England	2001
26 (inc 2st)	A.C.Gilchrist	Australia v England	2006-07
25 (inc 2st)	I.A.Healy	Australia v England	1994-95
25 (inc 2st)	A.C.Gilchrist	Australia v England	2002-03
25	A.C.Gilchrist	Australia v India	2007-08

TEN OR MORE DISMISSALS IN A TEST

11	R.C.Russell	England v South Africa	Johannesburg	1995-96
10	R.W.Taylor	England v India	Bombay	1979-80
10	A.C.Gilchrist	Australia v New Zealand	Hamilton	1999-00

SEVEN DISMISSALS IN AN INNINGS

7	Wasim Bari	Pakistan v New Zealand	Auckland	1978-79
7	R.W.Taylor	England v India	Bombay	1979-80
7	I.D.S.Smith	New Zealand v Sri Lanka	Hamilton	1990-91
7	R.D.Jacobs	West Indies v Australia	Melbourne	2000-01

FIVE STUMPINGS IN AN INNINGS

5	K.S.More	India v West Indies	Madras	1987-88

FIELDING RECORDS

100 CATCHES IN TESTS

Total			Tests	Total			Tests
210	R.S.Dravid	India/ICC	164	120	I.T.Botham	England	102
193	R.T.Ponting	Australia	162	120	M.C.Cowdrey	England	114
181	D.P.M.D.Jayawardena	Sri Lanka	128	115	C.L.Hooper	West Indies	102
181	M.E.Waugh	Australia	128	113	S.R.Tendulkar	India	188
180	J.H.Kallis	South Africa/ICC	150	112	S.R.Waugh	Australia	168
171	S.P.Fleming	New Zealand	111	110	R.B.Simpson	Australia	62
164	B.C.Lara	West Indies/ICC	131	110	W.R.Hammond	England	85
157	M.A.Taylor	Australia	104	109	A.J.Strauss	England	92
156	A.R.Border	Australia	156	109	G.St A.Sobers	West Indies	93
135	V.V.S.Laxman	India	134	108	S.M.Gavaskar	India	125
128	M.L.Hayden	Australia	103	105	I.M.Chappell	Australia	75
125	G.C.Smith	South Africa/ICC	96	105	M.Azharuddin	India	99
125	S.K.Warne	Australia	145	105	G.P.Thorpe	England	100
122	G.S.Chappell	Australia	87	103	G.A.Gooch	England	118
122	I.V.A.Richards	West Indies	121				

The most for Pakistan is 93 by Javed Miandad (124), for Zimbabwe 60 by A.D.R.Campbell (60) and for Bangladesh 24 by Mohammad Ashraful (57).

15 CATCHES IN A SERIES

15	J.M.Gregory	Australia v England	1920-21

SEVEN CATCHES IN A TEST

7	G.S.Chappell	Australia v England	Perth	1974-75
7	Yajurvindra Singh	India v England	Bangalore	1976-77
7	H.P.Tillekeratne	Sri Lanka v New Zealand	Colombo (SSC)	1992-93
7	S.P.Fleming	New Zealand v Zimbabwe	Harare	1997-98
7	M.L.Hayden	Australia v Sri Lanka	Galle	2003-04

FIVE CATCHES IN AN INNINGS

5	V.Y.Richardson	Australia v South Africa	Durban	1935-36
5	Yajurvindra Singh	India v England	Bangalore	1976-77
5	M.Azharuddin	India v Pakistan	Karachi	1989-90
5	K.Srikkanth	India v Australia	Perth	1991-92
5	S.P.Fleming	New Zealand v Zimbabwe	Harare	1997-98

APPEARANCE RECORDS
100 TEST MATCH APPEARANCES

			Opponents									
			E	A	SA	WI	NZ	I	P	SL	Z	B
188	S.R.Tendulkar	India	28	35	25	19	22	–	18	25	9	7
168	S.R.Waugh	Australia	46	–	16	32	23	18	20	8	3	2
164†	R.S.Dravid	India/ICC	21	32	21	23	15	–	15	20	9	7
162†	R.T.Ponting	Australia	35	–	23	21	17	29	15	14	3	4
156	A.R.Border	Australia	47	–	6	31	23	20	22	7	–	–
150†	J.H.Kallis	South Africa/ICC	28	25	–	24	14	16	15	15	6	6
145†	S.K.Warne	Australia	36	–	24	19	20	14	15	13	1	2
144†	M.V.Boucher	South Africa/ICC	25	20	–	24	14	14	15	17	6	8
137	S.Chanderpaul	West Indies	30	17	21	–	13	23	14	7	6	6
134	V.V.S.Laxman	India	17	29	19	22	10	–	15	13	6	3
133	A.J.Stewart	England	–	33	23	24	16	9	13	9	6	–
133†	M.Muralitharan	Sri Lanka/ICC	16	12	15	12	14	22	16	–	14	11
132	A.Kumble	India	19	20	21	17	11	–	15	18	7	4
132	C.A.Walsh	West Indies	36	38	10	–	10	15	18	3	2	–
131	Kapil Dev	India	27	20	4	25	10	–	29	14	2	–
131†	B.C.Lara	West Indies/ICC	30	30	18	–	11	17	12	8	2	2
128	M.E.Waugh	Australia	29	–	18	28	14	14	15	9	1	–
128	D.P.M.D.Jayawardena	Sri Lanka	19	13	16	11	11	18	21	–	8	11
125	S.M.Gavaskar	India	38	20	–	27	9	–	24	7	–	–
124†	G.D.McGrath	Australia	30	–	17	23	14	11	17	8	1	2
124	Javed Miandad	Pakistan	22	24	–	17	18	28	–	12	3	–
121	I.V.A.Richards	West Indies	36	34	–	–	7	28	16	–	–	–
120†	Inzamam-ul-Haq	Pakistan/ICC	19	13	15	15	12	10	–	20	11	6
119	I.A.Healy	Australia	33	–	12	28	11	9	14	11	1	–
118	G.A.Gooch	England	–	42	3	26	15	19	10	3	–	–
117	D.I.Gower	England	–	42	–	19	13	24	17	2	–	–
116	D.L.Haynes	West Indies	36	33	1	–	10	19	16	1	–	–
116	D.B.Vengsarkar	India	26	24	–	25	11	–	22	8	–	–
115	M.A.Atherton	England	–	33	18	27	11	7	11	4	4	–
114	M.C.Cowdrey	England	–	43	14	21	18	8	10	–	–	–
113	S.C.Ganguly	India	12	24	17	12	8	–	12	14	9	5
111	S.P.Fleming	New Zealand	19	14	15	11	–	13	9	13	11	6
111	W.P.J.U.C.Vaas	Sri Lanka	15	12	11	9	10	14	18	–	15	7
110	S.T.Jayasuriya	Sri Lanka	14	13	15	10	13	10	17	–	13	5
110	C.H.Lloyd	West Indies	34	29	–	–	8	28	11	–	–	–
108	G.Boycott	England	–	38	7	29	15	13	6	–	–	–
108	C.G.Greenidge	West Indies	29	32	–	–	10	23	14	–	–	–

			Opponents									
			E	A	SA	WI	NZ	I	P	SL	Z	B
108	S.M.Pollock	South Africa	23	13	–	16	11	12	12	13	5	3
108†	D.L.Vettori	New Zealand/ICC	17	18	11	9	–	15	8	11	9	9
107	D.C.Boon	Australia	31	–	6	22	17	11	11	9	–	–
106	K.C.Sangakkara	Sri Lanka	18	9	15	12	8	15	13	–	5	11
105†	J.L.Langer	Australia	21	–	11	18	14	14	13	8	3	2
104	M.A.Taylor	Australia	33	–	11	20	11	9	12	8	–	–
104	Wasim Akram	Pakistan	18	13	4	17	9	12	–	19	10	2
103†	M.L.Hayden	Australia	20	–	19	15	11	18	6	7	2	4
103	Salim Malik	Pakistan	19	15	1	7	18	22	–	15	6	–
102	I.T.Botham	England	–	36	–	20	15	14	14	3	–	–
102	C.L.Hooper	West Indies	24	25	10	–	2	19	14	6	2	–
101	G.Kirsten	South Africa	22	18	–	13	13	10	11	9	3	2
101	M.Ntini	South Africa	18	15	–	15	11	10	9	12	3	8
100	G.P.Thorpe	England	–	16	16	27	13	5	8	9	2	4

† Includes appearance in the Australia v ICC 'Test' in 2005-06. The most for Zimbabwe is 67 by G.W.Flower, and for Bangladesh 57 by Mohammad Ashraful.

100 CONSECUTIVE TEST APPEARANCES

153	A.R.Border	Australia	March 1979 to March 1994
107	M.E.Waugh	Australia	June 1993 to October 2002
106	S.M.Gavaskar	India	January 1975 to February 1987

50 TESTS AS CAPTAIN

			Won	*Lost*	*Drawn*	*Tied*
93	A.R.Border	Australia	32	22	38	1
88	G.C.Smith	South Africa	41	26	21	–
80	S.P.Fleming	New Zealand	28	27	25	–
77	R.T.Ponting	Australia	48	16	13	–
74	C.H.Lloyd	West Indies	36	12	26	–
57	S.R.Waugh	Australia	41	9	7	–
56	A.Ranatunga	Sri Lanka	12	19	25	–
54	M.A.Atherton	England	13	21	20	–
53	W.J.Cronje	South Africa	27	11	15	–
51	M.P.Vaughan	England	26	11	14	–
50	I.V.A.Richards	West Indies	27	8	15	–
50	M.A.Taylor	Australia	26	13	11	–

The most for India is 49 by S.C.Ganguly, for Pakistan 48 by Imran Khan, for Zimbabwe 21 by A.D.R.Campbell and H.H.Streak, and for Bangladesh 18 by Habibul Bashar.

50 TEST UMPIRING APPEARANCES

128	S.A.Bucknor	(West Indies)	28.04.1989 to 22.03.2009
106	R.E.Koertzen	(South Africa)	26.12.1992 to 19.02.2010
95	D.J.Harper	(Australia)	28.11.1998 to 23.06.2011
92	D.R.Shepherd	(England)	01.08.1985 to 07.06.2005
78	D.B.Hair	(Australia)	25.01.1992 to 08.06.2008
73	S.Venkataraghavan	(India)	29.01.1993 to 20.01.2004
71	S.J.A.Taufel	(Australia)	26.12.2000 to 06.02.2012
70	Alim Dar	(Pakistan)	21.10.2003 to 28.01.2012
70	B.F.Bowden	(New Zealand)	11.03.2000 to 19.01.2012
66	H.D.Bird	(England)	05.07.1973 to 24.06.1996

THE FIRST-CLASS COUNTIES REGISTER, RECORDS AND 2011 AVERAGES

Career best statistics are to 10 March 2012.
Test Match career bests have been updated to 6 March 2012 and LOI career bests to 10 March 2012.

ABBREVIATIONS – General

*	not out/unbroken partnership	IT20	International Twenty20
b	born	l-o	limited-overs
BB	Best innings bowling analysis	LOI	Limited-Overs Internationals
Cap	Awarded 1st XI County Cap	Tests	International Test Matches
f-c	first-class	F-c Tours	Overseas tours involving first-class appearances
HS	Highest Score		

Awards

PCA 2011	Professional Cricketers' Association Player of 2011
Wisden 2010	One of Wisden Cricketers' Almanack's Five Cricketers of 2010
YC 2011	Cricket Writers' Club Young Cricketer of 2011

ECB Competitions

BHC	Benson & Hedges Cup (1972-2002)
CB40	Clydesdale Bank 40 (2010-11)
CC	LV= County Championship
CGT	Cheltenham & Gloucester Trophy (2001-06)
FPT	Friends Provident Trophy (2007-09)
NL	National League (1999-2005)
NWT	NatWest Trophy (1981-2000)
P40	NatWest PRO 40 League (2006-09)
SL	Sunday League (1969-98)
T20	Twenty20 Competition

Education

ARU	Anglia Ruskin University
BHS	Boys' High School
C	College
CFE	College of Further Education
CHE	College of Higher Education
CS	Comprehensive School
GS	Grammar School
HS	High School
I	Institute
IHE	Institute of Higher Education
RGS	Royal Grammar School
S	School
SFC	Sixth Form College
SM	Secondary Modern School
SS	Secondary School
TC	Technical College
T(H)S	Technical (High) School
U	University
UMIST	University of Manchester Institute of Science and Technology
UWIC	University of Wales Institute, Cardiff

Playing Categories

LBG	Bowls right-arm leg-breaks and googlies
LF	Bowls left-arm fast
LFM	Bowls left-arm fast-medium
LHB	Bats left-handed
LM	Bowls left-arm medium pace
LMF	Bowls left-arm medium fast
OB	Bowls right-arm off-breaks
RF	Bowls right-arm fast
RFM	Bowls right-arm fast-medium
RHB	Bats right-handed
RM	Bowls right-arm medium pace
RMF	Bowls right-arm medium-fast

RSM	Bowls right-arm slow-medium
SLA	Bowls left-arm leg-breaks
SLC	Bowls left-arm 'Chinamen'
WK	Wicket-keeper

Teams (see also p 223)

ACT	Australian Capital Territory
ADBP	Agricultural Development Bank of Pakistan
B	Bangladesh
BS	Basnahira South
CC&C	Combined Campuses & Colleges
CD	Central Districts
EL	England Lions
EP	Eastern Province
FS	Free State
GW	Griqualand West
HK	Hong Kong
K	Kenya
KRL	Khan Research Laboratories
ME	Mashonaland Eagles
MT	Matabeleland Tuskers
MWR	Mid West Rhinos
NBP	National Bank of Pakistan
ND	Northern Districts
NSW	New South Wales
NT	Northern Transvaal
NW	North West
(O)FS	(Orange) Free State
PIA	Pakistan International Airlines
PNSC	Pakistan National Shipping Corporation
PTC	Pakistan Telecommunication Co
Q	Queensland
REDCO	Really Efficient Development Co
SAU	South African Universities
SNGPL	Sui Northern Gas Pipelines Limited
SR	Southern Rocks
SSGC	Sui Southern Gas Corporation
Tas	Tasmania
T&T	Trinidad & Tobago
Uni	Unicorns
UP	Uttar Pradesh
Vic	Victoria
WA	Western Australia
WAPDA	Water & Power Development Authority
WP	Western Province
ZTB	Zarai Taraqiati Bank Limited

DERBYSHIRE

Formation of Present Club: 4 November 1870
Inaugural First-Class Match: 1871
Colours: Chocolate, Amber and Pale Blue
Badge: Rose and Crown
County Champions: (1) 1936
Gillette/NatWest/C&G/FP Trophy Winners: (1) 1981
Benson and Hedges Cup Winners: (1) 1993
Pro 40/National League (Div 1) Winners: (0); best – 4th (Div 2) 2002
Sunday League Winners: (1) 1990
Clydesdale Bank 40 Winners: (0); best – 3rd Group A 2011
Twenty20 Cup Winners: (0) best – Quarter-Finalist 2005

Chief Executive: Keith Loring, Derbyshire County Cricket Club, Grandstand Road, Derby DE21 6AF • Tel: 01332 388101 • Fax: 0844 500 8322 • Email: info@derbyshireccc.com • Web: www. derbyshireccc.com

Head of Cricket: K.M.Krikken. **Captain:** W.L.Madsen. **Vice-Captain:** None. **Overseas Player:** M.J.Guptill, U.T.Khawaja and Naved-ul-Hasan (T20 only). **2012 Beneficiary:** None. **Head Groundsman:** Neil Godrich. **Scorer:** John M.Brown. ‡ New registration. NQ Not qualified for England.

BORRINGTON, Paul Michael (Repton S; Chellarton S; Loughborough U), b Nottingham 24 May 1988. Son of A.J.Borrington (Derbyshire 1971-80). 5'10". RHB, OB. Debut (Derbyshire) 2005. Loughborough UCCE 2008-09. HS 105 LU v Hants (Southampton) 2009. De HS 87 v Surrey (Oval) 2011. BB – . LO HS 25 v Glam (Derby) 2009 (P40).

BURGOYNE, Peter Ian (St John Houghton S, Ilkeston; Derby SFC), b Nottingham 11 Nov 1993. 6'2". RHB, OB. Awaiting f-c debut. Derbyshire 2nd XI debut 2011. LO HS 6* v Kent (Canterbury) 2011 (CB40). LO BB 2-36 v Middx (Chesterfield) 2011 (CB40).

CLARE, Jonathan Luke (St Theodore's HS), b Burnley, Lancs 14 Jun 1986. 6'4". RHB, RMF. Debut (Derbyshire) 2007, taking 5-90 v Notts (Chesterfield). Lancashire 2nd XI. Derbyshire 2nd XI debut 2006. HS 130 v Glamorgan (Derby) 2011. BB 7-74 v Northants (Northampton) 2008. LO HS 34 v Kent (Chesterfield) 2009 (P40). LO BB 3-39 v Scotland (Derby) 2008 (FPT). T20 HS 18. T20 BB 2-20.

DURHAM, Christopher Michael (Cheadle and Marple C), b Stockport, Cheshire 4 Mar 1992. RHB, WK. Derbyshire 2nd XI debut 2009. Awaiting 1st XI debut.

DURSTON, Wesley John (Millfield S; University C, Worcester), b Taunton, Somerset 6 Oct 1980. 5'10". RHB, OB. Somerset 2002-09. Derbyshire debut 2010. Unicorns 2010 (l-o only). 1000 runs (1): 1138 (2011). HS 151 v Glos (Derby) 2011. BB 4-45 v Kent (Derby) 2011. LO HS 117 Uni v Sussex (Arundel) 2010 (CB40). LO BB 3-7 v Worcs (Derby) 2011 (CB40). T20 HS 111 v Notts (Nottingham) 2010 – De record. T20 BB 3-25.

FOOTITT, Mark Harold Alan (Carlton le Willows S; West Notts C), b Nottingham 25 Nov 1985. 6'2". RHB, LFM. Nottinghamshire 2005-09. MCC 2006. No f-c appearances in 2008. Derbyshire debut 2010. HS 30 v Surrey (Oval) 2010. BB 5-45 Nt v West Indies A (Nottingham) 2006. De BB 5-53 v Northants (Chesterfield) 2011. LO HS 4 v Middx (Chesterfield) 2011 (CB40). LO BB 3-20 v Middx (Derby) 2010 (CB40). T20 HS – . T20 BB – .

GROENEWALD, Timothy Duncan (Maritzburg C; South Africa U), b Pietermaritzburg, South Africa 10 Jan 1984. 6'0". RHB, RFM. Debut Cambridge UCCE 2006. Warwickshire 2006-08. Derbyshire debut 2009; cap 2011. HS 78 Wa v Bangladesh A (Birmingham) 2008. CC HS 76 Wa v Durham (Chester-le-St) 2006. De HS 60* v Leics (Derby) 2011. BB 6-50 v Surrey (Croydon) 2009. LO HS 36 Wa v Lancs (Manchester) 2007 (FPT). LO BB 4-22 v Worcs (Worcester) 2011 (CB40). T20 HS 41. T20 BB 3-18.

^{NQ}**GUPTILL, Martin** James (Avondale C), b Auckland, New Zealand 30 Sep 1986. 6'3". RHB, OB. Auckland 2005-06 to date. Derbyshire debut 2011. **Tests** (NZ): 19 (2008-09 to 2011-12); HS 189 v B (Hamilton) 2009-10; BB 3-37 v P (Napier) 2009-10. **LOI** (NZ): 60 (2008-09 to 2011-12); HS 122* v WI (Auckland) 2008-09 – on debut; BB 2-7 v B (Napier) 2009-10. **IT20** (NZ): 29 (2008-90 to 2011-12); HS 91* v Z (Auckland) 2011-12; BB – . F-c Tours (NZ): A 2011-12; I 2008-09 (NZ A), 2010-11; SL 2009; Z 2010-11 (NZ A), 2011-12. HS 195* Auck v Canterbury (Rangiora) 2011-12. De HS 143 v Glos (Derby) 2011. BB 3-37 (*see* Tests). LO HS 156 Auck v Canterbury (Christchurch) 2009-10. LO BB 2-7 (*see LOI*). T20 HS 120*. T20 BB – .

HIGGINBOTTOM, Matthew (New Mills SS; Leeds Met U), b Stockport, Cheshire 20 Oct 1990. 6'2". LHB, RM. Derbyshire 2nd XI debut 2009. Bradford/Leeds MCCU 2009-11. Awaiting 1st XI debut.

HUGHES, Alex Lloyd (Ounsdale HS, Wolverhampton), b Wordsley, Staffs 29 Sep 1991. RHB, RM. Derbyshire 2nd XI debut 2009. Awaiting f-c debut. T20 HS 11*. T20 BB – .

^{NQ}**HUGHES, Chesney** Francis, b Anguilla 20 January 1991. 6'2''. LHB, SLA. British passport. Debut (Derbyshire) 2010. Derbyshire 2nd XI debut 2009. Leeward Is 2009-10 to date (l-o only). HS 167 v Glamorgan (Derby) 2011. BB 2-9 v Middx (Derby) 2011. LO HS 81 Leeward Is v Windward Is (Kingston) 2010-11. LO BB 3-19 v Sussex (Derby) 2011 (CB40). T20 HS 65. T20 BB 4-23.

^{NQ}**KHAWAJA, Usman** Tariq, b Islamabad, Pakistan 18 Dec 1986. 5'9''. LHB, RM. NSW 2007-08 to date. Derbyshire debut 2011. **Tests** (A): 6 (2010-11 to 2011-12); HS 65 v SA (Johannesburg) 2011-12. F-c Tours (A): SA 2011-12; SL 2011; Z 2011 (Aus A). HS 214 and BB 1-21 NSW v S Australia (Adelaide) 2010-11. De HS 135 v Kent (Canterbury) 2011. De BB – . LO HS 121 NSW v S Australia (Sydney) 2010-11. T20 HS 65.

KNIGHT, Thomas Craig ('**Tom**') (Eckington C), b Sheffield, Yorks 28 Jun 1993. 6'0½". RHB, SLA. Debut (Derbyshire) 2011. Derbyshire 2nd XI debut 2010 aged 16 years 311 days. HS 14 v Surrey (Oval) 2011. BB 2-32 v Glamorgan (Cardiff) 2011. LO HS 1* v Middx (Chesterfield) 2011 (CB40). LO BB 2-27 v Kent (Canterbury) 2011 (CB40). T20 HS 2*. T20 BB 3-16.

LINEKER, Matthew Steven (Swanwick Hall S), b Derby 22 Jan 1985. 6'5". LHB, SLA. Debut (Derbyshire) 2011. Derbyshire 2nd XI debut 2006. Nottinghamshire 2nd XI 2008. HS 71 v Kent (Derby) 2011. LO HS 13 v Kent (Canterbury) 2011.

^{NQ}**MADSEN, Wayne** Lee (Kearsney C, Durban; U of South Africa), b Durban, South Africa 2 Jan 1984. Nephew of M.B.Madsen (Natal 1967-68 to 1978-79), T.R.Madsen (Natal 1976-77 to 1989-90) and H.R.Fotheringham (Natal, Transvaal 1971-72 to 1989-90) and cousin of G.S.Fotheringham (KwaZulu-Natal 2008-09 to date). 5'11". RHB, OB. KwaZulu-Natal 2003-04 to 2007-08. Dolphins 2006-07 to 2007-08. Derbyshire debut 2009, scoring 170 v Glos (Cheltenham); cap 2011; captain 2012. HS 179 v Northants (Northampton) 2010. BB 3-45 KZ-Natal v EP (Pt Elizabeth) 2007-08. De BB 1-68 v Glam (Cardiff) 2010. LO HS 75 v Netherlands (Derby) 2011 (CB40). LO BB 2-18 v Glamorgan (Derby) 2009 (P40). T20 HS 61*.

‡**NQNAVED-UL-HASAN**, Rana (Government HS, Sheikhupura), b Sheikhupura, Pakistan 28 Feb 1978. 5'11". RHB, RMF. Debut Pakistan A v England A (Multan) 1995-96. Lahore 1999-00. Pakistan Customs 2000-01. Sheikhupura 2000-01 to 2001-02. Allied Bank 2001-02. WAPDA 2002-03 to date. Sialkot 2003-04 to 2005-06. Sussex 2005-07, 2010; cap 2005. Punjab 2006-07. Yorkshire 2008-09. Herefordshire 2002. Joins Derbyshire in 2012 for T20 only. **Tests** (P): 9 (2004-05 to 2006-07); HS 42* v E (Lahore) 2005-06; BB 3-30 v E (Faisalabad) 2005-06. **LOI** (P): 74 (2002-03 to 2009-10); HS 33 v SL (Colombo, RPS) 2009 and v A (Adelaide) 2009-10; BB 6-27 v I (Jamshedpur) 2004-05. **IT20** (P): 4 (2006 to 2009-10); HS 17* v SA (Johannesburg) 2006-07; BB 3-19 v SL (Colombo, RPS) 2009. F-c Tours (P): A 2004-05; SA 2006-07; WI 2004-05; I 2004-05. HS 139 Sx v Middx (Lord's) 2005. 50 wkts (2+3); most – 91 (2000-01). BB 7-49 Sheikhupura v Sialkot (Muridke) 2001-02. CC BB 7-62 (11-148 match) Sx v Yorks (Leeds) 2006. LO HS 74 Y v Derbys (Derby) 2008. LO BB 6-27 (*see LOI*). T20 HS 95. T20 BB 5-17.

NEEDHAM, Jake (Nottingham Bluecoat S, Aspley), b Portsmouth, Hants 30 Sep 1986. 6'1". RHB, OB. Debut (Derbyshire) 2005. No f-c appearances in 2010 and 2011. HS 48 v Notts (Chesterfield) 2007. BB 6-49 v Leics (Leicester) 2008. LO HS 42 v Somerset (Taunton) 2007 (P40). LO BB 3-36 v Essex (Colchester) 2010 (CB40). T20 HS 7*. T20 BB 4-21.

PALLADINO, Antonio Paul (Cardinal Pole SS; Anglia Polytechnic U), b Tower Hamlets, London 29 Jun 1983. 6'0". RHB, RMF. Cambridge UCCE 2003-05. Essex 2003-10. Namibia 2009-10. Derbyshire debut 2011. HS 66 Ex v Durham (Chelmsford) 2010. De HS 60 v Northants (Northampton) 2011. 50 wkts (1): 52 (2011). BB 6-41 Ex v Kent (Canterbury) 2003. De BB 5-39 v Middx (Derby) 2011. LO HS 31 Namibia v Boland (Windhoek) 2009-10. LO BB 4-32 v Kent (Canterbury) 2011 (CB40). T20 HS 8*. T20 BB 4-21.

PARK, Garry Terence (Eshowe HS, Natal; Anglia Ruskin U), b Empangeni, Zululand, South Africa 19 Apr 1983. Elder brother of C.M.Park (Cambridge MCCU 2010) and younger brother of S.M.Park (Unicorns 2010). 5'7". RHB, RM, occ WK. Cambridge UCCE 2003-05. Durham 2006-08. Derbyshire debut 2009. Cambridgeshire 2005. 1000 runs (1): 1059 (2009). HS 178* v Kent (Derby) 2009. BB 3-25 v Surrey (Derby) 2009. LO HS 64 v Surrey (Croydon) 2009 (P40). LO BB 2-21 v Yorks (Chesterfield) 2011 (CB40). T20 HS 66. T20 BB 3-11.

POYNTON, Thomas (John Taylor HS, Barton-under-Needwood; Repton S), b Burton upon Trent, Staffs 25 Nov 1989. 5'10". RHB, WK. Debut (Derbyshire) 2007. No f-c appearances in 2009 and 2011. HS 25 and BB 2-96 v Glamorgan (Cardiff) 2010. LO HS 40 v Middx (Chesterfield) 2011 (CB40). T20 HS 3.

REDFERN, Daniel James (Adam's GS, Newport, Shropshire), b Shrewsbury, Shropshire 18 Apr 1990. 5'9". LHB, OB. Debut (Derbyshire) 2007. HS 99 v Glamorgan (Derby) 2011. BB 1-7 (twice). LO HS 57* v Yorks (Derby) 2007 (P40). LO BB 2-10 v Kent (Chesterfield) 2009 (P40). T20 HS 9.

SIDDIQUE, Hamza Ghani (Denstone C; Repton S), b Stoke-on-Trent, Staffs 19 Jan 1991. RHB, OB. Derbyshire 2nd XI debut 2009. Awaiting 1st XI debut. Cardiff MCCU 2011 (not f-c).

SLATER, Benjamin Thomas (Netherthorpe S; Leeds Met U), b Chesterfield 26 Aug 1991. 5'10". LHB, LB. Derbyshire 2nd XI debut 2009. Awaiting 1st XI debut. Bradford/Leeds MCCU 2009-11 (not f-c).

TURNER, Mark Leif (Thornhill CS), b Sunderland, Co Durham 23 Oct 1984. 5'11". RHB, RMF. Durham 2005-06. Somerset 2007-09, no f-c appearances in 2010. Derbyshire debut 2011. HS 57 Sm v Derbys (Taunton) 2007. De HS 27* v Glamorgan (Derby) 2011. BB 5-32 v Northants (Northampton) 2011. LO HS 15* Sm v Essex (Taunton) 2009 (P40). LO BB 4-36 Sm v Worcs (Bath) 2010 (CB40). T20 HS 11*. T20 BB 3-25.

‡**WAINWRIGHT, David** John (Hemsworth HS and SFC; Loughborough U); b Pontefract, Yorks 21 Mar 1985. 5'9". LHB, SLA. Yorkshire 2004-11; cap 2010. Loughborough UCCE 2005-06. British U 2006. Police Sports Club 2011-12. HS 104* (batting at No 10) Y v Sussex (Hove) 2008. BB 6-40 Y v Durham MCCU (Durham) 2011. CC BB 5-134 Y v Sussex (Hove) 2009. LO HS 26 Y v Surrey (Scarborough) 2007 (P40). LO BB 3-26 EL v Pakistan A (Dubai) 2009-10. T20 HS 6*. T20 BB 3-6.

WHITELEY, Ross Andrew (Repton S), b Sheffield, Yorks 13 Sep 1988. 6'2". LHB, LMF. Debut (Derbyshire) 2008. No f-c appearances in 2009-10. Derbyshire 2nd XI debut 2006. HS 130* v Kent (Derby) 2011. BB 1-21 v Glamorgan (Derby) 2011. LO HS 40 v Kent (Canterbury) 2011 (CB40). LO BB 1-26 v Netherlands (Derby) 2011 (CB40). T20 HS 40*. T20 BB 1-12.

RELEASED/RETIRED
(Having made a County First-Class or List A appearance in 2011)

JONES, Philip Steffan (Stradey CS, Llanelli; Neath TC; Loughborough U; Homerton C, Cambridge), b Llanelli, Carms, Wales 9 Feb 1974. 6'2". RHB, RMF. Cambridge U 1997; blue 1997. Somerset 1997-2003, 2007-08; cap 2001. Northamptonshire 2004-05. Derbyshire 2006, 2009-11; cap 2010. Kent 2009. Wales MC 1994-97. HS 114 Sm v Leics (Leicester) 2007. De HS 86 v Worcs (Worcester) 2010. 50 wkts (2); most – 59 (2001, 2006). BB 6-25 v Glamorgan (Cardiff) 2006. LO HS 42 Sm v Glamorgan (Taunton) 2008 (FPT). LO BB 6-56 Nh v Ire (Clontarf) 2004 (CGT). T20 HS 40. T20 BB 3-20.

SMITH, G.M. – *see ESSEX.*

SUTTON, Luke David (Millfield S; Durham U), b Keynsham, Somerset 4 Oct 1976. 5'11". RHB, WK. Somerset 1997-98. Derbyshire 2000-05; cap 2002; captain 2004-05. Lancashire 2006-10; cap 2007. Derbyshire 2011; captain 2011. HS 151* La v Yorks (Manchester) 2006. De HS 140* v Sussex (Derby) 2001. LO HS 83 v Lancs (Derby) 2003 (NL). T20 HS 61*.

A.Sheikh left the staff without making a County First-Class or List A appearance for Derbyshire in 2011.

DERBYSHIRE 2011

RESULTS SUMMARY

	Place	Won	Lost	Tied	Drew	NR
LV= County Championship (2nd Division)	5th	5	6		5	
All First-Class Matches		5	6		5	
Clydesdale Bank 40 (Group A)	3rd	6	5	1		
Friends Life t20 (North Group)	7th	4	8	1		3

LV= COUNTY CHAMPIONSHIP AVERAGES

BATTING AND FIELDING

Cap		M	I	NO	HS	Runs	Avge	100	50	Ct/St
	W.J.Durston	16	31	3	151	1138	40.64	3	6	7
	R.A.Whiteley	11	20	4	130*	644	40.25	2	2	9
	U.T.Khawaja	4	8	–	135	319	39.87	1	–	5
	M.J.Guptill	8	16	2	143	537	38.35	1	4	9
	M.L.Turner	7	11	8	27*	113	37.66	–	–	–
2009	G.M.Smith	13	24	3	130	726	34.57	1	5	5
	J.L.Clare	14	23	2	130	688	32.76	1	3	7
	D.J.Redfern	13	25	–	99	775	31.00	–	7	6
	P.M.Borrington	2	4	–	87	114	28.50	–	1	3
	C.F.Hughes	14	27	–	167	741	27.44	2	2	13
2011	W.L.Madsen	14	27	–	140	727	26.92	2	4	9
2002	L.D.Sutton	16	26	1	56	573	22.92	–	1	59/2
2011	T.D.Groenewald	14	21	8	60*	281	21.61	–	1	3
2010	P.S.Jones	2	4	1	27	54	18.00	–	–	1
	M.S.Lineker	3	6	–	71	107	17.83	–	1	1
	Azeem Rafiq	3	4	1	25*	52	17.33	–	–	–
	A.P.Palladino	14	22	5	60	241	14.17	–	1	1
	M.H.A.Footitt	4	7	1	17	36	6.00	–	–	3

Also batted (2 matches): T.C.Knight 0, 1*, 14 (1 ct); G.T.Park 5, 14, 0 (2 ct).

BOWLING

	O	M	R	W	Avge	Best	5wI	10wM
M.H.A.Footitt	95.5	18	387	15	25.80	5-53	1	–
A.P.Palladino	435.1	94	1379	52	26.51	5-39	3	–
J.L.Clare	321.4	64	1165	43	27.09	5-50	1	–
T.D.Groenewald	469	107	1422	48	29.62	5-59	1	–
M.L.Turner	152	23	647	21	30.80	5-32	1	–
G.M.Smith	323.5	71	991	26	38.11	4-63	–	–
Also bowled:								
Azeem Rafiq	99	25	293	8	36.62	3-24	–	–
C.F.Hughes	108	16	370	9	41.11	2- 9	–	–
W.J.Durston	97.2	12	345	8	43.12	4-45	–	–
R.A.Whiteley	92	5	385	6	64.16	1-21	–	–

P.S.Jones 42.3-8-148-3; U.T.Khawaja 1-0-2-0; T.C.Knight 48-7-143-2; G.T.Park 4-0-16-0; D.J.Redfern 3-0-14-0.

Derbyshire played no first-class fixtures outside the County Championship in 2011. The First-Class Averages (pp 223–240) give the records of their players in all first-class county matches.

DERBYSHIRE RECORDS

FIRST-CLASS CRICKET

Highest Total	For 801-8d		v	Somerset	Taunton	2007
	V 662		by	Yorkshire	Chesterfield	1898
Lowest Total	For 16		v	Notts	Nottingham	1879
	V 23		by	Hampshire	Burton upon T	1958
Highest Innings	For 274	G.A.Davidson	v	Lancashire	Manchester	1896
	V 343*	P.A.Perrin	for	Essex	Chesterfield	1904

Highest Partnership for each Wicket

1st	322	H.Storer/J.Bowden	v	Essex	Derby	1929
2nd	417	K.J.Barnett/T.A.Tweats	v	Yorkshire	Derby	1997
3rd	316*	A.S.Rollins/K.J.Barnett	v	Leics	Leicester	1997
4th	328	P.Vaulkhard/D.Smith	v	Notts	Nottingham	1946
5th	302*†	J.E.Morris/D.G.Cork	v	Glos	Cheltenham	1993
6th	212	G.M.Lee/T.S.Worthington	v	Essex	Chesterfield	1932
7th	258	M.P.Dowman/D.G.Cork	v	Durham	Derby	2000
8th	198	K.M.Krikken/D.G.Cork	v	Lancashire	Manchester	1996
9th	283	A.Warren/J.Chapman	v	Warwicks	Blackwell	1910
10th	132	A.Hill/M.Jean-Jacques	v	Yorkshire	Sheffield	1986

† *346 runs were added for this wicket in two separate partnerships*

Best Bowling	For	10- 40	W.Bestwick	v	Glamorgan	Cardiff	1921
(Innings)	V	10- 45	R.L.Johnson	for	Middlesex	Derby	1994
Best Bowling	For	17-103	W.Mycroft	v	Hampshire	Southampton	1876
(Match)	V	16-101	G.Giffen	for	Australians	Derby	1886

Most Runs – Season	2165	D.B.Carr	(av 48.11)		1959
Most Runs – Career	23854	K.J.Barnett	(av 41.12)		1979-98
Most 100s – Season	8	P.N.Kirsten			1982
Most 100s – Career	53	K.J.Barnett			1979-98
Most Wkts – Season	168	T.B.Mitchell	(av 19.55)		1935
Most Wkts – Career	1670	H.L.Jackson	(av 17.11)		1947-63
Most Career W-K Dismissals	1304	R.W.Taylor	(1157 ct; 147 st)		1961-84
Most Career Catches in the Field	563	D.C.Morgan			1950-69

LIMITED-OVERS CRICKET

Highest Total	50ov	365-3		v	Cornwall	Derby	1986
	40ov	304-3		v	Kent	Maidstone	2005
	T20	222-5		v	Yorkshire	Leeds	2010
Lowest Total	50ov	79		v	Surrey	The Oval	1967
	40ov	60		v	Kent	Canterbury	2008
	T20	81-8		v	Lancashire	Manchester	2011
Highest Innings	50ov	173*	M.J.Di Venuto	v	Derbys CB	Derby	2000
	40ov	141*	C.J.Adams	v	Kent	Chesterfield	1992
	T20	111	W.J.Durston	v	Notts	Nottingham	2010
Best Bowling	50ov	8-21	M.A.Holding	v	Sussex	Hove	1988
	40ov	6- 7	M.Hendrick	v	Notts	Nottingham	1972
	T20	5-27	T.Lungley	v	Leics	Leicester	2009

DURHAM

Formation of Present Club: 23 May 1882
Inaugural First-Class Match: 1992
Colours: Navy Blue, Yellow and Maroon
Badge: Coat of Arms of the County of Durham
County Champions: (2) 2008, 2009
Gillette/NatWest/C&G/FP Trophy Winners: (1) 2007
Benson and Hedges Cup Winners: (0); best –
Quarter-Finalist 1998, 2000, 2001
Pro 40/National League (Div 1) Winners: (0); best – 6th
2009
Sunday League Winners: (0); best – 7th 1993
Clydesdale Bank 40 Winners: (0); best – Semi-Finalist 2011
Twenty20 Cup Winners: (0); best – Semi-Finalist 2008

Chief Executive: David Harker, Emirates Durham International Cricket Ground, Chester-le-Street, Co Durham DH3 3QR • Tel: 0191 387 1717 • Fax: 0191 387 1616 • Email: marketing@durhamccc.co.uk • Web: www.durhamccc.co.uk

Director of Cricket: G.Cook. **Assistant Coaches:** J.J.B.Lewis and A.Walker. **Captain:** P.Mustard (f-c) and D.M.Benkenstein (l-o). **Vice-Captain:** none. **Overseas Player:** H.H.Gibbs (T20 only). **2012 Beneficiary:** none. **Head Groundsman:** David Measor. **Scorer:** Brian Hunt. ‡ New registration. NQ Not qualified for England.

Durham initially awarded caps immediately after their players joined the staff but revised this policy in 1998, again capping players on merit, past 'awards' having been nullified. Durham abolished both their capping and 'awards' systems after the 2005 season.

BENKENSTEIN, Dale Martin (Durban HS; Michaelhouse HS), b Salisbury, Rhodesia 9 Jun 1974. Son of M.M.Benkenstein (Rhodesia, Natal B 1970-71 to 1980-81); brother of twins B.R. (Natal B 1993-94) and B.N. Benkenstein (Natal B, GW 1994-95 to 1996-97). 5'9". RHB, RM/OB. Natal/KwaZulu-Natal 1993-94 to 2003-04. Dolphins 2004-05 to 2007-08. MCC 2004. British passport. Durham debut/cap 2005; captain 2006-08, l-o captain 2011 to date. *Wisden* 2008. **LOI** (SA): 23 (1998-99 to 2002-03); HS 69 v WI (Cape Town) 1998-99; BB 3-5 v Kenya (Colombo) 2002-03. F-c Tours (SA A): WI 2000; NZ 1998-99 (SA); SL 1995 (SA U-24), 1998. 1000 runs (5); most – 1500 (2006). HS 259 KZ-Natal v Northerns (Durban) 2001-02. Du HS 181 v Somerset (Taunton) 2009. BB 4-16 Dolphins v Warriors (Durban) 2005-06. Du BB 4-29 v Northants (Northampton) 2005. LO HS 107* Natal v North West (Fochville) 1997-98. LO BB 4-16 v Surrey (Chester-le-St) 2005 (NL). T20 HS 60. T20 BB 3-10.

BLACKWELL, Ian David (Brookfield Community S), b Chesterfield, Derbys 10 Jun 1978. 6'2". LHB, SLA. Derbyshire 1997-99. Somerset 2000-08; cap 2001; captain 2006 (*part*). Durham debut 2009. **Tests:** 1 (2005-06); HS 4 and BB-v I (Nagpur) 2005-06. **LOI:** 34 (2002-03 to 2005-06); HS 82 v I (Colombo) 2002-03; BB 3-26 v A (Adelaide) 2002-03. F-c Tour: I 2005-06. 1000 runs (3); most – 1256 (2005). HS 247* Sm v Derbys (Taunton) 2003 – off 156 balls and including 204 off 98 balls in reduced post-lunch session. Won Walter Lawrence Trophy 2005 for 67-ball hundred v Derbys (Taunton). Du HS 158 v Warwks (Birmingham) 2009 and v Durham MCCU (Durham) 2011. BB 7-85 v Lancs (Manchester) 2009. LO HS 134* Sm v Sussex (Taunton) 2005 (NL). LO BB 5-26 Sm v Derbys (Taunton) 2005 (NL). T20 HS 82. T20 BB 4-26.

BORTHWICK, Scott George (Farringdon Community Sports C, Sunderland), b Sunderland 19 Apr 1990. 5'9". LHB, LBG. Debut (Durham) 2009. Durham 2nd XI debut 2006. England U19 2008-09 to 2009. **LOI**: 2 (2011 to 2011-12); HS 15 v Ireland (Dublin) 2011; BB – . **IT20**: 1 (2011); HS 14 and BB 1-15 v WI (Oval) 2011. HS 101 v Sri Lanka A (Chester-le-St) 2011. CC HS 68 v Notts (Chester-le-St) 2010. BB 5-80 v Sussex (Hove) 2011. LO HS 44 EL v Bangladesh A (Chittagong) 2011-12. LO BB 2-11 v Worcs (Chester-le-St) 2009 (P40). T20 HS 30. T20 BB 3-19.

BRATHWAITE, Ruel Marlon Ricardo (Queen's C, Barbados; Dulwich C; Loughborough U; Queens' C, Cambridge), b Bridgetown, Barbados 6 Sep 1985. 6'2". RHB, RFM. British passport. Loughborough UCCE 2006-08. British U 2006. MCC 2007. Cambridge U 2009. Durham debut 2010. HS 76* LU v Worcs (Worcester) 2007. Du HS 13 v Notts (Nottingham) 2011. BB 5-54 CU v Oxford U (Cambridge) 2009. Du BB 5-56 v Sussex (Chester-le-St) 2011. LO HS – . LO BB 1-19 WI v Eng Lions (Worcester) 2007. T20 HS 0. T20 BB 1-33.

BREESE, Gareth Rohan (Wolmer's BHS, Kingston; Kingston U of Technology, Jamaica), b Montego Bay, Jamaica 9 Jan 1976. 5'7". RHB, OB. Jamaica 1995-96 to 2005-06; captain/overseas player 2003-04 to 2005-06. British passport (Welsh father). Durham debut 2004; cap 2005. **Tests** (WI): 1 (2002-03); HS 5 and BB 2-108 v I (Madras) 2002-03. F-c Tours (WI): E 2002 (WI A); I 2002-03. HS 165* v Somerset (Taunton) 2004. BB 7-60 Jamaica v Barbados (Bridgetown) 2000-01. Du BB 5-41 (10-151 match) v Yorks (Scarborough) 2004 – scored 35 and 68 to complete match double. LO HS 68* v Notts (Chester-le-St) 2007 (FPT). LO BB 5-41 v Derbys (Chester-le-St) 2008 (FPT). T20 HS 37. T20 BB 4-14.

CLAYDON, Mitchell Eric (Westfield Sports HS, Sydney), b Fairfield, NSW, Australia 25 Nov 1982. 6'4". LHB, RMF. Yorkshire 2005-06. Durham debut 2007. Canterbury 2010-11. HS 40 v Lancs (Manchester) 2008. BB 6-104 v Somerset (Taunton) 2011. LO HS 19 v Glos (Bristol) 2009 (FPT). LO BB 4-39 Cant v Otago (Timaru) 2010-11. T20 HS 19. T20 BB 5-26.

COLLINGWOOD, Paul David (Blackfyne CS; Derwentside C), b Shotley Bridge 26 May 1976. 5'11". RHB, RM. Debut (Durham) 1996 v Northants (Chester-le-St) taking wicket of D.J.Capel with his first ball before scoring 91 and 16; cap 1998; benefit 2007. MBE 2005. *Wisden* 2007. **Tests**: 68 (2003-04 to 2010-11); HS 206 v A (Adelaide) 2006-07; BB 3-23 v NZ (Wellington) 2007-08. **LOI**: 197 (2001 to 2010-11, 25 as captain); HS 120* v A (Melbourne) 2006-07; BB 6-31 v B (Nottingham) 2005 – record analysis for E, and first to score a hundred (112*) and take six wickets in same LOI. **IT20**: 35 (2005 to 2010-11, 30 as captain); HS 79 v WI (Oval) 2007; BB 4-22 v SL (Southampton) 2006. F-c Tours: A 2006-07, 2010-11; SA 2009-10; WI 2003-04, 2008-09; NZ 2007-08; I 2005-06, 2008-09; P 2005-06; SL 2003-04, 2007-08; B 2009-10. 1000 runs (2); most – 1120 (2005), inc six hundreds (Du record). HS 206 (*see Tests*). Du HS 190 v SL (Chester-le-St) 2002 and 190 v Derbys (Derby) 2005, sharing Du record 4th wkt partnership of 250 with D.M.Benkenstein. BB 5-52 v Somerset (Stockton) 2005. LO HS 120* (*see LOI*). LO BB 6-31 (*see LOI*). T20 HS 79 (*see IT20*). T20 BB 5-6 v Northants (Chester-le-St) 2011 – Du record.

DAVIES, Anthony Mark (Northfield CS, Billingham; Stockton SFC), b Stockton-on-Tees 4 Oct 1980. 6'3". RHB, RMF. Debut (Durham) 2002; cap 2005. No f-c appearances in 2011. Nottinghamshire 2007 (on loan). F-c Tour (Eng A): NZ 2008-09. HS 62 v Somerset (Stockton) 2005. 50 wkts (1): 50 (2004). BB 8-24 (11-75 match) v Hants (Basingstoke) 2008. LO HS 31* v Warwks (Chester-le-St) 2002 (NL). LO BB 4-13 v Sussex (Chester-le-St) 2001 (NL). T20 HS 6. T20 BB 2-14.

^{NQ}**Di VENUTO, Michael** James (St Virgil's C; Hobart), b Hobart, Australia 12 Dec 1973. 6'0". LHB, RM/LBG. Tasmania 1991-92 to 2007-08. Sussex 1999; cap 1999. Derbyshire 2000-06; cap 2000; appointed captain for 2004 but missed entire season – back surgery. Durham debut 2007, carrying his bat for 155* v Worcs (Worcester) on debut. Italian passport 2008. **LOI** (A): 9 (1996-97 to 1997-98); HS 89 v SA (Johannesburg) 1996-97. F-c Tours: Z 1995-96 (Tas); Scotland/Ireland 1998 (Aus A). 1000 runs (10); most – 1654 (2009), inc six hundreds (Du record). HS 254* v Sussex (Chester-le-St) 2009. BB 1-0 Tas v Q (Brisbane) 1990-91. UK BB 1-3 Sx v Somerset (Taunton) 1999. LO HS 173* v Derbys CB (Derby) 2000 (NWT). LO BB 1-10 Tas v Q (Hobart) 1995-96. T20 HS 95*. T20 BB 3-19.

‡^{NQ}**GIBBS, Herschelle** Herman, b Green Point, Cape Town, South Africa 23 Feb 1974. RHB/RM. Western Province 1990-91 to 2004-05. Cape Cobras 2005-06 to date. Glamorgan 2009. Joins Durham in 2012 for T20 only. **Tests** (SA): 90 (1996-97 to 2007-08); HS 228 v P (Cape Town) 2002-03. BB – . **LOI** (SA): 248 (1996-97 to 2009-10); HS 175 v A (Johannesburg) 2005-06 in total of 438-9 – highest ever l-o run chase. **IT20** (SA): 23 (2005-06 to 2010); HS 90* v WI (Johannesburg) 2007. F-c Tours (SA): E 1995 (SA A), 2003; A 1997-98, 2001-02, 2005-06; WI 2000-01, 2004-05; NZ 1998-99, 2003-04; I 1996-97, 1999-00; P 2003-04, 2007-08; SL 2004, 2006; Z 2001-02; B 2003. HS (*see Tests*). CC HS 96 Gm v Glos (Bristol) 2009. BB 2-14 SA A v Somerset (Taunton) 1996. LO HS 175 (*see LOI*). LO BB 1-16 SA A v Essex (Chelmsford) 1996. T20 HS 101*.

HARMISON, Stephen James (Ashington HS), b Ashington, Northumb 23 Oct 1978. Elder brother of B.W.Harmison. 6'4". RHB, RF. Debut (Durham) 1996; cap 1999. ICC World XI 2005-06. Lions 2007-08. MCC 2007. *Wisden* 2004. MBE 2005. **Tests**: 63 (2002 to 2009); HS 49* v SA (Oval) 2008; BB 7-12 (9-73 match) v WI (Kingston) 2003-04. **LOI**: 58 (2002-03 to 2008-09); HS 18* v WI (Providence) 2008-09; BB 5-33 v A (Bristol) 2005; hat-trick v I (Nottingham) 2004. **IT20**: 2 (2005 to 2006); HS – ; BB 1-13 v A (Southampton) 2005. F-c Tours: A 2002-03, 2005-06 (RW), 2006-07; SA 1998-99 (Eng A), 2004-05; WI 2003-04, 2008-09; NZ 2007-08; I 2005-06, 2008-09; P 2005-06; SL 2007-08; Z 1998-99 (Eng A); B 2003-04. HS 49* (*see Tests*). Du HS 36* v Hants (Chester-le-St) 2008. 50 wkts (6); most – 65 (2008). BB 7-12 (*see Tests*). Du BB 7-29 (9-74 match) v Warwks (Chester-le-St) 2010. Hat-tricks (2): v Worcs (Chester-le-St) 2005 and v Sussex (Hove) 2008. LO HS 25* v Somerset (Chester-le-St) 2008 (P40). LO BB 5-33 (*see LOI*). T20 HS 6. T20 BB 5-41.

HARRISON, Jamie (Sedburgh S), b Whiston, Lancs 19 Nov 1990. 6'0". RHB, LMF. Durham 2nd XI debut 2009. Gloucestershire 2nd XI 2008. Awaiting 1st XI debut. Development contract in 2012.

MUCHALL, Gordon James (Durham S), b Newcastle upon Tyne, Northumb 2 Nov 1982. 6'0". RHB, RM. Northumberland 1999. Older brother of P.B.Muchall (*see KENT*). Debut (Durham) 2002; cap 2005. F-c Tour: SL 2002-03 (ECB Acad). HS 219 v Kent (Canterbury) 2006, sharing Du record 6th wkt partnership of 249 with P.Mustard (*see below*). HS BB 3-26 v Yorks (Leeds) 2003. LO HS 101* v Yorks (Leeds) 2005 (NL). LO BB 1-15 v Sussex (Hove) 2003 (NL). T20 HS 64*. T20 BB 1-8.

MUSTARD, Philip (Usworth CS), b Sunderland 8 Oct 1982. Cousin of C.Rushworth (*see below*). 5'11". LHB, WK. Debut (Durham) 2002; captain 2010 (*part*) to date. Mountaineers 2011-12. **LOI**: 10 (2007-08); HS 83 v NZ (Napier) 2007-08. **IT20**: 2 (2007-08); HS 40 v NZ (Christchurch) 2007-08. HS 130 v Kent (Canterbury) 2006. LO HS 139* v Northants (Northampton) 2011 (CB40). T20 HS 88*.

ONIONS, Graham (St Thomas More RC S, Blaydon), b Gateshead 9 Sep 1982. 6'1". RHB, RFM. Debut (Durham) 2004. MCC 2007-08. *Wisden* 2009. Missed entire 2010 season through back injury. **Tests**: 8 (2009 to 2009-10); HS 17* v A (Lord's) 2009; BB 5-38 v WI (Lord's) 2009 – on debut. **LOI**: 4 (2009 to 2009-10); HS 1 v A (Centurion) 2009-10; BB 2-58 v SL (Johannesburg) 2009-10. F-c Tours: SA 2009-10; I 2007-08 (Eng L); B 2006-07 (Eng A); UAE 2011-12 (part). HS 41 v Yorks (Leeds) 2007. 50 wkts (3); most – 69 (2009). BB 8-101 v Warwks (Birmingham) 2007. LO HS 19 v Derbys (Derby) 2008 (FPT). LO BB 3-39 v Derbys (Derby) 2005 (NL). T20 HS 31. T20 BB 3-25.

PLUNKETT, Liam Edward (Nunthorpe SS; Teesside Tertiary C), b Middlesbrough, Yorks 6 Apr 1985. 6'3". RHB, RFM. Debut (Durham) 2003. Dolphins 2007-08. **Tests**: 9 (2005-06 to 2007); HS 44* v WI (Leeds) 2007; BB 3-17 v SL (Birmingham) 2006. **LOI**: 29 (2005-06 to 2010-11); HS 56 v P (Lahore) 2005-06; BB 3-24 v A (Sydney) 2006-07. **IT20**: 1 (2006); HS – ; BB 1-37 v SL (Southampton) 2006. F-c Tours: WI 2010-11 (EL); NZ 2008-09 (EL); I 2005-06, 2007-08 (EL); P 2005-06. HS 107* v Durham MCCU (Durham) 2011. CC HS 94* v Sussex (Hove) 2009. 50 wkts (3); most – 60 (2009). BB 6-63 (11-119) v Worcs (Chester-le-St) 2009. LO HS 72 v Somerset (Chester-le-St) 2008 (P40). LO BB 4-15 v Essex (Chester-le-St) 2007 (FPT). T20 HS 41. T20 BB 5-31.

RAINE, Benjamin Alexander (St Aidan's RC SS, Sunderland) b Sunderland 14 Sep 1991. 6'0". LHB, RM. Debut (Durham) 2011. Durham 2nd XI debut 2010. Development contract for 2012. HS 7 v Sri Lanka A (Chester-le-St) 2011. BB – . LO HS – .

RAMANPREET SINGH (Gosforth HS), b Newcastle upon Tyne 19 Feb 1993. 5'11". RHB, OB. Durham 2nd XI debut 2009 aged 16y 181d. Northumberland 2009. Development contract in 2012.

RICHARDSON, Michael John (Rondebosch HS; Stonyhurst C, Nottingham U), b Pt Elizabeth, South Africa 4 Oct 1986. Son of D.J.Richardson (South Africa, EP and NT 1977-78 to 1997-98), grandson of J.H.Richardson (NE Transvaal and Transvaal B 1952-53 to 1960-61), nephew of R.P.Richardson (WP 1984-85 to 1988-89). 5'10". RHB, WK. MCC Young Cricketer 2008-09. Debut (Durham) 2010. HS 73* v Yorks (Leeds) 2011.

RUSHWORTH, Christopher (Castle View CS, Sunderland), b Sunderland 11 Jul 1986. Cousin of P.Mustard (*see above*). 6'2". RHB, RMF. Debut (Durham) 2010. Durham 2nd XI debut 2004. Northumberland 2004-05. HS 28 v Yorks (Chester-le-St) 2010. BB 4-90 v Essex (Chelmsford) 2010. LO HS 12* v Northants (Chester-le-St) 2011 (CB40). LO BB 3-6 v Scotland (Chester-le-St) 2010. T20 HS 2. T20 BB 3-20.

SMITH, William Rew (Bedford S; Collingwood C, Durham), b Luton, Beds 28 Sep 1982. 5'9". RHB, OB. Nottinghamshire 2002-06. Durham UCCE 2003-05; captain 2004-05. British U 2004-05. Durham debut 2007; captain 2009-10 (*part*). Bedfordshire 1999-2002. HS 201* v Surrey (Guildford) 2008. BB 3-34 DU v Leics (Leicester) 2005. CC BB 1-5 v Lancs (Chester-le-St) 2007. LO HS 103 v Worcs (Chester-le-St) 2007 (FPT). LO BB 1-6 v Derbys (Chester-le-St) 2008 (FPT). T20 HS 55. T20 BB 1-31.

STOKES, Benjamin Andrew (Cockermouth S), b Christchurch, Canterbury, New Zealand 4 Jun 1991. 6'0". LHB, RM. Debut (Durham) 2010. Durham 2nd XI debut 2007 when aged 16y 99d. England U19s 2009 to 2009-10. **LOI**: 5 (2011); HS 20 v I (Oval) 2011. **IT20**: 2 (2011); HS 31 v WI (Oval) 2011. F-c Tours (EL): WI 2010-11. HS 185 v Lancs (Chester-le-St) 2011. BB 6-68 v Hants (Southampton) 2011. LO HS 150* v Warwks (Chester-le-St) 2011 (CB40) – Du record. BB 4-29 v Hants (Chester-le-St) 2011 (CB40). T20 HS 44. T20 BB 1-23.

STONEMAN, Mark Daniel (Whickham CS), b Newcastle upon Tyne, Northumb 26 Jun 1987. 5'11". LHB, RM. Debut (Durham) 2007. HS 128 v Sussex (Hove) 2011. LO HS 73 v Leics (Chester-le-St) 2011 (CB40). T20 HS 46.

THORP, Callum David (Servite C, Tuart Hill, Perth), b Mount Lawley, Perth, Australia 11 Feb 1975. 6'3". British passport (English parents). RHB, RMF. W Australia 2002-03 to 2003-04. Durham debut 2005. HS 79* v MCC (Abu Dhabi) 2010. CC HS 75 v Hants (Southampton) 2006. 50 wkts (1): 50 (2008). BB 7-88 v Kent (Canterbury) 2008. LO HS 52 v Bangladesh (Chester-le-St) 2005. LO BB 6-17 v Scotland (Edinburgh) 2006 (CGT). T20 HS 13. T20 BB 2-32.

WOOD, Mark Andrew (Ashington HS; Newcastle C), b Ashington 11 Jan 1990. 5'11". RHB, RMF. Debut (Durham) 2011. Durham 2nd XI debut 2009. Northumberland 2008-10. HS 48 v Sri Lanka A (Chester-le-St) 2011. CC HS 45* and BB 3-72 v Notts (Nottingham) 2011. LO HS 5 v Northants (Chester-le-St) 2011 (CB40). LO BB 1-28 v Scotland (Edinburgh) 2011 (CB40).

RELEASED/RETIRED
(Having made a County First-Class or List A appearance in 2011)

COETZER, K.J. – *see NORTHAMPTONSHIRE.*

HARMISON, B.W. – *see KENT.*

D.A.Miller left the staff without making a County First-Class or List A appearance in 2011.

COUNTY CAPS AWARDED IN 2011

Derbyshire	T.D.Groenewald, W.L.Madsen
Durham	None
Essex	None
Glamorgan	A.N.Petersen, B.J.Wright
Gloucestershire	I.A.Cockbain, R.G.Coughtrie, J.K.Fuller, W.R.S.Gidman, C.N.Miles, L.C.Norwell, D.A.Payne, K.S.Williamson
Hampshire	None
Kent	None
Lancashire	S.C.Moore
Leicestershire	N.L.Buck
Middlesex	C.D.Collymore, S.A.Newman, C.J.L.Rogers, J.A.Simpson
Northamptonshire	J.D.Middlebrook, N.J.O'Brien, W.P.J.U.C.Vaas
Nottinghamshire	D.M.Bravo, A.D.Hales
Somerset	N.R.D.Compton
Surrey	G.J.Batty, S.M.Davies, J.W.Dernbach, R.J.Hamilton-Brown
Sussex	J.E.Anyon
Warwickshire	R.Clarke
Worcestershire (colours)	A.Kapil, J.K.Manuel, M.G.Pardoe, N.D.Pinner, K.A.J.Roach, Saeed Ajmal, A.Shankar, D.G.Wright
Yorkshire	J.M.Bairstow

Durham abolished their capping system after 2005. Gloucestershire award caps on first-class debut. Worcestershire award club colours on Championship debut. Glamorgan's capping system is now based on a player's number of appearances and not on his performances.

DURHAM 2011

RESULTS SUMMARY

	Place	Won	Lost	Tied	Drew	NR
LV= County Championship (1st Division)	3rd	8	4		4	
All First-Class Matches		10	4		4	
Clydesdale Bank 40 (Group B)	SF	9	3			1
Friends Life t20 (North Group)	4th	6	6			4

LV= COUNTY CHAMPIONSHIP AVERAGES

BATTING AND FIELDING

Cap		M	I	NO	HS	Runs	Avge	100	50	Ct/St
2005	D.M.Benkenstein	16	26	4	150	1353	61.50	4	9	7
	M.D.Stoneman	5	8	–	128	418	52.25	1	3	5
	P.Mustard	13	18	4	101	716	51.14	1	6	48/2
	B.A.Stokes	9	15	2	185	628	48.30	3	–	6
	I.D.Blackwell	16	25	1	134	905	39.34	2	6	2
	W.R.Smith	15	25	–	179	978	39.12	3	4	11
	M.J.Di Venuto	16	25	1	132	935	38.95	3	4	27
	M.J.Richardson	3	5	1	73*	154	38.50	–	2	18
1998	P.D.Collingwood	7	13	1	108	439	36.58	1	2	4
2005	G.J.Muchall	13	21	–	175	716	34.09	1	6	9
	S.G.Borthwick	12	17	5	67*	376	31.33	–	2	14
	C.D.Thorp	16	20	3	43	310	18.23	–	–	9
	M.E.Claydon	8	13	3	38	145	14.50	–	–	–
1999	S.J.Harmison	6	4	–	27	45	11.25	–	–	–
	G.Onions	11	14	5	28*	100	11.11	–	–	3
	R.M.R.Brathwaite	6	6	4	13	18	9.00	–	–	1

Also batted: L.E.Plunkett (2 matches) 5, 66* (1 ct); C.Rushworth (1) 21; M.A.Wood (1) 6, 45*.

BOWLING

	O	M	R	W	Avge	Best	5wI	10wM
R.M.R.Brathwaite	149.4	23	540	22	24.54	5- 56	2	–
S.J.Harmison	117.4	24	454	17	26.70	4- 67	–	–
G.Onions	365.3	72	1341	50	26.82	6- 95	2	–
M.E.Claydon	204.5	46	772	26	29.69	6-104	2	–
S.G.Borthwick	226	55	806	27	29.85	5- 80	1	–
C.D.Thorp	476.4	124	1412	46	30.69	6- 20	1	–
I.D.Blackwell	446.5	151	1113	36	30.91	5-102	1	–
B.A.Stokes	124.4	16	561	17	33.00	6- 68	1	–
Also bowled:								
M.A.Wood	24.3	2	129	5	25.80	3- 72	–	–
L.E.Plunkett	67.4	13	225	5	45.00	3- 75	–	–

D.M.Benkenstein 69-18-182-3; P.D.Collingwood 37-9-117-4; C.Rushworth 20-8-61-1; W.R.Smith 5-2-5-0.

The First-Class Averages (pp 223–240) give the records of Durham players in all first-class county matches (Durham's other opponents being Durham MCCU and Sri Lanka A), with the exception of G.Onions, whose first-class figures for Durham are as above, and:
    S.G.Borthwick 14-20-5-101-477-31.80-1-2-14ct. 273-66-958-35-27.37-5/80-1-0.

DURHAM RECORDS

FIRST-CLASS CRICKET

Highest Total	For	648-5d		v	Notts	Chester-le-St[2]	2009
	V	810-4d		by	Warwicks	Birmingham	1994
Lowest Total	For	67		v	Middlesex	Lord's	1996
	V	56		by	Somerset	Chester-le-St[2]	2003
Highest Innings	For	273	M.L.Love	v	Hampshire	Chester-le-St[2]	2003
	V	501*	B.C.Lara	for	Warwicks	Birmingham	1994

Highest Partnership for each Wicket

1st	334*	S.Hutton/M.A.Roseberry	v	Oxford U	Oxford	1996
2nd	258	J.J.B.Lewis/M.L.Love	v	Notts	Chester-le-St[2]	2001
3rd	205	G.Fowler/S.Hutton	v	Yorkshire	Leeds	1993
4th	331	B.A.Stokes/D.M.Benkenstein	v	Lancashire	Chester-le-St[2]	2011
5th	247	G.J.Muchall/I.D.Blackwell	v	Worcs	Worcester	2011
6th	249	G.J.Muchall/P.Mustard	v	Kent	Canterbury	2006
7th	315	D.M.Benkenstein/O.D.Gibson	v	Yorkshire	Leeds	2006
8th	147	P.Mustard/L.E.Plunkett	v	Yorkshire	Leeds	2009
9th	127	D.G.C.Ligertwood/S.J.E.Brown	v	Surrey	Stockton	1996
10th	103	M.M.Betts/D.M.Cox	v	Sussex	Hove	1996

Best Bowling	For	10- 47	O.D.Gibson		v	Hampshire	Chester-le-St[2]	2007
(Innings)	V	9- 36	M.S.Kasprowicz	for	Glamorgan	Cardiff		2003
Best Bowling	For	14-177	A.Walker		v	Essex	Chelmsford	1995
(Match)	V	13-110	M.S.Kasprowicz	for	Glamorgan	Chester-le-St[2]		2003

Most Runs – Season	1654	M.J.Di Venuto	(av 78.76)	2009
Most Runs – Career	7854	J.J.B.Lewis	(av 31.41)	1997-2006
Most 100s – Season	6	P.D.Collingwood		2005
	6	M.J.Di Venuto		2009
Most 100s – Career	21	D.M.Benkenstein		2005-11
Most Wkts – Season	80	O.D.Gibson	(av 20.75)	2007
Most Wkts – Career	518	S.J.E.Brown	(av 28.30)	1992-2002
Most Career W-K Dismissals	454	P.Mustard	(437 ct; 17 st)	2002-11
Most Career Catches in the Field	127	P.D.Collingwood		1996-2011

LIMITED-OVERS CRICKET

Highest Total	50ov	332-4		v	Worcs	Chester-le-St[2]	2007
	40ov	325-9		v	Surrey	The Oval	2011
	T20	225-2		v	Leics	Chester-le-St[2]	2010
Lowest Total	50ov	82		v	Worcs	Chester-le-St[1]	1968
	40ov	72		v	Warwicks	Birmingham	2002
	T20	93		v	Kent	Canterbury	2009
Highest Innings	50ov	138	M.J.Di Venuto	v	Derbyshire	Chester-le-St[2]	2008
	40ov	150*	B.A.Stokes	v	Warwicks	Birmingham	2011
	T20	80*	L.R.P.L.Taylor	v	Leics	Chester-le-St[2]	2010
Best Bowling	50ov	7-32	S.P.Davis	v	Lancashire	Chester-le-St[1]	1983
	40ov	6-31	N.Killeen	v	Derbyshire	Derby	2000
	T20	5- 6	P.D.Collingwood	v	Northants	Chester-le-St[2]	2011

[1] Chester-le-Street CC (Ropery Lane) [2] Emirates Durham International Cricket Ground

ESSEX

Formation of Present Club: 14 January 1876
Inaugural First-Class Match: 1894
Colours: Blue, Gold and Red
Badge: Three Seaxes above Scroll bearing 'Essex'
County Champions: (6) 1979, 1983, 1984, 1986, 1991, 1992
Gillette/NatWest/C&G/FP Trophy Winners: (3) 1985, 1997, 2008
Benson and Hedges Cup Winners: (2) 1979, 1998
Pro 40/National League (Div 1) Winners: (2) 2005, 2006
Sunday League Winners: (3) 1981, 1984, 1985
Clydesdale Bank 40 Winners: (0); best – Semi-Finalist 2010
Twenty20 Cup Winners: (0); best – Semi-Finalist 2006, 2008, 2010

Chief Executive: David E.East, The Ford County Ground, New Writtle Street, Chelmsford CM2 0PG • Tel: 01245 252420 • Fax: 01245 254030 • Email: administration@essexcricket.org.uk • Web: www.essexcricket.org.uk

First Team Coach: A.P.Grayson. **Assistant Coach:** M.J.Walker. **Bowling Coach:** C.E.W.Silverwood. **Captain:** J.S.Foster. **Vice-Captain:** R.S.Bopara. **Overseas Players:** A.N.Petersen and P.M.Siddle (T20 only). **2012 Beneficiary:** G.R.Napier. **Head Groundsman:** Stuart Kerrison. **Scorer:** A.E. (Tony) Choat. ‡ New registration. NQ Not qualified for England.

BOPARA, Ravinder Singh (Brampton Manor S; Barking Abbey Sports C), b Newham, London 4 May 1985. 5'8". RHB, RM. Debut (Essex) 2002; cap 2005. Auckland 2009-10. Dolphins 2010-11. MCC 2006, 2008. YC 2008. **Tests:** 12 (2007-08 to 2011); HS 143 v WI (Lord's) 2009; BB 1-39 v SL (Galle) 2007-08. **LOI:** 72 (2006-07 to 2011-12); HS 96 v I (Lord's) 2011; BB 4-38 v B (Birmingham) 2010. **IT20:** 19 (2008 to 2011-12); HS 55 v WI (Oval) 2009; BB 4-10 v WI (Oval) 2011 – England record. F-c Tours: WI 2008-09, 2010-11 (EL); SL 2007-08. 1000 runs (1): 1256 (2008). HS 229 v Northants (Chelmsford) 2007. BB 5-75 v Surrey (Chelmsford) 2006. LO HS 201* v Leics (Leicester) 2008 (FPT) – Ex record. LO BB 5-63 Dolphins v Warriors (Pietermaritzburg) 2010-11. T20 HS 105*. T20 BB 4-10.

CHAMBERS, Maurice Anthony (Homerton TC; Sir George Monoux C), b Port Antonio, Portland, Jamaica 14 Sep 1987. 6'3". RHB, RFM. Debut (Essex) 2005. No f-c appearances 2006-07 – stress fracture of the back. MCC YC 2004. F-c Tours (EL): WI 2010-11. HS 30 v Leics (Leicester) 2011. BB 6-68 (10-123 match) v Notts (Chelmsford) 2010. LO HS 1* v Leics (Leicester) 2008 (P40). LO BB 1-26 v Yorks (Chelmsford) 2008. T20 HS 10*. T20 BB 3-31.

COMBER, Michael Andrew (Clacton County HS), b Colchester 26 Oct 1989. 6'3". RHB, RMF. Debut (Essex) 2010. Essex 2nd XI debut 2007. HS 19 and BB 2-34 v Bangladeshis (Chelmsford) 2010. CC HS 0. CC BB 1-4 v Durham (Chelmsford) 2010. LO HS 52* v Northants (Southend) 2010 (CB40). LO BB –. T20 HS 5.

COOK, Alastair Nathan (Bedford S), b Gloucester 25 Dec 1984. 6'3". LHB, OB. Debut (Essex) 2003; cap 2005. MCC 2004-07. Essex 2nd XI debut 2000 when aged 15y 235d. England U19 captain 2003-04. YC 2005. **ECB central contract 2011-12. Tests**: 75 (2005-06 to 2011-12, 2 as captain); HS 294 v I (Birmingham) 2011. Scored 60 and 104* v I (Nagpur) 2005-06 on debut. Third, after D.G.Bradman and S.R.Tendulkar, to score seven Test hundreds before his 23rd birthday. Second, after M.A.Taylor, to score 1000 runs in the calendar year of his debut. BB – . **LOI**: 45 (2006 to 2011-12, 22 as captain); HS 137 v P (Abu Dhabi) 2011-12. **IT20**: 4 (2007 to 2009-10); HS 26 v SA (Centurion) 2009-10. F-c Tours (C=captain): A 2006-07, 2010-11; SA 2009-10; WI 2005-06 (Eng A), 2008-09; NZ 2007-08; I 2005-06, 2008-09; SL 2004-05 (Eng A), 2007-08; B 2009-10C; UAE 2011-12 (v P). 1000 runs (5+1); most – 1466 (2005). HS (*see Tests*). CC HS 195 v Northants (Northampton) 2005. Scored 214 v Australians (Chelmsford) 2005 in 2-day non-f-c match. BB 3-13 v Northants (Chelmsford) 2005. LO HS 137 (*see LOI*). BB – . T20 HS 100*.

CRADDOCK, Thomas Richard (Holmfirth HS; Huddersfield New C; Leeds Met U), b Huddersfield, Yorks 13 Jul 1989. 5'10". RHB, LB. Debut (Essex) 2011. Leeds/Bradford MCCU (not f-c) 2010-11. Northamptonshire 2nd XI 2010. Gloucestershire 2nd XI 2011. HS 21 and BB 4-59 v Leics (Southend) 2011. Joint BB 4-59 v Leics (Leicester) 2011. LO HS 5* and LO BB 2-38 v Somerset (Taunton) 2011 (CB40). T20 HS – . T20 BB – .

FOAKES, Benjamin Thomas (Tendring TC), b Colchester 15 Feb 1993. 6'1". RHB, WK. Debut (Essex) 2011. Essex 2nd XI debut 2008 when aged 15y 172d. England U19s 2010-11. HS 5 v Sri Lankans (Chelmsford) 2011 – only 1st XI match.

FOSTER, James Savin (Forest S, Snaresbrook; Collingwood C, Durham U), b Whipps Cross 15 Apr 1980. 6'0". RHB, WK. British U 2000-01. Essex debut 2000; cap 2001; captain 2010 (*part*) to date; benefit 2011. Durham UCCE 2001. MCC 2004, 2008-10. **Tests**: 7 (2001-02 to 2002-03); HS 48 v I (Bangalore) 2001-02. **LOI**: 11 (2001-02); HS 13 v I (Bombay) 2001-02. **IT20**: 5 (2009); HS 14* v P (Oval) 2009. F-c Tours: A 2002-03; WI 2000-01 (Eng A); NZ 2001-02; I 2001-02, 2007-08 (Eng A). 1000 runs (1): 1037 (2004). HS 212 v Leics (Chelmsford) 2004. BB 1-122 v Northants (Northampton) 2008 – in contrived circumstances. LO HS 83* v Durham, inc 5 sixes in 5 balls off S.G.Borthwick (Chester-le-St) 2009 (P40). T20 HS 62*.

GODLEMAN, Billy Ashley (Islington Green S), b Islington, London 11 Feb 1989. 6'3". LHB, LB. Middlesex 2005-09. Essex debut 2010. England U19s 2006 to 2007-08. HS 130 v Leics (Leicester) 2011. BB – . LO HS 82 M v Scotland (Lord's) 2009 (FPT). T20 HS 69.

MASTERS, David Daniel (Fort Luton HS; Mid Kent CHE), b Chatham, Kent 22 Apr 1978. Son of K.D.Masters (Kent 1983-84), elder brother of D.Masters (Leicestershire 2009-10). 6'4". RHB, RMF. Kent 2000-02. Leicestershire 2003-07; cap 2007. Essex debut/cap 2008. HS 119 Le v Sussex (Hove) 2003. Ex HS 67 v Leics (Chelmsford) 2009. 50 wkts (2); most – 93 (2011). BB 8-10 v Leics (Southend) 2011. LO HS 39 Le v Glos (Cheltenham) 2006 (P40). LO BB 5-17 v Surrey (Oval) 2008 (FPT). T20 HS 14. T20 BB 3-7.

MICKLEBURGH, Jaik Charles (Bungay HS), b Norwich, Norfolk 30 Mar 1990. 5'10". RHB, RM. Debut (Essex) 2008. Essex 2nd XI debut when aged 16y 160d. Norfolk 2007. England U19s 2009. HS 174 v Durham (Chester-le-St) 2010. BB – . LO HS 56 v Somerset (Taunton) 2011 (CB40). T20 HS 32.

MILLS, Tymal Solomon (Mildenhall C of T), b Dewsbury, Yorks 12 Aug 1992. 6'1". RHB, LMF. Debut (Essex) 2011. Essex 2nd XI debut 2010. England U19s 2010-11. HS 8 v Sri Lankans (Chelmsford) 2011. CC HS 7 v Surrey (Chelmsford) 2011. BB 3-48 v Leics (Leicester) 2011. LO HS 0 v Somerset (Taunton) 2011 (CB40). LO BB 2-40 Eng Development XI v Sri Lanka A (Manchester) 2011.

NAPIER, Graham Richard (The Gilberd S, Colchester), b Colchester 6 Jan 1980. 5'9½". RHB, RM. Debut (Essex) 1997; cap 2003; benefit 2012. Wellington 2008-09. MCC 2004. F-c Tour (Eng A): I 2003-04. HS 196 v Surrey (Croydon) 2011, hitting a world record-equalling 16 sixes and being dismissed just 28 balls after reaching his century. Won 2008 Walter Lawrence Trophy with 44-ball hundred v Sussex (Chelmsford). BB 6-53 v Surrey (Chelmsford) 2011. LO HS 79 Essex CB v Lancs CB (Chelmsford) 2000 (NWT). LO BB 6-29 v Worcs (Chelmsford) 2001 (NL). T20 HS 152* v Sussex (Chelmsford) 2008 – record T20 Cup score (58b, 10 fours, 16 sixes); 2nd highest score in all T20. T20 BB 4-10.

‡**ᴺᑫPETERSEN, Alviro** Nathan, Port Elizabeth, South Africa 25 November 1980. RHB, RM/OB. Northerns 2000-01 to 2005-06. Titans 2004-05 to 2005-06. Lions 2005-06 to date. North West 2008-09. Glamorgan 2011; cap/captain 2011. **Tests** (SA): 10 (2009-10 to 2011-12); HS 109 v SL (Cape Town) 2011-12; scored 100 v I (Kolkata) on debut; BB 1-2 v WI (Port-of-Spain) 2010. **LOI** (SA): 17 (2006-07 to 2011-12); HS 80 v Z (Potchefstroom) 2006-07; BB – . **IT20** (SA): 2 (2010); HS 8 v WI (North Sound) 2010. F-c Tours (SA): WI 2010; I 2007-08 (SA A), 2009-10; Z 2007 (SA A); B 2010 (SA A); UAE (v P) 2010-11. 1000 runs (1+1); most – 1376 (2008-09). HS 286 v Surrey (Oval) 2011. BB 2-7 Northerns v Easterns (Benoni) 2001-02. CC BB 1-37 Gm v Glos (Cardiff) 2011. LO HS 145* Lions v Dolphins (Potchefstroom) 2011-12. LO BB 2-48 Lions v Cape Cobras (Johannesburg) 2011-12. T20 HS 84*. T20 BB 1-5.

PETTINI, Mark Lewis (Comberton Village C; Hills Road SFC, Cambridge; Cardiff U), b Brighton, Sussex 7 Aug 1983. 5'10". RHB, RM. Debut (Essex) 2001; cap 2006; captain 2007 (*part*) to 2010 (*part*). Mountaineers 2011-12. MCC 2005. 1000 runs (1): 1218 (2006). HS 208* v Derbys (Chelmsford) 2006. BB – . LO 144 v Surrey (Oval) 2007 (FPT). T20 HS 87.

PHILLIPS, Timothy James (Felsted S; St Hild & St Bede C, Durham U), b Cambridge 13 Mar 1981. 6'1". LHB, SLA. Essex 1999, 2001-02, 2005 to date; cap 2006. Durham UCCE 2001-02. HS 89 v Worcs (Worcester) 2005. BB 5-41 v Derbys (Chelmsford) 2006. LO HS 58* v Glos (Cheltenham) 2011 (CB40). LO BB 5-28 v Unicorns (Bury St Edmunds) 2011 (CB40). T20 HS 57*. T20 BB 4-22.

RAMSDEN, Henry Douglas ('**Harry**') (Oundle S), b Wandsworth, Surrey 11 Nov 1992. LHB, OB. Hertfordshire 2011. Awaiting 1st XI debut.

SHAH, Owais Alam (Isleworth & Syon S), b Karachi, Pakistan 22 Oct 1978. 6'0". RHB, OB. Middlesex 1996-2010; cap 2000; captain 2004 (*part*); benefit 2008. Cape Cobras 2010-11. Essex debut 2011. MCC 2002-08. YC 2001. **Tests**: 6 (2005-06 to 2008-09); HS 88 v I (Bombay) 2005-06; BB – . **LOI**: 71 (2001 to 2009-10); HS 107* v I (Oval) 2007; BB 3-15 v Ire (Belfast) 2009. **IT20**: 17 (2007 to 2009); HS 55* v WI (Oval) 2007. F-c Tours (Eng A): A 1996-97; WI 2005-06 (*part*), 2008-09 (Eng); I 2005-06 (Eng – *part*); SL 1997-98, 2004-05, 2007-08 (Eng). 1000 runs (8); most – 1728 (2005). HS 203 M v Derbys (Southgate) 2001. Ex HS 118 v Glamorgan (Cardiff) 2011. BB 3-33 M v Glos (Bristol) 1999. Ex BB – . LO HS 134 M v Sussex (Arundel) 1999 (NL). LO BB 4-11 M v Leics (Lord's) 2009 (P40). T20 HS 80. T20 BB 2-26.

‡**ᴺᑫSIDDLE, Peter** Matthew, b Traralgon, Victoria, Australia 25 Nov 1984. 6'1½". RHB, RFM. Victoria 2005-06 to date. Joins Essex for T20 only in 2012. **Tests** (A): 31 (2008-09 to 2011-12); HS 43 v E (Sydney) 2010-11; BB 6-54 v E (Brisbane) 2010-11. **LOI** (A): 17 (2008-09 to 2010-11); HS 9* v SL (Sydney) 2010-11; BB 3-55 v E (Centurion) 2009-10. **IT20** (A): 2 (2008-09 to 2010-11); HS 1* and BB 2-24 v NZ (Sydney) 2008-09. F-c Tours (A): E 2009; SA 2008-09, 2011-12; I 2008-09 (Aus A), 2008-09; SL 2011; Z 2011 (Aus A). HS 45* Vic v NSW (Melbourne) 2010-11. BB 6-43 Vic v S Aus (Melbourne) 2011-12. LO HS 25* Vic v Tas (Hobart) 2010-11. LO BB 4-27 Vic v Tas (Hobart (2008-09. T20 HS 9*. T20 BB 4-29.

‡^{NO}SMITH, Gregory Marc (St Stithins C), b Johannesburg, South Africa 20 Apr 1983. 5'9". RHB, RM/OB. Debut (SA Academy) 2003-04. Griqualand West 2003-04. Derbyshire 2006-11 (Kolpak registration); cap 2009; captain 2010 (*part*). Mountaineers 2010-11. HS 165* De v Glamorgan (Derby) 2010. BB 5-54 De v Northants (Chesterfield) 2010. LO HS 88 De v Kent (Derby) 2007 (P40). LO BB 4-53 De v Lancs (Derby) 2009 (P40). T20 HS 100*. T20 BB 5-27.

^{NO}Ten DOESCHATE, Ryan Neil (Fairbairn C; Cape Town U), b Port Elizabeth, South Africa 30 Jun 1980. 5'10½". RHB, RMF. Debut (Essex) 2003; cap 2006. EU passport – Dutch ancestry. Netherlands 2005 to date. LOI (Ne): 33 (2006 to 2010-11); HS 119 v E (Nagpur) 2010-11; BB 4-31 v Canada (Nairobi) 2006-07. IT20 (Ne): 9 (2008 to 2009-10); HS 56 v Kenya (Belfast) 2008; BB 3-23 v Scotland (Belfast) 2008. F-c Tours (Ne): SA 2006-07, 2007-08; K 2005-06, 2009-10; Ireland 2005. HS 259* and BB 6-20 (9-112 match) Netherlands v Canada (Pretoria) 2006. Ex HS 164 v Sri Lankans (Chelmsford) 2011. CC HS 159* v Surrey (Guildford) 2009. Ex BB 6-57 v NZ (Chelmsford) 2008. CC BB 5-13 v Hants (Chelmsford) 2010. LO HS 134* Ne v Namibia (Benoni) 2008-09. LO BB 5-50 v Glos (Bristol) 2007 (FPT). T20 HS 121*. T20 BB 4-24.

TOPLEY, Reece James William (Royal Hospital S, Ipswich), b Ipswich, Suffolk 21 February 1994. Son of T.D.Topley (Surrey, Essex, GW 1985-94) and nephew of P.A.Topley (Kent 1972-75). 6'7". RHB, LMF. Debut (Essex) 2011. Essex 2nd XI debut 2010 when aged 16y 156d. HS 9 v Derbys (Chelmsford) 2011. BB 5-46 v Kent (Chelmsford) 2011 – on CC debut. LO HS 19 and LO BB 2-45 v Somerset (Taunton) 2011 (CB40).

VELANI, Kishen Shailesh (Brentwood S), b Newham, London 2 Sep 1994. RHB, RM. Awaiting 1st XI debut.

WALKER, Matthew Jonathan (King's S, Rochester), b Gravesend, Kent 2 Jan 1974. Grandson of Jack Walker (Kent 1949). 5'8". LHB, RM. Kent 1992-93 (Z tour) to 2008; UK debut 1994; cap 2000; benefit 2008. Essex debut 2009; cap 2010. F-c Tour: Z 1992-93 (K). 1000 runs (4); most – 1419 (2006). HS 275* K v Somerset (Canterbury) 1996. Ex HS 150 v Middx (Lord's) 2009. BB 3-35 v Kent (Canterbury) 2010. LO HS 117 K v Warwks (Canterbury) 1997 (BHC). LO BB 4-24 K v Yorks (Leeds) 2001 (NL). T20 HS 74*.

WESTLEY, Thomas (Linton Village C; Hills Road SFC), b Cambridge 13 March 1989. 6'2". RHB, OB. Debut (Essex) 2007. MCC 2007, 2009. Durham MCCU 2010-11. Essex 2nd XI debut 2004 when aged 15y 88d. Cambridgeshire 2005. HS 132 v Derbys (Derby) 2009 and v Kent (Chelmsford) 2010. BB 4-55 DU v Durham (Durham) 2010. CC BB 2-33 v Glamorgan (Cardiff) 2009. LO HS 50 v Glos (Colchester) 2011 (CB40). LO BB 1-18 v Somerset (Southend) 2011 (CB40).

WHEATER, Adam Jack (Millfield S), b Whipps Cross 13 Feb 1990. 5'6". RHB, WK. Debut (Essex) 2008. Cambridge MCCU 2010. Matabeleland Tuskers 2010-11 to date. Badureliya Sports Club 2011-12. Essex 2nd XI debut when aged 16y 190d. HS 164 v Northants (Chelmsford) 2011. LO HS 69 MT v SR (Bulawayo) 2010-11. T20 HS 29.

‡WILLOUGHBY, Charl Myles (Wynberg BHS; Stellenbosch U), b Cape Town, South Africa 3 Dec 1974. 6'2". LHB, LMF. Boland 1994-95 to 1999-00. W Province 2000-01 to 2003-04. MCC 2001, 2004. WP-Boland 2004-05. Leicestershire 2005-07 (Kolpak). Cape Cobras 2005-06 to date. Somerset 2006-11; cap 2007. Qualified as UK resident in 2011. Berkshire 2000. Tests (SA): 2 (2003); HS – ; BB 1-47 v B (Chittagong) 2002-03. LOI (SA): 3 (1999-00 to 2003); HS 0; BB 2-39 v P (Sharjah) 1999-00. F-c Tours (SA): E 2003; WI 2000 (SA A); Z 1998-99 (SA Acad), 2004 (SA A); B 2003. HS 47 Sm v Worcs (Taunton) 2006. 50 wkts (6+2); most – 66 (2006). BB 7-44 Sm v Glos (Taunton) 2006. LO HS 15 Sm v Kent (Canterbury) 2009 (FPT). LO BB 6-16 Le v Somerset (Leicester) 2005 (CGT) – Le record. T20 HS 11. T20 BB 4-9.

RELEASED/RETIRED continued on p 107

ESSEX 2011

RESULTS SUMMARY

	Place	Won	Lost	Tied	Drew	NR
LV= County Championship (2nd Division)	7th	4	4		8	
All First-Class Matches		4	4		10	
Clydesdale Bank 40 (Group C)	3rd	6	3			3
Friends Life t20 (South Group)	6th	7	7			2

LV= COUNTY CHAMPIONSHIP AVERAGES
BATTING AND FIELDING

Cap		M	I	NO	HS	Runs	Avge	100	50	Ct/St
2001	J.S.Foster	15	26	6	117*	931	46.55	2	4	46/4
2005	R.S.Bopara	9	17	1	178	683	42.68	3	2	1
	A.J.Wheater	11	20	1	164	804	42.31	2	4	5
2005	A.N.Cook	6	12	–	155	504	42.00	1	3	5
2003	G.R.Napier	7	12	1	196	383	34.81	1	1	3
	O.A.Shah	10	18	1	118	574	33.76	2	2	15
	B.A.Godleman	11	21	–	130	619	29.47	1	3	5
2010	M.J.Walker	10	19	1	97	529	29.38	–	4	13
2006	R.N.ten Doeschate	8	13	1	124*	337	28.08	1	2	8
	J.C.Mickleburgh	15	28	–	112	733	26.17	1	3	11
2006	M.L.Pettini	6	11	2	67*	232	25.77	–	2	4
	T.Westley	10	19	–	67	450	23.68	–	4	11
	C.J.C.Wright	4	7	–	34	115	16.42	–	–	–
2006	T.J.Phillips	8	14	2	58	186	15.50	–	1	5
	T.R.Craddock	7	10	4	21	65	10.83	–	–	1
2008	D.D.Masters	16	24	2	48	234	10.63	–	–	4
	M.A.Chambers	10	15	3	30	91	7.58	–	–	1
	L.L.Tsotsobe	3	4	3	6	6	6.00	–	–	1
	R.J.W.Topley	7	10	5	9	21	4.20	–	–	1
	T.S.Mills	3	5	2	7	11	3.66	–	–	1

BOWLING

	O	M	R	W	Avge	Best	5wI	10wM
D.D.Masters	637.1	169	1687	93	18.13	8- 10	8	–
G.R.Napier	192.4	37	690	28	24.64	6- 53	2	–
T.R.Craddock	197.2	34	579	22	26.31	4- 59	–	–
R.J.W.Topley	180.1	30	717	25	28.68	5- 46	2	–
C.J.C.Wright	118	16	420	12	35.00	3-109	–	–
R.S.Bopara	215	31	719	19	37.84	2- 50	–	–
M.A.Chambers	240.1	34	896	23	38.95	3- 34	–	–
T.J.Phillips	154	19	595	11	54.09	4- 97	–	–
Also bowled:								
R.N.ten Doeschate	65.3	3	249	9	27.66	2- 33	–	–
T.S.Mills	51	7	207	6	34.50	3- 48	–	–
L.L.Tsotsobe	84	8	388	5	77.60	2- 71	–	–

O.A.Shah 2.5-0-4-0; M.J.Walker 20-4-45-3; T.Westley 53.5-9-157-2.

The First-Class Averages (pp 223–240) give the records of Essex players in all first-class county matches (Essex's other opponents being Cambridge MCCU and the Sri Lankans), with the exception of:

A.N.Cook 7-14-0-155-634-45.28-2-3-5ct.
R.S.Bopara 11-20-1-178-776-40.84-3-3-1ct. 239-37-803-24-33.45-5/45-0-0.
T.Westley 11-20-0-99-549-27.45-0-5-11ct. 61.5-10-184-2-92.00-2/45-0-0.
C.J.C.Wright 5-9-0-77-217-24.11-0-1-0ct. 147-19-521-12-43.41-3/109-0-0.

ESSEX RECORDS

FIRST-CLASS CRICKET

Highest Total	For 761-6d		v	Leics	Chelmsford	1990
	V 803-4d		by	Kent	Brentwood	1934
Lowest Total	For 30		v	Yorkshire	Leyton	1901
	V 14		by	Surrey	Chelmsford	1983
Highest Innings	For 343*	P.A.Perrin	v	Derbyshire	Chesterfield	1904
	V 332	W.H.Ashdown	for	Kent	Brentwood	1934

Highest Partnership for each Wicket

1st	316	G.A.Gooch/P.J.Prichard	v	Kent	Chelmsford	1994
2nd	403	G.A.Gooch/P.J.Prichard	v	Leics	Chelmsford	1990
3rd	347*	M.E.Waugh/N.Hussain	v	Lancashire	Ilford	1992
4th	314	Salim Malik/N.Hussain	v	Surrey	The Oval	1991
5th	339	J.C.Mickleburgh/J.S.Foster	v	Durham	Chester-le-St[2]	2010
6th	253	A.J.Wheater/J.S.Foster	v	Northants	Chelmsford	2011
7th	261	J.W.H.T.Douglas/J.Freeman	v	Lancashire	Leyton	1914
8th	263	D.R.Wilcox/R.M.Taylor	v	Warwicks	Southend	1946
9th	251	J.W.H.T.Douglas/S.N.Hare	v	Derbyshire	Leyton	1921
10th	218	F.H.Vigar/T.P.B.Smith	v	Derbyshire	Chesterfield	1947

Best Bowling	For	10- 32	H.Pickett	v	Leics	Leyton	1895
(Innings)	V	10- 40	E.G.Dennett	for	Glos	Bristol	1906
Best Bowling	For	17-119	W.Mead	v	Hampshire	Southampton	1895
(Match)	V	17- 56	C.W.L.Parker	for	Glos	Gloucester	1925

Most Runs – Season	2559	G.A.Gooch	(av 67.34)		1984
Most Runs – Career	30701	G.A.Gooch	(av 51.77)		1973-97
Most 100s – Season	9	J.O'Connor			1929, 1934
	9	D.J.Insole			1955
Most 100s – Career	94	G.A.Gooch			1973-97
Most Wkts – Season	172	T.P.B Smith	(av 27.13)		1947
Most Wkts – Career	1610	T.P.B.Smith	(av 26.68)		1929-51
Most Career W-K Dismissals	1231	B.Taylor	(1040 ct; 191 st)		1949-73
Most Career Catches in the Field	519	K.W.R.Fletcher			1962-88

LIMITED-OVERS CRICKET

Highest Total	50ov	391-5		v	Surrey	The Oval	2008
	40ov	316-4		v	Glamorgan	Chelmsford	2004
	T20	242-3		v	Sussex	Chelmsford	2008
Lowest Total	50ov	57		v	Lancashire	Lord's	1996
	40ov	69		v	Derbyshire	Chesterfield	1974
	T20	82		v	Somerset	Chelmsford	2011
Highest Innings	50ov	201*	R.S.Bopara	v	Leics	Leicester	2008
	40ov	176	G.A.Gooch	v	Glamorgan	Southend	1983
	T20	152*	G.R.Napier	v	Sussex	Chelmsford	2008
Best Bowling	50ov	5- 8	J.K.Lever	v	Middlesex	Westcliff	1972
		5- 8	G.A.Gooch	v	Cheshire	Chester	1995
	40ov	8-26	K.D.Boyce	v	Lancashire	Manchester	1971
	T20	6-16	T.G.Southee	v	Glamorgan	Chelmsford	2011

103

GLAMORGAN

Formation of Present Club: 6 July 1888
Inaugural First-Class Match: 1921
Colours: Blue and Gold
Badge: Gold Daffodil
County Champions: (3) 1948, 1969, 1997
Gillette/NatWest/C&G/FP Trophy Winners: (0); best – Finalist 1977
Benson and Hedges Cup Winners: (0); best – Finalist 2000
Pro 40/National League (Div 1) Winners: (2) 2002, 2004
Sunday League Winners: (1) 1993
Clydesdale Bank 40 Winners: (0); best – 5th Group C 2011
Twenty20 Cup Winners: (0); best – Semi-Finalist 2004

Chief Executive: A.D.Hamer, SWALEC Stadium, Cardiff, CF11 9XR • Tel: 0871 282 3401 • Fax: 0871 282 3405 • email: info@glamorgancricket.co.uk • Web: www.glamorgancricket.com

Managing Director of Cricket: C.P.Metson. **1st XI Coach:** M.P.Mott. **Bowling Coach:** S.L.Watkin. **Player Development Manager:** R.V.Almond. **Captain:** M.A.Wallace. **Vice-Captain:** J.Allenby. **Overseas Players:** M.C.Henriques and M.J.North. **2012 Beneficiary:** R.D.B.Croft (testimonial). **Head Groundsman:** Keith Exton. **Scorer:** Andrew K.Hignell. ‡ New registration. ^{NQ} Not qualified for England.

ALLENBY, James (Christ Church GS, Perth), b Perth, W Australia 12 Sep 1982. 6'0". RHB, RM. Leicestershire 2006-09. Glamorgan debut 2009; cap 2010. HS 138* Le v Bangladesh A (Leicester) 2008. CC HS 137 v Surrey (Oval) 2009. BB 5-44 v Derbys (Cardiff) 2011. LO HS 91* Le v Middx (Lord's) 2007 (P40). LO BB 5-43 v Derbys (Leicester) 2007 (FPT). T20 HS 110. T20 BB 5-21 Le v Lancs (Manchester) 2008, inc 4 wkts in 4 balls.

ASHLING, Christopher Paul (Millfield S, UWIC), b Manchester 26 Nov 1988. 5'7". RHB, RMF. Debut (Glamorgan) 2009. Cardiff UCCE 2008. Wales MC 2008-09. Lancashire 2nd XI debut 2005. HS 20 v Derbys (Derby) 2010. BB 4-47 v Surrey (Oval) 2011. LO HS 6* v Leics (Leicester) 2009 (P40). LO BB 2-33 v Lancs (Cardiff) 2009 (P40). T20 HS 6. T20 BB 2-39.

BRAGG, William David (Rougemont S, Newport; UWIC), b Newport, Monmouthshire 24 Oct 1986. 5'9". LHB, WK. Debut (Glamorgan) 2007. 1000 runs (1): 1033 (2011). HS 110 v Leics (Colwyn Bay) 2011. BB 1-4 v Kent (Canterbury) 2011. LO HS 78 v Leics (Leicester) 2009 (P40). BB – . T20 HS 15.

COOKE, Christopher Barry (Bishops S, Cape Town; U of Cape Town), b Johannesburg, South Africa 30 May 1986. RHB, WK. W Province 2009-10. Glamorgan 2nd XI debut 2010. HS 44 WP v EP (Cape Town) 2009-10. LO HS WP v Boland (Cape Town) 2009-10. T20 HS 47.

COSKER, Dean Andrew (Millfield S), b Weymouth, Dorset 7 Jan 1978. 5'11". RHB, SLA. Debut (Glamorgan) 1996; cap 2000; benefit 2010. MCC 2010. F-c Tours (Eng A): SA 1998-99; SL 1997-98; Z 1998-99; K 1997-98. HS 52 v Glos (Bristol) 2005. 50 wkts (1): 51 (2010). BB 6-91 (11-126 match) v Essex (Cardiff) 2009. LO HS 50* v Northants (Northampton) 2009 (FPT). LO BB 5-54 v Essex (Chelmsford) 2003 (NL). T20 HS 21*. T20 BB 3-11.

CROFT, Robert Damien Bale (St John Lloyd Catholic CS, Llanelli; Neath Tertiary C; W Glamorgan IHE), b Morriston, Swansea 25 May 1970. 5'10½". RHB, OB. Debut (Glamorgan) 1989; cap 1992; benefit 2000; testimonial 2012; captain 2003 (*part*) and 2006 (*part*). MCC 1996. **Tests**: 21 (1996 to 2001); HS 37* v SA (Manchester) 1998; BB 5-95 v NZ (Christchurch) 1996-97. **LOI**: 50 (1996 to 2001); HS 32 v SL (Perth) 1998-99; BB 3-51 v SA (Oval) 1998. F-c Tours: A 1998-99; SA 1993-94 (Eng A), 1995-96 (Gm); WI 1991-92 (Eng A), 1997-98; NZ 1996-97; SL 2000-01, 2003-04; Z 1990-91 (Gm), 1994-95 (Gm), 1996-97. HS 143 v Somerset (Taunton) 1995. 50 wkts (10); most – 76 (1996). Took 1,000th f-c wicket 2007. BB 8-66 (14-169 match) v Warwks (Swansea) 1992. LO HS 143 v Lincs (Lincoln) 2004 (CGT). LO BB 6-20 v Worcs (Cardiff) 1994 (SL). T20 HS 62*. T20 BB 3-9.

GLOVER, John Charles (Llantarnam CS; St Aidan's C, Durham), b Cardiff 29 Aug 1989. 6'4". RHB, RMF. Durham MCCU 2008-10. Glamorgan debut 2011. Glamorgan 2nd XI debut 2009. Wales MC 2008-11. HS 16* and CC BB 4-49 v Kent (Canterbury) 2011. BB 5-38 DU v Durham (Durham) 2009.

HARRIS, James Alexander Russell (Pontardulais CS; Gorseinon C), b Morriston, Swansea 16 May 1990. 6'0". RHB, RFM. Debut (Glamorgan) 2007 – aged 16 years 351 days – youngest Glamorgan player to take a first-class wicket; cap 2010. Glamorgan 2nd XI debut 2005 when aged 14y 353d. Wales MC 2005-08. England U19s 2007. F-c Tour (Eng A): WI 2010-11. HS 87* v Notts (Swansea) 2007. 50 wkts (1): 63 (2010). BB 7-66 (12-118 match) v Glos (Bristol) 2007 – youngest (17y 3d) to take 10 wickets in any CC match. LO HS 29 EL v Sri Lanka A (Northampton) 2011. LO BB 4-48 v Kent (Canterbury) 2008 (P40). T20 HS 18. T20 BB 4-23.

‡**NQHENRIQUES, Moises** Constantino, b Funchal, Madeira 1 Feb 1987. 6'1½". RHB, RFM. New South Wales 2006-07 to date. Joins Glamorgan in 2012. **LOI** (A): 2 (2009-10); HS 12 and BB 1-51 v I (Delhi) 2009-10. **IT20** (A): 1 (2008-09); HS 1 v NZ (Sydney) 2008-09. HS 82 Australia A v Pakistan A (Townsville) 2009. BB 5-17 NSW v Q (Brisbane) 2006-07. LO HS 65* NSW v Tas (Canberra) 2011-12. LO BB 3-29 NSW v WA (Sydney) 2008-09. T20 HS 70. T20 BB 3-11.

JAMES, Nicholas Alexander (King Edward VI S, Aston), b Sandwell, Birmingham 17 Sep 1986. 5'9". LHB, SLA. Warwickshire 2008. Glamorgan debut 2010. Staffordshire 2006-07. England U19 2005 to 2005-06. HS 60* v West Indies A (Cardiff) 2010. CC HS 49 v Middx (Cardiff) 2011. BB 2-28 v Kent (Canterbury) 2011. LO HS 43 v Somerset (Cardiff) 2011 (CB40). LO BB 3-36 v Unicorns (Wormsley) 2011 (CB40). T20 HS 13. T20 BB 2-22.

JONES, Alexander John (Cowbridge CS), b Bridgend 10 Nov 1988. RHB, LMF. Debut (Glamorgan) 2011. Glamorgan 2nd XI debut 2008. Wales MC 2007-10. Cardiff MCCU 2009-10. HS 26 v Northants (Northampton) 2011. BB 1-50 v Surrey (Oval) 2011. LO HS 5 v Somerset (Taunton) 2010 (CB40). LO BB 1-38 v Notts (Nottingham) 2011. (CB40). T20 HS 4*. T20 BB 3-16.

JONES, Simon Philip (Coedcae CS; Millfield S), b Morriston, Swansea 25 Dec 1978. Son of I.J.Jones (Glamorgan and England 1960-68). 6'3½". LHB, RFM. Glamorgan 1998-2007; cap 2002. Worcestershire 2008 (no 1st XI appearances in 2009). Hampshire 2010-11. MCC 2002-04. MBE 2005. **Wisden** 2005. **Tests**: 18 (2002 to 2005); HS 44 v I (Lord's) 2002 – on debut; BB 6-53 v A (Manchester) 2005. **LOI**: 8 (2004-05 to 2005); HS 1; BB 2-43 v Z (Bulawayo) 2004-05 – on debut. F-c Tours: A 2002-03 (*part*); SA 2004-05; WI 2003-04; I 2003-04 (Eng A – *part*). HS 46 v Yorks (Scarborough) 2001. BB 6-45 v Derbys (Cardiff) 2002. LO HS 26 v Hants (Swansea) 2007 (FPT). LO BB 5-32 Wo v Hants (Worcester) 2008 (FPT). T20 HS 11*. T20 BB 4-10.

NORMAN, Aneurin John (Millfield S), b Cardiff 22 Mar 1991. RHB, RM. Debut (Glamorgan) 2011. Glamorgan 2nd XI debut 2008. Wales MC 2008-11. Development contract. HS 34 and BB-v Kent (Canterbury) 2011. LO HS 15 and BB-v Unicorns (Wormsley) 2011.

‡^{NQ}**NORTH, Marcus** James (Kent Street Sr HS), b Pakenham, Melbourne, Australia 28 Jul 1979. 6'1". LHB, OB. Debut (Aus Academy in Zim) 1998-99. W Australia 1999-00 to date; captain 2007-08 to date. Durham 2004. Lancashire 2005. Derbyshire 2006. Gloucestershire 2007-08; cap 2007. Hampshire 2009 (one match only). **Tests** (A): 21 (2008-09 to 2010-11); scored 117 v SA (Johannesburg) 2008-09 – on debut; HS 128 v I (Bangalore) 2010-11; BB 6-55 v P (Lord's) 2010. **LOI** (A): 2 (2009); HS 5 v P (Abu Dhabi) 2009; BB – . **IT20** (A): 1 (2009); HS 20 v P (Dubai) 2009. F-c Tours (Aus): E 2009, 2010 (v P); SA 2008-09; NZ 2009-10; I 2010-11; P 2005-06 (Aus A); Z 1998-99 (Aus Acad). 1000 runs (0+1): 1074 (2003-04). HS 239* WA v Vic (Perth) 2006-07. UK HS 219 Du v Glamorgan (Cardiff) 2004. Won Walter Lawrence Trophy 2007 for 73-ball hundred v Leics (Bristol). BB 6-55 (*see Tests*). CC BB 3-53 Gs v Leics (Bristol) 2007. LO HS 134* WA v Q (Perth) 2004-05. LO BB 4-26 Durham CB v Bucks (Beaconsfield) 2001 (CGT). T20 HS 70. T20 BB 2-19.

O'SHEA, Michael Peter (Barry CS; Millfield S), b Cardiff 4 Sep 1987. 5'11". RHB, OB. Debut (Glamorgan) 2005; no f-c appearances 2006, 2008, 2010-11. Wales MC 2005-08. England U19s 2004-05 to 2006. HS 50 v Kent (Canterbury) 2009. LO HS 90 Unicorns v Worcs (Kidderminster) 2010 (CB40). LO BB 2-32 v Somerset (Cardiff) 2011 (CB40). T20 HS 11. T20 BB 1-25.

OWEN, William Thomas (Prestatyn HS; UWIC), b St Asaph, Flintshire 2 Sep 1988. 6'0". RHB, RMF. Debut (Glamorgan) 2007. Wales MC 2007-10. HS 69 v Derbys (Derby) 2011. BB 5-124 v Middx (Cardiff) 2011. LO HS 12 and LO BB 5-49 v Unicorns (Bournemouth) 2010 (CB40). T20 HS 8. T20 BB 3-21.

REED, Michael Thomas (De Lisle S, Leicester; Cardiff U), b Leicester 10 Sep 1988. RHB, RFM. Glamorgan 2nd XI debut 2009. Wales MC 2009-10. Cardiff MCCU 2010-11 (not f-c). Awaiting 1st XI debut. Development contract.

REES, Gareth Peter (Coedcae CS; Bath U), b Swansea 8 Apr 1985. 6'1". LHB, LM. Wales MC 2003-05. Debut (Glamorgan) 2006; cap 2009. 1000 runs (2); most – 1088 (2008). HS 154 v Surrey (Oval) 2008. LO HS 123* v Essex (Chelmsford) 2009 (FPT). T20 HS 38.

SALTER, Andrew Graham (Milford Haven SFC), b Haverfordwest 1 Jun 1993. RHB, OB. Glamorgan 2nd XI debut 2010. Wales MC 2010-11. Awaiting 1st XI debut.

WAGG, Graham Grant (Ashlawn S, Rugby), b Rugby, Warwks 28 Apr 1983. 6'0". RHB, LM. Warwickshire 2002-04; contract terminated after ECB imposed a 15-month ban, expiring 1 Jan 2006, for taking cocaine. Derbyshire 2006-10; cap 2007. Glamorgan debut 2011. F-c Tour (Eng A): I 2003-04. HS 108 De v Northants (Northampton) 2008. Gm HS 70 v Glos (Bristol) 2011. 50 wkts (2); most – 58 (2007). Gm BB 6-35 De v Surrey (Derby) 2009. Gm BB 3-52 v Kent (Canterbury) 2011. LO HS 48* De v Middx (Lord's) 2010 (CB40). LO BB 4-35 De v Durham (Derby) 2008 (FPT). T20 HS 62. T20 BB 3-23.

WALLACE, Mark Alexander (Crickhowell HS), b Abergavenny, Monmouthshire 19 Nov 1981. 5'9". LHB, WK. Debut (Glamorgan) 1999; cap 2003; captain 2012. F-c Tour (ECB Acad): SL 2002-03. 1000 runs (1): 1020 (2011). HS 139 v Surrey (Oval) 2009. LO HS 85 v Surrey (Cardiff) 2008 (P40). T20 HS 42*.

^{NQ}**WALTERS, Stewart** Jonathan (Guildford GS, Perth, WA), b Mornington, Victoria, Australia 25 Jun 1983. 6'1". RHB, RM. Surrey 2006-10. Glamorgan debut 2011. HS 188 Sy v Leics (Oval) 2009. Gm HS 147 v Kent (Canterbury) 2011. BB 1-4 Sy v Durham (Chester-le-St) 2009. LO HS 91 Sy v Northants (Oval) 2008 (P40). LO BB 1-12 Sy v Yorks (Scarborough) 2007 (P40). T20 HS 53*. T20 BB 1-9.

WATERS, Huw Thomas (Llantaram CS; Monmouth S), b Cardiff 26 Sep 1986. 6'2". RHB, RMF. Debut (Glamorgan) 2005. No f-c appearances in 2009. Wales MC 2004-07. HS 54 v Surrey (Cardiff) 2011. BB 5-86 v Somerset (Taunton) 2006. LO HS 8 v Hants (Swansea) 2007 (FPT). LO BB 3-47 v Durham (Chester-le-St) 2007 (P40). T20 HS 11*. T20 BB 3-30.

WRIGHT, Ben James (Cowbridge CS), b Preston, Lancs 5 Dec 1987. 5'9". RHB, RM. Debut (Glamorgan) 2006; cap 2011. No f-c appearances in 2008. HS 172 v Glos (Cardiff) 2010. BB 1-14 v Essex (Chelmsford) 2007. LO HS 79 v Lancs (Colwyn Bay) 2010 (CB40). LO BB 1-19 v Derbys (Derby) 2009 (FPT). T20 HS 55*. T20 BB 1-16.

RELEASED/RETIRED
(Having made a County First-Class or List A appearance in 2011)

PETERSEN, A.N. – *see ESSEX.*

POWELL, M.J. – *see KENT.*

SHANTRY, Adam John (Priory S; Shrewsbury SFC), b Bristol 13 Nov 1982. 6'2½". Son of B.K.Shantry (Gloucestershire 1978-79), brother of J.D.Shantry (*see WORCESTERSHIRE*). LHB, LFM. Northamptonshire 2003-04. Warwickshire 2006-07. Glamorgan 2008-11. Shropshire 2001. HS 100 v Leics (Colwyn Bay) 2009. BB 5-49 Wa v West Indies A (Birmingham) 2006. Gm BB 5-52 (10-129 match) v Warwks (Birmingham) 2008. LO HS 19* v Northants (Northampton) 2009 (FPT). LO BB 5-37 Nh v New Zealanders (Northampton) 2004. T20 HS – . T20 BB – .

D.O.Brown and D.S.Harrison left the staff without making a County First-Class or List A appearance for Glamorgan in 2011.

ESSEX RELEASED/RETIRED (continued from p 101)
(Having made a County First-Class or List A appearance in 2011)

STYRIS, S.B. – *see SUSSEX.*

TSOTSOBE, Lonwabo Lopsy (Western HS; Russell Road C), b Port Elizabeth, South Africa 7 Mar 1984. 6'3". RHB, LFM. Eastern Province 2004-05 to 2006-07. Warriors 2006-07 to date. Essex 2011. Sussex 2nd XI 2008. **Tests** (SA): 5 (2010 to 2010-11); HS 8* v I (Cape Town) 2010-11; BB 3-43 v I (Durban) 2010-11. **LOI** (SA): 29 (2008-09 to 2011-12); HS 4* (twice); BB 4-22 v I (Johannesburg) 2010-11. **IT20** (SA): 9 (2008-09 to 2011-12); HS 1 v A (Melbourne) 2008-09; BB 3-16 v P (Abu Dhabi) 2010-11. F-c Tours (SA): WI 2010; B 2010 (SA A). HS 27* and BB 7-39 Warriors v Lions (Johannesburg) 2007-08. Ex HS 6 v Northants (Northampton) 2011. Ex BB 2-71 v Glamorgan (Chelmsford) 2011. LO HS 11* Warriors v Eagles (Port Elizabeth) 2007-08. LO BB 5-28 EP v Border (East London) 2005-06. T20 HS 3*. T20 BB 4-18.

WRIGHT, C.J.C. – *see WARWICKSHIRE.*

M.Osborne and T.G.Southee left the staff without making a County First-Class or List A appearance for Essex in 2011.

GLAMORGAN 2011

RESULTS SUMMARY

	Place	Won	Lost	Tied	Drew	NR
LV= County Championship (2nd Division)	6th	5	6		5	
All First-Class Matches		5	6		5	
Clydesdale Bank 40 (Group C)	5th	4	5			3
Friends Life t20 (South Group)	7th	5	9			2

LV= COUNTY CHAMPIONSHIP AVERAGES

BATTING AND FIELDING

Cap		M	I	NO	HS	Runs	Avge	100	50	Ct/St
	S.J.Walters	7	14	4	147	508	50.80	2	1	5
2011	A.N.Petersen	15	27	2	210	1069	42.76	2	5	6
2003	M.A.Wallace	16	29	4	107	1020	40.80	2	7	39/5
	W.D.Bragg	16	30	–	110	1033	34.43	1	8	6
2010	J.Allenby	9	17	1	113	517	32.31	1	4	6
2000	M.J.Powell	12	23	2	99	675	32.14	–	5	8
	H.T.Waters	3	5	2	54	93	31.00	–	1	–
2009	G.P.Rees	16	31	–	126	954	30.77	1	8	13
2011	B.J.Wright	9	16	1	101	460	30.66	1	3	3
2010	J.A.R.Harris	10	17	3	60*	403	28.78	–	3	6
	N.A.James	4	7	–	49	186	26.57	–	–	–
	W.T.Owen	9	11	4	69	167	23.85	–	1	1
	G.G.Wagg	14	23	1	70*	446	20.27	–	3	5
	J.C.Glover	3	4	2	16*	35	17.50	–	–	2
2000	D.A.Cosker	16	24	4	39	314	15.70	–	–	6
1992	R.D.B.Croft	9	14	2	33	182	15.16	–	–	–
	A.J.Shantry	3	6	4	14	25	12.50	–	–	2

Also batted: C.P.Ashling (2 matches) 0*, 2*, 7; Alex J.Jones (2) 0, 8, 26 (1 ct); A.J.Norman (1) 34.

BOWLING

	O	M	R	W	Avge	Best	5wI	10wM
J.Allenby	228.3	51	654	25	26.16	5- 44	1	–
J.A.R.Harris	340.2	63	1186	44	26.95	5- 39	3	–
D.A.Cosker	613.1	162	1650	49	33.67	5- 48	1	–
W.T.Owen	229.2	26	1041	30	34.70	5-124	1	–
G.G.Wagg	401.2	64	1380	33	41.81	3- 52	–	–
R.D.B.Croft	295.1	49	831	19	43.73	3- 80	–	–
Also bowled:								
N.A.James	24	2	79	5	15.80	2- 28	–	–
C.P.Ashling	44	2	183	6	30.50	4- 47	–	–
A.J.Shantry	93.5	20	291	9	32.33	3- 42	–	–
J.C.Glover	52	4	201	5	40.20	4- 49	–	–

W.D.Bragg 10-1-27-1; Alex J.Jones 36-4-158-2; A.J.Norman 17-4-49-0; A.N.Petersen 55-11-160-1; H.T.Waters 59-14-161-3.

Glamorgan played no first-class fixtures outside the County Championship in 2011. The First-Class Averages (pp 223–240) give the records of Glamorgan players in all first-class county matches, with the exception of J.A.R.Harris, whose first-class figures for Glamorgan are as above.

GLAMORGAN RECORDS

FIRST-CLASS CRICKET

Highest Total	For 718-3d		v	Sussex	Colwyn Bay	2000
	V 712		by	Northants	Northampton	1998
Lowest Total	For 22		v	Lancashire	Liverpool	1924
	V 33		by	Leics	Ebbw Vale	1965
Highest Innings	For 309*	S.P.James	v	Sussex	Colwyn Bay	2000
	V 322*	M.B.Loye	for	Northants	Northampton	1998

Highest Partnership for each Wicket

1st	374	M.T.G.Elliott/S.P.James	v	Sussex	Colwyn Bay	2000
2nd	252	M.P.Maynard/D.L.Hemp	v	Northants	Cardiff	2002
3rd	313	D.E.Davies/W.E.Jones	v	Essex	Brentwood	1948
4th	425*	A.Dale/I.V.A.Richards	v	Middlesex	Cardiff	1993
5th	264	M.Robinson/S.W.Montgomery	v	Hampshire	Bournemouth	1949
6th	240	J.Allenby/M.A.Wallace	v	Surrey	The Oval	2009
7th	211	P.A.Cottey/O.D.Gibson	v	Leics	Swansea	1996
8th	202	D.Davies/J.J.Hills	v	Sussex	Eastbourne	1928
9th	203*	J.J.Hills/J.C.Clay	v	Worcs	Swansea	1929
10th	143	T.Davies/S.A.B.Daniels	v	Glos	Swansea	1982

Best Bowling	For 10- 51	J.Mercer	v	Worcs	Worcester	1936
(Innings)	V 10- 18	G.Geary	for	Leics	Pontypridd	1929
Best Bowling	For 17-212	J.C.Clay	v	Worcs	Swansea	1937
(Match)	V 16- 96	G.Geary	for	Leics	Pontypridd	1929

Most Runs – Season	2276	H.Morris	(av 55.51)	1990
Most Runs – Career	34056	A.Jones	(av 33.03)	1957-83
Most 100s – Season	10	H.Morris		1990
Most 100s – Career	54	M.P.Maynard		1985-2005
Most Wkts – Season	176	J.C.Clay	(av 17.34)	1937
Most Wkts – Career	2174	D.J.Shepherd	(av 20.95)	1950-72
Most Career W-K Dismissals	933	E.W.Jones	(840 ct; 93 st)	1961-83
Most Career Catches in the Field	656	P.M.Walker		1956-72

LIMITED-OVERS CRICKET

Highest Total	50ov	429	v	Surrey	The Oval	2002
	40ov	328-4	v	Lancashire	Colwyn Bay	2011
	T20	206-6	v	Somerset	Taunton	2006
Lowest Total	50ov	76	v	Northants	Northampton	1968
	40ov	42	v	Derbyshire	Swansea	1979
	T20	94-9	v	Essex	Cardiff	2010
Highest Innings	50ov	162*	I.V.A.Richards	v	Oxfordshire	Swansea	1993
	40ov	155*	J.H.Kallis	v	Surrey	Pontypridd	1999
	T20	116*	I.J.Thomas	v	Somerset	Taunton	2004
Best Bowling	50ov	5-13	R.J.Shastri	v	Scotland	Edinburgh	1988
	40ov	7-16	S.D.Thomas	v	Surrey	Swansea	1998
	T20	5-16	R.E.Watkins	v	Glos	Cardiff	2009

GLOUCESTERSHIRE

Formation of Present Club: 1871
Inaugural First-Class Match: 1870
Colours: Blue, Gold, Brown, Silver, Green and Red
Badge: Coat of Arms of the City and County of Bristol
County Champions (since 1890): (0); best – 2nd 1930, 1931, 1947, 1959, 1969, 1986
Gillette/NatWest/C&G/FP Trophy Winners: (5) 1973, 1999, 2000, 2003, 2004
Benson and Hedges Cup Winners: (3) 1977, 1999, 2000
Pro 40/National League (Div 1) Winners: (1) 2000
Sunday League Winners: (0); best – 2nd 1988
Clydesdale Bank 40 Winners: (0); best – 3rd Group B 2010
Twenty20 Cup Winners: (0); best – Finalist 2007

Chief Executive: Tom E.M.Richardson, County Ground, Nevil Road, Bristol BS7 9EJ • Tel: 0117 910 8000 • Fax: 0117 924 1193 • Email: info@glosccc.co.uk • Web: www.glosccc.co.uk

Director of Cricket: J.G.Bracewell. **Assistant Coach**: S.N.Barnes. **Captain**: A.P.R.Gidman. **Vice-Captain**: H.J.H.Marshall. **Overseas Player**: M.Muralitharan (T20 only). **2012 Beneficiary**: A.P.R.Gidman. **Head Groundsman**: Sean Williams. **Scorer**: Adrian Bull. ‡ New registration. NQ Not qualified for England.

Gloucestershire revised their capping policy in 2004 and now award players with their County Caps when they make their first-class debut.

BATTY, Jonathan Neil (Wheatley Park S, Oxon; Repton S; Durham U; Keble C, Oxford), b Chesterfield, Derbys 18 Apr 1974. 5'10". RHB, WK. Comb U 1994-95. Oxford U 1996; blue 1996. Surrey 1997-2009; cap 2001; captain 2004; benefit 2009. Gloucestershire debut/cap 2010. Oxfordshire 1993-96. Minor C 1996. 1000 runs (1): 1025 (2006). HS 168* Sy v Essex (Chelmsford) 2003. Gs HS 70 v Derbys (Bristol) 2011. BB 1-21 Sy v Lancs (Manchester) 2000. LO HS 158* Sy v Hants (Oval) 2005 (CGT). T20 HS 59.

BEARD, Michael Adam (Lord Williams's S, Thame), b Oxford 24 Oct 1992. 6'5". LHB, LMF. Gloucestershire 2nd XI debut 2008 aged 15y 216d. Oxfordshire 2011. Awaiting 1st XI debut.

COCKBAIN, Ian Andrew (Maghull HS), b Bootle, Liverpool 17 Feb 1987. Son of I.Cockbain (Lancs and Minor Cos 1979-94). 6'0". RHB, RM. Lancashire 2nd XI 2006-08. MCC YC 2008-10. Debut (Gloucestershire) 2011; cap 2011. Gloucestershire 2nd XI debut 2010. HS 127 v Middx (Uxbridge) 2011. LO HS 79 v Notts (Cheltenham) 2011 (CB40). T20 HS 78.

COUGHTRIE, Richard George (Newcastle RGS; Oxford Brookes U), b North Shields, Co Durham 1 Sep 1988. 5'10". RHB, WK. Oxford MCCU 2009-11. Gloucestershire debut/cap 2011. Gloucestershire 2nd XI debut 2009. Durham 2nd XI 2006-08. Northumberland 2008-09. HS 54* v Derbys (Derby) 2011. T20 HS 18.

DENT, Christopher David James (Backwell CS; Alton C), b Bristol 20 Jan 1991. 5'9". LHB, WK, occ SLA. Debut (Gloucestershire) 2007. Gloucestershire 2nd XI debut 2007, aged 16y 80d. England U19s 2009-10. HS 100 v Surrey (Cheltenham) 2011. BB – . LO HS 25 v Essex (Cheltenham) 2011 (CB40). LO BB 1-17 v Neth (Rotterdam) 2010 (CB40). T20 HS 63.

NQFULLER, James Kerr (Otago U, NZ), b Cape Town, South Africa 24 Jan 1990. British passport. 6'3". RHB, RFM. Otago 2009-10. Gloucestershire debut/cap 2011. HS 24 Otago v Wellington (Wellington) 2009-10. Gs HS 4 and BB 1-49 v Glamorgan (Bristol) 2011. BB 1-33 Otago v ND (Whangarei) 2009-10. LO HS 33 v Essex (Colchester) 2011 (CB40). LO BB 4-33 v Essex (Cheltenham) 2011 (CB40). T20 BB – .

GIDMAN, Alex Peter Richard (Wycliffe C), b High Wycombe, Bucks 22 Jun 1981. Elder brother of W.R.S.Gidman (*see below*). 6'3". RHB, RM. Debut (Gloucestershire) 2002; cap 2004; captain 2009 to date; benefit 2012. Otago 2007-08. MCC YC 2001. MCC 2004, 2007, 2010. F-c Tour (Eng A): SL 2004-05. Appointed captain of Eng A tour to India 2003-04 but withdrew because of hand injury. 1000 runs (4); most – 1244 (2006). HS 176 v Surrey (Bristol) 2009. BB 4-47 v Glamorgan (Cardiff) 2005. LO HS 116 v Sussex (Hove) 2009 (FPT). LO BB 5-42 Eng A v Bangladesh A (Mirpur) 2006-07. T20 HS 64. T20 BB 2-24.

GIDMAN, William Robert Simon (Wycliffe C; Berkshire C of Agriculture), b High Wycombe, Bucks 14 Feb 1985. Younger brother of A.P.R.Gidman (*see above*). 6'2". LHB, RM. Durham 2007. No f-c appearances in 2008-10. Gloucestershire debut/cap 2011, becoming first player for Gs to score 1000 runs and take 50 wkts in debut season. MCC YC 2004-06. 1000 runs (1): 1006 (2011). HS 116* v Northants (Bristol) 2011. 50 wkts (1): 51 (2011). BB 6-92 v Derbys (Derby) 2011. LO HS 40* v Glamorgan (Cardiff) 2011 (CB40). LO BB 4-36 Du v Hants (Chester-le-St) 2010 (P40). T20 HS 40*. T20 BB 1-18.

‡HOUSEGO, Daniel Mark (Oratory S, Reading), b Windsor, Berkshire 12 Oct 1988. 5'8". RHB, LB. Middlesex 2008-11. Middlesex 2nd XI debut 2005. Berkshire 2006. HS 104 M v Sri Lankans (Uxbridge) 2011. CC HS 48 M v Derbys (Derby) 2011. BB – . T20 HS 18.

McCARTER, Graeme John (Foyle and Londonderry C), b Londonderry, N.Ireland 10 Oct 1992. RHB, RFM. Ireland 2011. Gloucestershire 2nd XI debut 2008, aged 15y 292d. Awaiting 1st XI debut. HS 10 and BB 1-47 Ire v Namibia (Belfast) 2011.

NQMARSHALL, Hamish John Hamilton (Mahurangi C, Warkworth; King C, Auckland), b Warkworth, New Zealand 15 Feb 1979. Twin brother of J.A.H.Marshall (ND and NZ 1997-98 to date). Irish passport, qualified to play in April 2011. 5'9". RHB, RM. N Districts 1998-99 to date. Gloucestershire debut 2006 (scoring 102 v Worcs on UK debut); cap 2006; Kolpak registration 2008-11. Buckinghamshire 2003. **Tests** (NZ): 13 (2000-01 to 2005-06); HS 160 v SL (Napier) 2004-05. **LOI** (NZ): 66 (2003-04 to 2006-07); HS 101* v P (Faisalabad) 2003-04. **IT20** (NZ): 3 (2004-05 to 2005-06); HS 8 v A (Auckland) 2004-05. F-c Tours (NZ): A 2004-05; SA 2000-01, 2005-06; Z 2005; B 2004-05. 1000 runs (1): 1218 (2006). HS 170 ND v Canterbury (Rangiora) 2009-10. Gs HS 168 v Leics (Cheltenham) 2006. BB 4-24 v Leics (Leicester) 2009. LO HS 122 v Sussex (Hove) 2007 (P40). LO BB 2-21 v Hants (Southampton) 2009 (P40). T20 HS 102.

MILES, Craig Neil (Bradon Forest S, Swindon; Filton C, Bristol), b Swindon, Wilts 20 July 1994. 6'4". RHB, RMF. Debut (Gloucestershire) 2011; cap 2011. Gloucestershire 2nd XI debut 2009, aged 14y 318d. HS 19 and BB 2-80 v Northants (Bristol) 2011 – only f-c game. LO BB 2-32 v Essex (Cheltenham) 2011 (CB40).

NQMURALITHARAN, Muttiah (St Anthony's C, Kandy), Kandy, Sri Lanka 17 Apr 1972. RHB, OB. Central Province 1989-90 to 2003-04. Tamil Union 1991-92 to 2003-04. Lancashire 1999 (taking 7-44 and 7-73 v Warwks at Southport on debut), 2001, 2005, 2007; cap 1999. Kent 2003; cap 2003. Gloucestershire 2011 (T20 only). *Wisden* 1998. **Tests** (SL): 133 (1992-93 to 2010); HS 67 v I (Kandy) 2001-02; BB 9-51 (13-115 match) v Z (Kandy) 2001-02. **LOI** (SL): 350 (1993 to 2010-11); HS 33* v B (Dhaka) 2008-09; BB 7-30 v I (Sharjah) 2000-01. **IT20** (SL): 12 (2006-07 to 2010-11); HS 1 v P (Colombo, RPS) 2009; BB 3-29 v WI (Oval) 2009. F-c Tours (SL): E 1991, 1998, 2002, 2006; A 1995-96, 2005-06, 2007-08; SA 1992-93 (SL U24), 1994-95, 1997-98, 2000-01, 2002-03; WI 1996-97, 2003, 2007-08; NZ 1994-95, 1996-97; I 1993-94, 1997-98, 2006-07, 2009-10; P 1995-96, 1999-00, 2001-02, 2008-09; Z 1994-95, 1999-00, 2004; B 2005-06, 2008-09. HS 67 (*see Tests*). CC HS 28 La v Sussex (Liverpool) 2007. 50 wkts (3+3); most – 96 (2003-04). BB 9-51 (*see Tests*). CC BB 7-39 (11-61 match) La v Derbys (Derby) 1999. LO HS 33* (*see LOI*). LO BB 7-30 (*see LOI*). T20 HS 11. T20 BB 4-16.

NORWELL, Liam Connor (Redruth SS), b Bournemouth, Dorset 27 Dec 1991. 6'3". RHB, RMF. Debut (Gloucestershire) 2011; cap 2011. Gloucestershire 2nd XI debut 2009. HS 26 v Middx (Bristol) 2011. BB 6-46 v Derbys (Bristol) 2011 – on debut.

PAYNE, David Alan (Lytchett Minster S), b Poole, Dorset, 15 Feb 1991. 6'2". RHB, LMF. Debut (Gloucestershire) 2011; cap 2011. Gloucestershire 2nd XI debut 2008. Dorset 2009. England U19s 2010. HS 62 v Glamorgan (Bristol) 2011. BB 6-26 v Leics (Bristol) 2011. LO HS 13 and BB 7-29 v Essex (Chelmsford) 2010 (CB40), inc 4 wkts in 4 balls and 6 wkts in 9 balls – Gs l-o record. T20 HS 10. T20 BB 3-20.

SAXELBY, Ian David (Oakham S), b Nottingham 22 May 1989. 6'2". RHB, RMF. Nephew of K.Saxelby (Nottinghamshire 1978-90) and M.Saxelby (Notts, Durham and Derbys 1989-2000). Debut (Gloucestershire) 2008; cap 2008. No 1st XI appearances in 2010. Nottinghamshire 2nd XI debut 2006. England U19s 2008. HS 60* v Northants (Northampton) 2009. BB 6-69 (10-142 match) v Surrey (Oval) 2011. LO HS 7* and BB 4-31 v Surrey (Bristol) 2009 (FPT). T20 HS 5. T20 BB 2-23.

TAYLOR, Jack Martin Robert (Chipping Norton S), b Banbury, Oxfordshire 12 Nov 1991. 5'11". RHB, OB. Elder brother of M.D.Taylor (*see below*). Debut (Gloucestershire) 2010; cap 2010. Gloucestershire 2nd XI debut 2007, aged 15y 191d. Oxfordshire 2009-11. HS 39 v Surrey (Cheltenham) 2011. BB 2-81 v Middx (Uxbridge) 2011. LO HS 9* v Glamorgan (Cardiff) 2011 (CB40). LO BB 3-37 v Unicorns (Exmouth) 2011 (CB40). T20 HS 38. T20 BB 4-16 v Somerset (Bristol) 2011 – Gs record.

TAYLOR, Matthew David (Chipping Norton S), b Banbury, Oxfordshire 8 Jul 1994. 6'0". RHB, LM. Younger brother of J.M.R.Taylor (*see above*). Gloucestershire 2nd XI debut 2011. Oxfordshire 2011. Awaiting f-c debut. LO HS 7* and LO BB 2-43 v Notts (Cheltenham) 2011 (CB40).

WADE, David Neil (Bishop Luffa C of E S, Chichester; Havant C), b Chichester, W Sussex 27 Sep 1983. RHB, RFM. Gloucestershire 2nd XI debut 2010. Awaiting 1st XI debut.

YOUNG, Edward George Christopher (Wellington C; Oxford Brookes U), b Chertsey, Surrey 21 May 1989. 6'1". RHB, SLA. Brother of P.J.W.Young (Oxford UCCE 2006-08). Oxford MCCU 2009-11. Gloucestershire debut/cap 2010. HS 133 OU v Lancs (Oxford) 2011. Gs HS 51* v Essex (Bristol) 2011. BB 2-74 OU v Notts (Oxford) 2009. Gs BB 1-75 v Leics (Leicester) 2010. LO HS 50 v Notts (Nottingham) 2011 (CB40). LO BB 2-32 v Somerset (Bristol) 2011 (CB40). T20 HS 28. T20 BB 2-14.

BANERJEE, Vikram (King Edward's S, Birmingham; Downing C, Cambridge), b Bradford, Yorks 20 Mar 1984. 6'0". LHB, SLA. Cambridge UCCE 2004-06; blue 2004-05-06. Gloucestershire 2006-11; cap 2006. Buckinghamshire 2011. HS 35 and BB 5-74 v Surrey (Oval) 2010. LO HS 6 v Surrey (Bristol) 2009 (FPT). LO BB 3-47 v Sussex (Bristol) 2009 (FPT). T20 HS 5*. T20 BB 2-30.

DAWSON, Richard Kevin James (Batley GS; Exeter U), b Doncaster, Yorks 4 Aug 1980. 6'3". RHB, OB. British U 2000. Yorkshire 2001-06; cap 2004. MCC 2002. Northamptonshire 2007. Gloucestershire 2008-09; cap 2008. No f-c appearances 2010-11. Devon 1999-2000. **Tests**: 7 (2001-02 to 2002-03); HS 19* v A (Perth) 2002-03; BB 4-134 v I (Chandigarh) 2001-02 – on debut. F-c Tours: A 2002-03; NZ 2001-02; I 2001-02; SL 2002-03 (ECB Acad), 2004-05 (Eng A). HS 87 Y v Kent (Canterbury) 2002. Gs HS 50 and Gs BB 4-76 v Glamorgan (Cardiff) 2009. BB 6-82 Y v Glamorgan (Scarborough) 2001. LO HS 41 Y v Leics (Scarborough) 2002 (NL). LO BB 4-13 Y v Derbys (Derby) 2002 (BHC). T20 HS 27*. T20 BB 3-24.

LEWIS, J. – see SURREY.

[NQ]**O'BRIEN, Kevin** Joseph (Marian C, Dublin; Tallaght I of T), b Dublin, Ireland 4 Mar 1984. RHB, RMF. Son of B.A.O'Brien (Ireland 1966-81) and younger brother of N.J.O'Brien (see NORTHAMPTONSHIRE). Ireland 2006-07 to date. Nottinghamshire 2009. Gloucestershire 2011 (l-o and T20 only). **LOI** (Ire): 66 (2006 to 2011-12); HS 142 v Kenya (Nairobi) 2006-07; BB 4-71 v WI (Mohali) 2010-11. **IT20** (Ire): 20 (2008 to 2011-12); HS 39* v B (Nottingham) 2009; BB 2-15 v Kenya (Belfast) 2008. HS 171* Ire v Kenya (Nairobi) 2008-09. BB 5-39 Ire v Canada (Toronto) 2010. LO HS 142 (see LOI). LO BB 4-31 Ire v Notts (Dublin) 2008 (FPT). T20 HS 119 v Middx (Uxbridge) 2011 – Gs record. T20 BB 2-14.

TAYLOR, Christopher Glyn (Colston's Collegiate S), b Southmead, Bristol 27 Sep 1976. 5'7". RHB, OB. Gloucestershire 2000-11, scoring 104 v Middx – first to score a hundred at Lord's in a Championship match on his f-c debut; cap 2001; captain 2004-05; benefit 2009. 1000 runs (3); most – 1139 (2011). HS 196 v Notts (Nottingham) 2001 and 196 v Kent (Cheltenham) 2011. BB 4-52 v Northants (Northampton) 2007. LO HS 105 v Northants (Northampton) 2010 (CB40). LO BB 2-5 v Northants (Northampton) 2004 (NL). T20 HS 83. T20 BB 1-22.

[NQ]**WILLIAMSON, Kane** Stuart, b Tauranga, New Zealand 8 Aug 1990. RHB, OB. Cousin of D.Cleaver (Central Districts 2010-11 to date). N Districts 2007-08 to date. Gloucestershire 2011; cap 2011. **Tests** (NZ): 9 (2010-11 to 2011-12); HS 131 v I (Ahmedabad) 2010-11 – on debut; BB 1-12 v Z (Napier) 2011-12. **LOI** (NZ): 24 (2010 to 2011-12); HS 108 v B (Dhaka) 2010-11; BB 2-13 v Z (Napier) 2011-12. **IT20** (NZ): 6 (2011-12); HS 48 and BB 1-6 v Z (Auckland) 2011-12. F-c Tours (NZ): A 2011-12; I 2010-11; Z 2011-12. HS 284* ND v Wellington (Lincoln) 2011-12. Gs HS 149 and Gs BB 2-39 v Leics (Leicester) 2011. BB 5-75 ND v Canterbury (Christchurch) 2008-09. LO HS 108* ND v Wellington (Wellington) 2009-10. LO BB 5-51 ND v Auckland (Auckland) 2009-10. T20 HS 53. T20 BB 3-33.

GLOUCESTERSHIRE 2011

RESULTS SUMMARY

	Place	Won	Lost	Tied	Drew	NR
LV= County Championship (2nd Division)	4th	6	5		5	
All First-Class Matches		6	5		5	
Clydesdale Bank 40 (Group C)	6th	4	8			
Friends Life t20 (South Group)	8th	4	11			1

LV= COUNTY CHAMPIONSHIP AVERAGES

BATTING AND FIELDING

Cap†		M	I	NO	HS	Runs	Avge	100	50	Ct/St
2011	W.R.S.Gidman	16	28	6	116*	1006	45.72	1	8	4
2010	E.G.C.Young	3	5	2	51*	129	43.00	–	1	–
2001	C.G.Taylor	16	29	1	196	1139	40.67	3	6	5
2004	A.P.R.Gidman	15	27	3	168	903	37.62	1	6	12
2011	K.S.Williamson	13	23	–	149	831	36.13	1	5	12
2010	C.D.J.Dent	12	21	2	100	649	34.15	1	3	17
2011	I.A.Cockbain	12	21	1	127	542	27.10	1	3	10
2011	R.G.Coughtrie	16	30	5	54*	632	25.28	–	2	36
1998	J.Lewis	16	25	2	71	525	22.82	–	4	5
2006	H.J.H.Marshall	11	19	1	72	401	22.27	–	2	9
2010	J.M.R.Taylor	3	5	–	39	111	22.20	–	–	1
2011	L.C.Norwell	3	5	2	26	59	19.66	–	–	–
2010	J.N.Batty	6	10	–	70	179	17.90	–	1	28
2006	V.Banerjee	3	5	2	25	52	17.33	–	–	–
2011	D.A.Payne	14	21	6	62	255	17.00	–	1	5
2008	I.D.Saxelby	15	23	6	34*	238	14.00	–	–	2

Also batted (1 match): J.K.Fuller (cap 2011) 4 (1 ct); C.N.Miles (cap 2011) 19, 5.

BOWLING

	O	M	R	W	Avge	Best	5wI	10wM
W.R.S.Gidman	375.2	84	1088	51	21.33	6-92	3	–
J.Lewis	513.3	109	1521	65	23.40	5-65	1	–
L.C.Norwell	86.5	16	341	12	28.41	6-46	1	–
D.A.Payne	345.2	61	1298	42	30.90	6-26	2	–
I.D.Saxelby	393.2	53	1529	49	31.20	6-69	2	1
Also bowled:								
H.J.H.Marshall	94.1	20	274	6	45.66	2-18	–	–
J.M.R.Taylor	78	4	355	6	59.16	2-81	–	–
K.S.Williamson	94	10	332	5	66.40	2-39	–	–

V.Banerjee 100-17-307-4; C.D.J.Dent 2-0-8-0; J.K.Fuller 19-3-62-1; A.P.R.Gidman 32-4-127-2; C.N.Miles 19-1-80-2; C.G.Taylor 5-1-11-1; E.G.C.Young 6-1-23-0.

Gloucestershire played no first-class fixtures outside the County Championship in 2011. The First-Class Averages (pp 223–240) give the records of their players in all first-class county matches, with the exception of R.G.Coughtrie and E.G.C.Young, whose first-class figures for Gloucestershire are as above.

  † Gloucestershire revised their capping policy in 2004 and now award players with their County Caps when they make their first-class debut.

GLOUCESTERSHIRE RECORDS

FIRST-CLASS CRICKET

Highest Total	For	695-9d		v	Middlesex	Gloucester	2004
	V	774-7d		by	Australians	Bristol	1948
Lowest Total	For	17		v	Australians	Cheltenham	1896
	V	12		by	Northants	Gloucester	1907
Highest Innings	For	341	C.M.Spearman	v	Middlesex	Gloucester	2004
	V	319	C.J.L.Rogers	for	Northants	Northampton	2006

Highest Partnership for each Wicket

1st	395	D.M.Young/R.B.Nicholls	v	Oxford U	Oxford	1962
2nd	256	C.T.M.Pugh/T.W.Graveney	v	Derbyshire	Chesterfield	1960
3rd	336	W.R.Hammond/B.H.Lyon	v	Leics	Leicester	1933
4th	321	W.R.Hammond/W.L.Neale	v	Leics	Gloucester	1937
5th	261	W.G.Grace/W.O.Moberley	v	Yorkshire	Cheltenham	1876
6th	320	G.L.Jessop/J.H.Board	v	Sussex	Hove	1903
7th	248	W.G.Grace/E.L.Thomas	v	Sussex	Hove	1896
8th	239	W.R.Hammond/A.E.Wilson	v	Lancashire	Bristol	1938
9th	193	W.G.Grace/S.A.P.Kitcat	v	Sussex	Bristol	1896
10th	131	W.R.Gouldsworthy/J.G.Bessant	v	Somerset	Bristol	1923

Best Bowling	For	10-40	E.G.Dennett	v	Essex	Bristol	1906
(Innings)	V	10-66	A.A.Mailey	for	Australians	Cheltenham	1921
		10-66	K.Smales	for	Notts	Stroud	1956
Best Bowling	For	17-56	C.W.L.Parker	v	Essex	Gloucester	1925
(Match)	V	15-87	A.J.Conway	for	Worcs	Moreton-in-M	1914

Most Runs – Season	2860	W.R.Hammond	(av 69.75)	1933
Most Runs – Career	33664	W.R.Hammond	(av 57.05)	1920-51
Most 100s – Season	13	W.R.Hammond		1938
Most 100s – Career	113	W.R.Hammond		1920-51
Most Wkts – Season	222	T.W.J.Goddard	(av 16.80)	1937
	222	T.W.J.Goddard	(av 16.37)	1947
Most Wkts – Career	3170	C.W.L.Parker	(av 19.43)	1903-35
Most Career W-K Dismissals	1054	R.C.Russell	(950 ct; 104 st)	1981-2004
Most Career Catches in the Field	719	C.A.Milton		1948-74

LIMITED-OVERS CRICKET

Highest Total	50ov	401-7		v	Bucks	Wing	2003
	40ov	344-6		v	Northants	Cheltenham	2001
	T20	254-3		v	Middlesex	Uxbridge	2011
Lowest Total	50ov	82		v	Notts	Bristol	1987
	40ov	49		v	Middlesex	Bristol	1978
	T20	68		v	Hampshire	Bristol	2010
Highest Innings	50ov	177	A.J.Wright	v	Scotland	Bristol	1997
	40ov	153	C.M.Spearman	v	Warwicks	Gloucester	2003
	T20	119	K.J.O'Brien	v	Middlesex	Uxbridge	2011
Best Bowling	50ov	6-21	C.A.Walsh	v	Kent	Bristol	1990
		6-21	C.A.Walsh	v	Cheshire	Bristol	1992
	40ov	7-29	D.A.Payne	v	Essex	Chelmsford	2010
	T20	4-16	J.M.R.Taylor	v	Somerset	Bristol	2011

HAMPSHIRE

Formation of Present Club: 12 August 1863
Inaugural First-Class Match: 1864
Colours: Blue, Gold and White
Badge: Tudor Rose and Crown
County Champions: (2) 1961, 1973
Gillette/NatWest/C&G/FP Trophy Winners: (3) 1991, 2005, 2009
Benson and Hedges Cup Winners: (2) 1988, 1992
Pro 40/National League (Div 1) Winners: (0); best – 2nd 2008
Sunday League Winners: (3) 1975, 1978, 1986
Clydesdale Bank 40 Winners: (0); best – 4th in Group 2010, 2011
Twenty20 Cup Winners: (1) 2010

Chairman and CEO: Rod Bransgrove, The Ageas Bowl, Botley Road, West End, Southampton SO30 3XH • Tel: 023 8047 2002 • Fax: 023 8047 2122 • Email: enquiries@ageasbowlplc.com • Web: www.ageasbowlplc.com

Cricket Secretary and Director of Rose Bowl Plc: T.M.Tremlett. **First XI Manager:** G.W.White. **Head Coach:** T.C.Middleton. **Assistant 1st XI/Bowling Coach:** C.White. **Captain:** J.H.K.Adams. **Vice-Captain:** none. **Overseas Players:** S.M.Katich and Shahid Afridi (T20 only). **2012 Beneficiary:** Nigel Gray (testimonial). **Head Groundsman:** Nigel Gray. **Scorer:** A.E. (Tony) Weld. ‡ New registration. ^{NQ} Not qualified for England.

ADAMS, James Henry Kenneth (Sherborne S; University C, London; Loughborough U), b Winchester 23 Sep 1980. 6'2". LHB, LM. British U 2002-04. Hampshire debut 2002; cap 2006; captain 2012. Loughborough UCCE 2003-04 – scoring 107 v Somerset (Taunton) on debut. Dorset 1998. F-c Tour (EL): WI 2010-11. 1000 runs (2); most – 1351 (2009). HS 262* v Notts (Nottingham) 2006. BB 2-16 v Durham (Chester-le-St) 2004. LO HS 131 v Warwks (Birmingham) 2010 (CB40). LO BB 1-34 v Essex (Chelmsford) 2007 (FPT). T20 HS 101*. T20 BB –.

ALI, Kabir (Moseley CS and SFC), b Moseley, Birmingham, Warwks 24 Nov 1980. 6'0". RHB, RMF. Worcestershire 1999-2009. Rajasthan 2006-07. Hampshire debut 2010. **Tests:** 1 (2003); HS 9 and BB 3-80 v SA (Leeds) 2003. **LOI:** 14 (2003 to 2006); HS 39* v P (Rawalpindi) 2005-06; BB 4-45 v I (Delhi) 2005-06. F-c Tours: WI 2005-06 (Eng A); SL 2002-03 (ECB Acad). HS 84* Wo v Durham (Stockton) 2003. H HS 32 v Sussex (Hove) 2011. 50 wkts (5); most – 71 (2002). BB 8-50 Wo v Lancs (Manchester) 2007. Took 8-53 before lunch first day Wo v Yorks (Scarborough) 2003. H BB 5-33 v Essex (Chelmsford) 2010 – on H debut. LO HS 92 Wo v Essex (Worcester) 2003 (NL). LO BB Wo 5-36 v Yorks (Leeds) 2002 (NL). T20 HS 49. T20 BB 4-44.

BALCOMBE, David John (St John's S, Leatherhead; St Hild & St Bede C, Durham), b City of London 24 Dec 1984. 6'4". RHB, RFM. Durham UCCE 2005-07. British U 2006. Hampshire debut 2007. Kent 2011 (on loan). HS 73 DU v Leics (Leicester) 2005. H HS 30 v Yorks (Southampton) 2010. BB 6-51 (10-102 match) v Essex (Canterbury) 2011. H BB 3-58 v Yorks (Leeds) 2007. LO HS 6 K v Netherlands (Rotterdam) 2011 (CB40). LO BB 4-38 v Worcs (Worcester) 2011 (CB40). T20 HS 3. T20 BB 1-23.

BATES, Michael David (Lord Wandsworth C, Hook), b Frimley, Surrey 10 Oct 1990. 5'10". RHB, WK. Debut (Hampshire) 2010. Hampshire 2nd XI debut 2007. Berkshire 2009. England U19s 2009-10. HS 58* v Durham (Chester-le-St) 2011. LO HS 24* v Warwks (Birmingham) 2011 (CB40). T20 HS 10.

116

BRIGGS, Danny Richard (Isle of Wight C), b Newport, IoW, 30 Apr 1991. 6'2". RHB, SLA. Debut (Hampshire) 2009. Hampshire 2nd XI debut 2007, aged 16y 120d. **LOI**: 1 (2011-12); HS-and BB 2-39 v P (Dubai) 2011-12. F-c Tour (EL): WI 2010-11. HS 38* EL v Barbados (Bridgetown) 2010-11. CC HS 36 v Somerset (Southampton) 2009 – on debut. BB 6-45 EL v Windward Is (Roseau) 2010-11. CC BB 6-65 v Notts (Southampton) 2011. LO HS 16 v Surrey (Southampton) 2011 (CB40). LO BB 3-27 EL v Sri Lanka A (Colombo, RPS) 2011-12. T20 HS 10. T20 BB 5-19.

CARBERRY, Michael Alexander (St John Rigby Catholic C), b Croydon, Surrey 29 Sep 1980. 6'0". LHB, OB. Surrey 2001-02. Kent 2003-05. Hampshire debut/cap 2006. MCC 2008. **Tests**: 1 (2009-10); HS 34 v B (Chittagong) 2009-10. F-c Tours: B 2006-07 (Eng A), 2009-10. 1000 runs (2); most – 1251 (2009). HS 300* v Yorks (Southampton) 2011, sharing in UK 3rd highest and UK record 3rd-wkt partnership of 523 with N.D.McKenzie. BB 2-85 v Durham (Chester-le-St) 2006. LO HS 121* v Ireland (Southampton) 2009 (FPT). LO BB 2-11 v Notts (Nottingham) 2009 (FPT). T20 HS 90. T20 BB 1-16.

DAWSON, Liam Andrew (John Bentley S, Calne), b Swindon, Wilts 1 Mar 1990. 5'8". RHB, SLA. Debut (Hampshire) 2007. Mountaineers 2011-12. England U19s 2007 to 2008. Wiltshire 2006-07. HS 169 v Somerset (Southampton) 2011. BB 7-51 Mountaineers v ME (Mutare) 2011-12 (also scored 110* in same match). BB 2-3 v Sussex (Southampton) 2009. LO HS 70 v Northants (Northampton) 2011 (CB40). BB 4-45 v Middx (Lord's) 2008 (P40). T20 HS 26. T20 BB 3-25.

NO**ERVINE, Sean** Michael (Lomagundi C, Chinhoyi), b Harare, Zimbabwe 6 Dec 1982. Elder brother of C.R.Ervine (Midlands, SR 2003-04 to date); son of R.M.Ervine (Rhodesia 1977-78); grandson of M.A.Den (Rhodesia 1935-36); nephew of N.B.Ervine (Rhodesia 1977-78) and G.M.Den (Rhodesia and Eastern Province 1963-64 to 1969-70). Irish passport. 6'2". LHB, RM. CFX Academy 2000-01 to 2001. Midlands 2001-02 to 2003-04. Hampshire debut/cap 2005 (Kolpak registration). W Australia 2006-07 to 2007-08. Southern Rocks 2009-10. Matabeleland Tuskers 2011-12. **Tests** (Z): 5 (2003 to 2003-04); HS 86 v B (Harare) 2003-04; BB 4-146 v A (Perth) 2003-04. **LOI** (Z): 42 (2001-02 to 2003-04); HS 100 v I (Adelaide) 2003-04; BB 3-29 v P (Sharjah) 2001-02. F-c Tours (Z): E 2003; A 2003-04. HS 237* v Somerset (Southampton) 2010. BB 6-82 Midlands v Mashonaland (Kwekwe) 2002-03. H BB 5-60 v Glamorgan (Cardiff) 2005. LO HS 167* v Ireland (Southampton) 2009 (FPT). LO BB 5-50 v Glamorgan (Cardiff) 2005 (CGT). T20 HS 74*. T20 BB 4-12.

GRIFFITHS, David Andrew (Sandown HS, IoW), b Newport, IoW 10 Sep 1985. 6'1". LHB, RFM. Debut (Hampshire) 2006. HS 31* v Surrey (Southampton) 2007. BB 6-85 v Notts (Nottingham) 2011. LO HS 7 v Durham (Southampton) 2011 (CB40). LO BB 4-29 v Glos (Southampton) (P40). T20 HS 4*. T20 BB 3-13.

NO**KATICH, Simon** Mathew (Trinity C, WA: U of WA), b Middle Swan, Midland, W Australia 21 Aug 1975. 6'0". LHB, SLC. W Australia 1996-97 to 2001-02. Durham 2000; cap 2000. Yorkshire (1 match) 2002. NSW 2002-03 to date. Hampshire 2003-05, cap 2003. Derbyshire 2007; cap/captain 2007. Lancashire (1 match) 2010. **Tests** (A): 56 (2001 to 2010-11); HS 157 v WI (Bridgetown) 2008; BB 6-65 v Z (Sydney) 2003-04. **LOI** (A): 45 (2000-01 to 2006-07); HS 107* v SL (Brisbane) 2005-06. **IT20** (A): 3 (2004-05 to 2005-06); HS 39 v SA (Johannesburg) 2005-06. F-c Tours (A): E 2001, 2005, 2009, 2010 (v P); SA 2008-09; WI 2008; NZ 2004-05, 2009-10; I 2004-05, 2008-09 (Aus A), 2008-09, 2010-11; SL 1999-00, 2003-04. 1000 runs (3+4); most – 1506 (2007-08). HS 306 NSW v Q (Sydney) 2007-08. UK HS 221 De v Somerset (Taunton) 2007. H HS 143* v Yorks (Scarborough) 2003. BB 7-130 NSW v Vic (Melbourne) 2002-03. UK BB 4-21 H v Northants (Southampton) 2003. LO HS 136* NSW v Vic (Bowral) 2003-04. LO BB 3-21 Aus A v SA (Adelaide) 2001-02. T20 HS 75.

^{NQ}**McKENZIE, Neil** Douglas (King Edward VII HS; Rand Afrikaans U), b Johannesburg, South Africa 24 Nov 1975. 5'9½". Son of K.A.McKenzie (N-E Transvaal and Transvaal 1966-67 to 1986-87). RHB, RM. Transvaal/Gauteng 1994-95 to 1998-99. Northerns 1999-00 to 2003-04. Lions 2004-05 to date; captain 2004-05 to 2009-10 (*part*). Somerset 2007. Durham 2008 (*part*). Hampshire debut/cap 2010 (Kolpak registration). *Wisden* 2008. **Tests** (SA): 58 (2000 to 2008-09); HS 226 v B (Chittagong) 2007-08, sharing Test record 1st wkt partnership of 415 with G.C.Smith; BB – . **LOI** (SA): 64 (1999-00 to 2008-09); HS 131* v Kenya (Cape Town) 2001-02; BB – . **IT20** (SA): 2 (2005-06 to 2008-09); HS 7* v A (Brisbane) 2008-09. F-c Tours (SA): E 2003, 2008; A 2001-02, 2008-09; WI 2000-01; NZ 2003-04; I 2007-08; P 2003-04; SL 2000; Z 2001-02, 2004 (SA A); B 2003, 2007-08. 1000 runs (1): 1120 (2011). HS 237 v Yorks (Southampton) 2011, sharing in UK 3rd highest and UK record 3rd-wkt partnership of 523 with M.A.Carberry. BB 2-13 Lions v Eagles (Kimberley) 2007-08. H BB 2-30 v Lancs (Liverpool) 2010. LO HS 131* (*see LOI*). LO BB 2-19 Gauteng v GW (Kimberley) 1997-98. T20 HS 89*. T20 BB 1-4.

MASCARENHAS, Adrian Dimitri (Trinity C, Perth, Australia), b Hammersmith, London 30 Oct 1977. 6'2". Resident in Australia 1979-96. RHB, RMF. Debut (Hampshire) 1996, taking 6-88 v Glamorgan (Southampton); took 14 wickets in first two CC matches; cap 1998; benefit 2007; captain 2008-10. No f-c or l-o appearances in 2010 after Achilles injury. Dorset 1996. **LOI**: 20 (2007 to 2009); HS 52 v I (Bristol) 2007; BB 3-23 v I (Lord's) 2007. **IT20**: 14 (2007 to 2009); HS 31 v NZ (Auckland) 2007-08; BB 3-18 v Z (Cape Town) 2007-08. HS 131 v Kent (Canterbury) 2006. 50 wkts (1): 56 (2004). BB 6-25 v Derbys (Southampton) 2004. LO HS 79 v Worcs (Southampton) 1999 (NL) and 79 v Kent (Canterbury) 2004 (NL). LO BB 5-27 v Glos (Southampton) 2002 (NL). T20 HS 57*. T20 BB 5-14 v Sussex (Hove) 2004 – H record.

RIAZUDDIN, Hamza (Bradfield C), b Chelsea, London 19 Dec 1989. 5'11". RHB, RMF. Debut (Hampshire) 2008. England U19s 2009. Berkshire 2008. HS 4 and CC BB 1-21 v Somerset (Taunton) 2008. LO BB 1-0 v OU (Oxford) 2010. LO HS 23* v Durham (Chester-le-St) 2010 (CB40). LO BB 3-37 v Scotland (Southampton) 2011 (CB40). T20 HS 13*. T20 BB 4-15.

ROUSE, Adam Paul (Perrins Community Sports C; Peter Symonds C, Winchester), b Harare, Zimbabwe 30 Jun 1992. 5'8". RHB, WK. Hampshire 2nd XI debut 2008, aged 15y 331d. England U19s 2010. Awaiting 1st XI debut. Development contract for 2012.

^{NQ}**SHAHID KHAN AFRIDI**, Sahibzada Mohammad (Ibrahim Alibhai S; Islamia Science C, Karachi) b Kohat, Pakistan, 1 Mar 1980. Brother of Tariq Afridi (Karachi 1999-00) and Ashfaq Afridi (Karachi Blues 2008-09). RHB, LBG. Debut Combined XI v Eng A 1995-96. Karachi 1995-96 to 2003-04. Habib Bank 1997-98 to 2008-09. Leicestershire 2001; cap 2001. Derbyshire 2003. GW 2003-04. Sind 2007-08 to 2008-09. MCC 2001. Hampshire T20 contract for 2011-12. **Tests** (P): 27 (1998-99 to 2010, 1 as captain); HS 156 v I (Faisalabad) 2005-06; BB 5-52 v A (Karachi) 1998-99 – on debut. **LOI** (P): 333 (1996-97 to 2011-12, 21 as captain); HS 124 v B (Dambulla) 2010; BB 6-38 v A (Dubai) 2009. Scored a 37-ball hundred (*LOI record*) which included then joint record 11 sixes v SL (Nairobi) 1996-97 in his first LOI innings. **IT20** (P): 48 (2006-07 to 2011-12, 19 as captain); HS 54* v SL (Lord's) 2009; BB 4-11 v Netherlands (Lord's) 2009. F-c Tours (P): E 2006, 2010; A 1996-97, 2004-05; WI 1999-00, 2005; I 1998-99, 2004-05; SL 2005-06; Z 2002-03; B 1998-99. HS 164 Le v Northants (Northampton) 2001. BB 6-101 Habib Bank v KRL (Rawalpindi) 1997-98. UK BB 5-84 Le v Essex (Chelmsford) 2001. LO HS 124 (*see LOI*). LO BB 6-38 (*see LOI*). T20 HS 80. T20 BB 5-20.

TERRY, Sean Paul (Aquinas C, Perth; Notre Dame U, Perth), b Southampton 1 Aug 1991. Son of V.P.Terry (Hampshire, England 1978-96). RHB, OB. Hampshire 2nd XI debut 2011. Awaiting 1st XI debut. Development contract for 2012.

TOMLINSON, James Andrew (Harrow Way S, Andover; Cardiff U), b Winchester 12 Jun 1982. 6'1". LHB, LMF. British U 2002-03. Hampshire debut 2002; cap 2008. Wiltshire 2001. HS 42 v Somerset (Southampton) 2010. 50 wkts (1): 67 (2008). BB 8-46 (10-194 match) v Somerset (Taunton) 2008. LO HS 14 v Durham (Chester-le-St) 2010 (CB40). LO BB 4-47 v Glamorgan (Southampton) 2006 (CGT). T20 HS 5. T20 BB 1-20.

VINCE, James Michael (Warminster S), b Cuckfield, Sussex 14 Mar 1991. 6'2". RHB, RM. Debut (Hampshire) 2009. Hampshire 2nd XI debut 2006. Wiltshire 2007-08. HS 180 v Yorks (Scarborough) 2010. BB – . LO HS 131 v Scotland (Southampton) 2011 (CB40). T20 HS 85*.

WOOD, Christopher Philip (Alton C), b Basingstoke 27 June 1990. 6'2". RHB, LM. Debut (Hampshire) 2010. Hampshire 2nd XI debut 2007. England U19s 2009. HS 56* and CC BB 4-35 v Worcs (Southampton) 2011. BB 5-54 v Oxford MCCU (Oxford) 2010. LO HS 14* v Northants (Northampton) 2011 (CB40). LO BB 4-33 v Scotland (Aberdeen) 2010 (CB40). T20 HS 18. T20 BB 3-27.

RELEASED/RETIRED
(Having made a County First-Class or List A appearance in 2011)

CORK, Dominic Gerald (St Joseph's C, Stoke-on-Trent; Newcastle CFE), b Newcastle-under-Lyme, Staffs 7 Aug 1971. 6'2". RHB, RFM. Derbyshire 1990-2003; cap 1993; captain 1998-2003; benefit 2001. Lancashire 2004-08; cap 2004. Hampshire 2009-11; cap 2009; captain 2010-11. *Wisden* 1995. PCA 1995. **Tests**: 37 (1995 to 2002); HS 59 v NZ (Auckland) 1996-97; BB 7-43 v WI (Lord's) 1995 – on debut (record England analysis by Test match debutant; hat-trick v WI (Manchester) 1995 – the first in Test history to occur in the opening over of a day's play. **LOI**: 32 (1992 to 2002-03); HS 31* v NZ (Napier) 1996-97; BB 3-27 v WI (Lord's) 1995. F-c Tours: A 1992-93 (Eng A), 1998-99; SA 1993-94 (Eng A), 1995-96; WI 1991-92 (Eng A); NZ 1996-97; I 1994-95 (Eng A); P 2000-01 (*part*). HS 200* De v Durham (Derby) 2000. H HS 55 v Essex (Southampton) 2010. 50 wkts (7); most – 90 (1995). BB 9-43 (13-93 match) De v Northants (Derby) 1995. H BB 5-14 v Worcs (Worcester) 2009. Took 8-53 before lunch on his 20th birthday for De v Essex (Derby) 1991. 2 hat-tricks: 1994 and 1995 (*see Tests*). LO HS 93 De v Derbys CB (Derby) 2000 (NWT). LO BB 6-21 De v Glamorgan (Chesterfield) 1997 (SL). T20 HS 28. T20 BB 4-16.

[NQ]**De WET, Friedel** (Grenswag Hoerskool; Pretoria TC), b Durban, South Africa 26 Jun 1980. 6'1". RHB, RFM. Northerns 2001-02 to 2002-03. North West 2004-05 to date. Lions 2005-06 to 2010-11. Hampshire 2011. Dolphins 2011-12. **Tests** (SA): 2 (2009-10); HS 20 and BB 4-55 v E (Pretoria) 2009-10. F-c Tour (SA A): I 2007-08. HS 73 Dolphins v Warriors (Port Elizabeth) 2011-12. H HS 16* v Notts (Nottingham) 2011. 50 wkts (0+1): 61 (2006-07). BB 7-61 Lions v Cape Cobras (Cape Town) 2005-06. H BB 2-78 v Somerset (Southampton) 2011. LO HS 56* NW v FS (Potchefstroom) 2005-06. LO BB 5-59 Lions v Eagles (Johannesburg) 2006-07. T20 HS 17. T20 BB 2-18.

HOWELL, Benny Alexander Cameron (The Oratory S), b Bordeaux, France 5 Oct 1988. Son of J.B.Howell (Warwickshire 2nd XI 1978). 5'11". RHB, RM. Hampshire 2011. Hampshire 2nd XI debut 2005. Berkshire 2007. HS 71 v Lancs (Southampton) 2011. LO HS 122 v Surrey (Croydon) 2011 (CB40). LO BB 1-23 v Leics (Southampton) 2010 (CB40). T20 HS 29*. T20 BB 2-14.

NQIMRAN TAHIR, Mohammad (Government Pakistan Angels HS and MAO College, Lahore), b Lahore, Pakistan 4 Jun 1979. 5'11". RHB, LB. Lahore City 1996-97 to 1997-98. WAPDA 1998-99. REDCO 1999-00. Lahore Whites 2000-01. SNGPL 2001-02 to 2003-04. Sialkot 2002-03. Middlesex 2003. Lahore Blues 2004-05. PIA 2004-05 to 2006-07. Lahore Ravi 2005-06. Yorkshire (1 match) 2007. Titans 2007-08 to 2009-10. Hampshire 2008-09, 2011; cap 2009. Easterns 2008-09 to 2009-10. Warwickshire 2010; cap 2010. Dolphins 2010-11 to date. Staffordshire 2004-05. Qualified for SA on 1 Apr 2009. **Tests** (SA): 5 (2011-12); HS 29* v SL (Centurion) 2011-12; BB 3-55 v A (Johannesburg) 2011-12. **LOI** (SA): 5 (2010-11); HS 1* and BB 4-38 v E (Chennai) 2010-11. F-c Tour (Pak A): SL 2004-05. HS 77* v Somerset (Southampton) 2009. 50 wkts (2+2); most – 74 (2004-05). BB 8-76 REDCO v Karachi Blues (Lahore) 1999-00. UK BB 7-66 (12-189 match) v Lancs (Manchester) 2008 – on H debut. LO HS 41* Staffs v Lancs (Stone) 2004 (CGT). LO BB 5-27 v Sussex (Southampton) 2008 (P40). T20 HS 17*. T20 BB 3-13.

JONES, S.P. – see GLAMORGAN.

LUMB, M.J. – see NOTTINGHAMSHIRE.

NQMYBURGH, Johannes Gerhardus (Pretoria BHS; U of SA), b Pretoria, South Africa 22 Oct 1980. 5'7". Elder brother of S.J.Myburgh (Northerns 2005-06 to 2009-10) and brother-in-law of F.de Wet (see above). RHB, OB. Northerns 1997-98 to 2006-07. Titans 2004-05. Canterbury 2007-08 to 2009-10. Hampshire 2011. EU qualified through wife's visa. HS 203 Northerns B v Easterns (Pretoria) 1997-98. H HS 80 v Sussex (Southampton) 2011. BB 4-56 Canterbury v ND (Hamilton) 2008-09. H BB 1-30 v Durham (Southampton) 2011. LO HS 112 Canterbury v Auckland (Christchurch) 2009-10. LO BB 2-22 Canterbury v CD (Christchurch) 2009-10. T20 HS 88. T20 BB 3-16.

POTHAS, Nic (King Edward VII S; Rand Afrikaans U), b Johannesburg, South Africa 18 Nov 1973. ECB qualified – EU (Greek) passport. 6'3". RHB, WK, occ RM. Transvaal 1993-94 to 1996-97. Gauteng 1997-98 to 2000-01. Hampshire 2002-11; cap 2003; benefit 2011. **LOI** (SA): 3 (2000-01); HS 24 v P (Singapore) 2000 – on debut. F-c Tours (SA): E 1996 (SA A); WI 2000 (SA A); SL 1998. HS 165 Gauteng v KZ-Natal (Johannesburg) 1998-99. H HS 146* v Worcs (Worcester) 2003. BB 1-16 v Middx (Lord's) 2006. Held 7 catches in an innings v Lancs (Manchester) 2006. LO HS 114* v Glamorgan (Cardiff) 2005 (CGT). T20 HS 59.

RAVENSCROFT, Timothy John (Elizabeth C, Guernsey), b Guernsey 21 Jan 1992. 5'10". RHB, OB. Hampshire 2nd XI debut 2011. LO HS 5 v Scotland (Southampton) 2011 (CB40) – only 1st XI appearance.

J.R.Miller left the staff, without making a County First-Class or List A appearance in 2011.

HAMPSHIRE 2011

RESULTS SUMMARY

	Place	Won	Lost	Tied	Drew	NR
LV= County Championship (1st Division)	9th	3	6		7	
All First-Class Matches		3	6		7	
Clydesdale Bank 40 (Group B)	4th	5	6			1
Friends Life t20 (South Group)	SF	12	3			3

LV= COUNTY CHAMPIONSHIP AVERAGES
BATTING AND FIELDING

Cap		M	I	NO	HS	Runs	Avge	100	50	Ct/St
2006	M.A.Carberry	9	15	1	300*	793	56.64	3	1	6
2010	N.D.McKenzie	16	28	2	237	1120	43.07	3	3	12
	L.A.Dawson	15	26	1	169	908	36.32	2	5	17
2006	J.H.K.Adams	15	26	–	207	935	35.96	2	4	13
2005	S.M.Ervine	14	24	2	128	663	30.13	1	3	6
	J.M.Vince	16	27	2	157	723	28.92	2	2	9
	J.G.Myburgh	6	11	–	80	287	26.09	–	2	2
	C.P.Wood	8	11	1	56*	259	25.90	–	1	4
2009	D.G.Cork	10	15	1	50	317	22.64	–	1	6
2003	N.Pothas	8	15	1	72	303	21.64	–	3	20
	Kabir Ali	5	9	4	32	98	19.60	–	–	1
	M.D.Bates	8	12	1	58*	204	18.54	–	1	18/4
	F.de Wet	4	6	3	16*	49	16.33	–	–	1
1998	A.D.Mascarenhas	8	14	2	50	190	15.83	–	1	2
2009	Imran Tahir	8	10	3	22*	74	10.57	–	–	4
2008	J.A.Tomlinson	6	10	6	12*	36	9.00	–	–	1
	D.R.Briggs	11	17	2	29*	103	6.86	–	–	2
	D.A.Griffiths	6	10	4	6*	19	3.16	–	–	–

Also played (1 match): B.A.C.Howell 0, 71; S.P.Jones 0; M.J.Lumb (cap 2008) 6, 11.

BOWLING

	O	M	R	W	Avge	Best	5wI	10wM
Imran Tahir	235.3	40	685	28	24.46	6-132	2	–
A.D.Mascarenhas	229.2	61	581	21	27.66	6- 62	1	–
C.P.Wood	192.4	39	671	24	27.95	4- 35	–	–
Kabir Ali	129	21	437	13	33.61	4- 43	–	–
D.A.Griffiths	172.5	41	607	18	33.72	6- 85	1	–
D.G.Cork	278.3	60	802	22	36.45	5- 75	1	–
D.R.Briggs	449.5	89	1393	38	36.65	6- 65	3	–
J.A.Tomlinson	173.1	39	573	15	38.20	4- 13	–	–
S.M.Ervine	220.2	33	896	15	59.73	3- 66	–	–

Also bowled:
| F.de Wet | 124 | 15 | 470 | 9 | 52.22 | 2- 78 | | |

M.A.Carberry 8.3-3-18-0; L.A.Dawson 61-9-231-3; S.P.Jones 18.3-1-65-1; N.D.McKenzie 2-0-23-0; J.G.Myburgh 15-1-66-1.

Hampshire played no first-class fixtures outside the County Championship in 2011. The First-Class Averages (pp 223–240) give the records of Hampshire players in all first-class county matches, with the exception of J.H.K.Adams, whose first-class figures for Hampshire are as above.

HAMPSHIRE RECORDS

FIRST-CLASS CRICKET

Highest Total	For 714-5d		v	Notts	Southampton	2005
	V 742		by	Surrey	The Oval	1909
Lowest Total	For 15		v	Warwicks	Birmingham	1922
	V 23		by	Yorkshire	Middlesbrough	1965
Highest Innings	For 316	R.H.Moore	v	Warwicks	Bournemouth	1937
	V 303*	G.A.Hick	for	Worcs	Southampton	1997

Highest Partnership for each Wicket

1st	347	V.P.Terry/C.L.Smith	v	Warwicks	Birmingham	1987
2nd	373	J.H.K.Adams/M.A.Carberry	v	Somerset	Taunton	2011
3rd	523	M.A.Carberry/N.D.McKenzie	v	Yorkshire	Southampton	2011
4th	278	J.H.K.Adams/J.M.Vince	v	Yorkshire	Scarborough	2010
5th	235	G.Hill/D.F.Walker	v	Sussex	Portsmouth	1937
6th	411	R.M.Poore/E.G.Wynyard	v	Somerset	Taunton	1899
7th	325	G.Brown/C.H.Abercrombie	v	Essex	Leyton	1913
8th	257	N.Pothas/A.J.Bichel	v	Glos	Cheltenham	2005
9th	230	D.A.Livingstone/A.T.Castell	v	Surrey	Southampton	1962
10th	192	H.A.W.Bowell/W.H.Livsey	v	Worcs	Bournemouth	1921

Best Bowling	For	9- 25	R.M.H.Cottam	v	Lancashire	Manchester	1965
(Innings)	V	10- 46	W.Hickton	for	Lancashire	Manchester	1870
Best Bowling	For	16- 88	J.A.Newman	v	Somerset	Weston-s-Mare	1927
(Match)	V	17-103	W.Mycroft	for	Derbyshire	Southampton	1876

Most Runs – Season	2854	C.P.Mead	(av 79.27)	1928
Most Runs – Career	48892	C.P.Mead	(av 48.84)	1905-36
Most 100s – Season	12	C.P.Mead		1928
Most 100s – Career	138	C.P.Mead		1905-36
Most Wkts – Season	190	A.S.Kennedy	(av 15.61)	1922
Most Wkts – Career	2669	D.Shackleton	(av 18.23)	1948-69
Most Career W-K Dismissals	700	R.J.Parks	(630 ct; 70 st)	1980-92
Most Career Catches in the Field	629	C.P.Mead		1905-36

LIMITED-OVERS CRICKET

Highest Total	50ov	371-4		v	Glamorgan	Southampton	1975
	40ov	353-8		v	Middlesex	Lord's	2005
	T20	225-2		v	Middlesex	Southampton	2006
Lowest Total	50ov	75		v	Essex	Chelmsford	2007
	40ov	43		v	Essex	Basingstoke	1972
	T20	85		v	Sussex	Southampton	2008
Highest Innings	50ov	177	C.G.Greenidge	v	Glamorgan	Southampton	1975
	40ov	172	C.G.Greenidge	v	Surrey	Southampton	1987
	T20	124*	M.J.Lumb	v	Essex	Southampton	2009
Best Bowling	50ov	7-30	P.J.Sainsbury	v	Norfolk	Southampton	1965
	40ov	6-20	T.E.Jesty	v	Glamorgan	Cardiff	1975
	T20	5-14	A.D.Mascarenhas	v	Sussex	Hove	2004

KENT

Formation of Present Club: 1 March 1859
Substantial Reorganisation: 6 December 1870
Inaugural First-Class Match: 1864
Colours: Maroon and White
Badge: White Horse on a Red Ground
County Champions: (6) 1906, 1909, 1910, 1913, 1970, 1978
Joint Champions: (1) 1977
Gillette/NatWest/C&G/FP Trophy Winners: (2) 1967, 1974
Benson and Hedges Cup Winners: (3) 1973, 1976, 1978
Pro 40/National League (Div 1) Winners: (1) 2001
Sunday League Winners: (4) 1972, 1973, 1976, 1995
Clydesdale Bank 40 Winners: (0); best – 2nd Group C 2010
Twenty20 Cup Winners: (1) 2007

Acting Chief Executive: Jamie Clifford, St Lawrence Ground, Canterbury, CT1 3NZ • Tel: 01227 456886 • Fax: 01227 762168 • Email: kent@ecb.co.uk • Web: www.kentcricket.co.uk

Head Coach: Jimmy C.Adams. **High Performance Director:** Simon Willis. **1st Team Assistant Coach:** Paul Relf. **Captain:** R.W.T.Key. **Vice-Captain:** tba. **Overseas Player:** Azhar Mahmood. **2012 Beneficiary:** G.O.Jones. **Head Groundsman:** Andrew Peirson. **Scorer:** Jack C.Foley. ‡ New registration. NQ Not qualified for England.

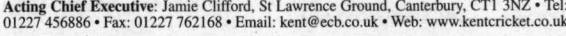

NQ**AZHAR MAHMOOD** Sagar (F.G. No. 1 HS, Islamabad), b Rawalpindi, Pakistan 28 Feb 1975. 5'11". RHB, RFM. Islamabad 1993-94 to 2006-07. United Bank 1995-96 to 1996-97. Rawalpindi 1998-99 to 2004-05. PIA 2001-02. Surrey 2002-07; cap 2004. Habib Bank 2006-07 to 2010-11. Kent debut 2008 (British passport holder) scoring 116 v Notts (Canterbury); cap 2008. MCC 2001. **Tests** (P): 21 (1997-98 to 2001); HS 136 v SA (Johannesburg) 1997-98; BB 4-50 v E (Lord's) 2001. Scored 128* and 50* v SA (Rawalpindi) 1997-98 on debut. **LOI** (P): 143 (1996-97 to 2006-07); HS 67 v I (Adelaide) 1999-00; BB 6-18 v WI (Sharjah) 1999-00. F-c Tours (P): E 1997 (Pak A), 2001; A 1999-00; SA 1997-98; I 1998-99; SL 2000; Z 1997-98. HS 204* Sy v Middx (Oval) 2005. K HS 116 (*see above*). 50 wkts (0+1): 59 (1996-97). BB 8-61 Sy v Lancs (Oval) 2002. K BB 6-36 v Middx (Lord's) 2011. LO HS 101* Sy v Glamorgan (Oval) 2006 (CGT). LO BB 6-18 (*see LOI*). T20 HS 106*. T20 BB 4-20.

BALL, Adam James (Beths GS, Bexley) b Greenwich, London 1 March 1993. 6'1". RHB, LFM. Debut (Kent) 2011. Kent 2nd XI debut 2009, aged 16y 117d. England U19s 2010 to 2010-11. HS 46 v Glos (Canterbury) 2011. BB 3-36 v Leics (Leicester) 2011. LO HS 19 v Middx (Canterbury) 2011 (CB40). LO BB 2-31 v Sussex (Hove) 2011 (CB40). T20 HS 15. T20 BB 2-28.

BELL-DRUMMOND, Daniel James (Millfield S), b Lewisham, London 4 Aug 1993. 6'0". RHB, RMF. Debut (Kent) 2011. Kent 2nd XI debut 2009, aged 16y 21d. England U19s 2010 to 2010-11. HS 80 v Loughborough MCCU (Canterbury) 2011. CC HS 29 v Glamorgan (Canterbury) 2011. LO HS 42 v Worcs (Worcester) 2011 (CB40). T20 HS 11.

BILLINGS, Samuel William (Haileybury S; Loughborough U), b Pembury 15 Jun 1991. 5'11". RHB, WK. Looughborough MCCU 2011, scoring 131 v Northants (Loughborough) on f-c debut. Kent debut 2011. Kent 2nd XI debut 2007, aged 15y 349d. HS 131 (see above). K HS 19 v Loughborough MCCU (Canterbury) 2011. LO HS 26 v Worcs (Worcester) 2011 (CB40). T20 HS 2.

123

BLAKE, Alexander James (Hayes SS; Leeds Met U), b Farnborough 25 Jan 1989. 6'1". LHB, RMF. Debut (Kent) 2008. Kent 2nd XI debut 2005. Leeds/Bradford UCCE 2009-11 (not f-c). HS 105* v Yorks (Leeds) 2010. BB 2-9 v Pakistanis (Canterbury) 2010. CC BB 1-60 v Hants (Southampton) 2010. LO HS 81* v Scotland (Canterbury) 2010 (CB40). LO BB 2-13 v Yorks (Leeds) 2011 (CB40). T20 HS 33.

COLES, Matthew Thomas (Maplesden Noakes S; Mid-Kent C), b Maidstone 26 May 1990. 6'3". LHB, RMF. Debut (Kent) 2009. Kent 2nd XI debut 2007. HS 51 v Lancs (Canterbury) 2010. BB 5-29 v Loughborough MCCU (Canterbury) 2011. CC BB 5-77 v Leics (Tunbridge Wells) 2011. LO HS 47 v Yorks (Leeds) 2011 (CB40). LO BB 4-47 v Hants (Southampton) 2010 (CB40). T20 HS 16*. T20 BB 3-30.

COOK, Simon James (Matthew Arnold S), b Oxford 15 Jan 1977. 6'4". RHB, RMF. Middlesex 1999-2004; cap 2003. Kent debut 2005; cap 2007. HS 93* M v Notts (Lord's) 2001. K HS 71 v Yorks (Leeds) 2006. BB 8-63 M v Northants (Northampton) 2002. K BB 6-35 v Sussex (Canterbury) 2007. LO HS 67* M v Durham (Lord's) 2003 (NL). LO BB 6-37 M v Leics (Leicester) 2004 (NL). T20 HS 25*. T20 BB 3-13.

COWDREY, Fabian Kruuse (Tonbridge S), b Canterbury 30 Jan 1993. Son of C.S.Cowdrey (Kent, Glamorgan, England 1977-92). Grandson of M.C.Cowdrey (Kent, Oxford U, England 1950-76). Nephew of G.R.Cowdrey (Kent 1984-97). 6'0". RHB, SLA. Kent 2nd XI debut 2009, aged 16y 207d. Awaiting 1st XI debut.

‡**HARMISON, Ben** William (Ashington HS), b Ashington, Northumb 9 Jan 1986. Younger brother of S.J.Harmison (*see DURHAM*). 6'5". LHB, RMF. Durham 2006-10, scoring 110 v Oxford U (Oxford) on debut. Scored 105 in his second match (v West Indies A) to emulate A.Fairbairn (Middlesex 1947) in scoring hundreds in first two f-c matches, those matches being in England. HS 110 (*see above*). CC HS 101 Du v Warwks (Chester-le-St) 2007. BB 4-27 Du v Surrey (Guildford) 2008. LO HS 67 Du v Notts (Chester-le-St) 2009 (P40). LO BB 3-43 Du v Scotland (Chester-le-St) 2008 (FPT). T20 HS 24. T20 BB 3-20.

JONES, Geraint Owen (Harristown State HS, Toowoomba and MacGregor State HS, Brisbane, Australia), b Kundiawa, Papua New Guinea 14 Jul 1976. Welsh parents. 5'10". RHB, WK. Debut (Kent) 2001; cap 2003; benefit 2012. MBE 2005. **Tests**: 34 (2003-04 to 2006-07); HS 100 v NZ (Leeds) 2004. **LOI**: 49 (2004 to 2006); HS 80 v Z (Bulawayo) 2004-05. **IT20**: 2 (2005 to 2006); HS 19 v A (Southampton) 2005. F-c Tours: A 2006-07; SA 2004-05; WI 2003-04; I 2005-06; P 2005-06; SL 2003-04. 1000 runs (2); most – 1345 (2009). HS 178 v Somerset (Canterbury) 2010. LO HS 86 v Surrey (Oval) 2008 (FPT). T20 HS 56.

KEMP, Benedict William (St Edmund's S, Canterbury), b Canterbury 26 May 1993. Son of N.J.Kemp (Kent, Middlesex 1977-82). 6'4". RHB, RFM. Kent 2nd XI debut 2010. Awaiting 1st XI debut.

KEY, Robert William Trevor (Colfe's S), b East Dulwich, London 12 May 1979. 6'1". RHB, RM/OB. Debut (Kent) 1998; cap 2001; captain 2006 to date; benefit 2011. MCC 2002-04, 2009. *Wisden* 2004. **Tests**: 15 (2002 to 2004-05); HS 221 v WI (Lord's) 2004. **LOI**: 5 (2003 to 2004); HS 19 v WI (Lord's) 2004. **IT20**: 1 (2009); HS 10* v Netherlands (Lord's) 2009. F-c Tours: A 2002-03; SA 1998-99 (Eng A), 2004-05; NZ 2008-09 (EL – captain); SL 2002-03 (ECB Acad); Z 1998-99 (Eng A). 1000 runs (6); most – 1896 (2004). HS 270* v Glamorgan (Cardiff) 2009. BB 2-31 v Somerset (Canterbury) 2010. LO HS 120* v Essex (Canterbury) 2008 (P40). T20 HS 98*.

NORTHEAST, Sam Alexander (Harrow S), b Ashford 16 Oct 1989. 5'11". RHB, OB. Debut (Kent) 2007. No 1st XI appearances in 2008. England U19s 2009. HS 176 v Loughborough MCCU (Canterbury) 2011. CC HS 128* v Glos (Bristol) 2009. BB – . LO HS 69 v Surrey (Canterbury) 2009 (P40). T20 HS 39*.

PIESLEY, Christopher Damien (Fulston Manor S, Sittingbourne), b Chatham 12 Mar 1992. 5'11½". LHB, OB. Debut (Kent) 2010. Kent 2nd XI debut 2008, aged 16y 126d. HS 43 v Pakistanis (Canterbury) 2010. CC HS 4 v Glos (Cheltenham) 2011. LO HS 4 v Netherlands (Rotterdam) 2011 (CB40).

‡POWELL, Michael John (Crickhowell SS; Pontypool CFE), b Abergavenny, Monmouth-shire 3 Feb 1977. 6'1". RHB, OB, occ WK. Glamorgan 1997-2011, scoring 200* v Oxford U (Oxford) on debut; cap 2000; benefit 2011. MCC 2005. 1000 runs (5); most – 1327 (2006). HS 299 Gm v Glos (Cheltenham) 2006 – record score for Glamorgan in England. BB 2-39 Gm v Oxford U (Oxford) 1999. CC BB – . LO HS 114* Gm v Hants (Cardiff) 2008 (FPT). LO BB 1-26 Gm v Lincs (Lincoln) 2004 (CGT). T20 HS 68*.

RILEY, Adam Edward Nicholas (Beths GS, Bexley), b Sidcup 23 Mar 1992. 6'2". RHB, OB. Debut (Kent) 2011. Kent 2nd XI debut 2010. HS 5 v Derbys (Derby) 2011. BB 5-76 v Loughborough MCCU (Canterbury) 2011. CC BB 4-145 v Northants (Canterbury) 2011. LO HS 3* and LO BB 2-32 v Sussex (Hove) 2011 (CB40). T20 HS – . T20 BB 1.34.

SHAW, Stuart **Ashley** (Shavington HS, Crewe), b Crewe, Cheshire 14 Apr 1991. 5'11". RHB, LFM. Debut (Kent) 2011. Kent 2nd XI debut 2010. HS 22* and BB 5-118 v Derbys (Canterbury) 2011. LO HS 4* v Yorks (Leeds) 2011 (CB40). LO BB 3-26 v Middx (Lord's) 2011 (CB40). T20 HS 3*. T20 BB 1-10.

‡SHRECK, Charles Edward (Truro S), b Truro, Cornwall 6 Jan 1978. 6'7". RHB, RFM. Nottinghamshire 2003-11; cap 2006. Wellington 2005-06 to 2007-08. MCC 2008. Cornwall 1997-2002. HS 19 Nt v Essex (Chelmsford) 2003. 50 wkts (2); most – 61 (2006, 2008). BB 8-31 (12-129 match) Nt v Middx (Nottingham) 2006. Hat-trick Nt v Middx (Lord's) 2006. LO HS 9* Wellington v CD (Palmerston N) 2005-06. LO BB 5-19 Cornwall v Worcs (Truro) 2002 (CGT). T20 HS 6*. T20 BB 4-22.

STEVENS, Darren Ian (Hinckley C), b Leicester 30 Apr 1976. 5'11". RHB, RM. Leicestershire 1997-2004; cap 2002. MCC 2002. Kent debut/cap 2005. F-c Tour (ECB Acad): SL 2002-03. 1000 runs (2); most – 1277 (2005). HS 208 v Glamorgan (Canterbury) 2005 and v Middx (Uxbridge) 2009. BB 7-21 (11-70 match) v Surrey (Canterbury) 2011. LO HS 133 Le v Northumb (Jesmond) 2000 (NWT). LO BB 5-32 v Scotland (Edinburgh) 2005 (NL). T20 HS 77. T20 BB 4-14.

THOMAS, Ivan Alfred (John Roan S, Blackheath; Leeds U), b Greenwich, London 25 Sep 1991. 6'4". RHB, RMF. Kent 2nd XI debut 2011. Awaiting 1st XI debut.

TREDWELL, James Cullum (Southlands Community CS, New Romney), b Ashford 27 Feb 1982. 6'0". LHB, OB. Debut (Kent) 2001; cap 2007. MCC 2004, 2008. **Tests**: 1 (2009-10); HS 37 and BB 4-82 v B (Dhaka) 2009-10. **LOI**: 5 (2009-10 to 2010-11); HS 16 v A (Hobart) 2010-11; BB 4-48 v WI (Chennai) 2010-11. F-c Tours: I 2003-04 (Eng A, captain); B 2009-10. HS 123* v New Zealanders (Canterbury) 2008. CC HS 116* v Yorks (Tunbridge W) 2007. 50 wkts (1): 69 (2009). BB 8-66 (11-120 match) v Glamorgan (Canterbury) 2009. LO HS 88 v Surrey (Oval) 2007 (FPT). LO BB 6-27 v Middx (Southgate) 2009 (FPT). T20 HS 34*. T20 BB 4-21.

RELEASED/RETIRED
(Having made a County First-Class or List A appearance in 2011)

DENLY, J.L. – *see MIDDLESEX.*

GOODMAN, James Elliot (St Olave's GS), b Farnborough 19 Nov 1990. 5'10". RHB, RM. Kent 2010-11. Kent 2nd XI debut 2006, aged 15y 194d. England U19s 2009-10. HS 59 and BB 1-16 v Pakistanis (Canterbury) 2010. CC HS 30 v Glamorgan (Cardiff) 2011. LO HS 26* v Surrey (Canterbury) 2009 (P40).

JOSEPH, R.H. – *see LEICESTERSHIRE.*

^{NQ}**NEL**, Johann **Dewald** (George Watson's C, Edinburgh), b Klerksdorp, Transvaal, South Africa 6 Jun 1980. 6'0". RHB, RMF. Scotland 2004-10. Worcestershire 2007. Kent 2010-11. **LOI** (Scot): 19 (2006 to 2010); HS 11* v Afghanistan (Ayr) 2010; BB 4-25 v Ireland (Aberdeen) 2008. **IT20** (Scot): 10 (2007-08 to 2009-10); HS 13* v P (Durban) 2007-08; BB 3-10 v Kenya (Belfast) 2008. HS 36 Scotland v Afghanistan (Ayr) 2010. CC HS 8 Wo v Yorks (Leeds) 2007. K HS 4 v Pakistanis (Canterbury) 2010. BB 6-62 (9-119 match) v Yorks (Leeds) 2010. LO HS 36* Scotland v Durham (Edinburgh) 2006 (CGT). LO BB 4-25 Scotland v Ireland (Aberdeen) 2008. T20 HS 13*. T20 BB 3-10.

SAKER, Neil Clifford (Raynes Park HS; Nescot C), b Tooting, London 20 Sep 1984. 6'4". RHB, RFM. Surrey 2003-08; no f-c appearances in 2008. Kent 2011. HS 58* Sy v Essex (Colchester) 2006. K HS 18 v Northants (Canterbury) 2011. BB 5-76 v Lancs (Manchester) 2007. K BB 5-112 v Glamorgan (Cardiff) 2011. LO HS 40* Unicorns v Surrey (Wormsley) 2010 (CB40). LO BB 4-43 Sy v Kent (Canterbury) 2005 (NL). T20 HS 0. T20 BB 1-28.

VAN JAARSVELD, Martin (Warmbaths S; Pretoria U), b Klerksdorp, South Africa 18 Jun 1974. 6'2". RHB, OB. N Transvaal/Northerns 1994-95 to 2003-04. Northamptonshire 2004. Titans 2004-05 to date. Kent 2005-11; cap 2005. Scored 118 and 111 v Warwks (Canterbury) on debut – second player after C.W.G.Bassano (Derbyshire) to score two hundreds on a county debut. PCA 2008. Qualified for England in 2010. **Tests** (SA): 9 (2002-03 to 2004-05); HS 73 v WI (Johannesburg) 2003-04. **LOI** (SA): 11 (2002-03 to 2004); HS 45 v E (Birmingham) 2003; BB 1-0 v B (Kimberley) 2002-03. Took wickets with his first and third balls in LOI. F-c Tours (SA): A 2002-03 (SA A); NZ 2003-04; I 2004-05; SL 1998-99 (SA A), 2004; Z 1998-99 (SA Acad). 1000 runs (6+1); most – 1509 (2009). HS 262* v Glamorgan (Cardiff) 2005. BB 5-33 v Surrey (Oval) 2008. LO HS 132* Titans v Eagles (Bloemfontein) 2008-09 and 132* v Somerset (Canterbury) 2009 (FPT). LO BB 3-13 Titans v Cape Cobras (Centurion) 2008-09. T20 HS 82. T20 BB 3-20.

^{NQ}**WAHAB RIAZ**, b Lahore, Pakistan 28 Jun 1985. RHB, LFM. Lahore 2001-02 to 2006-07. Karachi Port Trust 2003-04. Hyderabad 2003-04 to 2004-05. National Bank 2007-08 to date. Kent 2011. **Tests** (P): 7 (2010 to 2011); HS 27 and BB 5-63 v E (Oval) 2010. **LOI** (P): 24 (2007-08 to 2011-12); HS 21 v SA (Dubai) 2010-11; BB 5-46 v I (Mohali) 2010-11. **IT20** (P): 6 (2007-08 to 2011); HS 30* v NZ (Auckland) 2010-11; BB 2-24 v WI (Gros Islet) 2011. F-c Tours (P): E 2010; A 2009 (P A); WI 2011; NZ 2010-11; SL 2009 (P A). HS 84 NBP v WAPDA (Lahore) 2011-12. K HS 34 v Surrey (Canterbury) 2011. BB 7-74 NBP v ZTB (Lahore) 2011-12. K BB 4-94 v Leics (Leicester) 2011. LO HS 42* NBP v SNGPL (Sheikhupura) 2006-07. LO BB 5-24 NBP v SNGPL (Sargodha) 2008-09. T20 HS 32*. T20 BB 5-17.

KENT 2011

RESULTS SUMMARY

	Place	Won	Lost	Tied	Drew	NR
LV= County Championship (2nd Division)	8th	5	9		2	
All First-Class Matches		6	9		2	
Clydesdale Bank 40 (Group A)	4th	6	6			
Friends Life t20 (South Group)	QF	9	6			2

LV= COUNTY CHAMPIONSHIP AVERAGES
BATTING AND FIELDING

Cap		M	I	NO	HS	Runs	Avge	100	50	Ct/St
2008	Azhar Mahmood	7	13	3	97	521	52.10	–	5	9
2001	R.W.T.Key	12	24	2	162	895	40.68	2	5	11
2008	J.L.Denly	14	28	1	199	1024	37.92	2	5	4
2005	M.van Jaarsveld	14	28	3	95	755	30.20	–	6	24
2005	D.I.Stevens	16	31	–	143	819	26.41	1	4	13
	S.A.Shaw	3	5	3	22*	50	25.00	–	–	1
2003	G.O.Jones	16	31	1	99	699	23.30	–	4	57/4
	S.A.Northeast	16	32	–	112	704	22.00	1	4	7
2007	S.J.Cook	7	14	2	51	237	19.75	–	1	1
	M.T.Coles	9	15	3	50*	236	19.66	–	1	3
2007	J.C.Tredwell	12	22	2	47	362	18.10	–	–	14
	A.J.Blake	8	16	–	96	280	17.50	–	2	6
	A.J.Ball	9	15	1	46	184	13.14	–	–	5
	D.J.Bell-Drummond	3	6	–	29	67	11.16	–	–	2
	J.E.Goodman	3	6	–	30	65	10.83	–	–	3
	Wahab Riaz	5	9	1	34	85	10.62	–	–	1
	R.H.Joseph	6	11	6	19*	42	8.40	–	–	1
	D.J.Balcombe	5	8	2	12	40	6.66	–	–	1
	N.C.Saker	3	5	–	18	29	5.80	–	–	1
	A.E.N.Riley	5	8	4	17	17	4.25	–	–	1

Also batted (1 match each): J.D.Nel 2*, 0; C.D.Piesley 0, 4; C.E.Shreck 4, 0*.

BOWLING

	O	M	R	W	Avge	Best	5wI	10wM
D.J.Balcombe	174.5	40	588	33	17.81	6- 51	4	1
D.I.Stevens	288.2	74	862	41	21.02	7- 21	2	1
Azhar Mahmood	210.1	63	546	23	23.73	6- 36	1	–
J.C.Tredwell	394.5	78	1175	42	27.97	5- 35	2	–
R.H.Joseph	128.1	27	485	16	30.31	4- 25	–	–
S.A.Shaw	65.1	5	313	10	31.30	5-118	1	–
N.C.Saker	93	15	332	10	33.20	5-112	1	–
Wahab Riaz	121.4	24	436	13	33.53	4- 94	–	–
M.T.Coles	258.4	44	965	26	37.11	5- 77	1	–
A.J.Ball	143	25	560	15	37.33	3- 36	–	–
S.J.Cook	144.1	28	448	11	40.72	3- 40	–	–
Also bowled:								
J.L.Denly	92	10	305	7	43.57	3- 43	–	–
A.E.N.Riley	111.1	9	471	9	52.33	4-145	–	–

A.J.Blake 2-0-10-0; J.E.Goodman 7.5-0-21-0; R.W.T.Key 0.4-0-8-0; J.D.Nel 15-1-60-1;
C.E.Shreck 25-8-69-0; M.van Jaarsveld 14-0-60-2.

The First-Class Averages (pp 223–240) give the records of Kent players in all first-class
county matches (Kent's other opponents being Loughborough MCCU), with the exception
of C.E.Shreck, whose first-class figures for Kent are as above.

KENT RECORDS

FIRST-CLASS CRICKET

Highest Total	For 803-4d		v	Essex	Brentwood	1934
	V 676		by	Australians	Canterbury	1921
Lowest Total	For 18		v	Sussex	Gravesend	1867
	V 16		by	Warwicks	Tonbridge	1913
Highest Innings	For 332	W.H.Ashdown	v	Essex	Brentwood	1934
	V 344	W.G.Grace	for	MCC	Canterbury	1876

Highest Partnership for each Wicket

1st	300	N.R.Taylor/M.R.Benson	v	Derbyshire	Canterbury	1991
2nd	366	S.G.Hinks/N.R.Taylor	v	Middlesex	Canterbury	1990
3rd	323	R.W.T.Key/M.van Jaarsveld	v	Surrey	Tunbridge Wells	2005
4th	368	P.A.de Silva/G.R.Cowdrey	v	Derbyshire	Maidstone	1995
5th	277	F.E.Woolley/L.E.G.Ames	v	N Zealanders	Canterbury	1931
6th	315	P.A.de Silva/M.A.Ealham	v	Notts	Nottingham	1995
7th	248	A.P.Day/E.Humphreys	v	Somerset	Taunton	1908
8th	177	G.O.Jones/Yasir Arafat	v	Warwicks	Canterbury	2007
9th	171	M.A.Ealham/P.A.Strang	v	Notts	Nottingham	1997
10th	235	F.E.Woolley/A.Fielder	v	Worcs	Stourbridge	1909

Best Bowling	For 10- 30	C.Blythe	v	Northants	Northampton	1907
(Innings)	V 10- 48	C.H.G.Bland	for	Sussex	Tonbridge	1899
Best Bowling	For 17- 48	C.Blythe	v	Northants	Northampton	1907
(Match)	V 17-106	T.W.J.Goddard	for	Glos	Bristol	1939

Most Runs – Season	2894	F.E.Woolley	(av 59.06)	1928
Most Runs – Career	47868	F.E.Woolley	(av 41.77)	1906-38
Most 100s – Season	10	F.E.Woolley		1928, 1934
Most 100s – Career	122	F.E.Woolley		1906-38
Most Wkts – Season	262	A.P.Freeman	(av 14.74)	1933
Most Wkts – Career	3340	A.P.Freeman	(av 17.64)	1914-36
Most Career W-K Dismissals	1253	F.H.Huish	(901 ct; 352 st)	1895-1914
Most Career Catches in the Field	773	F.E.Woolley		1906-38

LIMITED-OVERS CRICKET

Highest Total	50ov	384-6		v	Berkshire	Finchampstead 1994
	40ov	327-6		v	Leics	Canterbury 1993
	T20	217		v	Glos	Gloucester 2010
Lowest Total	50ov	60		v	Somerset	Taunton 1979
	40ov	83		v	Middlesex	Lord's 1984
	T20	72		v	Hampshire	Southampton 2011
Highest Innings	50ov	136*	C.L.Hooper	v	Berkshire	Finchampstead 1994
	40ov	146	A.Symonds	v	Lancashire	Tunbridge Wells 2004
	T20	112	A.Symonds	v	Middlesex	Maidstone 2004
Best Bowling	50ov	8-31	D.L.Underwood	v	Scotland	Edinburgh 1987
	40ov	6- 9	R.A.Woolmer	v	Derbyshire	Chesterfield 1979
	T20	5-17	Wahab Riaz	v	Glos	Beckenham 2011

LANCASHIRE

Formation of Present Club: 12 January 1864
Inaugural First-Class Match: 1865
Colours: Red, Green and Blue
Badge: Red Rose
County Champions (since 1890): (8) 1897, 1904, 1926, 1927, 1928, 1930, 1934, 2011
Joint Champions: (1) 1950
Gillette/NatWest/C&G/FP Trophy Winners: (7) 1970, 1971, 1972, 1975, 1990, 1996, 1998
Benson and Hedges Cup Winners: (4) 1984, 1990, 1995, 1996
Pro 40/National League (Div 1) Winners: (1) 1999.
Sunday League Winners: (4) 1969, 1970, 1989, 1998
Clydesdale Bank 40 Winners: (0); best – 4th in Group 2010, 2011
Twenty20 Cup Winners: (0); best – Finalist 2005

Chief Executive: Jim Cumbes, Old Trafford, Manchester M16 0PX • Tel: 0161 282 4000 • Fax: 0161 282 4100 • Email: enquiries@lccc.co.uk • Web: www.lccc.co.uk

Director of Cricket: M.Watkinson. **Head Coach**: Peter Moores. **Assistant Coach**: G.Yates. **Captain**: G.Chapple. **Vice-Captain**: none. **Overseas Player**: A.G.Prince. **2012 Beneficiary**: J.M.Anderson. **Head Groundsman**: Matthew Merchant. **Scorer**: Alan West. ‡ New registration. ᴺᑫ Not qualified for England.

AGATHANGELOU, Andrea Peter (Fields C, Rustenburg), b Rustenburg, South Africa 16 Nov 1989. 6'3". RHB, LB. North West 2007-08 to 2010-11. Lions 2008-09. Lancashire debut 2011. HS 158 NW v KwaZulu-Natal (Potchefstroom) 2009-10. La HS 18 v Oxford MCCU (Oxford) 2011. BB 2-62 NW v KwaZulu-Natal Inland (Potchefstroom) 2009-10. LO HS 94 NW v EP (Port Elizabeth) 2010-11.

ANDERSON, James Michael (St Theodore RC HS and SFC, Burnley), b Burnley 30 Jul 1982. 6'2". LHB, RFM. Debut (Lancashire) 2002; cap 2003; benefit 2012. YC 2003. *Wisden* 2008. **ECB central contract 2011-12. Tests**: 66 (2003 to 2011-12); HS 34 v SA (Leeds) 2008; BB 7-43 v NZ (Nottingham) 2008. **LOI**: 154 (2002-03 to 2011-12); HS 20* v A (Brisbane) 2010-11; BB 5-23 v SA (Port Elizabeth) 2009-10. Hat-trick v P (Oval) 2003 – 1st for Eng in 373 LOI. **IT20**: 19 (2006-07 to 2009-10); HS 1* v A (Sydney) 2006-07; BB 3-23 v Netherlands (Lord's) 2009. F-c Tours: A 2006-07, 2010-11; SA 2004-05, 2009-10; WI 2003-04, 2005-06 (Eng A) (*part*), 2008-09; NZ 2007-08; I 2005-06 (*part*), 2008-09; SL 2003-04, 2007-08; UAE 2011-12 (v P). HS 37* v Durham (Manchester) 2005. 50 wkts (2); most – 60 (2005). BB 7-43 (*see Tests*). La BB 6-23 v Hants (Southampton) 2002. Hat-trick v Essex (Manchester) 2003. LO HS 20* (*see LOI*). LO BB 5-23 (*see LOI*). T20 HS 16. T20 BB 3-23.

BROWN, Karl Robert (Hesketh Fletcher HS, Atherton), b Bolton 17 May 1988. 5'10". RHB, RMF. Debut (Lancashire) 2006. Moors Sports Club 2011-12. HS 114 v Sussex (Liverpool) 2011. BB 2-30 v Notts (Nottingham) 2009. LO HS 101* v Essex (Manchester) 2011 (CB40). T20 HS 51.

CHAPPLE, Glen (West Craven HS; Nelson & Colne C), b Skipton, Yorks 23 Jan 1974. 6'1". RHB, RMF. Debut (Lancashire) 1992; cap 1994; benefit 2004; captain 2009 to date. **LOI**: 1 (2006); HS 14 and BB – v Ireland (Belfast) 2006. F-c Tours (Eng A): A 1996-97; WI 1995-96 (La); I 1994-95. HS 155 v Somerset (Manchester) 2001. Scored 100 off 27 balls in contrived circumstances v Glamorgan (Manchester) 1993. 50 wkts (6); most – 57 (2011). BB 7-53 v Durham (Blackpool) 2007. LO HS 81* v Derbys (Manchester) 2002 (CGT). LO BB 6-18 v Essex (Lord's) 1996 (NWT) – La record. T20 HS 55*. T20 BB 3-36.

CLARK, Jordan (Sedbergh S), b Whitehaven, Cumbria 14 Oct 1990. 6'4". RHB, RM, occ WK. Awaiting f-c debut. Lancashire 2nd XI debut 2008. Cumberland 2007-08. LO HS 32 v Worcs (Liverpool) 2010 (CB40). T20 HS 38.

CROFT, Steven John (Highfield HS, Blackpool; Myerscough C), b Blackpool 11 Oct 1984. 5'10". RHB, RMF. Debut (Lancashire) 2005; cap 2010. Auckland 2008-09. HS 122 v Notts (Manchester) 2008 and 122 v Warwks (Liverpool) 2011. BB 4-51 v Notts (Nottingham) 2008. LO HS 107 v Somerset (Taunton) 2011 (CB40). LO BB 4-24 v Scotland (Manchester) 2008 (FPT). T20 HS 88. T20 BB 3-6.

CROSS, Gareth David (Moorside S; Eccles C), b Bury 20 Jun 1984. 5'9". RHB, RMF, WK. Debut (Lancashire) 2005. No f-c appearances in 2009. HS 125 v Sussex (Hove) 2011. LO HS 76 v Warwks (Birmingham) 2007 (P40). LO BB 2-26 v Durham (Chester-le-St) 2008 (FPT). T20 HS 65*.

DAVIES, Alexander Luke (Queen Elizabeth GS, Blackburn), b Darwen 23 Aug 1994. 5'7". RHB, WK. Awaiting f-c debut. Lancashire 2nd XI debut 2011. LO HS 6* v Glamorgan (Colwyn Bay) 2011 (CB40).

HOGG, Kyle William (Saddleworth HS), b Birmingham, Warwks 2 Jul 1983. Son of W.Hogg (Lancashire and Warwickshire 1976-83); grandson of S.Ramadhin (Trinidad, Lancashire and West Indies 1949-50 to 1965). 6'4". LHB, RFM. Debut (Lancashire) 2001; cap 2010. Otago 2006-07. Worcestershire 2007 (on loan). Nottinghamshire 2007 (on loan). F-c Tour (ECB Acad): SL 2002-03. HS 88 v Yorks (Manchester) 2010. 50 wkts (1): 50 (2011). BB 7-28 (11-59 match) v Hants (Southampton) 2011. LO HS 66* v Scotland (Manchester) 2008 (FPT). LO BB 4-20 v Hants (Southampton) 2002 (NL). T20 HS 44. T20 BB 2-10.

HORTON, Paul James (St Margaret's HS, Liverpool), b Sydney, Australia 20 Sep 1982. 5'10". RHB, RM. UK resident since 1997. Debut (Lancashire) 2003; cap 2007. Matabeleland Tuskers 2010-11 to date. 1000 runs (3); most – 1116 (2007). HS 209 MT v SR (Masvingo) 2010-11. La HS 173 v Somerset (Taunton) 2009. LO HS 111* v Derbys (Manchester) 2009 (FPT). T20 HS 71.

KEEDY, Gary (Garforth CS), b Wakefield, Yorks 27 Nov 1974. 6'0". LHB, SLA. Yorkshire 1994 (one match). Lancashire debut 1995; cap 2000; benefit 2009. MCC 2011. F-c Tour: WI 1995-96 (La). HS 64 v Sussex (Hove) 2008. 50 wkts (4); most – 72 (2004). BB 7-68 (10-128 match) v Durham (Manchester) 2010. LO HS 33 v Derbys (Derby) 2008. LO BB 5-30 v Sussex (Manchester) 2000 (NL). T20 HS 9*. T20 BB 4-15.

KERRIGAN, Simon Christopher (Corpus Christi RC HS, Preston), b Preston 10 May 1989. 5'9". RHB, SLA. Debut (Lancashire) 2010. Lancashire 2nd XI debut 2007. HS 40 v Somerset (Taunton) 2011. BB 9-51 (12-192 match) v Hants (Liverpool) 2011. LO HS 5 v Glamorgan (Colwyn Bay) 2011 (CB40). LO BB 3-21 EL v Sri Lanka A (Northampton) 2011. T20 HS 4*. T20 BB 3-17.

MAHMOOD, Sajid Iqbal (North C, Bolton), b Bolton 21 Dec 1981. 6'4". RHB, RF. Debut (Lancashire) 2002; cap 2007. MCC 2005, 2009. **Tests**: 8 (2006 to 2006-07); HS 34 and BB 4-22 v P (Leeds) 2006. **LOI**: 26 (2004 to 2009-10); HS 22* v P (Birmingham) 2006; BB 4-50 v SL (North Shore, Antigua) 2006-07. **IT20**: 4 (2006 to 2009-10); HS 1* v SA (Centurion) 2009-10; BB 1-31 v SA (Johannesburg) 2009-10. F-c Tours (Eng A): A 2006-07 (Eng); WI 2005-06; NZ 2008-09; I 2003-04; SL 2004-05. HS 94 v Sussex (Manchester) 2004. BB 6-30 v Durham (Chester-le-St) 2009. LO HS 29 v Staffs (Stone) 2004 (CGT). LO BB 5-16 v Sri Lanka A (Liverpool) 2007. T20 HS 34. T20 BB 4-21.

MOORE, Stephen Colin (St Stithian's C, Johannesburg; Exeter U), b Johannesburg, South Africa 4 Nov 1980. 6'1". RHB, RM. Worcestershire 2003-09. Lancashire debut 2010; cap 2011. MCC 2009, 2011. F-c Tour (Eng A): NZ 2008-09. 1000 runs (4); most – 1451 (2008). HS 246 Wo v Derbys (Worcester) 2005. La HS 169* v Hants (Liverpool) 2011. HS 130 Wo v Lancs (Worcester) 2004. LO HS 118 v Surrey (Croydon) 2010 (CB40). LO BB 1-1 Wo v Scotland (Worcester) 2004 (NL). T20 HS 83*.

NEWBY, Oliver James (Ribblesdale HS; Myerscough C), b Blackburn 26 Aug 1984. 6'5". RHB, RMF. Debut (Lancashire) 2003. Nottinghamshire 2005 (on loan). Gloucestershire (on loan) 2008; cap 2008. No f-c appearances in 2010. HS 38* Nt v Kent (Nottingham) 2005 – on Notts debut. La HS 29* v Oxford MCCU (Oxford) 2011. BB 5-69 Gs v Northants (Bristol) 2008. La BB 4-21 v Durham MCCU (Durham) 2009. LO HS 35* v Glos (Cheltenham) 2009 (CB40). LO BB 4-41 v Glamorgan (Cardiff) 2009 (FPT). T20 HS 6*. T20 BB 2-34.

PARRY, Stephen David (Audenshaw HS), b Manchester 12 Jan 1986. 5'11". RHB, SLA. Debut (Lancashire) 2007, taking 5-23 v Durham U (Durham). No 1st XI appearances in 2008. Cumberland 2005-06. HS 2 and CC BB 2-51 v Durham (Manchester) 2009. BB 5-23 (*see above*). LO HS 31 v Essex (Chelmsford) 2009 (FPT). LO BB 3-40 v Glos (Manchester) 2011 (CB40). T20 HS 11. T20 BB 4-23.

NQ**PRINCE, Ashwell** Gavin (St Thomas Senior SS, UPE), b Port Elizabeth, South Africa, 28 May 1977. LHB, OB. E Province 1995-96 to 1997-98. W Province 1997-98 to 2003-04. W Province-Boland 2004-05. Cape Cobras 2005-06 to 2007-08. Nottinghamshire 2008. Warriors 2008-09 to date. Lancashire debut 2009. **Tests** (SA): 66 (2001-02 to 2011-12, 2 as captain); HS 162* v B (Centurion) 2008-09; BB 1-2 v NZ (Cape Town) 2006. **LOI** (SA): 52 (2002-03 to 2007); HS 89* v WI (Port of Spain) 2005; BB – . **IT20** (SA): 1 (2005-06); HS 5 v NZ (Johannesburg) 2005-06. F-c Tours (SA): E 2008; A 2005-06; WI 2000 (SA A), 2005, 2010; I 2007-08, 2009-10; P 2007-08; SL 2006; Z 2007 (SA A); B 2007-08; UAE 2010-11 (v P). 1000 runs (0+1): 1180 (2008-09). HS 254 Warriors v Titans (Centurion) 2008-09; CC HS 135* v Notts (Manchester) 2009. BB 2-11 SA v Middx (Uxbridge) 2008. CC BB – . LO HS 128 Warriors v Dolphins (East London) 2009-10. LO BB – . T20 HS 74. T20 BB – .

PROCTER, Luke Anthony (Counthill S, Oldham), b Oldham 24 June 1988. 5'11". LHB, RM. Debut (Lancashire) 2010. Lancashire 2nd XI debut 2006. Cumberland 2007. HS 89 v Sussex (Hove) 2011. BB 3-33 v Warwks (Birmingham) 2011. LO HS 97 v West Indies A (Manchester) 2010. LO BB 3-29 v Unicorns (Colwyn Bay) 2010 (CB40). T20 HS 25*. T20 BB 3-22.

SMITH, Thomas Christopher (Parkland HS, Chorley; Runshaw C, Leyland), b Liverpool 26 Dec 1985. 6'3". LHB, RMF. Debut (Lancashire) 2005; cap 2010. Leicestershire (on loan) 2008. F-c Tour (Eng A): B 2006-07. HS 128 v Hants (Southampton) 2010. BB 6-46 v Yorks (Manchester) 2009. LO HS 117 and LO BB 4-48 v Notts (Nottingham) 2011 (CB40). T20 HS 92*. T20 BB 3-12.

‡**TAHIR, Naqaash** Sarosh (Moseley S; Spring Hill C), b Birmingham 14 Nov 1983. 5'10", RHB, RFM. Warwickshire 2004-11. HS 53 Wa v Durham (Birmingham) 2011. BB 7-107 Wa v Lancs (Blackpool) 2006. LO HS 13* Wa v Leics (Oakham) 2008 (FPT). LO BB 2-47 Wa v Notts (Nottingham) 2008 (FPT).

RELEASED/RETIRED
(Having made a County First-Class or List A appearance in 2011)

CHILTON, Mark James (Manchester GS; Durham U), b Sheffield, Yorks 2 Oct 1976. 6'3". RHB, RM. Lancashire 1997-2011; cap 2002; captain 2005-07; benefit 2011. British U 1998. 1000 runs (1): 1154 (2003). HS 131 v Kent (Manchester) 2006. BB 2-3 v Durham UCCE (Durham) 2009. CC BB 1-1 (twice). LO HS 115 v Surrey (Croydon) 2004 (NL). LO BB 5-26 Brit U v Sussex (Cambridge) 1997 (BHC). T20 HS 38.

JUNAID KHAN, Mohammad, b Matra, NW Frontier, Pakistan 24 Dec 1989. RHB, LMF. Abbottabad 2006-07 to date. NW Frontier Province 2008-09. Khan Research Laboratories 2008-09. Lancashire 2011. **Tests** (P): 5 (2011 to 2011-12); HS 6 v Z (Bulawayo) 2011. BB 5-38 v SL (Abu Dhabi) 2011-12. **LOI** (P): 11 (2011 to 2011-12); HS 1* v WI (Bridgetown) 2011; BB 4-12 v Ireland (Belfast) 2011. **IT20** (P): 3 (2011 to 2011-12); HS 3* v WI (Gros Islet) 2011; BB 2-23 v Z (Harare) 2011. F-c Tours (P): WI 2010-11; SL 2010 (P A); Z 2011; UAE 2011-12 (v E). HS 71 Abbottabad v Rawalpindi (Abbottabad) 2007-08. La HS 16 and La BB 1-44 v Durham (Liverpool) 2011. BB 7-46 (13-77 match) Abbottabad v Peshawar (Peshawar) 2007-08. LO HS 32 Pakistan A v South Africa A (Colombo, PSS) 2010. LO BB 4-12 (*see LOI*). T20 HS 8. T20 BB 3-12.

MAHAROOF, Mohamed **Farveez**, b Colombo, Sri Lanka 7 Sep 1984. RHB, RMF. SL Schools 2001-02 to 2002-03. Bloomfield 2003-04 to 2006-07. Nondescripts 2007-08 to date. Wayamba 2009-10. Lancashire 2011. **Tests** (SL): 22 (2004 to 2011); HS 72 v B (Chittagong) 2005-06; BB 4-52 v P (Colombo, SSC) 2005-06. **LOI** (SL): 101 (2004 to 2011-12); HS 69* v P (Abu Dhabi) 2007; BB 6-14 v WI (Mumbai, BS) 2006-07). **IT20** (SL): 7 (2006 to 2008-09); HS 13* and BB 2-18 v Z (King City, NW) 2008-09. F-c Tours (SL): E 2006, 2011; A 2007-08; NZ 2004-05, 2006-07; I 2005-06; P 2004-05; Z 2004, 2008-09; B 2005-06. HS 118 Nondescripts v Bloomfield (Colombo) 2010-11. La HS 102 v Somerset (Liverpool) 2011. BB 7-73 Bloomfield v Ragama (Colombo) 2006-07. La BB 4-35 v Yorks (Liverpool) 2011. LO HS 70* Wayamba v Basnahira (Kurunegala) 2009-10. LO BB 6-14 (*see LOI*). T20 HS 55*. T20 BB 3-21.

S.P.Cheetham left the staff, without making a County First-Class or List A appearance in 2011.

LANCASHIRE 2011

RESULTS SUMMARY

	Place	Won	Lost	Tied	Drew	NR
LV= County Championship (1st Division)	**1st**	10	4		2	
All First-Class Matches		10	4		3	
Clydesdale Bank 40 (Group C)	4th	6	5			1
Friends Life t20 (North Group)	SF	10	6	1		1

LV= COUNTY CHAMPIONSHIP AVERAGES
BATTING AND FIELDING

Cap		M	I	NO	HS	Runs	Avge	100	50	Ct/St
	L.A.Procter	7	10	1	89	366	40.66	–	2	2
2011	S.C.Moore	16	28	3	169*	1013	40.52	2	5	8
	M.F.Maharoof	5	7	1	102	241	40.16	1	–	4
2007	P.J.Horton	16	29	1	99	1040	37.14	–	8	32
	K.R.Brown	16	28	2	114	888	34.15	1	6	7
2010	S.J.Croft	16	27	1	122	825	31.73	2	5	20
2010	T.C.Smith	12	19	1	89	459	25.50	–	4	22
2002	M.J.Chilton	13	21	–	87	478	22.76	–	2	8
	G.D.Cross	16	25	–	125	557	22.28	1	2	46/10
2010	K.W.Hogg	11	18	1	52	365	21.47	–	2	2
1994	G.Chapple	12	20	1	97	365	19.21	–	1	2
2007	S.I.Mahmood	10	15	–	50	256	17.06	–	1	3
	S.C.Kerrigan	4	6	2	40	66	16.50	–	–	1
2000	G.Keedy	16	24	15	20	111	12.33	–	–	5

Also batted: J.M.Anderson (2 matches – cap 2003) 5, 18*, 5* (3 ct); Junaid Khan 0, 16; O.J.Newby (3) 0*, 14, 9*.

BOWLING

	O	M	R	W	Avge	Best	5wI	10wM
S.C.Kerrigan	183	38	437	24	18.20	9- 51	2	1
K.W.Hogg	309	68	940	50	18.80	7- 28	3	1
G.Chapple	412.3	94	1090	55	19.81	6- 70	3	–
G.Keedy	562.4	110	1442	61	23.63	6-133	3	1
S.I.Mahmood	250.1	30	1045	35	29.85	5- 74	2	1
T.C.Smith	226.3	44	747	25	29.88	4- 32	–	–
Also bowled:								
S.J.Croft	68	16	193	6	32.16	2- 10	–	–
O.J.Newby	62	14	260	8	32.50	2- 26	–	–
J.M.Anderson	71.3	20	165	5	33.00	3- 57	–	–
L.A.Procter	83	8	332	9	36.88	3- 33	–	–
M.F.Maharoof	112.5	18	397	9	44.11	4- 35	–	–

Junaid Khan 27-4-90-1.

The First-Class Averages (pp 223–240) give the records of Lancashire players in all first-class county matches (Lancashire's other opponents being Oxford MCCU), with the exception of J.M.Anderson and M.F.Maharoof, whose first-class figures for Lancashire are as above.

LANCASHIRE RECORDS

FIRST-CLASS CRICKET

Highest Total	For 863		v	Surrey	The Oval	1990
	V 707-9d		by	Surrey	The Oval	1990
Lowest Total	For 25		v	Derbyshire	Manchester	1871
	V 22		by	Glamorgan	Liverpool	1924
Highest Innings	For 424	A.C.MacLaren	v	Somerset	Taunton	1895
	V 315*	T.W.Hayward	for	Surrey	The Oval	1898

Highest Partnership for each Wicket

1st	368	A.C.MacLaren/R.H.Spooner	v	Glos	Liverpool	1903
2nd	371	F.B.Watson/G.E.Tyldesley	v	Surrey	Manchester	1928
3rd	364	M.A.Atherton/N.H.Fairbrother	v	Surrey	The Oval	1990
4th	358	S.P.Titchard/G.D.Lloyd	v	Essex	Chelmsford	1996
5th	360	S.G.Law/C.L.Hooper	v	Warwicks	Birmingham	2003
6th	278	J.Iddon/H.R.W.Butterworth	v	Sussex	Manchester	1932
7th	248	G.D.Lloyd/I.D.Austin	v	Yorkshire	Leeds	1997
8th	158	J.Lyon/R.M.Ratcliffe	v	Warwicks	Manchester	1979
9th	142	L.O.S.Poidevin/A.Kermode	v	Sussex	Eastbourne	1907
10th	173	J.Briggs/R.Pilling	v	Surrey	Liverpool	1885

Best Bowling	For	10-46	W.Hickton	v	Hampshire	Manchester	1870
(Innings)	V	10-40	G.O.B.Allen	for	Middlesex	Lord's	1929
Best Bowling	For	17-91	H.Dean	v	Yorkshire	Liverpool	1913
(Match)	V	16-65	G.Giffen	for	Australians	Manchester	1886

Most Runs – Season	2633	J.T.Tyldesley	(av 56.02)	1901
Most Runs – Career	34222	G.E.Tyldesley	(av 45.20)	1909-36
Most 100s – Season	11	C.Hallows		1928
Most 100s – Career	90	G.E.Tyldesley		1909-36
Most Wkts – Season	198	E.A.McDonald	(av 18.55)	1925
Most Wkts – Career	1816	J.B.Statham	(av 15.12)	1950-68
Most Career W-K Dismissals	925	G.Duckworth	(635 ct; 290 st)	1923-38
Most Career Catches in the Field	556	K.J.Grieves		1949-64

LIMITED-OVERS CRICKET

Highest Total	50ov	381-3		v	Herts	Radlett	1999
	40ov	310-7		v	Somerset	Taunton	2003
	T20	220-5		v	Derbyshire	Derby	2009
Lowest Total	50ov	59		v	Worcs	Worcester	1963
	40ov	68		v	Yorkshire	Leeds	2000
		68		v	Surrey	The Oval	2002
	T20	91		v	Derbyshire	Manchester	2003
Highest Innings	50ov	162*	A.R.Crook	v	Bucks	Wormsley	2005
	40ov	143	A.Flintoff	v	Essex	Chelmsford	1999
	T20	102*	L.Vincent	v	Derbyshire	Manchester	2008
Best Bowling	50ov	6-18	G.Chapple	v	Essex	Lord's	1996
	40ov	6-25	G.Chapple	v	Yorkshire	Leeds	1998
	T20	4-12	A.Flintoff	v	Durham	Chester-le-St[2]	2008

LEICESTERSHIRE

Formation of Present Club: 25 March 1879
Inaugural First-Class Match: 1894
Colours: Dark Green and Scarlet
Badge: Gold Running Fox on Green Ground
County Champions: (3) 1975, 1996, 1998
Gillette/NatWest/C&G/FP Trophy Winners: (0); best –
Finalist 1992, 2001
Benson and Hedges Cup Winners: (3) 1972, 1975, 1985
Pro 40/National League (Div 1) Winners: (0); best – 2nd
2001
Sunday League Champions: (2) 1974, 1977
Clydesdale Bank 40 Winners: (0); best – 6th in Group
2010, 2011
Twenty20 Cup Winners: (3) 2004, 2006, 2011

Chief Executive: Mike Siddall, County Ground, Grace Road, Leicester LE2 8AD • Tel:
0871 282 1879 • Fax: 0871 282 1873 • Email: enquiries@leicestershireccc.co.uk • Web:
www.leicestershireccc.co.uk

Head Coach/Academy Director: Phil Whitticase. **Captain:** M.J.Hoggard. **Vice-Captain:**
tba. **Overseas Players:** Abdul Razzaq (T20 only) and R.R.Sarwan. **2012 Beneficiary:**
Leicestershire CCC. **Head Groundsman:** Andrew Ward. **Scorer:** Paul J.Rogers. ‡ New
registration. NQ Not qualified for England.

‡NQ**ABDUL RAZZAQ**, b Lahore, Pakistan 2 Dec 1979. 5'11". RHB, RFM. Lahore 1996-97
to 2006-07. Khan Research Labs 1997-98 to 1998-99. Pakistan Int Airlines 2001-02.
Middlesex 2002-03; cap 2002. Zarai Taraqiati Bank Ltd 2003-04 to date. Worcestershire
2007; cap 2007. Surrey 2008. Joins Leicestershire for T20 only in 2011. **Tests** (P): 46
(1999-00 to 2006-07); HS 134 v B (Dhaka) 2001-02; BB 5-35 v SL (Karachi) 2004-05. **LOI**
(P): 265 (1996-97 to 2011-12); HS 112 v SA (Port Elizabeth) 2002-03; BB 6-35 v B (Dhaka
) 2001-02. **IT20** (P): 26 (2006 to 2010-11); HS 46* v E (Dubai) 2009-10; BB 3-13 v NZ
(Christchurch) 2010-11. F-c Tours (P): E 1997 (P A), 2001, 2006; A 1999-00, 2004-05; SA
2002-03; WI 2000, 2005; NZ 1998-99 (P A), 2003-04; I 2004-05; SL 2000, 2005-06; B
2001-02; UAE 2001-02 (v WI). HS 203* M v Glamorgan (Cardiff) 2002. BB 7-51 Lahore
City v Karachi Whites (Thatta) 1996-97 – on debut. CC BB 7-133 M v Essex (Southgate)
2002. LO HS 112 (*see LOI*). LO BB 6-35 (*see LOI*). T20 HS 109. T20 BB 4-13.

BOYCE, Matthew Andrew Golding (Oakham S; Nottingham U), b Cheltenham, Glos
13 Aug 1985. 5'9". LHB, RM. Debut (Leicestershire) 2006. HS 119 v Glos (Leicester) 2011.
BB – . LO HS 80 v Hants (Leicester) 2009 (FPT). T20 HS 34.

BUCK, Nathan Liam (Newbridge HS; Ashby S), b Leicester 26 Apr 1991. 6'2" RHB, RMF.
Debut (Leicestershire) 2009; cap 2011. Leicestershire 2nd XI debut 2008. England U19s
2009 to 2009-10. F-c Tour (EL): WI 2010-11. HS 26 v Glos (Leicester) 2010 and 26 v
Middx (Leicester) 2011. BB 5-99 v Glos (Bristol) 2011. LO HS 21 v Glamorgan (Leicester)
2009 (P40). LO BB 2-16 v Hants (Southampton) 2010 (CB40). T20 HS 3*. T20 BB 3-16.

COBB, Joshua James (Oakham S), b Leicester 17 Aug 1990. Son of R.A.Cobb (Leics and
N Transvaal 1980-89). 5'11½". RHB, LB. Debut (Leicestershire) 2007. Leicestershire 2nd
XI debut 2006, aged 16y 5d. England U19s 2009. HS 148* v Middx (Lord's) 2008. BB 2-11
v Glos (Leicester) 2008. LO HS 91* v Northants (Leicester) 2011 (CB40). LO BB 2-35 v
Surrey (Oval) 2011 (CB40). T20 HS 60. T20 BB 4-22.

135

DIXEY, Paul Garrod (King's S, Canterbury; Hatfield C, Durham U), b Canterbury 2 Nov 1987. 5'8". RHB, WK. Kent 2005-10; no f-c appearances for K 2007-09. MCC 2007. Durham UCCE 2007-09. Leicestershire debut 2011. HS 103 DU v Lancs (Durham) 2009. Le HS 72* v Glos (Leicester) 2011. LO HS 42 v Surrey (Oval) 2011 (CB40).

Du TOIT, Jacques (Elspark S; Oosterlig C; Pretoria U), b Port Elizabeth, South Africa 2 Jan 1980. RHB, RMF. British passport. Easterns 1998-99 to 2004-05. Leicestershire debut 2008. Colombo CC 2010-11. HS 154 v Cambridge MCCU (Cambridge) 2010. CC HS 122 v Surrey (Leicester) 2010. BB 3-31 v Glos (Leicester) 2008. LO HS 144 v Glamorgan (Colwyn Bay) 2008 (P40). LO BB 2-30 Easterns v KZ-Natal (Benoni) 2004-05. T20 HS 69. T20 BB 2-15.

ECKERSLEY, Edmund John Holden ('Ned') (St Benedict's GS, Ealing), b Oxford 9 Aug 1989. 6'0". RHB, WK. Debut (Leicestershire) 2011. Mountaineers 2011-12. Middlesex 2nd XI 2008. Northamptonshire 2nd XI 2010. HS 106 v Middx (Leicester) 2011. LO HS 27* Mountaineers v MWR (Kwekwe) 2011-12. T20 HS 12*.

NOHENDERSON, Claude William (Worcester HS), b Worcester, Cape Province, South Africa 14 Jun 1972. Elder brother of J.M.Henderson (Boland, Transvaal, North West, Free State and Eagles 1994-95 to 2005-06). Applying for UK citizenship. 6'1½". RHB, SLA. Boland 1990-91 to 1997-98. W Province 1998-99 to 2003-04. Leicestershire debut/cap 2004 (the first Kolpak registration); benefit 2011. Lions 2006-07 to 2007-08. Cape Cobras 2008-09 to 2010-11. **Tests** (SA): 7 (2001-02 to 2002-03); HS 50 v A; BB 4-116 v A (Adelaide) 2001-02. **LOI** (SA): 4 (2001-02); HS – ; BB 4-17 v Z (Harare) 2001-02. F-c Tours (SA): A 2001-02; SL 1998 (SA A); Z 2001-02. HS 81 v Glos (Leicester) 2007. 50 wkts (1): 56 (2010). BB 7-57 Boland v EP (Paarl) 1994-95. Le BB 7-74 v Durham (Leicester) 2004. LO HS 45 Lions v Eagles (Johannesburg) 2006-07. LO BB 6-29 Boland v Easterns (Paarl) 1997-98. T20 HS 32. T20 BB 3-23.

HOGGARD, Matthew James (Grangefield S, Pudsey), b Leeds, Yorks 31 Dec 1976. 6'2". RHB, RMF. Yorkshire 1996-2009; cap 2000; benefit 2008. Free State 1998-99 to 1999-00. Leicestershire debut/cap 2010; captain 2010 to date. MCC 2004-07. MBE 2005. *Wisden* 2005. **Tests**: 67 (2000 to 2007-08); HS 38 v WI (Oval) 2004; BB 7-61 (12-205 match) v SA (Johannesburg) 2004-05; hat-trick v WI (Bridgetown) 2003-04. **LOI**: 26 (2001-02 to 2005-06); HS 7 v I (Cochin) 2005-06; BB 5-49 v Z (Harare) 2001-02. F-c Tours: A 2002-03, 2006-07; SA 2004-05; WI 2003-04; NZ 2001-02, 2007-08; I 2001-02, 2005-06; P 2000-01, 2005-06; SL 2000-01, 2003-04, 2007-08; B 2003-04. HS 89* v Glamorgan (Leeds) 2004. Le HS 19 v Kent (Tunbridge W) 2011. 50 wkts (3); most – 50 (2000, 2005, 2010). BB 7-49 Y v Somerset (Leeds) 2003. Le BB 6-63 v Middx (Lord's) 2010. Hat-tricks (3): (*see Tests*) and Y v Sussex (Hove) 2009; v Glamorgan (Leicester) 2011. LO HS 23 v Surrey (Oval) 2011 (CB40). LO BB 5-28 Y v Leics (Leicester) 2000 (NL). T20 HS 18. T20 BB 3-19.

JEFFERSON, William Ingleby (Beeston Hall S, Norfolk; Oundle S; St Hild & St Bede C, Durham U), b Derby 25 Oct 1979. Son of R.I.Jefferson (Cambridge U and Surrey 1961-66); grandson of J.Jefferson (Army 1919, Comb Services 1922). 6'10". RHB, RMF. British U 2000-02. Essex 2000-06; cap 2002. Durham UCCE 2001-02. Nottinghamshire 2007-09. Leicestershire debut 2010. F-c Tour (Eng A): B 2006-07. 1000 runs (2); most – 1555 (2004). HS 222 Ex v Hants (Southampton) 2004. Le HS 135 v Surrey (Oval) 2010. BB 1-16 Ex v Yorks (Leeds) 2005. LO HS 132 Ex v Essex CB (Chelmsford) 2003 (CGT). LO BB 2-9 Ex v Worcs (Worcester) 2005 (NL). T20 HS 83.

JONES, William Stephen (Harrow S; Cardiff U), b Perth, Australia 29 Mar 1990. 6'1". British citizen. RHB, LB. Debut (Leicestershire) 2011. Leicestershire 2nd XI debut 2010. Hertfordshire 2009. HS 10 v Sri Lanka A (Leicester) 2011. CC HS 2 v Middx (Leicester) 2011. BB – . LO HS 3 v Surrey (Oval) 2011 (CB40).

‡JOSEPH, Robert ('Robbie') Hartman (Sutton Valence S; St Mary's C, Twickenham), b Antigua 20 Jan 1982. Resided in England since 1997. 6'1". RHB, RFM. Debut (First-Class Counties XI v NZ) 2000. Kent 2004-11. Leeward Is 2008-09. F-c Tour (EL): NZ 2008-09. HS 36* K v Sussex (Hove) 2007. 50 wkts (1): 55 (2008). BB 6-32 (9-62 match) K v Durham (Chester-le-St) 2008. LO HS 15 K v (Canterbury) 2005 (NL). LO BB 5-13 K v Derbys (Canterbury) 2008 (P40). T20 HS 1*. T20 BB 2-14.

MALIK, Muhammad **Nadeem** (Wilford Meadows CS; Bilborough C), b Nottingham 6 Oct 1982. 6'5". RHB, RFM. Nottinghamshire 2001-03, 2007 – on loan. Worcestershire 2004-07. Leicestershire debut 2008, taking 5-51 (8-119 match) v Middx (Leicester). HS 41 v Essex (Leicester) 2008. BB 6-46 v Essex (Chelmsford) 2008. LO HS 11 Nt v Worcs (Nottingham) 2002 (NL). LO BB 4-40 v Hants (Southampton) 2010 (CB40). T20 HS 3*. T20 BB 4-16.

NAIK, Jigar Kumar Hakumatrai (Rushey Mead SS; Gateway SFC; Nottingham Trent U; Loughborough U), b Leicester 10 Aug 1984. 6'2". RHB, OB. Debut (Leicestershire) 2006. Loughborough UCCE 2007. Colombo CC 2010-11. HS 109* v Derbys (Leicester) 2009. BB 7-96 v Surrey (Oval) 2010. LO HS 18 v Derbys (Derby) 2009 (P40). LO BB 3-21 v Lancs (Leicester) 2009 (P40). T20 HS 7*. T20 BB 3-3.

RADFORD, Luke Anthony (Bromsgrove S; Loughborough U), b Worcester 3 Jun 1988. Son of N.V.Radford (Transvaal, Lancs, Worcs, England 1978-79 to 1995), nephew of W.R.Radford (OFS, Boland, E Transvaal, Easterns 1977-78 to 1997-98) and G.Radford (Transvaal and NW 1991-92 to 1996-97) RHB, RFM. Debut (Leicestershire) 2011. Warwickshire 2nd XI debut 2007. HS-and BB 2-47 v Loughborough MCCU (Leicester) 2011 – only 1st XI app to date.

‡NOSARWAN, Ramnaresh Ronnie (North Gromuel S), b Wakenaam Island, Essequibo, Guyana 23 Jun 1980. 5'7½". RHB, LB. Guyana 1995-96 to date (youngest to play f-c cricket in WI). Gloucestershire 2005; cap 2005. **Tests** (WI): 87 (2000 to 2011); HS 291 v E (Bridgetown) 2008-09; BB 4-37 v B (St Lucia) 2004. **LOI** (WI): 173 (2000 to 2011); HS 115* v I (Basseterre) 2006; BB 3-31 v NZ (Lord's) 2004. **IT20** (WI): 18 (2007 to 2011); HS 59 v E (Port of Spain) 2008-09; BB 2-10 v B (Johannesburg) 2007. F-c Tours (WI): E 2000, 2004, 2007, 2009; A 2000-01, 2005-06, 2009-10; SA 2003-04; NZ 2005-06, 2008-09; I 2002-03; P 2006-07; SL 2001-02; Z 2001, 2003-04; B 2002-03. HS 291 (*see Tests*). CC HS 117 Gs v Sussex (Hove) 2005. BB 6-62 Guyana v Leeward Is (Antigua) 2000-01. CC BB 2-38 Gs v Glamorgan (Bristol) 2005. LO HS 118* Gs v Lancs (Manchester) 2005 (NL). LO BB 5-10 Guyana v Bermuda (Hampton Court) 1998-99. T20 HS 70. T20 BB 2-10.

SMITH, Gregory Philip (Oundle S; St Hild & St Bede C, Durham U), b Leicester 16 Nov 1988. 6'0". RHB, LBG. Debut (Leicestershire) 2008. Durham MCCU 2009-11. England U19s 2008. HS 158* v Glos (Leicester) 2010. BB 1-64 v Glos (Leicester) 2008. LO HS 58 v Surrey (Oval) 2008 (P40).

SYKES, James Stuart (St Ives S, Huntingdon), b Hinchingbrooke, Cambs 26 Apr 1992. 6'2". LHB, SLA. Leicestershire 2nd XI debut 2009. Cambridgeshire 2010. Awaiting 1st XI debut.

TAYLOR, Robert Meadows Lombe (Harrow S; Loughborough U), b Northampton 21 Dec 1989. 6'3". LHB, LMF. Loughborough MCCU 2010-11. Leicestershire debut 2011. Leicestershire 2nd XI debut 2008. Northamptonshire 2nd XI debut 2010. HS 101* LU v Leics (Leicester) 2011. Le HS 70 and BB 3-53 v Surrey (Leicester) 2011.

THAKOR, Shivsinh Jaysinh (Loughborough GS), b Leicester 22 Oct 1993. RHB, RM. Debut (Leicestershire) 2011. Leicestershire 2nd XI debut 2008, aged 14y 218d. England U19s 2010-11. HS 134 v Loughborough MCCU (Leicester) 2011 – on debut. CC HS 34 v Kent (Leicester) 2011. BB 3-57 v Surrey (Leicester) 2011. LO HS 13 v Northants (Northampton) and v Scotland (Leicester) 2011 (CB40).

WHITE, Wayne Andrew (John Port S, Etwall; Nottingham Trent U), b Derby 22 Apr 1985. 6'2". RHB, RMF. Derbyshire 2005-08. Leicestershire debut 2009. HS 101* v Derbys (Derby) 2010. BB 5-87 De v Northants (Northampton) 2007. Le BB 4-37 v Sri Lanka A (Leicester) 2011. LO HS 46* v Glamorgan (Leicester) 2009 (P40). LO BB 6-29 v Notts (Leics) 2010 (CB40). T20 HS 26. T20 BB 3-27.

WYATT, Alexander Charles Frederick (Oakham S), b Roehampton 23 Jul 1990. 6'7". RHB, RMF. Debut (Leicestershire) 2009. Leicestershire 2nd XI debut 2007. HS 4* v Mddx (Leicester) 2011. BB 3-42 v West Indians (Leicester) 2009. BB 2-44 v Glos (Bristol) 2009. LO HS 2* v Hants (Southampton) 2011 (CB40). LO BB 2-36 v Durham (Leicester) 2011 (CB40). T20 HS – . T20 BB 3-14.

RELEASED/RETIRED
(Having made a County First-Class or List A appearance in 2011)

GURNEY, H.F. – *see NOTTINGHAMSHIRE.*

NQ**McDONALD, Andrew** Barry (Murray HS, Lavington, NSW), b Wodonga, Victoria, Australia, 15 Jun 1981. 6'4". RHB, RFM. Victoria 2001-02 to date. Leicestershire 2010-11. **Tests** (A): 4 (2008-09); HS 68 v SA (Cape Town) 2008-09; BB 3-25 v SA (Durban) 2008-09. F-c Tours (A): E 2009; SA 2008-09. HS 176* v Middx (Leicester) 2010. BB 6-34 Vic v Q (Brisbane) 2006-07. Le BB 5-40 v Worcs (Leicester) 2010. LO HS 67 Vic v WA (Melbourne) 2008-09. LO BB 5-38 Vic v Q (Melbourne) 2011-12. T20 HS 96*. T20 BB 5-13 v Notts (Nottingham) 2010 – Le record.

NEW, Thomas James (Quarrydale S), b Sutton in Ashfield, Notts 18 Jan 1985. 5'10". LHB, RM, WK. Leicestershire 2004-11; cap 2009. Derbyshire 2008 – on loan. HS 125 v Oxford U (Oxford) 2007. CC HS 109 v Middx (Leicester) 2008. BB 2-18 v Glos (Leicester) 2007. LO HS 68 v Northants (Oakham) 2006 (CGT). T20 HS 18.

NIXON, Paul Andrew (Ullswater HS, Penrith), b Carlisle, Cumberland 21 Oct 1970. 6'0". LHB, WK, occ RM. Leicestershire 1989-99, 2003-11; cap 1994; benefit 2007; captain 2007 (*part*) to 2009 (*part*). MCC 1999-00. Kent 2000-02; cap 2000. Cumberland 1987. **LOI:** 19 (2006-07); HS 49 v NZ (Perth) 2006-07. **IT20:** 1 (2006-07); HS 31* v A (Sydney) 2006-07. F-c Tours: SA 1996-97 (Le); I 1994-95 (Eng A); P 2000-01; B 1999-00 (MCC). 1000 runs (1): 1046 (1994). HS 173* v Kent (Canterbury) 2009. BB 1-7 v Glos (Bristol) 2010. LO HS 101 v Sri Lanka A (Galle) 1998-99. T20 HS 65.

TAYLOR, J.W.A. – *see NOTTINGHAMSHIRE.*

LEICESTERSHIRE 2011

RESULTS SUMMARY

	Place	Won	Lost	Tied	Drew	NR
LV= County Championship (2nd Division)	9th	1	11		4	
All First-Class Matches		2	11		5	
Clydesdale Bank 40 (Group B)	6th	2	8			2
Friends Life t20 (North Group)	Winners	13	2			4

LV= COUNTY CHAMPIONSHIP AVERAGES
BATTING AND FIELDING

Cap		M	I	NO	HS	Runs	Avge	100	50	Ct/St
	E.J.H.Eckersley	4	8	–	106	321	40.12	1	2	13
	A.B.McDonald	5	10	2	164	312	39.00	1	1	2
2009	J.W.A.Taylor	13	25	2	127*	889	38.65	1	7	11
	W.I.Jefferson	15	29	1	133	1007	35.96	3	3	24
	W.A.White	12	22	1	83*	666	31.71	–	5	3
	M.A.G.Boyce	14	28	–	119	772	27.57	2	–	11
	P.G.Dixey	5	9	1	72*	206	25.75	–	2	13/1
	G.P.Smith	11	22	–	108	541	24.59	1	2	8
2004	C.W.Henderson	13	22	3	80*	435	22.89	–	3	5
	J.K.H.Naik	15	28	4	77*	503	20.95	–	2	3
	R.M.L.Taylor	4	8	–	70	160	20.00	–	1	2
2009	T.J.New	8	15	–	76	261	17.40	–	2	15/1
	S.J.Thakor	2	4	–	34	56	14.00	–	–	–
1994	P.A.Nixon	4	7	–	46	97	13.85	–	–	–
	J.du Toit	5	9	–	42	120	13.33	–	–	2
	J.J.Cobb	7	14	–	44	177	12.64	–	–	3
	M.N.Malik	10	16	8	12	63	7.87	–	–	1
2011	N.L.Buck	12	20	5	26	110	7.33	–	–	–
2010	M.J.Hoggard	12	19	7	19*	68	5.66	–	–	2

Also batted: Kadeer Ali (1 match) 1, 33; H.F.Gurney (1) 2; W.S.Jones (1) 0, 2; A.C.F.Wyatt (2) 4, 4*, 1*.

BOWLING

	O	M	R	W	Avge	Best	5wI	10wM
C.W.Henderson	495.1	127	1269	40	31.72	4-43	–	–
J.K.H.Naik	415.1	69	1376	40	34.40	5-34	2	–
M.N.Malik	284.4	73	899	26	34.57	4-62	–	–
M.J.Hoggard	323	70	993	28	35.46	4-66	–	–
W.A.White	247.2	30	1004	28	35.85	4-66	–	–
N.L.Buck	320.4	78	1116	24	46.50	5-99	1	–
Also bowled:								
A.B.McDonald	87	11	303	8	37.87	3-51	–	–
A.C.F.Wyatt	58	13	233	5	46.60	2-65	–	–
R.M.L.Taylor	67.1	5	300	5	60.00	3-53	–	–

Kadeer Ali 1-1-0-0; J.J.Cobb 13-1-44-1; J.du Toit 2-1-10-0; H.F.Gurney 35.3-6-113-3; S.J.Thakor 17-2-74-3.

The First-Class Averages (pp 223–240) give the records of Leicestershire players in all first-class county matches (Leicestershire's other opponents being Loughborough MCCU and Sri Lanka A), with the exception of R.M.L.Taylor, whose first-class figures for Leicestershire are as above, and:

G.P.Smith 12-24-0-108-620-25.83-1-3-8ct.
J.W.A.Taylor 15-28-3-237-1335-53.40-3-7-12ct.

LEICESTERSHIRE RECORDS

FIRST-CLASS CRICKET

Highest Total	For 701-4d		v	Worcs	Worcester	1906
	V 761-6d		by	Essex	Chelmsford	1990
Lowest Total	For 25		v	Kent	Leicester	1912
	V 24		by	Glamorgan	Leicester	1971
	24		by	Oxford U	Oxford	1985
Highest Innings	For 309*	H.D.Ackerman	v	Glamorgan	Cardiff	2006
	V 341	G.H.Hirst	for	Yorkshire	Leicester	1905

Highest Partnership for each Wicket

1st	390	B.Dudleston/J.F.Steele	v	Derbyshire	Leicester	1979
2nd	289*	J.C.Balderstone/D.I.Gower	v	Essex	Leicester	1981
3rd	436*	D.L.Maddy/B.J.Hodge	v	L'boro UCCE	Leicester	2003
4th	360*	J.W.A.Taylor/A.B.McDonald	v	Middlesex	Leicester	2010
5th	330	J.W.A.Taylor/S.J.Thakor	v	L'boro MCCU	Leicester	2011
6th	284	P.V.Simmons/P.A.Nixon	v	Durham	Chester-le-St[2]	1996
7th	219*	J.D.R.Benson/P.Whitticase	v	Hampshire	Bournemouth	1991
8th	195	J.W.A.Taylor/J.K.H.Naik	v	Derbyshire	Leicester	2009
9th	160	R.T.Crawford/W.W.Odell	v	Worcs	Leicester	1902
10th	228	R.Illingworth/K.Higgs	v	Northants	Leicester	1977

Best Bowling	For 10- 18	G.Geary	v	Glamorgan	Pontypridd	1929
(Innings)	V 10- 32	H.Pickett	for	Essex	Leyton	1895
Best Bowling	For 16- 96	G.Geary	v	Glamorgan	Pontypridd	1929
(Match)	V 16-102	C.Blythe	for	Kent	Leicester	1909

Most Runs – Season	2446	L.G.Berry	(av 52.04)	1937
Most Runs – Career	30143	L.G.Berry	(av 30.32)	1924-51
Most 100s – Season	7	L.G.Berry		1937
	7	W.Watson		1959
	7	B.F.Davison		1982
Most 100s – Career	45	L.G.Berry		1924-51
Most Wkts – Season	170	J.E.Walsh	(av 18.96)	1948
Most Wkts – Career	2131	W.E.Astill	(av 23.18)	1906-39
Most Career W-K Dismissals	905	R.W.Tolchard	(794 ct; 111 st)	1965-83
Most Career Catches in the Field	426	M.R.Hallam		1950-70

LIMITED-OVERS CRICKET

Highest Total	50ov	406-5		v	Berkshire	Leicester	1996
	40ov	344-4		v	Durham	Chester-le-St[2]	1996
	T20	221-3		v	Yorkshire	Leeds	2004
Lowest Total	50ov	56		v	Northants	Leicester	1964
	40ov	36		v	Sussex	Leicester	1973
	T20	97-9		v	Durham	Leicester	2004
Highest Innings	50ov	201	V.J.Wells	v	Berkshire	Leicester	1996
	40ov	154*	B.J.Hodge	v	Sussex	Horsham	2004
	T20	111	D.L.Maddy	v	Yorkshire	Leeds	2004
Best Bowling	50ov	6-16	C.M.Willoughby	v	Somerset	Leicester	2005
	40ov	6-17	K.Higgs	v	Glamorgan	Leicester	1973
	T20	5-13	A.B.McDonald	v	Notts	Nottingham	2010

MIDDLESEX

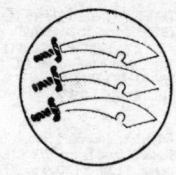

Formation of Present Club: 2 February 1864
Inaugural First-Class Match: 1864
Colours: Blue
Badge: Three Seaxes
County Champions (since 1890): (10) 1903, 1920, 1921, 1947, 1976, 1980, 1982, 1985, 1990, 1993
Joint Champions: (2) 1949, 1977
Gillette/NatWest/C&G/FP Trophy Winners: (4) 1977, 1980, 1984, 1988
Benson and Hedges Cup Winners: (2) 1983, 1986
Pro 40/National League (Div 1) Winners: (0); best – 1st (Div 2) 2004
Sunday League Winners: (1) 1992
Clydesdale Bank 40 Winners: (0); best – 2nd Group A 2011
Twenty20 Cup Winners: (1) 2008

Secretary: Vincent J.Codrington, Lord's Cricket Ground, London NW8 8QN • Tel: 020 7289 1300 • Fax: 020 7289 5831 • Email: enquiries@middlesexccc.com • Web: www.middlesexccc.com

Managing Director of Cricket: Angus R.C.Fraser. **Head Coach:** Richard J.Scott. **Assistant Coach:** Richard L.Johnson. **Captain:** N.J.Dexter. **Vice-Captain:** tba. **Overseas Player:** C.J.L.Rogers. **2012 Beneficiary:** none. **Head Groundsman:** Mick Hunt. **Scorer:** Don K.Shelley. ‡ New registration. NQ Not qualified for England.

NO**BALBIRNIE, Andrew** (St Andrew's C, Dublin; UWIC), b Dublin, Ireland 28 Dec 1990. 6'2". RHB, OB. Middlesex 2nd XI debut 2011. MCC YCs 2010. Cardiff MCCU 2011 (not f-c). Summer contract, awaiting 1st XI debut. **LOI** (Ire): 4 (2010); HS 17 v Canada (Amstelveen) 2010. LO HS 17 (*see LOI*).

BERG, Gareth Kyle (South African College S), b Cape Town, South Africa 18 Jan 1981. 6'0". RHB, RMF. England qualified through residency. Debut (Middlesex) 2008; cap 2010. WP Academy (1999-00) and WP B (2001-02 to 2002-03). Northants 2nd XI 2004. HS 130* v Leics (Leicester) 2011. BB 6-58 v Glamorgan (Cardiff) 2011. LO HS 65 v Surrey (Lord's) 2008 (FPT). LO BB 4-24 v Worcs (Worcester) 2011 (CB40). T20 HS 41. T20 BB 2-31.

NO**COLLYMORE, Corey** Dalanelo (Alexandra SS), b St Peter, Barbados 21 Dec 1977. 6'0". RHB, RFM. Barbados 1998-99 to 2008-09. Warwickshire 2003. Sussex 2008-10; cap 2008. Middlesex debut/cap 2011. Kolpak registration. **Tests** (WI): 30 (1998-99 to 2007); HS 16* v Z (Bulawayo) 2003-04 and 16* v E (Chester-le-St) 2007; BB 7-57 v SL (Kingston) 2003. **LOI** (WI): 84 (1999 to 2006-07); HS 13* v I (Toronto) 1999; BB 5-51 v SL (Colombo) 2001-02. F-c Tours (WI): E 2000, 2004, 2007; A 2005-06; SA 2003-04; P 2006-07; Z 2002, 2003-04; K 2000-01. HS 23 Sx v Notts (Horsham) 2009. M HS 8* v Derbys (Lord's) 2011. 50 wkts (1): 57 (2010). BB 7-57 (*see Tests*). CC BB 6-48 Sx v Leics (Leicester) 2010. M BB 4-28 v Surrey (Guildford) 2011. LO HS 13* (*see LOI*). LO BB 5-27 Barbados v Leeward Is (Weymouth) 2005-06. T20 HS 4. T20 BB 1-21.

CROOK, Steven Paul (Rostrevor C; Magill U), b Modbury, S Australia 28 May 1983. Younger brother of A.R.Crook (S Australia, Aus Academy, Lancashire, Northamptonshire 1998-99 to 2008). 5'11". RHB, RFM. British passport. Lancashire 2003-05. Northamptonshire 2005-09. Middlesex debut 2011. Aus Academy 2001-02. HS 97 Nh v Yorks (Northampton) 2005. M HS 13 v Surrey (Lord's) 2011. BB 5-71 Nh v Essex (Northampton) 2009. M BB 5-94 v Northants (Lord's) 2011. LO HS 72 Nh v Essex (Chelmsford) 2009 (FPT). LO BB 4-20 Nh v Sussex (Northampton) 2006 (P40). T20 HS 29. T20 BB 3-21.

141

DAVEY, Joshua Henry (Culford S), b Aberdeen, Scotland 3 Aug 1990. RHB, RM. Debut (Middlesex) 2010. Middlesex 2nd XI debut 2008. Suffolk 2009. **LOI** (Scot): 8 (2010 to 2011); HS 48* v Ireland (Edinburgh) 2011; BB 5-9 v Afghanistan (Ayr) 2010. HS 72 and BB 2-41 v Oxford MCCU (Oxford) 2010 – on debut. CC HS 61 v Glos (Bristol) 2010. CC BB – . LO HS 91 Scot v Warwks (Birmingham) 2011 (CB40). LO BB 5-9 (*see LOI*). T20 HS 18*. T20 BB – .

DENLY, Joseph Liam (Chaucer TC), b Canterbury, Kent 16 Mar 1986. 6'0". RHB, LB. Kent 2004-11; cap 2008. **LOI**: 9 (2009 to 2009-10); HS 67 v Ireland (Belfast) 2009 – on debut. **IT20**: 5 (2009 to 2009-10); HS 14 and BB 1-9 v SA (Centurion) 2009-10. F-c Tours (Eng A): NZ 2008-09; I 2007-08. 1000 runs (2); most – 1024 (2011). HS 199 K v Derbys (Derby) 2011. BB 3-43 K v Surrey (Oval) 2011. LO HS 115 K v Warwks (Birmingham) 2009 (FPT). LO BB 3-42 K v Netherlands (Rotterdam) 2011 (CB40). T20 HS 100. T20 BB 1-9.

DEXTER, Neil John (Northwood HS, Durban; Varsity C; U of South Africa), b Johannesburg, South Africa 21 Aug 1984. 6'0". RHB, RM. Kent 2005-08. Essex 2008. Middlesex debut 2009; cap 2010; captain 2010 (*part*) to date. Qualified for England in 2010. HS 146 (and 118) v Kent (Uxbridge) 2009. BB 3-46 v Surrey (Lord's) 2011. LO HS 135* K v Glamorgan (Cardiff) 2006 (CGT). LO BB 3-17 K v Leics (Canterbury) 2006 (P40). T20 HS 73. T20 BB 4-21.

FINN, Steven Thomas (Parmiter's S, Garston), b Watford, Herts 4 Apr 1989. 6'7½". RHB, RF. Debut (Middlesex) 2005; cap 2009. Otago 2011-12. YC 2010. **ECB central contract 2011-12. Tests**: 12 (2009-10 to 2011); HS 19 v SL (Lord's) 2011; BB 6-125 v A (Brisbane) 2010-11. **LOI**: 15 (2010-11 to 2011-12); HS 35 v A (Brisbane) 2010-11; BB 4-34 v P (Abu Dhabi) 2011-12 (twice). **IT20**: 5 (2011 to 2011-12); HS – ; BB 3-22 v I (Kolkata) 2011-12. F-c Tours: A 2010-11; B 2009-10; UAE 2011-12 (v P). HS 32 v Essex (Lord's) 2011. 50 wkts (2); most – 64 (2010). BB 9-37 (14-106 match) v Worcs (Worcester) 2010. LO HS 35 (*see LOI*). LO BB 5-33 v Derbys (Lord's) 2011 (CB40). T20 HS 8. T20 BB 3-22.

[NQ]**IRELAND, Anthony** John (Plumtree HS), b Masvingo, Zimbabwe 30 Aug 1984. RHB, RM. Midlands 2002-03 to 2004-05. Gloucestershire 2007-10; cap 2007. Middlesex debut 2011. Kolpak registration. **LOI** (Z): 26 (2005-06 to 2006-07); HS 8* v K (Bulawayo) 2005-06; BB 3-41 v B (Harare) (twice) – 2006 and 2006-07. **IT20** (Z): 1 (2006-07); HS 2* and BB 1-33 v B (Khulna) 2006-07. HS 29 and M BB 2-51 v Essex (Chelmsford) 2011. BB 7-36 Zimbabwe A v Bangladesh A (Mirpur) 2006-07. CC BB 6-31 Gs v Leics (Bristol) 2009. LO HS 22* v Kent (Lord's) 2011 (CB40). LO BB 4-16 Zimbabwe A v Kenya (Harare) 2005-06. T20 HS 8*. T20 BB 3-7.

LONDON, Adam Brian (Bishop Wand S, Sunbury), b Ashford 12 Oct 1988. 5'8". LHB, OB. Debut (Middlesex) 2009. No 1st XI appearances in 2011. Middlesex 2nd XI debut 2006. HS 77 v Northants (Northampton) 2010. BB 1-15 v Oxford MCCU (Oxford) 2010. CC BB – . LO HS and BB – .

MALAN, Dawid Johannes (Paarl HS), b Roehampton, Surrey 3 Sep 1987. Son of D.J.Malan (WP B and Transvaal B 1978-79 to 1981-82), elder brother of C.C.Malan (Loughborough UCCE 2009). 6'0". LHB, LB. Boland 2005-06. MCC YC 2006-07. Middlesex debut 2008, scoring 132* v Northants (Uxbridge); cap 2010. MCC 2010-11. 1000 runs (1): 1001 runs (2010). HS 143 v Derbys (Lord's) 2011. BB 4-80 v Cambridge MCCU (Cambridge) 2011. CC BB 2-10 v Essex (Chelmsford) 2011. LO HS 107 v Kent (Canterbury) 2011 (CB40). LO BB 2-4 v Scotland (Edinburgh) 2009 (FPT). T20 HS 103. T20 BB 2-10.

MORGAN, Eoin Joseph Gerard (Catholic University S), b Dublin, Ireland 10 Sep 1986. 6'0". LHB, RM. British passport. Ireland 2004 to 2007-08. Middlesex debut 2006; cap 2008. **ECB central contract 2011-12. Tests**: 16 (2010 to 2011-12); HS 130 v P (Nottingham) 2010. **LOI** (E/Ire): 75 (23 for Ire 2006 to 2008-09; 52 for E 2009 to 2011-12); HS 115 Ire v Canada (Nairobi) 2006-07. **IT20**: 21 (2009 to 2011-12); HS 85* v SA (Johannesburg) 2009-10 – E record. F-c Tours (Ire): A 2010-11 (E); NZ 2008-09 (Eng A); Namibia 2005-06; UAE 2006-07, 2007-08, 2011-12 (v P). 1000 runs (1): 1085 (2008). HS 209* Ire v UAE (Abu Dhabi) 2006-07. CC HS 137* v Glos (Bristol) 2008. BB 2-24 v Notts (Lord's) 2007. LO HS 161 v Kent (Canterbury) 2009 (FPT). LO BB – . T20 HS 85*.

MURTAGH, Timothy James (John Fisher S; St Mary's C), b Lambeth, London 2 Aug 1981. Elder brother of C.P.Murtagh (Loughborough UCCE and Surrey 2005-09); nephew of A.J.Murtagh (Hampshire and EP 1973-77). 6'0". LHB, RFM. British U 2000-03. Surrey 2001-06. Middlesex debut 2007; cap 2008. MCC 2010. HS 74* Sy v Middx (Oval) 2004 and 74* Sy v Warwks (Croydon) 2005. M HS 55 v Leics (Leicester) 2011. 50 wkts (3); most – 85 (2011). BB 7-82 v Derbys (Derby) 2009. M HS 5 v Leics (Leicester) v Surrey (Lord's) 2008 (FPT). LO BB 4-14 Sy v Derbys (Derby) 2005 (NL). T20 HS 40*. T20 BB 6-24 Sy v Middx (Lord's) 2005 – Sy record and 4th best UK figs.

NEWMAN, Scott Alexander (Trinity S, Croydon; Coulsdon C; Brighton U), b Epsom, Surrey 3 Nov 1979. 6'2". LHB, RM. Surrey 2002-09, scoring 99 v Hampshire on debut; cap 2005. Nottinghamshire 2009 (on loan). Middlesex debut 2010, cap 2011. Starts 2012 season on loan at Middx. MCC 2010. F-c Tour (Eng A): I 2003-04. 1000 runs (4); most – 1404 (2006). HS 219 (and 117) Sy v Glamorgan (Oval) 2005. M HS 126 v Derbys (Derby) 2010. BB – . LO HS 177 Sy v Yorks (Oval) 2009 (FPT). T20 HS 81*.

PATEL, Ravi Hasmukh (Merchant Taylors' S, Northwood; Loughborough U), b Harrow 4 Aug 1991. RHB, SLA. Debut (Middlesex) 2010. No 1st XI appearances in 2011. Loughborough MCCU 2011. Middlesex 2nd XI debut. HS 19* and M BB 3-52 v Oxford MCCU (Oxford) 2010. BB 3-25 LU v Leics (Leicester) 2011. LO HS and BB – .

RAYNER, Oliver Philip (St Bede's S, Sussex), b Fallingbostel, W Germany, 1 Nov 1985. 6'5". RHB, OB. Sussex 2006-11, scoring 101 v Sri Lankans (Hove) – first hundred on debut for Sussex since 1920. Middlesex debut 2011 (on loan). HS 101 (see above). CC HS 62* Sx v Hants (Hove) 2011. M HS 58* v Derbys (Derby) 2011. BB 5-49 Sx v Hants (Arundel) 2008. M BB 4-43 v Leics (Leicester) 2011. LO HS 61 Sx v Lancs (Hove) 2006 (P40). LO BB 2-20 v Netherlands (Deventer) 2011 (CB40). T20 HS 41*. T20 BB 5-18.

NQ ROBSON, Sam David (Marcellin C, Randwick), b Paddington, Sydney, NSW, Australia 1 Jul 1989. 6'0". RHB, LB. Debut (Middlesex) 2009. Middlesex 2nd XI debut 2008. HS 204 v Oxford MCCU (Oxford) 2010. CC HS 146 v Essex (Chelmsford) 2011. BB – . LO HS 65 v Sussex (Lord's) 2011 (CB40). T20 HS 28*.

NQ ROGERS, Christopher John Llewellyn (Wesley C, Perth; Curtin U, Perth), b St George, Sydney, Australia 31 Aug 1977. Son of W.J.Rogers (NSW 1968-69 to 1969-70). 5'10". LHB, LBG. W Australia 1998-99 to 2007-08. Derbyshire 2004, 2008-10; cap 2008; captain 2008 (part) to 2010 (part). Leicestershire 2005. Northamptonshire 2006. Victoria 2008-09 to date. Middlesex debut/cap 2011. MCC 2011. Shropshire 2003. Wiltshire 2005. **Tests** (A): 1 (2007-08); HS 15 v I (Perth) 2007-08. F-c Tour (Aus A): P 2007-08. 1000 runs (5+2); most – 1461 (2009). HS 319 Nh v Glos (Northampton) 2006. M HS 148 v Glos (Uxbridge) 2011. BB 1-16 Nh v Leics (Northampton) 2006. LO HS 140 Vic v S Aus (Melbourne) 2009-10. LO BB 2-22 Nh v Durham (Northampton) 2006. T20 HS 58.

ROLAND-JONES, Tobias Skelton ('Toby') (Hampton S; Leeds U), b Ashford 29 Jan 1988. 6'4". RHB, RMF. Debut (Middlesex) 2010. MCC 2011. Middlesex 2nd XI debut 2008. Leeds/Bradford UCCE 2010-11 (not f-c). HS 30* MCC v Notts (Abu Dhabi) 2011. M HS 28 v Northants (Northampton) 2011. BB 5-41 v Surrey (Lord's) 2010. LO HS 23* and LO BB 3-51 v Kent (Canterbury) 2011 (CB40). T20 HS 12. T20 BB 2-42.

ROSSINGTON, Adam Matthew (Mill Hill S), b Edgware 5 May 1993. 5'11". RHB, WK. Debut (Middlesex) 2010. Middlesex 2nd XI debut 2010. England U19s 2010-11, scoring 113 v SL on debut. Summer contract. HS 4 v Sri Lankans (Uxbridge) 2011. T20 HS 25.

SANDHU, Gurjit Singh (Isleworth & Syon S; Heathland S), b W Middlesex Hospital 24 Mar 1992. 6'4". RHB, LMF. Middlesex 2nd XI debut 2008, aged 16y 85d. HS 8 and BB – v Sri Lankans (Uxbridge) 2011 – only 1st XI appearance.

^{NQ}**SCOLLAY, Thomas** Edward (St Phillips C), b Alice Springs, Northern Territory, Australia 28 Nov 1987. RHB, OB. Awaiting f-c debut. Middlesex 2nd XI debut 2010. Hampshire 2nd XI 2008. LO HS 32 and LO BB 1-21 v Yorks (Lord's) 2010 (CB40). T20 HS 15.

SIMPSON, John Andrew (St Gabriel's RC HS), b Bury, Lancs 13 Jul 1988. 5'10". LHB, WK. Debut (Middlesex) 2009, cap 2011. Lancashire 2nd XI debut 2004. Cumberland 2007. MCC YCs 2008. England U19s 2004-05 to 2005. HS 143 v Surrey (Lord's) 2011. LO HS 82 v Glos (Cheltenham) 2010 (CB40). T20 HS 60*.

SMITH, Thomas Michael John (Seaford Head Community C; Sussex Downs C), b Eastbourne, Sussex 22 Aug 1987. 5'9". RHB, SLA. Sussex 2007-09. No f-c appearances in 2008. Surrey 2009 (l-o only). Middlesex debut 2010. HS 33 v Derbys (Derby) 2010. BB 3-38 v Derbys (Lord's) 2011. LO HS 65 Sy v Leics (Leicester) 2009 (P40). LO BB 3-26 v Derbys (Lord's) 2010 (CB40). T20 HS 36*. T20 BB 5-24.

^{NQ}**STIRLING, Paul** Robert (Belfast HS), b Belfast, N Ireland 3 Sep 1990. 5'10". RHB, OB. Ireland 2007-08 to date. Awaiting Middlesex f-c debut. **LOI** (Ire): 36 (2008 to 2011-12); HS 177 v Canada (Toronto) 2010; BB 4-11 v Netherlands (Amstelveen) 2010. **IT20** (Ire): 9 (2009 to 2011-12); HS 65* and BB 2-21 v Kenya (Mombasa) 2011-12. F-c Tour (Ire): WI 2009-10; Kenya 2011-12. HS 107 Ire v Canada (Dublin) 2011. BB 2-45 Ire v Jamaica (Spanish Town) 2009-10. LO HS 177 (*see LOI*). LO BB 4-11 (*see LOI*). T20 HS 65*. T20 BB 2-21.

STRAUSS, Andrew John (Radley C; Durham U), b Johannesburg, South Africa 2 Mar 1977. 5'11". LHB, LM. Debut (Middlesex) 1998; cap 2001; captain 2002 (*part*) to 2004 (*part*); benefit 2009. MCC 2002. N Districts 2007-08. Somerset (1 game) 2011. Oxfordshire 1996. British U (List A) 1997-98. *Wisden* 2004. MBE 2005. **ECB central contract 2011-12. Tests**: 92 (2004 to 2011-12, 42 as captain); HS 177 v NZ (Napier) 2007-08. Scored 112 & 83 (run out) v NZ (Lord's) on debut and 126 & 94* v SA (Port Elizabeth) 2004-05 on his debut overseas. **LOI**: 127 (2003-04 to 2010-11, 62 as captain); HS 158 v I (Bangalore) 2010-11; BB – . **IT20**: 4 (2005 to 2008-09); HS 33 v SL (Southampton) 2006. F-c Tours (C=captain): A 2006-07, 2010-11C; SA 2004-05, 2009-11C; WI 2008-09C; NZ 2007-08; I 2005-06, 2008-09C; P 2005-06; UAE 2011-12C (v P). 1000 runs (4); most – 1529 (2003). HS 241* v Leics (Lord's) 2011. BB 1-16 v Notts (Lord's) 2007. LO HS 163 v Surrey (Oval) 2008 (FPT) – M record. LO BB – . T20 HS 60.

WILKIN, Oliver (Loughborough U), b Ealing 6 Apr 1992. RHB, RM. Loughborough MCCU 2011. Summer contract. HS 38 LU v Northants (Loughborough) 2011. BB 2-63 v Kent (Canterbury) 2011.

WILLIAMS, Robert Edward Morgan (Marlborough C; St Mary's C, Durham U), b Pembury, Kent 19 Jan 1987. 6'0". RHB, RMF. Durham UCCE 2007-09. Middlesex debut 2007; no 1st XI appearances in 2008 after a stress fracture in his back. MCC 2007. HS 31 DU v Lancs (Durham) 2009. M HS 15 and M BB 5-112 v Essex (Chelmsford) 2007 – on M debut. BB 5-70 DU v Lancs (Durham) 2007. LO HS 2* and LO BB 2-60 v Bangladeshis (Lord's) 2010. T20 HS and BB – .

RELEASED/RETIRED continued on p 158

MIDDLESEX 2011

RESULTS SUMMARY

	Place	Won	Lost	Tied	Drew	NR
LV= County Championship (2nd Division)	**1st**	8	2		6	
All First-Class Matches		9	3		6	
Clydesdale Bank 40 (Group A)	2nd	8	4			
Friends Life t20 (South Group)	9th	2	12	1		1

LV= COUNTY CHAMPIONSHIP AVERAGES

BATTING AND FIELDING

Cap		M	I	NO	HS	Runs	Avge	100	50	Ct/St
2001	A.J.Strauss	5	8	2	241*	438	73.00	2	–	6
	S.D.Robson	11	18	3	146	885	59.00	2	4	12
2011	C.J.L.Rogers	15	25	3	148	1286	58.45	4	6	6
	O.P.Rayner	8	8	3	58*	266	53.20	–	3	14
2011	J.A.Simpson	16	22	4	143	768	42.66	1	6	64/1
2010	G.K.Berg	7	10	2	130*	418	41.87	1	1	4
2004	J.W.M.Dalrymple	11	17	3	122*	505	36.07	2	1	8
2010	D.J.Malan	15	25	1	143	745	31.04	2	2	23
2011	S.A.Newman	12	21	1	95	614	30.70	–	-3	11
2010	N.J.Dexter	12	21	3	145	470	26.11	1	2	10
	D.M.Housego	6	11	1	48	223	22.30	–	–	1
	T.S.Roland-Jones	6	7	2	28	103	20.60	–	–	3
2008	T.J.Murtagh	15	18	5	55	221	17.00	–	1	4
2009	S.T.Finn	7	8	1	32	108	15.42	–	–	1
	S.P.Crook	10	9	1	13	64	8.00	–	–	4
	T.M.J.Smith	3	4	–	13	26	6.50	–	–	–
2011	C.D.Collymore	16	15	7	8*	43	5.37	–	–	1

Also batted: A.J.Ireland (2 matches) 29, 1, 16.

BOWLING

	O	M	R	W	Avge	Best	5wI	10wM
G.K.Berg	164.5	27	519	26	19.96	6- 58	1	–
T.J.Murtagh	485.5	95	1679	80	20.98	5- 27	4	1
S.T.Finn	219.2	44	661	31	21.32	5-113	1	–
C.D.Collymore	456.2	100	1289	49	26.30	4- 28	–	–
T.S.Roland-Jones	166.5	19	620	22	28.18	5- 91	1	–
S.P.Crook	172.5	18	812	26	31.23	5- 94	1	–
O.P.Rayner	165.5	32	462	11	42.00	4- 43	–	–
J.W.M.Dalrymple	148.4	16	446	10	44.60	3- 21	–	–
Also bowled:								
T.M.J.Smith	80	12	243	6	40.50	3- 38	–	–
N.J.Dexter	118.1	25	411	9	45.66	3- 46	–	–

A.J.Ireland 52.3-12-171-4; D.J.Malan 43.4-8-127-3; S.A.Newman 1-0-2-0; S.D.Robson 1-0-8-0; A.J.Strauss 1-0-2-0.

The First-Class Averages (pp 223–240) give the records of Middlesex players in all first-class county matches (Middlesex's other opponents being Cambridge MCCU and the Sri Lankans), with the exception of:
S.T.Finn 8-9-1-32-108-13.50-0-0-1ct. 241.2-55-705-34-20.73-5/113-1-0.
O.P.Rayner 9-9-3-58*-269-44.83-0-3-15ct. 184.5-36-523-13-40.23-4/43-0-0.
A.J.Strauss 6-10-2-241*-614-76.75-3-0-6ct. 1-0-2-0.

MIDDLESEX RECORDS

FIRST-CLASS CRICKET

Highest Total	For 642-3d		v	Hampshire	Southampton	1923
	V 850-7d		by	Somerset	Taunton	2007
Lowest Total	For 20		v	MCC	Lord's	1864
	V 31		by	Glos	Bristol	1924
Highest Innings	For 331*	J.D.B.Robertson	v	Worcs	Worcester	1949
	V 341	C.M.Spearman	for	Glos	Gloucester	2004

Highest Partnership for each Wicket

1st	372	M.W.Gatting/J.L.Langer	v	Essex	Southgate	1998
2nd	380	F.A.Tarrant/J.W.Hearne	v	Lancashire	Lord's	1914
3rd	424*	W.J.Edrich/D.C.S.Compton	v	Somerset	Lord's	1948
4th	325	J.W.Hearne/E.H.Hendren	v	Hampshire	Lord's	1919
5th	338	R.S.Lucas/T.C.O'Brien	v	Sussex	Hove	1895
6th	270	J.D.Carr/P.N.Weekes	v	Glos	Lord's	1994
7th	271*	E.H.Hendren/F.T.Mann	v	Notts	Nottingham	1925
8th	182*	M.H.C.Doll/H.R.Murrell	v	Notts	Lord's	1913
9th	172	G.K.Berg/T.J.Murtagh	v	Leics	Leicester	2011
10th	230	R.W.Nicholls/W.Roche	v	Kent	Lord's	1899

Best Bowling	For 10- 40	G.O.B.Allen	v	Lancashire	Lord's	1929
(Innings)	V 9- 38	R.C.R-Glasgow†	for	Somerset	Lord's	1924
Best Bowling	16-114	G.Burton	v	Yorkshire	Sheffield	1888
(Match)	16-114	J.T.Hearne	v	Lancashire	Manchester	1898
	V 16-100	J.E.B.B.P.Q.C.Dwyer	for	Sussex	Hove	1906

Most Runs – Season	2669	E.H.Hendren	(av 83.41)	1923
Most Runs – Career	40302	E.H.Hendren	(av 48.81)	1907-37
Most 100s – Season	13	D.C.S.Compton		1947
Most 100s – Career	119	E.H.Hendren		1907-37
Most Wkts – Season	158	F.J.Titmus	(av 14.63)	1955
Most Wkts – Career	2361	F.J.Titmus	(av 21.27)	1949-82
Most Career W-K Dismissals	1223	J.T.Murray	(1024 ct; 199 st)	1952-75
Most Career Catches in the Field	561	E.H.Hendren		1907-37

LIMITED-OVERS CRICKET

Highest Total	50ov	341-7		v	Somerset	Lord's	2009
	40ov	337-5		v	Somerset	Southgate	2003
	T20	213-4		v	Glamorgan	Richmond	2010
Lowest Total	50ov	41		v	Essex	Westcliff	1972
	40ov	23		v	Yorkshire	Leeds	1974
	T20	102		v	Glamorgan	Richmond	2011
Highest Innings	50ov	163	A.J.Strauss	v	Surrey	The Oval	2008
	40ov	147*	M.R.Ramprakash	v	Worcs	Lord's	1990
	T20	106	A.C.Gilchrist	v	Kent	Canterbury	2010
Best Bowling	50ov	6-15	W.W.Daniel	v	Sussex	Hove	1980
	40ov	6- 6	R.W.Hooker	v	Surrey	Lord's	1969
	T20	5-13	M.Kartik	v	Essex	Lord's	2007

† R.C.Robertson-Glasgow

NORTHAMPTONSHIRE

Formation of Present Club: 31 July 1878
Inaugural First-Class Match: 1905
Colours: Maroon
Badge: Tudor Rose
County Champions: (0); best – 2nd 1912, 1957, 1965, 1976
Gillette/NatWest/C&G/FP Trophy Winners: (2) 1976, 1992
Benson and Hedges Cup Winners: (1) 1980
Pro 40/National League (Div 1) Winners: (0); best – 2nd 2006, 2007
Sunday League Winners: (0); best – 3rd 1991
Clydesdale Bank 40 Winners: (0); best – 3rd Group B 2011
Twenty20 Cup Winners: (0); best – Semi-Finalist 2009

Chief Executive: K.David Smith, County Ground, Wantage Road, Northampton, NN1 4TJ • Tel: 01604 514455 • Fax: 01604 609288 • Email: post@nccc.co.uk • Web: www.nccc.co.uk

First XI Coach: David J.Capel. **Captain**: A.J.Hall. **Vice-Captain**: N.J.O'Brien. **Overseas Player**: W.P.J.U.C.Vaas. **2012 Beneficiary**: none. **Head Groundsman**: Paul Marshall. **Scorer**: A.C. (Tony) Kingston. ‡ New registration. NQ Not qualified for England.

BROOKS, Jack Alexander (Wheatley Park S), b Oxford 4 Jun 1984. 6'2". RHB, RFM. Debut (Northamptonshire) 2009. Oxfordshire 2004-09. HS 53 v Glos (Bristol) 2010. BB 5-23 v Leics (Leicester) 2011. LO HS 10 v Middx (Uxbridge) 2009 (P40). LO BB 3-35 EL v Bangladesh A (Sylhet) 2011-12. T20 HS 33*. T20 BB 3-24.

BURTON, David Alexander (Sacred Heart RC SS; Lambeth C), b Dulwich, London 23 Aug 1985. 5'11". RHB, RMF. Gloucestershire 2006; cap 2006. Middlesex 2008-09. Northamptonshire debut 2010. MCC YC 2006. HS 52* Gs v Glamorgan (Cardiff) 2006 – on debut. Nh HS 6 v Surrey (Northampton) 2011. BB 5-68 v Glos (Bristol) 2009. Nh BB 5-75 v Leics (Northampton) 2010. LO HS 2 v Kent (Canterbury) 2009 (P40). LO BB 3-25 v Warwks (Birmingham) 2011 (CB40). T20 HS – . T20 BB 2-13.

COETZER, Kyle James (Aberdeen GS), b Aberdeen, Scotland 14 Apr 1984. 5'11". RHB, RM. Durham 2004-10. Northamptonshire debut 2011. Scotland 2004 to date. **LOI** (Scot): 9 (2008 to 2011); HS 89* and BB 1-35 v Netherlands (Aberdeen) 2011. **IT20** (Scot): 9 (2008 to 2009-10); HS 48* v Kenya (Belfast) 2008; BB 3-25 v Afghanistan (Abu Dhabi) 2009-10. F-c Tour (Scot): Kenya 2009-10. HS 172 Du v MCC (Abu Dhabi) 2010. CC HS 142 Du v Warwks (Chester-le-St) 2007. Nh HS 84 v Glos (Northampton) 2011. BB 2-16 Scot v Kenya (Nairobi) 2009-10. CC BB – . LO HS 127 Scot v Oman (Johannesburg) 2008-09. LO BB (see LOI). T20 HS 64. T20 BB 3-25.

DAGGETT, Lee Martin (Woodhey HS, and Holy Cross C, Bury; Durham U) b Bury, Lancs 1 Oct 1982. 6'0". RHB, RMF. Durham UCCE 2003-05. British U 2004. Warwickshire 2006-08. Leicestershire 2008. Northamptonshire debut 2009. HS 50* v Leics (Leicester) 2011. BB 8-94 DU v Durham (Chester-le-St) 2004. CC BB 6-30 Wa v Durham (Birmingham) 2006. Nh BB 4-25 v Worcs (Worcester) 2010. LO HS 14* and BB 4-17 v Netherlands (Northampton) 2010 (CB40). T20 HS 3*. T20 BB 2-17.

DAVIS, Christian Arthur Linghorne (Bedford S), b Milton Keynes, Bucks 11 Oct 1992. 6'0". RHB, LFM. Northamptonshire 2nd XI debut 2010. Bedfordshire 2010. England U19s 2010-11. Awaiting f-c debut. LO HS and BB – .

‡**DE LANGE, Con** de Wet, b Belville, South Africa 11 Feb 1981. Cousin of A.D.de Lange (Free State, Boland 2006-07 to 2008-09) and nephew of C.P.L.de Lange (N Transvaal 1981-82 to 1986-87). 5'8". RHB, SLA. Boland 1997-98 to 2006-07. Cape Cobras 2005-06 to 2007-08. Eagles 2008-09 to 2009-10. Free State 2009-10 to 2010-11. Knights 2010-11. Qualifies via UK residency. HS 109 Boland v Easterns (Paarl) 2003-04. BB 7-48 (12-116 match) Boland v Gauteng (Randjesfontein) 2003-04. LO HS 66 Boland v EP (Port Elizabeth) 2002-03. LO BB 4-8 Boland v EP (Port Elizabeth) 2006-07. T20 HS 8. T20 BB 2-14.

EVANS, Luke (St Aidan's S, Sunderland), b Sunderland 26 Apr 1987. 6'7". RHB, RMF. Durham 2007-10. No 1st XI appearances in 2008. Northamptonshire debut 2010 (on loan). HS 8* and CC BB 3-53 v Glos (Bristol) 2010. BB 3-21 v Loughborough MCCU (Loughborough) 2011. LO HS 18 v Hants (Northampton) 2011 (CB40). LO BB 2-53 Du v Notts (Chester-le-St) 2009 (P40). T20 HS – . T20 BB 1-15.

^NQ**HALL, Andrew** James (Alberton HS), b Alberton, Johannesburg, South Africa 31 Jul 1975. 6'0". RHB, RFM. Transvaal/Gauteng 1995-96 to 2000-01. Easterns 2001-02 to 2003-04. Worcestershire 2003-04. Lions 2004-05 to 2005-06. Kent 2005-07; cap 2005. Northamptonshire debut 2008 (Kolpak registration); cap 2009; captain 2010 (*part*) to date. Dolphins 2009-10. Mashonaland Eagles 2010-11. Durham CB 1999. Suffolk 2002. **Tests** (SA): 21 (2001-02 to 2006-07); HS 163 v I (Kanpur) 2004-05; BB 3-1 v SL (Johannesburg) 2002-03. **LOI** (SA): 88 (1998-99 to 2007); HS 81 v SL (Galle) 2000-01; BB 5-18 v E (Bridgetown) 2006-07. **IT20** (SA): 2 (2005-06); HS 11 v A (Brisbane) 2005-06; BB 3-22 v A Johannesburg) 2005-06. F-c Tours (SA): E 2003; WI 2004-05; I 2004-05; SL 2006; Z 1995-96 (Transvaal B), 2007-08 (SA A). 1000 runs (1): 1161 (2009). HS 163 (*see Tests*). UK HS 159 v Leics (Northampton) 2009. BB 6-77 (11-99 match) Easterns v WP (Pt Elizabeth) 2002-03. UK BB 5-29 v Essex (Northampton) 2009. LO HS 129* Gauteng v Border (E London) 1999-00. LO BB 5-18 (*see LOI*). T20 HS 66* and T20 BB 6-21 v Worcs (Northampton) 2008 (Nh record analysis, and 1st man in UK to score 50 and take 5 wkts in a game).

HOWGEGO, Benjamin Henry Nicholas (King's S, Ely; Stowe S; Exeter U), b King's Lynn, Norfolk 3 Mar 1988. 5'11". LHB, RM. Debut (Northamptonshire) 2008. Northamptonshire 2nd XI debut 2005. HS 80 v Derbys (Chesterfield) 2010. BB – . LO HS 12 v Scotland (Edinburgh) 2011 (CB40). T20 HS 3.

KEOGH, Robert Ian (Queensbury S; Dunstable C), b Luton, Beds 21 Oct 1991. 5'11". RHB, OB. Northamptonshire 2nd XI debut 2009. Bedfordshire 2009-10. Awaiting f-c debut. LO HS 11 v Yorks (Northampton) 2010 (CB40). T20 HS 1. T20 BB – .

MIDDLEBROOK, James Daniel (Pudsey Crawshaw S), b Leeds, Yorks 13 May 1977. 6'1". RHB, OB. Yorkshire 1998-2001. Essex 2002-09; cap 2003. Northamptonshire debut 2010, cap 2011. MCC 2010. HS 127 Ex v Middx (Lord's) 2007. Nh HS 109 v Glos (Bristol) 2011. 50 wkts (1): 56 (2003). BB 6-82 (10-170 match) Y v Hants (Southampton) 2000 – inc 4 wkts in 5 balls. Nh BB 5-123 v Middx (Northampton) 2011. Hat-trick Ex v Kent (Canterbury) 2003. LO HS 57* v Derbys (Derby) 2010 (CB40). LO BB 4-27 Ex v Somerset (Taunton) 2006 (CGT). T20 HS 43. T20 BB 3-13.

MURPHY, David (Richard Hale S, Hertford; Loughborough U), b Welwyn Garden City, Herts 24 June 1989. 5'11". RHB, WK. Loughborough MCCU 2009-11. Northamptonshire debut 2009. Northamptonshire 2nd XI debut 2007. HS 79 v Glamorgan (Northampton) 2011. LO HS 31* v Netherlands (Northampton) 2010 (CB40). T20 HS 20.

NEWTON, Robert Irving (Framlingham C), b Taunton, Somerset 18 Jan 1990. 5'8". RHB, OB. Debut (Northamptonshire) 2010. Northamptonshire 2nd XI debut 2006. HS 113 v Middx (Northampton) 2011. BB – . LO HS 66 v Essex (Northampton) 2010 (CB40). T20 HS 37.

O'BRIEN, Niall John (Marian C, Dublin), b Dublin, Ireland 8 Nov 1981. Son of B.A.O'Brien (Ireland 1966-81); elder brother of K.J.O'Brien (Nottinghamshire and Ireland 2006-07 to date). 5'6". LHB, WK. Kent 2004-06. Ireland 2005-06 to date. Northamptonshire debut 2007; cap 2011. **LOI** (Ire): 49 (2006 to 2011); HS 72 v P (Kingston) 2006-07 and 72 v Scotland (Belfast) 2007. **IT20** (Ire): 16 (2008 to 2009-10); HS 50 v Canada (Colombo, SSC) 20090-10. HS 176 Ireland v UAE (Windhoek) 2005. Nh HS 168 v Glamorgan (Northampton) 2008. BB 1-4 K v Cambridge UCCE (Cambridge) 2006. LO HS 121 v Hants (Southampton) 2011 (CB40). T20 HS 84.

PETERS, Stephen David (Coopers Coborn & Co S), b Harold Wood, Essex 10 Dec 1978. 5'11". RHB, occ LB. Essex 1996-2001, scoring 110 and 12* v Cambridge U (Cambridge) on debut. Worcestershire 2002-05. Northamptonshire debut 2006; cap 2007. MCC 2011. 1000 runs (4); most – 1320 (2010). HS 222 v Glamorgan (Swansea) 2011. BB 1-19 Ex v Oxford U (Chelmsford) 1999. LO HS 107 v Yorks (Leeds) 2007 (FPT). T20 HS 61*.

SALES, David John Grimwood (Caterham S; Cumnor House S), b Carshalton, Surrey 3 Dec 1977. 6'0". RHB, RM. Debut (Northamptonshire) 1996 v Worcs (Kidderminster) scoring 0 and 210* – record Championship score on f-c debut; youngest (18y 237d) to score 200 in a Championship match; cap 1999; captain 2004-07; benefit 2007. Missed entire 2009 season with knee injury. Wellington 2001-02. MCC 2010. F-c Tours (Eng A): NZ 1999-00; SL 1997-98; K 1997-98; B 1999-00. Sustained severe knee injury prior to start of England A tour of WI 2000-01 – no f-c appearances 2001. 1000 runs (6); most – 1384 (2007). HS 303* v Essex (Northampton) 1999 – youngest Englishman (21y 240d) to score a f-c 300. BB 4-25 v Sri Lanka A (Northampton) 1999. CC BB 2-7 v Yorks (Scarborough) 1999. LO HS 161 v Yorks (Northampton) 2006 (CGT) – Nh record. LO BB – . T20 HS 78*. T20 BB 1-10.

SWEENEY, Samuel Alan (Parklands HS, Chorley; Myerscough C, Manchester), b Preston, Lancs 15 Mar 1990. RHB, RM. Northamptonshire 2nd XI debut 2011. Awaiting f-c debut. LO BB – .

NQ**VAAS**, Warnakulasuriya Patabendige Joseph Ushantha **Chaminda** (St Joseph's C, Maradana), b Mattumagala, Sri Lanka 27 Jan 1974. LHB, LFM. Colts 1990-91 to date. Hampshire 2003. Worcestershire 2005. Middlesex 2007; cap 2007. Northamptonshire debut 2010; cap 2011. **Tests** (SL): 111 (1994-95 to 2009); HS 100* v B (Colombo, SSC) 2007; BB 7-71 (14-191 match) v WI (Colombo, SSC) 2001-02. **LOI** (SL): 322 (1993-94 to 2008, 1 as captain); HS 50* v P (Sharjah) 2000-01; BB 8-19 v Z (Colombo, SSC) 2001-02, world record LOI analysis and inc first of two LOI hat-tricks. **IT20** (6): (2006-07 to 2007-08); HS 21 v A (Cape Town) 2007-08; BB 2-14 v B (Johannesburg) 2007-08. F-c Tours (SL): E 2002, 2006; A 1995-96, 2004, 2007-08; SA 1994-95, 1997-98, 2000-01, 2002-03; WI 2003, 2007-08; NZ 1994-95, 1996-97, 2004-05, 2006-07; I 1993-94, 1997-98, 2005-06; P 1995-96, 1999-00, 2001-02, 2004-05, 2008-09; Z 1994-95, 1999-00, 2004; B 1998-99 (v P), 2008-09. HS 134 Colts v Burgher (Colombo, SSC) 2004-05. Nh HS 96 v Essex (Northampton) 2011. 50 wkts (1+2); most – 70 (2011). BB 7-54 (11-93 match) WP v S Province (Colombo, RPS) 2004-05. Nh BB 6-46 v Essex (Chelmsford) 2011. LO HS 76* Colts v Nondescripts (Colombo, NCC) 2009-10. LO BB (*see LOI*). T20 HS 73. T20 BB 3-16.

WAKELY, Alexander George (Bedford S), b Hammersmith, London 3 Nov 1988. 6'2".
RHB, OB. Debut (Northamptonshire) 2007. Bedfordshire 2004-05. Northamptonshire 2nd
XI debut, aged 15y 295d. HS 113* v Glamorgan (Cardiff) 2009. BB 2-62 v Somerset
(Taunton) 2007 – on debut. LO HS 94 v Surrey (Northampton) 2011 (CB40). BB 2-14 v
Lancs (Northampton) 2007 (P40). T20 HS 62. T20 BB – .

WHITE, Robert Allan (Stowe S; Durham U; Loughborough U), b Chelmsford, Essex
15 Oct 1979. 5'11". RHB, LB. Debut (Northamptonshire) 2000; cap 2008. Loughborough
UCCE 2003. British U 2003. 1000 runs (1): 1037 (2008). HS 277 and BB 2-30 v Glos
(Northampton) 2002 – highest maiden f-c hundred in UK; included 107 before lunch on first
day. LO HS 111 v Warwks (Northampton) 2008 (FPT). LO BB 2-18 v Sussex (Northampton) 2002 (NL). T20 HS 94*.

WILLEY, David Jonathan (Northampton S), b Northampton 28 Feb 1990. Son of P.Willey
(Northants, Leics, England 1966-91). 6'1". LHB, LFM. Debut (Northamptonshire) 2009.
Bedfordshire 2008. England U19s 2009. HS 64 and BB 5-29 (10-75 match) v Glos
(Northampton) 2011. LO HS 74 v Surrey (Oval) 2011 (CB40). LO BB 3-49 v Scotland
(Edinburgh) 2011 (CB40). T20 HS 22*. T20 BB 3-9.

RELEASED/RETIRED
(Having made a County First-Class or List A appearance in 2011)

BRETT, Thomas (Latimer Arts Community C), b Kettering 13 Nov 1989. 6'2". RHB, SLA.
Northamptonshire 2010-11. Northamptonshire 2nd XI debut 2007. Bedfordshire 2008-09.
HS 2 and BB 1-29 v Loughborough MCCU (Loughborough) 2011. LO HS 2* v Glos
(Northampton) 2010 (CB40). LO BB 2-29 v Warwks (Birmingham) 2011 (CB40).

LOYE, Malachy Bernhard (Moulton S), b Northampton 27 Sep 1972. 6'2". RHB, OB.
Northamptonshire 1991-2002 and 2010-11; cap 1994. PCA 1998. Lancashire 2003-09,
scoring 126 v Surrey (Oval) and 113 v Notts (Manchester) in his first two innings; cap 2003;
benefit 2008. Auckland 2006-07. **LOI**: 7 (2006-07); HS 45 v A (Sydney) 2006-07. F-c Tours
(Eng A): SA 1993-94, 1998-99; Z 1994-95 (Nh), 1998-99. 1000 runs (6); most – 1296
(2006). HS 322* v Glamorgan (Northampton) 1998 – record Nh score until 2001. BB 1-8 La
v Kent (Blackpool) 2003. Nh BB – . LO HS 127 La v Durham (Manchester) 2006 (CGT).
T20 HS 100.

LUCAS, D.S. – *see WORCESTERSHIRE.*

G.C.Baker and J.Botha left the staff without making a County First-Class or List A
appearance in 2011.

NORTHAMPTONSHIRE 2011

RESULTS SUMMARY

	Place	Won	Lost	Tied	Drew	NR
LV= County Championship (2nd Division)	3rd	7	2		7	
All First-Class Matches		7	2		8	
Clydesdale Bank 40 (Group B)	3rd	6	6			
Friends Life t20 (North Group)	9th	2	11			3

LV= COUNTY CHAMPIONSHIP AVERAGES
BATTING AND FIELDING

Cap		M	I	NO	HS	Runs	Avge	100	50	Ct/St
	D.Murphy	4	4	1	79	164	54.66	–	1	16
2009	A.J.Hall	16	23	4	146	960	50.52	2	5	31
2007	S.D.Peters	15	21	1	222	864	43.20	3	2	15
2011	J.D.Middlebrook	16	20	5	109	644	42.93	3	1	8
	A.G.Wakely	15	21	–	98	823	39.19	–	5	6
	R.I.Newton	7	13	1	113	454	37.83	1	2	2
2011	N.J.O'Brien	13	21	4	166	641	37.70	1	4	45/3
	K.J.Coetzer	4	7	1	84	214	35.66	–	2	1
2008	R.A.White	12	17	–	140	588	34.58	1	2	7
1994	M.B.Loye	8	12	–	87	393	32.75	–	4	–
2011	W.P.J.U.C.Vaas	14	16	1	96	403	26.86	–	2	–
	L.M.Daggett	14	16	9	50*	181	25.85	–	1	2
2009	D.S.Lucas	9	11	2	60	188	20.88	–	1	1
	J.A.Brooks	9	8	5	15*	58	19.33	–	–	2
	B.H.N.Howgego	5	7	–	41	132	18.85	–	–	5
1999	D.J.G.Sales	11	15	1	65	246	17.57	–	1	11

Also batted (one match each): P.M.Best 31* (1 ct); D.A.Burton 6, 2; L.Evans 5; D.J.Willey 64.

BOWLING

	O	M	R	W	Avge	Best	5wI	10wM
D.J.Willey	26.2	5	75	10	7.50	5- 29	2	1
W.P.J.U.C.Vaas	499	119	1501	70	21.44	6- 46	6	1
J.A.Brooks	289	68	942	43	21.90	5- 23	2	–
J.D.Middlebrook	426.4	86	1307	43	30.39	5-123	2	–
D.S.Lucas	206.4	39	822	27	30.44	5- 20	1	–
L.M.Daggett	408.5	81	1440	41	35.12	4- 35	–	–
A.J.Hall	351.1	66	1267	28	45.25	3- 8	–	–

Also bowled:
P.M.Best 47-12-153-2; D.A.Burton 30-9-142-2; L.Evans 22-4-104-2; D.Murphy 1-0-3-0; A.G.Wakely 4.2-0-21-1; R.A.White 64-4-262-4.

The First-Class Averages (pp 223–240) give the records of Northamptonshire players in all first-class county matches (Northamptonshire's other opponents being Loughborough MCCU), with the exception of P.M.Best and D.Murphy, whose first-class figures for Northamptonshire are as above.

NORTHAMPTONSHIRE RECORDS

FIRST-CLASS CRICKET

Highest Total	For 781-7d		v	Notts	Northampton	1995
	V 673-8d		by	Yorkshire	Leeds	2003
Lowest Total	For 12		v	Glos	Gloucester	1907
	V 33		by	Lancashire	Northampton	1977
Highest Innings	For 331*	M.E.K.Hussey	v	Somerset	Taunton	2003
	V 333	K.S.Duleepsinhji	for	Sussex	Hove	1930

Highest Partnership for each Wicket

1st	375	R.A.White/M.J.Powell	v	Glos	Northampton	2002
2nd	344	G.Cook/R.J.Boyd-Moss	v	Lancashire	Northampton	1986
3rd	393	A.Fordham/A.J.Lamb	v	Yorkshire	Leeds	1990
4th	370	R.T.Virgin/P.Willey	v	Somerset	Northampton	1976
5th	401	M.B.Loye/D.Ripley	v	Glamorgan	Northampton	1998
6th	376	R.Subba Row/A.Lightfoot	v	Surrey	The Oval	1958
7th	293	D.J.G.Sales/D.Ripley	v	Essex	Northampton	1999
8th	179	A.J.Hall/J.D.Middlebrook	v	Surrey	The Oval	2011
9th	156	R.Subba Row/S.Starkie	v	Lancashire	Northampton	1955
10th	148	B.W.Bellamy/J.V.Murdin	v	Glamorgan	Northampton	1925

Best Bowling	For	10-127	V.W.C.Jupp	v	Kent	Tunbridge W	1932
(Innings)	V	10- 30	C.Blythe	for	Kent	Northampton	1907
Best Bowling	For	15- 31	G.E.Tribe	v	Yorkshire	Northampton	1958
(Match)	V	17- 48	C.Blythe	for	Kent	Northampton	1907

Most Runs – Season	2198	D.Brookes	(av 51.11)		1952
Most Runs – Career	28980	D.Brookes	(av 36.13)		1934-59
Most 100s – Season	8	R.A.Haywood			1921
Most 100s – Career	67	D.Brookes			1934-59
Most Wkts – Season	175	G.E.Tribe	(av 18.70)		1955
Most Wkts – Career	1102	E.W.Clark	(av 21.26)		1922-47
Most Career W-K Dismissals	810	K.V.Andrew	(653 ct; 157 st)		1953-66
Most Career Catches in the Field	469	D.S.Steele			1963-84

LIMITED-OVERS CRICKET

Highest Total	50ov	360-2		v	Staffs	Northampton	1990
	40ov	319-7		v	Scotland	Northampton	2003
	T20	224-5		v	Glos	Milton Keynes	2005
Lowest Total	50ov	62		v	Leics	Leicester	1974
	40ov	41		v	Middlesex	Northampton	1972
	T20	47		v	Durham	Chester-le-St[2]	2011
Highest Innings	50ov	161	D.J.G.Sales	v	Yorkshire	Northampton	2006
	40ov	172*	W.Larkins	v	Warwicks	Luton	1983
	T20	111*	L.Klusener	v	Worcs	Kidderminster	2007
Best Bowling	50ov	7-10	C.Pietersen	v	Denmark	Brondby	2005
	40ov	7-39	A.Hodgson	v	Somerset	Northampton	1976
	T20	6-21	A.J.Hall	v	Worcs	Northampton	2008

NOTTINGHAMSHIRE

Formation of Present Club: March/April 1841
Substantial Reorganisation: 11 December 1866
Inaugural First-Class Match: 1864
Colours: Green and Gold
Badge: Badge of City of Nottingham
County Champions (since 1890): (6) 1907, 1929, 1981, 1987, 2005, 2010
Gillette/NatWest/C&G/FP Trophy Winners: (1) 1987
Benson and Hedges Cup Winners: (1) 1989
Pro 40/National League (Div 1) Winners: (0); best – 2nd 2007
Sunday League Winners: (1) 1991
Clydesdale Bank 40 Winners: (0); best – 2nd Group C 2011
Twenty20 Cup Winners: (0); best – Finalist 2006

Chief Executive: Lisa Pursehouse, Trent Bridge, Nottingham NG2 6AG • Tel: 0115 982 3000 • Fax: 0115 945 5730 • Email: administration@nottsccc.co.uk • Webs: www.nottsccc.co.uk • www.trentbridge.co.uk

Director of Cricket: Mick Newell. **Club Coach:** Paul Johnson. **Captain:** C.M.W.Read. **Vice-Captain:** P.J.Franks. **Overseas Player:** A.C.Voges. **2012 Beneficiary:** none. **Head Groundsman:** Steve Birks. **Scorer:** Roger Marshall. ‡ New registration. NQ Not qualified for England.

NQ**ADAMS, Andre** Ryan (Westlake BHS, Auckland), b Mangere, Auckland, New Zealand 17 Jul 1975. 5'9". RHB, RMF. Auckland 1997-98 to date. Essex 2004-06, scoring 124 on debut (*see below*); cap 2004. Nottinghamshire debut/cap 2007 (Kolpak registration). Herefordshire 2001. **Tests** (NZ): 1 (2001-02); HS 11 and BB 3-44 v E (Auckland) 2001-02. **LOI** (NZ): 42 (2000-01 to 2006-07); HS 45 v P (Rawalpindi) 2001-02; BB 5-22 v I (Queenstown) 2002-03. **IT20** (NZ): 4 (2004-05 to 2005-06); HS 7 v A (Auckland) 2004-05; BB 2-20 v SL (Auckland) 2006-07. HS 124 Ex v Leics (Leicester) 2004 (91 balls, 7 sixes, 13 fours; 100 off 80 balls) on UK debut. Nt HS 84 v Yorks (Scarborough) 2009. 50 wkts (2); most – 68 (2010). BB 6-25 Auckland v Wellington. UK BB 6-31 (11-85 match) v Hants (Nottingham) 2011. Hat-trick Ex v Somerset (Taunton) 2005. LO HS 90* North Is Selection XI v Sri Lankans (New Plymouth) 2000-01. LO BB 5-7 Auckland v ND (Auckland) 1999-00. T20 HS 54*. T20 BB 5-20.

BALL, Jacob Timothy ('**Jake**') (Meden CS), b Mansfield 14 Mar 1991. Nephew of B.N.French (Notts and England 1976-95). 6'0". RHB, RM. Debut (Nottinghamshire) 2011. Nottinghamshire 2nd XI debut 2008. England U19s 2010. HS 4 and BB 3-72 v MCC (Abu Dhabi) 2011 – only f-c match. LO HS 19* v Sri Lanka A (Nottingham) 2011. BB 3-32 v Leics (Nottingham) 2010 (CB40). T20 BB – .

BROAD, Stuart Christopher John (Oakham S), b Nottingham 24 Jun 1986. 6'6". LHB, RFM. Son of B.C.Broad (Glos, Notts, OFS and England 1979-94). Debut (Leicestershire) 2005; cap 2007. Nottinghamshire debut 2008. YC 2006. *Wisden* 2009. **ECB central contract 2011-12**. Tests: 44 (2007-08 to 2011-12); HS 169 v P (Lord's) 2010, sharing in record Test and UK f-c 8th-wkt partnership of 332 with I.J.L.Trott; BB 6-46 v I (Nottingham) 2011, inc hat-trick. **LOI**: 87 (2006 to 2011-12); HS 45* v I (Manchester) 2007; BB 5-23 v SA (Nottingham) 2008. **IT20**: 34 (2006 to 2011-12, 5 as captain); HS 10* v WI (Oval) 2009; BB 3-17 v P (Oval) 2009. F-c Tours: A 2010-11; SA 2009-10; WI 2005-06 (Eng A), 2008-09; NZ 2007-08; I 2008-09; SL 2007-08; B 2006-07 (Eng A), 2009-10; UAE 2011-12 (v P). HS 169 (*see Tests*). CC HS 91* Le v Derbys (Leicester) 2007. Nt HS 60 v Worcs (Nottingham) 2009. BB 8-52 (11-131 match) v Warwks (Birmingham) 2010. LO HS 45* (*see LOI*). LO BB 5-23 (*see LOI*). T20 HS 10*. T20 BB 3-13.

CARTER, Andrew (Lincoln C), b Lincoln 27 Aug 1988. 6'4". RHB, RM. Debut (Nottinghamshire) 2009. Essex 2010 (on loan). Nottinghamshire 2nd XI debut 2006. Lincolnshire 2007-10. HS 17 v Oxford MCCU (Oxford) 2011. CC HS 16* and BB 5-40 Ex v Kent (Canterbury) 2010. Nt BB 2-37 v Oxford MCCU (Oxford) 2011. LO HS 12 v Sussex (Hove) 2009 (P40). LO BB 3-32 v Essex (Southend) 2009 (P40). T20 HS – . T20 BB 4-20.

EDWARDS, Neil James (Cape Cornwall CS; Richard Huish C), b Treliske, Truro, Cornwall 14 Oct 1983. 6'3". LHB, RM. Somerset 2002-08. Nottinghamshire debut 2010. Cornwall 2000-06. 1000 runs (1): 1251 (2007). HS 212 Sm v Loughborough UCCE (Taunton) 2007. CC HS 160 Sm v Hants (Taunton) 2003. Nt HS 85 v Kent (Nottingham) 2010. BB 1-16 Sm v Derbys (Taunton) 2004. LO HS 65 Sm v Yorks (Taunton) 2006 (P40). T20 HS 1.

ELSTONE, Scott Liam (Friary Grange C), b Burton-on-Trent, Staffs 10 Jun 1990. 5'8". RHB, OB. Awaiting f-c debut. Nottinghamshire 2nd XI debut 2006, aged 16y 81d. LO HS 40 v Glamorgan (Nottingham) 2011 (CB40). LO BB 1-22 v Scotland (Nottingham) 2010 (CB40). T20 HS 21*.

FLETCHER, Luke Jack (Henry Mellish S, Nottingham), b Nottingham 18 Sep 1988. 6'6". RHB, RMF. Debut (Nottinghamshire) 2008. Nottinghamshire 2nd XI debut 2007. HS 92 v Hants (Southampton) 2009. BB 5-82 v Lancs (Nottingham) 2011. LO HS 40* v Durham (Chester-le-St) 2009 (P40). LO BB 3-27 v Somerset (Taunton) 2011 (CB40). T20 HS 5. T20 BB 4-30.

FRANKS, Paul John (Southwell Minster CS), b Mansfield 3 Feb 1979. 6'2". LHB, RMF. Debut (Nottinghamshire) 1996; cap 1999; benefit 2007. Canterbury 2002-03. MW Rhinos 2010-11. YC 2000. **LOI**: 1 (2000); HS 4 v WI (Nottingham) 2000. F-c Tours (Eng A): SA 1998-99; WI 2000-01; NZ 1999-00; SL 2004-05; B 1999-00. HS 123* v Leics (Leicester) 2003. 50 wkts (2); most – 63 (1999). BB 7-56 v Middx (Lord's) 2000. Hat-trick v Warwks (Nottingham) 1997. LO HS 84* v Lincs (Lincoln) 2003 (CGT). LO BB 6-27 v Durham (Chester-le-St) 2000 (NL). T20 HS 29*. T20 BB 2-12.

‡**GURNEY, Harry** Frederick (Garendon HS; Loughborough GS; Leeds U), b Nottingham 25 Oct 1986. 6'2". RHB, LFM. Leicestershire 2007-11. Bradford/Leeds UCCE 2006-07 (not f-c). HS 24* Le v Middx (Leicester) 2009. BB 5-82 Le v Surrey (Leicester) 2009. LO HS 7 Le v Kent (Canterbury) 2010 (CB40). LO BB 5-24 Le v Hants (Leicester) 2010 (CB40). T20 HS 5*. T20 BB 3-21.

HALES, Alexander Daniel (Chesham S), b Hillingdon, Middx 3 Jan 1989. 6'5". RHB, RM, occ WK. Debut (Nottinghamshire) 2008; cap 2011. Nottinghamshire 2nd XI debut 2007. Buckinghamshire 2006-07. MCC YCs 2006-07. England U19s 2008. **IT20**: 4 (2011 to 2011-12); HS 62* v WI (Oval) 2011. 1000 runs (1): 1127 (2011). HS 184 v Somerset (Nottingham) 2011. BB 2-63 v Yorks (Nottingham) 2009. LO HS 150* v Worcs (Nottingham) 2009 (P40). T20 HS 83.

HUTTON, Brett Alan (Worksop C), b Doncaster, Yorks 6 Feb 1993. 6'2". RHB, RM. Debut (Nottinghamshire) 2011. Nottinghamshire 2nd XI debut 2010. HS 9 and BB – v MCC (Abu Dhabi) 2011. LO HS 17* and LO BB 1-60 v Sri Lanka A (Nottingham) 2011.

KELSALL, Samuel (Trentham HS, Stoke), b Stoke-on-Trent, Staffs 14 Mar 1993. RHB, RM. Debut (Nottinghamshire) 2011. Nottinghamshire 2nd XI debut 2008, aged 15y 158d. HS 11 v Durham (Chester-le-St) 2011 – only f-c game. LO HS 40 v Sri Lanka A (Nottingham) 2011.

‡**LUMB, Michael** John (St Stithians C, Johannesburg), b Johannesburg, South Africa 12 Feb 1980. Son of R.G.Lumb (Yorkshire 1970-84); nephew of A.J.S.Smith (SAU and Natal 1972-73 to 1983-84). 6'0". LHB, RM. Yorkshire 2000-06; ECB qualified and CC debut 2001; cap 2003. Hampshire 2007-11; cap 2008. **IT20**: 8 (2009-10 to 2011); HS 33 v SL (Gros Islet) 2009-10. F-c Tour (Eng A): I 2003-04. 1000 runs (2); most – 1038 (2003). HS 219 H v Notts (Nottingham) 2009. BB 2-10 Y v Kent (Canterbury) 2001. LO HS 110 EL v Pakistan A (Dubai) 2009-10. LO BB – . T20 HS 124* H v Essex (Southampton) 2009 – H record. T20 BB 3-32.

MULLANEY, Steven John (St Mary's RC S, Astley), b Warrington, Cheshire 19 Nov 1986. 5'9". RHB, RM. Lancashire 2006-08. No f-c appearances in 2009. Nottinghamshire debut 2010, scoring 100* v Hants (Southampton). HS 165* La v Durham UCCE (Durham) 2007. Nt HS (*see above*). BB 4-31 v Essex (Nottingham) 2010. LO HS 61 v Sri Lanka A (Nottingham) 2011. LO BB 3-13 La v Derbys (Derby) 2007 (FPT). T20 HS 53. T20 BB 3-12.

PATEL, Samit Rohit (Worksop C), b Leicester 30 Nov 1984. Elder brother of A.Patel (*see below*). 5'8". RHB, SLA. Debut (Nottinghamshire) 2002; cap 2008. Nottinghamshire 2nd XI debut 1999, aged 14y 274d. **LOI**: 25 (2008 to 2011-12); HS 70* v I (Mohali) 2011-12. and BB 5-41 v SA (Oval) 2008. **IT20**: 8 (2011 to 2011-12); HS 25* v I (Manchester) 2011; BB 2-22 v WI (Oval) 2011. F-c Tour: NZ 2008-09 (Eng A). HS 176 v Glos (Nottingham) 2007. BB 7-68 (11-111 match) v Hants (Southampton) 2011. LO HS 114 v Durham (Chester-le-St) 2008 (FPT). LO BB 6-13 v Ireland (Dublin) 2009 (FPT). T20 HS 84*. T20 BB 3-11.

PATTINSON, Darren John, b Grimsby, Lincs 2 Aug 1979. Elder brother of J.L.Pattinson (Victoria 2008-09 to date). 6'1". RHB, RFM. Victoria 2006-07 to date. Nottinghamshire debut 2008 taking 5-22 (8-85 match) v Kent (Canterbury); cap 2008. **Tests**: 1 (2008); HS 13 and BB 2-95 v SA (Leeds) 2008. HS 59 v Durham (Chester-le-St) 2009. BB 8-35 Vic v WA (Perth) 2010-11. Nt BB 6-30 v Lancs (Nottingham) 2008. LO HS 13* v Lancs (Nottingham) 2008. LO BB 4-29 v Warwks (Nottingham) 2008. T20 HS 12*. T20 BB 5-25 v Warwks (Birmingham) 2011 – Nt record.

PHILLIPS, Ben James (Langley Park S and SFC, Beckenham), b Lewisham, London 30 Sep 1974. 6'6". RHB, RFM. Kent 1996-98. Northamptonshire 2002-06; cap 2005. Somerset 2008-10, having joined staff in 2007 but missed entire season through injury. Nottinghamshire debut 2011. HS 100* K v Lancs (Manchester) 1997. Nt HS 71 v Yorks (Nottingham) 2011. BB 6-29 Nh v Cambridge UCCE (Cambridge) 2006. CC BB 5-47 K v Sussex (Horsham) 1997. NT BB – . LO HS 51* Sm v Worcs (Bath) 2010 (CB40). LO BB 4-25 K v Northants (Canterbury) 2000 (NL). T20 HS 41*. T20 BB 4-18.

155

READ, Christopher Mark Wells (Torquay GS; Bath U), b Paignton, Devon 10 Aug 1978. 5'8". RHB, WK. Gloucestershire (l-o only) 1997. Debut 1997-98 for England A in Kenya. Nottinghamshire debut 1998; cap 1999; captain 2008 to date; benefit 2009. MCC 2002. Devon 1995-97. **Tests**: 15 (1999 to 2006-07); HS 55 v P (Leeds) 2006. Made six dismissals twice in successive innings 2006-07 to establish an Ashes record. **LOI**: 36 (1999-00 to 2006-07); HS 30* v SA (Manchester) 2003. **IT20**: 1 (2006); HS 13 v P (Bristol) 2006. F-c Tours: A 2006-07; SA 1998-99 (Eng A), 1999-00; WI 1998-99 (Eng A), 2003-04, 2005-06 (Eng A); SL 1997-98 (Eng A), 2002-03 (ECB Acad), 2003-04; Z 1998-99 (Eng A); B 2003-04; K 1997-98 (Eng A). 1000 runs (2); most – 1203 (2009). HS 240 v Essex (Chelmsford) 2007. BB – . LO HS 135 v Durham (Nottingham) 2006 (CGT). T20 HS 58*.

SWANN, Graeme Peter (Sponne S, Towcester), b Northampton 24 Mar 1979. Son of R.Swann (Northumberland 1969-72; Bedfordshire 1988-95); younger brother of A.J.Swann (Northamptonshire and Lancashire 1996-2004). 6'0". RHB, OB. Northamptonshire 1998-2004; cap 1999. Nottinghamshire debut/cap 2005. MCC 2005. Bedfordshire 1996. *Wisden* 2009. **ECB central contract 2011-12**. **Tests**: 39 (2008-09 to 2011-12); HS 85 v SA (Centurion) 2009-10. BB 6-65 v P (Birmingham) 2010. **LOI**: 67 (1999-00 to 2011-12); HS 34 v SL (Dambulla) 2007-08; BB 5-28 v A (Chester-le-St) 2009. **IT20**: 30 (2007-08 to 2011-12); HS 15* v NZ (Auckland) 2007-08; BB 3-13 v P (Dubai) 2011-12. F-c Tours: A 2010-11; SA 1998-99 (Eng A), 1999-00, 2009-10; WI 2000-01 (Eng A *part*), 2008-09; I 2008-09; SL 2004-05 (Eng A); Z 1998-99 (Eng A); B 2009-10; UAE 2011-12 (v P). HS 183 Nh v Glos (Bristol) 2002 – including 114 before lunch on third day. Nt HS 97 v Essex (Chelmsford) 2007. 50 wkts (1): 57 (1999). BB 7-33 Nh v Derbys (Northampton) 2003. Nt BB 7-100 v Glamorgan (Swansea) 2007. LO HS 83 Nh v Leics (Northampton) 2001 (NL). LO BB 5-17 v Glos (Nottingham) 2007 (P40). T20 HS 90*. T20 BB 3-13.

‡TAYLOR, James William Arthur (Shrewsbury S), b Nottingham 6 Jan 1990. 5'6". RHB, LB. Leicestershire 2008-11; cap 2009. MCC 2010. Shropshire 2007. England U19s 2008 to 2009. YC 2009. **LOI**: 1 (2011); HS 1 v Ireland (Dublin) 2011. F-c Tour (EL): WI 2010-11. 1000 runs (3); most – 1602 (2011). HS 237 Le v Loughborough MCCU (Leicester) 2011. CC HS 207* Le v Surrey (Oval) 2009. BB – . LO HS 111 EL v Sri Lanka A (Northampton) 2011. LO BB 4-61 Le v Warwks (Leicester) 2010 (CB40). T20 HS 62*. T20 BB 1-10.

TURNER, Karl (Deerness Valley CS, Ushaw Moor), b Dryburn, Durham 29 Nov 1987. 5'10". LHB, RM. Debut (Nottinghamshire) 2011. Durham 2nd XI debut 2005. HS 64 v Sussex (Nottingham) 2011. LO HS 18 v Sri Lanka A (Nottingham) 2011.

NQVOGES, Adam Charles (Edith Cowan U, Perth), b Perth, Australia 4 Oct 1979. 6'0". RHB, SLC. Western Australia 2002-03 to date. Hampshire (l-o only) 2007. Nottinghamshire debut/cap 2008. **LOI** (A): 15 (2006-07 to 2010-11); HS 80* v E (Perth) 2010-11. BB 1-22 v I (Vadodara) 2009-10. **IT20** (A): 4 (2007-08 to 2009); HS 26 v NZ (Perth) 2007-08 and 26 v NZ (Sydney) 2008-09; BB 2-5 v I (Melbourne) 2007-08. F-c Tours (Aus A): I 2008-09; P 2007-08. HS 180 WA v Tas (Hobart) 2007-08. Nt HS 165 v Oxford MCCU (Oxford) 2011. CC HS 139 v Sussex (Horsham) 2009. BB 4-92 WA v S Aus (Adelaide) 2006-07. Nt BB 3-21 v Durham (Nottingham) 2008. LO HS 104* WA v S Aus (Adelaide) 2008-09. LO BB 3-25 v Sussex (Hove) 2009 (P40). T20 HS 82*. T20 BB 2-4.

NQWESSELS, Mattheus Hendrik (**'Riki'**) (Woodridge C, Pt Elizabeth; Northampton U), b Marogudoore, Queensland, Australia 12 Nov 1985. Left Australia when 2 months old. Son of K.C.Wessels (OFS, Sussex, WP, NT, Q, EP, GW, Australia and South Africa 1973-74 to 1999-00). 5'11". RHB, WK. MCC 2004. Northamptonshire 2005-09 (Kolpak registration). Nondescripts 2007-08. Mid West Rhinos 2009-10 to date. Nottinghamshire debut 2011. HS 197 MWR v MT (Bulawayo) 2011-12. CC HS 109 v Surrey (Oval) 2009. Nt HS 84 v Durham (Nottingham) 2011. BB 1-10 MWR v MT (Bulawayo) 2009-10. LO HS 100 Nh v Surrey (Oval) 2008 (P40). LO BB 1-0 MWR v Matabeleland Tuskers (Bulawayo) 2009-10. T20 HS 86*.

WHITE, Graeme Geoffrey (Stowe S), b Milton Keynes, Bucks 18 Apr 1987. 5'11". RHB, SLA. Northamptonshire 2006-09. Nottinghamshire debut 2010. HS 65 Nh v Glamorgan (Colwyn Bay) 2007. Nt HS 54* v Lancs (Southport) 2011. BB 4-72 v Durham (Nottingham) 2011. LO HS 25 v Lancs (Nottingham) 2011 (CB40). LO BB 5-35 v Scotland (Edinburgh) 2010 (CB40). T20 HS 26*. T20 BB 3-22.

WOOD, Samuel Kenneth (Colonel Frank Seely S, Nottingham), b Nottingham 3 Apr 1993. LHB, OB. Debut (Nottinghamshire) 2011. Nottinghamshire 2nd XI debut 2008, aged 15y 40d. England U19s 2010-11. HS and BB – . LO HS 8 and LO BB 2-24 v Lancs (Manchester) 2011 (CB40).

RELEASED/RETIRED
(Having made a County First-Class or List A appearance in 2011)

BRAVO, Darren Michael, b Santa Cruz, Trinidad 6 Feb 1989. LHB, RM. Half-brother of D.J.Bravo (T&T, Kent, WI 2001-02 to date); cousin of B.C.Lara (T&T, Warwicks, WI 1987-88 to 2007-08). Trinidad & Tobago 2006-07 to date. Nottinghamshire 2011; cap 2011. **Tests** (WI): 13 (2010-11 to 2011-12); HS 195 v B (Dhaka) 2011-12. **LOI** (WI): 34 (2009 to 2011-12); HS 86 v I (Kingston) 2011. **IT20** (WI): 4 (2009-10 to 2011-12); HS 42 v P (Gros Islet) 2010-11. F-c Tours (WI): I 2011-12; SL 2010-11; B 2010 (WI A), 2011-12. HS 195 (*see Tests*). Nt HS 70 v Warwks (Birmingham) 2011. BB 1-9 T&T v Windward Is (Kingstown) 2008-09. LO HS 107* WI A v SA A (Mirpur) 2010. T20 HS 70.

BROWN, Alistair Duncan (Caterham S), b Beckenham, Kent 11 Feb 1970. 5'10". RHB, OB, occ WK. Surrey 1992-2008; cap 1994; benefit 2002. TCCB XI 1996. Walter Lawrence Trophy for fastest f-c hundred 1998. Nottinghamshire 2009-11; cap 2009. **LOI**: 16 (1996 to 2001); HS 118 v I (Manchester) 1996. 1000 runs (8); most – 1382 (1993). HS 295* Sy v Leics (Oakham) 2000 – record score (all levels) in Rutland. Nt HS 148 v Hants (Southampton) 2009. BB 3-25 Sy v Somerset (Guildford) 2006. Nt BB 1-16 v Yorks (Nottingham) 2009. LO HS 268 Sy v Glamorgan (Oval) 2002 (CGT) – world record l-o score (160 balls, 12 sixes, 30 fours). LO BB 3-39 Sy v Notts (Nottingham) 2000 (NL). T20 HS 83.

[NQ]**HUSSEY, David** John (Prendiville Catholic C; Edith Cowan U), b Morley, Perth, Australia 15 Jul 1977. Younger brother of M.E.K.Hussey (WA, Northants, Glos, Durham and Australia 1994-95 to date). 5'11". RHB, OB. Victoria 2002-03 to date. Nottinghamshire 2004-11; cap 2004; scored 107* v Oxford U (Oxford) – on UK debut. Sussex CB (List A) 2001. **LOI** (A): 50 (2008 to 2011-12); HS 111 v Scotland (Edinburgh) 2009; BB 4-21 v E (Adelaide) 2010-11. **IT20** (A): 34 (2007-08 to 2011-12); HS 88* v SA (Johannesburg) 2008-09; BB 3-25 v SA (Melbourne) 2008-09. F-c Tour (Aus A): P 2007-08. 1000 runs (4+1); most – 1315 (2004). HS 275 v Essex (Nottingham) 2007. Scored 170, 116 and 140 in successive innings 2004. BB 4-105 v Hants (Nottingham) 2005. LO HS 130 Vic v Q (Brisbane) 2005-06. LO BB 4-21 (*see LOI*). T20 HS 100*. T20 BB 3-25.

PATEL, Akhil (Kimberley CS, Nottingham), b Nottingham 18 Jun 1990. Younger brother of S.R.Patel (*see above*). 5'10". LHB, SLC. Derbyshire 2007. Nottinghamshire 2009-11, scoring 69* v Oxford UCCE (Oxford) on debut. HS (*see above*). CC HS 37 v Sussex (Nottingham) 2009. BB 1-34 v Oxford UCCE (Oxford) 2009. LO HS 41 v Glos (Nottingham) 2009 (P40). LO BB 2-34 v Hants (Southampton) 2009 (P40).

SHRECK, C.E. – *see KENT.*

WAGH, Mark Anant (King Edward's S, Birmingham; Keble C, Oxford), b Birmingham, Warwks 20 Oct 1976. 6'2". RHB, OB. Oxford U 1996-98; blue 1996-97-98; captain 1997. Warwickshire 1997-2006; cap 2000. British U 1996-1998. Mashonaland A 1998-99. Nottinghamshire 2007-11; cap 2007. 1000 runs (6); most – 1310 (2007). HS 315 Wa v Middx (Lord's) 2001. Nt HS 152 v Northants (Northampton) 2007. BB 7-222 Wa v Lancs (Birmingham) 2003. Nt BB 2-6 v Somerset (Taunton) 2007. LO HS 102* Wa v Kent (Birmingham) 2004 (NL). LO BB 4-35 Wa v Glamorgan (Birmingham) 2004 (NL). T20 HS 56. T20 BB 2-16.

MIDDLESEX RELEASED/RETIRED (continued from p 144)
(Having made a County First-Class or List A appearance in 2011)

DALRYMPLE, James William Murray (Radley C; St Peter's C, Oxford), b Nairobi, Kenya 21 Jan 1981. Brother of S.H.Dalrymple (Oxford U 2002-04). 5'11". RHB, OB. Oxford UCCE/U 2001-03; captain 2002; blue 2001-02-03. British U 2001-02. Middlesex 2001-07, 2011; cap 2004. Glamorgan 2008-10; cap 2008; captain 2009-10. **LOI**: 27 (2006 to 2006-07); HS 67 v SL (Lord's) 2006; BB 2-5 v I (Jaipur) 2006-07. **IT20**: 3 (2006 to 2006-07); HS 32 v A (Sydney) 2006-07; BB 1-10 v P (Bristol) 2006. F-c Tour (Eng A): WI 2005-06. 1000 runs (1): 1009 (2009). HS 244 v Surrey (Oval) 2004. BB 5-49 OU v CU (Cambridge) 2003. CC BB 4-53 v Hants (Southgate) 2005. LO HS 107 v Glamorgan (Lord's) 2004 (CGT). LO BB 4-14 v Essex (Southgate) 2001 (NL). T20 HS 63. T20 BB 3-25.

HOUSEGO, D.M. – *see GLOUCESTERSHIRE.*

SCOTT, B.J.M. – *see WORCESTERSHIRE.*

R.McLaren left the staff without making a County First-Class or List A appearance in 2011.

NOTTINGHAMSHIRE 2011

RESULTS SUMMARY

	Place	Won	Lost	Tied	Drew	NR
LV= County Championship (1st Division)	6th	5	6		5	
All First-Class Matches		5	6		6	
Clydesdale Bank 40 (Group C)	2nd	7	4			1
Friends Life t20 (North Group)	QF	11	3			3

LV= COUNTY CHAMPIONSHIP AVERAGES

BATTING AND FIELDING

Cap		M	I	NO	HS	Runs	Avge	100	50	Ct/St
2011	A.D.Hales	12	22	2	184	1023	51.15	3	7	14
2008	S.R.Patel	11	19	1	128	756	42.00	2	5	5
2008	A.C.Voges	11	19	1	80	680	37.77	–	7	18
1999	C.M.W.Read	16	28	4	133*	897	37.37	2	4	47/4
2011	D.M.Bravo	4	7	–	70	248	35.42	–	2	1
1999	P.J.Franks	13	23	2	96	576	27.42	–	4	5
	K.Turner	5	9	–	64	227	25.22	–	1	1
2007	A.R.Adams	16	27	4	64	551	23.95	–	5	5
2008	D.J.Pattinson	6	10	4	35*	136	22.66	–	–	1
	M.H.Wessels	10	19	–	84	384	20.21	–	3	6
	S.J.Mullaney	16	28	–	83	544	19.42	–	2	12
	S.C.J.Broad	3	5	–	26	97	19.40	–	–	–
2007	M.A.Wagh	7	14	2	48	195	16.25	–	–	2
	N.J.Edwards	7	14	3	64	172	15.63	–	1	6
	G.G.White	6	10	1	54*	140	15.55	–	1	4
	A.Patel	3	6	–	24	74	12.33	–	–	–
2005	G.P.Swann	2	4	–	25	42	10.50	–	–	1
	L.J.Fletcher	12	19	4	39	153	10.20	–	–	2
2006	C.E.Shreck	10	13	10	7*	25	8.33	–	–	2
2009	A.D.Brown	3	5	–	12	33	6.60	–	–	1

Also played (one match each): D.J.Hussey (cap 2004) 5, 13 (5 ct); S.Kelsall 11, 4 (1 ct); B.J.Phillips 71* (1 ct); S.K.W.Wood did not bat.

BOWLING

	O	M	R	W	Avge	Best	5wI	10wM
A.R.Adams	479.3	93	1515	67	22.61	6-31	7	2
S.R.Patel	265.4	47	798	31	25.74	7-68	1	1
D.J.Pattinson	158.5	34	503	19	26.47	5-44	1	–
C.E.Shreck	281.5	62	945	34	27.79	5-52	1	–
L.J.Fletcher	383.4	83	1186	36	32.94	5-82	1	–
S.C.J.Broad	111.3	24	384	11	34.90	5-95	1	–
G.G.White	119	19	463	13	35.61	4-72	–	–
P.J.Franks	307	53	1039	20	51.95	4-50	–	–

Also bowled:
S.J.Mullaney 114.5 25 351 5 70.20 1-13
A.Patel 1.5-0-10-0; B.J.Phillips 37.2-5-139-0; G.P.Swann 42-5-144-3; S.K.W.Wood 4-1-8-0.

The First-Class Averages (pp 223–240) give the records of Nottinghamshire players in all first-class county matches (Nottinghamshire's other opponents being Oxford MCCU), with the exception of S.C.J.Broad, C.E.Shreck and G.P.Swann, whose first-class figures for Nottinghamshire are as above, and:

    A.D.Hales 13-24-2-184-1035-47.04-3-7-14ct. 1-0-1-0.
    S.R.Patel 12-21-1-128-861-43.05-2-6-5ct. 305.4-54-915-32-28.59-7/68-1-1.

NOTTINGHAMSHIRE RECORDS

FIRST-CLASS CRICKET

Highest Total	For	791		v	Essex	Chelmsford	2007
	V	781-7d		by	Northants	Northampton	1995
Lowest Total	For	13		v	Yorkshire	Nottingham	1901
	V	16		by	Derbyshire	Nottingham	1879
		16		by	Surrey	The Oval	1880
Highest Innings	For	312*	W.W.Keeton	v	Middlesex	The Oval	1939
	V	345	C.G.Macartney	for	Australians	Nottingham	1921

Highest Partnership for each Wicket

1st	406*	D.J.Bicknell/G.E.Welton	v	Warwicks	Birmingham	2000
2nd	398	A.Shrewsbury/W.Gunn	v	Sussex	Nottingham	1890
3rd	367	W.Gunn/J.R.Gunn	v	Leics	Nottingham	1903
4th	361	A.O.Jones/J.R.Gunn	v	Essex	Leyton	1905
5th	359	D.J.Hussey/C.M.W.Read	v	Essex	Nottingham	2007
6th	372*	K.P.Pietersen/J.E.Morris	v	Derbyshire	Derby	2001
7th	301	C.C.Lewis/B.N.French	v	Durham	Chester-le-St[2]	1993
8th	220	G.F.H.Heane/R.Winrow	v	Somerset	Nottingham	1935
9th	170	J.C.Adams/K.P.Evans	v	Somerset	Taunton	1994
10th	152	E.B.Alletson/W.Riley	v	Sussex	Hove	1911
	152	U.Afzaal/A.J.Harris	v	Worcs	Nottingham	2000

Best Bowling	For	10-66	K.Smales	v	Glos	Stroud	1956
(Innings)	V	10-10	H.Verity	for	Yorkshire	Leeds	1932
Best Bowling	For	17-89	F.C.L.Matthews	v	Northants	Nottingham	1923
(Match)	V	17-89	W.G.Grace	for	Glos	Cheltenham	1877

Most Runs – Season	2620	W.W.Whysall	(av 53.46)	1929
Most Runs – Career	31592	G.Gunn	(av 35.69)	1902-32
Most 100s – Season	9	W.W.Whysall		1928
	9	M.J.Harris		1971
	9	B.C.Broad		1990
Most 100s – Career	65	J.Hardstaff jr		1930-55
Most Wkts – Season	181	B.Dooland	(av 14.96)	1954
Most Wkts – Career	1653	T.G.Wass	(av 20.34)	1896-1920
Most Career W-K Dismissals	957	T.W.Oates	(733 ct; 224 st)	1897-1925
Most Career Catches in the Field	466	A.O.Jones		1892-1914

LIMITED-OVERS CRICKET

Highest Total	50ov	346-9		v	Ireland	Nottingham	2009
	40ov	329-6		v	Derbyshire	Nottingham	1993
	T20	215-6		v	Yorkshire	Nottingham	2011
Lowest Total	50ov	123		v	Yorkshire	Scarborough	1969
	40ov	57		v	Glos	Nottingham	2009
	T20	91		v	Lancashire	Manchester	2006
Highest Innings	50ov	149*	D.W.Randall	v	Devon	Torquay	1988
	40ov	167*	P.Johnson	v	Kent	Nottingham	1993
	T20	91	M.A.Ealham	v	Yorkshire	Nottingham	2004
Best Bowling	50ov	6-10	K.P.Evans	v	Northumb	Jesmond	1994
	40ov	6-12	R.J.Hadlee	v	Lancashire	Nottingham	1980
	T20	5-25	D.J.Pattinson	v	Warwicks	Birmingham	2011

SOMERSET

Formation of Present Club: 18 August 1875
Inaugural First-Class Match: 1882
Colours: Black, White and Maroon
Badge: Somerset Dragon
County Champions: (0); best – 2nd (Div 1) 2001, 2010
Gillette/NatWest/C&G/FP Trophy Winners: (3) 1979, 1983, 2001
Benson and Hedges Cup Winners: (2) 1981, 1982
Pro 40/National League (Div 1) Winners: (0); best – 4th 2001
Sunday League Winners: (1) 1979
Clydesdale Bank 40 Winners: (0); best – Finalist 2010, 2011
Twenty20 Cup Winners: (1) 2005

Chief Executive: Guy Lavender, County Ground, Taunton TA1 1JT • Tel: 0845 337 1875 • Fax: 01823 332395 • Email: enquiries@somersetcountycc.co.uk • Web: www.somerset cricketclub.co.uk

Director of Cricket: Brian C.Rose. **Head Coach:** Andy Hurry. **Asst Coach:** Jason Kerr. **Captain:** M.E.Trescothick. **Vice-Captain:** A.C.Thomas. **Overseas Players:** C.H.Gayle (T20 only), J.A.Morkel (T20 only) and V.D.Philander. **2012 Beneficiary:** none. **Grounds-man:** Simon Lee. **Scorer:** Gerald A.Stickley. ‡ New registration. [NQ] Not qualified for England.

BARROW, Alexander William Rodgerson (King's C, Taunton), b Frome 6 May 1992. 5'7". RHB, RM/OB. Debut (Somerset) 2011. Somerset 2nd XI debut 2009. HS 69 v Yorks (Leeds) 2011. BB 1-4 v Hants (Southampton) 2011.

BUTTLER, Joseph Charles (King's C, Taunton), b Taunton 8 Sep 1990. 6'0". RHB, WK. Debut (Somerset) 2009. Somerset 2nd XI debut 2006. **LOI:** 1 (2011-12); HS 0 v P (Dubai) 2011-12. **IT20:** 7 (2011 to 2011-12); HS 13 v WI (Oval) 2011. HS 144 v Hants (Southampton) 2010. LO HS 119 EL v Sri Lanka A (Kurunegala) 2011-12. T20 HS 72*.

COMPTON, Nicholas Richard Denis (Harrow S; Durham U), b Durban, South Africa 26 Jun 1983. Son of R.Compton (Natal 1978-79 to 1980-81). Grandson of D.C.S.Compton (Middlesex, England, Holkar, Europeans, Commonwealth and Cavaliers 1936-64); great-nephew of L.H.Compton (Middlesex 1938-56). 6'1". RHB, OB. Middlesex 2004-09; cap 2006. Somerset debut 2010; cap 2011. Mashonaland Eagles 2010-11. MCC 2007. F-c Tour (Eng A): B 2006-07. 1000 runs (2); most – 1315 (2006). HS 254* v Durham (Chester-le-St) 2011. BB 1-1 v Hants (Southampton) 2010. LO HS 131 M v Kent (Canterbury) 2009 (FPT). LO BB 1-0 M v Scotland (Lord's) 2009 (FPT). T20 HS 74.

DIBBLE, Adam John (Taunton S), b Exeter, Devon 9 Mar 1991. 6'4". RHB, RMF. Debut (Somerset) 2011. Somerset 2nd XI debut 2009. Devon 2009. HS 39* v Notts (Nottingham) 2011. BB 1-26 v Yorks (Leeds) 2011. LO HS – . LO BB 3-52 v Glos (Taunton) 2011 (CB40). T20 HS – . T20 BB 1-20.

DOCKRELL, George Henry (Gonzaga C, Dublin), b Dublin, Ireland 22 Jul 1992. RHB, SLA. Ireland 2010 to date. Somerset debut 2011. **LOI:** (Ire): 28 (2009-10 to 2011-12); HS 19 v WI (Mohali) 2010-11; BB 4-35 v Netherlands (Amstelveen) 2010. **IT20:** (Ire): 10 (2009-10 to 2011-12); HS 2* v Kenya (Mombasa) 2011-12; BB 4-20 v Netherlands (Dubai) 2009-10. HS 53 Ire v Namibia (Belfast) 2011. Sm HS 14 and Sm BB 2-76 v Notts (Taunton) 2011. BB 5-37 (9-87 match) Ire v Kenya (Mombasa) 2011-12. LO HS 22* Ire v Namibia (Belfast) 2011. LO BB 4-35 (*see LOI*). T20 HS 2*. T20 BB 4-20.

161

‡NQGAYLE, Christopher Henry (Excelsior HS), b Kingston, Jamaica 21 Sep 1979. 6'3".
LHB, OB. Jamaica 1998-99 to date. Worcestershire 2005. Joins Somerset in 2012 for T20
only. Tests (WI): 91 (1999-00 to 2010-11, 20 as captain); HS 333 v SL (Galle) 2010-11; BB
5-34 v E (Birmingham) 2004. LOI (WI): 228 (1999 to 2010-11, 53 as captain); HS 153* v
Z (Bulawayo) 2003-04; BB 5-46 v A (St George's) 2003. IT20 (WI): 20 (2005-06 to 2010,
17 as captain); HS 117 v SA (Johannesburg) 2007, 2nd highest score in all IT20s; BB 2-15
v A (Hobart) 2009-10. F-c Tours (WI) (C=captain): E 2000, 2002 (WI A), 2004, 2007,
2009C; A 2005-06, 2009-10C; SA 2003-04, 2007-08C; NZ 2005-06, 2008-09C; I 2002-03,
2005-06; P 2006-07; SL 2001-02, 2010-11; Z 2001, 2003-04; B 2002-03. HS 333 (see
Tests). CC HS 57 and CC BB 2-18 Wo v Leics (Worcester) 2005. BB 5-34 (see Tests). LO
HS 153* (see LOI). LO BB 5-46 (see LOI). T20 HS 117. T20 BB 4-22.

GREGORY, Lewis (Hele's S, Plympton), b Plymouth, Devon 24 May 1992. 6'0". RHB,
RMF. Debut (Somerset) 2011. Somerset 2nd XI debut 2008, aged 16y and 87d. Devon 2008.
England U19s 2010 to 2010-11. HS 48 v Warwks (Birmingham) 2011. BB 1-15 v Durham
(Chester-le-St) 2011. LO HS 11 v Unicorns (Wormsley) 2011 (CB40). LO BB 4-27 v Glos
(Taunton) 2011 (CB40). T20 HS 15. T20 BB 4-15.

HILDRETH James Charles (Millfield S), b Milton Keynes, Bucks 9 Sep 1984. 5'10",
RHB, RMF. Debut (Somerset) 2003; cap 2007. F-c Tour (EL): WI 2010-11. 1000 runs (2);
most – 1440 (2010). HS 303* v Warwks (Taunton) 2009. BB 2-39 v Hants (Taunton) 2004.
LO HS 151 v Scotland (Taunton) 2009 (FPT). LO BB 2-26 v Worcs (Worcester) 2008
(FPT). T20 HS 77*. T20 BB 3-24.

HUSSAIN, Gemaal Maqsood (Top Valley CS, Nottingham; High Pavement SFC, Nottingham), b Whipps Cross, London, 10 Oct 1983. 6'5". RHB, RMF. Gloucestershire 2009-10;
cap 2009. Somerset debut 2011. Bradford/Leeds UCCE 2003 (not f-c). HS 42 v Lancs
(Liverpool) 2011. 50 wkts (1): 67 (2010). BB 6-33 v Worcs (Taunton) 2011. LO HS 16* v
Glamorgan (Cardiff) 2011 (CB40). BB 2-17 Gs v Notts (Nottingham) 2009 (P40). T20 HS
8. T20 BB 3-22.

JONES, Chris Robert (Poole GS; Richard Huish C, Taunton), b Harold Wood, Essex 5 Nov
1990. 6'3". RHB, RM. Debut (Somerset) 2010. Durham MCCU 2011. Somerset 2nd XI
debut 2006, aged 15y 290d. Dorset 2008-11. HS 69 DU v Yorks (Durham) 2011. Sm HS 55
v Notts (Nottingham) 2011. LO HS 45* v Essex (Taunton) 2011 (CB40). T20 HS 16.

KIESWETTER, Craig (Diocesan C; Millfield S), b Johannesburg, South Africa 18 Nov
1987. 6'1". RHB, WK. Debut (Somerset) 2007; cap 2009. Represented South Africa in U19
World Cup 2006. Qualified for England Feb 2010. LOI: 32 (2009-10 to 2011-12); HS 107 v
B (Chittagong) 2009-10. IT20: 17 (2009-10 to 2011-12); HS 63 v A (Bridgetown) 2009-10.
F-c Tour (EL): WI 2010-11. 1000 runs (1): 1242 (2009). HS 164 v Notts (Nottingham)
2011. LO HS 143 England XI v Bangladesh CB (Fatullah) 2009-10. T20 HS 84.

KIRBY, Steven Paul (Elton HS; Bury C), b Ainsworth, nr Bolton, Lancs 4 Oct 1977. 6'3½".
RHB, RFM. Leicestershire staff 1998 – no f-c appearances. Yorkshire 2001-04, debut as sub
for M.J.Hoggard (England duty) taking 7-50; cap 2003. Gloucestershire 2005-10; cap 2005.
Somerset debut 2011. MCC 2008, 2010-11. F-c Tour (Eng A): I 2003-04 (part). Hs 57 Y v
Hants (Leeds) 2002. Sm HS 19 v Durham (Taunton) 2011. 50 wkts (3); most – 67 (2003).
BB 8-80 (13-154 match) Y v Somerset (Taunton) 2003. Sm BB 6-115 v Lancs (Liverpool)
2011. LO HS 15 Y v Leics (Leicester) 2003 (NL). LO BB 5-36 Gs v Middx (Lord's) 2007
(FPT). T20 HS 25. T20 BB 3-17.

LEACH, Matthew Jack (UWIC), b Taunton 22 Jun 1991. RHB, SLA. Somerset 2nd XI
debut 2009. Dorset 2011. Cardiff MCCU 2011 (not f-c). Awaiting 1st XI debut.

MESCHEDE, Craig Anthony Joseph (King's C, Taunton), b Johannesburg, South Africa 21 Nov 1991. 6'1". RHB, RMF. Debut (Somerset) 2011. Somerset 2nd XI debut 2008, aged 16y 244d. HS 53 v Hants (Taunton) 2011. BB 1-14 v Indians (Taunton) 2011. CC BB 1-24 v Lancs (Taunton) 2011. LO HS 19 v Notts (Taunton) 2011 (CB40). LO BB 2-16 v Essex (Taunton) 2011 (CB40). T20 HS 53. T20 BB 3-9.

‡^{NQ}**MORKEL**, Johannes Albertus ('**Albie**') (Hoërskool Vereeniging), b Vereeniging, Transvaal, South Africa 10 June 1981. 6'1". Brother of M.Morkel (Easterns, Titans, Yorkshire, South Africa 2003-04 to date). LHB, RM. Easterns 1999-00 to 2005-06. Titans 2004-05 to date. Durham 2008. Joins Somerset in 2012 for T20 only. **Tests** (SA): 1 (2008-09); HS 58 and BB 1-44 v A (Cape Town) 2008-09. **LOI** (SA): 58 (2003-04 to 2011-12); HS 97 v Z (Harare) 2007; BB 4-29 v B (Dhaka) 2007-08. **IT20** (SA): 34 (2005-06 to 2011-12); HS 43 and BB 2-12 v E (Cape Town) 2007-08. HS 204* Titans v WP (Paarl) 2004-05. CC HS 37 Du v Yorks (Leeds) 2008. BB 6-36 EP v GW (Kimberley) 1999-00. LO HS 97 (*see LOI*). LO BB 4-23 EP v FS (Bloemfontein) 1999-00. T20 HS 71*. T20 BB 4-30.

‡^{NQ}**PHILANDER, Vernon** Darryl, b Bellville, Cape Province, South Africa 24 Jun 1985. RHB, RMF. Western Province 2003-04 to 2009-10. WP Boland 2004-05. Cape Cobras 2005-06 to date. Middlesex 2008. Devon 2004. **Tests** (SA): 4 (2011-12); HS 23 v A (Johannesburg) 2011-12; BB 5-15 v A (Cape Town) 2011-12. **LOI** (SA): 8 (2007 to 2011-12); HS 23 v E (Leeds) 2008; BB 4-12 v Ireland (Belfast) 2007 – on debut. **IT20** (SA): 7 (2007-08); HS 6 v E (Cape Town) 2007-08; BB 2-23 v B (Cape Town) 2007-08. F-c Tours (SA A): SL 2010; B 2010. HS 168 WP v GW (Kimberley) 2004-05. CC HS 30 and BB 3-45 M v Essex (Chelmsford) 2008. 50 wkts (0+2); most – 59 (2009-10). BB 7-61 (9-89 match) Cape Cobras v Knights (Cape Town) 2011-12. LO HS 79* SA A v Bangladesh A (East London) 2010-11. LO BB 4-12 (*see LOI*). T20 HS 56*. T20 BB 5-17.

^{NQ}**SUPPIAH, Arul** Vivasvan (Millfield S; Exeter U), b Kuala Lumpur, Malaysia 30 Aug 1983. Son of R.Suppiah (Kuala Lumpur). Brother of R.V.Suppiah (Malaysia 1997-98 to 2006; f-c 2004). 6'0". RHB, SLA. Debut (Somerset) 2002; cap 2009. Malaysia 2000-01 to 2005 (not f-c). Devon 2003-05. 1000 runs (1): 1201 (2009). HS 156 v Indians (Taunton) 2011. CC HS 151 v Notts (Taunton) 2009. BB 3-46 v West Indies A (Taunton) 2002. CC BB 3-58 v Hants (Taunton) 2009. LO HS 80 v Lancs (Manchester) 2010 (CB40). LO BB 4-39 v Surrey (Oval) 2006 (CGT). T20 HS 32*. T20 BB 6-5 v Glamorgan (Cardiff) 2011 – world record T20 analysis.

^{NQ}**THOMAS, Alfonso** Clive (Ravensmead SS; Parow HS), b Cape Town, South Africa 9 Feb 1977. 5'10". RHB, RFM. W Province 1998-99. North West 2000-01 to 2002-03. Northerns 2003-04 to 2005-06. Titans 2004-05 to 2007-08. Warwickshire 2007. Somerset debut 2008; cap 2008 (Kolpak registration). **IT20** (SA): 1 (2006-07); HS-and BB 3-25 v P (Johannesburg) 2006-07. F-c Tour (SA A): Z 2004. HS 119* North West v Northerns (Pretoria) 2002-03. UK HS 94 v Hants (Taunton) 2011. BB 7-54 Titans v Cape Cobras (Cape Town) 2005-06. UK BB 6-60 (10-88 match) v Sussex (Taunton) 2011. LO HS 28* v Scotland (Edinburgh) 2009 (FPT). LO BB 4-18 v Glos (Bristol) 2009 (P40). T20 HS 30*. T20 BB 4-27.

TREGO, Peter David (Wyvern CS, W-s-M), b Weston-super-Mare 12 Jun 1981. 6'0". RHB, RMF. Somerset 2000-02, 2006 to date; cap 2007; 2nd XI debut 1997, aged 16y 20d. Kent 2003. Middlesex 2005. Herefordshire 2005. HS 140 v West Indies A (Taunton) 2002. CC HS 135 v Derbys (Taunton) 2006. BB 6-59 M v Notts (Nottingham) 2005. Sm BB 4-22 v Worcs (Worcester) 2011. LO HS 147 v Glamorgan (Taunton) 2010 (CB40). LO BB 5-40 EL v West Indies A (Worcester) 2010. T20 HS 79. T20 BB 4-27.

TRESCOTHICK, Marcus Edward (Sir Bernard Lovell S), b Keynsham 25 Dec 1975. 6'2". LHB, RM, occ WK. Debut (Somerset) 1993; cap 1999; joint captain 2002; benefit 2008; captain 2010 to date. PCA 2000, 2009, 2011. *Wisden* 2004. MBE 2005. **Tests**: 76 (2000 to 2006, 2 as captain); HS 219 v SA (Oval) 2003; BB 1-34 v P (Karachi) 2000-01. **LOI**: 123 (2000 to 2006, 10 as captain); HS 137 v P (Lord's) 2001; BB 2-7 v Z (Manchester) 2000. **IT20**: 3 (2005 to 2006); HS 72 v SL (Southampton) 2006. F-c Tours: A 2002-03; SA 2004-05; WI 2003-04; NZ 1999-00 (Eng A), 2001-02; I 2001-02, 2005-06 (*part*); P 2000-01, 2005-06; SL 2000-01, 2003-04; B 1999-00 (Eng A), 2003-04. 1000 runs (5); most – 1817 (2009). HS 284 v Northants (Northampton) 2007. BB 4-36 (inc hat-trick) v Young A (Taunton) 1995. CC BB 4-82 v Yorks (Leeds) 1998. Hat-trick 1995 (*see above*). LO HS 184 v Glos (Taunton) 2008 (P40) – Sm record. LO BB 4-50 v Northants (Northampton) 2000 (NL). T20 HS 108*.

WALLER, Maximilian Thomas Charles (Millfield S; Bournemouth U), b Salisbury, Wiltshire 3 March 1988. 6'0". RHB, LB. Debut (Somerset) 2009. Somerset 2nd XI debut 2006. Dorset 2007-08. HS 28 v Hants (Southampton) 2009. BB 2-27 v Sussex (Hove) 2009. LO HS 5 v Lancs (Manchester) 2010 (CB40). LO BB 2-24 v Unicorns (Exmouth) 2010 (CB40). T20 HS 3. T20 BB 3-16.

RELEASED/RETIRED
(Having made a County First-Class or List A appearance in 2011)

KARTIK, M. – *see SURREY*.

NQMENDIS, Balapuwaduge **Ajantha** Winslo, b Moratuwa, Sri Lanka, 11 March 1985. RHB, LBG. Sri Lanka Army 2006-07 to date. Somerset 2011. **Tests** (SL): 16 (2008 to 2011); HS 78 v I (Colombo, PSS) 2010; BB 6-117 (match 10-209) v I (Galle) 2008. **LOI** (SL): 59 (2007-08 to 2011-12); HS 15* v B (Lahore) 2008 and v UAE (Lahore) 2008; BB 6-13 v I (Karachi) 2008. **IT20** (SL): 21 (2008-09 to 2011-12); HS 4* v Ireland (Lord's) 2009; BB 6-16 v A (Pallekele) 2011 – record IT20 analysis. F-c Tours (SL): E 2011; SA 2011-12; I 2009-10; P 2008-09; Z 2008-09; B 2008-09. HS 78 (*see Tests*). Sm HS 28 and Sm BB 4-183 v Warwks (Taunton) 2011. 50 wkts (0+1): 68 (2007-08). BB 7-37 SL Army v Lankan (Panagoda) 2007-08. LO HS 71* SL Army v Kurunegala Youth (Welisara) 2006-07. LO BB 6-12 SL Army v Seeduwa Raddoluwa (Panagoda) 2010-11. T20 HS 15. T20 BB 6-16.

WILLOUGHBY, C.M. – *see ESSEX*.

J.E.Burke, C.J.Haggett and K.A.Pollard left the staff, without making a County First-Class or List A appearance in 2011.

SOMERSET 2011

RESULTS SUMMARY

	Place	Won	Lost	Tied	Drew	NR
LV= County Championship (1st Division)	4th	6	7		3	
All First-Class Matches		6	7		4	
Clydesdale Bank 40 (Group C)	Finalist	10	3			1
Friends Life t20 (South Group)	Finalist	9	5	1		4

LV= COUNTY CHAMPIONSHIP AVERAGES

BATTING AND FIELDING

Cap		M	I	NO	HS	Runs	Avge	100	50	Ct/St
1999	M.E.Trescothick	13	23	2	227	1673	79.66	6	6	29
2011	N.R.D.Compton	13	22	4	254*	1010	56.11	2	5	5
2009	C.Kieswetter	9	14	–	164	572	40.85	2	3	27/1
2007	J.C.Hildreth	15	23	–	186	893	38.82	2	4	21
2008	A.C.Thomas	7	10	–	94	333	33.30	–	1	–
	J.C.Buttler	12	18	1	100	524	30.82	1	3	28/1
2009	A.V.Suppiah	16	29	3	95	760	29.23	–	6	11
	M.Kartik	8	13	3	65*	285	28.50	–	2	4
2007	P.D.Trego	16	25	4	120	591	28.14	1	4	10
	C.A.J.Meschede	4	8	1	53	149	21.28	–	1	–
	A.J.Dibble	2	4	2	39*	40	20.00	–	–	–
	A.W.R.Barrow	7	11	–	69	218	19.81	–	1	4
	L.Gregory	5	8	1	48	98	14.00	–	–	–
	B.A.W.Mendis	2	4	–	28	51	12.75	–	–	–
	C.R.Jones	7	11	–	55	118	10.72	–	1	4
	S.P.Kirby	16	24	3	19	143	6.80	–	–	5
	G.M.Hussain	9	14	2	42	75	6.25	–	–	2
2007	C.M.Willoughby	14	19	8	23*	51	4.63	–	–	2

Also played (one match each): G.H.Dockrell 14; S.D.Snell 4.

BOWLING

	O	M	R	W	Avge	Best	5wI	10wM
A.C.Thomas	219.5	42	752	32	23.50	6- 60	2	1
S.P.Kirby	490.5	89	1672	53	31.54	6-115	1	–
M.Kartik	322.2	75	893	26	34.34	5-137	1	–
C.M.Willoughby	482.3	97	1629	47	34.65	4- 40	–	–
P.D.Trego	282.4	41	1039	27	38.48	4- 22	–	–
A.V.Suppiah	149.1	29	447	10	44.70	2- 16	–	–
G.M.Hussain	247.1	41	987	22	44.86	6- 33	1	–

Also bowled:
A.W.R.Barrow 7-0-36-1; A.J.Dibble 36-4-142-2; G.H.Dockrell 18-1-76-2; L.Gregory 48-2-222-4; B.A.W.Mendis 66.1-3-285-4; C.A.J.Meschede 23.1-3-100-1.

The First-Class Averages (pp 223–240) give the records of Somerset players in all first-class county matches (Somerset's other opponents being the Indians), with the exception of C.Kieswetter and B.A.W.Mendis, whose first-class figures for Somerset are as above, and:
J.C.Hildreth 16-25-1-186-923-38.45-2-4-22ct.
C.R.Jones 8-12-1-55-169-15.36-0-2-5ct.

SOMERSET RECORDS

FIRST-CLASS CRICKET

Highest Total	For 850-7d		v	Middlesex	Taunton	2007
	V 811		by	Surrey	The Oval	1899
Lowest Total	For 25		v	Glos	Bristol	1947
	V 22		by	Glos	Bristol	1920
Highest Innings	For 342	J.L.Langer	v	Surrey	Guildford	2006
	V 424	A.C.MacLaren	for	Lancashire	Taunton	1895

Highest Partnership for each Wicket

1st	346	L.C.H.Palairet/ H.T.Hewett	v	Yorkshire	Taunton	1892
2nd	290	J.C.W.MacBryan/M.D.Lyon	v	Derbyshire	Burton upon T	1924
3rd	319	P.M.Roebuck/M.D.Crowe	v	Leics	Taunton	1984
4th	310	P.W.Denning/I.T.Botham	v	Glos	Taunton	1980
5th	320	J.D.Francis/I.D.Blackwell	v	Durham UCCE	Taunton	2005
6th	265	W.E.Alley/K.E.Palmer	v	Northants	Northampton	1961
7th	279	R.J.Harden/G.D.Rose	v	Sussex	Taunton	1997
8th	172	I.V.A.Richards/I.T.Botham	v	Leics	Leicester	1983
	172	A.R.K.Pierson/P.S.Jones	v	N Zealanders	Taunton	1999
9th	183	C.H.M.Greetham/H.W.Stephenson	v	Leics	Weston-s-Mare	1963
	183	C.J.Tavaré/N.A.Mallender	v	Sussex	Hove	1990
10th	163	I.D.Blackwell/N.A.M.McLean	v	Derbyshire	Taunton	2003

Best Bowling	For 10- 49	E.J.Tyler	v	Surrey	Taunton	1895
(Innings)	V 10- 35	A.Drake	for	Yorkshire	Weston-s-Mare	1914
Best Bowling	For 16- 83	J.C.White	v	Worcs	Bath	1919
(Match)	V 17-137	W.Brearley	for	Lancashire	Manchester	1905

Most Runs – Season	2761	W.E.Alley	(av 58.74)	1961
Most Runs – Career	21142	H.Gimblett	(av 36.96)	1935-54
Most 100s – Season	11	S.J.Cook		1991
Most 100s – Career	49	H.Gimblett		1935-54
Most Wkts – Season	169	A.W.Wellard	(av 19.24)	1938
Most Wkts – Career	2165	J.C.White	(av 18.03)	1909-37
Most Career W-K Dismissals	1007	H.W.Stephenson	(698 ct; 309 st)	1948-64
Most Career Catches in the Field	381	J.C.White		1909-37

LIMITED-OVERS CRICKET

Highest Total	50ov	413-4		v	Devon	Torquay	1990
	40ov	377-9		v	Sussex	Hove	2003
	T20	250-3		v	Glos	Taunton	2006
Lowest Total	50ov	58		v	Middlesex	Southgate	2000
	40ov	58		v	Essex	Chelmsford	1977
	T20	82		v	Kent	Taunton	2010
Highest Innings	50ov	162*	C.J.Tavaré	v	Devon	Torquay	1990
	40ov	184	M.E.Trescothick	v	Glos	Taunton	2008
	T20	141*	C.L.White	v	Worcs	Worcester	2006
Best Bowling	50ov	8-66	S.R.G.Francis	v	Derbyshire	Derby	2004
	40ov	6-24	I.V.A.Richards	v	Lancashire	Manchester	1983
	T20	6- 5	A.V.Suppiah	v	Glamorgan	Cardiff	2011

SURREY

Formation of Present Club: 22 August 1845
Inaugural First-Class Match: 1864
Colours: Chocolate
Badge: Prince of Wales' Feathers
County Champions (since 1890): (18) 1890, 1891, 1892, 1894, 1895, 1899, 1914, 1952, 1953, 1954, 1955, 1956, 1957, 1958, 1971, 1999, 2000, 2002
Joint Champions: (1) 1950
Gillette/NatWest/C&G/FP Trophy Winners: (1) 1982
Benson and Hedges Cup Winners: (3) 1974, 1997, 2001
Pro 40/National League (Div 1) Winners: (1) 2003
Sunday League Winners: (1) 1996
Clydesdale Bank 40 Winners: (1) 2011
Twenty20 Cup Winners: (1) 2003

Chief Executive: Richard Gould, The Kia Oval, London, SE11 5SS • Tel: 0871 246 1100 • Fax: 020 7820 5601 • E-mail: enquiries@surreyccc.com • Web: www.kiaoval.com

Team Director: Chris Adams. **First XI Coach:** Ian D.K.Salisbury. **Captain:** R.J.Hamilton-Brown. **Vice-Captain:** tba. **Overseas Players:** M.Kartik, D.P.Nannes (T20 only) and J.A.Rudolph. **2012 Beneficiary:** none. **Head Groundsman:** Scott Patterson. **Scorer:** Keith R.Booth. ‡ New registration. NQ Not qualified for England.

ANSARI, Zafar Shahaan (Hampton S; Cambridge U), b Ascot, Berks 10 Dec 1991. Younger brother of A.S.Ansari (Cambridge U 2008-10). 5'11". LHB, SLA. Cambridge MCCU 2011. Surrey debut 2011. Surrey 2nd XI debut 2008, aged 16y 133d. Summer contract. HS 41 and BB 5-33 CU v Surrey (Cambridge) 2011. Sy HS 21 v Kent (Canterbury) 2011. Sy BB 2-39 v Glos (Cheltenham) 2011. LO HS 23* England Dev XI v Sri Lanka A (Manchester) 2011. LO BB 1-22 v Warwks (Birmingham) 2011 (CB40). T20 HS 34*. T20 BB 1-19.

BATTY, Gareth Jon (Bingley GS), b Bradford, Yorks 13 Oct 1977. Younger brother of J.D.Batty (Yorkshire and Somerset 1989-96). 5'11". RHB, OB. Yorkshire 1997. Surrey 1999-2001, rejoined in 2010; cap 2011. Worcestershire 2002-09. **Tests:** 7 (2003-04 to 2005); HS 38 v SL (Kandy) 2003-04; BB 3-55 v SL (Galle) 2003-04. Took wicket with his third ball in Test cricket. **LOI:** 10 (2002-03 to 2008-09); HS 17 v WI (Bridgetown) 2008-09; BB 2-40 v WI (Gros Islet, St Lucia) 2003-04. **IT20:** 1 (2008-09); HS 4 v WI (Port-of-Spain) 2008-09. F-c Tours: WI 2003-04, 2005-06; NZ 2008-09 (Eng A); SL 2002-03 (ECB Acad); SL 2003-04; B 2003-04. HS 133 Wo v Surrey (Oval) 2004. Sy HS 79 v Essex (Croydon) 2011. 50 wkts (2); most – 60 (2003). BB 7-52 (10-113 match) Wo v Northants (Northampton) 2004. Sy BB 5-76 v Northants (Oval) 2010 and 5-76 v Middx (Lord's) 2011. LO HS 83* v Yorks (Oval) 2001 (NL). LO BB 5-35 Wo v Hants (Southampton) 2009 (FPT). T20 HS 87. T20 BB 4-23.

BURNS, Rory Joseph (City of London Freemen's S), b Epsom 26 Aug 1990. 5'9". LHB, WK. Debut (Surrey) 2011. Surrey 2nd XI debut 2009. MCC Univs 2010. Hampshire 2nd XI 2010. HS 26 v Cambridge MCCU (Cambridge) 2011 – only 1st XI game.

DAVIES, Steven Michael (King Charles I S, Kidderminster), b Bromsgrove, Worcs 17 Jun 1986. 5'10". LHB, WK. Worcestershire 2005-09. Surrey debut 2010; cap 2011. Worcs 2nd XI debut 2001, aged 15y 8d. MCC 2006-07, 2011. **LOI:** 8 (2009-10 to 2010-11); HS 87 v P (Chester-le-St) 2010. **IT20:** 5 (2008-09 to 2010-11); HS 33 v P (Cardiff) 2010. F-c Tours: A 2010-11; B 2006-07 (Eng A); UAE 2011-12 (v P). 1000 runs (4); most – 1090 (2010). HS 192 Wo v Glos (Bristol) 2006. Sy HS 156 v Northants (Northampton) 2011. LO HS 119 Wo v Glos (Worcester) 2008 (P40). T20 HS 99*.

NQDE BRUYN, Zander (Helpmekaar HS; Randburg HS; Rand Afrikaans U, Jo'burg), b Johannesburg, South Africa 5 Jul 1975. 6'0". RHB, RMF. Transvaal B 1995-96 to 1996-97. Gauteng 1996-97 to 2001-02. Easterns 2002-03 to 2005-06. Titans 2004-05 to 2005-06. Worcestershire 2005. Warriors 2006-07 to 2008-09. Somerset 2008-10; cap 2008. Lions 2009-10 to date. Surrey debut 2011 (Kolpak registration) **Tests** (SA): 3 (2004-05); HS 83 v I (Kanpur) 2004-05 – on debut; BB 2-32 v I (Calcutta) 2004-05. F-c Tours (SA): I 2004-05; SL 2005-06 (SA A). 1000 runs (1+1): 1383 (2011). HS 266* Easterns v GW (Kimberley) 2003-04. UK HS 179 v Kent (Oval) 2011. BB 7-67 Warriors v Titans (Port Elizabeth) 2007-08. UK BB 4-23 Sm v Essex (Colchester) 2010. Sy BB 3-39 v Glos (Oval) 2011. LO HS 122* Sm v Pakistanis (Taunton) 2010. LO BB 5-44 Easterns v WP (Cape Town) 2003-04. T20 HS 95*. T20 BB 4-18.

DERNBACH, Jade Winston (St John the Baptist S), b Johannesburg, South Africa 3 Mar 1986. 6'1½". RHB, RFM. Italian passport. UK resident since 1998. Debut (Surrey) 2003; cap 2011. **LOI:** 14 (2011 to 2011-12); HS 5 v SL (Leeds) 2011; BB 4-45 v P (Dubai) 2011-12. **IT20:** 8 (2011 to 2011-12); HS 3 v WI (Oval) 2011; BB 4-22 v I (Manchester) 2011. F-c Tour (Eng A): WI 2010-11. HS 56* v Northants (Northampton) 2010. 50 wkts (1): 51 (2010). BB 6-47 v Leics (Leicester) 2009. LO HS 31 v Somerset (Taunton) 2010 (CB40). LO BB 5-31 v Derbys (Chesterfield) 2009 (P40). T20 HS 12. T20 BB 4-22.

DUNN, Matthew Peter (Bearwood C, Wokingham), b Egham 5 May 1992. 6'2". LHB, RFM. Debut (Surrey) 2010. Surrey 2nd XI debut 2009. England U19s 2010. HS 2* v Cambridge MCCU (Cambridge) 2011. CC HS 0*. BB 5-56 v Derbys (Derby) 2011. LO HS and LO BB 2-32 England Dev XI v Sri Lanka A (Manchester) 2011.

EDWARDS, George Alexander (St Joseph C, Croydon), b King's College H, Camberwell, London 29 Jul 1992. 6'3". RHB, RMF. Debut (Surrey) 2011. Surrey 2nd XI debut 2009, aged 16y 322d. HS 19 and BB – v Cambridge MCCU (Cambridge) 2011 – only 1st XI appearance.

HAMILTON-BROWN, Rory James (Millfield S), b St John's Wood, London 3 Sep 1987. 6'0". RHB, OB. Surrey 2005; rejoined as captain 2010; cap 2011. No f-c appearances 2006-07. Sussex 2008-09. 1000 runs (1): 1039 (2011). HS 171* and BB 2-49 Sx v Yorks (Hove) 2009. Sy HS 159 v Essex (Croydon) 2011. Sy BB 1-17 v Cambridge MCCU (Cambridge) 2010. LO HS 115 v Glamorgan (Oval) 2010 (CB40). LO BB 3-28 v Leics (Leicester) 2007 (P40). T20 HS 87*. T20 BB 4-15.

HARINATH, Arun (Whitgift S; Loughborough U), b Sutton 26 Mar 1987. 5'11". LHB, OB. Loughborough UCCE 2007-09. MCC 2008. Surrey debut 2009. Surrey 2nd XI debut 2003. Buckinghamshire 2007-08. HS 80 v Cambridge MCCU (Cambridge) 2011. CC HS 63 v Middx (Oval) 2010. BB – . LO HS 21* v Warwks (Oval) 2009 (P40).

JEWELL, Thomas Melvin (Bradfield C), b Reading, Berkshire 13 Jan 1991. 6'1". RHB, RMF. Debut (Surrey) 2008. Surrey 2nd XI debut 2007. HS 61 and BB 5-49 v Cambridge MCCU (Cambridge) 2011. CC HS 6 v Derbys (Derby) 2011. CC BB 1-56 v Northants (Northampton) 2010. LO HS 1 v Northants (Northampton) 2009 (P40). LO BB – .

NQJORDAN, Christopher James (Comber Mere S, Barbados; Dulwich C), b Christ Church, Barbados 4 Oct 1988. 6'0". RHB, RFM. Debut (Surrey) 2007. Missed entire 2010 season with back injury. Barbados 2011-12. HS 79* and Sy BB 4-57 v Essex (Chelmsford) 2011. BB 5-77 Barbados v Guyana (Bridgetown) 2011-12. LO HS 38 v Yorks (Guildford) 2008 (P40). LO BB 3-28 v Yorks (Scarborough) 2007 (P40). T20 HS 31. T20 BB 2-34.

‡^{NQ}**KARTIK, Murali** (educated in New Delhi), b Madras, India 11 Sep 1976. 6'0". LHB, SLA. Railways 1996-97 to date. Central Zone 1997-98 to date. Lancashire 2005-06. Middlesex 2007-09; cap 2007. Somerset 2010-11. **Tests** (I): 8 (1999-00 to 2004-05); HS 43 v B (Dhaka) 2000-01; BB 4-44 v A (Bombay) 2004-05. **LOI** (I): 37 (2001-02 to 2007-08); HS 32* v A (Perth) 2003-04; BB 6-27 v A (Bombay) 2007-08. **IT20** (I): 1 (2007-08); HS and BB-v P (Jaipur) 2007-08. F-c Tours (I A): E 2003; A 2003-04 (I); SA 2001-02; WI 1999-00, 2002-03; P 1997-98; SL 2002; B 2000-01 (I). HS 96 Railways v Rest of India (Delhi) 2005-06. CC HS 65* Sm v Lancs (Taunton) 2011. 50 wkts (1): 51 (2007). BB 9-70 Rest of India v Bombay (Bombay) 2000-01. CC BB 6-21 M v Glamorgan (Lord's) 2007. LO HS 44 Railways v Rajasthan (Indore) 2008-09. LO BB 6-27 (*see LOI*). T20 HS 28. T20 BB 5-13 M v Essex (Lord's) 2007 – M record.

LANCEFIELD, Thomas John (Whitgift S), b Epsom 8 Oct 1990. 5'9". LHB, LM. Debut (Surrey) 2010. Tamil Union 2010-11. Surrey 2nd XI debut 2009. HS 74 v Worcs (Worcester) 2010. BB 1-12 Tamil Union v Colts (Colombo, CCC) 2010-11. Sy BB – . LO HS 20 v Leics (Leicester) 2009 (P40). T20 HS 27.

‡**LEWIS, Jonathan** (Churchfields S, Swindon; Swindon C), b Aylesbury, Bucks 26 Aug 1975. 6'2". RHB, RMF. Gloucestershire 1995-2011; cap 1998; captain 2006-08; benefit 2007. MCC 2005, 2010. Wiltshire 1993, 1995. Northamptonshire staff 1994. **Tests**: 1 (2006); HS 20 and BB 3-68 v SL (Nottingham) 2006. **LOI**: 13 (2005 to 2007); HS 17 v I (Leeds) 2007; BB 4-36 v A (Brisbane) 2006-07. **IT20**: 2 (2005 to 2006-07); HS 1 v A (Sydney) 2006-07; BB 4-24 v A (Southampton) 2005. F-c Tours (Eng A): WI 2000-01; SL 2004-05. HS 71 Gs v Middx (Uxbridge) 2011. 50 wkts (9); most – 74 (2003). BB 8-95 Gs v Z (Gloucester) 2000. CC BB 7-38 (10-75 match) Gs v Somerset (Bristol) 2006. Hat-trick Gs v Notts (Nottingham) 2000. LO HS 54 Gs v Durham (Cheltenham) 2009 (P40). LO BB 5-19 Gs v Hants (Southampton) 2005 (NL). T20 HS 43. T20 BB 4-24.

LINLEY, Timothy Edward (St Mary's RC CS, Menston; Notre Dame SFC; Oxford Brookes U), b Leeds, Yorks 23 Mar 1982. 6'2". RHB, RFM. Oxford UCCE 2003-05. British U 2004. Sussex 2006 (1 match). Surrey debut 2009. HS 42 OU v Derbys (Oxford) 2005. Sy HS 36 v Kent (Canterbury) 2009. 50 wkts (1): 73 (2011). BB 6-57 (9-79 match) v Leics (Leicester) 2011. LO HS 20* v Warwks (Oval) 2009 (P40). LO BB 3-50 v Hants (Croydon) 2011 (CB40). T20 HS 8. T20 BB 2-28.

MAYNARD, Thomas Lloyd (Millfield S; Whitchurch HS, Cardiff), b Cardiff 25 Mar 1989. Son of M.P.Maynard (Glamorgan and England 1985-2005). 6'3". RHB, OB. Glamorgan 2007-10. Surrey debut 2011. Wales MC 2006-08. England U19s 2007 to 2008. 1000 runs (1): 1022 (2011). HS 141 v Middx (Guildford) 2011. BB – . LO HS 108 Gm v Northants (Colwyn Bay) 2009 (P40). LO BB – . T20 HS 78*.

MEAKER, Stuart Christopher (Cranleigh S), b Durban, South Africa 21 Jan 1989. Moved to UK in 2001. 6'1". RHB, RFM. Debut (Surrey) 2008. Surrey 2nd XI debut 2007. **LOI**: 2 (2011-12); HS 1 and BB 1-45 v I (Mumbai) 2011-12. HS 94 v Bangladeshis (Oval) 2010. CC HS 72 v Essex (Colchester) 2009. BB 5-48 v Northants (Northampton) 2011. LO HS 10* v Kent (Canterbury) 2009 (P40). LO BB EL v Bangladesh A (Chittagong) 2011-12. T20 HS 17. T20 BB 2-16.

^{NQ}**NANNES, Dirk** Peter (Wesley C and Monash U, Melbourne), b Mount Waverley, Victoria, Australia 16 May 1976. 6'3". RHB, LFM. Victoria 2005-06 to 2009-10. Middlesex 2008; cap 2008. Dutch passport. Rejoins Surrey for T20 only in 2012. **LOI** (A): 1 (2009); HS 1 and BB 1-20 v Scotland (Edinburgh) 2009. **IT20** (Neth/A): 17 (2 for Neth 2009; 15 for A 2009 to 2010-11); HS 12* A v P (Birmingham) 2010; BB 4-18 A v B (Bridgetown) 2010. HS 31* Vic v S Australia (Adelaide) 2007-08. CC HS 5 and CC BB 6-32 M v Worcs (Kidderminster) 2008. BB 7-50 (11-95 match) Vic v Q (Brisbane) 2008-09. LO HS 5* M v Somerset (Lord's) 2008. LO BB 4-38 M v Worcs (Kidderminster) 2008 (P40). T20 HS 12*. T20 BB 5-40.

PIETERSEN, Kevin Peter (Maritzburg C; Natal U), b Pietermaritzburg, South Africa 27 Jun 1980. British passport (English mother) – qualified for England Oct 2004. 6'4". RHB, OB. MBE 2005. *Wisden* 2005. Natal/KwaZulu-Natal 1997-98 to 1999-00. Nottinghamshire 2001-04; cap 2002. MCC 2004. Hampshire 2005-08; cap 2005 (no f-c appearances 2006-07, 2009-10). Surrey debut 2010 (initially on loan). Dolphins 2010-11. **ECB central contract 2011-12**. **Tests**: 81 (2005 to 2011-12, 3 as captain); HS 227 v A (Adelaide) 2010-11; BB 1-0 v SA (Lord's) 2008. **LOI**: 127 (2004-05 to 2011-12, 12 as captain); HS 130 v P (Dubai) 2011-12; scored 454 runs (av 151.33) in 7-match series, including fastest England 100 off 69 balls (E London), v SA 2004-05; BB 2-22 v SA (Leeds) 2008. **IT20**: 36 (2005 to 2011-12); HS 79 v Z (Cape Town) 2007-08; BB 1-27 v SA (Centurion) 2009-10. F-c Tours: A 2006-07, 2010-11; SA 2009-10; WI 2008-09; NZ 2007-08; I 2003-04 (Eng A), 2005-06, 2008-09 (Captain); P 2005-06; SL 2007-08; B 2009-10; UAE 2011-12 (v P). 1000 runs (3); most – 1546 (2003). HS 254* Nt v Middx (Nottingham) 2002. Sy HS 58 and Sy BB 1-24 v Essex (Croydon) 2011. BB 4-31 Nt v Durham U (Nottingham) 2003. CC BB 3-72 Nt v Hants (Nottingham) 2004. LO HS 147 Nt v Somerset (Taunton) 2002 (NL). LO BB 3-14 Nt v Middx (Lord's) 2004 (NL). T20 HS 79. T20 BB 3-33.

RAMPRAKASH, Mark Ravin (Gayton HS; Harrow Weald SFC), b Bushey, Herts 5 Sep 1969. 5'9". RHB, OB. Middlesex 1987-2000; cap 1990; captain 1997-99. Surrey debut 2001 – scoring 146 v Kent (Oval); cap 2002; joint Testimonial 2008. YC 1991. *Wisden* 2006. PCA 2006. **Tests**: 52 (1991 to 2001-02); HS 154 v WI (Bridgetown) 1997-98; BB 1-2 v WI (Georgetown) 1997-98. **LOI**: 18 (1991 to 2001-02); HS 51 v WI (Port-of-Spain) 1997-98; BB 3-28 v Z (Harare) 2001-02. F-c Tours: A 1994-95 (*part*), 1998-99; SA 1995-96; WI 1991-92 (Eng A), 1993-94, 1997-98; NZ 1991-92, 2001-02; I 1994-95 (Eng A), 2001-02; P 1990-91 (Eng A). SL 1990-91 (Eng A). 1000 runs (20, inc 2000 (3): 2258 (1995), 2278 (2006), 2026 (2007)). Averaged 103.54 in f-c matches 2006, the second-highest average by any batsman scoring 1000 runs in a season (105.28 in CC), setting world records by scoring 2000 runs in only 20 innings, posting scores of at least 150 in five successive matches and reaching double figures in each of his 24 innings. In 2007 he became the first to score 2000 f-c runs in a season and average over 100 (101.30) twice. Ten hundreds in a season (2): 1995, 2007. HS 301* v Northants (Oval) 2006. BB 3-32 M v Glamorgan (Lord's) 1998. Sy BB 2-35 v Northants (Northampton) 2004. LO HS 147* M v Worcs (Lord's) 1990 (SL) – M record. LO BB 5-38 M v Leics (Lord's) 1993 (SL). T20 HS 85*.

ROY, Jason Jonathan (Whitgift S), b Durban, South Africa 21 Jul 1990. 6'0". RHB, RM. Debut (Surrey) 2010. Surrey 2nd XI debut 2008. HS 106* and BB 2-29 v Glamorgan (Oval) 2011. LO HS 131 v Leics (Leicester) 2011 (CB40). LO BB – . T20 HS 101* v Kent (Beckenham) 2010 – Sy record.

^{NQ}**RUDOLPH, Jacobus** Andries ('**Jacques**') (Afrikaanse Hoer Seunskool), b Springs, Transvaal, South Africa 4 May 1981. Elder brother of G.J.Rudolph (Limpopo and Namibia 2006-07 to date). 5'11". LHB, LBG. Northerns 1997-98 to 2003-04. Titans 2004-05, 2008-09 to date. Eagles 2005-06 to 2007-08. Yorkshire 2007-11 (Kolpak registration); scored 122 v Surrey (Oval) on debut; cap 2007. **Tests** (SA): 40 (2003 to 2011-12); HS 222* v B (Chittagong) 2003 – on debut; BB 1-1 v E (Leeds) 2003. **LOI** (SA): 45 (2003 to 2005-06); HS 81 v B (Dhaka) 2003. **IT20** (SA): 1 (2005-06); HS 6* v A (Brisbane) 2005-06. F-c Tours (SA): E 2003; A 2001-02, 2005-06; WI 2004-05; NZ 2003-04; I 2004-05; SL 2004, 2005-06, 2006; B 2003. 1000 runs (4+1); most – 1375 (2010). HS 228* Y v Durham (Leeds) 2010. BB 5-80 Eagles v Cape Cobras (Cape Town) 2007-08. CC BB 1-13 Y v Somerset (Scarborough) 2008. LO HS 134* South Africa A v Kenya (Laudium) 2001-02. LO BB 4-41 South Africa A v New Zealand A (Colombo) 2005-06. T20 HS 71. T20 BB 3-16.

SPRIEGEL, Matthew Neil William (Whitgift S; Loughborough U), b Epsom 4 Mar 1987. 6'3". LHB, OB. Loughborough UCCE 2007-08; captain 2007-08. Surrey debut 2008. Surrey 2nd XI debut 2004. HS 108* v Bangladeshis (Oval) 2010. CC HS 103 v Northants (Oval) 2010. BB 2-28 v Hants (Oval) 2008. LO HS 86 v Durham (Oval) 2011 (CB40). LO BB 3-39 v Warwks (Birmingham) 2011 (CB40). T20 HS 25*. T20 BB 4-33.

TREMLETT, Christopher Timothy (Thornden S, Chandler's Ford; Taunton's C, Southampton), b Southampton, Hampshire 2 Sep 1981. Son of T.M.Tremlett (Hampshire 1976-91); grandson of M.F.Tremlett (Somerset, CD and England 1947-60). 6'7". RHB, RFM. Hampshire 2000-09, taking wicket of M.H.Richardson (NZ A) with his first ball; cap 2004. Surrey debut 2010. **ECB central contract 2011-12**. **Tests**: 11 (2007 to 2011-12); HS 25* v I (Oval) 2007; BB 6-48 v SL (Southampton) 2011. **LOI**: 15 (2005 to 2010-11); HS 19* v I (Birmingham) 2007; BB 4-32 v B (Nottingham) 2005 – on debut (hat-trick ball hit stump without dislodging bails). **IT20**: 1 (2007-08); BB 2-45 v I (Durban) 2007-08. F-c Tours: A 2010-11; SL 2002-03 (ECB Acad); UAE 2011-12 (v P). HS 64 H v Glos (Southampton) 2005. Sy HS 53* v Middx (Lord's) 2010. BB 6-44 H v Sussex (Hove) 2005. Sy BB 4-29 v Glos (Bristol) 2010. Hat-trick: H v Notts (Nottingham) 2005. LO HS 38* H v Cheshire (Alderley Edge) 2004 (CGT). LO BB 4-25 H v Essex (Southend) 2002 (NL). T20 HS 13. T20 BB 4-16.

VAN DEN BERGH, Frederick Oliver Edward (Whitgift S, Croydon; Durham U), b Farnborough, Kent 4 Jun 1992. 6'2". RHB, SLA. Debut (Surrey) 2011. Surrey 2nd XI debut, aged 16y 326d. Summer contract. HS 0 and BB 3-79 v Cambridge MCCU (Cambridge) 2011.

[NQ]**WILSON, Gary** Craig (Methodist C, Belfast; Manchester Met), b Dundonald, N Ireland 5 Feb 1986. 5'10". RHB, WK. Ireland 2005 to date. Surrey debut 2010. MCC YC 2005. Surrey 2nd XI debut 2006. **LOI** (Ire): 37 (2007 to 2011-12); HS 13 v Netherlands (Dublin) 2010. **IT20** (Ire): 17 (2008 to 2011-12); HS 32 v Kenya (Mombasa) 2011-12. HS 125 v Leics (Leicester) 2010. BB – . LO HS 113 (*see LOI*). T20 HS 49.

RELEASED/RETIRED
(Having made a County First-Class or List A appearance in 2011)

BROWN, Michael James (Queen Elizabeth GS, Blackburn; Collingwood C, Durham U), b Burnley, Lancs 9 Feb 1980. Elder brother of D.O.Brown (Durham U, Glamorgan, Glos 2003-10). 6'0". RHB, OB. Middlesex 1999-2003. Durham UCCE 2001-02. British U 2001-02. Hampshire 2004-08; cap 2007. Surrey 2009-11. 1000 runs (1): 1078 (2007). HS 133 H v Loughborough UCCE (Southampton) 2006. CC HS 126* H v Durham (Chester-le-St) 2007. Sy HS 120 v Derbys (Croydon) 2009. LO HS 96* H v Worcs (Southampton) 2008 (FPT). T20 HS 77.

KING, Simon James (Warlingham S; John Fisher S), b Warlingham 4 Sep 1987. 6'1". RHB, OB. Surrey 2009-11. Surrey 2nd XI debut 2005. HS 13 v Cambridge MCCU (Cambridge) 2011. CC HS 8 v Derbys (Croydon) 2009. BB 3-61 v Middx (Lord's) 2009 – on debut. LO HS 5* v Kent (Beckenham) 2009.

[NQ]**OJHA, Pragyan** Prayash (DAV Public S, Chandrasekharpur), b Khurda, Orissa, India 5 Sep 1986. 6'0". LHB, SLA. Hyderabad (Ind) 2004-05 to date. South Zone 2005-06 to date. Surrey 2011. **Tests** (I): 14 (2009-10 to 2011-12); HS 18* v SL (Colombo, SSC) 2010; BB 6-47 v WI (Mumbai) 2011-12. **LOI** (I): 16 (2008 to 2011); HS 16* v SL (Dambulla) 2008; BB 4-38 v SL (Colombo, RPS) 2008-09. **IT20** (I): 6 (2009 to 2010); HS 10* v SL (Nagpur) 2009-10; BB 4-21 v B (Nottingham) 2009. F-c Tours (I): SL 2010; Z/Kenya 2007 (I A); B 2009-10. HS 35 Hyderabad v Bengal (Kolkata) 2007-08. Sy HS 5* v Leics (Leicester) 2011. BB 7-114 Hyderabad v Rajasthan (Jaipur) 2006-07. Sy BB 6-8 v Northants (Northampton) 2011. LO HS 20 India Red v India Blue (Ahmedabad) 2007-08. LO BB 5-19 Hyderabad v Andhra (Bangalore) 2011-12. T20 HS 11*. T20 BB 4-21.

SCHOFIELD, Christopher Paul (Wardle HS), b Birch Hill, Rochdale, Lancs 6 Oct 1978. 6'2". LHB, LBG. Lancashire 1998-2004; cap 2002. Surrey 2006-11. **Tests**: 2 (2000); HS 57 v Z (Nottingham) 2000. BB – . **IT20**: 4 (2007-08); HS 9* and BB 2-15 v Z (Cape Town) 2007-08. F-c Tours (Eng A): WI 2000-01; NZ 1999-00; B 1999-00. HS 144 v Essex (Colchester) 2009. BB 6-120 Eng A v Bangladesh (Chittagong) 1999-00. Sy BB 5-40 v Northants (Northampton) 2009. LO HS 75* v Hants (Southampton) 2007 (FPT). LO BB 5-31 La v Derbys (Manchester) 2001 (NL). T20 HS 30*. T20 BB 4-12.

RELEASED/RETIRED continued on p 191

SURREY 2011

RESULTS SUMMARY

	Place	Won	Lost	Tied	Drew	NR
LV= County Championship (2nd Division)	2nd	8	4		4	
All First-Class Matches		8	5		4	
Clydesdale Bank 40 (Group B)	**Winners**	12	1			1
Friends Life t20 (South Group)	5th	7	6			3

LV= COUNTY CHAMPIONSHIP AVERAGES
BATTING AND FIELDING

Cap		M	I	NO	HS	Runs	Avge	100	50	Ct/St
	C.P.Schofield	3	4	1	99	179	59.66	–	1	–
	Z.de Bruyn	16	27	2	179	1383	55.32	4	9	7
	T.L.Maynard	16	28	3	141	1022	40.88	3	3	14
2011	S.M.Davies	16	27	1	156	1035	39.80	2	5	53/2
2011	R.J.Hamilton-Brown	16	30	2	159	1039	37.10	1	5	12
2002	M.R.Ramprakash	13	23	2	141	700	33.33	1	3	10
	J.J.Roy	12	22	1	106*	623	29.66	1	1	11
	C.J.Jordan	7	9	1	79*	228	28.50	–	2	3
	Yasir Arafat	8	11	2	65	255	28.33	–	1	2
2011	G.J.Batty	16	24	4	79	532	26.60	–	4	20
	G.C.Wilson	3	5	–	42	110	22.00	–	–	1
	C.T.Tremlett	3	4	1	17	47	15.66	–	–	–
	M.J.Brown	3	5	–	46	78	15.60	–	–	–
	S.C.Meaker	10	12	1	55*	143	13.00	–	1	2
2011	J.W.Dernbach	9	11	4	19	51	7.28	–	–	3
	Z.S.Ansari	3	6	–	21	43	7.16	–	–	1
	T.E.Linley	14	24	5	21	122	6.42	–	–	4
	P.P.Ojha	4	5	3	5*	12	6.00	–	–	–

Also batted: M.P.Dunn (2 matches) 0*, 0*, 0*; A.Harinath (1) 1, 6; T.M.Jewell (1) 6; K.P.Pietersen (1) 58 (1 ct).

BOWLING

	O	M	R	W	Avge	Best	5wI	10wM
P.P.Ojha	150.4	52	311	24	12.95	6- 8	2	1
T.E.Linley	482.3	102	1339	73	18.34	6-57	2	1
S.C.Meaker	279.1	48	993	44	22.56	5-37	3	–
G.J.Batty	390.5	69	1200	36	33.33	5-76	1	–
Z.de Bruyn	189	38	589	15	39.26	3-39	–	–
J.W.Dernbach	307.1	71	872	22	39.63	5-41	1	–
Yasir Arafat	276	56	948	20	47.40	5-86	1	–
C.J.Jordan	144	26	528	11	48.00	4-57	–	–
Also bowled:								
M.P.Dunn	21.1	2	101	6	16.83	5-56	1	–
Z.S.Ansari	50	6	158	6	26.33	2-39	–	–
C.P.Schofield	72	13	230	5	46.00	2-57	–	–
C.T.Tremlett	96	20	306	6	51.00	2-19	–	–

R.J.Hamilton-Brown 25.5-2-107-1; T.M.Jewell 16-3-68-1; T.L.Maynard 2-0-7-0; K.P.Pietersen 13-3-24-1; J.J.Roy 6.2-0-43-2.

The First-Class Averages (pp 223–240) give the records of Surrey players in all first-class county matches (Surrey's other opponents being Cambridge MCCU), with the exception of Z.S.Ansari, J.W.Dernbach, S.C.Meaker and C.T.Tremlett, whose first-class figures for Surrey are as above, and:
   K.P.Pietersen 2-3-0-58-136-45.33-0-1-1ct. 14-3-27-1-27.00-1/24-0-0.

SURREY RECORDS

FIRST-CLASS CRICKET

Highest Total	For 811		v	Somerset	The Oval	1899
	V 863		by	Lancashire	The Oval	1990
Lowest Total	For 14		v	Essex	Chelmsford	1983
	V 16		by	MCC	Lord's	1872
Highest Innings	For 357*	R.Abel	v	Somerset	The Oval	1899
	V 366	N.H.Fairbrother	for	Lancashire	The Oval	1990

Highest Partnership for each Wicket

1st	428	J.B.Hobbs/A.Sandham	v	Oxford U	The Oval	1926
2nd	371	J.B.Hobbs/E.G.Hayes	v	Hampshire	The Oval	1909
3rd	413	D.J.Bicknell/D.M.Ward	v	Kent	Canterbury	1990
4th	448	R.Abel/T.W.Hayward	v	Yorkshire	The Oval	1899
5th	318	M.R.Ramprakash/Azhar Mahmood	v	Middlesex	The Oval	2005
6th	298	A.Sandham/H.S.Harrison	v	Sussex	The Oval	1913
7th	262	C.J.Richards/K.T.Medlycott	v	Kent	The Oval	1987
8th	205	I.A.Greig/M.P.Bicknell	v	Lancashire	The Oval	1990
9th	168	E.R.T.Holmes/E.W.J.Brooks	v	Hampshire	The Oval	1936
10th	173	A.Ducat/A.Sandham	v	Essex	Leyton	1921

Best Bowling	For 10-43	T.Rushby	v	Somerset	Taunton	1921
(Innings)	V 10-28	W.P.Howell	for	Australians	The Oval	1899
Best Bowling	For 16-83	G.A.R.Lock	v	Kent	Blackheath	1956
(Match)	V 15-57	W.P.Howell	for	Australians	The Oval	1899

Most Runs – Season	3246	T.W.Hayward	(av 72.13)	1906
Most Runs – Career	43554	J.B.Hobbs	(av 49.72)	1905-34
Most 100s – Season	13	T.W.Hayward		1906
	13	J.B.Hobbs		1925
Most 100s – Career	144	J.B.Hobbs		1905-34
Most Wkts – Season	252	T.Richardson	(av 13.94)	1895
Most Wkts – Career	1775	T.Richardson	(av 17.87)	1892-1904
Most Career W-K Dismissals	1221	H.Strudwick	(1035 ct; 186 st)	1902-27
Most Career Catches in the Field	605	M.J.Stewart		1954-72

LIMITED-OVERS CRICKET

Highest Total	50ov	496-4		v	Glos	The Oval	2007
	40ov	386-3		v	Glamorgan	The Oval	2010
	T20	224-5		v	Glos	Bristol	2006
Lowest Total	50ov	74		v	Kent	The Oval	1967
	40ov	64		v	Worcs	Worcester	1978
	T20	94		v	Essex	Chelmsford	2008
Highest Innings	50ov	268	A.D.Brown	v	Glamorgan	The Oval	2002
	40ov	203	A.D.Brown	v	Hampshire	Guildford	1997
	T20	101*	J.J.Roy	v	Kent	Beckenham	2010
Best Bowling	50ov	7-33	R.D.Jackman	v	Yorkshire	Harrogate	1970
	40ov	7-30	M.P.Bicknell	v	Glamorgan	The Oval	1999
	T20	6-24	T.J.Murtagh	v	Middlesex	Lord's	2005

SUSSEX

Formation of Present Club: 1 March 1839
Substantial Reorganisation: August 1857
Inaugural First-Class Match: 1864
Colours: Dark Blue, Light Blue and Gold
Badge: County Arms of Six Martlets
County Champions: (3) 2003, 2006, 2007
Gillette/NatWest/C&G/FP Trophy Winners: (5) 1963, 1964, 1978, 1986, 2006
Benson and Hedges Cup Winners: (0); best – Semi-Finalist 1982, 1999
Pro 40/National League (Div 1) Winners: (2) 2008, 2009
Sunday League Winners: (1) 1982
Clydesdale Bank Winners: (0); best – Semi-Finalist 2011
Twenty20 Cup Winners: (1) 2009

Chief Executive: David Brooks, the PROBIZ County Ground, Eaton Road, Hove BN3 3AN • Tel: 0844 264 0202 • Fax: 01273 771549 • Email: info@sussexcricket.co.uk • Web: www.sussexcricket.co.uk

Professional Cricket Manager: Mark A.Robinson. **Club Coach:** Mark J.G.Davis and Carl Robinson. **Captain:** M.H.Yardy. **Vice-Captain:** E.C.Joyce. **Overseas Player:** S.B.Styris (T20 only). **2012 Beneficiary:** M.J.Prior. **Head Groundsman:** Andy Mackay. **Scorer:** M.J. (Mike) Charman. ‡ New registration. NQ Not qualified for England.

ADKIN, William Anthony (Sackville S, E Grinstead; Southampton Solent C), b Redhill, Surrey 9 Apr 1990. 6'8½". LHB, RM. Debut (Sussex) 2010. Sussex 2nd XI debut 2006, aged 16y 88d. HS 45 v Surrey (Guildford) 2010. BB 1-28 v Worcs (Worcester) 2011. LO HS 30 and LO BB 1-16 v Bangladeshis (Hove) 2010. T20 HS 8*. T20 BB 1-28.

ANYON, James Edward (Garstang HS; Preston C; Loughborough U), b Lancaster, Lancs 5 May 1983. 6'1". LHB, RFM. Loughborough U 2003-04. Warwickshire 2005-09. Surrey 2009 (on loan). Sussex debut 2010; cap 2011. Cumberland 2003. HS 53 v Yorks (Scarborough) 2011. 50 wkts (1): 55 (2011). BB 6-82 Wa v Glamorgan (Cardiff) 2008. Sx BB 5-136 v Warwks (Birmingham) 2011. LO HS 12 Wa v Worcs (Birmingham) 2006 (CGT). LO BB 3-6 Wa v Notts (Nottingham) 2008 (FPT). T20 HS 8*. T20 BB 3-6.

BEER, William Andrew Thomas (Reigate GS; Collyer's C, Horsham), b Crawley 8 Oct 1988. RHB, LB. Debut (Sussex) 2008. No f-c appearances in 2009. Sussex 2nd XI debut 2006. HS 37* and BB 3-31 v Worcs (Worcester) 2010. LO HS 27* v Derbys (Derby) 2011 (CB40). LO BB 2-17 v Durham (Hove) 2009 (P40). T20 HS 22. T20 BB 3-19.

BROWN, Ben Christopher (Ardingly C), b Crawley 23 Nov 1988. RHB, WK. Debut (Sussex) 2007. No f-c appearances in 2008 or 2009. HS 112 v Derbys (Horsham) 2010 and 112 v Oxford MCCU (Oxford) 2011. LO HS 60 v Yorks (Scarborough) 2011 (CB40). T20 HS 68.

GATTING, Joe Stephen (Cardinal Newman C; Brighton C), b Brighton 25 Nov 1987. Son of S.P.Gatting (Middlesex 2nd XI, football for Arsenal, Brighton & Hove Albion, Charlton Athletic), nephew of M.W.Gatting (Middlesex and England 1975-98). 6'0". RHB, OB. Debut (Sussex) 2009, scoring 152 v Cambridge UCCE (Cambridge). Sussex 2nd XI debut 2005. HS 152 (*see above*). CC HS 116* v Worcs (Worcester) 2011. BB 1-8 v Notts (Nottingham) 2011. LO HS 122 v Worcs (Horsham) 2011 (CB40). LO BB – . T20 HS 37. LO BB 1-12.

GLOVER, John Andrew (Hove Park S; Brighton & Hove SFC), b Shoreham-by-Sea 10 Oct 1992. 6'2". RHB, RFM. Debut (Sussex) 2011. Sussex 2nd XI debut 2010. HS- and BB 1-52 v Oxford MCCU (Oxford) 2011 – only 1st XI game.

NQGONDAL, Naveed Arif (Mandi Baha u Din S), Mandi Baha u Din, Pakistan 2 Nov 1981. EU qualification via Danish wife. 5'10½". LHB, LMF. Gujranwala 2001-02 to 2002-03. Sialkot 2008-09 to date. Sussex debut 2011. F-c Tours (Pak A): A 2009; SL 2009. HS 100* v Lancs (Hove) 2011. BB 7-66 v Sialkot v Abbottabad (Abbottabad) 2009-10. Sx BB 4-41 v Notts (Nottingham) 2011. LO HS 49 v Gujranwala v Sargodha (Sargodha) 2002-03. LO BB 3-19 Sialkot v Peshawar (Sialkot) 2008-09. T20 HS 12. T20 BB 3-12.

NQGOODWIN, Murray William (Newton Moore HS, Bunbury, WA), b Salisbury, Rhodesia 11 Dec 1972. Younger brother of D.G.Goodwin (Zimbabwe 1986-87 to 1989-90). Migrated to Australia in Nov 1986 and gained Australian citizenship in Sep 1997. Kolpak registration 2005 to date. 5'9". RHB, LB. WA 1994-95 to 1996-97, 2000-01 to 2005-06. Mashonaland 1997-98 to 1998-99. Sussex debut/cap 2001. Warriors 2006-07. Netherlands 1997. **Tests** (Z): 19 (1997-98 to 2000); HS 166* v P (Bulawayo) 1997-98. **LOI** (Z): 71 (1997-98 to 2000); HS 112* v WI (Chester-le-St) 2000; BB 1-12 v SL (Sharjah) 1998-99. F-c Tours (Z): E 2000, SA 1999-00; WI 1999-00; NZ 1997-98; P 1998-99; SL 1997-98. 1000 runs (9+1); most – 1654 (2001). HS 344* (Sx record) v Somerset (Taunton) 2009, sharing record Sx 4th wkt partnership of 363 with C.D.Hopkinson. BB 2-23 Z v Lahore City (Lahore) 1998-99. Sx BB – . LO HS 167 WA v NSW (Perth) 2000-01. LO BB 1-9 Mashonaland v Eng A (Harare) 1998-99. T20 HS 102*.

HATCHETT, Lewis James (Steyning GS), b Shoreham-by-Sea 21 Jan 1990. 6'3". LHB, LMF. Debut (Sussex) 2010. Sussex 2nd XI debut 2009. HS 20 v Middx (Uxbridge) 2010. BB 5-47 v Leics (Leicester) 2010.

HODD, Andrew John (Bexhill C), b Chichester 12 Jan 1984. 5'9". RHB, WK. Sussex 2003 (1 match), 2006 to date. Surrey 2005 (1 match). HS 123 v Yorks (Hove) 2007. LO HS 91 v Lancs (Hove) 2010 (CB40). T20 HS 26.

JOYCE, Edmund Christopher (Presentation C, Bray, Co Wicklow; Trinity C, Dublin), b Dublin, Ireland 22 Sep 1978. Brother of four Ireland cricketers: Augustine (2000), Dominick (2004-06), Cecilia (2001-07) and Isobel, her twin (1999-2007). 5'11". LHB, RM. Ireland 1997-98. Middlesex 1999-2008; cap 2002. Sussex debut/cap 2009. Qualified for England 2005. MCC 2006, 2008. **LOI** (E/Ire): 30 (17 for E 2006 to 2006-07; 13 for Ire 2010-11 to 2011-12); HS 107 E v A (Sydney) 2006-07. **IT20** (E/Ire): 4 (2 for E 2006 to 2006-07; 2 for Ire 2011-12) HS 38 Ire v Kenya (Mombasa) 2011-12. F-c Tour (Eng A): WI 2005-06. 1000 runs (6); most – 1668 (2005). HS 211 M v Warwks (Birmingham) 2006. Sx HS 183 v Notts (Horsham) 2009. BB M 2-34 v Cambridge U (Cambridge) 2004. CC BB 1-4 M v Glamorgan (Cardiff) 2005. Sx BB 1-9 v Hants (Southampton) 2009. LO HS 146 v Glos (Hove) 2009 (FPT). LO BB 2-10 M v Notts (Nottingham) 2003 (NL). T20 HS 47.

KHAN, Amjad (Skolenpa Duevej, Denmark), b Copenhagen, Denmark 14 Oct 1980. 6'0". RHB, RFM. Kent 2001-10. Sussex debut 2011. Denmark 1998-2000. Qualified for England Dec 2006. Missed 2007 season following reconstructive knee surgery. **Tests**: 1 (2008-09); HS-and BB 1-111 v WI (Port-of-Spain) 2008-09. **IT20**: 1 (2008-09); HS 2 and BB 2-34 v WI (Port-of-Spain) 2008-09. F-c Tours: WI 2008-09 (*part*); NZ 2008-09 (Eng A – *part*). HS 78 K v Middx (Lord's) 2003. Sx HS 65 v Notts (Nottingham) 2011. 50 wkts (2); most – 63 (2002). BB 6-52 K v Yorks (Canterbury) 2002. Sx BB 4-70 v Yorks (Scarborough) 2011. LO HS 65* Denmark v Ireland (Harare) 1999-00. LO BB 4-26 v Leics (Leicester) 2003 (NL). T20 HS 15. T20 BB 3-11.

LIDDLE, Christopher John (Nunthorpe CS), b Middlesbrough, Yorks 1 Feb 1984. 6'5". RHB, LFM. Leicestershire 2005-06. Sussex debut 2007. Missed entire 2009 season with a stress fracture of the right ankle. HS 53 v Worcs (Hove) 2007. BB 3-42 Le v Somerset (Leicester) 2006. Sx BB 2-43 v Sri Lanka A (Hove) 2007. LO HS 11 v Essex (Arundel) 2007 (FPT). LO BB 5-18 v Netherlands (Amstelveen) 2011 (CB40). T20 HS 16. T20 BB 4-15.

MACHAN, Matthew William (Hurstpierpoint C; Brighton C), b Brighton 15 Feb 1991. 5'8". LHB, RM/OB. Debut (Sussex) 2010. Sussex 2nd XI debut 2006, aged 15y 153d. HS 99 v Oxford MCCU (Oxford) 2011. CC HS 71 v Notts (Nottingham) 2011. LO HS 56 v Indians (Hove) 2011. T20 HS 6.

NASH, Christopher David (Collyer's SFC; Loughborough U), b Cuckfield 19 May 1983. 5'11". RHB, OB. Debut (Sussex) 2002 – no f-c appearances 2003-04; cap 2008. Loughborough UCCE 2003-04. British U 2004. 1000 runs (1): 1321 (2009). HS 184 v Leics (Leicester) 2010. BB 4-12 v Glamorgan (Cardiff) 2010. LO HS 124* v Kent (Canterbury) 2011 (CB40). LO BB 4-40 v Yorks (Hove) 2009 (FPT). T20 HS 64*. T20 BB 4-7.

PANESAR, Mudhsuden Singh ('Monty') (Stopsley HS; Bedford Modern S; Loughborough U), b Luton, Beds 25 Apr 1982. 6'0". LHB, SLA. Northamptonshire 2001-09; cap 2006. British U 2002-05. Loughborough UCCE 2004. Lions 2009-10. Sussex debut/cap 2010. MCC 2006. Bedfordshire 1998-99. *Wisden* 2007. **Tests**: 41 (2005-06 to 2011-12); HS 26 v SL (Nottingham) 2006; BB 6-37 v NZ (Manchester) 2008. **LOI**: 26 (2006-07 to 2007-08); HS 13 v WI (Nottingham) 2007; BB 3-25 v B (Bridgetown) 2006-07. **IT20**: 1 (2006-07); HS 1 and BB 2-40 v A (Sydney) 2006-07. F-c Tours: A 2006-07, 2010-11; WI 2008-09; NZ 2007-08; I 2005-06, 2008-09; SL 2002-03 (ECB Acad), 2007-08; UAE 2011-12 (v P). HS 46* v Middx (Hove) 2010. 50 wkts (5); most – 71 (2006). BB 7-181 Nh v Essex (Chelmsford) 2005. Sx BB 5-44 v Glos (Arundel) 2010. LO HS 17* Nh v Leics (Northampton) 2008 (FPT). LO BB 5-20 ECB Acad v SL Acad XI (Colombo) 2002-03. T20 HS 3*. T20 BB 3-14.

PRIOR, Matthew James (Brighton C), b Johannesburg, South Africa 26 Feb 1982. 5'11". RHB, WK. Debut (Sussex) 2001; cap 2003; benefit 2012. MCC 2005. *Wisden* 2009. **ECB central contract 2011-12**. **Tests**: 50 (2007 to 2011-12); HS 131* v WI (Port-of-Spain) 2008-09 (scored 126* v WI on debut – first instance while keeping wicket for England). **LOI**: 68 (2004-05 to 2010-11); HS 87 v WI (Birmingham) 2009. **IT20**: 10 (2007 to 2009-10); HS 32 v SA (Cape Town) 2007-08. F-c Tours: A 2010-11; SA 2009-10; WI 2008-09; I 2003-04 (Eng A), 2008-09; SL 2004-05 (Eng A), 2007-08; B 2006-07 (Eng A), 2009-10; UAE 2011-12 (v P). 1000 runs (3); most – 1158 (2004). HS 201* v Loughborough U (Hove) 2004. CC HS 153* v Essex (Colchester) 2003. LO HS 144 v Warwks (Hove) 2005 (NL). T20 HS 117 v Glamorgan (Hove) 2010 – Sx record.

‡NO**STYRIS, Scott** Bernard (Hamilton HBS), b Brisbane, Australia 10 Jul 1975. 5'10". RHB, RMF. N Districts 1994-95 to date. Middlesex 2005-06; cap 2006. Auckland 2005-06 to 2009-10. Durham 2007. Essex l-o and T20 only 2010-11. Joins Sussex for T20 only in 2012. **Tests** (NZ): 29 (2002-2007-08); HS 170 v SA (Auckland) 2003-04; BB 3-28 v I (Wellington) 2002-03. **LOI** (NZ): 188 (1999-00 to 2010-11); HS 141 v SL (Bloemfontein) 2002-03; BB 6-25 v WI (Port-of-Spain) 2002. **IT20** (NZ): 31 (2004-05 to 2010-11); HS 66 v A (Auckland) 2004-05; BB 3-5 v Z (Providence) 2009-10. F-c Tours (NZ): E 2000 (NZ A), 2004; A 2004-05; SA 2000-01, 2005-06, 2007-08; WI 2002; I 2003-04; SL 2002-03; Z 2005; B 2004-05. HS 212* ND v Otago (Hamilton) 2001-02. UK HS 133 and UK BB 6-71 M v Lancs (Lord's) 2006. LO HS 141 (*see LOI*). LO BB 6-25 (*see LOI*). T20 HS 106*. T20 BB 3-5.

WELLS, Luke William Peter (St Bede's S), b Eastbourne 29 Dec 1990. Son of A.P.Wells (Border, Kent, Sussex and England 1981-2000) and nephew of C.M.Wells (Border, Derbyshire, Sussex and WP 1979-96). 6'4". LHB, OB. Debut (Sussex) 2010. Colombo CC 2011-12. Sussex 2nd XI debut 2008. England U19s 2009 to 2010. HS 174 v Yorks (Hove) 2011. BB 2-28 v Yorks (Horsham) 2011. LO HS 17 v Yorks (Hove) 2011 (CB40). BB 3-19 v Netherlands (Amstelveen) 2011 (CB40). T20 HS 3.

NO**WERNARS, Kirk** Ogilvy, b Constantiaberg, Cape Town, South Africa 14 Jun 1991. EU passport. 6'3". LHB, RMF. W Province 2009-10 to 2010-11. Sussex debut 2011. HS 53 v Worcs (Horsham) 2011. BB 2-11 WP v Boland (Cape Town) 2009-10. Sx BB 2-13 v Yorks (Hove) 2011. LO HS 37* WP v Namibia (Windhoek) 2010-11. LO BB 6-27 WP v Gauteng (Johannesburg) 2010-11. T20 HS 9. T20 BB 1-21.

WRIGHT, Luke James (Belvoir HS; Ratcliffe C; Loughborough U), b Grantham, Lincs 7 Mar 1985. Younger brother of A.S.Wright (Leicestershire 2001-02). 5'11". RHB, RMF. Leicestershire 2003 (one f-c match). Sussex debut 2004; cap 2007. **LOI**: 46 (2007 to 2010-11); HS 52 v NZ (Birmingham) 2008; BB 2-34 v NZ (Bristol) 2008. **IT20**: 30 (2007-08 to 2011); HS 71 v Netherlands (Lord's) 2009; BB 1-5 v A (Bridgetown) 2009-10. F-c Tour (EL): NZ 2008-09. HS 155* v MCC (Lord's) 2008. CC HS 134 v Middx (Uxbridge) 2010. BB 5-65 v Derbys (Derby) 2010. LO HS 125 v Glos (Hove) 2007 (P40). LO BB 4-12 v Middx (Hove) 2004 (NL). T20 HS 117. T20 BB 3-17.

YARDY, Michael Howard (William Parker S, Hastings), b Pembury, Kent 27 Nov 1980. 6'0". LHB, LM/SLA. Debut (Sussex) 2000; cap 2005; captain 2009 to date. **LOI**: 28 (2006 to 2010-11); HS 60* v A (Perth) 2010-11; BB 3-24 v P (Nottingham) 2006 – on debut. **IT20**: 14 (2006 to 2010-11); HS 35* v P (Cardiff) 2010; BB 2-19 v P (Bridgetown) 2009-10. F-c Tours (Eng A, C=Captain): WI 2005-06; I 2007-08C; B 2006-07C. 1000 runs (2); most – 1520 (2005). HS 257 (record Sx score v touring team) and BB 5-83 v Bangladeshis (Hove) 2005. CC HS 179 v Middx (Lord's) 2005. CC BB 3-15 v Yorks (Leeds) 2009. LO HS 98* v Surrey (Oval) 2006 (CGT). LO BB 6-27 v Warwks (Birmingham) 2005 (NL). T20 HS 76*. T20 BB 3-21.

RELEASED/RETIRED
(Having made a County First-Class or List A appearance in 2011)

NAVED-UL-HASAN – *see DERBYSHIRE.*

NO**PARNELL, Wayne** Dillon (Grey HS), b Port Elizabeth, South Africa, 30 Jul 1989. 6'1". LHB, LFM. EP 2006-07 to date. Warriors 2008-09 to date. Kent 2009. Sussex 2011. **Tests** (SA): 3 (2009-10); HS 22 v I (Kolkata) 2009-10; BB 2-17 v E (Johannesburg) 2009-10. **LOI** (SA): 22 (2008-09 to 2011-12); HS 49 v I (Jaipur) 2009-10; BB 5-48 v E (Cape Town) 2009-10. **IT20** (SA): 14 (2008-09 to 2011); HS 29* v A (Johannesburg) 2011-12; BB 4-13 v WI (Oval) 2009. F-c Tour (SA): I 2009-10. HS 90 K v Glamorgan (Canterbury) 2009. Sx HS 44 v Durham (Hove) 2011. BB 4-7 EP v KwaZulu Natal (Port Elizabeth) 2006-07. CC BB 4-78 K v Essex (Chelmsford) 2009. Sx BB 3-60 v Yorks (Hove) 2011. LO HS 104 Warriors v Lions (Potchefstroom) 2011-12. LO BB 5-48 (*see LOI*). T20 HS 29*. T20 BB 4-13.

RAYNER, O.P. – *see MIDDLESEX.*

NQ**VINCENT, Lou** (Westlake BHS; Adelaide S), b Warkworth, Auckland, New Zealand 11 Nov 1978. RHB, RM. Auckland 1997-98 to date. NZ Academy 1998-99. North Is 1999-00. Worcestershire 2006. Lancashire 2008. Sussex 2011. Suffolk 2005. **Tests** (NZ): 23 (2001-02 to 2007-08); HS 224 v SL (Wellington) 2004-05. **LOI** (NZ): 102 (2000-01 to 2007-08); HS 172 v Z (Bulawayo) 2005-06; BB 1-0 v SA (Cape Town) 2007-08. **IT20** (NZ): 9 (2005-06 to 2007-08); HS 42 v WI (Auckland) 2005-06. F-c Tours (NZ): A 2001-02; SA 2004-05 (NZ A), 2007-08; WI 2002; I 2003-04; P 2002; Z 2005-06. HS 224 (*see Tests*). CC HS 141 Wo v Leics (Worcester) 2006. Sx HS 36 v Oxford MCCU (Oxford) 2011. BB 2-37 Auckland v Wellington (Auckland) 1999-00. UK BB 1-12 Wo v Leics (Leicester) 2006. LO HS 172 (*see LOI*). LO BB 3-7 Auckland v Otago (Auckland) 2010-11. T20 HS 105*. T20 BB 3-28.

SUSSEX 2011

RESULTS SUMMARY

	Place	Won	Lost	Tied	Drew	NR
LV= County Championship (1st Division)	5th	6	6		4	
All First-Class Matches		6	6		5	
Clydesdale Bank 40 (Group A)	SF	8	5			
Friends Life t20 (South Group)	QF	9	6			2

LV= COUNTY CHAMPIONSHIP AVERAGES

BATTING AND FIELDING

Cap		M	I	NO	HS	Runs	Avge	100	50	Ct/St
2001	M.W.Goodwin	16	29	3	274*	1372	52.76	4	4	6
2009	E.C.Joyce	16	29	1	140	1269	45.32	2	9	22
	J.S.Gatting	6	10	1	116*	407	45.22	1	3	3
2005	M.H.Yardy	10	16	2	130	617	44.07	2	3	17
2003	M.J.Prior	5	8	1	97*	284	40.57	–	2	16/2
	K.O.Wernars	3	4	1	53	104	34.66	–	1	3
2007	L.J.Wright	4	7	–	116	237	33.85	1	–	–
2008	C.D.Nash	15	28	–	120	928	33.14	1	7	9
	N.A.Gondal	4	7	2	100*	165	33.00	1	–	–
	L.W.P.Wells	14	27	2	174	824	32.96	3	–	6
	O.P.Rayner	4	8	2	62*	191	31.83	–	2	3
	A.J.Hodd	8	14	3	67	270	24.54	–	1	19/1
	B.C.Brown	10	18	2	108	392	24.50	1	2	14/2
	W.D.Parnell	5	7	1	44	143	23.83	–	–	3
	Naved-ul-Hasan	9	13	1	43*	186	15.50	–	–	1
	W.A.Adkin	3	5	1	29*	62	15.50	–	–	3
	A.Khan	13	18	5	65	186	14.30	–	1	9
2011	J.E.Anyon	15	22	3	53	269	14.15	–	2	5
2010	M.S.Panesar	16	22	8	20	120	8.57	–	–	2

Also batted: M.W.Machan (1 match) 71.

BOWLING

	O	M	R	W	Avge	Best	5wI	10wM
N.A.Gondal	98.4	12	388	15	25.86	4- 41	–	–
C.D.Nash	92	18	291	11	26.45	4-103	–	–
M.S.Panesar	750.3	223	1880	69	27.24	5- 58	3	–
A.Khan	381.5	72	1259	39	32.28	4- 70	–	–
J.E.Anyon	450.1	50	1785	55	32.45	5-136	1	–
Naved-ul-Hasan	279.4	58	921	27	34.11	5- 79	2	1
W.D.Parnell	154	20	611	15	40.73	3- 60	–	–
Also bowled:								
L.J.Wright	49	8	146	5	29.20	3- 54	–	–

W.A.Adkin 63-17-174-1; J.S.Gatting 5-2-9-1; O.P.Rayner 76.1-19-241-4; L.W.P.Wells 44-7-170-2; K.O.Wernars 29.5-7-109-4; M.H.Yardy 3-0-7-0.

The First-Class Averages (pp 223–240) give the records of Sussex players in all first-class county matches (Sussex's other opponents being Oxford MCCU), with the exception of M.J.Prior, whose full first-class figures for Sussex are as above, and:
O.P.Rayner 5-10-3-62*-240-34.28-0-2-3ct. 99.1-26-284-6-47.33-2/38-0-0.

SUSSEX RECORDS

FIRST-CLASS CRICKET

Highest Total	For 742-5d		v	Somerset	Taunton	2009
	V 726		by	Notts	Nottingham	1895
Lowest Total	For 19		v	Surrey	Godalming	1830
	19		v	Notts	Hove	1873
	V 18		by	Kent	Gravesend	1867
Highest Innings	For 344*	M.W.Goodwin	v	Somerset	Taunton	2009
	V 322	E.Paynter	for	Lancashire	Hove	1937

Highest Partnership for each Wicket

1st	490	E.H.Bowley/J.G.Langridge	v	Middlesex	Hove	1933
2nd	385	E.H.Bowley/M.W.Tate	v	Northants	Hove	1921
3rd	385*	M.H.Yardy/M.W.Goodwin	v	Warwicks	Hove	2006
4th	363	M.W.Goodwin/C.D.Hopkinson	v	Somerset	Taunton	2009
5th	297	J.H.Parks/H.W.Parks	v	Hampshire	Portsmouth	1937
6th	255	K.S.Duleepsinhji/M.W.Tate	v	Northants	Hove	1930
7th	344	K.S.Ranjitsinhji/W.Newham	v	Essex	Leyton	1902
8th	291	R.S.C.Martin-Jenkins/M.J.G.Davis	v	Somerset	Taunton	2002
9th	178	H.W.Parks/A.F.Wensley	v	Derbyshire	Horsham	1930
10th	156	G.R.Cox/H.R.Butt	v	Cambridge U	Cambridge	1908

Best Bowling	For 10- 48	C.H.G.Bland	v	Kent	Tonbridge	1899
(Innings)	V 9- 11	A.P.Freeman	for	Kent	Hove	1922
Best Bowling	For 17-106	G.R.Cox	v	Warwicks	Horsham	1926
(Match)	V 17- 67	A.P.Freeman	for	Kent	Hove	1922

Most Runs – Season	2850	J.G.Langridge	(av 64.77)	1949
Most Runs – Career	34150	J.G.Langridge	(av 37.69)	1928-55
Most 100s – Season	12	J.G.Langridge		1949
Most 100s – Career	76	J.G.Langridge		1928-55
Most Wkts – Season	198	M.W.Tate	(av 13.47)	1925
Most Wkts – Career	2211	M.W.Tate	(av 17.41)	1912-37
Most Career W-K Dismissals	1176	H R Butt	(911 ct; 265 st)	1890-1912
Most Career Catches in the Field	779	J.G.Langridge		1928-55

LIMITED-OVERS CRICKET

Highest Total	50ov	384-9		v	Ireland	Belfast	1996
	40ov	399-4		v	Worcs	Horsham	2011
	T20	239-5		v	Glamorgan	Hove	2010
Lowest Total	50ov	49		v	Derbyshire	Chesterfield	1969
	40ov	59		v	Glamorgan	Hove	1996
	T20	67		v	Hampshire	Hove	2004
Highest Innings	50ov	158*	M.W.Goodwin	v	Essex	Chelmsford	2006
	40ov	163	C.J.Adams	v	Middlesex	Arundel	1999
	T20	117	M.J.Prior	v	Glamorgan	Hove	2010
Best Bowling	50ov	6- 9	A.I.C.Dodemaide	v	Ireland	Downpatrick	1990
	40ov	7-41	A.N.Jones	v	Notts	Nottingham	1986
	T20	5-11	Mushtaq Ahmed	v	Essex	Hove	2005

WARWICKSHIRE

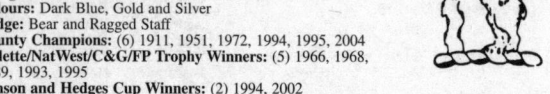

Formation of Present Club: 8 April 1882
Substantial Reorganisation: 19 January 1884
Inaugural First-Class Match: 1894
Colours: Dark Blue, Gold and Silver
Badge: Bear and Ragged Staff
County Champions: (6) 1911, 1951, 1972, 1994, 1995, 2004
Gillette/NatWest/C&G/FP Trophy Winners: (5) 1966, 1968, 1989, 1993, 1995
Benson and Hedges Cup Winners: (2) 1994, 2002
Pro 40/National League (Div 1) Winners: (0); best – 3rd 2001, 2002
Sunday League Winners: (3) 1980, 1994, 1997
Clydesdale Bank 40 Winners: (1) 2010
Twenty20 Cup Winners: (0); best – Finalist 2003

Chief Executive: Colin Povey, County Ground, Edgbaston, Birmingham, B5 7QU • Tel: 0121 446 4422 • Fax: 0121 446 4544 • Email: info@edgbaston.com • Web: www.edgbaston.com

Director of Coaching/First XI Coach: Ashley F.Giles. **Assistant Coach:** Dougie Brown. **Captain:** J.O.Troughton. **Vice-Captain:** tba. **Overseas Player:** J.S.Patel. **2012 Beneficiary:** N.M.Carter. **Head Groundsman:** Gary Barwell. **Scorer:** David E.Wainwright. ‡ New registration. NQ Not qualified for England.

ALLIN, Thomas William (Cardiff U), b Devon 27 Nov 1987. Son of A.W.Allin (Glamorgan 1976) and brother of M.L.Allin (Devon 2003). RHB, RMF. Cardiff UCCE (not f-c) 2008-10. Warwickshire 2nd XI debut 2008. Devon 2007. Awaiting f-c debut. LO HS 2* and BB – v Surrey (Birmingham) 2011 (CB40) – only 1st XI game.

AMBROSE, Timothy Raymond (Merewether HS, NSW; TAFE C), b Newcastle, NSW, Australia 1 Dec 1982. ECB qualified – British/EU passport. 5'7". RHB, WK. Sussex 2001-05; cap 2003. Warwickshire debut 2006; cap 2007. **Tests:** 11 (2007-08 to 2008-09); HS 102 v NZ (Wellington) 2007-08. **LOI:** 5 (2008); HS 6 v NZ (Oval) 2008. **IT20:** 1 (2008); HS – . F-c Tours: WI 2008-09; NZ 2007-08. HS 251* v Worcs (Worcester) 2007. LO HS 135 v Durham (Birmingham) 2007 (FPT). T20 HS 77.

BARKER, Keith Hubert Douglas (Moorhead HS; Fulwood C, Preston), b Manchester 21 Oct 1986. Son of K.H.Barker (British Guiana 1960-61 to 1963-64). Played football for Blackburn Rovers and Rochdale. 6'3". LHB, LM. Debut (Warwickshire) 2009. Warwickshire 2nd XI debut 2008. HS 118 v Sussex (Birmingham) 2011. BB 5-31 v Durham MCCU (Durham) 2011. CC BB 4-56 v Yorks (Leeds) 2011. LO HS 56 v Scotland (Birmingham) 2011. LO BB 4-33 v Scotland (Birmingham) 2010 (CB40). T20 HS 46. T20 BB 4-19.

BELL, Ian Ronald (Princethorpe C), b Walsgrave-on-Stowe 11 Apr 1982. 5'9". RHB, RM. Debut (Warwickshire) 1999; cap 2001; benefit 2011. MCC 2004. YC 2004. MBE 2005. **ECB central contract 2011-12. Tests:** 72 (2004 to 2011-12); HS 235 v I (Oval) 2011; BB 1-33 v P (Faisalabad) 2005-06. **LOI:** 108 (2004-05 to 2011-12); HS 126* v I (Southampton) 2007; BB 3-9 v Z (Bulawayo) 2004-05 – taking a wicket with his third ball in LOI. **IT20:** 7 (2006 to 2010-11); HS 60* v NZ (Manchester) 2008. F-c Tours: A 2006-07, 2010-11; SA 2009-10; WI 2000-01 (Eng A – *part*), 2008-09; NZ 2007-08; I 2005-06, 2008-09; P 2005-06; SL 2002-03 (ECB Acad), 2004-05, 2007-08; B 2009-10; UAE 2011-12 (v P). 1000 runs (4); most – 1714 (2004). HS 262* v Sussex (Horsham) 2004. BB 4-4 v Middx (Lord's) 2004. LO HS 158 EL v India A (Worcester) 2010. LO BB 5-41 v Essex (Chelmsford) 2003 (NL). T20 HS 85. T20 BB 1-12.

180

BEST, Paul Merwood (Bablake S, Coventry; Cambridge U), b Nuneaton 8 Mar 1991. LHB, SLA. Cambridge MCCU 2011 (blue 2011). Warwickshire debut 2011. Northamptonshire 2011. Warwickshire 2nd XI debut 2009. England U19s 2009-10 to 2010. HS 150 CU v Surrey (Cambridge) 2011. CC HS 31* Nh v Glamorgan (Swansea) 2011. Wa HS 2 and CC BB 2-69 v Durham (Chester-le-St) 2011. BB 6-86 (9-131 match) CU v Oxford U (Cambridge) 2011. LO HS 12 v Northants (Birmingham) 2011 (CB40). LO BB 3-53 Nh v Surrey (Northampton) 2011 (CB40).

CARTER, Neil Miller (Hottentots Holland HS; Cape Technicon), b Cape Town, South Africa 29 Jan 1975. British passport. 6'2". LHB, LMF. Boland 1999-00 to 2000-01. Warwickshire debut 2001; cap 2005; benefit 2012. PCA 2010. HS 103 v Sussex (Hove) 2002 – completed maiden hundred off 67 balls. 50 wkts (1): 51 (2010). BB 6-30 v Lancs (Liverpool) 2011. LO HS 135 v Scotland (Birmingham) 2006 (CGT). LO BB 5-31 v Durham (Birmingham) 2002 (NL). T20 HS 58. T20 BB 5-19 v Worcs (Birmingham) 2005 – Wa record.

CHOPRA, Varun (Ilford County HS), b Barking, Essex 21 Jun 1987. 6'1". RHB, LB. Essex 2006-09. Warwickshire debut 2010. Tamil Union 2011-12. England U19s 2005 to 2006. 1000 runs (1): 1203 (2011). HS 233* Tamil Union v Sinhalese (Colombo, PSS) 2011-12. Wa HS 228 v Worcs (Worcester) 2011 (in 2nd CC game of season, having scored 210 v Somerset in 1st). Scored 106 Ex v Glos (Chelmsford) 2006 – on CC debut. BB – . LO HS 115 v Leics (Birmingham) 2011 (CB40). T20 HS 51.

CLARKE, Rikki (Broadwater SS; Godalming C), b Orsett, Essex 29 Sep 1981. 6'4". RHB, RFM. Surrey 2002-07, scoring 107* v Cambridge U (Cambridge) on debut; cap 2005. Derbyshire cap/captain 2008. Warwickshire debut 2008; cap 2011. MCC 2006. YC 2002. **Tests**: 2 (2003-04); HS 55 and BB 2-7 v B (Chittagong) 2003-04. **LOI**: 20 (2003 to 2006); HS 39 v P (Lord's) 2006; BB 2-28 v B (Dhaka) 2003-04. F-c Tours: WI 2003-04, 2005-06; SL 2002-03 (ECB Acad), 2004-05; B 2003-04. 1000 runs (1): 1027 (2006). HS 214 Sy v Somerset (Guildford) 2006. Wa HS 127* v Yorks (Leeds) 2010. BB 6-63 v Kent (Canterbury) 2010. Took seven catches in an innings v Lancs (Liverpool) 2011 to equal world record. LO HS 98* Sy v Derbys (Derby) 2002 (NL). LO BB 4-28 v Northants (Birmingham) 2011 (CB40). T20 HS 79*. T20 BB 3-11.

EVANS, Laurie John (Whitgift S; The John Fisher S; St Mary's C, Durham U), b Lambeth, London 12 Oct 1987. 6'0". RHB, RFM. Durham UCCE 2007. MCC 2007. Surrey 2009-10. Warwickshire debut 2010. HS 133* DU v Lancs (Durham) 2007. Wa HS 52 v Sussex (Birmingham) 2011. BB 1-30 Sy v Bangladeshis (Oval) 2010. LO HS 36* v Derbys (Croydon) 2009 (P40). T20 HS 7.

GORDON, Recordo Olton (Aston Manor S; Hamstead Hall SFC), b St Elizabeth, Jamaica 12 Oct 1991. RHB, RFM. Warwickshire 2nd XI debut 2011. Awaiting 1st XI debut.

JAVID, Ateeq (Aston Manor S), b Birmingham 15 Oct 1991. RHB, RM. Debut (Warwick-shire) 2009. Warwickshire 2nd XI debut 2008. England U19s 2010 to 2010-11. HS 48 v Yorks (Leeds) 2010. BB – . LO HS 34 v Northants (Birmingham) 2011 (CB40). BB – .

JOHNSON, Richard Matthew, b Solihull 1 Sep 1988. RHB, WK. Debut (Warwickshire) 2008. Warwickshire 2nd XI debut 2007. Herefordshire 2006. HS 72 v Cambridge UCCE (Cambridge) 2008 – on debut. CC HS 39 v Essex (Birmingham) 2010. LO HS 20 v Northants (Birmingham) 2008 (FPT). T20 HS 6*.

MADDY, Darren Lee (Wreake Valley C), b Leicester 23 May 1974. 5'9". RHB, RM/OB. Leicestershire 1994-2006; cap 1996; benefit 2006. Warwickshire debut/cap 2007; captain 2007-08. **Tests**: 3 (1999 to 1999-00); HS 24 v SA (Durban) 1999-00; BB – . **LOI**: 8 (1998 to 1999-00); HS 53 v Z (Harare) 1999-00. **IT20**: 4 (2007-08); HS 50 and BB 2-6 v NZ (Durban) 2007-08. F-c Tours (Eng A): SA 1996-97 (Le), 1998-99, 1999-00 (Eng); SL 1997-98; Z 1998-99; K 1997-98. 1000 runs (4); most – 1187 (2002). HS 229* Le v Loughborough U (Leicester) 2003. CC HS 162 Le v Durham (Darlington) 1998. Wa HS 148* v Kent (Canterbury) 2007. BB 5-37 Le v Hants (Southampton) 2002. Wa BB 5-63 v Durham (Chester-le-St) 2007. LO HS 167* Le v Scotland (Edinburgh) 2006 (CGT). LO BB 4-16 Le v Somerset (Taunton) 2000 (NL). T20 HS 111 Le v Yorks (Leeds) 2004 – Le record. T20 BB 3-10.

METTERS, Christopher Liam (Coombeshead C; Exeter C), b Torquay, Devon 12 Sep 1990. 6'2". RHB, SLA. Debut (Warwickshire) 2011, taking 6-65 v Worcs (Birmingham). Warwickshire 2nd XI debut 2010. Essex 2nd XI 2010. Devon 2008-10. HS 30 v Hants (Southampton) 2011. BB (*see above*). LO HS 2 v Northants (Birmingham) 2011 (CB40). LO BB 2-41 v Durham (Chester-le-St) 2011 (CB40).

MILLER, Andrew Stephen (St Cecilia's RC HS; Preston C), b Preston, Lancs 27 Sep 1987. 6'4". RHB, RFM. Debut (Warwickshire) 2008. Lancashire 2nd XI 2005. Warwickshire 2nd XI debut 2006. England U19s 2004-05 to 2006. HS 35 v Durham (Birmingham) 2010. BB 5-58 v Lancs (Birmingham) 2010. LO HS 2* v Scotland (Birmingham) 2011 (CB40). LO BB 2-31 v Durham (Birmingham) 2011 (CB40). T20 HS 0*. T20 BB 2-16.

MILNES, Thomas Patrick, b Stourbridge, Worcs 6 Oct 1992. RHB, RFM. Debut (Warwickshire) 2011. Warwickshire 2nd XI debut 2009. England U19s 2010-11. HS 23 and BB 4-15 v Durham MCCU (Durham) 2011 – only 1st XI game.

[NQ]**PATEL, Jeetan** Shashi, b Wellington, New Zealand 7 May 1980. RHB, OB. Wellington 1999-00 to date. **Tests** (NZ): 13 (2006-07 to 2011-12); HS 27* v SA (Cape Town) 2006-07; BB 5-110 v WI (Napier) 2008-09. **LOI** (NZ): 39 (2005 to 2009-10); HS 34 v SL (Kingston) 2006-07; BB 3-11 v SA (Mumbai, BS) 2006-07. **IT20** (NZ): 11 (2005-06 to 2008-09); HS 5 v E (Auckland) 2007-08; BB 3-20 v SA (Johannesburg) 2005-06. F-c Tours (NZ): E 2008; SA 2005-06; I 2010-11; SL 2009; Z 2010-11, 2011-12; B 2008-09. HS 120 v Yorks (Birmingham) 2009. BB 6-32 Wellington v Otago (Queenstown) 2004-05. Wa BB 6-111 (10-163 match) v Sussex (Birmingham) 2011. LO HS 34 (*see LOI*). LO BB 4-16 NZ A v Aus A (Hyderabad) 2008-09. T20 HS 12. T20 BB 4-27.

PIOLET, Steffan Andrew (Warden Park S; Central Sussex C), b Redhill, Surrey 8 Aug 1988. 6'1". RHB, RM. Debut (Warwickshire) 2009. Sussex 2nd XI 2006-08. Warwickshire 2nd XI debut 2008. HS 26* and BB 6-17 (10-43 match) v Durham UCCE (Durham) 2009 – on debut. CC HS 6 and CC BB 1-67 v Yorks (Leeds) 2010. LO HS 39 v Yorks (Birmingham) 2011 (CB40). LO BB 3-34 v Northants (Northampton) 2009 (P40). T20 HS 21. T20 BB 3-25.

PORTERFIELD, William Thomas Stuart (Strabane GS; Leeds Met U), b Londonderry, N.Ireland 6 Sep 1984. 5'11". LHB, OB. Ireland 2006 to date. MCC 2007. Gloucestershire 2008-10; cap 2008. Warwickshire debut 2011. **LOI** (Ire): 58 (2006 to 2011-12); HS 112* v Bermuda (Nairobi) 2006-07. **IT20** (Ire): 20 (2008 to 2011-12); HS 46 v Afghanistan (Colombo, PSS) 2009-10. F-c Tour (Ire, C=captain): WI 2009-10C. HS 175 Gs v Worcs (Cheltenham) 2010. Wa HS 87 v Durham (chester-le-St) 2011. BB 1-29 Ire v Jamaica (Spanish Town) 2009-10. UK BB 1-57 Gs v Loughborough UCCE (Bristol) 2008. LO HS 112* (*see LOI*). T20 HS 83.

182

RANKIN, William Boyd (Strabane GS; Harper Adams UC), b Londonderry, Co Derry, N Ireland 5 Jul 1984. 6'8". LHB, RMF. Brother of R.J.Rankin (Ireland U19 2003-04). Ireland 2006-07 to 2008. Derbyshire 2007. Warwickshire debut 2008. Middlesex summer contract 2004-05. **LOI** (Ireland): 37 (2006-07 to 2011-12); HS 7* v SL (St George's) 2006-07; BB 3-32 v P (Kingston) 2006-07. **IT20** (Ire): 8 (2009 to 2011-12); HS 7* and joint BB 2-25 v Kenya (Mombasa) 2011-12; BB 2-25 v E (Providence) 2009-10. HS 43 ICC Combined XI v England XI (Dubai) 2011-12. Wa HS 28 v Durham (Chester-le-St) 2011. 50 wkts (1): 55 (2011). BB 5-16 v Essex (Birmingham) 2010. LO HS 9 v Kent (Canterbury) 2009 (FPT). LO BB 4-34 v Kent (Birmingham) 2010 (CB40). T20 HS 7*. T20 BB 2-25.

TROTT, Ian Jonathan Leonard (Rondebosch BHC; Stellenbosch U), b Cape Town, South Africa 22 Apr 1981. Stepbrother of K.C.Jackson (WP and Boland 1988-89 to 2001-02). 6'0". RHB, RM. Boland 2000-01. W Province 2001-02. EU/British passport. Warwickshire debut 2003, scoring 134 v Sussex (Birmingham); cap 2005. Otago 2005-06. **ECB central contract 2011-12. Tests**: 26 (2009 to 2011-12); HS 226 v B (Lord's) 2011; scored 119 v A (Oval) 2009 on debut. BB 1-5 v SL (Lord's) 2011. **LOI**: 44 (2009 to 2011-12); HS 137 v A (Sydney) 2010-11. BB 2-31 v A (Adelaide) 2010-11. **IT20**: 7 (2007 to 2009-10); HS 51 v SA (Centurion) 2009. F-c Tours: A 2010-11; SA 2009-10; NZ 2008-09 (EL); I 2007-08 (EL); B 2009-10; UAE 2011-12 (v P). 1000 runs (6); most – 1400 (2009). HS 226 (*see Tests*). CC HS 210 v Sussex (Birmingham) 2005. BB 7-39 v Kent (Canterbury) 2003. LO HS 137 (*see LOI*). LO BB 4-55 v Hants (Lord's) 2011. T20 HS 86*. T20 BB 2-19.

TROUGHTON, Jamie Oliver ('Jim') (Trinity S, Leamington Spa; Birmingham U), b Camden, London 2 Mar 1979. Great-grandson of H.T.Crichton (Warwicks 1908). 5'11". LHB, SLA. Debut (Warwickshire) 2001; cap 2002; captain 2011 to date. **LOI**: 6 (2003); HS 20 v P (Lord's) 2003. F-c Tour (ECB Acad): SL 2002-03. 1000 runs (1): 1067 (2002). HS 223 v Hants (Birmingham) 2009. BB 3-1 v Cambridge U (Cambridge) 2004. CC BB 2-26 v Lancs (Birmingham) 2006. LO HS 115* and BB 4-23 Wa CB v Cumberland (Millom) 2001 (CGT). T20 HS 66. T20 BB 2-10.

WESTWOOD, Ian James (Wheelers Lane S; Solihull SFC), b Birmingham 13 Jul 1982. 5'7½". LHB, OB. Debut (Warwickshire) 2003; cap 2008; captain 2009-10. HS 178 v West Indies A (Birmingham) 2006. CC HS 176 v Glamorgan (Cardiff) 2008. BB 2-39 v Hants (Southampton) 2009. LO HS 65 v Northants (Northampton) 2008 (FPT). BB 1-28 Wa CB v Cambs (March) 2001 (CGT). T20 HS 49*. T20 BB 3-29.

WOAKES, Christopher Roger (Barr Beacon Language S, Walsall), b Birmingham 2 March 1989. 6'2". RHB, RMF. Debut (Warwickshire) 2006; cap 2009. MCC 2009. Herefordshire 2006-07. **LOI**: 4 (2010-11 to 2011); HS 19* v Ireland (Dublin) 2011; BB 6-45 v A (Brisbane) 2010-11. **IT20**: 3 (2010-11 to 2011); HS 19* v A (Adelaide) 2010-11; BB 1-29 v A (Melbourne) 2010-11. F-c Tour (EL): WI 2010-11. HS 136* v Hants (Birmingham) 2010. 50 wkts (2); most – 58 (2010). BB 7-20 (10-123 match) v Hants (Birmingham) 2011. LO HS 49* v Leics (Birmingham) 2010 (CB40). LO BB 6-45 (*see LOI*). T20 HS 44*. T20 BB 4-21.

WRIGHT, Christopher Julian Clement (Eggars S, Alton; Anglia Ruskin U), b Chipping Norton, Oxon 14 Jul 1985. 6'3". RHB, RFM. Cambridge UCCE 2004-05. Middlesex 2004-07. Tamil Union 2005-06. Essex 2008-11. Warwickshire debut (on loan) 2011; joins on a permanent basis in 2012. HS 77 Ex v Cambridge MCCU (Cambridge) 2011. CC HS 71* Ex v Middx (Chelmsford) 2008. Wa HS 13* and Wa BB 5-31 v Yorks (Leeds) 2011. BB 6-22 Ex v Leics (Leicester) 2008. LO HS 42 Ex v Glos (Cheltenham) 2011 (CB40). LO BB 4-20 Ex v Unicorns (Chelmsford) 2011 (CB40). T20 HS 6*. T20 BB 4-24.

BOTHA, Anthony Greyvensteyn (Maritzburg C; Maritzburg Technikon), b Pretoria, South Africa 17 Nov 1976. 6'0". LHB, SLA. Natal/KwaZulu Natal 1995-96 to 1998-99. EP/Easterns 1999-00 to 2002-03. British passport. Derbyshire 2004-07; cap 2004. Warwickshire 2007-11. HS 156* De v Yorks (Derby) 2005. Wa HS 76 v Kent (Nottingham) 2010. 50 wkts (1): 55 (2007). BB 8-53 Natal B v Northerns B (Pretoria) 1997-98. CC BB 6-101 De v Somerset (Derby) 2007. Wa BB 4-77 v Worcs (Birmingham) 2008. LO HS 60* Easterns v EP (Benoni) 2001-02. LO BB 5-43 v Leics (Leicester) 2008. T20 HS 35*. T20 BB 4-14.

NQ**CHANDERPAUL, Shivnarine** (Cove and John SS, Unity Village), b Unity Village, Demerara, Guyana 16 Aug 1974. 5'6". LHB, LB. Guyana 1991-92 to date. Durham 2007-09. Lancashire 2010; cap 2010. Warwickshire 2011. **Tests** (WI): 137 (1993-94 to 2011-12, 14 as captain); HS 203* v SA (Georgetown) 2004-05; BB 1-2 v A (Adelaide) 1996-97. **LOI** (WI): 268 (1994-95 to 2010-11, 16 as captain); HS 150 v SA (E London) 1998-99; BB 3-18 v I (Sharjah) 1997-98. **IT20** (WI): 22 (2005-06 to 2010); HS 41 v E (Oval) 2007. F-c Tours (WI) (C=Captain): E 1995, 2000, 2004, 2007, 2009; A 1995-96, 1996-97, 2000-01, 2005-06C, 2009-10; SA 1998-99, 2003-04, 2007-08; NZ 1994-95, 1999-00, 2005-06C, 2008-09; I 1994-95, 2002-03, 2011-12; P 1997-98, 2001-02 (Sharjah), 2006-07; SL 2005C, 2010-11; Z 2001, 2003-04; B 1999-00, 2002-03, 2011-12; K 2001. 1000 runs (1+1); most – 1107 (2004-05). HS 303* Guyana v Jamaica (Kingston) 1995-96. CC HS 201* Du v Worcs (Worcester) 2009. Wa HS 193 v Yorks (Leeds) 2011. BB 4-48 Guyana v Leeward Is (Basseterre) 1992-93. LO HS 150 (see LOI). LO BB 4-22 Guyana v Trinidad (Hampton Court) 1995-96. T20 HS 87*.

HOLMES, Maurice Gibson (Loughborough U), b Tenterden, Kent 19 May 1990. RHB, OB. Kent 2nd XI 2009. Loughborough MCCU 2011. Warwickshire 2011. Warwickshire 2nd XI debut 2010. HS 4* LU v Leics (Leicester) 2011. Wa HS 1* and CC BB 1-10 v Lancs (Birmingham) 2011. BB 3-46 LU v Northants (Loughborough) 2011. Wa BB 2-54 v Durham MCCU (Durham) 2011.

NQ**MOHAMMAD YOUSUF** Youhana, b Lahore, Pakistan 27 Aug 1974. RHB. Debut 1996-97. Bahawalpur 1996-97. Lahore 1997-98 to 2003-04. WAPDA 1997-98 to 2006-07. PIA 2001-02. Punjab 2007-08. Lancashire 2008. Lahore Shalimar 2010-11. Warwickshire 2011. Wisden 2007. **Tests** (P): 90 (1997-98 to 2010, 9 as captain); HS 223 v E (Lahore) 2005-06. BB – . **LOI** (P): 288 (1997-98 to 2010-11, 8 as captain); HS 141* v Z (Bulawayo) 2002-03; BB 1-0 v Z (Kingston) 2006-07. **IT20** (P): 3 (2006 to 2010); HS 26 v E (Cardiff) 2010. Tours (P) (C=captain): E 2001, 2006, 2010; A 1999-00, 2005-06, 2009-10C; WI 1999-00; SA 1997-98, 2002-03, 2006-07; NZ 2000-01, 2003-04, 2009-10C; I 1998-99, 2004-05, 2007-08; SL 2000-01, 2006, 2009; Z 1997-98, 2002-03; B 2001-02. HS 223 (see Tests). CC HS 205* v Yorkshire (Leeds) 2008. Wa 109 v Worcs (Birmingham) 2011. LO HS 141* (see LOI). LO BB 1-0 (see LOI). T20 HS 57*.

TAHIR, N.S. – see LANCASHIRE.

WARWICKSHIRE 2011

RESULTS SUMMARY

	Place	Won	Lost	Tied	Drew NR
LV= County Championship (1st Division)	2nd	9	4		3
All First-Class Matches		10	4		3
Clydesdale Bank 40 (Group B)	5th	5	7		
Friends Life t20 (North Group)	8th	4	10		2

LV= COUNTY CHAMPIONSHIP AVERAGES
BATTING AND FIELDING

Cap		M	I	NO	HS	Runs	Avge	100	50	Ct/St
	S.Chanderpaul	5	7	1	193	539	89.83	3	1	2
2001	I.R.Bell	3	6	1	139	256	51.20	1	–	1
2009	C.R.Woakes	11	16	4	129	579	48.25	1	5	6
	V.Chopra	16	27	1	228	1178	45.30	3	4	16
	K.H.D.Barker	9	11	1	118	442	44.20	2	2	5
2007	D.L.Maddy	7	10	1	76	318	35.33	–	2	6
2008	I.J.Westwood	12	18	1	171	591	34.76	2	2	13
2007	T.R.Ambrose	15	21	2	73	649	34.15	–	7	36/2
2002	J.O.Troughton	13	20	2	151	583	32.38	1	2	12
	Mohammad Yousuf	6	11	–	109	353	32.09	1	2	–
	L.J.Evans	3	4	–	52	124	31.00	–	1	1
	J.S.Patel	3	4	–	65	114	28.50	–	1	2
2011	R.Clarke	15	22	1	126	558	26.57	1	2	39
	W.T.S.Porterfield	15	24	1	87	583	25.34	–	5	18
	C.L.Metters	10	12	5	30	167	23.85	–	–	15
2005	I.J.L.Trott	3	5	–	39	93	18.60	–	–	4
	N.S.Tahir	3	5	–	53	90	18.00	–	1	–
	W.B.Rankin	13	16	7	28	133	14.77	–	–	3
	A.S.Miller	6	9	4	8	15	3.00	–	–	–

Also batted: P.M.Best (1 match) 1, 2 (1 ct); A.G.Botha (2) 64, 0, 28* (5 ct); N.M.Carter (2 – cap 2005) 1, 25, 40 (1 ct); M.G.Holmes (1) 1*, 0; R.M.Johnson (1) 5, 5 (6 ct); C.J.C.Wright (4) 13*, 5*, 1.

BOWLING

	O	M	R	W	Avge	Best	5wI	10wM
N.M.Carter	60.4	11	197	10	19.70	6- 30	1	–
J.S.Patel	117.1	20	344	17	20.23	6-111	2	–
C.R.Woakes	406.4	90	1220	56	21.78	7- 20	3	1
C.L.Metters	221.4	32	695	29	23.96	6- 65	2	–
C.J.C.Wright	167.1	35	535	22	24.31	5- 31	2	–
W.B.Rankin	387.5	42	1419	55	25.80	5- 57	2	–
R.Clarke	410.5	70	1225	46	26.63	5- 10	1	–
K.H.D.Barker	214	41	712	18	39.55	4- 56	–	–
Also bowled:								
A.G.Botha	32	8	80	5	16.00	3- 39	–	–
N.S.Tahir	84	19	297	9	33.00	4- 36	–	–
D.L.Maddy	99	22	306	9	34.00	3- 29	–	–
A.S.Miller	124	25	434	7	62.00	2- 15	–	–

P.M.Best 15-1-82-3; M.G.Holmes 8.3-1-32-1; I.J.L.Trott 6-0-18-0; I.J.Westwood 2-0-13-0.

The First-Class Averages (pp 223–240) give the records of Warwickshire players in all first-class county matches (Warwickshire's other opponents being Durham MCCU), with the exception of I.R.Bell, P.M.Best, I.J.L.Trott and C.J.C.Wright, whose full first-class figures for Warwickshire are as above, and:

M.G.Holmes 2-3-1-1*-1-0.50-0-0-1ct. 33.3-8-118-4-29.50-2/54-0-0.

WARWICKSHIRE RECORDS

FIRST-CLASS CRICKET

Highest Total	For	810-4d		v	Durham	Birmingham	1994
	V	887		by	Yorkshire	Birmingham	1896
Lowest Total	For	16		v	Kent	Tonbridge	1913
	V	15		by	Hampshire	Birmingham	1922
Highest Innings	For	501*	B.C.Lara	v	Durham	Birmingham	1994
	V	322	I.V.A.Richards	for	Somerset	Taunton	1985

Highest Partnership for each Wicket

1st	377*	N.F.Horner/K.Ibadulla	v	Surrey	The Oval	1960
2nd	465*	J.A.Jameson/R.B.Kanhai	v	Glos	Birmingham	1974
3rd	327	S.P.Kinneir/W.G.Quaife	v	Lancashire	Birmingham	1901
4th	470	A.I.Kallicharran/G.W.Humpage	v	Lancashire	Southport	1982
5th	335	J.O.Troughton/T.R.Ambrose	v	Hampshire	Birmingham	2009
6th	226	T.R.Ambrose/H.H.Streak	v	Worcs	Worcester	2007
7th	289*	I.R.Bell/T.Frost	v	Sussex	Horsham	2004
8th	228	A.J.W.Croom/R.E.S.Wyatt	v	Worcs	Dudley	1925
9th	233	I.J.L.Trott/J.S.Patel	v	Yorkshire	Birmingham	2009
10th	214	N.V.Knight/A.Richardson	v	Hampshire	Birmingham	2002

Best Bowling	For	10-41	J.D.Bannister	v	Comb Servs	Birmingham	1959
(Innings)	V	10-36	H.Verity	for	Yorkshire	Leeds	1931
Best Bowling	For	15-76	S.Hargreave	v	Surrey	The Oval	1903
(Match)	V	17-92	A.P.Freeman	for	Kent	Folkestone	1932

Most Runs – Season	2417	M.J.K.Smith	(av 60.42)	1959
Most Runs – Career	35146	D.L.Amiss	(av 41.64)	1960-87
Most 100s – Season	9	A.I.Kallicharran		1984
	9	B.C.Lara		1994
Most 100s – Career	78	D.L.Amiss		1960-87
Most Wkts – Season	180	W.E.Hollies	(av 15.13)	1946
Most Wkts – Career	2201	W.E.Hollies	(av 20.45)	1932-57
Most Career W-K Dismissals	800	E.J.Smith	(662 ct; 138 st)	1904-30
Most Career Catches in the Field	422	M.J.K.Smith		1956-75

LIMITED-OVERS CRICKET

Highest Total	50ov	392-5		v	Oxfordshire	Birmingham	1984
	40ov	321-7		v	Leics	Birmingham	2010
	T20	205-2		v	Northants	Birmingham	2005
		205-7		v	Glamorgan	Swansea	2005
Lowest Total	50ov	98		v	Leics	Leicester	1998
	40ov	59		v	Yorkshire	Leeds	2001
	T20	106-8		v	Worcs	Worcester	2011
Highest Innings	50ov	206	A.I.Kallicharran	v	Oxfordshire	Birmingham	1984
	40ov	137	I.R.Bell	v	Yorkshire	Birmingham	2005
	T20	89	N.V.Knight	v	Worcs	Worcester	2003
Best Bowling	50ov	6-32	K.Ibadulla	v	Hampshire	Birmingham	1965
		6-32	A.I.Kallicharran	v	Oxfordshire	Birmingham	1984
	40ov	6-15	A.A.Donald	v	Yorkshire	Birmingham	1995
	T20	5-19	N.M.Carter	v	Worcs	Birmingham	2005

WORCESTERSHIRE

Formation of Present Club: 11 March 1865
Inaugural First-Class Match: 1899
Colours: Dark Green and Black
Badge: Shield Argent a Fess between three Pears Sable
County Championships: (5) 1964, 1965, 1974, 1988, 1989
Gillette/NatWest/C&G/FP Trophy Winners: (1) 1994
Benson and Hedges Cup Winners: (1) 1991
Pro 40/National League (Div 1) Winners: (1) 2007
Sunday League Winners: (3) 1971, 1987, 1988
Clydesdale Bank 40 Winners: (0); best – 5th Group A
2010
Twenty20 Cup Winners: (0); best – Quarter-Finalist 2004,
2007

Chief Executive: David Leatherdale, County Ground, New Road, Worcester, WR2 4QQ • Tel:
01905 748474 • Fax: 01905 748005 • Email: admin@wccc.co.uk • Web: www.wccc.co.uk

Director of Cricket: Steve J.Rhodes. **Academy Director**: Damian D'Oliveira. **Assistant
Coach**: Matt Mason. **Captain**: D.K.H.Mitchell. **Vice-Captain**: tba. **Overseas Players**:
P.J.Hughes, M.Klinger and Saeed Ajmal (T20 only). **2012 Beneficiary**: M.S.Mason
(testimonial). **Head Groundsman**: Tim Packwood. **Scorer**: Dawn Pugh. ‡ New registration.
NQ Not qualified for England.

*Worcestershire revised their capping policy in 2002 and now award players with their
County Colours when they make their Championship debut.*

ALI, Moeen Munir (Moseley S), b Birmingham, Warwks 18 Jun 1987. Brother of A.K.Ali
(Worcs, Glos 2005-10) and cousin of Kabir Ali (*see HAMPSHIRE*). 6'0". LHB, OB.
Warwickshire 2005-06, having joined staff when aged 15. Worcestershire debut 2007. HS
158 v Somerset (Worcester) 2011. BB 5-36 v Middx (Lord's) 2010. LO HS 158 v Sussex
(Horsham) 2011 (CB40). LO BB 3-32 v Yorks (Worcester) 2009 (P40). T20 HS 72. T20 BB
3-19.

ANDREW, Gareth Mark (Ansford Community S; Richard Huish C), b Yeovil, Somerset
27 Dec 1983. 6'0". LHB, RMF. Somerset 2003-05; 2nd XI debut 1999, aged 15y 247d.
Worcestershire debut 2008. HS 92* v Notts (Worcester) 2009. 50 wkts (1): 52 (2011). BB
5-58 v Middx (Kidderminster) 2008. LO HS 104 v Surrey (Oval) 2010 (CB40). LO BB 5-31
v Yorks (Worcester) 2009 (P40). T20 HS 65*. T20 BB 4-22.

BLOFIELD, Alexander David (Shrewsbury S), b Shrewsbury, Shropshire 28 Oct 1991.
6'2". RHB, OB. Worcestershire 2nd XI debut 2009. Shropshire 2009. Awaiting 1st XI debut.

CAMERON, James Gair (St George's C, Harare; U of WA), b Harare, Zimbabwe 31 Jan
1986. LHB, RM. British passport holder. Debut (Worcestershire) 2010. HS 105 v Sussex
(Worcester) 2010. BB 2-18 v Northants (Worcester) 2010. LO HS 69 v Derbys (Worcester)
2011 (CB40). LO BB 4-44 v Glamorgan (Cardiff) 2010 (CB40). T20 HS 55. T20 BB 3-22.

CHOUDHRY, Shaaiq Hussain (Fir Vale S; Bradford U), b Sheffield, Yorkshire 3 Nov 1985.
5'10". RHB, SLA. MCC 2007. Warwickshire 2009. Worcestershire debut 2010. Bradford/
Leeds UCCE 2006-08 (not f-c). HS 75 Wa v Durham UCCE (Durham) 2009. CC HS 63 v
Sussex (Hove) 2010. BB 1-14 v Lancs (Blackpool) 2011. LO HS 39 v Sussex (Hove) 2010
(CB40). LO BB 4-54 v Surrey (Oval) 2010 (CB40). T20 HS 26*. T20 BB 2-24.

COX, Oliver Ben (Bromsgrove S), b Wordsley, Stourbridge 2 Feb 1992. 5'10". RHB, WK. Debut (Worcestershire) 2009, scoring 61 v Somerset (Taunton). Worcestershire 2nd XI debut 2009. HS 61 (*see above*). LO HS 9* v Somerset (Worcester) 2010 (CB40). T20 HS 6*.

D'OLIVEIRA, Brett Louis (Worcester SFC), b Worcester 28 Feb 1992. Son of D.B.D'Oliveira (Worcs 1982-95), grandson of B.L.D'Oliveira (Worcs, EP and England 1964-80). RHB, LB. Worcestershire 2nd XI debut 2010. Awaiting f-c debut. LO HS- and LO BB 1-40 v Yorks (Leeds) 2011 (CB40) – only 1st XI game.

HARRISON, Nicholas Luke (Hardenhuish S, Chippenham), b Bath, Somerset 3 Feb 1992. RHB, RMF. Worcestershire 2nd XI debut 2010. Wiltshire 2009-10. Awaiting f-c debut. LO HS 2* v Sussex (Horsham) 2011 (CB40). LO BB 2-43 v Yorks (Leeds) 2011 (CB40).

‡NO**HUGHES, Phillip** Joel, b Macksville, NSW, Australia 30 Nov 1988. LHB, OB. New South Wales 2007-08 to date. Middlesex 2009, scoring 118 and 65* on debut. Hampshire 2010. **Tests** (A): 17 (2008-09 to 2011-12); HS 160 (and 115) v SA (Durban) 2008-09. F-c Tours (A): E 2009; SA 2008-09, 2011-12; NZ 2009-10; I 2008-09 (Aus A); SL 2011. HS 198 NSW v S Australia (Adelaide) 2008-09. UK HS 195 M v Surrey (Oval) 2009. LO HS 138 Australia A v South Africa A (Harare) 2011. T20 HS 83.

JONES, Richard Alan (Grange HS and King Edward VI C, Stourbridge; Loughborough U), b Wordsley, Stourbridge 6 Nov 1986. 6'2". RHB, RMF. Debut (Worcestershire) 2007. Matabeleland Tuskers 2011-12. HS 62 MT v SR (Bulawayo) 2011-12. Wo HS 53* v Durham (Worcester) 2009. BB 7-115 v Sussex (Hove) 2010. LO HS 11* v Sussex (Worcester) 2010 (CB40). LO BB 1-25 MT v ME (Bulawayo) 2011-12. T20 HS 9. T20 BB 1-17.

KAPIL, Aneesh (Denstone C), b Wolverhampton 3 Aug 1993. 5'8". RHB, RFM. Worcestershire 2nd XI debut 2008, aged 15y 10d. Debut (Worcestershire) 2011. HS 54 v Sussex (Horsham) 2011 – on debut. BB 2-38 v Lancs (Blackpool) 2011. LO HS 44 v Yorks (Worcester) 2011 (CB40). LO BB 1-18 v Netherlands (Worcester) 2011 (CB40). T20 HS 13. T20 BB 3-9.

NO**KERVEZEE, Alexei** Nicolaas (Duneside HS, Namibia; Grenoobi HS, SA; Segbroek C, Holland), b Walvis Bay, Namibia 11 Sep 1989. 5'8". RHB, OB. Netherlands 2005 to 2009-10. Worcestershire debut 2008. Worcestershire 2nd XI debut 2007. **LOI** (Ne): 37 (2006 to 2011); HS 92 v Kenya (Voorburg) 2010; BB – . **IT20** (Ne): 6 (2009 to 2009-10); HS 39 v Canada (Dubai) 2009-10 and 39 v Afghanistan (Dubai) 2009-10). HS 155 v Derbys (Derby) 2010. BB 1-14 Netherlands v Namibia (Windhoek) 2007-08. LO HS 121* Netherlands v Denmark (Potchefstroom) 2008-09. LO BB – . T20 HS 56.

‡NO**KLINGER, Michael**, b Kew, Melbourne, Australia 4 Jul 1980. 5'10½". RHB. Victoria 1999-00 to 2007-08. S Australia 2008-09 to date. HS 255 S Aus v WA (Adelaide) 2008-09. LO HS 133* S Aus v Tas (Adelaide) 2008-09. T20 HS 78.

LEACH, Joseph (Shrewsbury S), b Stafford 30 Oct 1990. 6'1". RHB, RMF. Worcestershire 2nd XI debut 2008. Staffordshire 2008-09. Awaiting 1st XI debut.

‡**LUCAS, David** Scott (Djanogly CTC, Nottingham), b Nottingham 19 Aug 1978. 6'2". RHB, LMF. Nottinghamshire 1999-2002. Yorkshire 2005. Northamptonshire 2007-11; cap 2009. Lincolnshire 2006. HS 60 Nh v Leics (Leicester) 2011. 50 wkts (1): 60 (2009). BB 7-24 (12-73 match) Nh v Glos (Cheltenham) 2009. LO HS 32* Nh v Lancs (Manchester) 2009 (FPT). LO BB 5-48 Nh v Hants (Northampton) 2011 (CB40). T20 HS 5*. T20 BB 3-19.

MANUEL, Jack Kenneth (Wilncote HS, Tamworth), b Sutton Coldfield, Warwks 13 Feb 1991. 6'1". LHB, OB. Debut (Worcestershire) 2011. Worcestershire 2nd XI debut 2008. England U19s 2009 to 2010. HS 5 v Somerset (Worcester) 2011 – only f-c game. LO HS 48 v Sussex (Worcester) 2011 (CB40). T20 HS 31.

MITCHELL, Daryl Keith Henry (Prince Henry's HS; University C, Worcester), b Badsey, near Evesham 25 Nov 1983. 5'10". RHB, RM. Debut (Worcestershire) 2005; captain 2011 to date. Mountaineers 2011-12. 1000 runs (2); most – 1180 (2010). HS 298 v Somerset (Taunton) 2009. BB 4-49 v Yorks (Leeds) 2010. LO HS 92 v Somerset (Taunton) 2008 (FPT). LO BB 4-42 v Lancs (Worcester) 2006 (CGT). T20 HS 45. T20 BB 4-11 v Glos (Bristol) 2008 – Wo record.

PARDOE, Matthew Graham (Haybridge HS), b Stourbridge 5 Jan 1991. 6'1". LHB, LM. Debut (Worcestershire) 2011. Worcestershire 2nd XI debut 2007. HS 74 v Notts (Nottingham) 2011. LO HS 11 v Middx (Worcester) 2011 (CB40).

PINNER, Neil Douglas (RGS Worcester), b Wordsley, Stourbridge 29 Sep 1990. 5'11". RHB, OB. Debut (Worcestershire) 2011. Worcestershire 2nd XI debut 2008. HS 0 v Notts (Worcester) 2011 – only f-c game. LO HS 37 v Kent (Canterbury) 2011 (CB40). LO BB – .

RICHARDSON, Alan (Alleyne's HS, Stone; Stafford CFE; Durham U), b Newcastle-under-Lyme, Staffs 6 May 1975. 6'2". RHB, RMF. Derbyshire 1995 (one match). Warwickshire 1999-2004; cap 2002. Middlesex 2005-09; cap 2005, taking 7-113 v Notts (Lord's) on debut. Worcestershire debut 2010. Staffordshire 1996-98. Minor Counties 1998. HS 91 Wa v Hants (Birmingham) 2002 – adding Wa record 214 for 10th wicket with N.V.Knight. Wo HS 41 v Sussex (Horsham) 2011. 50 wkts (3); most – 73 (2011). BB 8-46 Wa v Sussex (Birmingham) 2002. Wo BB 6-22 v Lancs (Worcester) 2011. LO HS 21* M v Lancs (Lord's) 2005 (NL). LO BB 5-35 Wa v Staffs (Stone) 2002 (CGT). T20 HS 6*. T20 BB 3-13.

RUSSELL, Christopher James (Medina HS), b Newport, I-o-W 16 Feb 1989. 6'1". RHB, RMF. Worcestershire 2nd XI debut 2008. Awaiting f-c debut. LO HS-and LO BB 1-23 v Unicorns (Worcester) 2010 (CB40).

NQ**SAEED AJMAL**, b Faisalabad, Pakistan 14 Oct 1977. RHB, OB. Faisalabad 1996-97 to 2006-07. KRL 2000-01 to 2008-09. Islamabad 2001-02. Federal Areas 2007-08. ZT Bank 2009-10 to date. Worcestershire 2011. Returns in 2012 for T20 only. **Tests** (P): 20 (2009 to 2011-12); HS 50 v E (Birmingham) 2010. BB 7-55 (10-97 match) v E (Dubai) 2011-12. **LOI** (P): 61 (2008 to 2011-12); HS 33 v NZ (Abu Dhabi) 2009-10. BB 5-43 v E (Abu Dhabi) 2011-12. **IT20** (P): 37 (2009 to 2011-12); HS 21* v WI (Gros Islet) 2010-11; BB 4-19 v Ireland (Oval) 2009. F-c Tours (P): E 2010; A 2009-10; WI 2011; NZ 2009-10; SL 2009; Z 2011; B 2011-12; UAE 2010-11 (v SA), 2011-12 (v SL), 2011-12 (v E). HS 53 Faisalabad v Quetta (Sargodha) 2003-04. Wo HS 47 v Yorks (Scarborough) 2011. 50 wkts (0+1); 62 (2006-07). BB 7-55 (see Tests). Wo BB 6-124 v Sussex (Horsham) 2011. LO HS 33 (see LOI). LO BB 5-18 Faisalabad v Karachi (Karachi) 2003-04. T20 HS 21*. T20 BB 4-14.

SCOTT, Ben James Matthew (Whitton S, Richmond; Richmond C), b Isleworth 4 Aug 1981. 5'8". RHB, WK. Surrey 2003. Middlesex 2004-09; cap 2007. Worcestershire 2010-11 (on loan). Joins permanently in 2012. MCC YC 2000. F-c Tour (Eng A): NZ 2008-09. HS 164* M v Northants (Uxbridge) 2008. Wo HS 98* v Sussex (Hove) 2010. LO HS 73* M v Surrey (Southgate) 2006 (CGT). T20 HS 43*.

SHANTRY, Jack David (Priory SS; Shrewsbury SFC; Liverpool U), b Shrewsbury, Shropshire 29 Jan 1988. Son of B.K.Shantry (Gloucestershire 1978-79) and brother of A.J.Shantry (see GLAMORGAN). 6'4". LHB, LM. Debut (Worcestershire) 2009. Shropshire 2007-09. HS 47* v Yorks (Scarborough) 2011. BB 5-49 v Leics (Leicester) 2010. LO HS 18 v Sussex (Hove) 2010 (CB40). LO BB 3-33 v Unicorns (Worcester) 2010 (CB40). T20 HS 6*. T20 BB 3-23.

SOLANKI, Vikram Singh (Regis S, Wolverhampton), b Udaipur, India 1 Apr 1976. 6'0". RHB, OB, occ WK. Debut (Worcestershire) 1995; cap 1998; captain 2005-10; benefit 2007. Rajasthan 2006-07. **LOI**: 51 (1999-00 to 2006); HS 106 v SA (Oval) 2003; BB 1-17 v SL (Leeds) 2006. **IT20**: 3 (2005 to 2007-08); HS 43 v I (Durban) 2007-08. F-c Tours (Eng A): SA 1998-99, 1999-00 (Eng – part); WI 2000-01, 2005-06 (Captain); NZ 1999-00; SL 2004-05; Z 1996-97 (Wo), 1998-99; B 1999-00. 1000 runs (6); most – 1339 (1999). HS 270 v Glos (Cheltenham) 2008, sharing Wo 2nd wkt record partnership of 316 with S.C.Moore. Won Walter Lawrence Trophy 2009 with 49-ball hundred v Glamorgan (Worcester). BB 5-40 v Middx (Lord's) 2004. LO HS 164* v Worcs CB (Worcester) 2003 (CGT). LO BB 4-14 v Somerset (Taunton) 2006 (P40). T20 HS 100. T20 BB 1-6.

RELEASED/RETIRED
(Having made a County First-Class or List A appearance in 2011)

MASON, Matthew Sean (Mazenod C, Lesmurdie, WA), b Claremont, Perth, Australia 20 Mar 1974. British passport. 6'5". RHB, RFM. W Australia 1996-97 to 1997-98. Worcestershire 2002-11; benefit 2012. HS 63 v Warwks (Worcester) 2004. 50 wkts (3); most – 53 (2003, 2005). BB 8-45 (10-117) v Glos (Worcester) 2006. LO HS 25 v Durham (Worcester) 2004 (NL). LO BB 4-34 v Surrey (Guildford) 2003 (NL). T20 HS 8*. T20 BB 3-42.

[NQ]**ROACH, Kemar** Andre Jamal, b St Lucy, Barbados 30 Jun 1988. RHB, RF. Barbados 2007-08 to date. Worcestershire 2011. **Tests** (WI): 14 (2009 to 2011-12); HS 29 v P (Basseterre) 2011; BB 6-48 v B (St George's) 2009. **LOI** (WI): 36 (2008 to 2011-12); HS 24* v I (Visakhapatnam) 2011-12; BB 6-27 v Netherlands (Delhi) 2010-11. **IT20** (WI): 10 (2008 to 2010); HS 3* and BB 2-25 v SA (North Sound) 2010. F-c Tours (WI): A 2009-10; NZ 2008-09; I 2011-12; SL 2010-11; B 2011-12. HS 52* Barbados v Windward Is (St Andrew's) 2008-09. Wo HS 6 and Wo BB 3-44 v Lancs (Worcester) 2011. BB 7-23 Barbados v CC&C (Charlestown) 2009-10. LO HS (see LOI). LO BB (see LOI). T20 HS 10. T20 BB 2-25.

[NQ]**SHAKIB AL HASAN**, b Magura, Jessore, Bangladesh 24 Mar 1987. LHB, SLA. Debut Bangladesh CB President's XI 2004-05. Khulna Division 2004-05 to date. Worcestershire 2010-11. **Tests** (B): 26 (2007 to 2011-12, 9 as captain); HS 144 v P (Dhaka) 2011-12; BB 7-36 (9-115 match) v NZ (Chittagong) 2008-09. **LOI** (B): 122 (2006 to 2011-12, 47 as captain); HS 134* v Canada (St John's) 2006-07; BB 4-16 v WI (Chittagong) 2011-12. **IT20** (B): 16 (2006-07 to 2011-12, 4 as captain); HS 47 v P (Gros Islet) 2009-10; BB 4-34 v WI (Johannesburg) 2007-08. F-c Tours (B) (C=captain): E 2008 (B A), 2010C; SA 2008-09; WI 2009C; NZ 2007-08, 2009-10C; SL 2007; Z 2004-05 (B A), 2006 (B A), 2011C. HS 144 (see Tests). Wo HS 90 v Derbys (Derby) 2010. BB 7-32 v Middx (Lord's) 2010. LO HS 134* (see LOI). LO BB 4-16 (see LOI). T20 HS 86*. T20 BB 4-31.

SHANKAR, Adrian (Bedford S; Queens C, Cambridge U), b Ascot, Berks 7 May 1982. RHB, OB. Cambridge U 2002-05; blue 2002-03-04-05. Worcestershire 2011. Lancashire 2nd XI 2008-10. Bedfordshire 2000-06. HS 143 CU v Oxford U (Oxford) 2002. Wo HS 10* v Durham (Worcester) 2011. LO HS 27 Beds v Sussex (Luton) 2005 (CGT).

WHELAN, Christopher David (St Margaret's HS), b Liverpool, Lancs 8 May 1986. 6'2". RHB, RMF. Middlesex 2005-07. Worcestershire 2008-11. HS 58 v Middx (Kidderminster) 2008. BB 5-95 v Lancs (Worcester) 2009. LO HS 11 v Yorks (Worcester) 2009 (P40). LO BB 4-27 v Hants (Worcester) 2009 (FPT). T20 HS 2*. T20 BB 4-21.

^{NQ}**WRIGHT, Damien** Geoffrey (Terrigal HS, NSW), b Casino, NSW, Australia 25 Jul 1975. 6'1". RHB, RFM. Tasmania 1997-98 to 2006-07. Scotland 2001 (CGT). Northamptonshire 2003, 2005. Glamorgan 2007. Victoria 2008-09 to date. Sussex 2009. Somerset 2010. Worcestershire 2011. HS 111 Tas v Vic (Hobart) 2004-05. UK HS 85 Nh v Worcs (Worcester) 2005. Wo HS 65 v Notts (Nottingham) 2011. 50 wkts (1): 53 (2005). BB 8-60 Nh v Yorks (Leeds) 2005. Wo BB 6-56 v Somerset (Taunton) 2011. LO HS 55 Scotland v Middx CB (Southgate) 2001 (CGT). LO BB 5-37 Nh v Notts (Northampton) 2005. T20 HS 38*. T20 BB 3-17.

D.A.Wheeldon left the staff, without making a First-Class County or List A appearance in 2011.

SURREY RELEASED/RETIRED (continued from p 171)

^{NQ}**YASIR ARAFAT** Satti (Gordon C, Rawalpindi), b Rawalpindi, Pakistan 12 Mar 1982. 5'9½". RHB, RFM. Rawalpindi 1997-98 to 2006-07. Pakistan Reserves 1999-00. KRL 2000-01 to date. National Bank 2005-06. Sussex 2006, 2009-10; cap 2006. Kent 2007-08; cap 2007. Federal Areas 2007-08 to 2008-09. Surrey 2011. Scotland (not f-c) 2004-05. **Tests** (P): 3 (2007-08 to 2008-09); HS 50* v SL (Karachi) 2008-09; BB 5-161 v I (Bangalore) 2007-08 – on debut. **LOI** (P): 11 (1999-00 to 2009); HS 27 v SA (Chandigarh) 2006-07; BB 1-28 v SL (Karachi) 1999-00. **IT20** (P): 7 (2007-08 to 2009-10); HS 17 v Scotland (Durban) 2007-08; BB 3-32 v E (Dubai) 2009-10. F-c Tours (P): WI 2010-11 (Pak A); I 2007-08; SL 2001 (Pak A), 2004-05 (Pak A). HS 170 KRL v Multan (Multan) 2011-12. CC HS 122 K v Sussex (Canterbury) 2007. Sy HS 65 and Sy BB 5-86 v Glos (Cheltenham) 2011. 50 wkts (0+4); most – 91 (2001-02). BB 9-35 KRL v SSGC (Rawalpindi) 2008-09. CC BB 6-86 K v Hants (Canterbury) 2008. LO HS 110* Otago v Auckland (Oamaru) 2009-10. LO BB 6-24 Pakistan A v England A (Colombo) 2004-05. T20 HS 49. T20 BB 4-17.

WORCESTERSHIRE 2011

RESULTS SUMMARY

	Place	Won	Lost	Tied	Drew	NR
LV= County Championship (1st Division)	7th	4	11		1	
All First-Class Matches		4	11		1	
Clydesdale Bank 40 (Group A)	7th	2	9			1
Friends Life t20 (North Group)	5th	6	7			3

LV= COUNTY CHAMPIONSHIP AVERAGES

BATTING AND FIELDING

Cap†		M	I	NO	HS	Runs	Avge	100	50	Ct/St
1998	V.S.Solanki	16	30	3	173	1148	42.51	3	6	23
2008	M.M.Ali	16	29	1	158	930	33.21	1	5	12
2005	D.K.H.Mitchell	13	25	2	66	751	32.65	–	5	33
2010	B.J.M.Scott	12	20	5	73	463	30.86	–	2	31/4
2009	A.N.Kervezee	16	29	1	128	800	28.57	1	6	4
2010	J.G.Cameron	12	23	1	98	578	26.27	–	3	7
2008	G.M.Andrew	16	29	2	67	666	24.66	–	4	8
2009	J.D.Shantry	7	11	4	47*	148	21.14	–	–	1
2011	M.G.Pardoe	13	26	–	74	507	19.50	–	4	3
2011	A.Kapil	5	8	–	54	139	17.37	–	1	2
2011	Saeed Ajmal	3	6	1	47	86	17.20	–	–	–
2011	D.G.Wright	7	13	–	65	212	16.30	–	1	3
2009	O.B.Cox	4	8	1	23	86	12.28	–	–	15
2002	M.S.Mason	3	6	–	63	67	11.16	–	1	–
2010	A.Richardson	16	26	11	41	151	10.06	–	–	5
2007	R.A.Jones	6	10	2	23*	51	6.37	–	–	–
2010	S.H.Choudhry	2	4	–	9	23	5.75	–	–	1
2011	K.A.J.Roach	4	6	1	6	17	3.40	–	–	–

Also batted (one match each): J.K.Manuel (cap 2011) 5, 0; N.D.Pinner (cap 2011) 0 (1 ct); Shakib Al Hasan (cap 2010) 54 (1 ct); A.Shankar (cap 2011) 10*; C.D.Whelan (cap 2008) 11*.

BOWLING

	O	M	R	W	Avge	Best	5wI	10wM
A.Richardson	663.1	179	1783	73	24.42	6- 22	3	–
D.G.Wright	272.4	55	827	31	26.67	6- 56	3	–
Saeed Ajmal	164.1	31	471	17	27.70	6-124	2	–
G.M.Andrew	384.1	63	1545	52	29.71	5- 59	1	–
R.A.Jones	109.4	14	500	16	31.25	3- 38	–	–
K.A.J.Roach	133	25	550	14	39.28	3- 44	–	–
J.D.Shantry	204.1	42	634	14	45.28	3- 65	–	–
M.M.Ali	267.2	21	925	18	51.38	4- 53	–	–
Also bowled:								
Shakib Al Hasan	38.2	5	127	7	18.14	4- 42	–	–
M.S.Mason	95.3	19	290	7	41.42	3- 72	–	–

J.G.Cameron 7-0-42-0; S.H.Choudhry 11-2-70-1; A.Kapil 30.2-1-138-4; D.K.H.Mitchell 28-6-82-1; C.D.Whelan 8-0-35-0.

Worcestershire played no first-class fixtures outside the County Championship in 2011. The First-Class Averages (pp 223–240) give the records of Worcestershire players in all first-class county matches.

† Worcestershire revised their capping policy in 2002 and now award players with their County Colours when they make their Championship debut.

WORCESTERSHIRE RECORDS

FIRST-CLASS CRICKET

Highest Total	For 701-6d		v	Surrey	Worcester	2007
	V 701-4d		by	Leics	Worcester	1906
Lowest Total	For 24		v	Yorkshire	Huddersfield	1903
	V 30		by	Hampshire	Worcester	1903
Highest Innings	For 405*	G.A.Hick	v	Somerset	Taunton	1988
	V 331*	J.D.B.Robertson	for	Middlesex	Worcester	1949

Highest Partnership for each Wicket

1st	309	H.K.Foster/F.L.Bowley	v	Derbyshire	Derby	1901
2nd	316	S.C.Moore/V.S.Solanki	v	Glos	Cheltenham	2008
3rd	438*	G.A.Hick/T.M.Moody	v	Hampshire	Southampton	1997
4th	330	B.F.Smith/G.A.Hick	v	Somerset	Taunton	2006
5th	393	E.G.Arnold/W.B.Burns	v	Warwicks	Birmingham	1909
6th	265	G.A.Hick/S.J.Rhodes	v	Somerset	Taunton	1988
7th	256	D.A.Leatherdale/S.J.Rhodes	v	Notts	Nottingham	2002
8th	184	S.J.Rhodes/S.R.Lampitt	v	Derbyshire	Kidderminster	1991
9th	181	J.A.Cuffe/R.D.Burrows	v	Glos	Worcester	1907
10th	119	W.B.Burns/G.A.Wilson	v	Somerset	Worcester	1906

Best Bowling	For	9- 23	C.F.Root	v	Lancashire	Worcester	1931
(Innings)	V	10- 51	J.Mercer	for	Glamorgan	Worcester	1936
Best Bowling	For	15- 87	A.J.Conway	v	Glos	Moreton-in-M	1914
(Match)	V	17-212	J.C.Clay	for	Glamorgan	Swansea	1937

Most Runs – Season	2654	H.H.I.H.Gibbons	(av 52.03)	1934
Most Runs – Career	34490	D.Kenyon	(av 34.18)	1946-67
Most 100s – Season	10	G.M.Turner		1970
	10	G.A.Hick		1988
Most 100s – Career	106	G.A.Hick		1984-2008
Most Wkts – Season	207	C.F.Root	(av 17.52)	1925
Most Wkts – Career	2143	R.T.D.Perks	(av 23.73)	1930-55
Most Career W-K Dismissals	1095	S.J.Rhodes	(991 ct; 104 st)	1985-2004
Most Career Catches in the Field	528	G.A.Hick		1984-2008

LIMITED-OVERS CRICKET

Highest Total	50ov	404-3		v	Devon	Worcester	1987
	40ov	376-6		v	Surrey	Oval	2010
	T20	227-6		v	Northants	Kidderminster	2007
Lowest Total	50ov	58		v	Ireland	Worcester	2009
	40ov	86		v	Yorkshire	Leeds	1969
	T20	86		v	Northants	Worcester	2006
Highest Innings	50ov	180*	T.M.Moody	v	Surrey	The Oval	1994
	40ov	160	T.M.Moody	v	Kent	Worcester	1991
	T20	116*	G.A.Hick	v	Northants	Luton	2004
Best Bowling	50ov	7-19	N.V.Radford	v	Beds	Bedford	1991
	40ov	6-16	Shoaib Akhtar	v	Glos	Worcester	2005
	T20	4-11	D.K.H.Mitchell	v	Glos	Bristol	2008

YORKSHIRE

Formation of Present Club: 8 January 1863
Substantial Reorganisation: 10 December 1891
Inaugural First-Class Match: 1864
Colours: Dark Blue, Light Blue and Gold
Badge: White Rose
County Championships (since 1890): (30) 1893, 1896,
1898, 1900, 1901, 1902, 1905, 1908, 1912, 1919, 1922,
1923, 1924, 1925, 1931, 1932, 1933, 1935, 1937, 1938,
1939, 1946, 1959, 1960, 1962, 1963, 1966, 1967, 1968,
2001
Joint Champions: (1) 1949
Gillette/NatWest/C&G/FP Trophy Winners: (3) 1965,
1969, 2002
Benson and Hedges Cup Winners: (1) 1987
Pro 40/National League (Div 1) Winners: (0); best – 2nd
2000
Sunday League Winners: (1) 1983
Clydesdale Bank 40 Winners: (0); best – Semi-Finalist
2010
Twenty20 Cup Winners: (0); best – Quarter-Finalist 2007

Chairman: Colin Graves, Carnegie Pavilion, Kirkstall Lane, Headingley, Leeds, LS6 3BU •
Tel: 0871 971 1222 • Fax: 0113 278 4099 • Email: cricket@yorkshireccc.com • Web:
www.yorkshireccc.com

Director of Professional Cricket: Martyn D.Moxon. **Senior Coach:** Jason N.Gillespie.
Captain: A.W.Gale. **Vice-Captain:** tba. **Overseas Players:** none. **2012 Beneficiary:** none.
Head Groundsman: Andy Fogarty. **Scorer:** John T.Potter. ‡ New registration. NQ Not
qualified for England.

ASHRAF, Moin Aqeeb (Dixons City Academy, Bradford), b Bradford 5 Jan 1992. 6'4".
RHB, RMF. Debut (Yorkshire) 2010. Yorkshire 2nd XI debut 2009. HS 10 and BB 5-32 v
Kent (Leeds) 2010. LO HS-. LO BB 2-25 England Dev XI v Sri Lanka A (Manchester)
2011.

AZEEM Muhammad **RAFIQ** (Holgate S Sports C; Barnsley C), b Karachi, Pakistan 27 Feb
1991. 5'11". RHB, OB. Debut (Yorkshire) 2009. Derbyshire (on loan) 2011. Yorkshire 2nd
XI debut 2008. England U19s 2009 to 2010. HS 100 v Worcs (Worcester) 2009. BB 4-92 v
Lancs (Manchester) 2010. LO HS 18 De v Netherlands (Deventer) 2011 (CB40). LO BB
1-29 De v Worcs (Worcester) 2011 (CB40). T20 HS 11*. T20 BB 3-15.

BAIRSTOW, Jonathan Marc (St Peter's S, York; Leeds Met U), b Bradford 26 Sep 1989.
Son of D.L.Bairstow (Yorkshire, GW, England 1970-90) and brother of A.D.Bairstow
(Derbyshire 1995). 6'0". RHB, WK. Debut (Yorkshire) 2009; cap 2011. Yorkshire 2nd XI
debut 2007. YC 2011. Inaugural winner of Young Wisden Schools Cricketer of the Year 2008.
LOI: 6 (2011 to 2011-12); HS 41* v I (Cardiff) 2011. IT20: 6 (2011 to 2011-12): HS 60* v
P (Dubai) 2011-12. F-c Tour (EL): WI 2010-11. 1000 runs (1): 1213 (2011). HS 205 v Notts
(Nottingham) 2011. LO HS 114 v Middx (Lord's) 2011 (CB40). T20 HS 60*.

BALLANCE, Gary Simon (Peterhouse S, Marondera, Zimbabwe; Harrow S; Leeds Met
U), b Harare, Zimbabwe 22 Nov 1989. Nephew of G.S.Ballance (Rhodesia B 1978-79) and
D.L.Houghton (Rhodesia/Zimbabwe 1978-79 to 1997-98). 6'0". LHB, LB. Debut (York-
shire) 2008. Mid West Rhinos 2010-11 to date. Derbyshire (List A) 2006-07. HS 210 MWR
v SR (Masvingo) 2011-12. Y HS 111 v Warwks (Birmingham) 2011. LO HS 135* MWR v
ME (Kwekwe) 2010-11. T20 HS 67.

194

BRESNAN, Timothy Thomas (Castleford HS and TC; Pontefract New C), b Pontefract 28 Feb 1985. 6'0". RHB, RFM. Debut (Yorkshire) 2003; cap 2006. MCC 2006, 2009. **ECB central contract 2011-12. Tests:** 10 (2009 to 2011); HS 91 v B (Dhaka) 2009-10; BB 5-48 v I (Nottingham) 2011. **LOI:** 58 (2006 to 2011-12); HS 80 v SA (Centurion) 2009-10; BB 5-48 v I (Bangalore) 2010-11. **IT20:** 20 (2006 to 2011-12); HS 23* v NZ (Gros Islet) 2009-10; BB 3-10 v P (Cardiff) 2010. F-c Tours: A 2010-11; B 2006-07 (Eng A), 2009-10. HS 126* Eng A v Indians (Chelmsford) 2007. Y HS 116 v Surrey (Oval) 2007, sharing in Y record 9th wicket partnership of 246 with J.N.Gillespie. BB 5-42 v Worcs (Worcester) 2005. LO HS 80 (*see LOI*). BB 5-48 (*see LOI*). T20 HS 42. T20 BB 3-10.

BROPHY, Gerard Louis (Christian Brothers C, Boksburg; Witwatersrand TC), b Welkom, OFS, South Africa 26 Nov 1975. British/EU passport. Qualified for England 2006. 5'11". RHB, WK, RM. Transvaal/Gauteng 1996-97 to 1998-99. Free State 1999-00 to 2000-01. Northamptonshire 2002-05. Yorkshire debut 2006; cap 2008; benefit 2011. F-c Tour (SA Acad): Z 1998. HS 185 SA Academy v Zim President's XI (Harare) 1998-99. UK HS 181 Nh v Sussex (Hove) 2004. Y HS 177* v Worcs (Worcester) 2011. LO HS 93* v Derbys (Leeds) 2010 (CB40). T20 HS 57*.

GALE, Andrew William (Whitcliffe Mount S; Heckmondwike GS), b Dewsbury 28 Nov 1983. 6'2". LHB, LB. Debut (Yorkshire) 2004, 2006 to date; cap 2008; captain 2010 to date. F-c Tour (EL): WI 2010-11. HS 151* v Notts (Nottingham) 2010. BB 1-33 v Loughborough UCCE (Leeds) 2007. LO HS 125* v Essex (Chelmsford) 2010 (CB40). T20 HS 91.

GELDART, Callum John (Huddersfield New C), b Huddersfield 17 Dec 1991. 5'11". LHB, RM. Debut (Yorkshire) 2010. Yorkshire 2nd XI debut 2009. HS 34 v Durham MCCU (Durham) 2011 – awaiting CC debut.

GIBSON, Barney Peter (Crawshaw HS, Pudsey), b Leeds 31 Mar 1996. 5'8½". RHB, WK. Debut (Yorkshire) 2011, aged 15y 27d, becoming youngest player to play f-c cricket, beating a record set in 1867. HS 1* v Durham MCCU (Durham) 2011.

HANNON-DALBY, Oliver James (Brooksbank S, Leeds Met U), b Halifax 20 Jun 1989. 6'7". LHB, RMF. Debut (Yorkshire) 2008. No 1st XI appearances in 2009. Yorkshire 2nd XI debut 2006. HS 11* v Lancs (Manchester) 2010. BB 5-68 v Warwks (Birmingham) and 5-68 v Somerset (Leeds) 2010 – in consecutive matches. LO HS – . LO BB 2-22 v Worcs (Worcester) 2011 (CB40).

HODGSON, Daniel Mark (Richmond S; Leeds U), b Northallerton 26 Feb 1990. RHB, WK. Yorkshire 2nd XI debut 2011. Leeds/Bradford MCCU 2009-11 (not f-c). Awaiting 1st XI debut.

JAQUES, Philip Anthony (Fig Tree HS, Wollongong; Australian C of PE, Homebush), b Wollongong, NSW, Australia 3 May 1979. 6'1". LHB, SLC. British passport (English parents). New South Wales 2000-01 to date. Northamptonshire 2002; cap 2003. Yorkshire 2004-05; cap 2005. Worcestershire 2006-07, 2010. Returns to Yorkshire in 2012 as UK qualified, subject to ECB approval. **Tests** (A): 11 (2005-06 to 2008); HS 150 v SL (Hobart) 2007-08. **LOI** (A): 6 (2005-06 to 2006-07); HS 94 v SA (Melbourne) 2005-06. F-c Tours (A): WI 2008; P 2005-06 (Aus A), 2007-08 (Aus A); B 2005-06. 1000 runs (4+2); most – 1409 (2003). HS 244 v Essex (Chelmsford) 2006. BB – . LO HS 171* NSW v Q (Sydney) 2009-10. T20 HS 62.

LEES, Alexander Zak (Holy Trinity SS, Halifax), b Halifax 14 Apr 1993. 6'3". LHB, LB. Debut (Yorkshire) 2010. Yorkshire 2nd XI debut 2010. HS 38 v India A (Leeds) 2010. Awaiting CC debut. LO HS 12* v Worcs (Leeds) 2011 (CB40).

LILLEY, Alexander Edward (St Aidan's C of E HS, Harrogate), b Halifax 17 Apr 1992. 5'10". RHB, LM. Debut (Yorkshire) 2011. Yorkshire 2nd XI debut 2010. HS 0 and BB – v Durham MCCU (Durham) 2011 – only 1st XI game.

LYTH, Adam (Caedmon S, Whitby; Whitby Community C), b Whitby 25 Sep 1987. 5'8". LHB, RM. Debut (Yorkshire) 2007; cap 2010. F-c Tour (EL): WI 2010-11. 1000 runs (1): 1509 (2010). HS 142 v Somerset (Taunton) 2010. BB 1-12 v Loughborough UCCE (Leeds) 2007. CC BB 1-20 v Somerset (Scarborough) 2008. LO HS 109* v Sussex (Scarborough) 2009 (P40). LO BB – . T20 HS 59.

McGRATH, Anthony (Yorkshire Martyrs Collegiate S), b Bradford 6 Oct 1975. 6'2". RHB, RM. Debut (Yorkshire) 1995; cap 1999; captain 2003, 2009; benefit 2009. MCC 1999-00. **Tests:** 4 (2003); HS 81 v Z (Chester-le-St) 2003; BB 3-16 v Z (Lord's) 2003. **LOI:** 14 (2003 to 2004); HS 52 v SA (Manchester) 2003; BB 1-13 v WI (Nottingham) 2004. F-c Tours (Eng A): A 1996-97; P 1995-96; Z 1995-96 (Y); B 1999-00 (MCC). 1000 runs (3); most – 1425 (2005). HS 211 v Warwks (Birmingham) 2009. BB 5-39 v Derbys (Derby) 2004. LO HS 148 v Somerset (Taunton) 2006 (P40). LO BB 4-41 v Surrey (Leeds) 2003 (NL). T20 HS 73*. T20 BB 3-17.

PATTERSON, Steven Andrew (Malet Lambert CS; St Mary's SFC, Hull; Leeds U), b Hull 3 Oct 1983.6'4". RHB, RMF. Debut (Yorkshire) 2005. Bradford/Leeds UCCE 2003 (not f-c). HS 53 v Sussex (Hove) 2011. BB 5-50 v Essex (Scarborough) 2010. LO HS 25* v Worcs (Leeds) 2006 (P40). LO BB 6-32 v Derbys (Leeds) 2010. T20 HS 3*. T20 BB 4-30.

PYRAH, Richard Michael (Ossett S; Wakefield C), b Dewsbury 1 Nov 1982. 6'0". RHB, RM. Debut (Yorkshire) 2004; cap 2010. HS 134* v Loughborough MCCU (Leeds) 2010. CC HS 117 v Lancs (Leeds) 2011. BB 5-58 v Notts (Leeds) 2011. LO HS 69 v Netherlands (Leeds) 2011 (CB40). LO BB 5-50 Yorks CB v Somerset (Scarborough) 2002 (CGT). T20 HS 33*. T20 BB 5-16 v Durham (Scarborough) 2011 – Y record.

RANDHAWA, Gurman Singh (Newsome HS; Huddersfield New C), b Huddersfield 25 Jan 1992. 5'10". LHB, SLA. Debut (Yorkshire) 2011. Yorkshire 2nd XI debut 2009. England U19s 2010-11. HS 5 and BB 2-54 v Durham MCCU (Durham) 2011 – only 1st XI game.

RASHID, Adil Usman (Belle Vue S, Bradford), b Bradford 17 Feb 1988. 5'8". RHB, LBG. Debut (Yorkshire) 2006; cap 2008. MCC 2007-09. YC 2007. Match double (114, 48, 8-157 and 2-45) for England U19 v India U19 (Taunton) 2006. **LOI:** 5 (2009 to 2009-10); HS 31* v A (Oval) 2009; BB 1-16 v Ireland (Belfast) 2009. **IT20:** 5 (2009 to 2009-10); HS 9* v SA (Nottingham) 2009; BB 1-11 v WI (Oval) 2009. F-c Tours (EL): WI 2010-11; I 2007-08; B 2006-07 (Eng A). HS 157* v Lancs (Leeds) 2009. 50 wkts (2); most – 65 (2008). BB 7-107 v Hants (Southampton) 2008. LO HS 43 v Netherlands (Amstelveen) 2011 (CB40). BB 3-28 v Middx (Scarborough) 2010 (CB40). T20 HS 34. T20 BB 4-20.

ROOT, Joseph Edward (King Ecgbert S, Sheffield; Worksop C), b Sheffield 30 Dec 1990. 6'0". RHB, OB. Debut (Yorkshire) 2010. Yorkshire 2nd XI debut 2007. England U19s 2009-10 to 2010. 1000 runs (1): 1013 (2011). HS 160 v Sussex (Scarborough) 2011. BB 3-33 v Warwks (Leeds) 2011. LO HS 110* EL v Sri Lanka A (Colombo, RPS) 2011-12. LO BB 2-10 EL v Bangladesh A (Sylhet) 2011-12. T20 HS 46*. T20 BB 1-12.

SAYERS, Joseph John (St Mary's RC CS, Menston; Worcester C, Oxford) b Leeds 5 Nov 1983. 6'0". LHB, OB. Oxford U 2002-04; blue 2002-03-04. Yorkshire debut 2004; cap 2007. 1000 runs (1): 1150 (2009). HS 187 v Kent (Tunbridge W) 2007. BB 3-15 v Durham MCCU (Durham) 2011. CC BB 3-20 v Warwks (Scarborough) 2009. LO HS 62 v Glos (Leeds) 2003 (NL). LO BB 1-31 v Warwks (Birmingham) 2005 (NL). T20 HS 44.

SHAHZAD, Ajmal (Woodhouse Grove S; Bradford U), b Huddersfield 27 Jul 1985. 6'0". RHB, RFM. Debut (Yorkshire) 2006 (first British-born Asian to play for Yorkshire); cap 2010. **Tests:** 1 (2010); HS 5 and BB 3-45 v B (Manchester) 2010. **LOI:** 11 (2009-10 to 2010-11); HS 9 v A (Brisbane) 2010-11; BB 3-41 v B (Bristol) 2010. **IT20:** 3 (2009-10 to 2010-11); HS 0*; BB 2-38 v P (Dubai) 2009-10. F-c Tours: A 2010-11; B 2009-10. HS 88 v Sussex (Hove) 2009. BB 5-51 v Durham (Chester-le-St) 2010. LO HS 59* v Kent (Leeds) 2011 (CB40). LO BB 5-51 v Sri Lanka A (Leeds) 2007. T20 HS 20. T20 BB 3-30.

SIDEBOTTOM, Ryan Jay (King James's GS, Almondbury), b Huddersfield 15 Jan 1978. Son of A.Sidebottom (Yorks, OFS and England 1973-91). 6'3". LHB, LFM. Yorkshire 1997-2003; cap 2000. Returned to Yorkshire in 2011. Nottinghamshire 2004-10; cap 2004; benefit 2010. **Tests**: 22 (2001 to 2009-10); HS 31 v SL (Kandy) 2007-08; BB 7-47 v NZ (Napier) 2007-08. Hat-trick v NZ (Hamilton) 2007-08. **LOI**: 25 (2001-02 to 2009-10); HS 24 v A (Southampton) 2009; BB 3-19 v SL (Dambulla) 2007-08. **IT20**: 18 (2007 to 2010); HS 5* and BB 3-16 v NZ (Auckland) 2007-08. F-c Tours: SA 2009-10; WI 2000-01 (Eng A), 2008-09; NZ 2007-08; SL 2007-08. HS 61 v Worcs (Worcester) 2011. 50 wkts (3); most – 62 (2011). BB 7-37 (11-98 match) v Somerset (Leeds) 2011. LO HS 32 Nt v Middx (Nottingham) 2005 (NL). LO BB 6-40 v Glamorgan (Cardiff) 1998 (SL). T20 HS 17*. T20 BB 3-16.

WAINMAN, James Charles (Leeds GS), b Harrogate 25 Jan 1993. 6'4". LHB, LMF. Yorkshire 2nd XI debut 2010. Awaiting 1st XI debut.

WARDLAW, Iain (Whitcliffe Mount HS, Cleckheaton; Huddersfield U), b Dewsbury 29 Jun 1985. 6'2". RHB, RMF. Debut (Yorkshire) 2011. BB 1-68 v Lancs (Leeds) 2011. LO HS 1 and LO BB – v Netherlands (Amstelveen) 2011 (CB40). T20 HS – . T20 BB 2-17.

RELEASED/RETIRED
(Having made a County First-Class or List A appearance in 2011)

HODGSON, Lee John (De Brus SS), b Middlesbrough 29 Jun 1986. 5'11". RHB, RFM. Surrey 2008 (1 match). Yorkshire 2009-10. HS 63 Sy v Notts (Oval) 2008 – on debut. Y HS 34 v India A (Leeds) 2010. BB 1-42 v Loughborough MCCU (Leeds) 2010. LO HS 9 v Essex (Leeds) 2009 (P40). LO BB 2-44 v Glos (Leeds) 2009 (P40). T20 HS 39*. T20 BB 2-29.

SANDERSON, Ben William (Ecclesfield CS), b Sheffield 3 Jan 1989. RHB, RMF. Yorkshire 2008-10. Yorkshire 2nd XI debut 2006. HS 6 and CC BB 1-87 v Lancs (Leeds) 2008. BB 5-50 v Loughborough MCCU (Leeds) 2010. LO HS 12* v Essex (Leeds) 2010 (CB40). LO BB 2-17 v Derbys (Leeds) 2010 (CB40). T20 HS – . T20 BB 4-21.

WAINWRIGHT, D.J. – see DERBYSHIRE.

J.A.R.Blain and J.E.Lee left the staff, without making a County First-Class or List A appearance in 2011.

YORKSHIRE 2011

RESULTS SUMMARY

	Place	Won	Lost	Tied	Drew	NR
LV= County Championship (1st Division)	8th	3	6		7	
All First-Class Matches		4	6		7	
Clydesdale Bank 40 (Group A)	6th	5	7			
Friends Life t20 (North Group)	6th	6	7			3

LV= COUNTY CHAMPIONSHIP AVERAGES

BATTING AND FIELDING

Cap		M	I	NO	HS	Runs	Avge	100	50	Ct/St
2011	J.M.Bairstow	13	24	2	205	1015	46.13	2	6	43
2007	J.A.Rudolph	4	8	1	120	318	45.42	1	1	2
2008	G.L.Brophy	7	11	3	177*	355	44.37	1	1	7/1
2006	T.T.Bresnan	3	5	1	87	175	43.75	–	1	1
	G.S.Ballance	11	21	4	111	717	42.17	1	8	6
2008	A.W.Gale	12	22	3	145*	769	40.47	2	4	3
	J.E.Root	15	30	4	160	937	36.03	1	4	5
2007	J.J.Sayers	10	20	1	84	581	30.57	–	5	4
2010	A.Lyth	11	22	1	74	553	26.33	–	6	20
2010	R.M.Pyrah	11	16	1	117	376	25.06	1	1	2
2008	A.U.Rashid	16	26	3	82	556	24.17	–	3	9
2010	A.Shahzad	10	15	2	70	307	23.61	–	1	–
1999	A.McGrath	12	23	–	115	485	21.08	1	1	12
2010	D.J.Wainwright	3	5	1	32	84	21.00	–	–	–
2000	R.J.Sidebottom	16	25	6	61	389	20.47	–	2	2
	S.A.Patterson	11	16	6	53	130	13.00	–	1	4
	M.A.Ashraf	6	8	1	8*	21	3.00	–	–	–
	O.J.Hannon-Dalby	4	7	2	6*	10	2.00	–	–	–

Also played (one match each): S.M.Guy 8, 7 (1 ct); I.Wardlaw did not bat.

BOWLING

	O	M	R	W	Avge	Best	5wI	10wM
T.T.Bresnan	97	27	252	13	19.38	4- 50	–	–
R.J.Sidebottom	467.4	107	1364	62	22.00	7- 37	3	1
R.M.Pyrah	266.4	54	956	29	32.96	5- 58	1	–
A.Shahzad	272.2	42	1025	25	41.00	5- 65	1	–
A.U.Rashid	448.3	56	1692	39	43.38	6- 77	2	1
S.A.Patterson	294.5	55	973	21	46.33	4- 51	–	–
M.A.Ashraf	135	23	498	10	49.80	3- 71	–	–
Also bowled:								
J.E.Root	84.3	13	319	7	45.57	3- 33	–	–
D.J.Wainwright	92.5	18	336	5	67.20	3-111	–	–

G.S.Ballance 2-0-11-0; G.L.Brophy 2-0-6-0; O.J.Hannon-Dalby 97-7-325-2; A.Lyth 2-1-10-0; A.McGrath 21-2-56-1; J.A.Rudolph 6-0-28-0; J.J.Sayers 5-1-16-0; I.Wardlaw 13-0-68-1.

The First-Class Averages (pp 223–240) give the records of Yorkshire players in all first-class county matches (Yorkshire's other opponents being Durham MCCU), with the exception of J.M.Bairstow, T.T.Bresnan and J.E.Root, whose first-class figures for Yorkshire are as above, and:

A.Shahzad 11-16-2-70-320-22.85-0-1-0ct. 301.3-46-1116-30-37.20-5/61-2-0.

YORKSHIRE RECORDS

FIRST-CLASS CRICKET

Highest Total	For 887		v	Warwicks	Birmingham	1896
	V 681-7d		by	Leics	Bradford	1996
Lowest Total	For 23		v	Hampshire	Middlesbrough	1965
	V 13		by	Notts	Nottingham	1901
Highest Innings	For 341	G.H.Hirst	v	Leics	Leicester	1905
	V 318*	W.G.Grace	for	Glos	Cheltenham	1876

Highest Partnership for each Wicket

1st	555	P.Holmes/H.Sutcliffe	v	Essex	Leyton	1932
2nd	346	W.Barber/M.Leyland	v	Middlesex	Sheffield	1932
3rd	346	J.J.Sayers/A.McGrath	v	Warwicks	Birmingham	2009
4th	358	D.S.Lehmann/M.J.Lumb	v	Durham	Leeds	2006
5th	340	E.Wainwright/G.H.Hirst	v	Surrey	The Oval	1899
6th	276	M.Leyland/E.Robinson	v	Glamorgan	Swansea	1926
7th	254	W.Rhodes/D.C.F.Burton	v	Hampshire	Dewsbury	1919
8th	292	R.Peel/Lord Hawke	v	Warwicks	Birmingham	1896
9th	246	T.T.Bresnan/J.N.Gillespie	v	Surrey	The Oval	2007
10th	149	G.Boycott/G.B.Stevenson	v	Warwicks	Birmingham	1982

Best Bowling	For 10-10	H.Verity	v	Notts	Leeds	1932
(Innings)	V 10-37	C.V.Grimmett	for	Australians	Sheffield	1930
Best Bowling	For 17-91	H.Verity	v	Essex	Leyton	1933
(Match)	V 17-91	H.Dean	for	Lancashire	Liverpool	1913

Most Runs – Season	2883	H.Sutcliffe	(av 80.08)	1932
Most Runs – Career	38558	H.Sutcliffe	(av 50.20)	1919-45
Most 100s – Season	12	H.Sutcliffe		1932
Most 100s – Career	112	H.Sutcliffe		1919-45
Most Wkts – Season	240	W.Rhodes	(av 12.72)	1900
Most Wkts – Career	3597	W.Rhodes	(av 16.02)	1898-1930
Most Career W-K Dismissals	1186	D.Hunter	(863 ct; 323 st)	1888-1909
Most Career Catches in the Field	665	J.Tunnicliffe		1891-1907

LIMITED-OVERS CRICKET

Highest Total	50ov	411-6		v	Devon	Exmouth	2004
	40ov	352-6		v	Notts	Scarborough	2001
	T20	213-7		v	Worcs	Leeds	2010
Lowest Total	50ov	76		v	Surrey	Harrogate	1970
	40ov	54		v	Essex	Leeds	2003
	T20	90-9		v	Durham	Chester-le-St[2]	2009
Highest Innings	50ov	160	M.J.Wood	v	Devon	Exmouth	2004
	40ov	191	D.S.Lehmann	v	Notts	Scarborough	2001
	T20	109	I.J.Harvey	v	Derbyshire	Leeds	2005
Best Bowling	50ov	7-27	D.Gough	v	Ireland	Leeds	1997
	40ov	7-15	R.A.Hutton	v	Worcs	Leeds	1969
	T20	5-16	R.M.Pyrah	v	Durham	Scarborough	2011

FIRST-CLASS UMPIRES 2012

† New appointment. See page 84 for key to abbreviations.

BAILEY, Robert John (Biddulph HS), b Biddulph, Staffs 28 Oct 1963. 6'3". RHB, OB. Northamptonshire 1982-99; cap 1985; benefit 1993; captain 1996-97. Derbyshire 2000-01; cap 2000. Staffordshire 1980. YC 1984. **Tests:** 4 (1988 to 1989-90); HS 43 v WI (Oval) 1988. **LOI:** 4 (1984-85 to 1989-90); HS 43* v SL (Oval) 1988. F-c Tours: SA 1991-92 (Nh); WI 1989-90; Z 1994-95 (Nh). 1000 runs (13); most – 1987 (1990). HS 224* Nh v Glamorgan (Swansea) 1986. BB 5-54 Nh v Notts (Northampton) 1993. F-c career: 374 matches; 21844 runs @ 40.52, 47 hundreds; 121 wickets @ 42.51; 272 ct. Appointed 2006. Umpired 1 LOI (2011). **ICC International Panel (Third Umpire) 2011 to date.**

BAINTON, Neil Laurence, b Romford, Essex 2 October 1970. No f-c appearances. Appointed 2006.

BENSON, Mark Richard (Sutton Valence S), b Shoreham, Sussex 6 Jul 1958. 5'10". LHB, OB. Kent 1980-95; cap 1981; captain 1991-96 (did not play in 1996); benefit 1991. **Tests:** 1 (1986); HS 30 v I (Birmingham) 1986. **LOI:** 1 (1986); HS 24 v NZ (Leeds) 1986. 1000 runs (11); most – 1725 (1987). HS 257 K v Hants (Southampton) 1991. BB 2-55 K v Surrey (Dartford) 1986. F-c career: 292 matches; 18387 runs @ 40.23, 48 hundreds; 5 wickets @ 98.60; 140 ct. Appointed 2000. Umpired 27 Tests (2004-05 to 2009-10) and 72 LOI (2004 to 2008-09). **ICC Elite Panel 2006-09.**

BODENHAM, Martin John Dale, b Brighton, Sussex 23 Apr 1950. No f-c appearances. Former football referee who officiated at the 1997 League Cup final and four internationals. Appointed 2009.

COOK, Nicholas Grant Billson (Lutterworth GS), b Leicester 17 Jun 1956. 6'0". RHB, SLA. Leicestershire 1978-85; cap 1982. Northamptonshire 1986-94; cap 1987; benefit 1993. **Tests:** 15 (1983 to 1989); HS 31 v A (Oval) 1989. BB 6-65 (11-83 match) v P (Karachi) 1983-84. **LOI:** 3 (1983-84 to 1989-90); HS – ; BB 2-18 v P (Peshawar) 1987-88. F-c Tours: NZ 1979-80 (DHR), 1983-84; P 1983-84, 1987-88; SL 1985-86 (Eng B); Z 1980-81 (Le), 1984-85 (EC). HS 75 Le v Somerset (Taunton) 1980. 50 wkts (8); most – 90 (1982). BB 7-34 (10-97 match) Nn v Essex (Chelmsford) 1992. F-c career: 356 matches; 3137 runs @ 11.66; 879 wickets @ 29.01; 197 ct. Appointed 2009.

COWLEY, Nigel Geoffrey (Dutchy Manor SS, Mere), b Shaftesbury, Dorset 1 Mar 1953. 5'7". RHB, OB. Dorset 1972. Hampshire 1974-89; cap 1978; benefit 1988. Glamorgan 1990. 1000 runs (1): 1042 (1984). HS 109* H v Somerset (Taunton) 1977. BB 6-48 H v Leics (Southampton) 1982. F-c career: 271 matches; 7309 runs @ 23.35, 2 hundreds; 437 wickets @ 34.04; 105 ct. Appointed 2000.

EVANS, Jeffery Howard, b Llanelli, Carms 7 Aug 1954. No f-c appearances. Appointed 2001. Umpired in Indian Cricket League 2007-08.

GALE, Stephen Clifford, b Shrewsbury, Shropshire 3 Jun 1952. No f-c appearances. Shropshire (list A only) 1976-85. Reserve List 2008-10. Appointed 2011.

GARRATT, Steven Arthur, b Nottingham 5 Jul 1953. No f-c appearances. Reserve List 2003-07 standing in 20 f-c matches. Appointed 2008.

GOUGH, Michael Andrew (English Martyrs RCS; Hartlepool SFC), b Hartlepool, Co Durham 18 Dec 1979. Son of M.P.Gough (Durham 1974-77). 6'5". RHB, OB. Durham 1998-2003. F-c Tours (Eng A): NZ 1999-00; B 1999-00. HS 123 Du v CU (Cambridge) 1998. CC HS 103 Du v Essex (Colchester) 2002. BB 5-56 Du v Middx (Chester-le-St) 2001. F-c career: 67 matches; 2952 runs @ 25.44, 2 hundreds; 30 wickets @ 45.00; 57 ct. Reserve List 2006-08. Appointed 2009.

GOULD, Ian James (Westgate SS, Slough), b Taplow, Bucks 19 Aug 1957. 5'8". LHB, WK. Middlesex 1975 to 1980-81, 1996; cap 1977. Auckland 1979-80. Sussex 1981-90; cap 1981; captain 1987; benefit 1990. MCC YC. **LOI:** 18 (1982-83 to 1983); HS 42 v A (Sydney) 1982-83. F-c Tours: A 1982-83; P 1980-81 (Int); Z 1980-81 (M). HS 128 M v Worcs

(Worcester) 1978. BB 3-10 Sx v Surrey (Oval) 1989. Middlesex coach 1991-2000. Reappeared in one match (v OU) 1996. F-c career: 298 matches; 8756 runs @ 26.05, 4 hundreds; 7 wickets @ 52.14; 603 dismissals (536 ct, 67 st). Appointed 2002. Umpired 25 Tests (2008-09 to 2011-12) and 67 LOI (2006 to 2011-12), including 2010-11 World Cup. **ICC Elite Panel 2009 to date.**

HARTLEY, Peter John (Greenhead GS; Bradford C), b Keighley, Yorks 18 Apr 1960. 6'0". RHB, RMF. Warwickshire 1982. Yorkshire 1985-97; cap 1987; benefit 1996. Hampshire 1998-2000; cap 1998. F-c Tours (Y): SA 1991-92; WI 1986-87. HS 127* Y v Lancs (Manchester) 1988. 50 wkts (7); most – 81 (1995). BB 9-41 (inc hat-trick, 4 wkts in 5 balls and 5 in 9; 11-68 match) Y v Derbys (Chesterfield) 1995. Hat-trick 1995. F-c career: 232 matches; 4321 runs @ 19.91, 2 hundreds; 683 wickets @ 30.21; 68 ct. Appointed 2003. Umpired 6 LOI (2007 to 2009). **ICC International Panel 2006-09.**

ILLINGWORTH, Richard Keith (Salts GS), b Bradford, Yorks 23 Aug 1963. 5'11". RHB, SLA. Worcestershire 1982-2000; cap 1986; benefit 1997. Natal 1988-89. Derbyshire 2001. Wiltshire 2005. **Tests:** 9 (1991 to 1995-96); HS 28 v SA (Pt Elizabeth) 1995-96; BB 4-96 v WI (Nottingham) 1995. Took wicket of P.V.Simmons with his first ball in Tests – v WI (Nottingham) 1991. **LOI:** 25 (1991 to 1995-96); HS 14 v P (Melbourne) 1991-92; BB 3-33 v Z (Albury) 1991-92. F-c Tours: SA 1995-96; NZ 1991-92; P 1990-91 (Eng A); SL 1990-91 (Eng A); Z 1989-90 (Eng A), 1990-91 (Wo), 1993-94 (Wo), 1996-97 (Wo). HS 120* Wo v Warwks (Worcester) 1987 – as night-watchman. Scored 106 for England A v Z (Harare) 1989-90 – also as night-watchman. 50 wkts (5); most – 75 (1990). BB 7-50 Wo v OU (Oxford) 1985. F-c career: 376 matches; 7027 runs @ 22.45, 4 hundreds; 831 wickets @ 31.54; 161 ct. Appointed 2006. Umpired 10 LOI (2010 to 2011-12). **ICC International Panel 2011 to date.**

JESTY, Trevor Edward (Privet County SS, Gosport), b Gosport, Hants 2 Jun 1948. 5'8½". RHB, RM. Hampshire 1966-84; cap 1971; benefit 1982. Surrey 1985-87; cap 1985; captain 1985. Lancashire 1987-88 to 1991; cap 1989. Border 1973-74. GW 1974-75 to 1980-81. Canterbury 1979-80. *Wisden* 1982. **LOI:** 10 (1982-83); HS 52* v NZ (Adelaide) 1982-83; BB 1-23 v A (Sydney) 1982-83. F-c Tours (La): WI 1987-88, 1982-83 (Int); Z 1988-89. 1000 runs (10); most – 1645 (1982). HS 248 H v CU (Cambridge) 1984. Scored 122* La v OU (Oxford) 1991 in his final f-c innings. 50 wkts (2); most – 52 (1981). BB 7-75 H v Worcs (Southampton) 1976. F-c career: 490 matches; 21916 runs @ 32.71, 35 hundreds; 585 wickets @ 27.47; 265 ct, 1 st. Appointed 1994. Umpired in Indian Cricket League 2007-08.

KETTLEBOROUGH, Richard Allan (Worksop C), b Sheffield, Yorks 15 Mar 1973. 6'0". LHB, RM. Yorkshire 1994-97. Middlesex 1998-99. F-c Tour (Y): Z 1995-96. HS 108 Y v Essex (Leeds) 1996. BB 2-26 Y v Notts (Scarborough) 1996. F-c career: 33 matches; 1258 runs @ 25.16, 1 hundred; 3 wickets @ 81.00; 20 ct. Appointed 2006. Umpired 7 Tests (2010-11 to 2011-12) and 18 LOI (2009 to 2011-12), including 2010-11 World Cup. **ICC Elite Panel 2011 to date.**

LLONG, Nigel James (Ashford North S), b Ashford, Kent 11 Feb 1969. 6'0". LHB, OB. Kent 1990-98; cap 1993. F-c Tour (K): Z 1992-93. HS 130 K v Hants (Canterbury) 1996. BB 5-21 K v Middx (Canterbury) 1996. F-c career: 68 matches; 3024 runs @ 31.17, 6 hundreds; 35 wickets @ 35.97; 59 ct. Appointed 2002. Umpired 12 Tests (2007-08 to 2011-12) and 55 LOI (2006 to 2011-12), including 2010-11 World Cup. **ICC International Panel 2004 to date.**

LLOYDS, Jeremy William (Blundell's S), b Penang, Malaya 17 Nov 1954. 6'0". LHB, OB. Somerset 1979-84; cap 1982. Gloucestershire 1985-91; cap 1985. OFS 1983-84 to 1987-88. F-c Tour (Gl): SL 1986-87. 1000 runs (1); most – 1295 (1986). HS 132* Sm v Northants (Northampton) 1982. BB 7-88 Sm v Essex (Chelmsford) 1982. F-c career: 267 matches; 10679 runs @ 31.04, 10 hundreds; 333 wickets @ 38.86; 229 ct. Appointed 1998. Umpired 5 Tests (2003-04 to 2004-05) and 18 LOI (2000 to 2005-06). **ICC International Panel 2003-06.**

MALLENDER, Neil Alan (Beverley GS), b Kirk Sandall, Yorks 13 Aug 1961. 6'0". RHB, RFM. Northamptonshire 1980-86 and 1995-96; cap 1984. Somerset 1987-94; cap 1987; benefit 1994. Otago 1983-84 to 1992-93; captain 1990-91 to 1992-93. **Tests:** 2 (1992); HS 4 v P (Oval) 1992; BB 5-50 v P (Leeds) 1992 – on debut. F-c Tour (Nh): Z 1994-95. HS 100*

Otago v CD (Palmerston N) 1991-92. UK HS 87* Sm v Sussex (Hove) 1990. 50 wkts (6); most – 56 (1983). BB 7-27 Otago v Auckland (Auckland) 1984-85. UK BB 7-41 Nh v Derbys (Northampton) 1982. F-c career: 345 matches; 4709 runs @ 17.18, 1 hundred; 937 wickets @ 26.31; 111 ct. Appointed 1999. Umpired 3 Tests (2003-04) and 22 LOI (2001 to 2003-04), including 2002-03 World Cup. **ICC Elite Panel 2004.**

MILLNS, David James (Garibaldi CS; N Notts C; Nottingham Trent U), b Clipstone, Notts 27 Feb 1965. 6'3". LHB, RF. Nottinghamshire 1988-89, 2000-01; cap 2000. Leicestershire 1990-99; cap 1991; benefit 1999. Tasmania 1994-95. Boland 1996-97. F-c Tours: A 1992-93 (Eng A); SA 1996-97 (Le). HS 121 Le v Northants (Northampton) 1997. 50 wkts (4); most – 76 (1994). BB 9-37 (12-91 match) Le v Derbys (Derby) 1991. F-c career: 171 matches; 3082 runs @ 22.01, 3 hundreds; 553 wickets @ 27.35; 76 ct. Reserve List 2007-08. Appointed 2009.

O'SHAUGHNESSY, Steven Joseph (Harper Green SS, Franworth), b Bury, Lancs 9 Sep 1961. 5'10½". RHB, RM. Lancashire 1980-87; cap 1985. Worcestershire 1988-89. Scored 100 in 35 min to equal world record for La v Leics (Manchester) 1983. 1000 runs (1): 1167 (1984). HS 159* La v Somerset (Bath) 1984. BB 4-66 La v Notts (Nottingham) 1982. F-c career: 112 matches; 3720 runs @ 24.31, 5 hundreds; 114 wickets @ 36.03; 57 ct. Reserve List 2009-10. Appointed 2011.

ROBINSON, Robert Timothy (Dunstable GS; High Pavement SFC; Sheffield U), b Sutton in Ashfield, Notts 21 Nov 1958. 6'0". RHB, RM. Nottinghamshire 1978-99; cap 1983; captain 1988-95; benefit 1992. *Wisden* 1985. **Tests:** 29 (1984-85 to 1989); HS 175 v A (Leeds) 1985. **LOI:** 26 (1984-85 to 1988); HS 83 v P (Sharjah) 1986-87. F-c Tours: A 1987-88; SA 1989-90 (Eng XI), 1996-97 (Nt); NZ 1987-88; WI 1985-86; I/SL 1984-85; P 1987-88. 1000 runs (14) inc 2000 (1): 2032 (1984). HS 220* Nt v Yorks (Nottingham) 1990. BB 1-22. F-c career: 425 matches; 27571 runs @ 42.15, 63 hundreds; 4 wickets @ 72.25; 257 ct. Appointed 2007.

†SAGGERS, Martin John (Springwood HS; King's Lynn; Huddersfield U), b King's Lynn, Norfolk 23 May 1972. 6'2". RHB, RMF. Durham 1996-98. Kent 1999-2009; cap 2001; benefit 2009. MCC 2004. Essex 2007 (on loan). Norfolk 1995-96. **Tests:** 3 (2003-04 to 2004); HS 1 and BB 2-29 v B (Chittagong) 2003-04 – on debut. F-c Tour: B 2003-04. HS 64 K v Worcs (Canterbury) 2004. 50 wkts (4); most – 83 (2002). BB 7-79 K v Durham (Chester-le-St) 2000. F-c career: 119 matches; 1165 runs @ 11.20; 415 wickets @ 25.33; 27 ct. Reserve List 2010-11. Appointed 2012.

SHARP, George (Elwick Road SS, Hartlepool), b West Hartlepool, Co Durham 12 Mar 1950. 5'11". RHB, WK, occ LM. Northamptonshire 1968-85; cap 1973; benefit 1982. HS 98 Nh v Yorks (Northampton) 1983. BB 1-47. F-c career: 306 matches; 6254 runs @ 19.85; 1 wicket @ 70.00; 655 dismissals (565 ct, 90 st). Appointed 1992. Umpired 15 Tests (1996 to 2001-02) and 31 LOI (1995-96 to 2001-02). **ICC International Panel 1996 to 2001-02.**

WILLEY Peter (Seaham SS), b Sedgefield, Co Durham 6 Dec 1949. 6'1". RHB, OB. Northamptonshire 1966-83; cap 1971; benefit 1981. Leicestershire 1984-91; cap 1984; captain 1987. EP 1982-83 to 1984-85. Northumberland 1992. **Tests:** 26 (1976 to 1986); HS 102* v WI (St John's) 1980-81; BB 2-73 v WI (Lord's) 1980. **LOI:** 26 (1977 to 1985-86); HS 64 v A (Sydney) 1979-80; BB 3-33 v A (Melbourne) 1979-80. F-c Tours: A 1979-80; SA 1972-73 (DHR), 1981-82 (SAB); WI 1980-81, 1985-86; I 1979-80; SL 1977-78 (DHR). 1000 runs (10); most – 1783 (1982). HS 227 Nh v Somerset (Northampton) 1976. 50 wkts (3); most – 52 (1979). BB 7-37 Nh v OU (Oxford) 1975. F-c career: 559 matches; 24361 runs @ 30.56, 44 hundreds; 756 wickets @ 30.95; 235 ct. Appointed 1993. Umpired 25 Tests (1995-96 to 2003-04) and 34 LOI (1996 to 2003), including 1999 and 2002-03 World Cups. **ICC International Panel 1996 to 2001-02 and 2003-04.**

RESERVE FIRST-CLASS LIST: Paul K.Baldwin, Mike Burns, Ismail Dawood, Ben J.Debenham, Mark A.Eggleston, Russell J.Evans, Graham D.Lloyd, Paul R.Pollard, Billy V.Taylor, Alex G.Wharf.

Test Match statistics to 6 March 2012; LOI statistics to 10 March 2012.

UNIVERSITY FIRST-CLASS REGISTER 2011

CAMBRIDGE († Blue 2011)

Full Names	Birthdate	Birthplace	College	Bat/Bowl	F-C Debut
ACKLAND, Ben James	26.10.89	Nuneaton	(Anglia RU)	RHB/OB	2010
ANSARI, Zafar Shahaan	10.12.91	Ascot	Trinity Hall	LHB/SLA	2011
†ASHOK, Anand	28.11.88	Hyderabad, India	Queens'	RHB/RM	2009
†ASHTON, Philip Peter	02.08.88	Cambridge	Queens'	RHB/LB	2009
BELL, Dean William	03.05.92	Blackpool	(Anglia RU)	RHB/WK	2011
†BEST, Paul Merwood	08.03.91	Nuneaton	Homerton	LHB/SLA	2011
†BROWN, Francis Andrew	21.03.90	Nottingham	Jesus	RHB/SLA	2009
COWAN, James Daniel	17.08.89	Cambridge	(Anglia RU)	LHB/LMF	2011
†DEASY, Thomas James	29.09.91	London	Peterhouse	RHB/OB	2011
GUPTA, Amit	29.05.84	Delhi, India	(Anglia RU)	RHB/RM	2011
†HICKEY, Matthew Robert	23.09.91	Wandsworth	Trinity Hall	RHB/LM	2011
HUGHES, Philip Heywood	17.06.91	Southampton	Downing	RHB/RM	2010
†KENNEDY, Augustus Damian John	10.08.90	London	Corpus Christi	RHB/WK	2010
McCLUSKIE, Joseph James	07.12.91	Burnley	(Anglia RU)	RHB/RMF	2011
PARK, Craig Mitchell	01.03.86	Natal, South Africa	(Anglia RU)	RHB/RMF	2010
POYSDEN, Joshua Edward	08.08.91	Shoreham-by-Sea	(Anglia RU)	LHB/LB	2011
†PROBERT, Thomas John William	26.09.86	Pembury	Peterhouse	LHB/RM	2009
†SADLER, Patrick Thomas	28.09.91	Waltham Forest	Churchill	RHB/RFM	2011
†TIMMS, Richard Thomas	09.09.84	Bristol	Clare	RHB/RFM	2005
TURNBULL, Peter Thomas	20.05.89	Pontypridd	(Anglia RU)	RHB/RMF	2009
WOOLLEY, Robert James Joseph	06.08.90	Tameside	(Anglia RU)	RHB/RM	2009

DURHAM

Full Names	Birthdate	Birthplace	College	Bat/Bowl	F-C Debut
ATKINSON, James John	24.08.90	Hong Kong	St Mary's	RHB/WK	2009
BLACKABY, Luke Alexander	01.02.91	Farnborough, Kent	Grey	LHB/LM	2010
DEUCHAR, Alexander John Wilfred	10.12.87	Darlington	St Cuthbert's	RHB/RM	2011
DURANDT, Luc Etienne	01.09.89	Johannesburg, SA	Collingwood	LHB/RM	2010
JONES, Christopher Robert	05.11.90	Harold Wood	Grey	RHB/OB	2010
PATEL, Luke Adam	06.10.90	Wakefield	Grey	LHB/OB	2011
ROPER, Christopher George William	20.05.91	Bristol	Collingwood	RHB/RM	2010
SALT, Jonathan David	06.01.91	Chester	Van Mildert	RHB/RM	2011
SCARR, Max James Liam	08.09.91	Oxford		LHB/SLA	
SHAH, Rishabh Arjun Chandra	11.09.91	Whipps Cross		RHB/SLA	
SHAN MASOOD Khan	14.10.89	Kuwait		LHB/RMF	2007-08
SMITH, Gregory Philip	16.11.88	Leicester	St Hild & St Bede	RHB/SLA	2008
SMITH, Joshua William George	30.05.92	Oxford	Grey	LHB/WK	2011
WATKINS, Nathaniel Ashley Thomas	07.11.91	Oxford	Hatfield	RHB/SLA	2011
WESTLEY, Thomas	13.03.89	Cambridge	St Cuthbert's	RHB/OB	2007

LOUGHBOROUGH

Full Names	Birthdate	Birthplace		Bat/Bowl	F-C Debut
BILLINGS, Samuel William	15.06.91	Pembury		RHB/WK	2011
COX, DannyJo McEvoy	30.07.92	Wolverhampton		RHB/OB	2011
D'SOUZA, Darius	11.10.89	Mumbai, India		RHB/RM	2011
FEARON, Richard Martin	30.07.91	South Shields		RHB/OB	2011
GANDAM, Harvey Singh	21.01.90	Slough		RHB/RFM	2010
HOLMES, Maurice Gibson	19.05.90	Tenterden		RHB/OB	2011
JAMES, Oliver Richard	03.10.90	Neath		RHB/OB	2011
MURPHY, David	24.06.89	Welwyn Garden City		RHB/WK	2009
PATEL, Nitesh	31.10.89	Stourbridge		RHB/OB	2011
PATEL, Ravi Hasmukh	04.08.91	Harrow		RHB/SLA	2010
RATNAYAKE, Dimitri Eranga Mahen	09.03.90	Kandy, Sri Lanka		RHB/RM	2011

Full Names	Birthdate	Birthplace		Bat/Bowl	F-C Debut
SOILLEUX, Adam Charles	29.11.91	Southend-on-Sea		RHB/RMF	2011
STURMER, Ian William	23.08.91	Chiddingly, Lewes		RHB/RM	2011
TAVARÉ, William Andrew	01.01.90	Bristol		RHB/RMF	2010
TAYLOR, Robert Meadows Lombe	21.12.89	Northampton		LHB/LM	2010
TURNS, Michael	14.11.90	Sunderland		RHB/RM	2011
WILKIN, Oliver	06.04.92	Ealing		RHB/RM	2011

OXFORD († Blue 2011)

Full Names	Birthdate	Birthplace	College	Bat/Bowl	F-C Debut
†AGARWAL, Samridh Sunil	13.07.90	Agra, India	Queens	RHB/OB	2010
†BRYAN, Thomas Edward	31.10.88	Colchester	Worcester	RHB/RMF	2009
†CHADWICK, Thomas Robert	21.10.91	Norwich	Worcester	RHB/RM	2011
CONWAY, Danny Oliver	01.05.85	Stockton-on-Tees	(Brookes U)	RHB/RM	2010
COUGHTRIE, Richard George	01.09.88	North Shields	(Brookes U)	RHB/WK	2009
ELLISON, Charlie Peter	26.01.91	Canterbury	(Brookes U)	RHB/RM	2011
FLEMING, Joshua David	29.06.89	Crawley	(Brookes U)	RHB/RM	2011
GORDON, Donald Ashley	03.10.90	Isle of Wight	Keble	RHB/RFM	2011
†HIGHAM, Paul Sephton	20.08.90	London	Pembroke	RHB/RM	2011
†JEFFERY, Benjamin Anthony	31.07.91	Camden	St John's	RHB/LB	2011
KRUGER, Neil	15.08.81	Cape Town, SA	Green Templeton	RHB/RM	2008
MILLIGAN, Marc Jon	01.08.87	Pretoria, SA	(Brookes U)	RHB/RMF	2009
†PASCOE, Daniel Charles	14.05.83	Canberra, Australia	Lincoln	RHB/SLA	2011
†RICHARDS, Oliver Benjamin	08.12.90	Lambeth	St Anne's	RHB/RM	2011
†SCOTT, Alex James Dennis	04.05.90	Hong Kong	Keble	RHB/LB	2010
†SHARMA, Rajiv	10.06.84	Auckland, NZ	Mansfield	RHB/RMF	2009
SMITH, David Thomas	13.09.89	Canterbury	(Brookes U)	RHB/RM	2009
STEBBINGS, Benjamin Robert William	06.10.89	Oxford	(Brookes U)	RHB/RM	2010
WALKER, Charles Aubrey Mark	21.05.92	Bristol	(Brookes U)	RHB/OB	2011
†WESTAWAY, Samuel Alexander	29.07.92	Welwyn Garden City	Pembroke	RHB/WK	2011
†WILLIAMS, Ben	24.06.92	Knowsley	Hertford	RHB/RM	2011
YOUNG, Edward George Christopher	21.05.89	Chertsey	(Brookes U)	RHB/SLA	2009

TOURING TEAMS REGISTER 2011

INDIA

Full Names	Birthdate	Birthplace	Team	Type	F-C Debut
DHONI, Mahendra Singh	07.07.81	Ranchi	Chennai SK	RHB/WK	1999-00
DRAVID, Rahul Sharad	11.01.73	Indore	Karnataka	RHB/OB	1990-91
GAMBHIR, Gautam	14.10.81	Delhi	Delhi	LHB/LB	1999-00
HARBHAJAN SINGH	03.07.80	Jullundur	Mumbai Indians	RHB/OB	1997-98
KHAN, Zaheer	07.10.78	Shrirampur	Mumbai	RHB/LFM	1999-00
KUMAR, Praveen	02.10.86	Meerut	Uttar Pradesh	RHB/RM	2005-06
LAXMAN, Vangipurappu Venkata Sai	01.11.74	Hyderabad	Hyderabad	RHB/OB	1992-93
MISHRA, Amit	24.11.82	Delhi	Haryana	RHB/LB	2000-01
MUKUND, Abhinav	06.01.90	Madras	Tamil Nadu	LHB/LBG	2007-08
PATEL, Munaf Musa	12.07.83	Ikhar	Baroda	RHB/RMF	2003-04
RAINA, Suresh Kumar	27.11.86	Ghaziabad	Uttar Pradesh	LHB/OB	2002-03
SAHA, Wriddhaman Prasanta	24.10.84	Shaktigarh	Bengal	RHB/WK	2007-08
SEHWAG, Virender	20.10.78	Delhi	Delhi	RHB/OB	1997-98
SHARMA, Ishant	02.09.88	Delhi	Delhi	RHB/RFM	2006-07
SINGH, Rudra Pratap	06.12.85	Rae Bareli	Uttar Pradesh	RHB/LMF	2003-04
SREESANTH, Shanthakumaran	06.02.83	Kothamangalam	Kerala	RHB/RFM	2002-03
TENDULKAR, Sachin Ramesh	24.04.73	Bombay	Mumbai	RHB/OB	1988-89
YUVRAJ SINGH	12.12.81	Chandigarh	Punjab	LHB/SLA	1996-97

SRI LANKA

Full Names	Birthdate	Birthplace	Team	Type	F-C Debut
CHANDIMAL, L.Dinesh	18.11.89	Balapitiya	Nondescripts	RHB/WK	2009
DILSHAN, Tillekeratne M.	14.10.76	Kalutara	Bloomfield	RHB/OB	1993-94
FERNANDO, A.Nuwan Pradeep R.	19.10.86	Negombo	Bloomfield	RHB/RFM	2007-08
FERNANDO, C.R.Dilhara	19.07.79	Colombo	Sinhalese	RHB/RFM	1997-98
HERATH, H.M.Rangana K.B.	19.03.78	Kurunegala	Wayamba	LHB/SLA	1996-97
JAYAWARDENA, D.P.Mahela D.	27.05.77	Colombo	Sinhalese	RHB/RM	1995-96
JAYAWARDENA, H.A.Prasanna W.	09.10.79	Colombo	Bloomfield	RHB/WK	1997-98
KALUHALAMULLA, H.K.Suraj Randiv	30.01.85	Matara	Bloomfield	RHB/OB	2002-03
LAKMAL, R.A.Suranga	10.03.87	Matara	Tamil Union	RHB/RMF	2007-08
MAHAROOF, Mohamed Farveez	07.09.84	Colombo	Nondescripts	RHB/RMF	2001-02
MENDIS, B.Ajantha W.	11.03.85	Moratuwa	Sri Lanka Army	RHB/LBG	2006-07
PARANAVITANA, N.Tharanga	15.04.82	Kegalle	Sinhalese	LHB/OB	2001-02
PERERA, N.L.Tissara C.	03.04.89	Colombo	Colts	LHB/RFM	2008-09
SAMARAWEERA, Thilan T.	22.09.76	Colombo	Sinhalese	RHB/OB	1995-96
SANGAKKARA, Kumar C.	27.10.77	Matale	Kandurata	LHB/WK	1997-98
THIRIMANNE, H.D.R.Lahiru	08.09.89	Moratuwa	Ragama	LHB/RMF	2008-09
WELAGEDARA, U.W.M.B.Chanaka A.	20.03.81	Matale	Tamil Union	RHB/LFM	2002-03

NB: A.N.P.R.Fernando is also known as Nuwan Pradeep; H.K.S.R.Kaluhalamulla is also known as S.Randiv.

SRI LANKA A

Full Names	Birthdate	Birthplace	Team	Type	F-C Debut
ALWITIGALA, Kanishka G.	08.06.86	Homagama	Colts	RHB/RMF	2007-08
ERANGA, R.M.Shaminda	23.06.86	Chilaw	Chilaw Marians	RHB/RMF	2006-07
KARUNARATNE, F.Dimuth M.	21.04.88	Colombo	Sinhalese	LHB/RM	2008-09
KULASEKARA, C.Kosala B.	15.07.85	Mavanalle	Nondescripts	RHB/RFM	2002-03
LAKSHITHA, A.B.Tharanga	30.04.82	Matara	Bloomfield	RHB/RMF	1999-00
PERERA, M.D.Kushal Janith	17.08.90	Kalubovila	Colts	LHB/WK	2009-10
PRASANNA, Seekkuge	27.06.85	Balapitiya	Sri Lanka Army	RHB/LB	2006-07
PREMARATNE, W.G.H.Nilanka	17.06.88	Kandy	Ragama	RHB/LMF	2009-10
RAJAPASKA, P.Bhanuka B.	24.10.91	Colombo	Sinhalese	LHB/RM	2010-11
SENANAYAKE, S.M.Sachithra M.	09.02.85	Colombo	Sinhalese	RHB/OB	2006-07
SERASINGHE, S.P.Sachithra	13.04.87	Colombo	Tamil Union	RHB/OB	2006-07
SILVA, A.Roshen S.	17.11.88	Colombo	Colts	RHB/OB	2006-07
SILVA, Jayan Kaushal	27.05.86	Colombo	Sinhalese	RHB/WK	2001-02
THIRIMANNE, H.D.R.Lahiru	08.09.89	Moratuwa	Ragama	RHB/RMF	2008-09
WARNAPURA, Shalith Malinda	26.05.79	Colombo	Colts	LHB/OB	1998-99
WEERAKOON, Sajeewa	17.02.78	Galle	Colts	LHB/SLA	1995-96

THE 2011 FIRST-CLASS SEASON STATISTICAL HIGHLIGHTS

FIRST TO INDIVIDUAL TARGETS

1000 RUNS	A.N.Cook	Essex and England	18 June
2000 RUNS	–	Most 1673 – M.E.Trescothick (Somerset)	
50 WICKETS	D.D.Masters	Essex	12 July
100 WICKETS	–	Most 93 – D.D.Masters (Essex)	

TEAM HIGHLIGHTS

HIGHEST INNINGS TOTALS

710-7d	England v India (*3rd Test*)	Birmingham
642	Warwickshire v Somerset	Taunton
627-9d	Hampshire v Somerset	Taunton
610-6d	Somerset v Durham	Chester-le-Street
602-6d	Durham v Warwickshire	Birmingham

HIGHEST FOURTH INNINGS TOTALS

360-4	Essex (set 360) v Glamorgan	Chelmsford

LOWEST INNINGS TOTALS († *One man absent hurt*)

34	Leicestershire v Essex	Southend
48	Leicestershire v Northamptonshire	Leicester
50	Somerset v Warwickshire	Taunton
72	Glamorgan v Northamptonshire	Northampton
80†	Lancashire v Worcestershire	Worcester
82	Sri Lanka v England (*1st Test*)	Cardiff
84	Lancashire v Durham	Liverpool
86	Yorkshire v Nottinghamshire	Leeds
87	Kent v Middlesex	Lord's
95	Worcestershire v Somerset	Worcester
97	Warwickshire v Lancashire	Birmingham
98	Warwickshire v Hampshire	Birmingham
99	Derbyshire v Surrey	Derby
99	Northamptonshire v Essex	Chelmsford

MATCH AGGREGATES OF 1400 RUNS

1443-31	Essex (548 & 324) v Surrey (506 & 65-1)	Croydon
1431-32	Sussex (398 & 333-6d) v Yorks (388 & 312-6)	Scarborough
1427-30	England (486 & 335-7d) v Sri Lanka (479 & 127-3)	Lord's
1422-28	Durham (473 & 310-3d) v Hampshire (294 & 345-5)	Southampton
1410-40	Derbyshire (360 & 438) v Glamorgan (445 & 167)	Derby

BATSMEN'S MATCH (Qualification: 1200 runs, average 60 per wicket)

60.72 (1336-22)	Somerset (610-6d) v Durham (237 & 489-6)	Chester-le-St

LARGE MARGINS OF VICTORY

Inns & 382 runs	Warwickshire (642) v Somerset (210 & 50)	Taunton
Inns & 242 runs	England (710-7d) v India (224 & 244) (*3rd Test*)	Birmingham
333 runs	Surrey (269 & 410-6d) v Northants (194 & 152)	Northampton
319 runs	England (221 & 544) v India (288 & 158) (*2nd Test*)	Nottingham

NARROW MARGINS OF VICTORY

2 wkts	Sussex (194 & 309-8) beat Durham (292 & 210)	Chester-le-Street
2 wkts	Surrey (423 & 186-8) beat Glos (286 & 320)	Cheltenham
2 wkts	Durham (303 & 222-8) beat Sri Lanka A (203 & 319)	Chester-le-Street
21 runs	Surrey (387 & 184) beat Kent (250 & 300)	The Oval
23 runs	Lancashire (328 & 194) beat Yorks (239 & 260)	Leeds

ALL ELEVEN SCORING DOUBLE FIGURES

Lancashire (480) v Somerset	Taunton

SIX FIFTIES IN AN INNINGS

Warwickshire (481) v Sussex	Arundel
Warwickshire (521) v Sussex	Birmingham

60 EXTRAS IN AN INNINGS

	B	LB	W	NB	P		
66	11	15	1	34	5	Sussex (459-9) v Lancashire	Hove
65	–	21	–	44	–	Somerset (513) v Hampshire	Southampton
63	11	34	3	15	–	England (710-7d) v India (3rd Test)	Birmingham
62	6	19	5	32	–	Essex (548) v Surrey	Croydon

Under ECB regulations, Test matches excluded, two penalty extras were scored for each no-ball.

BATTING HIGHLIGHTS
TRIPLE HUNDREDS

M.A.Carberry	300*	Hampshire v Yorkshire	Southampton

DOUBLE HUNDREDS

J.H.K.Adams	207	Hampshire v Somerset	Taunton
J.M.Bairstow	205	Yorkshire v Nottinghamshire	Nottingham
I.R.Bell	235	England v India (4th Test)	The Oval
V.Chopra (2)	210	Warwickshire v Somerset	Taunton
	228	Warwickshire v Worcestershire	Worcester
N.R.D.Compton	254*	Somerset v Durham	Chester-le-Street
A.N.Cook	294	England v India (3rd Test)	Birmingham
M.W.Goodwin	274	Sussex v Yorkshire	Hove
N.D.McKenzie	237	Hampshire v Yorkshire	Southampton
S.D.Peters	222	Northamptonshire v Glamorgan	Swansea
A.N.Petersen	210	Glamorgan v Surrey	The Oval
K.P.Pietersen	202*	England v India (1st Test)	Lord's
A.J.Strauss	241*	Middlesex v Leicestershire	Lord's
J.W.A.Taylor	237	Leicestershire v Loughborough MCCU	Leicester
M.E.Trescothick (2)	227	Somerset v Hampshire	Southampton
	203	Somerset v Worcestershire	Worcester
I.J.L.Trott	203	England v Sri Lanka (1st Test)	Cardiff

HUNDRED IN EACH INNINGS OF A MATCH

M.E.Trescothick	189 151*	Somerset v Yorkshire	Taunton
M.H.Yardy	130 122	Sussex v Yorkshire	Scarborough

FASTEST HUNDRED AGAINST GENUINE BOWLING

T.L.Maynard (141)	67 balls Surrey v Middlesex	Guildford

HUNDRED BEFORE LUNCH

Day

G.R.Napier 25* – 150* 2 Essex v Surrey Croydon

MOST SIXES IN AN INNINGS

16† G.R.Napier (196) Essex v Surrey Croydon
† Equalled the world record for most sixes in an innings.

150 OR MORE RUNS FROM BOUNDARIES IN AN INNINGS

Runs	6s	4s			
184	2	43	M.A.Carberry (300*)	Hampshire v Yorkshire	Southampton
172	16	19	G.R.Napier (196)	Essex v Surrey	Croydon
150	5	30	E.J.G.Morgan (193)	England Lions v Sri Lankans	Derby

HUNDRED ON FIRST-CLASS DEBUT

S.W.Billings 131 Loughborough MCCU v Northants Loughborough

HUNDRED ON FIRST-CLASS DEBUT IN BRITAIN

N.T.Paranavitana 103 Sri Lankans v Middlesex Uxbridge
S.K.Raina 103* Indians v Somerset Taunton
S.J.Thakor 134 Leicestershire v Loughborough MCCU Leicester

CARRYING BAT THROUGH COMPLETED INNINGS

L.A.Dawson 152* Hampshire (324) v Warwickshire Southampton
R.S.Dravid 146* India (300) v England (*4th Test*) The Oval
A.D.Hales 106* Nottinghamshire (222) v Warwicks Birmingham
R.W.T.Key 110* Kent (230) v Surrey Canterbury

LONG INNINGS (Qualification 600 mins and/or 400 balls)

Mins	Balls			
520	410	J.H.K.Adams (207)	Hampshire v Somerset	Taunton
512	427	M.A.Carberry (300*)	Hampshire v Yorkshire	Southampton
544	434	N.R.D.Compton (254*)	Somerset v Durham	Chester-le-Street
773	545	A.N.Cook (294)	England v India (*3rd Test*)	Birmingham
475	412	N.D.McKenzie (237)	Hampshire v Yorkshire	Southampton
517	409	I.J.L.Trott (203)	England v Sri Lanka (*1st Test*)	Cardiff

UNUSUAL DISMISSAL – OBSTRUCTING THE FIELD

M.R.Ramprakash Surrey v Gloucestershire Cheltenham

FIRST-WICKET PARTNERSHIP OF 100 IN EACH INNINGS

118/129* G.S.Ballance/J.J.Sayers Yorkshire v Durham MCCU Durham
136/181 J.H.K.Adams/L.A.Dawson Hampshire v Somerset Southampton
100/119 E.C.Joyce/C.D.Nash Sussex v Nottinghamshire Hove
257/228* M.E.Trescothick/A.V.Suppiah Somerset v Yorkshire Taunton
101/131 A.J.Strauss/A.V.Suppiah Somerset v Indians Taunton
104/131 P.J.Horton/S.C.Moore Lancashire v Somerset Taunton

OTHER NOTABLE PARTNERSHIPS († County record)

Qualifications: 1ˢᵗ-4ᵗʰ wkts: 250 runs; 5ᵗʰ-6ᵗʰ: 225; 7ᵗʰ: 200; 8ᵗʰ: 175; 9ᵗʰ: 150; 10ᵗʰ: 100.

First Wicket

323[1]	A.J.Strauss/S.D.Robson/J.W.M.Dalrymple	Middlesex v Leicestershire	Lord's
257	M.E.Trescothick/A.V.Suppiah	Somerset v Yorkshire	Taunton

[1] *S.D.Robson retired not out with the score on 231.*

Second Wicket

373†	J.H.K.Adams/M.A.Carberry	Hampshire v Somerset	Taunton
258	A.N.Cook/J.C.Mickleburgh	Essex v Northamptonshire	Northampton

Third Wicket

523†	M.A.Carberry/N.D.McKenzie	Hampshire v Yorkshire	Southampton
350	I.R.Bell/K.P.Pietersen	England v India (*4th Test*)	The Oval
304	L.W.P.Wells/M.W.Goodwin	Sussex v Yorkshire	Hove
266	M.J.Guptill/W.J.Durston	Derbyshire v Gloucestershire	Derby
251	A.N.Cook/I.J.L.Trott	England v Sri Lanka (*1st Test*)	Cardiff

Fourth Wicket

331†	B.A.Stokes/D.M.Benkenstein	Durham v Lancashire	Chester-le-Street
273	W.R.Smith/D.M.Benkenstein	Durham v Warwickshire	Birmingham

Fifth Wicket

330†	J.W.A.Taylor/S.J.Thakor	Leics v Loughborough MCCU	Leicester
290	J.C.Hildreth/C.Kieswetter	Somerset v Nottinghamshire	Nottingham
266	E.J.G.Morgan/S.R.Patel	England Lions v Sri Lankans	Derby
254	N.J.Dexter/J.A.Simpson	Middlesex v Surrey	Lord's
247†	G.J.Muchall/I.D.Blackwell	Durham v Worcestershire	Worcester

Sixth Wicket

253†	A.J.Wheater/J.S.Foster	Essex v Northamptonshire	Chelmsford

Seventh Wicket

232	I.D.Blackwell/L.E.Plunkett	Durham v Durham MCCU	Durham

Eighth Wicket

179†	A.J.Hall/J.D.Middlebrook	Northamptonshire v Surrey	The Oval

Ninth Wicket

190	G.R.Napier/C.J.C.Wright	Essex v Surrey	Croydon
172†	G.K.Berg/T.J.Murtagh	Middlesex v Leicestershire	Leicester
155	K.H.D.Barker/J.S.Patel	Warwickshire v Sussex	Birmingham
154	R.M.Pyrah/R.J.Sidebottom	Yorkshire v Lancashire	Leeds
151	J.M.Bairstow/R.J.Sidebottom	Yorkshire v Nottinghamshire	Nottingham

Tenth Wicket

121	J.A.R.Harris/W.T.Owen	Glamorgan v Derbyshire	Derby
109	A.Shahzad/R.J.Sidebottom	Yorkshire v Worcestershire	Scarborough
104	J.L.Clare/M.L.Turner	Derbyshire v Glamorgan	Derby

BOWLING HIGHLIGHTS

EIGHT OR MORE WICKETS IN AN INNINGS

S.C.Kerrigan	9-51	Lancashire v Hampshire	Liverpool
D.D.Masters	8-10	Essex v Leicestershire	Southend

TEN OR MORE WICKETS IN A MATCH

A.R.Adams (2)	11- 85	Nottinghamshire v Hampshire	Nottingham
	10-122	Nottinghamshire v Lancashire	Southport
D.J.Balcombe	10-102	Kent v Essex	Canterbury
K.W.Hogg	11- 59	Lancashire v Hampshire	Southampton
G.Keedy	10-177	Lancashire v Yorkshire	Liverpool
S.C.Kerrigan	12-192	Lancashire v Hampshire	Liverpool
T.E.Linley	10-107	Surrey v Derbyshire	Derby
S.I.Mahmood	10-186	Lancashire v Nottinghamshire	Nottingham
T.J.Murtagh	10-128	Middlesex v Surrey	Guildford
Naved-ul-Hasan	10-161	Sussex v Somerset	Hove
P.P.Ojha	10- 90	Surrey v Derbyshire	The Oval
J.S.Patel	10-163	Warwickshire v Sussex	Birmingham
S.R.Patel	11-111	Nottinghamshire v Hampshire	Southampton
A.U.Rashid	11-114	Yorkshire v Worcestershire	Worcester
I.D.Saxelby	10-142	Gloucestershire v Surrey	The Oval
R.J.Sidebottom	11- 98	Yorkshire v Somerset	Leeds
D.I.Stevens	11- 70	Kent v Surrey	Canterbury
A.C.Thomas	10- 88	Somerset v Sussex	Taunton
W.P.J.U.C.Vaas	10- 82	Northamptonshire v Glamorgan	Northampton
D.J.Willey	10- 75	Northamptonshire v Gloucestershire	Northampton
C.R.Woakes	10-123	Warwickshire v Hampshire	Birmingham

OUTSTANDING INNINGS ANALYSIS

P.P.Ojha	16.3-10-8-6	Surrey v Northamptonshire	Northampton

BOWLING UNCHANGED THROUGHOUT INNINGS

D.S.Lucas (13-5-20-5)/J.A.Brooks (12.1-4-23-5)	Northants v Leics	Leicester

HAT-TRICKS

S.C.J.Broad	England v India (*2nd Test*)	Nottingham
M.J.Hoggard	Leicestershire v Glamorgan	Leicester
H.K.S.R.Kaluhalamulla	Sri Lankans v Essex	Chelmsford

MOST RUNS CONCEDED IN AN INNINGS

G.Keedy	55-7-200-4	Lancashire v Sussex	Hove

MOST OVERS BOWLED IN AN INNINGS

G.Keedy	55-7-200-4	Lancashire v Sussex	Hove

SEASON DOUBLE (1000 RUNS AND 50 WICKETS)

W.R.S.Gidman (Gloucestershire)	1006 runs @ 45.72 and 51 wkts @ 21.33

WICKET-KEEPING HIGHLIGHTS

SIX WICKET-KEEPING DISMISSALS IN AN INNINGS

J.N.Batty	6ct	Gloucestershire v Middlesex	Bristol
J.C.Buttler	6ct	Somerset v Hampshire	Taunton
R.G.Coughtrie	6ct	Gloucestershire v Glamorgan	Bristol
G.D.Cross	4ct, 2st	Lancashire v Somerset	Liverpool
E.J.Eckersley †	6ct	Leicestershire v Middlesex	Leicester
A.J.Hodd	6ct	Sussex v Hampshire	Southampton

† *Also scored 106 and 50 in the match.*

NINE WICKET-KEEPING DISMISSALS IN A MATCH

G.D.Cross	6ct, 3st	Lancashire v Somerset	Liverpool
J.A.Simpson	9ct	Middlesex v Gloucestershire	Bristol

NO BYES CONCEDED IN AN INNINGS OF 600 OR MORE

642	C.Kieswetter	Somerset v Warwickshire	Taunton

FIELDING HIGHLIGHTS

FIVE OR MORE CATCHES IN THE FIELD IN AN INNINGS

R.Clarke	7ct†	Warwickshire v Lancashire	Liverpool
M.E.Trescothick	5ct	Somerset v Lancashire	Liverpool

† *This equalled the world record for the most catches in an innings in the field.*

SIX OR MORE CATCHES IN THE FIELD IN A MATCH

R.Clarke	9ct	Warwickshire v Lancashire	Liverpool
D.K.H.Mitchell	6ct	Worcestershire v Hampshire	Worcester

COUNTY CHAMPIONSHIP 2011
LV FINAL TABLES

DIVISION 1

	P	W	L	D	Bonus Points Bat	Points Bowl	Deduct Points	Total Points
1 LANCASHIRE (4)	16	10	4	2	37	44	1	246
2 Warwickshire (6)	16	9	4	3	46	45	9	235
3 Durham (5)	16	8	4	4	47	45	–	232
4 Somerset (2)	16	6	7	3	45	39	–	189
5 Sussex (1)	16	6	6	4	34	40	–	182
6 Nottinghamshire (1)	16	5	6	5	35	43	–	173
7 Worcestershire (-)	16	4	11	1	31	44	–	142
8 Yorkshire (3)	16	3	6	7	34	37	2	138
9 Hampshire (7)	16	3	6	7	30	36	8	127

DIVISION 2

	P	W	L	D	Bonus Points Bat	Points Bowl	Deduct Points	Total Points
1 Middlesex (8)	16	8	2	6	50	44	–	240
2 Surrey (7)	16	8	4	4	43	44	–	227
3 Northamptonshire (6)	16	7	2	7	48	45	–	226
4 Gloucestershire (5)	16	6	5	5	41	47	1	198
5 Derbyshire (9)	16	5	6	5	42	44	–	181
6 Glamorgan (3)	16	5	6	5	44	40	1	178
7 Essex (-)	16	4	4	8	29	44	2	159
8 Kent (-)	16	5	9	2	30	42	9	149
9 Leicestershire (4)	16	1	11	4	24	31	–	88

SCORING OF CHAMPIONSHIP POINTS 2011 and 2012

(a) For a win, 16 points, plus any points scored in the first innings.

(b) In a tie, each side to score eight points, plus any points scored in the first innings.

(c) In a drawn match, each side to score three points, plus any points scored in the first innings (see also paragraph (f) below).

(d) If the scores are equal in a drawn match, the side batting in the fourth innings to score eight points plus any points scored in the first innings, and the opposing side to score three points plus any points scored in the first innings.

(e) **First Innings Points** (awarded only for performances **in the first 110 overs** of each first innings and retained whatever the result of the match).

    (i) A maximum of five batting points to be available as under:
        200 to 249 runs – 1 point; 250 to 299 runs – 2 points; 300 to 349 runs – 3 points; 350 to 399 runs – 4 points; 400 runs or over – 5 points.

    (ii) A maximum of three bowling points to be available as under:
        3 to 5 wickets taken – 1 point; 6 to 8 wickets taken – 2 points; 9 to 10 wickets taken – 3 points.

(f) If a match is abandoned without a ball being bowled, each side to score three points.

(g) The side which has the highest aggregate of points gained at the end of the season shall be the Champion County of their respective Division. Should any sides in the Championship table be equal on points, the following tie-breakers will be applied in the order stated: most wins, fewest losses, team achieving most points in contests between teams level on points, most wickets taken, most runs scored. At the end of the season, the top two teams from the Second Division will be promoted and the bottom two teams from the First Division will be relegated.

COUNTY CHAMPIONS

The English County Championship was not officially constituted until December 1889. Prior to that date there was no generally accepted method of awarding the title; although the 'least matches lost' method existed, it was not consistently applied. Rules governing playing qualifications were agreed in 1873 and the first unofficial points system 15 years later.

Research has produced a list of champions dating back to 1826, but at least seven different versions exist for the period from 1864 to 1889 (see *The Wisden Book of Cricket Records*). Only from 1890 can any authorised list of county champions commence.

That first official Championship was contested between eight counties: Gloucestershire, Kent, Lancashire, Middlesex, Nottinghamshire, Surrey, Sussex and Yorkshire. The remaining counties were admitted in the following seasons: 1891 – Somerset, 1895 – Derbyshire, Essex, Hampshire, Leicestershire and Warwickshire, 1899 – Worcestershire, 1905 – Northamptonshire, 1921 – Glamorgan, and 1992 – Durham.

The Championship pennant was introduced by the 1951 champions, Warwickshire, and the Lord's Taverners' Trophy was first presented in 1973. The first sponsors, Schweppes (1977-83), were succeeded by Britannic Assurance (1984-98), PPP Healthcare (1999-2000), CricInfo (2001), Frizzell (2002-05) and Liverpool Victoria (2006 to date). Based on their previous season's positions, the 18 counties were separated into two divisions in 2000. From 2000 to 2005 the bottom three Division 1 teams were relegated and the top three Division 2 sides promoted. This was reduced to two teams from the end of the 2006 season.

1890	Surrey	1933	Yorkshire	1973	Hampshire
1891	Surrey	1934	Lancashire	1974	Worcestershire
1892	Surrey	1935	Yorkshire	1975	Leicestershire
1893	Yorkshire	1936	Derbyshire	1976	Middlesex
1894	Surrey	1937	Yorkshire	1977	{ Kent
1895	Surrey	1938	Yorkshire		{ Middlesex
1896	Yorkshire	1939	Yorkshire	1978	Kent
1897	Lancashire	1946	Yorkshire	1979	Essex
1898	Yorkshire	1947	Middlesex	1980	Middlesex
1899	Surrey	1948	Glamorgan	1981	Nottinghamshire
1900	Yorkshire	1949	{ Middlesex	1982	Middlesex
1901	Yorkshire		{ Yorkshire	1983	Essex
1902	Yorkshire	1950	{ Lancashire	1984	Essex
1903	Middlesex		{ Surrey	1985	Middlesex
1904	Lancashire	1951	Warwickshire	1986	Essex
1905	Yorkshire	1952	Surrey	1987	Nottinghamshire
1906	Kent	1953	Surrey	1988	Worcestershire
1907	Nottinghamshire	1954	Surrey	1992	Essex
1908	Yorkshire	1955	Surrey	1993	Middlesex
1909	Kent	1956	Surrey	1994	Warwickshire
1910	Kent	1957	Surrey	1995	Warwickshire
1911	Warwickshire	1958	Surrey	1996	Leicestershire
1912	Yorkshire	1959	Yorkshire	1997	Glamorgan
1913	Kent	1989	Worcestershire	1998	Leicestershire
1914	Surrey	1990	Middlesex	1999	Surrey
1919	Yorkshire	1991	Essex	2000	Surrey
1920	Middlesex	1960	Yorkshire	2001	Yorkshire
1921	Middlesex	1961	Hampshire	2002	Surrey
1922	Yorkshire	1962	Yorkshire	2003	Sussex
1923	Yorkshire	1963	Yorkshire	2004	Warwickshire
1924	Yorkshire	1964	Worcestershire	2005	Nottinghamshire
1925	Yorkshire	1965	Worcestershire	2006	Sussex
1926	Lancashire	1966	Yorkshire	2007	Sussex
1927	Lancashire	1967	Yorkshire	2008	Durham
1928	Lancashire	1968	Yorkshire	2009	Durham
1929	Nottinghamshire	1969	Glamorgan	2010	Nottinghamshire
1930	Lancashire	1970	Kent	2011	Lancashire
1931	Yorkshire	1971	Surrey		
1932	Yorkshire	1972	Warwickshire		

COUNTY CHAMPIONSHIP RESULTS 2011

DIVISION 1

	DURHAM	HANTS	LANCS	NOTTS	SOM'T	SUSSEX	WARWKS	WORCS	YORKS
DURHAM	–	C-le-St H 50	C-le-St D I/125	C-le-St Drawn	C-le-St Drawn	C-le-St Sx 2w	C-le-St D 8w	C-le-St D 151	C-le-St Drawn
HANTS	So'ton Drawn	–	So'ton La 10w	So'ton Drawn	So'ton Sm 9w	So'ton Drawn	So'ton Drawn	So'ton Drawn	So'ton Drawn
LANCS	L'pool D 5w	L'pool L 222	–	S'port N 129	L'pool L I/20	L'pool L I/55	L'pool Drawn	B'pool L 98	L'pool L 6w
NOTTS	N'ham N 67	N'ham N 9w	N'ham L 6w	–	N'ham Drawn	N'ham Sx I/5	N'ham Wa 9w	N'ham N 3w	N'ham Drawn
SOM'T	Taunton Sm 9w	Taunton H I/61	Taunton L 8w	Taunton Drawn	–	Taunton Sm 9w	Taunton Wa I/382	Taunton Sm 91	Taunton Sm 10w
SUSSEX	Hove D 208	Hove Sx 5w	Hove Drawn	Hove Sx 9w	Hove Sx 8w	–	Arundel Wa 8w	Horsham Wo 34	Hove Drawn
WARWKS	B'ham D I/103	B'ham H 209	B'ham L 147	B'ham Wa I/114	B'ham Wa I/43	B'ham Wa 8w	–	B'ham Wa 218	B'ham Drawn
WORCS	Worcs D I/25	Worcs Wo 9w	Worcs Wo 10w	Worcs Wo 6w	Worcs Sm I/8	Worcs Sx 251	Worcs Wa 88	–	Worcs Y 9w
YORKS	Leeds D 146	Leeds Drawn	Leeds L 23	Leeds N 58	Leeds Y 6w	Scar Drawn	Leeds Wa I/58	Scar Y 6w	–

DIVISION 2

	DERBYS	ESSEX	GLAM	GLOS	KENT	LEICS	MIDDX	N'HANTS	SURREY
DERBYS	–	Derby Drawn	Derby D 186	Derby D 7w	Derby D 101	Derby D I/32	Derby M 3w	C'field N 165	Derby S 7w
ESSEX	C'ford Drawn	–	C'ford E 6w	Colch'r Drawn	C'ford K 57	Southend E 280	C'ford Drawn	C'ford E 171	C'ford S 109
GLAM	Cardiff D 6w	Cardiff Drawn	–	Cardiff Gm 189	Cardiff Gm I/8	Col B Gm 108	Cardiff Drawn	Swansea Drawn	Cardiff Drawn
GLOS	Bristol Gs 7w	Bristol Drawn	Bristol Gs 5w	–	Chelt'm Gs I/142	Bristol Gs 10w	Bristol Drawn	Bristol N I/6	Chelt'm S 2w
KENT	Cant Drawn	Cant K 6w	Cant Gm 8w	Cant Gs 45	–	Tun W K 5w	Cant K 69	Cant N 5w	Cant K 265
LEICS	Leics Drawn	Leics E 254	Leics L 89	Leics Drawn	Leics Drawn	–	Leics M 5w	Leics N I/155	Leics S 10w
MIDDX	Lord's M 7w	Lord's M 8w	Lord's Gm 9w	Uxbridge Drawn	Lord's M 9w	Lord's M 10w	–	Lord's Drawn	Lord's M I/42
N'HANTS	No'ton Drawn	No'ton Drawn	No'ton N I/177	No'ton N 9w	No'ton N I/159	No'ton Drawn	No'ton Drawn	–	No'ton S 333
SURREY	Oval S I/126	Croydon Drawn	Oval Drawn	Oval Gs 4w	Oval S 21	Oval S 215	Guildford M 6w	Oval Drawn	–

COUNTY CHAMPIONSHIP RESULTS 2012

KEEP YOUR OWN RECORD (see page 214)

DIVISION 1

	DURHAM	LANCS	MIDDX	NOTTS	SOM'T	SURREY	SUSSEX	WARWKS	WORCS
DURHAM	–	C-le-St	C-le-St	C-le-St	C-le-St	C-le-St	C-le-St	C-le-St	C-le-St
LANCS	Man	–	L'pool	Man	L'pool	Man	L'pool	L'pool	Man
MIDDX	Lord's	Lord's	–	Uxbridge	Lord's	Lord's	Lord's	Uxbridge	Lord's
NOTTS	N'ham	N'ham	N'ham	–	N'ham	N'ham	N'ham	N'ham	N'ham
SOM'T	Taunton	Taunton	Taunton	Taunton	–	Taunton	Taunton	Taunton	Taunton
SURREY	Oval	Guildford	Oval	Oval	Oval	–	Oval	Oval	Oval
SUSSEX	Arundel	Hove	Hove	Hove	Hove	Horsham	–	Hove	Hove
WARWKS	B'ham	B'ham	B'ham	B'ham	B'ham	B'ham	B'ham	–	B'ham
WORCS	Worcs	Worcs	Worcs	Worcs	Worcs	Worcs	Worcs	Worcs	–

DIVISION 2

	DERBYS	ESSEX	GLAM	GLOS	HANTS	KENT	LEICS	N'HANTS	YORKS
DERBYS	–	Derby	Derby	Derby	Derby	Derby	Derby	Derby	C'field
ESSEX	C'ford	–	Colch'r	C'ford	C'ford	C'ford	C'ford	C'ford	C'ford
GLAM	Cardiff	Cardiff	–	Swansea	Cardiff	Cardiff	Cardiff	Cardiff	Col B
GLOS	Bristol	Chelt'm	Bristol	–	Bristol	Bristol	Chelt'm	Bristol	Bristol
HANTS	So'ton	So'ton	So'ton	So'ton	–	So'ton	So'ton	So'ton	So'ton
KENT	Cant	Cant	Cant	Cant	Tun W	–	Cant	Cant	Cant
LEICS	Leics	Leics	Leics	Leics	Leics	Leics	–	Leics	Leics
N'HANTS	No'ton	No'ton	No'ton	No'ton	No'ton	No'ton	No'ton	–	No'ton
YORKS	Leeds	Leeds	Leeds	Scar	Leeds	Leeds	Scar	Leeds	–

CLYDESDALE BANK 40 2011

This latest format of the 40-over competition was launched in 2010, and is now the only List-A tournament played in the UK. The three Group winners, plus the runner-up with the most points, met in the semi-finals, with the winner decided in the final at Lord's.

GROUP A	P	W	L	T	NR	Pts	Net RR
1 Sussex (2)	12	8	4	–	–	16	+1.07
2 Middlesex (6)	12	8	4	–	–	16	+0.21
3 Derbyshire (4)	12	6	5	1	–	13	–0.07
4 Kent (2)	12	6	6	–	–	12	+0.01
5 Netherlands (7)	12	5	5	1	1	12	–0.36
6 Yorkshire (1)	12	5	7	–	–	10	–0.14
7 Worcestershire (5)	12	2	9	–	1	5	–0.71

GROUP B	P	W	L	T	NR	Pts	Net RR
1 Surrey (3)	12	10	1	–	1	21	+1.04
2 Durham (5)	12	9	2	–	1	19	+0.90
3 Northamptonshire (5)	12	6	6	–	–	12	–0.30
4 Hampshire (4)	12	5	6	–	1	11	+0.22
5 Warwickshire (1)	12	5	7	–	–	10	–0.27
6 Leicestershire (6)	12	2	8	–	2	6	–0.83
7 Scotland (7)	12	2	9	–	1	5	–0.85

GROUP C	P	W	L	T	NR	Pts	Net RR
1 Somerset (1)	12	9	2	–	1	19	+1.00
2 Nottinghamshire (3)	12	7	4	–	1	15	+0.26
3 Essex (2)	12	6	3	–	3	15	+0.25
4 Lancashire (4)	12	6	5	–	1	12	–0.17
5 Glamorgan (7)	12	4	5	–	3	11	+0.16
6 Gloucestershire (3)	12	4	8	–	–	8	–0.48
7 Unicorns (6)	12	1	10	–	1	3	–0.64

Win = 2 points. Tie (T)/No Result (NR) = 1 point. (Last year's positions in brackets.)

Positions of counties finishing equal on points are decided by most wins or, if equal, the team that achieved the most points in the matches played between them; if still equal, the team with the higher net run rate (ie deducting from the average runs per over scored by that team in matches where a result was achieved, the average runs per over scored against that team).

Statistical Highlights in 2011

Highest total	399-4	Sussex v Worcestershire	Horsham
Biggest victory (runs)	174	Hampshire beat Northants	Northampton
Biggest victory (wkts)	9	Sussex beat Middlesex	Hove
Most runs	649 (ave 72.11) C.D.Nash (Sussex)		
Highest innings	158	M.M.Ali	Worcestershire v Sussex	Horsham
Most sixes	10	A.N.Petersen	Glamorgan v Lancashire	Colwyn Bay
Highest partnership	233	J.H.K.Adams/J.M.Vince Hampshire v Scotland	Southampton
Most wickets	23 (ave 14.08) J.W.Dernbach (Surrey)		
Best bowling	5-18	C.J.Liddle	Sussex v Netherlands	Amstelveen
Most economical	8-1-12-1	D.D.Masters	Essex v Unicorns	Bury St Edmunds
Most expensive	8-0-77-3	M.E.Claydon	Durham v Surrey	The Oval
Most w/k dismissals	4	J.C.Buttler	Somerset v Gloucestershire	Bristol
Most catches	4	P.D.Collingwood	Durham v Leicestershire	Chester-le-St
	4	D.J.G.Sales	Northamptonshire v Surrey	Northampton

2011 CLYDESDALE BANK 40 FINAL

SOMERSET v SURREY

At Lord's, London, on 17 September (floodlit).
Result: **SURREY** won by five wickets (D/L method – target 186 in 30 overs).
Toss: Somerset. Award: J.W.Dernbach.

SOMERSET		Runs	Balls	4/6	Fall
* M.E.Trescothick	st Davies b Spriegel	15	17	2	1- 24
† C.Kieswetter	c Davies b Yasir Arafat	16	23	1	2- 36
P.D.Trego	c Ansari b Dernbach	16	14	3	3- 56
N.R.D.Compton	b Ansari	26	41	1	6-124
J.C.Hildreth	b Schofield	3	9	–	4- 66
A.V.Suppiah	lbw b Batty	11	16	–	5- 79
J.C.Buttler	b Dernbach	86	72	7/2	10-214
C.A.J.Meschede	c and b Batty	10	16	–	7-146
A.C.Thomas	c Davies b Dernbach	8	20	–	8-178
M.Kartik	b Dernbach	5	3	1	9-200
S.P.Kirby	not out	0	5	–	
Extras	(LB 5, W 13)	18			
Total	**(39.2 overs)**	**214**			

SURREY		Runs	Balls	4/6	Fall
* R.J.Hamilton-Brown	run out	78	62	7/1	5-147
† S.M.Davies	c Kartik b Kirby	8	11	1	1- 19
J.J.Roy	c Kieswetter b Kirby	11	9	2	2- 35
T.L.Maynard	c Kieswetter b Suppiah	17	16	2	3- 77
C.P.Schofield	c Trescothick b Thomas	26	31	3	4-135
Z.de Bruyn	not out	17	20	1	
M.N.W.Spriegel	not out	24	16	4	
Z.S.Ansari					
G.J.Batty					
Yasir Arafat					
J.W.Dernbach					
Extras	(LB 4, W 4)	8			
Total	**(5 wkts; 27.3 overs)**	**189**			

SURREY	O	M	R	W	SOMERSET	O	M	R	W
Spriegel	6	0	34	1	Thomas	5	0	25	1
Yasir Arafat	8	0	50	1	Kirby	5.3	0	39	2
Dernbach	7.2	0	30	4	Trego	3	0	21	0
Schofield	5	1	32	1	Meschede	3	0	24	0
Batty	8	0	35	2	Kartik	6	0	49	0
Ansari	5	0	28	1	Suppiah	5	0	27	1

Umpires: T.E.Jesty and R.T.Robinson

SEMI-FINALS

At County Ground, Taunton, on 4 September. Toss: Somerset. **SOMERSET** won by 39 runs (D/L method). Durham 219 (38.5/40; D.M.Benkenstein 82, S.P.Kirby 3-31). Somerset 165-3 (27/27; A.V.Suppiah 57). Award: P.D.Trego.

At The Oval, London, on 4 September. Toss: Surrey. **SURREY** won by 71 runs. Surrey 228-7 (24/24; T.L.Maynard 60, C.J.Liddle 4-38). Sussex 157 (22/24; C.D.Nash 55, C.P.Schofield 4-22). Award: T.L.Maynard.

CLYDESDALE BANK/PRO40/NATIONAL/SUNDAY LEAGUE CHAMPIONS

1969	Lancashire	1984	Essex	1999	Lancashire
1970	Lancashire	1985	Essex	2000	Gloucestershire
1971	Worcestershire	1986	Hampshire	2001	Kent
1972	Kent	1987	Worcestershire	2002	Glamorgan
1973	Kent	1988	Worcestershire	2003	Surrey
1974	Leicestershire	1989	Lancashire	2004	Glamorgan
1975	Hampshire	1990	Derbyshire	2005	Essex
1976	Kent	1991	Nottinghamshire	2006	Essex
1977	Leicestershire	1992	Middlesex	2007	Worcestershire
1978	Hampshire	1993	Glamorgan	2008	Sussex
1979	Somerset	1994	Warwickshire	2009	Sussex
1980	Warwickshire	1995	Kent	2010	Warwickshire
1981	Essex	1996	Surrey	2011	Surrey
1982	Sussex	1997	Warwickshire		
1983	Yorkshire	1998	Lancashire		

PRINCIPAL PRO40 RECORDS 1969-2011

Highest Total		399-4	Sussex v Worcs	Horsham	2011
Highest Total Batting Second		327-4	Unicorns v Sussex	Arundel	2010
Lowest Total		23	Middlesex v Yorks	Leeds	1974
Largest Victory (Runs)		249	Somerset beat Glamorgan	Taunton	2010
Highest Scores	203	A.D.Brown	Surrey v Hampshire	Guildford	1997
	191	D.S.Lehmann	Yorks v Notts	Scarborough	2001
	184	M.E.Trescothick	Somerset v Glos	Taunton	2008
	176	G.A.Gooch	Essex v Glamorgan	Southend	1983
	175*	I.T.Botham	Somerset v Northants	Wellingborough	1986
Fastest Hundred	44 balls	M.A.Ealham	Kent v Derbyshire	Maidstone	1995
Most Sixes (Inns)	13	I.T.Botham	Somerset v Northants	Wellingborough	1986
Highest Partnership for each Wicket					
1st	239	G.A.Gooch/B.R.Hardie	Essex v Notts	Nottingham	1985
2nd	302	M.E.Trescothick/C.Kieswetter	Somerset v Glos	Taunton	2008
3rd	228*	M.W.Goodwin/C.J.Adams	Sussex v Middlesex	Hove	2003
4th	219	C.G.Greenidge/C.L.Smith	Hampshire v Surrey	Southampton	1987
5th	221*	R.R.Sarwan/M.A.Hardinges	Glos v Lancashire	Manchester	2005
6th	167	C.L.Cairns/C.M.W.Read	Notts v Sussex	Nottingham	2003
7th	164	J.N.Snape/M.A.Hardinges	Glos v Notts	Nottingham	2001
8th	116*	N.D.Burns/P.A.J.DeFreitas	Leics v Northants	Leicester	2001
9th	105	D.G.Moir/R.W.Taylor	Derbyshire v Kent	Derby	1984
10th	82	G.Chapple/P.J.Martin	Lancashire v Worcs	Manchester	1996
Best Bowling	8-26	K.D.Boyce	Essex v Lancashire	Manchester	1971
	7-15	R.A.Hutton	Yorkshire v Worcs	Leeds	1969
	7-16	S.D.Thomas	Glamorgan v Surrey	Swansea	1998
	7-29	D.A.Payne	Gloucestershire v Essex	Chelmsford	2010
	7-30	M.P.Bicknell	Surrey v Glamorgan	The Oval	1999
	7-39	A.Hodgson	Northants v Somerset	Northampton	1976
	7-41	A.N.Jones	Sussex v Notts	Nottingham	1986
Four Wkts in Four Balls		A.Ward	Derbyshire v Sussex	Derby	1970
		V.C.Drakes	Notts v Derbys	Nottingham	1999
		D.A.Payne	Gloucestershire v Essex	Chelmsford	2010
Most Economical Analysis					
	8-8-0-0	B.A.Langford	Somerset v Essex	Yeovil	1969
Most Expensive Analysis					
	8-0-100-0	D.S.Harrison	Glamorgan v Somerset	Taunton	2010
Most Wicket-Keeping Dismissals in an Innings					
	7 (6 ct, 1 st)	R.W.Taylor	Derbyshire v Lancs	Manchester	1975
Most Catches in an Innings by a Fielder					
	5	J.M.Rice	Hampshire v Warwicks	Southampton	1978
	5	D.J.G.Sales	Northants v Essex	Northampton	2007

FRIENDS LIFE t20 2011

In 2011, the Twenty20 competition was sponsored by Friends Life. Between 2003 and 2009, three regional leagues competed to qualify for the knockout stages, but this was reduced to two leagues in 2010. (2010's positions in brackets.)

NORTH

	P	W	L	T	NR	Pts	Net RR
Nottinghamshire (2)	16	11	2	–	3	25	+1.09
Leicestershire (7)	16	10	2	–	4	24	+0.54
Lancashire (3)	16	9	5	1	1	20	+0.46
Durham (8)	16	6	6	–	4	16	+0.68
Worcestershire (9)	16	6	7	–	3	15	–0.09
Yorkshire (6)	16	6	7	–	3	15	–0.55
Derbyshire (5)	16	4	8	1	3	12	–0.49
Warwickshire (1)	16	4	10	–	2	10	–0.60
Northamptonshire (4)	16	2	11	–	3	7	–0.91

SOUTH

	P	W	L	T	NR	Pts	Net RR
Hampshire (4)*	16	11	2	–	3	23	+1.09
Sussex (3)	16	9	5	–	2	20	+0.06
Kent (7)	16	9	5	–	2	20	–0.21
Somerset (1)	16	7	4	1	4	19	+0.98
Surrey (5)	16	7	6	–	3	17	+0.13
Essex (2)	16	7	7	–	2	16	–0.09
Glamorgan (8)	16	5	9	–	2	12	+0.05
Gloucestershire (9)	16	4	11	–	1	9	–0.47
Middlesex (6)	16	2	12	1	1	6	–1.25

* Hampshire were deducted two points from last season for a poor pitch.

QUARTER-FINALS: LEICESTERSHIRE beat Kent by three wickets at Leicester.
SOMERSET beat Nottinghamshire by six wickets at Nottingham.
HAMPSHIRE beat Durham by 55 runs at Southampton.
LANCASHIRE beat Sussex by 20 runs at Hove.

SEMI-FINALS: LEICESTERSHIRE beat Lancashire in one-over eliminator after match tied (D/L method) at Birmingham.
SOMERSET beat Hampshire in one-over eliminator after match tied (D/L method) at Birmingham.

LEADING AGGREGATES AND RECORDS 2011

BATTING (500 runs)

		M	I	NO	HS	Runs	Avge	100	50	R/100b	Sixes
A.B.McDonald	(Leics)	18	17	6	96*	584	53.09	–	7	128.3	9
A.D.Hales	(Notts)	16	16	–	78	544	34.00	–	5	146.6	14
S.C.Moore	(Lancashire)	17	17	2	76	522	34.80	–	4	133.1	13
M.E.Trescothick	(Somerset)	16	16	3	108*	507	39.00	1	3	162.5	19

BOWLING (23 wkts)

		O	M	R	W	Avge	BB	4w	R/Over
T.J.Phillips	(Essex)	49.0	–	344	26	13.23	4-22	3	7.02
D.R.Briggs	(Hampshire)	50.1	–	343	23	14.91	5-19	3	6.83
H.F.Gurney	(Leics)	49.5	2	354	23	15.39	3-25	–	7.10
D.J.Pattinson	(Notts)	49.1	–	400	23	17.39	5-25	1	8.13

Highest total	254-3	Gloucestershire v Middlesex	Uxbridge
Highest innings	119 K.J.O'Brien	Gloucestershire v Middlesex	Uxbridge
Most sixes	11 K.J.O'Brien	Gloucestershire v Middlesex	Uxbridge
Best bowling	6-5 A.V.Suppiah	Somerset v Glamorgan	Cardiff
Most economical	4-1-7-3 A.J.Ireland	Middlesex v Kent	Canterbury
Most expensive	4-0-61-2 N.M.Carter	Warwickshire v Notts	Birmingham
Most w/k dismissals	5 B.J.M.Scott	Worcestershire v Yorkshire	Worcester
Most catches	4 G.R.Breese	Durham v Yorkshire	Scarborough

2011 FRIENDS LIFE t20 FINAL

LEICESTERSHIRE v SOMERSET

At Edgbaston, Birmingham, on 27 August.
Result: **LEICESTERSHIRE** won by 18 runs.
Toss: Somerset. Award: J.J.Cobb.

LEICESTERSHIRE		Runs	Balls	4/6	Fall
Abdul Razzaq	c and b Pollard	33	33	5	2- 94
J.J.Cobb	c Pollard b Kirby	18	10	2/1	1- 24
W.I.Jefferson	lbw b Suppiah	35	29	2/2	3- 96
J.du Toit	c Kirby b Suppiah	2	8	–	5-102
† P.A.Nixon	c Pollard b Meschede	4	5	1	4-101
A.B.McDonald	c Thomas b Pollard	14	15	–	6-127
J.W.A.Taylor	not out	18	15	1	
W.A.White	not out	10	5	1	
C.W.Henderson					
* M.J.Hoggard					
J.K.H.Naik					
Extras	(B 1, LB 3, W 7)	11			
Total	**(6 wkts; 20 overs)**	**145**			

SOMERSET		Runs	Balls	4/6	Fall
* M.E.Trescothick	c Cobb b Hoggard	16	14	3	1- 31
† C.Kieswetter	b McDonald	17	20	3	2- 42
P.D.Trego	c sub (M.A.G.Boyce) b Cobb	35	25	5	5- 95
J.C.Hildreth	c sub (M.A.G.Boyce) b Cobb	20	21	1	3- 84
K.A.Pollard	c Nixon b White	1	3	–	4- 89
J.C.Buttler	c sub (M.A.G.Boyce) b Cobb	12	11	1	7-103
A.V.Suppiah	run out	0	–	–	6- 97
C.A.J.Meschede	c Taylor b Razzaq	9	11	–	9-122
A.C.Thomas	c sub (M.A.G.Boyce) b Cobb	7	8	–	8-115
M.Kartik	not out	7	6	–	
S.P.Kirby	not out	1	1	–	
Extras	(B 1, W 1)	2			
Total	**(9 wkts; 20 overs)**	**127**			

SOMERSET	O	M	R	W	LEICESTERSHIRE	O	M	R	W
Kartik	4	0	14	0	Hoggard	3	0	17	1
Thomas	4	0	47	0	Abdul Razzaq	3.2	0	26	1
Kirby	2	0	17	1	Henderson	4	0	11	0
Pollard	4	0	24	2	McDonald	3.4	0	32	1
Suppiah	4	0	27	2	Naik	1	0	10	0
Meschede	2	0	12	2	Cobb	4	0	22	4
					White	1	0	8	1

Umpires: R.J.Bailey and N.A.Mallender

TWENTY20 CUP WINNERS

2003	Surrey	2006	Leicestershire	2009	Sussex
2004	Leicestershire	2007	Kent	2010	Hampshire
2005	Somerset	2008	Middlesex	2011	Leicestershire

PRINCIPAL TWENTY20 CUP RECORDS 2003-11

Highest Total	254-3		Gloucestershire v Middx	Uxbridge	2011
Highest Total Batting 2nd	222-3		Northants v Worcs	Kidderminster	2007
Lowest Total	47		Northants v Durham	Chester-le-St	2011
Largest Victory (Runs)	143		Somerset v Essex	Chelmsford	2011
Largest Victory (Balls)	75		Hampshire v Glos	Bristol	2010
Highest Scores	152*	G.R.Napier	Essex v Sussex	Chelmsford	2008
	141*	C.L.White	Somerset v Worcs	Worcester	2006
	124*	M.J.Lumb	Hampshire v Essex	Southampton	2009
	119	K.J.O'Brien	Gloucestershire v Middx	Uxbridge	2011
Fastest Hundred	34 balls	A.Symonds	Kent v Middlesex	Maidstone	2004
Most Sixes (Innings)	16	G.R.Napier	Essex v Sussex	Chelmsford	2008
Most Runs in Career	2002	D.I.Stevens	Kent, Leicestershire		2003-11

Highest Partnership for each Wicket

1st	192	K.J.O'Brien/H.J.H.Marshall	Gloucestershire v Middx	Uxbridge	2011
2nd	186	J.L.Langer/C.L.White	Somerset v Glos	Taunton	2006
3rd	144*	J.H.K.Adams/S.M.Ervine	Hampshire v Surrey	Southampton	2010
4th	139	M.R.Ramprakash/R.Clarke	Surrey v Glos	Bristol	2006
5th	117	M.van Jaarsveld/M.J.Walker	Kent v Leicestershire	Leicester	2006
6th	98*	R.W.T.Key/M.J.Walker	Kent v Middlesex	Beckenham	2006
7th	67	O.A.C.Banks/B.J.Phillips	Somerset v Northants	Northampton	2008
8th	68	M.W.Alleyne/J.Lewis	Glos v Glamorgan	Cardiff	2005
9th	59*	G.Chapple/P.J.Martin	Lancashire v Leics	Leicester	2003
9th	59*	D.J.Willey/J.A.Brooks	Northants v Warwickshire	Birmingham	2011
10th	59	H.H.Streak/J.E.Anyon	Warwickshire v Worcs	Birmingham	2005

Best Bowling	6- 5	A.V.Suppiah	Somerset v Glamorgan	Cardiff	2011
	6-16	T.G.Southee	Essex v Glamorgan	Chelmsford	2011
	6-21	A.J.Hall	Northants v Worcs	Northampton	2008
	6-24	T.J.Murtagh	Surrey v Middlesex	Lord's	2005
Most Wkts in Career	95	A.J.Hall	Worcs, Kent, Northants		2003-11

Most Economical Innings Analyses (Qualification: 4 overs)

4-2-5-2	A.C.Thomas	Somerset v Hampshire	Southampton	2010
4-0-5-3	D.R.Briggs	Hampshire v Kent	Canterbury	2010
4-1-6-2	J.Louw	Northants v Warwicks	Birmingham	2004
4-0-6-1	M.W.Alleyne	Glos v Worcs	Worcester	2005

Most Maiden Overs in an Innings

4-2-9-1	M.Morkel	Kent v Surrey	Beckenham	2007
4-2-5-2	A.C.Thomas	Somerset v Hampshire	Southampton	2010

Most Expensive Innings Analyses

4-0-67-1	R.J.Kirtley	Sussex v Essex	Chelmsford	2008
4-0-65-2	M.J.Hoggard	Yorkshire v Lancs	Leeds	2005
4-0-64-0	Abdul Razzaq	Hampshire v Somerset	Taunton	2010
4-0-63-1	R.J.Kirtley	Sussex v Surrey	Hove	2004

Most Wicket-Keeping Dismissals in an Innings

5 (5 ct)	M.J.Prior	Sussex v Middlesex	Richmond	2006
5 (4 ct, 1 st)	G.L.Brophy	Yorkshire v Durham	Chester-le-St	2008
5 (3 ct, 2 st)	B.J.M.Scott	Worcs v Yorkshire	Worcester	2011

Most Catches in an Innings by a Fielder

4	D.Pretorius	Warwicks v Glamorgan	Swansea	2005
4	W.R.Smith	Notts v Surrey	Nottingham	2006
4	D.J.G.Sales	Northants v Worcs	Northampton	2008
4	G.D.Elliott	Surrey v Kent	The Oval	2009
4	G.R.Breese	Durham v Yorkshire	Scarborough	2011

YOUNG CRICKETER OF THE YEAR

This annual award, made by The Cricket Writers' Club, is currently restricted to players qualified for England, Andrew Symonds meeting that requirement at the time of his award, and under the age of 23 on 1st May. In 1986 their ballot resulted in a dead heat. Up to 1 March 2012 their selections have gained a tally of 2,171 international Test match caps (shown in brackets).

Year	Player	Year	Player	Year	Player
1950	R.Tattersall (16)	1971	J.Whitehouse	1991	M.R.Ramprakash (52)
1951	P.B.H.May (66)	1972	D.R.Owen-Thomas	1992	I.D.K.Salisbury (15)
1952	F.S.Trueman (67)	1973	M.Hendrick (30)	1993	M.N.Lathwell (2)
1953	M.C.Cowdrey (114)	1974	P.H.Edmonds (51)	1994	J.P.Crawley (37)
1954	P.J.Loader (13)	1975	A.Kennedy	1995	A.Symonds (26 – Australia)
1955	K.F.Barrington (82)	1976	G.Miller (34)	1996	C.E.W.Silverwood (6)
1956	B.Taylor	1977	I.T.Botham (102)	1997	B.C.Hollioake (2)
1957	M.J.Stewart (8)	1978	D.I.Gower (117)	1998	A.Flintoff (79)
1958	A.C.D.Ingleby-Mackenzie	1979	P.W.G.Parker (1)	1999	A.J.Tudor (10)
1959	G.Pullar (28)	1980	G.R.Dilley (41)	2000	P.J.Franks
1960	D.A.Allen (39)	1981	M.W.Gatting (79)	2001	O.A.Shah (6)
1961	P.H.Parfitt (37)	1982	N.G.Cowans (19)	2002	R.Clarke (2)
1962	P.J.Sharpe (12)	1983	N.A.Foster (29)	2003	J.M.Anderson (66)
1963	G.Boycott (108)	1984	R.J.Bailey (4)	2004	I.R.Bell (72)
1964	J.M.Brearley (39)	1985	D.V.Lawrence (5)	2005	A.N.Cook (75)
1965	A.P.E.Knott (95)	1986 {	A.A.Metcalfe	2006	S.C.J.Broad (44)
1966	D.L.Underwood (86)		J.J.Whitaker (1)	2007	A.U.Rashid
1967	A.W.Greig (58)	1987	R.J.Blakey (2)	2008	R.S.Bopara (12)
1968	R.M.H.Cottam (4)	1988	M.P.Maynard (4)	2009	J.W.A.Taylor
1969	A.Ward (5)	1989	N.Hussain (96)	2010	S.T.Finn (12)
1970	C.M.Old (46)	1990	M.A.Atherton (115)	2011	J.M.Bairstow

THE PROFESSIONAL CRICKETERS' ASSOCIATION

PLAYER OF THE YEAR

Founded in 1967, the Professional Cricketers' Association introduced this award, decided by their membership, in 1970. The NatWest-sponsored award is presented at the PCA's Annual Awards Dinner in London.

Year	Player	Year	Player	Year	Player
1970 {	M.J.Procter	1984	R.J.Hadlee	1999	S.G.Law
	J.D.Bond	1985	N.V.Radford	2000	M.E.Trescothick
1971	L.R.Gibbs	1986	C.A.Walsh	2001	D.P.Fulton
1972	A.M.E.Roberts	1987	R.J.Hadlee	2002	M.P.Vaughan
1973	P.G.Lee	1988	G.A.Hick	2003	Mushtaq Ahmed
1974	B.Stead	1989	S.J.Cook	2004	A.Flintoff
1975	Zaheer Abbas	1990	G.A.Gooch	2005	A.Flintoff
1976	P.G.Lee	1991	Waqar Younis	2006	M.R.Ramprakash
1977	M.J.Procter	1992	C.A.Walsh	2007	O.D.Gibson
1978	J.K.Lever	1993	S.L.Watkin	2008	M.van Jaarsveld
1979	J.K.Lever	1994	B.C.Lara	2009	M.E.Trescothick
1980	R.D.Jackman	1995	D.G.Cork	2010	N.M.Carter
1981	R.J.Hadlee	1996	P.V.Simmons	2011	M.E.Trescothick
1982	M.D.Marshall	1997	S.P.James		
1983	K.S.McEwan	1998	M.B.Loye		

2011 FIRST-CLASS AVERAGES

These averages involve the 513 players who appeared in the 171 first-class matches played by 27 teams in England and Wales during the 2011 season.

'Cap' denotes the season in which the player was awarded a 1st XI cap by the county he represented in 2011. If he played for more than one county in 2011, the county(ies) who awarded him his cap is (are) underlined. Durham abolished both their capping and 'awards' system after the 2005 season. Glamorgan's capping system is based on a player's number of appearances. Gloucestershire now cap players on first-class debut. Worcestershire now award county colours when players make their Championship debut.

Team abbreviations: CU – Cambridge University/Cambridge MCCU; De – Derbyshire; Du – Durham; DU – Durham MCCU; E – England; EL – England Lions; Ex – Essex; Gm – Glamorgan; Gs – Gloucestershire; H – Hampshire; I – India(ns); K – Kent; La – Lancashire; Le – Leicestershire; LU – Loughborough MCCU; M – Middlesex; Nh – Northamptonshire; Nt – Nottinghamshire; OU – Oxford University/Oxford MCCU; Sm – Somerset; SL – Sri Lanka(ns); SL A – Sri Lanka A; Sy – Surrey; Sx – Sussex; Wa – Warwickshire; Wo – Worcestershire; Y – Yorkshire.

† Left-handed batsman. Cap: a dash (–) denotes a non-county player. A blank denotes uncapped by his current county.

BATTING AND FIELDING

	Cap	M	I	NO	HS	Runs	Avge	100	50	Ct/St
B.J.Ackland (CU)	–	3	6	2	74	200	50.00	–	2	1
A.R.Adams (Nt)	2007	16	27	4	64	551	23.95	–	5	5
† J.H.K.Adams (EL/H)	2006	16	28	–	207	950	33.92	2	4	16
† W.A.Adkin (Sx)		4	6	2	29*	74	18.50	–	–	4
S.S.Agarwal (OU)		4	7	–	71	138	19.71	–	1	1
A.P.Agathangelou (La)		1	2	–	18	18	9.00	–	–	4
Kabir Ali (H)		5	9	4	32	98	19.60	–	–	1
Kadeer Ali (Le)		1	2	–	33	34	17.00	–	–	–
† M.M.Ali (Wo)	2007	16	29	1	158	930	33.21	1	4	12
J.Allenby (Gm)	2010	9	17	1	113	517	32.31	1	4	6
K.G.Alwitigala (SL A)		1	1	–	36	36	36.00	–	–	–
T.R.Ambrose (Wa)	2007	16	22	3	95*	744	39.15	–	8	39/2
† J.M.Anderson (E/La)	2003	8	8	4	27	76	19.00	–	–	8
G.M.Andrew (Wo)	2008	16	29	2	67	666	24.66	–	4	8
† Z.S.Ansari (CU/Sy)		6	10	–	41	90	9.00	–	–	4
† J.E.Anyon (Sx)	2011	15	22	3	53	269	14.15	–	2	5
C.P.Ashling (Gm)		2	3	2	7	9	9.00	–	–	–
A.Ashok (CU)	–	1	2	–	39	40	20.00	–	–	–
M.A.Ashraf (Y)		7	9	1	8*	27	3.37	–	–	–
P.P.Ashton (CU)	–	1	2	–	36	43	21.50	–	–	–
J.J.Atkinson (DU)		3	6	–	34	105	17.50	–	–	3/1
Azeem Rafiq (De)		3	4	1	25*	52	17.33	–	–	–
Azhar Mahmood (K)	2008	7	13	3	97	521	52.10	–	5	9
J.M.Bairstow (EL/Y)	2011	15	28	3	205	1213	48.52	3	7	47
D.J.Balcombe (H)		5	8	2	12	40	6.66	–	–	1
A.J.Ball (K)		9	15	1	46	184	13.14	–	–	5
† G.S.Ballance (Y)		12	23	5	111	862	47.88	1	10	7
† V.Banerjee (Gs)	2006	3	5	2	25	52	17.33	–	–	–
† K.H.D.Barker (Wa)		10	12	1	118	473	43.00	2	5	2
A.W.R.Barrow (Sm)		7	11	–	69	218	19.81	–	1	4
M.D.Bates (H)		8	12	1	58*	204	18.54	–	1	18/4
G.J.Batty (Sy)	2011	16	24	4	79	532	26.60	–	4	20

F-C	Cap	M	I	NO	HS	Runs	Avge	100	50	Ct/St
J.N.Batty (Gs)	2010	6	10	–	70	179	17.90	–	1	28
W.A.T.Beer (Sx)		1	1	–	33	33	33.00	–	–	–
D.W.Bell (CU)	–	3	4	1	23*	50	16.66	–	–	5/6
I.R.Bell (E/Wa)	2001	10	16	4	235	1091	90.91	5	2	5
D.J.Bell-Drummond (K)		4	7	–	80	147	21.00	–	1	3
D.M.Benkenstein (Du)	2005	17	27	4	150	1366	59.39	4	9	7
G.K.Berg (M)	2010	8	11	2	130*	406	45.11	1	2	7
† P.M.Best (CU/Nh/Wa)		6	9	2	150	305	43.57	1	1	4
S.W.Billings (K/LU)		3	5	–	131	222	44.40	1	–	2
L.A.Blackaby (DU)	–	3	6	–	34	78	13.00	–	–	1
† I.D.Blackwell (Du)		17	26	2	158	1063	44.29	3	6	2
† A.J.Blake (K)		9	17	–	96	345	20.29	–	3	6
R.S.Bopara (E/EL/Ex)	2005	15	26	2	178	917	38.20	3	3	2
P.M.Borrington (De)		2	4	–	87	114	28.50	–	1	3
S.G.Borthwick (Du/EL)		15	21	5	101	480	30.00	1	2	14
† A.G.Botha (Wa)		2	3	1	64	92	46.00	–	1	5
† M.A.G.Boyce (Le)		15	30	–	119	815	27.16	2	–	13
† W.D.Bragg (Gm)		16	30	–	110	1033	34.43	1	8	6
R.M.R.Brathwaite (Du)		7	7	4	13	27	9.00	–	–	1
† D.M.Bravo (Nt)	2011	4	7	–	70	248	35.42	–	2	1
G.R.Breese (Du)	2005	1	2	–	38	42	21.00	–	–	3
T.T.Bresnan (E/Y)	2006	6	8	2	90	329	54.83	–	3	1
T.Brett (Nh)		1	1	–	2	2	2.00	–	–	–
D.R.Briggs (H)		11	17	2	29	103	6.86	–	–	2
† S.C.J.Broad (E/Nt)		10	12	1	74*	336	30.54	–	3	4
J.A.Brooks (Nh)		9	8	5	15*	58	19.33	–	–	2
G.L.Brophy (Y)	2008	7	11	3	177*	355	44.37	1	1	7/1
A.D.Brown (Nt)		4	7	2	128*	174	34.80	1	–	2
B.C.Brown (Sx)		11	19	2	112	504	29.64	2	2	14/2
F.A.Brown (CU)	–	3	5	–	31	87	17.40	–	–	1
† K.R.Brown (La)		17	30	2	114	997	35.60	1	7	8
M.J.Brown (Sy)		3	5	–	46	78	15.60	–	–	–
T.E.Bryan (OU)		1	2	–	20	33	16.50	–	–	–
N.L.Buck (Le)	2011	13	22	5	26	124	7.29	–	–	2
† R.J.Burns (Sy)		1	2	–	26	35	17.50	–	–	2
D.A.Burton (Nh)		1	2	–	6	8	4.00	–	–	–
J.C.Buttler (Sm)		13	18	1	100	524	30.82	1	3	31/1
J.G.Cameron (Wo)	2010	12	23	1	98	578	26.27	–	3	7
† M.A.Carberry (H)	2006	9	15	1	300*	793	56.64	3	1	6
A.Carter (Nt)		1	1	–	17	17	17.00	–	–	–
† N.M.Carter (Wa)	2005	2	3	–	40	66	22.00	–	–	1
T.R.Chadwick (OU)	–	1	2	–	1	1	0.50	–	–	–
M.A.Chambers (Ex)		12	17	4	30	108	8.30	–	–	1
† S.Chanderpaul (Wa)		5	7	1	193	539	89.83	3	1	2
L.D.Chandimal (SL)	–	3	6	1	42*	103	20.60	–	–	3/1
G.Chapple (La)	1994	13	22	1	97	380	18.09	–	1	2
M.J.Chilton (La)	2002	14	23	1	117	647	29.40	1	3	8
V.Chopra (Wa)		17	28	1	228	1203	44.55	3	4	16
S.H.Choudhry (Wo)	2010	2	4	–	9	23	5.75	–	–	1
J.L.Clare (De)		14	23	2	130	688	32.76	1	3	7
R.Clarke (Wa)	2011	15	22	1	126	558	26.57	1	2	39
† M.E.Claydon (Du)		9	14	4	38	150	15.00	–	–	1

F-C	Cap	M	I	NO	HS	Runs	Avge	100	50	Ct/St
S.J.Cliff (Le)		1			–	–	–	–	–	–
J.J.Cobb (Le)		9	18	–	44	215	11.94	–	–	6
I.A.Cockbain (Gs)	2011	12	21	1	127	542	27.10	1	3	10
† K.J.Coetzer (Nh)		4	7	1	84	214	35.66	–	2	1
M.T.Coles (K)		10	16	4	50*	242	20.16	–	1	3
P.D.Collingwood (D)	1998	7	13	1	108	439	36.58	1	2	4
C.D.Collymore (M)	2011	16	15	7	8*	43	5.37	–	–	1
N.R.D.Compton (Sm)	2011	14	23	4	254*	1098	47.51	2	6	5
D.O.Conway (OU)	–	3	3	–	20	28	9.33	–	–	2
† A.N.Cook (E/Ex)	2005	14	24	–	294	1372	54.29	5	5	12
S.J.Cook (K)	2007	7	14	2	51	237	19.75	–	1	1
D.G.Cork (H)	2009	10	15	1	50	317	22.64	–	1	6
D.A.Cosker (Gm)	2000	16	24	4	39	314	15.70	–	–	6
R.G.Coughtrie (Gs/OU)	2011	18	33	5	54*	669	23.89	–	2	36/1
† J.D.Cowan (CU)		1	2	–	11	18	9.00	–	–	–
D.J.M.Cox (LU)	–	2	4	–	18	32	8.00	–	–	–
O.B.Cox (Wo)	2009	4	8	1	23	86	12.28	–	–	15
T.R.Craddock (Ex)		8	11	4	21	65	9.28	–	–	1
R.D.B.Croft (Gm)	1992	9	14	2	33	182	15.16	–	–	–
S.J.Croft (La)	2010	17	29	1	122	842	30.07	2	5	21
S.P.Crook (M)		10	9	1	13	64	8.00	–	–	4
G.D.Cross (La)		17	27	–	125	611	22.62	1	2	48/10
L.M.Daggett (Nh)		15	17	9	50*	189	23.62	–	1	2
J.W.M.Dalrymple (M)	2004	12	19	3	122*	531	33.18	2	1	9
† S.M.Davies (Sy)	2011	16	27	1	156	1035	39.80	2	5	53/2
L.A.Dawson (H)		15	26	1	169	908	36.32	2	5	17
T.J.Deasy (CU)	–	1	2	–	41	41	20.50	–	–	1
Z.de Bruyn (Sy)		16	27	2	179	1383	55.32	4	9	7
J.L.Denly (K)	2008	14	28	1	199	1024	37.92	2	5	4
† C.D.J.Dent (Gs)	2010	12	21	2	100	649	34.15	1	3	17
J.W.Dernbach (EL/Sy)	2011	11	14	6	19	60	7.50	–	–	3
A.J.W.Deuchar (DU)	–	2	4	2	0*	0	0.00	–	–	1
F.de Wet (H)		4	6	3	16*	49	16.33	–	–	5
N.J.Dexter (M)	2010	13	22	3	145	561	29.52	1	3	11
M.S.Dhoni (I)		4	8	1	77	220	31.42	–	2	13
A.J.Dibble (Sm)		2	4	2	39*	40	20.00	–	–	–
T.M.Dilshan (SL)		4	7	–	193	553	79.00	3	1	1
† M.J.Di Venuto (Du)		16	25	1	132	935	38.95	3	4	27
P.G.Dixey (Le)		6	10	1	72*	228	25.33	–	2	15/1
G.H.Dockrell (Sm)		1	1	–	14	14	14.00	–	–	–
R.S.Dravid (I)	–	5	9	2	146*	478	68.28	3	–	5
D.D'Souza (LU)	–	1	2	–	18	19	9.50	–	–	–
† M.P.Dunn (Sy)		3	5	5	2*	2	–	–	–	–
† L.E.Durandt (DU)	–	3	6	–	131	227	37.83	1	–	–
W.J.Durston (De)		16	31	3	151	1138	40.64	3	6	7
J.du Toit (Le)		6	11	–	97	217	19.72	–	1	4
E.J.Eckersley (Le)		4	8	–	106	321	40.12	1	2	13
G.A.Edwards (Sy)		1	2	–	19	29	14.50	–	–	1
N.J.Edwards (Nt)		7	14	3	64	172	15.63	–	1	6
C.P.Ellison (OU)	–	2	2	–	1	2	1.00	–	–	–
R.M.S.Eranga (SL A)	–	2	4	2	50*	125	62.50	–	1	–
† S.M.Ervine (H)	2005	14	24	2	128	663	30.13	1	3	6

225

F-C	Cap	M	I	NO	HS	Runs	Avge	100	50	Ct/St
L.Evans (Nh)		2	1	–	5	5	5.00	–	–	–
L.J.Evans (Wa)		3	4	–	52	124	31.00	–	1	1
R.M.Fearon (LU)		1	2	–	8	8	4.00	–	–	1
A.N.P.R.Fernando (SL)	–	1	2	–	4	4	2.00	–	–	1
C.R.D.Fernando (SL)	–	4	4	2	39*	49	24.50	–	–	1
S.T.Finn (E/EL/M)	2009	10	11	1	32	133	13.30	–	–	1
J.D.Fleming (OU)	–	1	2	–	13	23	11.50	–	–	–
L.J.Fletcher (Nt)		13	21	5	39	166	10.37	–	–	3
B.T.Foakes (Ex)		1	1	–	5	5	5.00	–	–	3
M.H.A.Footitt (De)		4	7	1	17	36	6.00	–	–	3
J.S.Foster (Ex)	2001	16	28	7	117*	964	45.90	2	4	48/4
† P.J.Franks (Nt)	1999	14	25	2	96	592	25.73	–	4	5
J.K.Fuller (Gs)		1	1	–	4	4	4.00	–	–	1
† A.W.Gale (Y)	2008	12	22	3	145*	769	40.47	2	4	3
G.Gambhir (I)	–	4	8	1	38	159	22.71	–	1	3
H.S.Gandam (LU)	–	1	2	–	25	25	12.50	–	–	–
J.S.Gatting (Sx)		7	11	1	116*	513	51.30	2	3	3
† C.J.Geldart (Y)		1	1	–	34	34	34.00	–	–	1
B.P.Gibson (Y)		1	1	1	1*	1	–	–	–	6
A.P.R.Gidman (Gs)	2004	15	27	3	168	903	37.62	1	6	12
† W.R.S.Gidman (Gs)	2011	16	28	6	116*	1006	45.72	1	8	4
J.A.Glover (Sx)		1	–	–	–	–	–	–	–	–
J.C.Glover (Gm)		3	4	2	16*	35	17.50	–	–	2
† B.A.Godleman (Ex)		13	24	–	130	634	26.41	1	3	5
† N.A.Gondal (Sx)		4	7	2	100*	165	33.00	1	–	–
J.E.Goodman (K)		4	7	–	56	121	17.28	–	1	5
M.W.Goodwin (Sx)	2001	16	29	3	274*	1372	52.76	4	4	6
D.A.Gordon (OU)	–	3	3	2	1*	1	1.00	–	–	–
L.Gregory (Sm)		5	8	1	48	98	14.00	–	–	–
† D.A.Griffiths (H)		6	10	4	6*	19	3.16	–	–	–
T.D.Groenewald (De)	2011	14	21	8	60*	281	21.61	–	1	3
A.Gupta (CU)	–	1	1	–	10	10	10.00	–	–	–
† M.J.Guptill (De)		8	16	2	143	537	38.35	1	4	9
H.F.Gurney (Le)		1	1	–	2	2	2.00	–	–	–
S.M.Guy (Y)		1	2	–	8	15	7.50	–	–	–
A.D.Hales (EL/Nt)	2011	14	26	2	184	1127	46.95	3	8	14
A.J.Hall (Nh)	2009	16	23	4	146	960	50.52	2	5	31
R.J.Hamilton-Brown (Sy)	2011	16	30	2	159	1039	37.10	1	5	12
† O.J.Hannon-Dalby (Y)		5	8	2	6*	10	1.66	–	–	–
Harbhajan Singh (I)	–	2	4	–	46	58	14.50	–	–	–
† A.Harinath (Sy)		2	4	–	80	128	32.00	–	1	–
S.J.Harmison (Du)	1999	6	4	–	27	45	11.25	–	–	–
J.A.R.Harris (EL/Gm)	2010	11	18	4	60*	410	29.28	–	3	6
† L.J.Hatchett (Sx)		1	–	–	–	–	–	–	–	–
C.W.Henderson (Le)	2004	13	22	3	80*	435	22.89	–	3	5
† H.M.R.K.B.Herath (SL)	–	4	6	1	36	113	22.60	–	–	–
M.R.Hickey (CU)	–	2	4	–	53	101	25.25	–	1	–
P.S.Higham (OU)	–	1	2	1	14	14	14.00	–	–	–
J.C.Hildreth (EL/Sm)	2007	17	27	1	186	996	38.30	2	4	26
A.J.Hodd (Sx)		9	16	4	67	320	26.66	–	1	20/1
† K.W.Hogg (La)	2010	12	19	1	52	370	20.55	–	2	2
M.J.Hoggard (Le)	2010	12	19	7	19*	68	5.66	–	–	2

F-C	Cap	M	I	NO	HS	Runs	Avge	100	50	Ct/St
M.G.Holmes (LU/Wa)		4	6	3	4*	7	2.33	–	–	1
P.J.Horton (La)	2007	17	30	1	99	1099	37.89	–	9	32
D.M.Housego (M)		8	15	2	104	407	31.30	1	–	2
B.A.C.Howell (H)		1	2	–	71	71	35.50	–	1	–
† B.H.N.Howgego (Nh)		6	8	–	41	142	17.75	–	–	5
† C.F.Hughes (De)		14	27	–	167	741	27.44	2	2	13
P.H.Hughes (CU)	–	4	8	2	25	72	12.00	–	–	1
G.M.Hussain (Sm)		9	14	2	42	75	6.25	–	–	2
D.J.Hussey (Nt)	2004	1	2	–	13	18	9.00	–	–	5
Imran Tahir (H)	2009	8	10	3	22*	74	10.57	–	–	4
A.J.Ireland (M)		3	5	–	29	75	15.00	–	–	–
† N.A.James (Gm)		4	7	–	49	186	26.57	–	–	–
O.R.James (LU)	–	1	1	–	8	8	8.00	–	–	1
D.M.P.D.Jayawardena (SL)	–	4	8	–	49	130	16.25	–	–	4
H.A.P.W.Jayawardena (SL)	–	6	10	2	112	232	29.00	1	–	12/2
W.I.Jefferson (Le)		15	29	1	133	1007	35.96	3	3	24
B.A.Jeffery (OU)	–	1	2	–	16	17	8.50	–	–	3
T.M.Jewell (Sy)		2	3	–	61	92	30.66	–	1	–
R.M.Johnson (Wa)		1	2	–	5	10	5.00	–	–	6
A.J.Jones (Gm)		2	3	–	26	34	11.33	–	–	1
C.R.Jones (DU/Sm)		11	18	1	69	304	17.88	–	3	6
G.O.Jones (K)	2003	16	31	1	79	699	23.30	–	4	57/4
P.S.Jones (De)	2010	2	4	1	27	54	18.00	–	–	1
R.A.Jones (Wo)	2007	6	10	2	23*	51	6.37	–	–	–
† S.P.Jones (H)		1	1	–	0	0	0.00	–	–	–
W.S.Jones (Le)		2	4	–	10	12	3.00	–	–	–
C.J.Jordan (Sy)		7	9	1	79*	228	28.50	–	2	3
R.H.Joseph (K)		7	12	6	19*	42	7.00	–	–	1
† E.C.Joyce (Sx)	2009	16	29	1	140	1269	45.32	2	9	22
Junaid Khan (La)		1	2	–	16	16	8.00	–	–	–
H.K.S.R.Kaluhalamulla (SL)	–	2	3	1	76*	108	54.00	–	1	3
A.Kapil (Wo)	2011	5	8	–	54	139	17.37	–	1	2
† M.Kartik (Sm)		8	13	3	65*	285	28.50	–	2	4
† F.D.M.Karunaratne (SL A)	–	2	3	–	43	92	30.66	–	–	7
† G.Keedy (La)	2000	16	24	15	20	111	12.33	–	–	5
S.Kelsall (Nt)		1	2	–	11	15	7.50	–	–	1
A.D.J.Kennedy (CU)	–	1	2	–	61	81	40.50	–	1	6
S.C.Kerrigan (La)		5	7	3	40	80	20.00	–	–	1
A.N.Kervezee (Wo)	2009	16	29	1	128	800	28.57	1	6	4
R.W.T.Key (K)	2001	12	24	2	162	895	40.68	2	5	11
A.Khan (Sx)		13	18	5	65	186	14.30	–	1	9
Z.Khan (I)	–	2	3	1	15	15	7.50	–	–	–
† U.T.Khawaja (De)		4	8	–	135	319	39.87	1	–	5
C.Kieswetter (EL/Sm)	2009	10	16	–	164	604	37.75	2	3	31/1
S.J.King (Sy)		1	2	–	13	13	6.50	–	–	–
S.P.Kirby (Sm)		16	24	3	19	143	6.80	–	–	5
T.C.Knight (De)		2	3	1	14	15	7.50	–	–	1
N.Kruger (OU)	–	3	5	2	32*	76	25.33	–	–	1
C.K.B.Kulasekara (SL A)	–	3	5	1	41*	113	28.25	–	–	–
P.Kumar (I)	–	3	6	–	40	110	18.33	–	–	–
R.A.S.Lakmal (SL)	–	4	4	1	2	2	0.66	–	–	–
A.B.T.Lakshitha (SL A)	–	1	2	–	18	23	11.50	–	–	–

F-C	Cap	M	I	NO	HS	Runs	Avge	100	50	Ct/St
† T.J.Lancefield (Sy)		1	2	–	35	35	17.50	–	–	1
V.V.S.Laxman (I)	–	4	8	–	56	182	22.75	–	2	3
† A.Z.Lees (Y)		1	1	–	0	0	0.00	–	–	–
J.Lewis (Gs)	1998	16	25	2	71	525	22.82	–	4	5
C.J.Liddle (Sx)		1	–	–	–	–	–	–	–	–
A.E.Lilley (Y)		1	1	–	0	0	0.00	–	–	–
† M.S.Lineker (De)		3	6	–	71	107	17.83	–	1	1
T.E.Linley (Sy)		14	24	5	21	122	6.42	–	–	4
M.B.Loye (Nh)	1994	8	12	–	87	393	32.75	–	4	–
D.S.Lucas (Nh)	2009	10	12	2	60	199	19.90	–	1	1
† M.J.Lumb (H)	2008	1	2	–	11	17	8.50	–	–	–
† A.Lyth (Y)	2010	11	22	1	74	553	26.33	–	6	20
J.J.McCluskie (CU)	–	1	–	–	–	–	–	–	–	–
A.B.McDonald (Le)		5	10	2	164	312	39.00	1	1	2
A.McGrath (Y)	1999	12	23	–	115	485	21.08	1	1	12
N.D.McKenzie (H)	2010	16	28	2	237	1120	43.07	3	3	12
† M.W.Machan (Sx)		2	4	–	99	170	85.00	–	2	–
D.L.Maddy (Wa)	2007	8	11	1	76	354	35.40	–	2	8
W.L.Madsen (De)	2011	14	27	–	140	727	26.92	2	4	9
M.F.Maharoof (La/SL)		9	12	3	102	281	31.22	1	–	6
S.I.Mahmood (La)	2007	11	17	–	50	287	16.88	–	1	3
† D.J.Malan (M)	2010	17	28	2	143	947	36.42	3	2	25
M.N.Malik (Le)		11	17	8	12	71	7.88	–	–	1
† J.K.Manuel (Wo)		1	2	–	5	5	2.50	–	–	–
H.J.H.Marshall (Gs)	2006	11	19	1	72	401	22.27	–	2	9
A.D.Mascarenhas (H)	1998	8	14	2	50	190	15.83	–	1	2
M.S.Mason (Wo)	2002	3	6	–	63	67	11.16	–	1	–
D.D.Masters (Ex)	2008	16	24	2	48	234	10.63	–	–	4
T.L.Maynard (Sy)		16	28	3	141	1022	40.88	3	3	14
S.C.Meaker (EL/Sy)		11	13	1	55*	155	12.91	–	1	2
B.A.W.Mendis (Sm/SL)		5	7	2	28	64	12.80	–	–	–
C.A.J.Meschede (Sm)		5	8	1	53	149	21.28	–	1	–
C.L.Metters (Wa)		10	12	5	30	167	23.85	–	–	15
J.C.Mickleburgh (Ex)		16	30	–	112	793	26.43	1	4	11
J.D.Middlebrook (Nh)	2011	16	20	5	109	644	42.93	3	1	8
C.N.Miles (Gs)	2011	1	2	–	19	24	12.00	–	–	–
A.S.Miller (Wa)		6	9	4	8	15	3.00	–	–	–
M.J.Milligan (OU)	–	3	3	–	13	26	8.66	–	–	2
T.S.Mills (Ex)		4	6	2	8	19	4.75	–	–	2
T.P.Milnes (Wa)		1	1	–	23	23	23.00	–	–	–
A.Mishra (I)		3	5	–	84	159	31.80	–	1	–
D.K.H.Mitchell (Wo)	2005	13	25	2	66	751	45.98	–	5	33
Mohammad Yousuf (Wa)		6	11	–	109	353	32.09	1	2	–
S.C.Moore (La)	2011	16	28	3	169*	1013	40.52	2	5	8
† E.J.G.Morgan (E/EL)	–	8	12	1	193	559	50.81	2	3	7
G.J.Muchall (Du)	2005	15	24	1	175	836	36.34	1	7	11
† A.Mukund (I)	–	3	6	1	49	115	23.00	–	–	2
S.J.Mullaney (Nt)		17	30	–	83	587	19.56	–	2	14
D.Murphy (LU/Nh)		7	10	1	79	261	29.00	–	2	24/2
† T.J.Murtagh (M)	2008	16	19	5	55	269	19.21	–	1	4
† P.Mustard (Du)		13	18	4	101	716	51.14	1	6	48/2
J.G.Myburgh (H)		6	11	–	80	287	26.09	–	2	2

F-C	Cap	M	I	NO	HS	Runs	Avge	100	50	Ct/St
J.K.H.Naik (Le)		17	32	7	77*	545	21.80	–	2	6
G.R.Napier (Ex)	2003	7	12	1	196	383	34.81	1	1	3
C.D.Nash (Sx)	2008	15	28	–	120	928	33.14	1	7	9
Naved-ul-Hasan (Sx)		9	13	1	43*	186	15.50	–	–	1
J.D.Nel (K)		1	2	1	2*	2	2.00	–	–	–
† T.J.New (Le)	2009	10	19	–	76	412	21.68	–	4	20/1
O.J.Newby (La)		4	5	3	29*	75	37.50	–	–	1
† S.A.Newman (M)	2011	13	22	1	95	694	33.04	–	4	11
R.I.Newton (Nh)		8	14	1	113	478	36.76	1	2	3
† P.A.Nixon (Le)	1994	4	7	–	46	97	13.85	–	–	–
A.J.Norman (Gm)		1	1	–	34	34	34.00	–	–	–
S.A.Northeast (K)		17	33	–	176	880	26.66	2	4	9
L.C.Norwell (Gs)	2011	3	5	2	26	59	19.66	–	–	–
† N.J.O'Brien (Nh)	2011	14	22	4	166	676	37.55	1	4	49/4
† P.P.Ojha (Sy)		4	5	3	5*	12	6.00	–	–	1
G.Onions (Du)		12	16	5	28*	110	10.00	–	–	4
W.T.Owen (Gm)		9	11	4	69	167	23.85	–	1	1
A.P.Palladino (De)		14	22	5	60	241	14.17	–	1	1
† M.S.Panesar (Sx)	2010	16	22	–	120	188	8.57	–	–	2
† N.T.Paranavitana (SL)	–	6	12	–	125	506	42.16	2	2	9
† M.G.Pardoe (Wo)	2011	13	26	–	74	507	19.50	–	4	3
C.M.Park (CU)	–	3	4	–	81	188	47.00	–	2	2
G.T.Park (De)		2	3	–	14	19	6.33	–	–	2
† W.D.Parnell (Sx)		5	7	1	44	143	23.83	–	–	3
T.W.Parsons (Mx)		1	1	1	7*	7	–	–	–	–
D.C.Pascoe (OU)	–	2	3	–	23	35	11.66	–	–	2
† A.Patel (Nt)		3	6	–	24	74	12.33	–	–	–
J.S.Patel (Wa)		3	4	–	65	114	28.50	–	1	2
† L.A.Patel (DU)	–	2	4	–	32	64	16.00	–	–	1
M.M.Patel (I)	–	1	1	–	6	6	6.00	–	–	–
N.Patel (LU)	–	3	6	–	27	55	9.16	–	–	2
R.H.Patel (LU)	–	3	5	2	9*	23	11.50	–	–	–
S.R.Patel (EL/Nt)	2008	14	25	2	128	1094	47.56	3	7	6
S.A.Patterson (Y)		11	16	6	53	130	13.00	–	1	4
D.J.Pattinson (Nt)	2008	7	10	4	35*	136	22.66	–	–	1
D.A.Payne (Gs)	2011	14	21	6	62	255	17.00	–	1	5
† M.D.K.J.Perera (SL A)	–	1	1	–	1	1	1.00	–	–	1
† N.L.T.C.Perera (SL)	–	4	6	–	47	113	18.83	–	–	–
S.D.Peters (Nh)	2007	15	21	1	222	864	43.20	3	2	15
A.N.Petersen (Gm)	2011	15	27	–	210	1069	42.76	2	5	6
M.L.Pettini (Ex)	2006	8	14	2	67*	285	23.75	–	2	4
B.J.Phillips (Nt)		1	1	1	71*	71	–	–	1	1
† T.J.Phillips (Ex)	2006	10	16	4	58	273	22.75	–	2	7
† C.D.Piesley (K)		2	3	–	22	26	8.66	–	–	–
K.P.Pietersen (E/Sy)		9	13	1	202*	831	69.25	2	5	6
N.D.Pinner (Wo)	2011	1	1	–	0	0	0.00	–	–	1
S.A.Piolet (Wa)		1	1	–	6	6	6.00	–	–	1
L.E.Plunkett (Du)		4	5	3	107*	248	124.00	1	2	1
† W.T.S.Porterfield (Wa)		16	25	1	87	583	24.29	–	5	18
N.Pothas (H)	2003	8	15	1	72	303	21.64	–	3	20
M.J.Powell (Gm)	2000	12	23	2	99	675	32.14	–	5	8
† J.E.Poysden (CU)	–	2	1	–	47	47	47.00	–	–	2

F-C	Cap	M	I	NO	HS	Runs	Avge	100	50	Ct/St
S.Prasanna (SL A)	–	1	2	–	10	10	5.00	–	–	1
W.G.H.N.Premaratne (SL A)	–	2	3	1	11	12	6.00	–	–	–
M.J.Prior (E/Sx)	2003	12	17	3	126	685	48.92	2	4	43/4
† T.J.W.Probert (CU)	–	1	2	2	4*	6	–	–	–	–
† L.A.Procter (La)	7	10	1	89	366	40.66	–	2	2	
R.M.Pyrah (Y)	2010	11	16	1	117	376	25.06	1	1	2
L.A.Radford (Le)	1	–	–	–	–	–	–	–	–	
† S.K.Raina (I)	–	5	9	1	103*	208	26.00	1	1	4
† B.A.Raine (Du)	1	2	–	7	11	5.50	–	–	1	
† P.B.B.Rajapaksa (SL A)	–	3	5	–	76	190	38.00	–	1	1
M.R.Ramprakash (Sy)	2002	13	23	2	141	700	33.33	1	3	10
† G.S.Randhawa (Y)	1	1	–	5	5	5.00	–	–	–	
† W.B.Rankin (Wa)	13	16	7	28	133	14.77	–	–	3	
A.U.Rashid (Y)	2008	16	26	3	82	556	24.17	–	3	9
D.E.M.Ratnayake (LU)	–	3	6	–	43	104	17.33	–	–	1
O.P.Rayner (M/Sx)	14	19	6	62*	509	39.15	–	5	18	
C.M.W.Read (Nt)	1999	17	30	4	133*	942	36.23	2	4	48/4
† D.J.Redfern (De)	13	25	–	99	775	31.00	–	7	6	
† G.P.Rees (Gm)	2009	16	31	–	126	954	30.77	1	8	13
O.B.Richards (OU)	–	1	2	–	42	49	24.50	–	–	–
A.Richardson (Wo)	2010	16	26	11	41	151	10.06	–	–	5
M.J.Richardson (Du)	–	5	8	1	73*	167	23.85	–	2	27/1
A.E.N.Riley (K)	6	8	4	5	17	4.25	–	–	2	
K.A.J.Roach (Wo)	2011	4	6	1	6	17	3.40	–	–	–
S.D.Robson (M)	12	20	3	146	903	53.11	2	4	12	
C.J.L.Rogers (M)	2011	16	27	3	148	1303	54.29	4	6	7
T.S.Roland-Jones (M)	7	8	2	28	109	18.16	–	–	3	
J.E.Root (EL/Y)	16	32	4	160	1013	36.17	1	5	5	
C.G.W.Roper (DU)	–	2	4	1	6	7	2.33	–	–	–
A.M.Rossington (M)	1	2	–	4	4	2.00	–	–	1	
J.J.Roy (Sy)	12	22	1	106*	623	29.66	1	1	11	
† J.A.Rudolph (Y)	2007	4	8	1	120	318	45.42	1	1	2
C.Rushworth (Du)	3	3	1	21	28	14.00	–	–	1	
P.T.Sadler (CU)	–	2	3	1	34	36	18.00	–	–	1
Saeed Ajmal (Wo)	2011	3	6	1	47	86	17.20	–	–	–
W.P.Saha (I)	–	1	1	–	0	0	0.00	–	–	2
N.C.Saker (K)	4	5	–	18	29	5.80	–	–	2	
D.J.G.Sales (Nh)	1999	12	16	1	65	267	17.80	–	1	13
J.D.Salt (DU)	–	1	2	2	1*	1	–	–	–	–
T.T.Samaraweera (SL)	–	6	11	3	87*	377	47.12	–	3	4
G.S.Sandhu (M)	1	2	1	8	15	15.00	–	–	–	
† K.C.Sangakkara (SL)	–	5	10	1	153	389	43.22	2	1	1
I.D.Saxelby (Gs)	2008	15	23	6	34*	238	14.00	–	–	2
† J.J.Sayers (Y)	2007	11	22	2	139	773	38.65	1	6	5
† M.J.L.Scarr (DU)	–	2	4	–	16	31	7.75	–	–	–
† C.P.Schofield (Sy)	3	4	1	99	179	59.66	–	1	–	
A.J.D.Scott (OU)	–	2	3	–	27	49	16.33	–	–	1
B.J.M.Scott (Wo)	2010	12	20	5	73	463	30.86	–	2	31/4
V.Sehwag (I)	–	2	4	–	33	41	10.25	–	–	2
S.M.S.M.Senanayake (SL A)	–	3	5	1	48	108	27.00	–	–	1
S.C.Serasinghe (SL A)	–	3	5	–	44	105	21.00	–	–	2
O.A.Shah (Ex)	10	18	1	118	574	33.76	2	2	15	

F-C	Cap	M	I	NO	HS	Runs	Avge	100	50	Ct/St
R.A.C.Shah (DU)	–	3	6	–	45	99	16.50	–	–	2
A.Shahzad (EL/Y)	2010	12	18	3	70	341	22.73	–	1	–
† Shakib Al Hasan (Wo)	2010	1	1	–	54	54	54.00	–	1	1
† Shan Masood (DU)	–	3	6	1	58*	131	26.20	–	1	3
A.Shankar (Wo)	2011	1	1	1	10*	10	–	–	–	–
† A.J.Shantry (Gm)		3	6	4	14	25	12.50	–	–	2
† J.D.Shantry (Wo)	2009	7	11	4	47*	148	21.14	–	–	1
I.Sharma (I)	–	4	8	2	8*	24	4.00	–	–	1
R.Sharma (OU)	–	3	4	–	114	158	39.50	1	–	2
S.A.Shaw (K)		4	5	3	22*	50	25.00	–	–	3
C.E.Shreck (K/Nt)	2006	11	15	11	7*	29	7.25	–	–	2
† R.J.Sidebottom (Y)	2000	16	25	6	61	389	20.47	–	2	2
A.R.S.Silva (SL A)	–	1	2	–	17	21	10.50	–	–	–
J.K.Silva (SL A)	–	3	5	–	89	126	25.20	–	1	7/1
J.A.Simpson (M)	2011	18	26	6	143	869	43.45	1	7	67/1
R.P.Singh (I)	–	1	2	–	25	25	12.50	–	–	–
D.T.Smith (OU)	–	1	1	1	14*	14	–	–	–	2
G.M.Smith (De)	2009	13	24	3	130	726	34.57	1	5	5
G.P.Smith (DU/Le)		14	28	–	108	773	27.60	1	4	9
† J.W.G.Smith (Du)	–	1	2	–	3	4	2.00	–	–	–
† T.C.Smith (La)	2010	12	19	1	89	459	25.50	–	4	22
T.M.J.Smith (M)		4	6	–	16	42	7.00	–	–	–
W.R.Smith (Du)		15	25	–	179	978	38.12	3	4	11
S.D.Snell (Sm)		1	1	–	4	4	4.00	–	–	–
A.C.Soilleux (LU)	–	1	2	–	6	9	4.50	–	–	–
V.S.Solanki (Wo)	1998	16	30	3	173	1148	42.51	3	6	23
† M.N.W.Spriegel (Sy)		1	2	–	30	34	17.00	–	–	1
S.Sreesanth (I)	–	4	7	2	7*	19	3.80	–	–	–
B.R.W.Stebbings (OU)	–	1	2	–	29	46	23.00	–	–	2
D.I.Stevens (K)	2005	16	31	–	143	819	26.41	1	4	13
B.A.Stokes (Du)		11	18	2	185	734	45.87	3	2	7
† M.D.Stoneman (Du)		7	11	–	128	556	50.54	1	5	6
† A.J.Strauss (E/M/Sm)	2001	14	22	3	241*	1057	55.63	4	2	19
I.W.Sturmer (LU)	–	1	2	1	5	7	7.00	–	–	–
A.V.Suppiah (Sm)	2009	17	31	3	156	961	34.32	1	6	11
L.D.Sutton (De)	2002	16	26	1	56	573	22.92	–	1	59/2
G.P.Swann (E/Nt)	2005	9	8	–	28	101	12.62	–	–	8
N.S.Tahir (Wa)		4	6	–	53	93	15.50	–	1	–
W.A.Tavaré (LU)	–	1	2	–	59	112	56.00	–	2	–
C.G.Taylor (Gs)	2001	16	29	1	196	1139	40.67	3	6	5
J.M.R.Taylor (Gs)	2010	3	5	–	39	111	22.20	–	–	1
J.W.A.Taylor (EL/Le)	2009	17	32	3	237	1602	55.24	3	10	13
† R.M.L.Taylor (Le/LU)		7	14	1	101*	358	27.53	1	1	2
R.N.ten Doeschate (Ex)	2006	9	14	1	164	501	38.53	2	2	10
S.R.Tendulkar (I)	–	5	9	–	91	299	33.22	–	2	2
S.J.Thakor (Le)	–	3	5	–	134	190	38.00	1	–	1
† H.D.R.L.Thirimanne (SL/SL A)	–	6	12	2	104	390	39.00	1	1	7
A.C.Thomas (Sm)	2008	8	10	–	94	333	33.30	–	1	–
C.D.Thorp (Du)		16	20	3	43	310	18.23	–	–	9
R.T.Timms (CU)	–	1	2	–	7	11	5.50	–	–	–
† J.A.Tomlinson (H)	2008	6	10	6	12*	36	9.00	–	–	1
R.J.W.Topley (Ex)		9	11	5	9	21	3.50	–	–	1

F-C	Cap	M	I	NO	HS	Runs	Avge	100	50	Ct/St
† J.C.Tredwell (K)	2007	12	22	2	47	362	18.10	–	–	14
P.D.Trego (Sm)	2007	17	26	5	120	676	32.19	1	5	10
C.T.Tremlett (E/Sy)		7	6	3	24*	75	25.00	–	–	3
† M.E.Trescothick (Sm)	1999	13	23	2	227	1673	79.66	6	6	29
I.J.L.Trott (E/Wa)	2005	8	13	–	203	458	35.23	1	2	6
† J.O.Troughton (Wa)	2002	14	21	2	151	634	33.36	1	3	13
L.L.Tsotsobe (Ex)		3	4	3	6	6	6.00	–	–	1
P.T.Turnbull (CU)	–	3	4	–	33	43	10.75	–	–	–
K.Turner (Nt)		5	9	–	64	227	25.22	–	1	1
M.L.Turner (De)		7	11	8	27*	113	37.66	–	–	–
M.Turns (LU)	–	2	4	2	80	120	60.00	–	1	2
† W.P.J.U.C.Vaas (Nh)	2011	14	16	1	96	403	26.86	–	2	–
F.O.E.van der Bergh (Sy)		1	1	–	0	0	0.00	–	–	–
M.van Jaarsveld (K)	2005	14	28	3	95	755	30.20	–	6	24
J.M.Vince (H)		16	27	2	157	723	28.92	2	2	9
L.Vincent (Sx)		1	2	–	36	49	24.50	–	–	2
A.C.Voges (Nt)	2008	12	20	1	165	845	44.47	1	7	20
G.G.Wagg (Gm)		14	23	1	70*	446	20.27	–	3	5
M.A.Wagh (Nt)	2007	8	16	2	48	251	17.92	–	–	3
Wahab Riaz (K)		5	9	1	34	85	10.62	–	–	1
† D.J.Wainwright (Y)		4	6	1	62	146	29.20	–	1	–
A.G.Wakely (Nh)		16	22	–	98	869	39.50	–	5	8
C.A.M.Walker (OU)	–	2	2	–	43	69	34.50	–	–	–
† M.J.Walker (Ex)	2010	11	21	2	97	587	30.89	–	4	13
† M.A.Wallace (Gm)	2003	16	29	4	107	1020	27.21	2	7	39/5
M.T.C.Waller (Sm)		1	–	–	–	–	–	–	–	–
S.J.Walters (Gm)		7	14	4	147	508	50.80	2	1	5
I.Wardlaw (Y)		1	–	–	–	–	–	–	–	–
† S.M.Warnapura (SL A)	–	3	6	1	79*	189	37.80	–	1	2
H.T.Waters (Gm)		3	5	2	54	93	31.00	–	1	–
N.A.T.Watkins (DU)	–	1	2	–	4	4	2.00	–	–	2
† S.Weerakoon (SL A)	–	1	2	–	18	22	11.00	–	–	–
U.W.M.B.C.A.Welagedara (SL)	–	3	2	–	7	13	6.50	–	–	–
† L.W.P.Wells (Sx)		14	27	2	174	824	32.96	3	–	6
† K.D.Wernars (Sx)		3	4	1	53	104	34.66	–	1	3
M.H.Wessels (Nt)		10	19	–	84	384	20.21	–	3	6
S.A.Westaway (OU)	–	1	2	1	63*	63	63.00	–	1	4
T.Westley (DU/Ex)		13	24	–	127	700	29.16	1	5	12
† I.J.Westwood (Wa)	2008	13	19	1	171	693	38.50	3	2	15
A.J.Wheater (Ex)		11	20	1	164	804	42.31	2	4	5
C.D.Whelan (Wo)	2008	1	1	1	11*	11	–	–	–	–
G.G.White (Nt)		6	10	1	54*	140	15.55	–	1	4
R.A.White (Nh)	2008	13	18	–	140	599	33.27	1	2	9
W.A.White (Le)		14	26	1	83*	789	31.56	–	6	5
R.A.Whiteley (De)		11	20	4	130*	644	40.25	2	2	9
O.Wilkin (LU)	–	3	6	–	38	138	23.00	–	–	1
D.J.Willey (Nh)		2	2	1	64	118	118.00	–	2	–
B.Williams (OU)	–	4	7	2	41	116	23.20	–	–	4
K.S.Williamson (Gs)	2011	13	23	–	149	831	36.13	1	5	12
† C.M.Willoughby (Sm)	2007	15	19	8	23*	51	4.63	–	–	2
G.C.Wilson (Sy)		4	7	–	42	110	15.71	–	–	3
C.R.Woakes (Wa)	2009	11	16	4	129	579	48.25	1	5	6

F-C	Cap	M	I	NO	HS	Runs	Avge	100	50	Ct/St
C.P.Wood (H)		8	11	1	56*	259	25.90	–	1	4
M.A.Wood (Du)		3	5	1	48	118	29.50	–	–	2
† S.K.W.Wood (Nt)		1	–	–	–	–	–	–	–	–
R.J.J.Woolley (CU)	–	3	4	2	89*	148	74.00	–	1	4
B.J.Wright (Gm)	2011	9	16	1	101	460	30.66	1	3	3
C.J.C.Wright (Ex/Wa)		9	12	2	77	236	23.60	–	1	–
D.G.Wright (Wo)	2011	7	13	–	65	212	16.30	–	1	3
L.J.Wright (Sx)	2007	4	7	–	116	237	33.85	1	–	–
A.C.F.Wyatt (Le)		4	4	2	4*	10	5.00	–	–	–
† M.H.Yardy (Sx)	2005	10	16	2	130	617	44.07	2	3	17
Yasir Arafat (Sy)		8	11	2	65	255	28.33	–	1	2
E.G.C.Young (Gs/OU)	2010	5	9	2	133	393	56.14	1	2	2
† Yuvraj Singh (I)	–	2	3	–	62	70	23.33	–	1	2

BOWLING

See BATTING AND FIELDING section for details of matches and caps

	Cat	O	M	R	W	Avge	Best	5wI	10wM
A.R.Adams (Nt)	RMF	479.3	93	1515	67	22.61	6- 31	7	2
W.A.Adkin (Sx)	RM	63	17	174	1	174.00	1- 28	–	–
S.S.Agarwal (OU)	OB	95.2	20	313	4	78.25	2- 86	–	–
A.P.Agathangelou (La)	LB	4	0	12	0				
Kabir Ali (H)	RMF	129	21	437	13	33.61	4- 43	–	–
Kadeer Ali (Le)	RM/LB	1	1	0	0				
M.M.Ali (Wo)	OB	267.2	21	925	18	51.38	4- 53	–	–
J.Allenby (Gm)	RM	228.3	51	654	25	26.16	5- 44	1	–
K.G.Alwitigala (SL A)	RMF	33	2	137	1	137.00	1- 70	–	–
J.M.Anderson (E/La)	RFM	319.4	85	908	33	27.51	5- 65	1	–
G.M.Andrew (Wo)	RMF	384.1	63	1545	52	29.71	5- 59	1	–
Z.S.Ansari (CU)	SLA	127.3	18	402	12	33.50	5- 33	1	–
J.E.Anyon (Sx)	RFM	450.1	50	1785	55	32.45	5-136	1	–
C.P.Ashling (Gm)	RMF	44	2	183	6	30.50	4- 47	–	–
M.A.Ashraf (Y)	RMF	158	28	561	11	51.00	3- 71	–	–
Azeem Rafiq (De)	OB	99	25	293	8	36.62	3- 24	–	–
Azhar Mahmood (K)	RFM	210.1	63	546	23	23.73	6- 36	1	–
D.J.Balcombe (K)	RFM	174.5	40	588	33	17.81	6- 51	4	1
A.J.Ball (K)	LFM	143	25	560	15	37.33	3- 36	–	–
G.S.Ballance (Y)	LB	2	0	11	0				
V.Banerjee (Gs)	SLA	100	17	307	4	76.75	3-134	–	–
K.H.D.Barker (Wa)	LM	250	46	803	25	32.12	5- 31	1	–
A.W.R.Barrow (Sm)	RM/OB	7	0	36	1	36.00	1- 4	–	–
G.J.Batty (Sy)	OB	390.5	69	1200	36	33.33	5- 76	1	–
W.A.T.Beer (Sx)	LB	16	8	36	3	12.00	3- 36	–	–
D.M.Benkenstein (Du)	RM/OB	80	25	193	3	64.33	1- 6	–	–
G.K.Berg (M)	RMF	17.5	30	564	28	20.14	6- 58	1	–
P.M.Best (CU/Nh/Wa)	SLA	269.1	58	901	26	34.65	6- 86	2	–
L.A.Blackaby (DU)	LM	33	4	122	1	122.00	1- 41	–	–
I.D.Blackwell (Du)	SLA	482.5	167	1172	38	30.84	5-102	1	–
A.J.Blake (K)	RMF	6	0	27	0				
R.S.Bopara (E/EL/Ex)	RM	276	40	958	25	38.32	3- 45	–	–
S.G.Borthwick (Du/EL)	LBG	301	69	1059	35	30.25	5- 80	1	–
A.G.Botha (Wa)	SLA	32	8	80	5	16.00	3- 39	–	–

F-C	Cat	O	M	R	W	Avge	Best	5wI	10wM
W.D.Bragg (Gm)	(WK)	10	1	27	1	27.00	1- 4	–	–
R.M.R.Brathwaite (Du)	RFM	177.4	27	656	26	25.23	5- 56	2	–
G.R.Breese (Du)	OB	12	1	21	1	21.00	1- 19	–	–
T.T.Bresnan (E/Y)	RFM	188.3	47	513	29	17.68	5- 48	1	–
T.Brett (Nh)	SLA	30.4	8	94	2	47.00	1- 29	–	–
D.R.Briggs (H)	SLA	449.5	89	1393	38	36.65	6- 65	3	–
S.C.J.Broad (E/Nt)	RFM	381.5	87	1120	44	25.45	6- 46	2	–
J.A.Brooks (Nh)	RFM	289	68	942	43	21.90	5- 23	2	–
G.L.Brophy (Y)	RM	2	0	6	0				
F.A.Brown (CU)	SLA	16.2	3	33	2	16.50	2- 30	–	–
N.L.Buck (Le)	RMF	345.4	83	1197	25	47.88	5- 99	1	–
D.A.Burton (Nt)	RMF	30	9	142	2	71.00	2- 55	–	–
J.G.Cameron (Wo)	RM	7	0	42	0				
M.A.Carberry (H)	OB	8.3	3	18	0				
A.Carter (Nt)	RM	25	9	63	3	21.00	2- 37	–	–
N.M.Carter (Wa)	LMF	60.4	11	197	10	19.70	6- 30	1	–
M.A.Chambers (Ex)	RFM	292.1	45	1059	26	40.73	3- 34	–	–
G.Chapple (La)	RMF	434.3	104	1126	57	19.75	6- 70	3	–
S.H.Choudhry (Wo)	SLA	11	2	70	1	70.00	1- 14	–	–
J.L.Clare (De)	RMF	321.4	64	1165	43	27.09	5- 50	1	–
R.Clarke (Wa)	RFM	410.5	70	1225	46	26.63	5- 10	1	–
M.E.Claydon (Du)	RMF	226.5	50	824	28	29.42	6-104	2	–
S.J.Cliff (Le)	RMF	17	3	56	2	28.00	1- 17	–	–
J.J.Cobb (Le)	LB	24	3	79	1	79.00	1- 41	–	–
M.T.Coles (K)	RMF	284.3	51	1020	32	31.87	5- 29	1	–
P.D.Collingwood (Du)	RM	37	9	117	4	29.25	2- 22	–	–
C.D.Collymore (M)	RFM	456.2	100	1289	49	26.30	4- 28	–	–
D.O.Conway (OU)	RMF	75	12	310	8	38.75	4- 48	–	–
S.J.Cook (K)	RMF	144.1	28	448	11	40.72	3- 40	–	–
A.C.Cope (LU)	RM	4	0	24	0				
D.G.Cork (H)	RFM	278.3	60	802	22	36.45	5- 75	1	–
D.A.Cosker (Gm)	SLA	613.1	162	1650	49	33.67	5- 48	1	–
J.D.Cowan (CU)	LMF	16	1	65	1	65.00	1- 19	–	–
T.R.Craddock (Ex)	LB	205.2	35	632	22	28.72	4- 59	–	–
R.D.B.Croft (Gm)	OB	295.1	49	831	19	43.73	3- 80	–	–
S.J.Croft (La)	RMF	83	17	242	6	40.33	2- 10	–	–
S.P.Crook (M)	RFM	172.5	18	812	26	31.23	5- 94	1	–
L.M.Daggett (Nh)	RMF	451.5	91	1551	46	33.71	4- 35	–	–
J.W.M.Dalrymple (M)	OB	174.4	18	553	12	46.08	3- 64	–	–
L.A.Dawson (H)	SLA	61	9	231	3	77.00	1- 5	–	–
Z.de Bruyn (Sy)	RMF	189	38	589	15	39.26	3- 39	–	–
J.L.Denly (K)	LB	92	10	305	7	43.57	3- 43	–	–
C.D.J.Dent (Gs)	SLA	2	0	8	0				
J.W.Dernbach (EL/Sy)	RFM	375.3	82	1125	34	33.08	5- 41	2	–
A.J.W.Deuchar (DU)	RM	44	6	150	5	30.00	4- 50	–	–
F.de Wet (H)	RFM	124	15	470	9	52.22	2- 78	–	–
N.J.Dexter (M)	RM	118.1	25	411	9	45.66	3- 46	–	–
M.S.Dhoni (I)	RM	10	1	39	0				
A.J.Dibble (Sm)	RMF	36	4	142	2	71.00	1- 26	–	–
T.M.Dilshan (SL)	OB	41	3	154	2	77.00	1- 14	–	–
G.H.Dockrell (Sm)	SLA	18	1	76	2	38.00	2- 76	–	–
D.D'Souza (LU)	RM	2	0	7	0				

F-C	Cat	O	M	R	W	Avge	Best	5wI	10wM
M.P.Dunn (Sy)	RFM	39.1	4	193	6	32.16	5- 56	1	–
L.E.Durandt (DU)	RM	29.5	1	126	3	42.00	3- 65	–	–
W.J.Durston (De)	OB	97.2	12	345	8	32.12	4- 61	–	–
J.du Toit (Le)	RMF	7	2	27	1	27.00	1- 17	–	–
G.A.Edwards (Sy)	RFM	18.3	3	82	0			–	–
C.P.Ellison (OU)	RM	29.5	2	136	4	34.00	3- 69	–	–
R.M.S.Eranga (SL A)	RMF	71.1	13	227	12	18.91	4- 55	–	–
S.M.Ervine (H)	RM	220.2	33	896	15	59.73	3- 66	–	–
L.Evans (Nh)	RMF	35	8	125	5	25.00	3- 21	–	–
R.M.Fearon (LU)	RM	15	0	76	0			–	–
A.N.P.R.Fernando (SL)	RFM	35	3	130	5	26.00	4- 29	–	–
C.R.D.Fernando (SL)	RFM	89.3	8	410	11	37.27	3- 33	–	–
S.T.Finn (E/EL/M)	RF	319.2	68	993	41	24.21	5-113	1	–
L.J.Fletcher (Nt)	RMF	409	89	1247	40	31.17	5- 82	1	–
M.H.A.Footitt (De)	LFM	95.5	18	387	15	25.80	5- 53	1	–
P.J.Franks (Nt)	RMF	330	60	1123	22	51.04	4- 50	–	–
J.K.Fuller (Gs)	RFM	19	3	62	1	62.00	1- 49	–	–
H.S.Gandam (LU)	RFM	1	0	10	0			–	–
J.S.Gatting (Sx)	OB	12	3	36	1	36.00	1- 8	–	–
A.P.R.Gidman (Gs)	RM	32	4	127	2	63.50	2- 33	–	–
W.R.S.Gidman (Gs)	RM	375.2	84	1088	51	21.33	6- 92	3	–
J.A.Glover (Sx)	RFM	14	4	52	1	52.00	1- 52	–	–
J.C.Glover (Gm)	RMF	52	4	201	5	40.20	4- 49	–	–
N.A.Gondal (Sx)	LMF	98.4	12	388	15	25.86	4- 41	–	–
J.E.Goodman (K)	RM	7.5	0	21	0			–	–
D.A.Gordon (OU)	RFM	56.1	4	247	5	49.40	2- 27	–	–
L.Gregory (Sm)	RMF	48	2	222	4	55.50	1- 15	–	–
D.A.Griffiths (H)	RFM	172.5	41	607	18	33.72	6- 85	1	–
T.D.Groenewald (De)	RFM	469	107	1422	48	29.62	5- 59	1	–
H.F.Gurney (Le)	LFM	35.3	6	113	3	37.66	2- 64	–	–
A.D.Hales (EL/Nt)	RM	1	0	1	0			–	–
A.J.Hall (Nh)	RFM	351.1	66	1267	28	45.25	3- 8	–	–
R.J.Hamilton-Brown (Sy)	OB	25.5	2	107	1	107.00	1- 19	–	–
O.J.Hannon-Dalby (Y)	RMF	121	10	398	4	99.50	1- 28	–	–
Harbhajan Singh (I)	OB	69.4	5	287	2	143.50	1- 22	–	–
S.J.Harmison (Du)	RF	117.4	24	454	17	26.70	4- 67	–	–
J.A.R.Harris (EL/Gm)	RMF	371.2	68	1289	47	27.42	5- 39	3	–
L.J.Hatchett (Sx)	LMF	20	6	45	2	22.50	2- 45	–	–
C.W.Henderson (Le)	SLA	495.1	127	1269	40	31.72	4- 43	–	–
H.M.R.K.B.Herath (SL)	SLA	125.5	13	396	9	44.00	3- 87	–	–
M.R.Hickey (CU)	LM	37	5	138	4	34.50	2- 63	–	–
P.S.Higham (OU)	RM	30	8	76	3	25.33	3- 36	–	–
K.W.Hogg (La)	RFM	311	68	953	50	19.06	7- 28	3	1
M.J.Hoggard (Le)	RMF	323	70	993	28	35.46	4- 66	–	–
M.G.Holmes (LU/Wa)	RM	78.3	14	301	7	43.00	3- 46	–	–
C.F.Hughes (De)	SLA	108	16	370	9	41.11	2- 9	–	–
G.M.Hussain (Sm)	RMF	247.1	41	987	22	44.86	6- 33	1	–
Imran Tahir (H)	LBG	235.3	40	685	28	24.46	6-132	2	–
A.J.Ireland (M)	RM	80.3	14	285	5	57.00	2- 51	–	–
N.A.James (SL)	SLA	24	2	79	5	15.80	2- 28	–	–
O.R.James (LU)	OB	22.2	0	102	1	102.00	1- 91	–	–
D.P.M.D.Jayawardena (SL)	RM	1	0	5	0			–	–

235

F-C	Cat	O	M	R	W	Avge	Best	5wI	10wM
T.M.Jewell (Sy)	RMF	30.4	5	117	6	19.50	5- 49	1	–
A.J.Jones (Gm)	LMF	36	4	158	2	79.00	1- 50	–	–
P.S.Jones (De)	RMF	42.3	8	148	3	49.33	3- 56	–	–
R.A.Jones (Wo)	RMF	109.4	14	500	16	31.25	3- 38	–	–
S.P.Jones (H)	RFM	18.3	1	65	1	65.00	1- 59	–	–
W.S.Jones (Le)	LB	3	1	6	0			–	–
C.J.Jordan (Sy)	RFM	144	26	528	11	48.00	4- 57	–	–
R.H.Joseph (K)	RFM	145.1	30	552	20	27.60	4- 25	–	–
Junaid Khan (La)	LMF	27	4	90	1	90.00	1- 44	–	–
H.K.S.R.Kaluhalamulla (SL)	OB	57.3	5	260	6	43.33	4- 76	–	–
A.Kapil (Wo)	RFM	30.2	1	138	4	34.50	2- 38	–	–
M.Kartik (Sm)	SLA	322.2	75	893	26	34.34	5-137	1	–
G.Keedy (La)	SLA	562.4	110	1442	61	23.63	6-133	3	1
S.C.Kerrigan (La)	SLA	213	49	494	26	19.00	9- 51	2	1
R.W.T.Key (K)	RM/OB	0.4	0	8	0			–	–
A.Khan (Sx)	RFM	381.5	72	1259	39	32.28	4- 70	–	–
Z.Khan (I)	LFM	33.3	10	90	2	45.00	2- 18	–	–
U.T.Khawaja (De)	RM	1	0	2	0			–	–
S.J.King (Sy)	OB	18	2	81	0			–	–
S.P.Kirby (Sm)	RFM	490.5	89	1672	53	31.54	6-115	1	–
T.C.Knight (De)	SLA	48	7	143	2	71.50	2- 32	–	–
C.K.B.Kulasekara (SL A)	RFM	92	14	364	8	45.50	5- 69	1	–
P.Kumar (I)	RMF	158.3	38	443	15	29.53	5-106	1	–
R.A.S.Lakmal (SL)	RMF	112.2	11	452	10	45.20	3- 99	–	–
A.B.T.Lakshitha (SL A)	RMF	22	0	111	2	55.50	2- 65	–	–
J.Lewis (Gs)	RMF	513.3	109	1521	65	23.40	5- 65	1	–
C.J.Liddle (Sx)	LFM	15	7	14	1	14.00	1- 14	–	–
A.E.Lilley (Y)	LM	13	4	34	0			–	–
T.E.Linley (Sy)	RFM	482.3	102	1339	73	18.34	6- 57	2	1
D.S.Lucas (Nh)	LMF	242.4	48	915	32	28.59	5- 20	1	–
A.Lyth (Y)	RM	2	1	10	0			–	–
J.J.McCluskie (CU)	RMF	11	2	48	1	48.00	1- 25	–	–
A.B.McDonald (Le)	RFM	87	11	303	8	37.87	3- 51	–	–
A.McGrath (Y)	RM	21	2	56	1	56.00	1- 14	–	–
N.D.McKenzie (H)	RM	2	0	23	0			–	–
M.W.Machan (Sx)	RM/OB	1	0	4	0			–	–
D.L.Maddy (Wa)	RM/OB	116	29	336	11	30.54	3- 29	–	–
M.F.Maharoof (La/SL)	RMF	199.5	30	708	14	50.57	4- 35	–	–
S.I.Mahmood (La)	RF	270.4	36	1093	39	28.02	5- 74	2	1
D.J.Malan (M)	LB	62.5	11	212	7	30.28	4- 80	–	–
M.M.Malik (Le)	RFM	314.4	78	1006	29	34.68	4- 62	–	–
H.J.H.Marshall (Gs)	RM	94.1	20	274	6	45.66	2- 18	–	–
A.D.Mascarenhas (H)	RMF	229.2	61	581	21	27.66	6- 62	1	–
M.S.Mason (Wo)	RMF	95.3	19	290	7	41.42	3- 72	–	–
D.D.Masters (Ex)	RMF	637.1	169	1687	93	18.13	8- 10	8	–
T.L.Maynard (Sy)	OB	2	0	7	0			–	–
S.C.Meaker (EL/Sy)	RMF	297.4	54	1072	47	22.80	5- 37	3	–
B.A.W.Mendis (Sm/SL)	LBG	135.4	12	544	11	49.45	4-183	–	–
C.A.J.Meschede (Sm)	RMF	34.1	5	141	2	70.50	1- 14	–	–
C.L.Metters (Wa)	SLA	221.4	32	695	29	23.96	6- 65	2	–
J.D.Middlebrook (Nh)	OB	426.4	86	1307	43	30.39	5-123	2	–
C.N.Miles (Gs)	RMF	19	1	80	2	40.00	2- 80	–	–

F-C	Cat	O	M	R	W	Avge	Best	5wI	10wM
A.S.Miller (Wa)	RFM	124	25	434	7	62.00	2- 15	–	–
M.J.Milligan (OU)	RMF	78.1	11	313	12	26.08	3- 31	–	–
T.S.Mills (Ex)	LMF	65	11	241	7	34.42	3- 48	–	–
T.P.Milnes (Wa)	RFM	12	3	39	4	9.75	4- 15	–	–
A.Mishra (I)	LB	114.5	5	542	6	90.33	3-150	–	–
D.K.H.Mitchell (Wo)	RM	28	6	82	1	82.00	1- 11	–	–
S.J.Mullaney (Nt)	RM	131.3	29	395	6	65.83	1- 13	–	–
D.Murphy (LU/Nh)	(WK)	1	0	3	0				
T.J.Murtagh (M)	RFM	514.5	103	1774	85	20.87	5- 27	4	1
J.G.Myburgh (H)	OB	15	1	66	1	66.00	1- 30	–	–
J.K.H.Naik (Le)	OB	462.4	73	1528	49	31.18	5- 34	2	–
G.R.Napier (Ex)	RM	192.4	37	690	28	24.64	6- 53	2	–
C.D.Nash (Sx)	OB	92	18	291	11	26.45	4-103	–	–
Naved-ul-Hasan (Sx)	RMF	279.4	58	921	27	34.11	5- 79	2	–
J.D.Nel (K)	RMF	15	1	60	1	60.00	1- 60	–	–
O.J.Newby (La)	RMF	78	17	323	12	26.91	4- 63	–	–
S.A.Newman (M)	RM	1	0	2	0				
A.J.Norman (Gm)	RM	17	4	49	0				
L.C.Norwell (Gs)	RMF	86.5	16	341	12	28.41	6- 46	1	–
P.P.Ojha (Sy)	SLA	150.4	52	311	24	12.95	6- 8	2	1
G.Onions (Du/EL)	RFM	397.3	73	1479	53	27.90	6- 95	2	–
W.T.Owen (Gm)	RMF	229.2	26	1041	30	34.70	5-124	1	–
A.P.Palladino (De)	RMF	435.1	94	1379	52	26.51	5- 39	3	–
M.S.Panesar (Sx)	SLA	750.3	223	1880	69	27.24	5- 58	3	–
N.T.Paranavitana (SL)	OB	1	0	10	0				
C.M.Park (CU)	RMF	15	2	76	0				
G.T.Park (De)	RM	4	0	16	0				
W.D.Parnell (Sx)	LFM	154	20	611	15	40.73	3- 60	–	–
T.W.Parsons (M)	RFM	21	1	83	0				
D.C.Pascoe (OU)	SLA	59	25	126	6	21.00	3- 41	–	–
A.Patel (Nt)	SLC	1.5	0	10	0				
J.S.Patel (Wa)	OB	117.1	20	344	17	20.23	6-111	2	1
L.A.Patel (DU)	OB	30	4	75	1	75.00	1- 57	–	–
M.M.Patel (I)	RMF	29.1	10	81	0				
R.H.Patel (LU)	SLA	67.4	9	234	7	33.42	3- 25	–	–
S.R.Patel (EL/Nt)	SLA	333.4	57	1017	33	30.81	7- 68	1	1
S.A.Patterson (Y)	RMF	294.5	55	973	21	46.33	4- 51	–	–
D.J.Pattinson (Nt)	RFM	167.1	36	529	20	26.45	5- 44	1	–
D.A.Payne (Gs)	LMF	345.2	61	1298	42	30.90	6- 26	2	–
N.L.T.C.Perera (SL)	RMF	94	18	362	8	45.25	3- 88	–	–
A.N.Petersen (Gm)	RM/OB	55	11	160	1	160.00	1- 37	–	–
B.J.Phillips (Nt)	RFM	37.2	5	139	0				
T.J.Phillips (Ex)	SLA	181.3	29	657	11	59.72	4- 97	–	–
K.P.Pietersen (E/Sy)	OB	47	5	165	1	165.00	1- 24	–	–
S.A.Piolet (Wa)	RM	13	0	59	2	29.50	2- 26	–	–
L.E.Plunkett (Du)	RFM	113.4	20	428	11	38.90	3- 70	–	–
J.E.Poysden (CU)	LB	24.1	6	69	4	17.25	3- 20	–	–
S.Prasanna (SL A)	LB	34	5	109	2	54.50	2- 57	–	–
W.G.H.N.Prematarne (SL A)	LMF	50	8	190	3	63.33	2- 51	–	–
T.J.W.Probert (CU)	RM	22.4	2	70	4	17.50	4- 20	–	–
L.A.Procter (La)	RM	83	8	332	9	36.88	3- 33	–	–
R.M.Pyrah (Y)	RM	266.4	54	956	29	32.96	5- 58	1	–

237

F-C	Cat	O	M	R	W	Avge	Best	5wI	10wM
L.A.Radford (Le)	RFM	15	3	64	2	32.00	2- 47	–	–
S.K.Raina (I)	OB	79.4	5	335	5	67.00	2- 58	–	–
B.A.Raine (Du)	OB	3	1	7	0				
G.S.Randhawa (Y)	SLA	21	4	62	2	31.00	2- 54	–	–
W.B.Rankin (Wa)	RMF	387.5	82	1419	55	25.80	5- 57	2	–
A.U.Rashid (Y)	LB	448.3	56	1692	39	43.38	6- 77	2	1
D.E.M.Ratnayake (LU)	RM	15	1	46	1	46.00	1- 46	–	–
O.P.Rayner (M/Sx)	OB	284	62	807	19	42.47	4- 43	–	–
D.J.Redfern (De)	OB	3	0	14	0				
A.Richardson (Wo)	RMF	663.1	179	1783	73	24.42	6- 22	3	–
A.E.N.Riley (K)	OB	131.2	14	547	14	39.07	5- 76	1	–
K.A.J.Roach (Wo)	RF	133	25	550	14	39.28	3- 44	–	–
S.D.Robson (M)	LBG	1	0	8	0				
T.S.Roland-Jones (M)	RMF	188.5	25	684	26	26.30	5- 91	1	–
J.E.Root (EL/Y)	OB	84.3	13	319	7	45.57	3- 33	–	–
C.G.W.Roper (DU)	RM	40.4	5	207	4	51.75	3-110	–	–
J.J.Roy (Sy)	RM	6.2	0	43	2	21.50	2- 29	–	–
J.A.Rudolph (Y)	LBG	6	0	28	0				
C.Rushworth (Du)	RMF	55	16	169	5	33.80	2- 15	–	–
P.T.Sadler (CU)	RFM	49	9	106	2	53.00	2- 38	–	–
Saeed Ajmal (Wo)	OB	164.1	31	471	17	27.70	6-124	2	–
N.C.Saker (K)	RM	111	18	392	13	30.15	5-112	1	–
J.D.Salt (DU)	RM	26	5	93	1	93.00	1- 71	–	–
T.T.Samaraweera (SL)	OB	6	0	32	0				
G.S.Sandhu (M)	LMF	13	0	69	0				
I.D.Saxelby (Gs)	RMF	393.2	53	1529	49	31.20	6- 69	2	1
J.J.Sayers (Y)	OB	13.2	3	31	3	10.33	3- 15	–	–
M.J.L.Scarr (DU)	SLA	14	0	70	0				
C.P.Schofield (Sy)	LBG	72	13	230	5	46.00	2- 57	–	–
A.J.D.Scott (OU)	LB	37.3	5	156	7	22.28	3- 86	–	–
S.M.S.M.Senanayake (SL A)	OB	113.5	15	408	15	27.20	5- 47	1	–
S.C.Serasinghe (SL A)	OB	38	6	119	3	39.66	2- 75	–	–
O.A.Shah (Ex)	OB	2.5	0	4	0				
A.Shahzad (EL/Y)	RFM	325.3	46	1220	33	36.96	5- 61	2	–
Shakib Al Hasan (Wo)	SLA	38.2	5	127	7	18.14	4- 42	–	–
Shan Masood (DU)	RMF	43	4	180	4	45.00	2- 52	–	–
A.J.Shantry (Gm)	LFM	93.5	20	291	9	32.33	3- 42	–	–
J.D.Shantry (Wo)	LM	204.1	42	634	14	45.28	3- 65	–	–
I.Sharma (I)	RFM	173.3	33	640	11	58.18	4- 59	–	–
R.Sharma (OU)	RMF	54	20	132	5	26.40	4- 50	–	–
S.A.Shaw (K)	LFM	81.1	5	400	11	36.36	5-118	1	–
C.E.Shreck (K/Nt)	RFM	306.5	70	1014	34	29.82	5- 52	1	–
R.J.Sidebottom (Y)	LFM	467.4	107	1364	62	22.00	7- 37	3	1
R.P.Singh (I)	LFM	34	7	118	0				
D.T.Smith (OU)	RM	12	1	59	1	59.00	1- 29	–	–
G.M.Smith (De)	OB/RM	323.5	71	991	26	38.11	4- 63	–	–
T.C.Smith (La)	RMF	226.3	44	747	25	29.88	4- 32	–	–
T.M.J.Smith (M)	SLA	103	13	369	8	46.12	3- 38	–	–
W.R.Smith (Du)	OB	5	2	5	0				
A.C.Soilleux (LU)	RMF	17	2	56	2	28.00	2- 56	–	–
M.N.W.Spriegel (Sy)	OB	17	1	56	2	28.00	2- 56	–	–
S.Sreesanth (I)	RFM	139	16	634	9	70.44	3- 77	–	–

F-C	Cat	O	M	R	W	Avge	Best	5wI	10wM
D.I.Stevens (K)	RM	288.2	74	862	41	21.02	7- 21	2	1
B.A.Stokes (Du)	RM	146.3	20	621	21	29.57	6- 68	1	–
A.J.Strauss (E/M/Sm)	LM	.1	0	2	0				
I.W.Sturmer (LU)	RM	7	0	43	0				
A.V.Suppiah (Sm)	SLA	149.1	29	447	10	44.70	2- 16	–	–
G.P.Swann (E/Nt)	OB	287.2	39	956	28	34.14	6-106	1	–
N.S.Tahir (Wa)	RFM	119	33	348	11	31.63	4- 36	–	–
C.G.Taylor (Gs)	OB	5	1	11	1	11.00	1- 7	–	–
J.M.R.Taylor (Gs)	OB	78	4	355	6	59.16	2- 81	–	–
R.M.L.Taylor (Le/LU)	LM	115.4	10	532	11	48.36	3- 53	–	–
R.N.ten Doeschate (Ex)	RMF	69.3	3	270	9	30.00	2- 33	–	–
S.R.Tendulkar (I)	OB	6	0	28	0				
S.J.Thakor (Le)	RM	17	2	74	3	24.66	3- 57	–	–
H.D.R.L.Thirimanne (SL/SL A)	RMF	7	0	30	0				
A.C.Thomas (Sm)	RFM	236.5	44	840	33	25.45	6- 60	2	1
C.D.Thorp (Du)	RMF	476.4	124	1412	46	30.69	6- 20	1	–
J.A.Tomlinson (H)	LMF	173.1	39	573	15	38.20	4- 13	–	–
R.J.W.Topley (Ex)	LMF	222.5	44	801	34	23.55	5- 46	2	–
J.C.Tredwell (K)	OB	394.5	78	1175	42	27.97	5- 35	2	–
P.D.Trego (Sm)	RMF	293.4	43	1078	28	38.50	4- 22	–	–
C.T.Tremlett (E/Sy)	RFM	257	59	781	25	31.24	6- 48	1	–
I.J.L.Trott (E/Wa)	RM	31	3	117	1	117.00	1- 5	–	–
L.L.Tsotsobe (Ex)	LFM	84	8	388	5	77.60	2- 71	–	–
P.T.Turnbull (CU)	RMF	75	15	255	10	25.50	4- 40	–	–
M.L.Turner (De)	RMF	152	23	647	21	30.80	5- 32	1	–
M.Turns (LU)	RM	24	5	108	3	36.00	1- 22	–	–
W.P.J.U.C.Vaas (Nh)	LMF	499	119	1501	70	21.44	6- 46	6	1
F.O.E.van den Bergh (Sy)	SLA	24	5	79	3	26.33	3- 79	–	–
M.van Jaarsveld (K)	OB	14	0	60	2	30.00	2- 33	–	–
G.G.Wagg (Gm)	LM	401.2	64	1380	33	41.81	3- 52	–	–
Wahab Riaz (K)	LFM	121.4	24	436	13	33.53	4- 94	–	–
D.J.Wainwright (Y)	SLA	143.5	31	451	12	37.58	6- 40	1	–
A.G.Wakely (Nh)	OB	8.2	0	32	2	16.00	1- 0	–	–
M.J.Walker (Ex)	RM	25	5	60	3	20.00	2- 15	–	–
M.T.C.Waller (Sm)	LB	5.2	0	28	1	28.00	1- 7	–	–
I.Wardlaw (Y)	RMF	13	0	68	1	68.00	1- 68	–	–
S.M.Warnapura (SL A)	OB	3	0	15	1	15.00	1- 15	–	–
H.T.Waters (Gm)	RMF	59	14	161	3	53.66	2- 16	–	–
N.A.T.Watkins (DU)	SLA	35	2	129	5	25.80	5- 88	1	–
S.Weerakoon (SL A)	SLA	30	5	90	1	90.00	1- 62	–	–
U.W.M.B.C.A.Welagedara (SL)	LFM	98	16	393	12	32.75	4-122	–	–
L.W.P.Wells (Sx)	OB	44	7	170	2	85.00	2- 28	–	–
K.O.Wernars (Sx)	RMF	29.5	7	109	4	27.25	2- 13	–	–
T.Westley (DU/Ex)	OB	110.5	18	345	6	57.50	3- 64	–	–
I.J.Westwood (Wa)	ON	3	0	16	0				
C.D.Whelan (Wo)	RMF	8	0	35	0				
G.G.White (Nt)	SLA	119	19	463	13	35.61	4- 72	–	–
R.A.White (Nh)	LB	65	4	264	4	66.00	2- 51	–	–
W.A.White (Le)	RMF	295	45	1134	38	29.84	4- 37	–	–
R.A.Whiteley (De)	LMF	92	5	385	6	64.16	1- 21	–	–
O.Wilkin (LU)	RM	50	6	213	4	53.25	2- 63	–	–
D.J.Willey (Nh)	LFM	59.2	12	168	13	12.92	5- 29	2	1

F-C	Cat	O	M	R	W	Avge	Best	5wI	10wM
B.Williams (OU)	RSM	14	0	85	1	85.00	1-55	–	–
K.S.Williamson (Gs)	OB	94	10	332	5	66.40	2-39	–	–
C.M.Willoughby (Sm)	LMF	507.3	106	1721	53	32.47	6-76	1	–
C.R.Woakes (Wa)	RMF	406.4	90	1220	56	21.78	7-20	3	1
C.P.Wood (H)	LM	192.4	39	671	24	27.95	4-35	–	–
M.A.Wood (Du)	RMF	57	8	264	10	26.40	3-72	–	–
S.K.W.Wood (Nt)	OB	4	1	8	0				
R.J.J.Woolley (CU)	RM	80	17	281	8	35.12	3-54	–	–
C.J.C.Wright (Ex/Wa)	RFM	314.1	54	1056	34	31.05	5-31	2	–
D.G.Wright (Wo)	RFM	272.4	55	827	31	26.67	6-56	3	–
L.J.Wright (Sx)	RM	49	8	146	5	29.20	3-54	–	–
A.C.F.Wyatt (Le)	RMF	111	29	395	13	30.38	2-28	–	–
M.H.Yardy (Sx)	LM/SLA	3	0	7	0				
Yasir Arafat (Sy)	RFM	276	56	948	20	47.40	5-86	1	–
E.G.C.Young (Gs/OU)	SLA	50.5	6	240	2	120.00	1-29	–	–
Yuvraj Singh (I)	SLA	22	0	128	1	128.00	1-51	–	–

FIRST-CLASS CAREER RECORDS

Compiled by Philip Bailey

The following career records are for all players who appeared in first-class cricket during the 2011 season, and are complete to the end of that season. Some players who did not appear in 2011 but may do so in 2012 are included.

BATTING AND FIELDING

'1000' denotes instances of scoring 1000 runs in a season. Where these have been achieved outside the British Isles they are shown after a plus sign.

	M	I	NO	HS	Runs	Avge	100	50	1000	Ct/St
Abdul Razzaq	117	183	27	203*	5254	33.67	8	28	–	32
Ackland, B.J.	5	10	3	74	293	41.85	–	3	–	2
Adams, A.R.	135	187	20	124	3793	22.71	3	17	–	91
Adams, J.H.K.	126	224	16	262*	7772	37.36	13	42	3	113
Adkin, W.A.	5	7	2	45	119	23.80	–	–	–	4
Agarwal, S.S.	7	11	2	117	272	30.22	1	1	–	2
Agathangelou, A.P.	27	53	2	158	1831	35.90	4	11	0+1	41
Ali, Kabir	122	173	27	84*	2481	16.99	–	7	–	33
Ali, Kadeer	100	182	10	161	4940	28.72	6	26	–	54
Ali, M.M.	65	113	8	158	3627	34.54	6	23	1	33
Allenby, J.	72	113	16	138*	3692	38.06	5	29	–	66
Alwitigala, K.G.	25	28	2	60	317	12.19	–	2	–	23
Ambrose, T.R.	136	207	18	251*	6277	33.21	9	39	–	318/21
Anderson, J.M.	126	146	58	37*	894	10.15	–	–	–	58
Andrew, G.M.	58	88	12	92*	1844	24.26	–	11	–	20
Ansari, Z.S.	6	10	–	41	90	9.00	–	–	–	4
Anyon, J.E.	73	96	28	53	807	11.86	–	2	–	23
Ashling, C.P.	6	9	4	20	58	11.60	–	–	–	1
Ashok, A.	4	8	1	112	328	46.85	1	1	–	2
Ashraf, M.A.	11	13	1	10	42	3.50	–	–	–	1
Ashton, P.P.	2	3	–	36	47	15.66	–	–	–	1
Atkinson, J.J.	6	10	–	34	126	12.60	–	–	–	6/1
Azeem Rafiq	10	12	2	100	198	19.80	1	–	–	1
Azhar Mahmood	175	272	32	204*	7654	31.89	9	42	–	141
Bairstow, J.M.	46	81	17	205	2889	45.14	3	22	1	99/5
Balcombe, D.J.	34	44	9	73	462	13.20	–	1	–	9
Ball, A.J.	9	15	1	46	184	13.14	–	–	–	5
Ball, J.T.	1	2	1	4	4	4.00	–	–	–	–
Ballance, G.S.	25	44	7	132	1670	45.13	5	11	–	22
Banerjee, V.	43	67	22	35	438	9.73	–	–	–	14
Barker, K.H.D.	17	21	2	118	558	29.36	2	2	–	6
Barrow, A.W.R.	7	11	–	69	218	19.81	–	1	–	4
Bates, M.D.	16	23	4	58*	296	15.57	–	1	–	46/4
Batty, G.J.	166	252	42	133	5384	25.63	2	28	–	123
Batty, J.N.	212	334	36	168*	9417	31.60	20	40	1	581/67
Beer, W.A.T.	5	4	2	37*	76	38.00	–	–	–	1
Bell, D.W.	3	4	1	23*	50	16.66	–	–	–	5/6
Bell, I.R.	190	318	34	262*	13368	47.07	38	67	4	135
Bell-Drummond, D.J.	4	7	–	80	147	21.00	–	1	–	3
Benkenstein, D.M.	243	370	42	259	15107	46.05	38	81	5	160
Berg, G.K.	39	65	9	130*	1953	34.87	2	12	–	24
Best, P.M.	6	9	2	150	305	43.57	1	1	–	4
Billings, S.W.	3	5	–	131	222	44.40	1	–	–	2

F-C	M	I	NO	HS	Runs	Avge	100	50	1000	Ct/St
Blackaby, L.A.	5	7	–	38	116	16.57	–	–	–	1
Blackwell, I.D.	198	297	23	247*	10999	40.14	26	61	4	63
Blake, A.J.	23	39	1	105*	829	21.81	1	3	–	12
Bopara, R.S.	121	203	24	229	7452	41.63	20	29	1	72
Borrington, P.M.	28	46	5	105	1223	29.82	2	6	–	19
Borthwick, S.G.	28	39	9	101	821	27.36	1	4	–	23
Botha, A.G.	137	212	28	156*	4403	23.92	4	21	–	107
Botha, J.	67	111	18	109	3218	34.60	1	22	–	50
Boyce, M.A.G.	64	115	6	119	3003	27.55	3	15	–	39
Bragg, W.D.	30	52	–	110	1507	28.98	1	10	1	13/1
Brathwaite, R.M.R.	20	21	8	76*	171	13.15	–	1	–	1
Bravo, D.M.	30	48	2	111	1684	36.60	3	10	–	24
Breese, G.R.	117	187	20	165*	4401	26.35	4	27	–	99
Bresnan, T.T.	106	139	24	126*	3305	28.73	3	17	–	42
Brett, T.	2	1	–	2	2	2.00	–	–	–	–
Briggs, D.R.	33	40	6	38*	322	9.47	–	–	–	9
Broad, S.C.J.	87	109	20	169	2295	25.78	1	15	–	26
Brooks, J.A.	26	31	11	53	255	12.75	–	1	–	5
Brophy, G.L.	122	195	25	185	5473	32.19	8	27	–	293/22
Brown, A.D.	285	447	51	295*	16898	42.67	47	75	8	278/1
Brown, B.C.	21	34	4	112	1065	35.50	4	4	–	23/4
Brown, D.O.	24	41	4	99	1089	29.43	–	8	–	13
Brown, F.A.	7	9	–	31	148	16.44	–	–	–	2
Brown, K.R.	26	45	3	114	1178	28.04	1	7	–	15
Brown, M.J.	96	171	16	133	5273	34.01	9	28	1	71
Bryan, T.E.	3	4	–	20	50	12.50	–	–	–	1
Buck, N.L.	36	49	14	26	265	7.57	–	–	–	6
Burns, R.J.	1	2	–	26	35	17.50	–	–	–	2
Burton, D.A.	6	10	4	52*	66	11.00	–	1	–	1
Buttler, J.C.	27	39	4	144	1123	32.08	2	5	–	54/1
Cameron, J.G.	22	40	2	105	1154	30.36	1	6	–	14
Carberry, M.A.	121	213	19	300*	8625	44.45	26	37	3	56
Carter, A.	7	8	2	17	71	11.83	–	–	–	2
Carter, N.M.	109	151	24	103	2938	23.13	1	13	–	25
Chadwick, T.R.	1	2	–	1	1	0.50	–	–	–	–
Chambers, M.A.	36	49	20	30	195	6.72	–	–	–	8
Chanderpaul, S.	273	443	79	303*	19944	54.79	59	99	1+1	150
Chandimal, L.D.	35	55	7	244	2809	58.52	9	14	0+1	63/12
Chapple, G.	265	368	66	155	7484	24.78	6	34	–	85
Chilton, M.J.	196	320	28	131	9556	32.72	21	39	1	140
Chopra, V.	74	127	7	228	3864	32.20	5	21	–	65
Choudhry, S.H.	5	8	2	75	222	37.00	–	3	–	2
Clare, J.L.	38	55	7	130	1343	27.97	2	8	–	17
Clarke, R.	133	210	20	214	6581	34.63	13	30	1	200
Claydon, M.E.	41	48	10	40	554	14.57	–	–	–	6
Cliff, S.J.	8	7	2	26	71	14.20	–	–	–	1
Cobb, J.J.	37	66	5	148*	1320	21.63	1	7	–	18
Cockbain, I.A.	12	21	1	127	542	27.10	1	3	–	10
Coetzer, K.J.	48	84	10	172	2525	34.12	5	10	–	27
Coles, M.T.	26	41	10	51	650	20.96	–	2	–	7
Collingwood, P.D.	204	350	28	206	11749	36.48	25	60	2	232
Collymore, C.D.	150	202	92	23	862	7.83	–	–	–	46
Comber, M.A.	2	3	–	19	19	6.33	–	–	–	1
Compton, N.R.D.	82	143	17	254*	4760	37.77	11	20	2	40
Conway, D.O.	6	5	1	20	34	8.50	–	–	–	2
Cook, A.N.	156	276	21	294	12094	47.42	35	60	5+1	147

F-C	M	I	NO	HS	Runs	Avge	100	50	1000	Ct/St
Cook, S.J.	139	184	31	93*	2549	16.66	–	7	–	34
Cooke, C.B.	6	11	1	44*	186	18.60	–	–	–	12/1
Cork, D.G.	322	465	61	200*	10114	25.03	8	54	–	237
Cosker, D.A.	194	256	75	52	2488	13.74	–	1	–	116
Coughtrie, R.G.	23	40	6	54*	784	23.05	–	2	–	42/1
Cowan, J.D.	1	2	–	11	18	9.00	–	–	–	–
Cox, D.J.M.	2	4	–	18	32	8.00	–	–	–	–
Cox, O.B.	14	25	5	61	365	18.25	–	2	–	37/2
Craddock, T.R.	8	11	4	21	65	9.28	–	–	–	1
Croft, R.D.B.	400	590	105	143	12791	26.37	8	54	–	175
Croft, S.J.	76	119	10	122	3351	30.74	3	22	–	69
Crook, S.P.	45	56	8	97	1325	27.60	–	9	–	16
Cross, G.D.	32	51	2	125	1210	24.69	2	6	–	87/18
Daggett, L.M.	54	67	30	50*	491	13.27	–	1	–	7
Dalrymple, J.W.M.	135	211	19	244	6544	34.08	12	33	1	91
Davey, J.H.	4	7	–	72	220	31.42	–	3	–	3
Davies, S.M.	109	182	19	192	6518	39.98	10	34	4	331/16
Dawson, L.A.	44	70	7	169	2020	32.06	3	12	–	34
Deasy, T.J.	1	2	–	41	41	20.50	–	–	–	–
de Bruyn, Z.	192	321	33	266*	12152	42.19	27	67	1+1	114
Denly, J.L.	84	149	6	199	4930	34.47	12	24	2	37
Dent, C.D.J.	28	52	5	100	1374	29.23	1	7	–	41
Dernbach, J.W.	65	78	29	56*	478	9.75	–	1	–	8
Deuchar, A.J.W.	2	4	2	0*	0	0.00	–	–	–	1
de Wet, F.	56	77	18	56	982	16.64	–	1	–	27
Dexter, N.J.	64	103	15	146	3516	39.95	8	18	–	55
Dhoni, M.S.	102	161	13	148	5420	36.62	7	37	–	280/46
Dibble, A.J.	2	4	2	39*	40	20.00	–	–	–	–
Dilshan, T.M.	208	336	22	200*	12348	39.32	33	51	0+2	336/27
Di Venuto, M.J.	331	581	42	254*	24909	46.21	60	145	10	406
Dixey, P.G.	19	32	2	103	562	18.73	1	2	–	42/7
Dockrell, G.H.	6	7	1	53	111	18.50	–	1	–	3
Dravid, R.S.	291	484	67	270	23281	55.82	67	114	1+3	350/1
D'Souza, D.	1	2	–	18	19	9.50	–	–	–	–
Dunn, M.P.	4	5	5	2*	3	–	–	–	–	–
Durandt, L.E.	5	9	1	131	280	40.00	1	–	–	1
Durston, W.J.	56	99	15	151	3104	36.95	4	20	1	50
du Toit, J.	35	55	3	154	1817	34.94	4	10	–	28
Eckersley, E.J.	4	8	–	106	321	40.12	1	2	–	13
Edwards, G.A.	1	2	–	19	29	14.50	–	–	–	1
Edwards, N.J.	64	109	3	212	3337	31.48	3	17	1	61
Ellison, C.P.	2	2	–	1	2	1.00	–	–	–	–
Eranga, R.M.S.	35	48	19	78*	694	23.93	–	4	–	19
Ervine, S.M.	131	209	21	237*	6526	34.71	12	33	–	102
Evans, L.	6	7	4	8*	26	8.66	–	–	–	1
Evans, L.J.	12	22	1	133*	667	31.76	1	4	–	7
Fearon, R.M.	1	2	–	8	8	4.00	–	–	–	–
Fernando, A.N.P.R.	35	44	19	16	86	3.44	–	–	–	17
Fernando, C.R.D.	105	102	30	42	554	7.69	–	–	–	39
Finn, S.T.	61	76	24	32	381	7.32	–	–	–	14
Fleming, J.D.	1	2	–	13	23	11.50	–	–	–	–
Fletcher, L.J.	29	40	11	92	406	14.00	–	1	–	5
Foakes, B.T.	1	1	–	5	5	5.00	–	–	–	3
Footitt, M.H.A.	22	26	9	30	154	9.05	–	–	–	7
Foster, J.S.	190	291	37	212	9177	36.12	16	45	1	532/48
Franks, P.J.	195	282	49	123*	6473	27.78	4	35	–	65

F-C	M	I	NO	HS	Runs	Avge	100	50	1000	Ct/St
Fuller, J.K.	3	4	–	24	35	8.75	–	–	–	2
Gale, A.W.	79	128	8	151*	4470	37.25	12	20	–	32
Gambhir, G.	126	215	21	233*	10398	53.59	32	45	–	79
Gandam, H.S.	3	4	–	33	69	17.25	–	–	–	1
Gatting, J.S.	19	28	1	152	978	36.22	3	4	–	9
Geldart, C.J.	2	2	–	34	51	25.50	–	–	–	1
Gibbs, H.H.	193	331	13	228	13425	42.21	31	60	–	176
Gibson, B.P.	1	1	1	1*	1	–	–	–	–	6
Gidman, A.P.R.	145	254	23	176	8251	35.71	16	46	4	92
Gidman, W.R.S.	17	30	6	116*	1014	42.25	1	8	1	4
Glover, J.A.	1	–	–	–	–	–	–	–	–	–
Glover, J.C.	11	14	4	16*	76	7.60	–	–	–	3
Godleman, B.A.	61	105	3	130	3010	29.50	4	15	–	47
Gondal, N.A.	34	45	14	100*	575	18.54	1	–	–	11
Goodman, J.E.	5	9	1	59	180	22.50	–	2	–	5
Goodwin, M.W.	282	490	41	344*	21753	48.44	67	88	9+1	150
Gordon, D.A.	3	3	2	1*	1	1.00	–	–	–	2
Gregory, L.	5	8	1	48	98	14.00	–	–	–	–
Griffiths, D.A.	28	42	18	31*	160	6.66	–	–	–	2
Groenewald, T.D.	53	72	22	78	1059	21.18	–	4	–	19
Gupta, A.	1	1	–	10	10	10.00	–	–	–	–
Guptill, M.J.	47	84	5	189	2575	32.59	3	16	–	35
Gurney, H.F.	17	18	8	24*	63	6.30	–	–	–	2
Guy, S.M.	37	52	6	52*	742	16.13	–	1	–	98/12
Hales, A.D.	35	60	4	184	2259	40.33	4	16	1	29
Hall, A.J.	198	292	39	163	9100	35.96	12	54	1	196
Hamilton-Brown, R.J.	41	72	5	171*	2316	34.56	5	9	1	29
Hannon-Dalby, O.J.	23	24	9	11*	40	2.66	–	–	–	1
Harbhajan Singh	162	219	39	115	3572	19.84	2	13	–	75
Harinath, A.	26	44	1	80	1129	26.25	–	8	–	7
Harmison, B.W.	37	62	5	110	1488	26.10	3	7	–	23
Harmison, S.J.	205	262	74	49*	1857	9.87	–	–	–	29
Harris, J.A.R.	59	84	16	87*	1474	21.67	–	7	–	16
Hatchett, L.J.	5	4	–	20	30	7.50	–	–	–	1
Henderson, C.W.	259	354	74	81	5293	18.90	–	18	–	88
Henriques, M.C.	23	40	4	82	1013	28.13	–	6	–	12
Herath, H.M.R.K.B.	193	273	62	80*	3486	16.52	–	12	–	88
Hickey, M.R.	2	4	–	53	101	25.25	–	1	–	–
Higham, P.S.	1	2	1	14	14	14.00	–	–	–	–
Hildreth, J.C.	134	217	17	303*	8658	43.29	23	41	2	111
Hodd, A.J.	57	84	15	123	2006	29.07	4	9	–	113/12
Hodgson, L.J.	4	5	–	63	165	33.00	–	1	–	3
Hogg, K.W.	76	97	12	88	2019	23.75	–	13	–	18
Hoggard, M.J.	222	282	84	89*	1752	8.84	–	4	–	62
Holmes, M.G.	4	6	3	4*	7	2.33	–	–	–	1
Horton, P.J.	101	170	13	209	6191	39.43	12	34	3	106/1
Housego, D.M.	15	29	1	104	703	27.03	2	–	–	5
Howell, B.A.C.	1	2	–	71	71	35.50	–	1	–	–
Howgego, B.H.N.	20	34	4	80	669	22.30	–	1	–	11
Hughes, C.F.	26	48	2	167	1525	33.15	4	6	–	25
Hughes, P.H.	6	12	2	87	270	27.00	–	2	–	1
Hughes, P.J.	60	108	6	198	5210	51.07	17	26	–	38
Hussain, G.M.	25	42	12	42	244	8.13	–	–	–	4
Hussey, D.J.	155	242	25	275	11903	54.85	40	52	4+1	200
Hutton, B.A.	1	2	–	9	9	4.50	–	–	–	1

F-C	M	I	NO	HS	Runs	Avge	100	50	1000	Ct/St
Imran Tahir	136	171	37	77*	1919	14.32	–	3	–	63
Ireland, A.J.	39	58	16	29	210	5.00	–	–	–	9
James, N.A.	6	10	1	60*	295	32.77	–	1	–	1
James, O.R.	1	1	–	8	8	8.00	–	–	–	1
Jaques, P.A.	158	282	11	244	13482	49.74	38	62	4+2	123
Javid, A.	7	13	–	48	146	11.23	–	–	–	6
Jayawardena, D.P.M.D.	205	326	22	374	15648	51.47	46	68	0+2	268
Jayawardena, H.A.P.W.	200	305	36	229*	7733	28.74	12	32	–	455/91
Jefferson, W.I.	117	208	14	222	7021	36.19	17	27	2	126
Jeffery, B.A.	1	2	–	16	17	8.50	–	–	–	3
Jewell, T.M.	6	5	1	61	97	24.25	–	1	–	–
Johnson, R.M.	8	13	1	72	233	19.41	–	1	–	26/2
Jones, A.J.	2	3	–	26	34	11.33	–	–	–	1
Jones, C.R.	12	18	1	69	304	17.88	–	3	–	6
Jones, G.O.	159	249	21	178	7398	32.44	15	36	2	488/36
Jones, P.S.	148	179	44	114	2709	20.06	2	8	–	34
Jones, R.A.	29	46	7	53*	400	10.25	–	1	–	11
Jones, S.P.	90	111	37	46	899	12.14	–	–	–	17
Jones, W.S.	2	4	–	10	12	3.00	–	–	–	–
Jordan, C.J.	28	34	8	79*	661	25.42	–	3	–	10
Joseph, R.H.	53	71	28	36*	456	10.60	–	–	–	10
Joyce, E.C.	168	280	22	211	11613	45.01	26	65	6	148
Junaid Khan	38	51	16	71	441	12.60	–	2	–	7
Kaluhalamulla, H.K.S.R.	80	112	21	112	1715	18.84	1	6	–	59
Kapil, A.	5	8	–	54	139	17.37	–	1	–	2
Kartik, M.	177	224	36	96	3776	20.08	–	19	–	126
Karunaratne, F.D.M.	38	57	2	185	2395	43.54	6	13	0+1	47
Katich, S.M.	231	397	48	306	18608	53.31	51	99	3+4	206
Keedy, G.	211	245	121	64	1415	11.41	–	2	–	51
Kelsall, S.	1	2	–	11	15	7.50	–	–	–	1
Kennedy, A.D.J.	2	4	1	61	143	47.66	–	1	–	8
Kerrigan, S.C.	18	22	8	40	125	8.92	–	–	–	4
Kervezee, A.N.	52	91	6	155	2926	34.42	4	17	1	25
Key, R.W.T.	238	414	30	270*	15934	41.49	45	61	6	138
Khan, A.	100	120	37	78	1324	15.95	–	5	–	25
Khan, Z.	144	188	38	75	2094	13.96	–	4	–	42
Khawaja, U.T.	38	63	5	214	2665	45.94	8	10	–	21
Kieswetter, C.	76	111	13	164	3765	38.41	8	20	1	219/3
King, S.J.	4	4	–	13	21	5.25	–	–	–	–
Kirby, S.P.	147	206	61	57	1212	8.35	–	1	–	29
Knight, T.C.	2	3	1	14	15	7.50	–	–	–	1
Kruger, N.	7	11	2	172	548	60.88	1	2	–	6
Kulasekara, C.K.B.	71	109	6	129	2718	26.38	2	14	–	33
Kumar, P.	44	70	4	98	1579	23.92	–	8	–	7
Lakmal, R.A.S.	42	45	10	31	294	8.40	–	–	–	12
Lakshitha, A.B.T.	99	139	36	47	1093	10.61	–	–	–	41
Lancefield, T.J.	11	18	1	74	464	27.29	–	2	–	5
Laxman, V.V.S.	258	420	52	353	19067	51.81	53	95	0+4	269/1
Lees, A.Z.	2	2	–	38	38	19.00	–	–	–	–
Lewis, J.	228	327	63	71	4191	15.87	–	13	–	58
Liddle, C.J.	15	14	5	53	113	12.55	–	1	–	5
Lilley, A.E.	1	1	–	0	0	0.00	–	–	–	–
Lineker, M.S.	3	6	–	71	107	17.83	–	1	–	1
Linley, T.E.	34	48	10	42	350	9.21	–	–	–	10
Loye, M.B.	264	422	38	322*	15329	39.91	42	65	6	119
Lucas, D.S.	85	110	27	60	1590	19.15	–	2	–	15

F-C	M	I	NO	HS	Runs	Avge	100	50	1000	Ct/St
Lumb, M.J.	135	226	15	219	7283	34.51	12	45	2	92
Lyth, A.	52	88	1	142	3176	36.50	4	24	1	44
McCluskie, J.J.	1	–	–	–	–	–	–	–	–	–
McDonald, A.B.	80	130	29	176*	4000	39.60	10	20	–	59
McGrath, A.	243	412	27	211	14050	36.49	33	67	3	176
McKenzie, N.D.	232	392	45	237	15454	44.53	41	73	1	205
Machan, M.W.	3	4	–	99	181	45.25	–	2	–	–
Maddy, D.L.	266	433	29	229*	13161	32.57	26	62	4	277
Madsen, W.L.	63	113	7	179	3784	35.69	10	18	–	60
Maharoof, M.F.	64	92	10	118	2039	24.86	4	6	–	39
Mahmood, S.I.	107	139	18	94	1985	16.40	–	9	–	25
Malan, D.J.	64	112	10	143	3717	36.44	7	21	1	72
Malik, M.N.	85	113	41	41	717	9.95	–	–	–	11
Manuel, J.K.	1	2	–	5	5	2.50	–	–	–	–
Marshall, H.J.H.	170	287	19	170	9467	35.32	18	49	1	97
Mascarenhas, A.D.	189	285	32	131	6375	25.19	8	23	–	74
Mason, M.S.	101	133	31	63	1387	13.59	–	5	–	27
Masters, D.D.	148	189	29	119	2273	14.20	1	5	–	49
Maynard, T.L.	40	63	4	141	1749	29.64	3	8	1	36
Meaker, S.C.	29	38	3	94	566	16.17	–	4	–	5
Mendis, B.A.W.	44	58	6	78	687	13.21	–	1	–	12
Meschede, C.A.J.	5	8	1	53	149	21.28	–	1	–	–
Metters, C.L.	10	12	5	30	167	23.85	–	–	–	15
Mickleburgh, J.C.	41	76	–	174	2080	27.36	2	11	–	28
Middlebrook, J.D.	172	245	37	127	5528	26.57	7	20	–	86
Miles, C.N.	1	2	–	19	24	12.00	–	–	–	–
Miller, A.S.	17	25	11	35	85	6.07	–	–	–	4
Miller, D.A.	27	42	4	149	1142	30.05	2	5	–	22
Milligan, M.J.	8	6	–	13	35	5.83	–	–	–	4
Mills, T.S.	4	6	2	8	19	4.75	–	–	–	2
Milnes, T.P.	1	1	–	23	23	23.00	–	–	–	–
Mishra, A.	105	143	20	84	2506	20.37	–	11	–	56
Mitchell, D.K.H.	77	142	18	298	4753	38.33	9	23	2	108
Mohammad Yousuf	141	239	20	223	10505	47.96	30	51	–	84
Moore, S.C.	129	234	19	246	8384	38.99	17	41	4	64
Morgan, E.J.G.	64	104	13	209*	3495	38.40	9	16	1	54/1
Morkel, J.A.	70	100	17	204*	3720	44.81	7	21	–	28
Muchall, G.J.	130	224	11	219	6412	30.10	11	33	–	88
Mukund, A.	46	73	4	300*	3708	53.73	13	10	0+1	35
Mullaney, S.J.	33	54	5	165*	1418	28.93	2	6	–	25
Muralitharan, M.	232	276	83	67	2192	11.35	–	1	–	123
Murphy, D.	23	34	9	79	783	31.32	–	7	–	65/3
Murtagh, T.J.	114	158	48	74*	2437	22.15	–	10	–	33
Mustard, P.	131	200	24	130	5487	31.17	5	33	–	437/17
Myburgh, J.G.	79	143	18	203	5467	43.73	13	32	–	52
Naik, J.K.H.	41	64	16	109*	1165	24.27	1	3	–	18
Nannes, D.P.	23	24	8	31*	108	6.75	–	–	–	7
Napier, G.R.	110	154	31	196	3733	30.34	4	21	–	42
Nash, C.D.	94	162	11	184	5662	37.49	10	31	2	41
Naved-ul-Hasan	139	197	21	139	3875	22.01	5	10	–	60
Needham, J.	19	31	12	48	384	20.21	–	–	–	6
Nel, J.D.	19	25	11	36	156	11.14	–	–	–	10
New, T.J.	95	160	18	125	4338	30.54	2	33	–	161/8
Newby, O.J.	47	42	11	38*	313	10.09	–	–	–	8
Newman, S.A.	129	221	4	219	8415	38.77	16	50	4	96
Newton, R.I.	14	25	1	113	835	34.79	2	4	–	4

246

F-C	M	I	NO	HS	Runs	Avge	100	50	1000	Ct/St
Nixon, P.A.	355	533	111	173*	14498	34.35	21	72	1	889/67
Norman, A.J.	1	1	–	34	34	34.00	–	–	–	–
North, M.J.	166	291	28	239*	11222	42.66	32	56	0+1	130
Northeast, S.A.	46	84	2	176	2271	27.69	3	11	–	25
Norwell, L.C.	3	5	2	26	59	19.66	–	–	–	–
O'Brien, K.J.	20	28	2	171*	863	33.19	1	6	–	14
O'Brien, N.J.	98	150	18	176	4705	35.64	10	20	–	290/30
Ojha, P.P.	54	71	28	35	453	10.53	–	–	–	18
Onions, G.	84	109	37	41	868	12.05	–	–	–	21
O'Shea, M.P.	6	9	–	50	137	15.22	–	1	–	1
Owen, W.T.	13	15	5	69	205	20.50	–	1	–	1
Palladino, A.P.	66	88	23	66	861	13.24	–	3	–	25
Panesar, M.S.	149	191	61	46*	1154	8.87	–	–	–	32
Paranavitana, N.T.	126	209	20	236	8084	42.77	21	36	0+2	130
Pardoe, M.G.	13	26	–	74	507	19.50	–	4	–	3
Park, C.M.	6	8	–	81	279	34.87	–	3	–	4
Park, G.T.	47	79	10	178*	2354	34.11	4	14	1	43
Parnell, W.D.	30	37	4	90	715	21.66	–	3	–	9
Parry, S.D.	3	2	–	2	3	1.50	–	–	–	1
Parsons, T.W.	7	7	2	12	31	6.20	–	–	–	–
Pascoe, D.C.	5	7	2	37	166	33.20	–	–	–	5
Patel, A.	6	12	2	69*	227	22.70	–	1	–	2
Patel, J.S.	103	126	36	120	1821	20.23	1	7	–	34
Patel, L.A.	3	5	–	32	90	18.00	–	–	–	1
Patel, M.M.	54	62	21	78	617	15.04	–	1	–	14
Patel, N.	3	6	–	27	55	9.16	–	–	–	2
Patel, R.H.	4	6	3	19*	42	14.00	–	–	–	–
Patel, S.R.	92	145	10	176	5550	41.11	13	31	1	50
Patterson, S.A.	40	49	15	53	480	14.11	–	–	–	10
Pattinson, D.J.	61	73	15	59	746	12.86	–	1	–	6
Payne, D.A.	14	21	6	62	255	17.00	–	1	–	5
Perera, M.D.K.J.	18	28	1	114	750	27.77	1	4	–	33/6
Perera, N.L.T.C.	19	31	6	113*	894	35.76	1	5	–	10
Peters, S.D.	210	357	28	222	11610	35.28	27	56	4	169
Petersen, A.N.	123	221	12	210	7984	38.20	21	36	1+1	92
Pettini, M.L.	101	172	22	208*	4948	32.98	5	28	1	71
Philander, V.D.	65	91	13	168	2153	27.60	2	6	–	17
Phillips, B.J.	109	151	27	100*	2652	21.38	1	15	–	32
Phillips, T.J.	71	101	15	89	1709	19.87	–	6	–	47
Piesley, C.D.	3	5	–	43	69	13.80	–	–	–	–
Pietersen, K.P.	173	281	19	254*	13084	49.93	41	56	3	134
Pinner, N.D.	1	1	–	0	0	0.00	–	–	–	1
Piolet, S.A.	3	5	1	26*	47	11.75	–	–	–	3
Plunkett, L.E.	106	144	28	107*	2621	22.59	1	12	–	64
Pollard, K.A.	21	34	1	174	1247	37.78	3	5	–	32
Porterfield, W.T.S.	60	102	3	175	3131	31.62	4	20	–	63
Pothas, N.	218	340	60	165	11438	40.85	24	61	–	612/45
Powell, M.J.	212	358	33	299	12461	38.34	25	64	5	130
Poynton, T.	7	11	–	25	105	9.54	–	–	–	12/2
Poysden, J.E.	2	1	–	47	47	47.00	–	–	–	2
Prasanna, S.	57	86	5	70	1273	15.71	–	3	–	32
Premaratne, W.G.H.N.	19	19	11	28	71	8.87	–	–	–	5
Prince, A.G.	198	317	44	254	12034	44.08	31	55	0+1	136
Prior, M.J.	194	299	35	201*	10739	40.67	26	60	3	495/32
Probert, T.J.W.	2	3	3	4*	6	–	–	–	–	–
Procter, L.A.	9	13	1	89	430	35.83	–	2	–	2

F-C	M	I	NO	HS	Runs	Avge	100	50	1000	Ct/St
Pyrah, R.M.	33	44	5	134*	1177	30.17	3	5	–	15
Radford, L.A.	1	–	–	–	–	–	–	–	–	–
Raina, S.K.	67	113	6	203	4497	42.02	8	31	–	73
Raine, B.A.	1	2	–	7	11	5.50	–	–	–	1
Rajapaksa, P.B.B.	7	11	2	166	459	51.00	1	2	–	3
Ramprakash, M.R.	455	752	93	301*	35539	53.92	114	147	20	259
Randhawa, G.S.	1	1	–	5	5	5.00	–	–	–	–
Rankin, W.B.	47	58	24	28	261	7.67	–	–	–	15
Rashid, A.U.	89	129	24	157*	3580	34.09	4	22	–	47
Ratnayake, D.E.M.	3	6	–	43	104	17.33	–	–	–	1
Rayner, O.P.	52	64	15	101	1291	26.34	1	8	–	60
Read, C.M.W.	257	386	65	240	11693	36.42	20	62	2	759/44
Redfern, D.J.	45	76	4	99	2113	29.34	–	15	–	23
Rees, G.P.	79	137	8	154	4534	35.14	11	26	2	63
Riazuddin, H.	3	2	–	4	7	3.50	–	–	–	–
Richards, O.B.	1	2	–	42	49	24.50	–	–	–	–
Richardson, A.	138	153	64	91	983	11.04	–	1	–	43
Richardson, M.J.	6	9	1	73*	169	21.12	–	2	–	27/1
Riley, A.E.N.	6	8	4	5	17	4.25	–	–	–	2
Roach, K.A.J.	35	47	10	52*	366	9.89	–	1	–	16
Robson, S.D.	27	48	3	204	1857	41.26	4	8	–	32
Rogers, C.J.L.	194	342	25	319	16331	51.51	49	75	5+2	182
Roland-Jones, T.S.	16	22	4	30*	263	14.61	–	–	–	6
Root, J.E.	18	35	5	160	1051	35.03	1	5	1	6
Roper, C.G.W.	4	5	1	6	7	1.75	–	–	–	1
Rossington, A.M.	2	3	–	4	5	1.66	–	–	–	2
Roy, J.J.	15	27	1	106*	793	30.50	1	3	–	11
Rudolph, J.A.	202	345	23	228*	14681	45.59	43	65	4+1	189
Rushworth, C.	12	17	3	28	155	11.07	–	–	–	2
Sadler, P.T.	2	3	1	34	36	18.00	–	–	–	1
Saeed Ajmal	98	133	44	53	1106	12.42	–	3	–	31
Saha, W.P.	34	51	6	178*	1712	38.04	4	8	–	79/4
Saker, N.C.	22	28	4	58*	301	12.54	–	1	–	7
Sales, D.J.G.	216	345	29	303*	12412	39.27	24	60	6	202
Salt, J.D.	1	2	2	1*	1	–	–	–	–	–
Samaraweera, T.T.	231	325	59	231	12901	48.50	33	65	0+1	183
Sanderson, B.W.	3	2	1	6	6	6.00	–	–	–	–
Sandhu, G.S.	1	2	1	8	15	15.00	–	–	–	–
Sangakkara, K.C.	187	300	23	287	13240	47.79	34	60	0+1	328/33
Sarwan, R.R.	191	322	22	291	11822	39.40	31	62	–	137
Saxelby, I.D.	27	39	10	60*	426	14.68	–	1	–	8
Sayers, J.J.	96	161	12	187	5133	34.44	11	28	1	56
Scarr, M.J.L.	2	4	–	16	31	7.75	–	–	–	–
Schofield, C.P.	103	147	19	144	3823	29.86	1	27	–	57
Scott, A.J.D.	3	3	–	27	49	16.33	–	–	–	1
Scott, B.J.M.	89	139	27	164*	3173	28.33	3	18	–	242/26
Sehwag, V.	153	255	10	319	12240	49.95	36	45	0+2	127
Senanayake, S.M.S.M.	59	73	21	89	1023	19.67	–	3	–	48
Serasinghe, S.C.	45	69	12	126	2518	44.17	6	11	–	27
Shafayat, B.M.	123	207	8	161	5937	29.83	9	31	–	111/9
Shah, O.A.	237	404	36	203	15461	42.01	42	76	8	187
Shah, R.A.C.	3	6	–	45	99	16.50	–	–	–	2
Shahid Afridi	111	183	4	164	5631	31.45	12	30	–	75
Shahzad, A.	46	59	16	88	1155	26.86	–	3	–	8
Shakib Al Hasan	56	103	9	129	3119	33.18	4	16	–	30
Shankar, A.	13	21	1	143	394	19.70	1	–	–	5

F-C	M	I	NO	HS	Runs	Avge	100	50	1000	Ct/St
Shan Masood	24	39	3	127	1096	30.44	1	7	–	17
Shantry, A.J.	32	43	16	100	469	17.37	1	–	–	8
Shantry, J.D.	22	31	10	47*	215	10.23	–	–	–	6
Sharma, I.	60	76	35	31*	416	10.14	–	–	–	17
Sharma, R.	11	16	2	114	445	31.78	1	1	–	4
Shaw, S.A.	4	5	3	22*	50	25.00	–	–	–	3
Shreck, C.E.	96	112	65	19	183	3.89	–	–	–	33
Siddle, P.M.	48	65	14	45*	828	16.23	–	–	–	26
Sidebottom, R.J.	163	209	65	61	1981	13.75	–	3	–	51
Silva, A.R.S.	35	53	10	189	2043	47.51	6	7	–	27
Silva, J.K.	99	155	24	173	6033	46.05	15	29	0+1	249/36
Simpson, J.A.	37	59	8	143	1696	33.25	2	10	–	114/3
Singh, R.P.	63	86	17	47	692	10.02	–	–	–	30
Smith, D.T.	3	4	2	14*	36	18.00	–	–	–	4
Smith, G.M.	88	152	13	165*	4299	30.92	5	29	–	27
Smith, G.P.	34	64	6	158*	1871	32.25	4	9	–	20
Smith, J.W.G.	1	2	–	3	4	2.00	–	–	–	–
Smith, T.C.	68	97	17	128	2085	26.06	3	9	–	72
Smith, T.M.J.	10	16	1	33	165	11.00	–	–	–	3
Smith, W.R.	91	147	8	201*	4606	33.13	11	16	–	47
Snell, S.D.	42	70	7	127	1683	26.71	1	13	–	96/3
Soilleux, A.C.	1	2	–	6	9	4.50	–	–	–	–
Solanki, V.S.	283	476	29	270	16187	36.21	30	85	6	299
Southee, T.G.	35	47	7	77*	662	16.55	–	3	–	8
Spiegel, M.N.W.	32	52	3	108*	1237	25.24	3	3	–	24
Sreesanth, S.	68	92	28	35	592	9.25	–	–	–	15
Stebbings, B.R.W.	4	5	–	29	90	18.00	–	–	–	2
Stevens, D.I.	186	307	20	208	9655	33.64	22	46	2	141
Stirling, P.R.	11	17	–	107	518	30.47	2	2	–	7
Stokes, B.A.	28	42	5	185	1615	43.64	5	6	–	17
Stoneman, M.D.	52	86	3	128	2345	28.25	3	14	–	34
Strauss, A.J.	222	390	23	241*	15772	42.97	42	69	5	205
Sturmer, I.W.	1	2	1	5	7	7.00	–	–	–	–
Styris, S.B.	128	213	20	212*	6048	31.33	10	30	–	103
Suppiah, A.V.	77	130	8	156	4257	34.89	6	24	1	45
Sutton, L.D.	176	280	40	151*	7353	30.63	11	20	–	467/24
Swann, G.P.	216	291	24	183	6991	26.18	4	35	–	163
Tahir, N.S.	56	65	16	53	751	15.32	–	1	–	7
Tavaré, W.A.	3	5	–	59	172	34.40	–	2	–	–
Taylor, C.G.	160	279	19	196	9083	34.93	20	43	3	101
Taylor, J.M.R.	5	9	–	39	122	13.55	–	–	–	3
Taylor, J.W.A.	63	106	15	237	4534	49.82	10	23	3	48
Taylor, R.M.L.	9	16	1	101*	397	26.46	1	1	–	4
ten Doeschate, R.N.	90	132	16	259*	5451	46.99	18	19	–	54
Tendulkar, S.R.	285	451	48	248*	23884	59.26	78	107	1+3	176
Thakor, S.J.	3	5	–	134	190	38.00	1	–	–	–
Thirimanne, H.D.R.L.	47	81	9	148	3169	44.01	9	16	0+1	43
Thomas, A.C.	120	168	33	119*	3491	25.85	2	12	–	31
Thorp, C.D.	72	94	12	79*	1286	15.68	–	3	–	42
Timms, R.T.	9	17	–	57	319	18.76	–	2	–	6
Tomlinson, J.	71	95	41	42	566	10.48	–	–	–	17
Topley, R.J.W.	9	11	5	9	21	3.50	–	–	–	1
Tredwell, J.C.	113	167	21	123*	3366	23.05	3	13	–	120
Trego, P.D.	116	169	25	140	5028	34.91	9	31	–	47
Tremlett, C.T.	116	150	41	64	1978	18.14	–	7	–	32
Trescothick, M.E.	284	489	29	284	19715	42.85	49	97	5	369

F-C	M	I	NO	HS	Runs	Avge	100	50	1000	Ct/St
Trott, I.J.L.	169	282	34	226	11206	45.18	26	54	6	157
Troughton, J.O.	140	217	17	223	7132	35.66	17	34	1	71
Tsotsobe, L.L.	55	72	30	27*	256	6.09	–	–	–	13
Turnbull, P.T.	7	9	1	33	68	8.50	–	–	–	1
Turner, K.	5	9	–	64	227	25.22	–	1	–	1
Turner, M.L.	16	19	10	57	202	22.44	–	1	–	3
Turns, M.	2	4	2	80	120	60.00	–	1	–	2
Vaas, W.P.J.U.C.	220	294	58	134	6128	25.96	4	28	–	57
van den Bergh, F.O.E.	1	1	–	0	0	0.00	–	–	–	–
van der Merwe, R.E.	19	28	6	81	667	30.31	–	4	–	11
van Jaarsveld, M.	253	430	39	262*	17530	44.83	51	87	6+1	388
Vince, J.M.	41	67	7	180	1915	31.91	3	7	–	23
Vincent, L.	93	153	11	224	4971	35.00	10	29	–	111
Voges, A.C.	105	179	23	180	6363	40.78	12	37	–	132
Wagg, G.G.	82	117	12	108	2470	23.52	1	13	–	28
Wagh, M.A.	212	350	29	315	12455	38.80	31	58	6	91
Wahab Riaz	77	107	19	68	1269	14.42	–	3	–	24
Wainwright, D.J.	35	43	12	104*	1071	34.54	2	3	–	10
Wakely, A.G.	50	80	2	113*	2240	28.71	2	14	–	29
Walker, C.A.M.	2	2	–	43	69	34.50	–	–	–	–
Walker, M.J.	223	377	39	275*	12197	36.08	28	51	4	155
Wallace, M.A.	183	294	21	139	7868	28.82	11	39	1	457/42
Waller, M.T.C.	5	6	1	28	67	13.40	–	–	–	1
Walters, S.J.	41	68	5	188	1844	29.26	4	5	–	43
Wardlaw, I.	1	–	–	–	–	–	–	–	–	–
Warnapura, B.S.M.	165	255	24	242	8431	36.49	20	41	–	111
Waters, H.T.	37	55	24	54	305	9.83	–	1	–	7
Watkins, N.A.T.	1	2	–	4	4	2.00	–	–	–	2
Weerakoon, S.	152	180	51	90	1917	14.86	–	4	–	90
Welagedara, U.W.M.B.C.A.	84	100	36	76	612	9.56	–	1	–	17
Wells, L.W.P.	15	29	2	174	894	33.11	3	1	–	6
Wernars, K.O.	5	8	3	53	181	36.20	–	1	–	4
Wessels, M.H.	93	155	12	146	4469	31.25	9	25	–	171/12
Westaway, S.A.	1	2	1	63*	63	63.00	–	1	–	4
Westley, T.	48	85	9	132	2217	29.17	3	12	–	27
Westwood, I.J.	95	163	17	178	4842	33.16	10	25	–	55
Wheater, A.J.	28	42	5	164	1669	45.10	3	10	–	42
Whelan, C.D.	23	28	7	58	313	14.90	–	1	–	4
White, G.G.	15	21	3	65	309	17.16	–	2	–	6
White, R.A.	110	187	16	277	5644	33.00	8	28	1	67
White, W.A.	46	74	8	101*	1669	25.28	1	8	–	19
Whiteley, R.A.	12	22	4	130*	689	38.27	2	2	–	9
Wilkin, O.	3	6	–	38	138	23.00	–	–	–	1
Willey, D.J.	15	23	4	64	490	25.78	–	3	–	4
Williams, B.	4	7	2	41	116	23.20	–	–	–	4
Williams, R.E.M.	9	15	5	31	119	11.90	–	–	–	4
Williamson, K.S.	38	65	2	192	2558	40.60	6	13	–	37
Willoughby, C.M.	224	252	110	47	852	6.00	–	–	–	44
Wilson, G.C.	23	35	3	125	863	26.96	1	3	–	40/1
Woakes, C.R.	61	81	21	136*	2002	33.36	4	8	–	32
Wood, C.P.	11	15	1	56*	327	23.35	–	1	–	4
Wood, M.A.	3	5	1	48	118	29.50	–	–	–	2
Wood, S.K.W.	1	–	–	–	–	–	–	–	–	–
Woolley, R.J.J.	9	10	3	89*	283	40.42	–	2	–	8
Wright, B.J.	47	76	4	172	1987	27.59	4	10	–	28
Wright, C.J.C.	63	82	20	77	1152	18.58	–	4	–	13

F-C	M	I	NO	HS	Runs	Avge	100	50	1000	Ct/St
Wright, D.G.	123	188	25	111	3824	23.46	1	20	–	57
Wright, L.J.	70	100	15	155*	3104	36.51	9	15	–	29
Wyatt, A.C.F.	7	7	3	4*	14	3.50	–	–	–	1
Yardy, M.H.	139	233	23	257	8223	39.15	17	41	2	116
Yasir Arafat	184	269	40	122	6139	26.80	4	32	–	50
Young, E.G.C.	12	18	3	133	658	43.86	1	4	–	8
Yuvraj Singh	97	155	18	209	6114	44.62	18	30	–	94

BOWLING

'50wS' denotes instances of taking 50 or more wickets in a season. Where these have been achieved outside the British Isles they are shown after a plus sign.

	Runs	Wkts	Avge	Best	5wI	10wM	50wS
Abdul Razzaq	10818	340	31.81	7-51	11	2	–
Ackland, B.J.	3	0	–				
Adams, A.R.	13004	546	23.81	6-25	25	4	2
Adams, J.H.K.	662	11	60.18	2-16	–	–	–
Adkin, W.A.	212	2	106.00	1-28	–	–	–
Agarwal, S.S.	562	9	62.44	5-78	1	–	–
Agathangelou, A.P.	311	6	51.83	2-62	–	–	–
Ali, Kabir	12445	461	26.99	8-50	23	4	5
Ali, Kadeer	304	3	101.33	1- 4	–	–	–
Ali, M.M.	2584	45	57.42	5-36	1	–	–
Allenby, J.	3431	124	27.66	5-44	3	–	–
Alwitigala, K.G.	1650	51	32.35	5-34	1	–	–
Ambrose, T.R.	1	0	–				
Anderson, J.M.	13045	472	27.63	7-43	23	3	2
Andrew, G.M.	5199	153	33.98	5-58	3	–	1
Ansari, Z.S.	402	12	33.50	5-33	1	–	–
Anyon, J.E.	7061	196	36.02	6-82	3	–	1
Ashling, C.P.	499	15	33.26	4-47	–	–	–
Ashok, A.	82	1	82.00	1-15	–	–	–
Ashraf, M.A.	773	22	35.13	5-32	1	–	–
Azeem Rafiq	1048	23	45.56	4-92	–	–	–
Azhar Mahmood	15266	609	25.06	8-61	27	3	0+1
Balcombe, D.J.	3420	105	32.57	6-51	5	1	–
Ball, A.J.	560	15	37.33	3-36	–	–	–
Ball, J.T.	106	3	35.33	3-72	–	–	–
Ballance, G.S.	14	0	–				
Banerjee, V.	4491	97	46.29	5-74	2	–	–
Barker, K.H.D.	1113	28	39.75	5-31	1	–	–
Barrow, A.W.R.	36	1	36.00	1- 4	–	–	–
Batty, G.J.	15276	446	34.25	7-52	17	1	2
Batty, J.N.	61	1	61.00	1-21	–	–	–
Beer, W.A.T.	228	9	25.33	3-31	–	–	–
Bell, I.R.	1564	47	33.27	4- 4	–	–	–
Benkenstein, D.M.	3568	100	35.68	4-16	–	–	–
Berg, G.K.	2498	80	31.22	6-58	3	–	–
Best, P.M.	901	26	34.65	6-86	2	–	–
Blackaby, L.A.	133	1	133.00	1-41	–	–	–
Blackwell, I.D.	13603	371	36.66	7-85	13	–	–
Blake, A.J.	128	3	42.66	2- 9	–	–	–
Bopara, R.S.	5715	134	42.64	5-75	1	–	–
Borrington, P.M.	5	0	–				
Borthwick, S.G.	1856	61	30.42	5-80	1	–	–
Botha, A.G.	10576	307	34.44	8-53	9	1	1

F-C	Runs	Wkts	Avge	Best	5wI	10wM	50wS
Botha, J.	4953	156	31.75	6- 42	4	1	–
Boyce, M.A.G.	63	0	–		–	–	–
Bragg, W.D.	50	1	50.00	1- 4	–	–	–
Brathwaite, R.M.R.	1950	56	34.82	5- 54	3	–	–
Bravo, D.M.	9	1	9.00	1- 9	–	–	–
Breese, G.R.	8390	281	29.85	7- 60	12	3	–
Bresnan, T.T.	9072	297	30.54	5- 42	5	–	–
Brett, T.	132	2	66.00	1- 29	–	–	–
Briggs, D.R.	3605	113	31.90	6- 45	5	–	–
Broad, S.C.J.	8750	305	28.68	8- 52	14	1	–
Brooks, J.A.	2527	89	28.39	5- 23	2	–	–
Brophy, G.L.	7	0	–		–	–	–
Brown, A.D.	775	6	129.16	3- 25	–	–	–
Brown, D.O.	1251	28	44.67	5- 38	1	–	–
Brown, F.A.	363	10	36.30	3- 26	–	–	–
Brown, K.R.	44	2	22.00	2- 30	–	–	–
Brown, M.J.	20	0	–		–	–	–
Bryan, T.E.	17	0	–		–	–	–
Buck, N.L.	3057	82	37.28	5- 99	1	–	–
Burton, D.A.	692	16	43.25	5- 68	2	–	–
Cameron, J.G.	374	8	46.75	2- 18	–	–	–
Carberry, M.A.	891	13	68.53	2- 85	–	–	–
Carter, A.	571	21	27.19	5- 40	1	–	–
Carter, N.M.	10455	307	34.05	6- 30	14	–	1
Chambers, M.A.	3006	90	33.40	6- 68	2	1	–
Chanderpaul, S.	2491	57	43.70	4- 48	–	–	–
Chandimal, L.D.	5	0	–		–	–	–
Chapple, G.	22250	837	26.58	7- 53	34	2	6
Chilton, M.J.	667	12	55.58	2- 3	–	–	–
Chopra, V.	78	0	–		–	–	–
Choudhry, S.H.	156	2	78.00	1- 14	–	–	–
Clare, J.L.	2970	105	28.28	7- 74	3	–	–
Clarke, R.	7823	214	36.55	6- 63	2	–	–
Claydon, M.E.	3372	104	32.42	6-104	2	–	–
Cliff, S.J.	569	16	35.56	4- 42	–	–	–
Cobb, J.J.	322	6	53.66	2- 11	–	–	–
Coetzer, K.J.	129	3	43.00	2- 16	–	–	–
Coles, M.T.	2190	61	35.90	5- 29	2	–	–
Collingwood, P.D.	5184	132	39.27	5- 52	1	–	–
Collymore, C.D.	12006	455	26.38	7- 57	12	2	1
Comber, M.A.	94	4	23.50	2- 34	–	–	–
Compton, N.R.D.	215	3	71.66	1- 1	–	–	–
Conway, D.O.	559	14	39.92	4- 48	–	–	–
Cook, A.N.	205	6	34.16	3- 13	–	–	–
Cook, S.J.	10974	341	32.18	8- 63	12	–	–
Cork, D.G.	26439	989	26.73	9- 43	36	5	7
Cosker, D.A.	17540	494	35.50	6- 91	8	1	1
Cowan, J.D.	65	1	65.00	1- 19	–	–	–
Craddock, T.R.	628	22	28.54	4- 59	–	–	–
Croft, R.D.B.	40826	1152	35.43	8- 66	49	9	10
Croft, S.J.	1617	37	43.70	4- 51	–	–	–
Crook, S.P.	3654	85	42.98	5- 71	2	–	–
Daggett, L.M.	4879	137	35.61	8- 94	2	–	–
Dalrymple, J.W.M.	7446	172	43.29	5- 49	1	–	–
Davey, J.H.	107	2	53.50	2- 41	–	–	–
Dawson, L.A.	972	20	48.60	2- 3	–	–	–

252

F-C	Runs	Wkts	Avge	Best	5wI	10wM	50wS
de Bruyn, Z.	8751	225	38.89	7- 67	3	–	–
Denly, J.L.	967	20	48.35	3- 43	–	–	–
Dent, C.D.J.	51	0	–				
Dernbach, J.W.	5927	182	32.56	6- 47	9	–	1
Deuchar, A.J.W.	150	5	30.00	4- 50	–	–	–
de Wet, F.	5374	215	24.99	7- 61	10	2	0+1
Dexter, N.J.	1578	37	42.64	3- 46	–	–	–
Dhoni, M.S.	78	0	–				
Dibble, A.J.	142	2	71.00	1- 26	–	–	–
Dilshan, T.M.	2217	68	32.60	5- 49	1	–	–
Di Venuto, M.J.	484	5	96.80	1- 0	–	–	–
Dockrell, G.H.	530	19	27.89	5- 71	1	–	–
Dravid, R.S.	273	5	54.60	2- 16	–	–	–
D'Souza, D.	7	0	–				
Dunn, M.P.	241	9	26.77	5- 56	1	–	–
Durandt, L.E.	126	3	42.00	3- 65	–	–	–
Durston, W.J.	1841	33	55.78	4- 45	–	–	–
du Toit, J.	382	6	63.66	3- 31	–	–	–
Edwards, G.A.	82	0	–				
Edwards, N.J.	194	2	97.00	1- 16	–	–	–
Ellison, C.P.	136	4	34.00	3- 69	–	–	–
Eranga, R.M.S.	2237	66	33.89	5- 86	1	–	–
Ervine, S.M.	8734	196	44.56	6- 82	5	–	–
Evans, L.	452	14	32.28	3- 21	–	–	–
Evans, L.J.	30	1	30.00	1- 30	–	–	–
Fearon, R.M.	76	0	–				
Fernando, A.N.P.R.	2085	60	34.75	5- 36	1	–	–
Fernando, C.R.D.	8461	281	30.11	6- 29	6	–	–
Finn, S.T.	6219	222	28.01	9- 37	7	1	2
Fletcher, L.J.	2811	90	31.23	5- 82	1	–	–
Footitt, M.H.A.	1902	61	31.18	5- 45	3	–	–
Foster, J.S.	128	1	128.00	1-122	–	–	–
Franks, P.J.	16161	496	32.58	7- 56	11	–	2
Fuller, J.K.	293	3	97.66	1- 33	–	–	–
Gale, A.W.	47	1	47.00	1- 33	–	–	–
Gambhir, G.	277	7	39.57	3- 12	–	–	–
Gandam, H.S.	10	0	–				
Gatting, J.S.	55	2	27.50	1- 8	–	–	–
Gayle, C.H.	5015	129	38.87	5- 34	2	–	–
Gibbs, H.H.	78	3	26.00	2- 14	–	–	–
Gidman, A.P.R.	4378	99	44.22	4- 47	–	–	–
Gidman, W.R.S.	1174	55	21.34	6- 92	3	–	1
Glover, J.A.	52	1	52.00	1- 52	–	–	–
Glover, J.C.	802	20	40.10	5- 38	1	–	–
Godleman, B.A.	35	0	–				
Gondal, A.N.	3763	160	23.51	7- 66	10	1	0+1
Goodman, J.E.	37	1	37.00	1- 16	–	–	–
Goodwin, M.W.	376	7	53.71	2- 23	–	–	–
Gordon, D.A.	247	5	49.40	2- 27	–	–	–
Gregory, L.	222	4	55.50	1- 15	–	–	–
Griffiths, D.A.	2910	83	35.06	6- 85	2	–	–
Groenewald, T.D.	4767	146	32.65	6- 50	5	–	–
Guptill, M.J.	216	4	54.00	3- 37	–	–	–
Gurney, H.F.	1447	31	46.67	5- 82	1	–	–
Guy, S.M.	8	0	–				
Hales, A.D.	167	3	55.66	2- 63	–	–	–

F-C	Runs	Wkts	Avge	Best	5wI	10wM	50wS
Hall, A.J.	14588	533	27.36	6- 77	15	1	–
Hamilton-Brown, R.J.	485	8	60.62	2- 49	–	–	–
Hannon-Dalby, O.J.	1884	39	48.30	5- 68	2	–	–
Harbhajan Singh	19605	683	28.70	8- 84	39	7	0+2
Harinath, A.	30	0	–				
Harmison, B.W.	1144	33	34.66	4- 27	–	–	–
Harmison, S.J.	20381	730	27.91	7- 12	27	1	6
Harris, J.A.R.	5741	211	27.20	7- 66	7	1	1
Hatchett, L.J.	301	14	21.50	5- 47	1	–	–
Henderson, C.W.	26597	869	30.60	7- 57	33	2	1
Henriques, M.C.	1225	39	31.41	5- 17	2	–	–
Herath, H.M.R.K.B.	17571	703	24.99	8- 43	40	5	0+2
Hickey, M.R.	138	4	34.50	2- 63	–	–	–
Higham, P.S.	76	3	25.33	3- 36	–	–	–
Hildreth, J.C.	414	5	82.80	2- 39	–	–	–
Hodd, A.J.	7	0	–				
Hodgson, L.J.	216	2	108.00	1- 42	–	–	–
Hogg, K.W.	5359	174	30.79	7- 28	4	1	1
Hoggard, M.J.	20503	746	27.48	7- 49	25	1	3
Holmes, M.G.	301	7	43.00	3- 46	–	–	–
Horton, P.J.	16	0	–				
Housego, D.M.	17	0	–				
Howgego, B.H.N.	16	0	–				
Hughes, C.F.	451	10	45.10	2- 9	–	–	–
Hughes, P.J.	9	0	–				
Hussain, G.M.	2591	91	28.47	6- 33	3	–	1
Hussey, D.J.	1639	25	65.56	4-105	–	–	–
Hutton, B.A.	69	0	–				
Imran Tahir	14326	575	24.91	8- 76	43	9	2+2
Ireland, A.J.	3556	118	30.13	7- 36	4	1	–
James, N.A.	86	6	14.33	2- 28	–	–	–
James, O.R.	102	1	102.00	1- 91	–	–	–
Jaques, P.A.	87	0	–				
Javid, A.	78	0	–				
Jayawardena, D.P.M.D.	1616	52	31.07	5- 72	1	–	–
Jayawardena, H.A.P.W.	9	0	–				
Jefferson, W.I.	60	1	60.00	1- 16	–	–	–
Jewell, T.M.	260	10	26.00	5- 49	1	–	–
Jones, A.J.	158	2	79.00	1- 50	–	–	–
Jones, G.O.	26	0	–				
Jones, P.S.	14270	387	36.87	6- 25	10	1	2
Jones, R.A.	2961	84	35.25	7-115	3	–	–
Jones, S.P.	8072	265	30.46	6- 45	15	1	–
Jones, W.S.	6	0	–				
Jordan, C.J.	2352	56	42.00	4- 57	–	–	–
Joseph, R.H.	4810	150	32.06	6- 32	5	–	1
Joyce, E.C.	1025	11	93.18	2- 34	–	–	–
Junaid Khan	3771	171	22.05	7- 46	13	3	0+1
Kaluhalamulla, H.K.S.R.	8661	338	25.62	9- 62	24	6	0+3
Kapil, A.	138	4	34.50	2- 38	–	–	–
Kartik, M.	15378	586	26.24	9- 70	33	5	1
Karunaratne, F.D.M.	58	0	–				
Katich, S.M.	3480	95	36.63	7-130	3	–	–
Keedy, G.	20020	648	30.89	7- 68	32	7	4
Kerrigan, S.C.	1461	56	26.08	9- 51	5	1	–
Kervezee, A.N.	145	2	72.50	1- 14	–	–	–

F-C	Runs	Wkts	Avge	Best	5wI	10wM	50wS
Key, R.W.T.	206	3	68.66	2- 31	–	–	–
Khan, A.	10410	325	32.03	6- 52	8	–	2
Khan, Z.	16270	592	27.48	9-138	32	8	1
Khawaja, U.T.	47	1	47.00	1- 21	–	–	–
King, S.J.	371	5	74.20	3- 61	–	–	–
Kirby, S.P.	14709	522	28.17	8- 80	17	4	3
Knight, T.C.	143	2	71.50	2- 32	–	–	–
Kulasekara, C.K.B.	3913	148	26.43	6- 13	3	–	–
Kumar, P.	4665	199	23.44	8- 68	14	1	–
Lakmal, R.A.S.	3828	115	33.28	5- 78	1	–	–
Lakshitha, A.B.T.	6998	242	28.91	7- 59	10	–	–
Lancefield, T.J.	21	1	21.00	1- 12	–	–	–
Laxman, V.V.S.	754	22	34.27	3- 11	–	–	–
Lewis, J.	20623	798	25.84	8- 95	34	5	9
Liddle, C.J.	976	18	54.22	3- 42	–	–	–
Lilley, A.E.	34	0	–				
Linley, T.E.	2800	111	25.22	6- 57	3	1	1
Loye, M.B.	61	1	61.00	1- 8	–	–	–
Lucas, D.S.	7529	239	31.50	7- 24	9	1	1
Lumb, M.J.	242	6	40.33	2- 10	–	–	–
Lyth, A.	181	3	60.33	1- 12	–	–	–
McCluskie, J.J.	48	1	48.00	1- 25	–	–	–
McDonald, A.B.	5176	178	29.07	6- 34	4	–	–
McGrath, A.	4290	115	37.30	5- 39	1	–	–
McKenzie, N.D.	501	10	50.10	2- 13	–	–	–
Machan, M.W.	4	0	–				
Maddy, D.L.	7544	238	31.69	5- 37	5	–	–
Madsen, W.L.	372	7	53.14	3- 45	–	–	–
Maharoof, M.F.	4044	117	34.56	7- 73	1	–	–
Mahmood, S.I.	9847	303	32.49	6- 30	9	2	–
Malan, D.J.	1364	31	44.00	4- 20	–	–	–
Malik, M.N.	8072	229	35.24	6- 46	7	–	–
Marshall, H.J.H.	1757	36	48.80	4- 24	–	–	–
Mascarenhas, A.D.	12399	439	28.24	6- 25	17	–	1
Mason, M.S.	8700	318	27.35	8- 45	10	1	3
Masters, D.D.	12579	469	26.82	8- 10	20	–	2
Maynard, T.L.	45	0	–				
Meaker, S.C.	2707	90	30.07	5- 37	5	–	–
Mendis, B.A.W.	4542	211	21.52	7- 37	12	2	0+1
Meschede, C.A.J.	141	2	70.50	1- 14	–	–	–
Metters, C.L.	695	29	23.96	6- 65	2	–	–
Mickleburgh, J.C.	50	0	–				
Middlebrook, J.D.	14620	384	38.07	6- 82	10	1	1
Miles, C.N.	80	2	40.00	2- 80	–	–	–
Miller, A.S.	1216	34	35.76	5- 58	2	–	–
Miller, D.A.	23	0	–				
Milligan, M.J.	593	14	42.35	3- 31	–	–	–
Mills, T.S.	241	7	34.42	3- 48	–	–	–
Milnes, T.P.	39	4	9.75	4- 15	–	–	–
Mishra, A.	11323	391	28.95	6- 66	19	1	–
Mitchell, D.K.H.	678	17	39.88	4- 49	–	–	–
Mohammad Yousuf	24	0	–				
Moore, S.C.	321	5	64.20	1- 13	–	–	–
Morgan, E.J.G.	83	2	41.50	2- 24	–	–	–
Morkel, J.A.	5508	185	29.77	6- 36	5	–	–
Muchall, G.J.	617	15	41.13	3- 26	–	–	–

F-C	Runs	Wkts	Avge	Best	5wI	10wM	50wS
Mukund, A.	346	9	38.44	3- 5	–	–	–
Mullaney, S.J.	841	16	52.56	4- 31	–	–	–
Muralitharan, M.	26997	1374	19.64	9- 51	119	34	3+3
Murphy, D.	3	0	–				
Murtagh, T.J.	10415	365	28.53	7- 82	16	2	3
Myburgh, J.G.	1392	31	44.90	4- 56	–	–	–
Naik, J.K.H.	3146	101	31.14	7- 96	3	–	–
Nannes, D.P.	2327	93	25.02	7- 50	2	1	–
Napier, G.R.	8824	238	37.07	6- 53	5	–	–
Nash, C.D.	1458	38	38.36	4- 12	–	–	–
Naved-ul-Hasan	14387	584	24.63	7- 49	30	5	2+3
Needham, J.	1268	35	36.22	6- 49	1	–	–
Nel, J.D.	1434	52	27.57	6- 62	2	–	–
New, T.J.	211	5	42.20	2- 18	–	–	–
Newby, O.J.	3828	117	32.71	5- 69	1	–	–
Newman, S.A.	59	0	–				
Newton, R.I.	19	0	–				
Nixon, P.A.	157	1	157.00	1- 7	–	–	–
Norman, A.J.	49	0	–				
North, M.J.	5245	128	40.97	6- 55	2	–	–
Northeast, S.A.	10	0	–				
Norwell, L.C.	341	12	28.41	6- 46	1	–	–
O'Brien, K.J.	583	24	24.29	5- 39	1	–	–
O'Brien, N.J.	16	2	8.00	1- 4	–	–	–
Ojha, P.P.	6300	225	28.00	7-114	12	1	–
Onions, G.	8402	283	29.68	8-101	11	–	3
Owen, W.T.	1310	33	39.69	5-124	1	–	–
Palladino, A.P.	5373	169	31.79	6- 41	5	–	1
Panesar, M.S.	15689	494	31.75	7-181	24	3	5
Paranavitana, N.T.	843	22	38.31	4- 39	–	–	–
Park, C.M.	295	2	147.50	1- 34	–	–	–
Park, G.T.	974	18	54.11	3- 25	–	–	–
Parnell, W.D.	2709	76	35.64	4- 7	–	–	–
Parry, S.D.	256	9	28.44	5- 23	1	–	–
Parsons, T.W.	458	11	41.63	3- 39	–	–	–
Pascoe, D.C.	450	20	22.50	6- 68	2	–	–
Patel, A.	86	1	86.00	1- 34	–	–	–
Patel, J.S.	9828	237	41.46	6- 32	7	1	–
Patel, L.A.	75	1	75.00	1- 57	–	–	–
Patel, M.M.	4661	192	24.27	6- 50	7	1	0+1
Patel, R.H.	368	12	30.66	3- 25	–	–	–
Patel, S.R.	4949	131	37.77	7- 68	3	1	–
Patterson, S.A.	3157	88	35.87	5- 50	1	–	–
Pattinson, D.J.	5551	168	33.04	8- 35	8	–	–
Payne, D.A.	1298	42	30.90	6- 26	2	–	–
Perera, N.L.T.C.	1255	33	38.03	5- 69	1	–	–
Peters, S.D.	31	1	31.00	1- 19	–	–	–
Petersen, A.N.	419	7	59.85	2- 7	–	–	–
Pettini, M.L.	191	0	–				
Philander, V.D.	4673	235	19.88	7- 64	8	–	0+1
Phillips, B.J.	7260	238	30.50	6- 29	5	–	–
Phillips, T.J.	5703	121	47.13	5- 41	1	–	–
Pietersen, K.P.	3460	63	54.92	4- 31	–	–	–
Piolet, S.A.	182	13	14.00	6- 17	1	1	–
Plunkett, L.E.	10123	321	31.53	6- 63	8	1	3
Pollard, K.A.	349	7	49.85	2- 29	–	–	–

F-C	Runs	Wkts	Avge	Best	5wI	10wM	50wS
Porterfield, W.T.S.	138	2	69.00	1- 29	–	–	–
Pothas, N.	63	1	63.00	1- 16	–	–	–
Powell, M.J.	132	2	66.00	2- 39	–	–	–
Poynton, T.	96	2	48.00	2- 96	–	–	–
Poysden, J.E.	69	4	17.25	3- 20	–	–	–
Prasanna, S.	5594	278	20.12	8- 59	19	5	0+3
Premaratne, W.G.H.N.	1612	53	30.41	6- 61	2	–	–
Prince, A.G.	166	4	41.50	2- 11	–	–	–
Probert, T.J.W.	113	6	18.83	4- 20	–	–	–
Procter, L.A.	379	10	37.90	3- 33	–	–	–
Pyrah, R.M.	1773	45	39.40	5- 58	1	–	–
Radford, L.A.	64	2	32.00	2- 47	–	–	–
Raina, S.K.	1012	26	38.92	3- 31	–	–	–
Raine, B.A.	7	0	–				
Ramprakash, M.R.	2202	34	64.76	3- 32	–	–	–
Randhawa, G.S.	62	2	31.00	2- 54	–	–	–
Rankin, W.B.	4286	156	27.47	5- 16	5	–	1
Rashid, A.U.	9650	280	34.46	7-107	15	1	2
Ratnayake, D.E.M.	46	1	46.00	1- 46	–	–	–
Rayner, O.P.	3893	108	36.04	5- 49	3	–	–
Read, C.M.W.	90	0	–				
Redfern, D.J.	269	5	53.80	1- 7	–	–	–
Rees, G.P.	3	0	–				
Riazuddin, H.	200	5	40.00	1- 0	–	–	–
Richardson, A.	12482	442	28.23	8- 46	14	1	3
Riley, A.E.N.	547	14	39.07	5- 76	1	–	–
Roach, K.A.J.	3339	101	33.05	7- 23	4	–	–
Robson, S.D.	30	0	–				
Rogers, C.J.L.	131	1	131.00	1- 16	–	–	–
Roland-Jones, T.S.	1498	68	22.02	5- 41	3	–	–
Root, J.E.	346	7	49.42	3- 33	–	–	–
Roper, C.G.W.	456	6	76.00	3-110	–	–	–
Roy, J.J.	61	2	30.50	2- 29	–	–	–
Rudolph, J.A.	2572	58	44.34	5- 80	3	–	–
Rushworth, C.	990	26	38.07	4- 90	–	–	–
Sadler, P.T.	106	2	53.00	2- 38	–	–	–
Saeed Ajmal	9464	342	27.67	7- 63	22	2	0+1
Saker, N.C.	1970	44	44.77	5- 76	2	–	–
Sales, D.J.G.	184	9	20.44	4- 25	–	–	–
Salt, J.D.	93	1	93.00	1- 71	–	–	–
Samaraweera, T.T.	8194	348	23.54	6- 55	15	2	0+1
Sanderson, B.W.	190	6	31.66	5- 50	1	–	–
Sandhu, G.S.	69	0	–				
Sangakkara, K.C.	112	1	112.00	1- 13	–	–	–
Sarwan, R.R.	2224	54	41.18	6- 62	1	–	–
Saxelby, I.D.	2367	71	33.33	6- 69	2	1	–
Sayers, J.J.	178	6	29.66	3- 15	–	–	–
Scarr, M.J.L.	70	0	–				
Schofield, C.P.	8629	237	36.40	6-120	6	–	–
Scott, A.J.D.	303	15	20.20	4- 52	–	–	–
Scott, B.J.M.	1	0	–				
Sehwag, V.	4143	104	39.83	5-104	1	–	–
Senanayake, S.M.S.M.	6091	297	20.50	8- 70	23	4	0+3
Serasinghe, S.C.	1994	64	31.15	4- 23	–	–	–
Shafayat, B.M.	645	8	80.62	2- 25	–	–	–
Shah, O.A.	1493	26	57.42	3- 33	–	–	–

F-C	Runs	Wkts	Avge	Best	5wI	10wM	50wS
Shahid Afridi	7023	258	27.22	6-101	8	–	–
Shahzad, A.	4354	127	34.28	5- 51	3	–	–
Shakib Al Hasan	5147	175	29.41	7- 32	12	–	–
Shan Masood	207	4	51.75	2- 52	–	–	–
Shantry, A.J.	2214	90	24.60	5- 49	4	1	–
Shantry, J.D.	1961	49	40.02	5- 49	1	–	–
Sharma, I.	6275	207	30.31	7- 24	5	2	–
Sharma, R.	530	14	37.85	5- 81	1	–	–
Shaw, S.A.	400	11	36.36	5-118	1	–	–
Shreck, C.E.	10404	341	30.51	8- 31	19	2	2
Siddle, P.M.	4748	168	28.26	6- 54	9	–	–
Sidebottom, R.J.	13470	537	25.08	7- 37	23	3	3
Silva, A.R.S.	79	2	39.50	2- 22	–	–	–
Silva, J.K.	12	0	–				
Singh, R.P.	6536	215	30.40	6- 50	8	1	–
Smith, D.T.	64	1	64.00	1- 29	–	–	–
Smith, G.M.	5229	146	35.81	5- 54	2	–	–
Smith, G.P.	64	1	64.00	1- 64	–	–	–
Smith, T.C.	4539	141	32.19	6- 46	2	–	–
Smith, T.M.J.	780	11	70.90	3- 38	–	–	–
Smith, W.R.	557	8	69.62	3- 34	–	–	–
Snell, S.D.	15	0	–				
Soilleux, A.C.	56	2	28.00	2- 56	–	–	–
Solanki, V.S.	4120	86	47.90	5- 40	4	1	–
Southee, T.G.	3570	116	30.77	8- 27	5	–	–
Spriegel, M.N.W.	823	19	43.31	2- 28	–	–	–
Sreesanth, S.	7132	200	35.66	5- 40	6	–	–
Stevens, D.I.	4269	135	31.62	7- 21	2	1	–
Stirling, P.R.	179	4	44.75	2- 45	–	–	–
Stokes, B.A.	1046	28	37.35	6- 68	1	–	–
Strauss, A.J.	142	3	47.33	1- 16	–	–	–
Sturmer, I.W.	43	0	–				
Styris, S.B.	6440	204	31.56	6- 32	9	1	–
Suppiah, A.V.	2379	42	56.64	3- 46	–	–	–
Swann, G.P.	19390	605	32.04	7- 33	26	4	1
Tahir, N.S.	4163	139	29.94	7-107	2	–	–
Taylor, C.G.	1463	28	52.25	4- 52	–	–	–
Taylor, J.M.R.	368	7	52.57	2- 81	–	–	–
Taylor, J.W.A.	160	0	–				
Taylor, R.M.L.	734	16	45.87	3- 53	–	–	–
ten Doeschate, R.N.	5528	167	33.10	6- 20	7	–	–
Tendulkar, S.R.	4308	70	61.54	3- 10	–	–	–
Thakor, S.J.	74	3	24.66	3- 57	–	–	–
Thirimanne, H.D.R.L.	56	0	–				
Thomas, A.C.	10495	386	27.18	7- 54	18	2	–
Thorp, C.D.	5580	205	27.21	7- 88	8	1	1
Timms, R.T.	126	0	–				
Tomlinson, J.A.	7308	205	35.64	8- 46	8	1	1
Topley, R.J.W.	801	34	23.55	5- 46	2	–	–
Tredwell, J.C.	10709	309	34.65	8- 66	11	3	1
Trego, P.D.	7334	194	37.80	6- 59	1	–	–
Tremlett, C.T.	10608	386	27.48	6- 44	9	–	–
Trescothick, M.E.	1551	36	43.08	4- 36	–	–	–
Trott, I.J.L.	2588	57	45.40	7- 39	1	–	–
Troughton, J.O.	1416	22	64.36	3- 1	–	–	–
Tsotsobe, L.L.	4879	178	27.41	7- 39	5	1	–

F-C	Runs	Wkts	Avge	Best	5wI	10wM	50wS
Turnbull, P.T.	724	21	34.47	5- 92	1	–	–
Turner, M.L.	1500	38	39.47	5- 32	1	–	–
Turns, M.	108	3	36.00	1- 22	–	–	–
Vaas, W.P.J.U.C.	18704	765	24.44	7- 28	34	4	1+2
van den Bergh, F.O.E.	79	3	26.33	3- 79	–	–	–
van der Merwe, R.E.	1412	35	40.34	4- 59	–	–	–
van Jaarsveld, M.	1908	49	38.93	5- 33	1	–	–
Vince, J.M.	61	0	–				
Vincent, L.	527	10	52.70	2- 37	–	–	–
Voges, A.C.	1375	40	34.37	4- 92	–	–	–
Wagg, G.G.	8404	249	33.75	6- 35	8	1	2
Wagh, M.A.	4611	100	46.11	7-222	2	–	–
Wahab Riaz	7400	251	29.48	6- 64	10	2	0+1
Wainwright, D.J.	3003	82	36.62	6- 40	2	–	–
Wakely, A.G.	284	6	47.33	2- 62	–	–	–
Walker, M.J.	1274	28	45.50	3- 35	–	–	–
Wallace, M.A.	3	0	–				
Waller, M.T.C.	348	6	58.00	2- 27	–	–	–
Walters, S.J.	239	3	79.66	1- 4	–	–	–
Wardlaw, I.	68	1	68.00	1- 68	–	–	–
Warnapura, B.S.M.	3406	125	27.24	6- 22	4	–	–
Waters, H.T.	2538	68	37.32	5- 86	1	–	–
Watkins, N.A.T.	129	5	25.80	5- 88	1	–	–
Weerakoon, S.	13075	649	20.14	7- 40	41	12	0+5
Welagedara, U.W.M.B.C.A.	6972	231	30.18	5- 34	6	1	–
Wells, L.W.P.	186	2	93.00	2- 28	–	–	–
Wernars, K.O.	153	7	21.85	2- 11	–	–	–
Wessels, M.H.	42	2	21.00	1- 10	–	–	–
Westley, T.	760	20	38.00	4- 55	–	–	–
Westwood, I.J.	238	6	39.66	2- 39	–	–	–
Whelan, C.D.	1750	44	39.77	5- 95	1	–	–
White, G.G.	961	19	50.57	4- 72	–	–	–
White, R.A.	1071	18	59.50	2- 30	–	–	–
White, W.A.	3717	96	38.71	5- 87	1	–	–
Whiteley, R.A.	423	6	70.50	1- 21	–	–	–
Wilkin, O.	213	4	53.25	2- 63	–	–	–
Willey, D.J.	681	25	27.24	5- 29	2	1	–
Williams, B.	85	1	85.00	1- 55	–	–	–
Williams, R.E.M.	755	23	32.82	5- 70	2	–	–
Williamson, K.S.	1790	37	48.37	5- 75	1	–	–
Willoughby, C.M.	21367	827	25.83	7- 44	32	3	6+2
Wilson, G.C.	46	0	–				
Woakes, C.R.	5490	223	24.61	7- 20	12	3	2
Wood, C.P.	911	37	24.62	5- 54	1	–	–
Wood, M.A.	264	10	26.40	3- 72	–	–	–
Wood, S.K.W.	8	0	–				
Woolley, R.J.J.	970	19	51.05	3- 54	–	–	–
Wright, B.J.	137	2	68.50	1- 14	–	–	–
Wright, C.J.C.	6166	157	39.27	6- 22	4	–	–
Wright, D.G.	11623	406	28.62	8- 60	16	–	1
Wright, L.J.	4070	106	38.39	5- 65	3	–	–
Wyatt, A.C.F.	554	20	27.70	3- 42	–	–	–
Yardy, M.H.	2010	26	77.30	5- 83	1	–	–
Yasir Arafat	17765	733	24.23	9- 35	43	5	0+4
Young, E.G.C.	619	5	123.80	2- 74	–	–	–
Yuvraj Singh	1211	21	57.66	3- 25	–	–	–

LEADING CURRENT FIRST-CLASS PLAYERS

These are the leading career batting/bowling averages and wicket-keeping/fielding aggregates among players currently registered for first-class county cricket at the time of going to press. All figures are to the end of the 2011 English season.

BATTING (Qualification: 100 innings)

	Runs	Avge		Runs	Avge
M.R.Ramprakash	35539	53.92	C.H.Gayle	12127	44.74
S.M.Katich	18608	53.31	N.D.McKenzie	15454	44.53
C.J.L.Rogers	16331	51.51	M.A.Carberry	8625	44.45
P.J.Hughes	5210	51.07	A.G.Prince	12034	44.08
K.P.Pietersen	13084	49.93	J.C.Hildreth	8658	43.29
J.W.A.Taylor	4534	49.82	A.J.Strauss	15772	42.97
P.A.Jaques	13482	49.74	M.E.Trescothick	19715	42.85
M.W.Goodwin	21753	48.44	M.J.North	11222	42.66
A.N.Cook	12094	47.42	H.H.Gibbs	13425	42.21
I.R.Bell	13368	47.07	Z.de Bruyn	12152	42.19
R.N.ten Doeschate	5451	46.99	O.A.Shah	15461	42.01
M.J.Di Venuto	24909	46.21	R.S.Bopara	7452	41.63
D.M.Benkenstein	15107	46.05	R.W.T.Key	15934	41.49
J.A.Rudolph	14681	45.59	S.R.Patel	5550	41.11
I.J.L.Trott	11206	45.18	A.C.Voges	6363	40.78
E.C.Joyce	11613	45.01	M.J.Prior	10739	40.67
J.A.Morkel	3720	44.81	I.D.Blackwell	10999	40.14

BOWLING (Qualification: 100 wickets)

	Wkts	Avge		Wkts	Avge
M.Muralitharan	1374	19.64	C.D.Collymore	455	26.38
V.D.Philander	235	19.88	G.Chapple	837	26.58
A.M.Davies	253	22.63	D.D.Masters	469	26.82
N.A.Gondal	160	23.51	Kabir Ali	461	26.99
A.R.Adams	546	23.81	A.C.Thomas	386	27.18
W.P.J.U.C.Vaas	765	24.44	J.A.R.Harris	211	27.20
C.R.Woakes	223	24.61	C.D.Thorp	205	27.21
Naved-ul-Hasan	584	24.63	A.J.Hall	533	27.36
Azhar Mahmood	609	25.06	W.B.Rankin	156	27.47
R.J.Sidebottom	537	25.08	M.J.Hoggard	746	27.48
T.E.Linley	111	25.22	C.T.Tremlett	386	27.48
C.M.Willoughby	827	25.83	J.M.Anderson	472	27.63
J.Lewis	798	25.84	J.Allenby	124	27.66
M.Kartik	586	26.24	Saeed Ajmal	342	27.67

WICKET-KEEPING (Qualification: 400 dismissals, exc catches taken in the field)

	Total	Ct	St		Total	Ct	St
C.M.W.Read	803	759	44	M.J.Prior	502	468	34
J.N.Batty	648	581	67	M.A.Wallace	499	457	42
J.S.Foster	580	532	48	P.Mustard	454	437	17
G.O.Jones	524	488	36				

FIELDING (Qualification: 200 catches)

M.J.Di Venuto	406	S.M.Katich	206
M.E.Trescothick	369	N.D.McKenzie	205
V.S.Solanki	299	A.J.Strauss	205
D.L.Maddy	277	D.J.G.Sales	202
M.R.Ramprakash	259	R.Clarke	200
P.D.Collingwood	232		

LIMITED-OVERS CAREER RECORDS

Compiled by Philip Bailey

The following career records, to the end of the 2011 season, include all players currently registered with first-class counties. These records are restricted to performances in limited-overs matches of 'List A' status as defined by the Association of Cricket Statisticians and Historians now incorporated by ICC into their Classification of Cricket. The following matches qualify for List A status and are included in the figures that follow: Limited-Overs Internationals; Other International matches (e.g. Commonwealth Games, 'A' team internationals); Premier domestic limited-overs tournaments in Test status countries; Official tourist matches against the main first-class teams.

The following matches do NOT qualify for inclusion: World Cup warm-up games; Tourist matches against first-class teams outside the major domestic competitions (e.g. Universities, Minor Counties etc.); Festival, pre-season friendly games and Twenty20 Cup matches.

	M	Runs	Avge	HS	100	50	Wkts	Avge	Best	Econ
Adams, A.R.	149	1437	17.74	90*	–	1	180	29.89	5- 7	4.76
Abdul Razzaq	322	6342	30.20	112	3	33	364	30.30	6-35	4.81
Adams, A.R.	161	1458	16.75	90*	–	1	199	29.45	5- 7	4.76
Adams, J.H.K.	57	1868	38.12	131	2	13	1	105.00	1-34	7.97
Adkin, W.A.	3	40	20.00	30	–	–	2	40.00	1-16	5.00
Agathangelou, A.P.	23	654	32.70	94	–	5	0	–	–	7.00
Ali, Kabir	157	1092	15.16	92	–	3	227	25.33	5-36	5.16
Ali, Kadeer	64	1817	30.28	114	3	12	1	68.00	1- 4	5.44
Ali, M.M.	75	2119	30.71	158	6	9	24	53.66	3-32	5.75
Allenby, J.	68	1358	24.25	91*	–	6	54	31.51	5-43	5.20
Allin, T.W.	1	2	–	2*	–	–	0	–	–	14.50
Ambrose, T.R.	120	2351	27.65	135	3	8	–	–	–	120/22
Anderson, J.M.	204	292	8.84	20*	–	–	278	29.12	5-23	4.90
Andrew, G.M.	93	816	17.00	104	1	1	94	34.41	5-31	6.30
Ansari, Z.S.	9	76	25.33	23*	–	–	6	37.50	1-22	6.42
Anyon, J.E.	38	34	5.66	12	–	–	41	30.58	3- 6	5.47
Ashling, C.P.	8	11	5.50	6*	–	–	5	60.80	2-33	6.65
Ashraf, M.A.	4	–	–	–	–	–	4	38.50	2-25	6.46
Azeem Rafiq	7	30	30.00	18	–	–	3	50.33	1-29	5.00
Azhar Mahmood	301	4192	21.49	101*	2	17	328	31.57	6-18	4.67
Bairstow, J.M.	31	676	29.39	114	1	3	–	–	–	21/3
Balcombe, D.J.	12	10	2.00	6	–	–	16	29.00	4-38	5.76
Ball, A.J.	10	66	22.00	19	–	–	13	23.00	2-31	5.20
Ball, J.T.	7	41	20.50	19*	–	–	6	42.33	3-32	6.19
Ballance, G.S.	19	669	47.78	135*	1	3	–	–	–	–
Barker, K.H.D.	34	356	19.77	56	–	1	36	33.61	4-33	6.21
Bates, M.D.	17	36	7.20	24*	–	–	–	–	–	10/4
Batty, G.J.	204	2079	16.50	83*	–	5	185	32.92	5-35	4.57
Batty, J.N.	197	2970	22.16	158*	1	14	–	–	–	204/36
Beer, W.A.T.	16	63	12.60	27*	–	–	8	64.50	2-17	4.82
Bell, I.R.	231	7535	37.86	158	7	53	33	34.48	5-41	5.29
Bell-Drummond, D.J.	5	111	22.20	42	–	–	–	–	–	–
Benkenstein, D.M.	290	7134	35.31	107*	1	44	87	30.81	4-16	5.03
Berg, G.K.	39	679	25.14	65	–	3	31	28.25	4-24	5.50
Best, P.M.	6	15	7.50	12	–	–	5	56.00	3-53	6.66
Billings, S.W.	3	54	18.00	26	–	–	–	–	–	3/2
Blackwell, I.D.	250	5760	27.29	134*	3	34	203	34.32	5-26	4.79
Blake, A.J.	25	357	27.46	81*	–	2	3	24.66	2-13	5.28
Bopara, R.S.	192	5516	38.57	201*	6	32	144	25.77	5-63	5.37
Borrington, P.M.	1	25	25.00	25	–	–	–	–	–	–

L-O	M	Runs	Avge	HS	100	50	Wkts	Avge	Best	Econ
Borthwick, S.G.	21	93	15.50	32	–	–	13	45.92	2-11	6.31
Botha, J.	151	1604	21.10	55*	–	3	138	37.68	4-19	4.53
Boyce, M.A.G.	41	864	26.18	80	–	4	–	–	–	–
Bragg, W.D.	14	283	23.58	78	–	1	0	–	–	8.50
Brathwaite, R.M.R.	2	–	–	–	–	–	1	68.00	1-19	7.55
Breese, G.R.	161	1899	20.86	68*	–	3	168	28.27	5-41	4.70
Bresnan, T.T.	189	1792	19.06	80	–	4	207	33.88	5-48	5.08
Briggs, D.R.	19	47	7.83	16	–	–	15	49.40	3-30	5.19
Broad, S.C.J.	101	438	11.83	45*	–	–	162	27.15	5-23	5.23
Brooks, J.A.	13	16	5.33	10	–	–	11	40.90	3-41	5.11
Brophy, G.L.	118	2045	26.21	93*	–	13	–	–	–	115/24
Brown, B.C.	20	299	37.37	60	–	3	–	–	–	16/3
Brown, K.R.	23	687	34.35	101*	1	3	–	–	–	–
Buck, N.L.	14	40	10.00	21	–	–	16	36.87	3-54	6.04
Burgoyne, P.I.	2	6	6.00	6*	–	–	2	31.00	2-36	6.20
Burton, D.A.	5	2	2.00	2	–	–	5	28.20	3-25	5.87
Buttler, J.C.	29	854	71.16	94*	–	8	–	–	–	18/1
Cameron, J.G.	24	689	38.27	69	–	5	8	37.62	4-44	6.51
Carberry, M.A.	124	2930	28.17	121*	2	21	4	51.50	2-11	5.72
Carter, A.	10	25	5.00	12	–	–	12	23.25	3-32	5.69
Carter, N.M.	173	2965	22.29	135	3	13	223	26.86	5-31	4.88
Chambers, M.A.	3	1	–	1*	–	–	3	31.00	1-26	6.20
Chapple, G.	272	2004	17.57	81*	–	9	302	29.03	6-18	4.51
Chopra, V.	49	1783	38.76	115	3	15	0	–	–	6.00
Choudhry, S.H.	16	146	20.85	39	–	–	11	47.63	4-54	6.55
Clare, J.L.	32	225	9.78	34	–	–	25	39.88	3-39	5.62
Clark, J.	4	40	20.00	32	–	–	–	–	–	–
Clarke, R.	162	2982	25.93	98*	–	15	92	39.41	4-28	5.66
Claydon, M.E.	45	113	6.64	19	–	–	61	26.55	4-39	4.99
Cliff, S.J.	10	10	5.00	9	–	–	10	37.90	4-26	5.26
Cobb, J.J.	29	742	32.26	91*	–	5	8	49.00	2-35	6.12
Cockbain, I.A.	12	309	34.33	79	–	3	–	–	–	–
Coetzer, K.J.	72	2123	35.38	127	3	14	1	209.00	1-35	5.97
Coles, M.T.	15	81	10.12	47	–	–	23	21.43	4-45	7.04
Collingwood, P.D.	373	9826	34.00	120*	8	56	229	34.61	6-31	4.84
Collymore, C.D.	136	154	6.16	13*	–	–	147	30.94	5-27	4.29
Comber, M.A.	6	52	–	52*	–	1	0	–	–	5.41
Compton, N.R.D.	86	2441	39.37	131	6	13	1	53.00	1- 0	5.21
Cook, A.N.	89	3104	39.29	125	6	18	0	–	–	3.33
Cook, S.J.	183	1253	16.93	67*	–	2	229	27.72	6-37	4.74
Cooke, C.B.	21	541	33.81	109*	1	2	–	–	–	10/2
Cosker, D.A.	212	697	11.61	50*	–	1	216	32.87	5-54	4.79
Cox, O.B.	12	25	8.33	9*	–	–	–	–	–	9/2
Craddock, T.R.	6	9	–	5*	–	–	4	45.50	2-38	4.43
Croft, R.D.B.	407	6490	23.42	143	4	32	410	32.66	6-20	4.34
Croft, S.J.	88	2157	34.23	107	1	14	40	33.82	4-24	5.40
Crook, S.P.	36	352	16.00	72	–	2	27	47.44	4-20	5.97
Cross, G.D.	53	834	21.94	76	–	3	2	13.00	2-26	31/15
Daggett, L.M.	49	78	26.00	14*	–	–	60	28.16	4-17	5.00
Davey, J.H.	22	432	22.73	91	–	2	24	21.66	5- 9	5.43
Davies, A.L.	1	6	–	6*	–	–	–	–	–	–/–
Davies, S.M.	122	3620	36.20	119	5	21	–	–	–	109/31
Davis, C.A.L.	1	–	–	–	–	–	0	–	–	5.86
Dawson, L.A.	50	914	27.69	70	–	3	28	38.46	4-45	5.45
de Bruyn, Z.	203	5502	37.42	122*	6	34	139	31.09	5-44	5.50
Denly, J.L.	83	2419	32.68	115	4	11	4	30.50	3-42	6.10

L-O	M	Runs	Avge	HS	100	50	Wkts	Avge	Best	Econ
Dent, C.D.J.	8	49	9.80	25	–	–	1	17.00	1-17	8.50
Dernbach, J.W.	79	155	8.61	31	–	–	133	25.66	5-31	6.14
Dexter, N.J.	62	1464	34.04	135*	2	6	24	49.45	3-17	5.27
Dibble, A.J.	4	–	–	–	–	–	5	34.00	3-52	6.53
Di Venuto, M.J.	302	9217	33.15	173*	15	48	5	36.20	1-10	5.43
Dixey, P.G.	10	95	13.57	42	–	–	–	–	–	–
Dockrell, G.H.	35	101	14.42	22*	–	–	41	28.43	4-35	4.23
D'Oliveira, B.L.	1	–	–	–	–	–	1	40.00	1-40	6.66
Dunn, M.P.	1	–	–	–	–	–	2	16.00	2-32	5.33
Durston, W.J.	80	1833	34.58	117	1	12	32	37.25	3- 7	5.74
du Toit, J.	47	1147	27.30	144	2	4	2	33.00	2-30	6.00
Eckersley, E.J.	1	1	1.00	1	–	–	–	–	–	–
Edwards, N.J.	10	195	21.66	65	–	1	–	–	–	–
Elstone, S.L.	13	251	22.81	40	–	–	1	22.00	1-22	6.00
Ervine, S.M.	179	4308	31.91	167*	7	17	172	34.04	5-50	5.58
Evans, L.	7	19	9.50	18	–	–	5	45.40	2-53	7.09
Evans, L.J.	2	39	39.00	36*	–	–	–	–	–	–
Finn, S.T.	45	86	7.81	35	–	–	57	28.08	5-33	5.13
Fletcher, L.J.	27	97	10.77	40*	–	–	28	36.75	3-27	5.55
Footitt, M.H.A.	11	5	2.50	4	–	–	10	36.30	3-20	6.25
Foster, J.S.	172	2622	28.50	83*	–	14	–	–	–	198/53
Franks, P.J.	180	1899	20.86	84*	–	5	194	28.48	6-27	5.01
Fuller, J.K.	8	86	21.50	33	–	–	16	20.37	4-33	5.82
Gale, A.W.	101	2601	31.33	125*	2	14	–	–	–	–
Gatting, J.S.	31	832	30.81	122	1	4	0	–	–	6.60
Gayle, C.H.	290	10312	39.66	153*	21	59	210	32.30	5-46	4.53
Gibbs, H.H.	386	11937	35.42	175	27	62	2	28.50	1-16	5.18
Gidman, A.P.R.	166	3883	27.53	116	5	20	65	40.55	5-42	5.19
Gidman, W.R.S.	26	213	17.75	40*	–	–	23	28.39	4-36	4.80
Godleman, B.A.	17	342	21.37	82	–	1	–	–	–	–
Gondal, N.A.	22	141	17.62	49	–	–	18	42.94	3-19	5.89
Goodwin, M.W.	353	10654	35.99	167	14	66	7	43.71	1- 9	5.23
Gregory, L.	8	12	4.00	11	–	–	17	14.29	4-27	5.65
Griffiths, D.A.	8	10	10.00	7	–	–	10	31.30	4-29	5.90
Groenewald, T.D.	55	345	13.26	36	–	–	50	35.64	4-22	5.56
Guptill, M.J.	91	3006	38.53	156	7	16	2	26.50	2- 7	4.89
Gurney, H.F.	19	9	1.80	7	–	–	15	43.00	5-24	5.45
Guy, S.M.	32	282	14.84	40	–	–	–	–	–	34/11
Hales, A.D.	35	1068	34.45	150*	3	5	–	–	–	–
Hall, A.J.	303	5732	29.54	129*	6	31	352	27.31	5-18	4.75
Hamilton-Brown, R.J.	61	1392	26.76	115	1	7	31	36.29	3-28	5.73
Hannon-Dalby, O.J.	4	–	–	–	–	–	5	28.80	2-22	6.64
Harinath, A.	1	21	–	21*	–	–	–	–	–	–
Harmison, B.W.	51	953	24.43	67	–	3	24	35.62	3-43	5.93
Harmison, S.J.	143	267	8.09	25*	–	–	184	30.75	5-33	4.96
Harris, J.A.R.	30	175	11.66	29	–	–	40	25.15	4-48	5.34
Harrison, N.L.	4	2	–	2*	–	–	3	60.00	2-43	6.20
Henderson, C.W.	253	1160	15.06	45	–	–	317	25.62	6-29	4.34
Henriques, M.C.	44	753	22.81	59	–	1	35	41.48	3-29	5.42
Hildreth, J.C.	138	3600	32.72	151	4	15	6	30.83	2-26	7.40
Hodd, A.J.	42	566	23.58	91	–	1	–	–	–	34/8
Hogg, K.W.	129	950	16.66	66*	–	1	133	29.59	4-20	4.81
Hoggard, M.J.	147	130	5.65	23	–	–	201	25.69	5-28	4.53
Horton, P.J.	72	1866	32.17	111*	2	10	–	–	–	–
Howgego, B.H.N.	3	19	9.50	12	–	–	–	–	–	–
Hughes, C.F.	37	855	24.42	81	–	7	16	32.81	3-19	5.00

L-O	M	Runs	Avge	HS	100	50	Wkts	Avge	Best	Econ
Hughes, P.J.	44	1471	37.71	138	2	9	–	–	–	–
Hussain, G.M.	5	16	–	16*	–	–	5	39.80	2-17	6.63
Hutton, B.A.	2	20	20.00	17*	–	–	1	101.00	1-60	7.21
Ireland, A.J.	70	116	6.82	22*	–	–	89	29.78	4-16	5.41
James, N.A.	16	174	19.33	43	–	–	14	20.21	3-36	4.79
Jaques, P.A.	146	5657	42.21	171*	14	30	0	–	–	6.33
Javid, A.	2	58	29.00	34	–	–	0	–	–	6.75
Jefferson, W.I.	101	3144	34.17	132	4	18	2	4.50	2- 9	2.25
Jewell, T.M.	2	1	1.00	1	–	–	0	–	–	9.33
Johnson, R.M.	11	46	11.50	20	–	–	–	–	–	9/2
Jones, A.J.	4	8	4.00	5	–	–	3	67.33	1-38	7.76
Jones, C.R.	2	78	78.00	45*	–	–	–	–	–	–
Jones, G.O.	170	2861	23.64	86	–	11	–	–	–	183/39
Jones, R.A.	9	23	7.66	11*	–	–	2	177.50	1-33	7.47
Jones, S.P.	43	77	15.40	26	–	–	42	36.59	5-32	5.21
Jones, W.S.	1	3	3.00	3	–	–	–	–	–	–
Jordan, C.J.	20	74	6.72	38	–	–	23	32.47	3-28	5.87
Joseph, R.H.	33	43	21.50	15	–	–	39	28.56	5-13	5.11
Joyce, E.C.	215	6886	37.42	146	10	41	6	51.50	2-10	7.02
Kapil, A.	6	105	21.00	44	–	–	3	53.00	1-18	7.22
Kartik, M.	185	743	12.18	44	–	–	238	28.75	6-27	4.39
Katich, S.M.	219	6922	37.01	136*	7	54	24	34.08	3-21	5.59
Keedy, G.	79	143	8.93	33	–	–	94	26.95	5-30	4.68
Kelsall, S.	1	40	40.00	40	–	–	–	–	–	–
Keogh, R.I.	1	11	11.00	11	–	–	–	–	–	–
Kerrigan, S.C.	12	9	3.00	5	–	–	9	40.44	3-21	5.17
Kervezee, A.N.	68	1804	29.09	121*	2	7	0	–	–	9.12
Key, R.W.T.	199	5593	31.24	120*	5	35	–	–	–	–
Khan, A.	66	295	11.80	65*	–	1	66	34.34	4-26	5.24
Khawaja, U.T.	14	432	33.23	121	1	2	–	–	–	–
Kieswetter, C.	90	3112	39.89	143	8	13	–	–	–	88/19
Kirby, S.P.	86	88	4.19	15	–	–	117	28.13	5-36	5.66
Knight, T.C.	3	1	–	1*	–	–	5	22.60	2-27	4.70
Lancefield, T.J.	1	20	20.00	20	–	–	–	–	–	–
Lees, A.Z.	1	12	–	12*	–	–	–	–	–	–
Lewis, J.	213	879	11.12	54	–	1	285	26.21	5-19	4.57
Liddle, C.J.	29	36	4.00	11	–	–	36	28.83	5-18	6.07
Lineker, M.S.	1	13	13.00	13	–	–	–	–	–	–
Linley, T.E.	18	37	37.00	20*	–	–	12	46.16	3-50	5.61
Lucas, D.S.	73	212	10.09	32*	–	–	87	30.52	5-48	5.75
Lumb, M.J.	164	4752	32.32	110	3	37	0	–	–	14.00
Lyth, A.	53	1197	27.20	109*	1	5	0	–	–	4.66
McGrath, A.	293	7548	32.81	148	7	45	80	33.12	4-41	5.06
McKenzie, N.D.	243	6844	36.40	131*	8	48	4	62.00	2-19	5.83
Machan, M.W.	2	66	33.00	56	–	1	–	–	–	–
Maddy, D.L.	343	8681	31.00	167*	11	51	209	29.21	4-16	5.16
Madsen, W.L.	36	1105	38.10	75	–	9	5	14.80	2-18	4.35
Mahmood, S.I.	142	477	8.83	29	–	–	199	27.26	5-16	5.21
Malan, D.J.	54	1252	25.04	107	1	5	14	36.07	2- 4	6.02
Malik, M.N.	80	107	8.91	11	–	–	83	33.63	4-40	5.30
Manuel, J.K.	7	142	20.28	48	–	–	–	–	–	–
Marshall, H.J.H.	246	5931	28.24	122	6	40	4	68.75	2-21	6.34
Mascarenhas, A.D.	251	4171	24.97	79	–	27	290	26.38	5-27	4.28
Masters, D.D.	139	487	12.48	39	–	–	134	32.19	5-17	4.47
Maynard, T.L.	55	1624	33.14	108	2	12	0	–	–	16.00
Meaker, S.C.	21	30	6.00	10*	–	–	19	37.89	3-22	6.28

L-O	M	Runs	Avge	HS	100	50	Wkts	Avge	Best	Econ
Meschede, C.A.J.	9	66	13.20	19	–	–	5	32.00	2-16	5.71
Metters, C.L.	3	3	1.50	2	–	–	2	47.00	2-41	5.22
Mickleburgh, J.C.	7	141	23.50	56	–	1	–	–	–	–
Middlebrook, J.D.	168	1507	20.09	57*	–	1	131	35.77	4-27	4.68
Miles, C.N.	2	–	–	–	–	–	2	31.50	2-32	5.72
Miller, A.S.	4	4	4.00	2*	–	–	6	24.16	2-31	4.67
Mills, T.S.	2	0	0.00	0	–	–	3	30.66	2-40	6.57
Mitchell, D.K.H.	64	1280	31.21	92	–	8	34	40.23	4-42	5.82
Moore, S.C.	115	2836	28.36	118	4	16	1	53.00	1- 1	7.75
Morkel, J.A.	169	2625	26.78	97	–	11	184	29.88	4-23	5.03
Muchall, G.J.	106	2558	31.97	101*	1	15	1	144.00	1-15	5.14
Mullaney, S.J.	31	438	19.04	61	–	2	31	24.61	3-13	5.28
Muralitharan, M.	453	945	7.32	33*	–	–	682	22.39	7-30	3.86
Murphy, D.	12	81	40.50	31*	–	–	–	–	–	7/3
Murtagh, T.J.	125	614	12.03	35*	–	–	172	27.90	4-14	5.22
Mustard, P.	140	3552	30.10	139*	4	23	–	–	–	142/33
Naik, J.K.H.	27	100	9.09	18	–	–	22	41.72	3-21	5.31
Napier, G.R.	208	2523	18.28	79	–	12	237	25.67	6-29	5.17
Nash, C.D.	66	2013	33.55	124*	2	13	24	28.50	4-40	5.49
Naved-ul-Hasan	178	2166	21.87	74	–	10	274	26.71	6-27	5.25
Needham, J.	42	224	13.17	42	–	–	26	46.46	3-36	5.19
Newby, O.J.	24	73	10.42	35*	–	–	21	43.09	4-41	6.41
Newman, S.A.	106	2967	29.96	177	4	17	–	–	–	–
Newton, R.I.	14	324	24.92	66	–	1	–	–	–	–
Norman, A.J.	1	15	15.00	15	–	–	0	–	–	4.42
North, M.J.	141	4201	35.90	134*	8	28	67	30.44	4-26	5.05
Northeast, S.A.	23	467	25.94	69	–	4	–	–	–	–
O'Brien, K.J.	116	2749	30.88	142	3	11	79	35.18	4-31	5.20
O'Brien, N.J.	135	2949	29.49	121	1	20	–	–	–	117/31
Onions, G.	62	112	6.58	19	–	–	68	32.72	3-39	5.18
O'Shea, M.P.	26	557	26.52	90	–	3	10	49.10	2-32	6.03
Owen, W.T.	17	38	7.60	12	–	–	28	19.75	5-49	6.21
Palladino, A.P.	40	153	8.50	31	–	–	39	34.56	4-32	5.43
Panesar, M.S.	79	136	9.06	17*	–	–	78	34.61	5-20	4.63
Pardoe, M.G.	1	11	11.00	11	–	–	–	–	–	–
Park, G.T.	47	730	23.54	64	–	1	10	61.30	2-21	5.69
Parry, S.D.	34	117	11.70	31	–	–	40	29.77	3-40	4.96
Parsons, T.W.	1	–	–	–	–	–	2	20.50	2-41	6.83
Patel, J.S.	113	359	9.97	34	–	–	115	37.27	4-16	4.73
Patel, S.R.	129	2907	31.25	114	2	15	110	28.84	6-13	5.20
Patterson, S.A.	45	83	41.50	25*	–	–	56	29.23	6-32	5.12
Pattinson, D.J.	53	78	7.09	13	–	–	68	26.83	4-29	5.32
Payne, D.A.	19	28	14.00	13	–	–	35	19.85	7-29	5.69
Peters, S.D.	169	3284	22.49	107	2	20	–	–	–	–
Petersen, A.N.	133	4012	33.71	144	6	24	3	49.00	1-13	5.28
Pettini, M.L.	124	2826	27.17	144	5	18	–	–	–	–
Philander, V.D.	94	1179	25.08	79*	–	4	88	35.31	4-12	4.74
Phillips, B.J.	137	1042	18.60	51*	–	1	153	30.21	4-25	4.99
Phillips, T.J.	60	343	18.05	58*	–	1	69	23.11	5-28	5.06
Piesley, C.D.	1	4	4.00	4	–	–	–	–	–	–
Pietersen, K.P.	232	7332	40.73	147	13	43	41	51.34	3-14	5.32
Pinner, N.D.	9	122	13.55	37	–	–	0	–	–	6.66
Piolet, S.A.	19	56	14.00	39	–	–	18	30.05	3-34	5.70
Plunkett, L.E.	113	927	18.91	72	–	2	132	32.09	4-15	5.39
Porterfield, W.T.S.	125	4049	33.74	112*	5	25	–	–	–	–
Powell, M.J.	204	4665	26.96	114*	1	25	1	26.00	1-26	6.50

265

L-O	M	Runs	Avge	HS	100	50	Wkts	Avge	Best	Econ
Poynton, T.	10	96	24.00	40	–	–		–	–	7/2
Prince, A.G.	208	4611	31.36	128	2	22	0	–	–	5.67
Prior, M.J.	218	4946	27.02	144	4	27	–	–	–	185/31
Procter, L.A.	16	244	30.50	97	–	2	11	31.45	3-29	5.96
Pyrah, R.M.	89	868	19.72	69	–	2	107	24.97	5-50	5.73
Raine, B.A.	1	–	–	–	–	–		–	–	–
Ramprakash, M.R.	407	13273	40.22	147*	17	85	46	29.43	5-38	4.68
Rankin, W.B.	69	66	7.33	9	–	–	84	28.69	4-34	5.08
Rashid, A.U.	66	467	16.67	43	–	–	64	32.98	3-28	5.10
Rayner, O.P.	26	293	29.30	61	–	1	20	42.30	2-20	5.67
Read, C.M.W.	274	4674	28.15	135	2	18	–	–	–	262/61
Redfern, D.J.	28	496	20.66	57*	–	2	5	37.60	2-10	4.99
Rees, G.P.	33	1123	40.10	123*	3	8	0	–	–	4.00
Riazuddin, H.	21	64	16.00	23*	–	–	16	42.75	3-37	4.99
Richardson, A.	64	105	10.50	21*	–	–	62	35.46	5-35	4.70
Riley, A.E.N.	6	3	–	3*	–	–	5	39.40	2-32	5.47
Robson, S.D.	6	165	41.25	65	–	1	–	–	–	–
Rogers, C.J.L.	138	4411	35.28	140	4	30	2	13.00	2-22	6.50
Roland-Jones, T.S.	13	56	9.33	23*	–	–	19	29.26	3-51	5.81
Root, J.E.	10	309	34.33	63	–	3	2	44.50	1- 1	4.76
Roy, J.J.	23	694	31.54	131	2	5	0	–	–	12.00
Rudolph, J.A.	214	8399	48.54	134*	13	57	12	32.41	4-40	5.58
Rushworth, C.	14	28	9.33	12*	–	–	22	18.27	3- 6	4.70
Saker, N.C.	37	219	14.60	40*	–	–	30	46.26	4-43	5.84
Sales, D.J.G.	249	6937	34.17	161	4	49	0	–	–	4.78
Sarwan, R.R.	242	7824	41.39	118*	8	48	35	28.60	5-10	5.31
Saxelby, I.D.	10	27	5.40	7*	–	–	15	27.80	4-31	6.81
Sayers, J.J.	27	515	20.60	62	–	4	1	79.00	1-31	7.90
Scollay, T.E.	9	115	12.77	32	–	–	1	21.00	1-21	5.25
Scott, B.J.M.	111	926	18.89	73*	–	4	–	–	–	84/32
Shafayat, B.M.	107	2027	22.27	104	1	7	24	30.41	4-33	5.54
Shah, O.A.	338	9865	35.35	134	14	63	27	33.70	4-11	5.90
Shahid Afridi	416	9345	25.25	124	8	50	419	33.27	6-38	4.60
Shahzad, A.	46	288	13.71	59*	–	–	58	32.15	5-51	5.11
Shantry, A.J.	41	48	16.00	19*	–	–	13	25.00	5-37	4.77
Shantry, J.D.	28	62	12.40	18	–	–	37	30.83	3-33	5.91
Shaw, S.A.	6	9	4.50	4*	–	–	5	36.80	3-26	6.81
Shreck, C.E.	52	45	6.42	9*	–	–	63	31.90	5-19	5.22
Siddle, P.M.	36	88	12.57	25*	–	–	38	34.63	4-27	4.64
Sidebottom, R.J.	180	540	11.48	32	–	–	189	30.93	6-40	4.40
Simpson, J.A.	27	363	21.35	82	–	1	–	–	–	19/4
Smith, G.M.	78	1694	23.20	88	–	7	62	33.01	4-53	5.63
Smith, G.P.	12	141	14.10	58	–	1	–	–	–	–
Smith, T.C.	52	1024	29.25	117	1	7	64	26.65	4-48	5.18
Smith, T.M.J.	25	153	15.30	65	–	1	20	42.30	3-26	5.49
Smith, W.R.	74	1538	24.80	103	1	11	2	37.00	1- 6	6.25
Snell, S.D.	26	346	20.35	95	–	2	–	–	–	34/1
Solanki, V.S.	370	10064	32.05	164*	14	59	28	35.25	4-14	5.27
Spriegel, M.N.W.	49	1218	42.00	86	–	9	31	40.03	3-39	5.46
Stevens, D.I.	236	6026	30.58	133	4	40	64	36.45	5-32	5.05
Stirling, P.R.	65	2234	36.03	177	5	11	48	45.94	4-11	4.78
Stokes, B.A.	29	694	28.91	150*	1	3	14	14.78	4-29	5.26
Stoneman, M.D.	9	224	24.88	73	–	1	–	–	–	–
Strauss, A.J.	254	7631	32.75	163	10	49	0	–	–	3.00
Suppiah, A.V.	82	1478	27.88	80	–	6	44	31.75	4-39	5.55
Sutton, L.D.	167	2080	19.25	83	–	6	–	–	–	185/27

L-O	M	Runs	Avge	HS	100	50	Wkts	Avge	Best	Econ
Swann, G.P.	247	3080	19.01	83	–	14	288	25.63	5-17	4.39
Sweeney, S.A.	1	–	–	–	–	–	–	–	–	10.33
Taylor, C.G.	181	3716	26.73	105	2	21	16	38.31	2- 5	5.25
Taylor, J.M.R.	5	18	9.00	9*	–	–	7	21.57	3-37	5.88
Taylor, J.W.A.	49	1786	49.61	111	5	10	5	34.00	4-61	7.39
Taylor, M.D.	2	7	–	7*	–	–	4	22.25	2-43	6.43
ten Doeschate, R.N.	139	3667	45.83	134*	7	20	133	28.30	5-50	5.57
Thakor, S.J.	2	26	13.00	13	–	–	–	–	–	–
Thomas, A.C.	143	550	14.86	28*	–	–	185	27.94	4-18	5.09
Thorp, C.D.	42	323	17.00	52	–	1	53	27.13	6-17	4.54
Tomlinson, J.A.	27	34	3.77	14	–	–	29	31.37	4-47	5.01
Topley, R.J.W.	3	19	19.00	19	–	–	3	36.33	2-45	5.45
Tredwell, J.C.	167	1399	17.70	88	–	4	159	33.47	6-27	4.70
Trego, P.D.	122	2025	24.39	147	2	8	121	32.07	5-40	5.60
Tremlett, C.T.	125	521	10.01	38*	–	–	170	27.75	4-25	4.89
Trescothick, M.E.	346	11474	37.61	184	28	57	57	28.84	4-50	4.90
Trott, I.J.L.	198	7065	46.48	137	14	49	54	27.01	4-55	5.64
Troughton, J.O.	148	3365	29.00	115*	2	20	25	25.76	4-23	5.25
Turner, K.	2	22	11.00	18	–	–	–	–	–	–
Turner, M.L.	24	51	10.20	15*	–	–	23	27.03	4-36	6.16
Vaas, W.P.J.U.C.	409	3220	16.59	76*	–	8	505	26.54	8-19	4.15
Vince, J.M.	29	993	35.46	131	1	5	–	–	–	–
Voges, A.C.	122	3967	44.07	104*	3	32	22	50.27	3-25	5.25
Wagg, G.G.	87	1096	17.67	48*	–	–	93	32.74	4-35	5.63
Wainwright, D.J.	51	153	15.30	26	–	–	43	35.67	3-26	4.87
Wakely, A.G.	31	632	24.30	94	–	3	4	22.50	2-14	4.50
Walker, M.J.	285	6269	29.15	117	3	37	30	25.30	4-24	5.03
Wallace, M.A.	165	1940	18.65	85	–	3	–	–	–	150/41
Waller, M.T.C.	22	13	13.00	5	–	–	16	38.81	2-24	5.51
Walters, S.J.	56	1302	29.59	91	–	9	3	59.66	1-12	6.50
Wardlaw, I.	1	1	1.00	1	–	–	0	–	–	3.75
Waters, H.T.	21	24	4.80	8	–	–	14	59.71	3-47	6.28
Wells, L.W.P.	6	28	9.33	17	–	–	3	20.33	3-19	4.75
Wernars, K.O.	12	115	19.16	37*	–	–	7	34.14	6-27	5.75
Wessels, M.H.	92	2172	27.84	100	1	13	1	48.00	1- 0	5.87
Westley, T.	11	106	13.25	50	–	1	2	38.50	1-18	4.52
Westwood, I.J.	59	929	23.22	65	–	3	3	71.66	1-28	5.11
Wheater, A.J.	25	324	24.92	69	–	2	–	–	–	–
White, G.G.	27	104	10.40	25	–	–	24	30.00	5-35	5.45
White, R.A.	92	1992	23.71	111	2	10	21	39.50	2-18	7.64
White, W.A.	47	468	18.72	46*	–	–	40	40.37	6-29	6.36
Whiteley, R.A.	11	147	16.33	40	–	–	1	70.00	1-26	5.83
Willey, D.J.	30	348	19.33	74	–	2	20	36.75	3-49	5.84
Williams, R.E.M.	7	2	–	2*	–	–	2	152.50	2-60	8.06
Willoughby, C.M.	209	147	5.06	15	–	–	255	27.81	6-16	4.18
Wilson, G.C.	87	1691	23.81	113	1	12	–	–	–	59/17
Woakes, C.R.	55	402	18.27	49*	–	–	56	33.50	6-45	5.38
Wood, C.P.	20	49	6.12	14*	–	–	36	20.19	4-33	5.56
Wood, M.A.	3	6	3.00	5	–	–	1	62.00	1-28	4.42
Wood, S.K.W.	4	8	2.66	8	–	–	3	24.00	2-24	6.54
Wright, B.J.	54	1037	23.56	79	–	5	1	126.00	1-19	5.72
Wright, C.J.C.	67	183	10.76	42	–	–	60	39.16	4-20	5.57
Wright, L.J.	147	2305	24.26	125	1	6	102	38.95	4-12	5.26
Wyatt, A.C.F.	9	4	4.00	2*	–	–	7	40.57	2-36	6.26
Yardy, M.H.	186	3233	24.30	98*	–	21	127	37.97	6-27	5.09
Young, E.G.C.	19	155	14.09	50	–	1	12	50.25	2-32	4.91

FIRST-CLASS CRICKET RECORDS

To the end of the 2011 season

TEAM RECORDS

HIGHEST INNINGS TOTALS

1107	Victoria v New South Wales	Melbourne	1926-27
1059	Victoria v Tasmania	Melbourne	1922-23
952-6d	Sri Lanka v India	Colombo	1997-98
951-7d	Sind v Baluchistan	Karachi	1973-74
944-6d	Hyderabad v Andhra	Secunderabad	1993-94
918	New South Wales v South Australia	Sydney	1900-01
912-8d	Holkar v Mysore	Indore	1945-46
910-6d	Railways v Dera Ismail Khan	Lahore	1964-65
903-7d	England v Australia	The Oval	1938
900-6d	Queensland v Victoria	Brisbane	2005-06
887	Yorkshire v Warwickshire	Birmingham	1896
863	Lancashire v Surrey	The Oval	1990
860-6d	Tamil Nadu v Goa	Panjim	1988-89
850-7d	Somerset v Middlesex	Taunton	2007

Excluding penalty runs in India, there have been 34 innings totals of 800 runs or more in first-class cricket. Tamil Nadu's total of 860-6d was boosted to 912 by 52 penalty runs.

HIGHEST SECOND INNINGS TOTAL

770	New South Wales v South Australia	Adelaide	1920-21

HIGHEST FOURTH INNINGS TOTAL

654-5	England (set 696 to win) v South Africa	Durban	1938-39

HIGHEST MATCH AGGREGATE

2376-37	Maharashtra v Bombay	Poona	1948-49

RECORD MARGIN OF VICTORY

Innings and 851 runs: Railways v Dera Ismail Khan	Lahore	1964-65

MOST RUNS IN A DAY

721	Australians v Essex	Southend	1948

MOST HUNDREDS IN AN INNINGS

6	Holkar v Mysore	Indore	1945-46

LOWEST INNINGS TOTALS

12	†Oxford University v MCC and Ground	Oxford	1877
12	Northamptonshire v Gloucestershire	Gloucester	1907
13	Auckland v Canterbury	Auckland	1877-78
13	Nottinghamshire v Yorkshire	Nottingham	1901
14	Surrey v Essex	Chelmsford	1983
15	MCC v Surrey	Lord's	1839
15	†Victoria v MCC	Melbourne	1903-04
15	†Northamptonshire v Yorkshire	Northampton	1908
15	Hampshire v Warwickshire	Birmingham	1922

† *Batted one man short*

There have been 27 instances of a team being dismissed for under 20.

LOWEST MATCH AGGREGATE BY ONE TEAM

34 (16 and 18)	Border v Natal	East London	1959-60

LOWEST COMPLETED MATCH AGGREGATE BY BOTH TEAMS

105   MCC v Australians   Lord's   1878

FEWEST RUNS IN AN UNINTERRUPTED DAY'S PLAY

95   Australia (80) v Pakistan (15-2)   Karachi   1956-57

TIED MATCHES

Before 1949 a match was considered to be tied if the scores were level after the fourth innings, even if the side batting last had wickets in hand when play ended. Law 22 was amended in 1948 and since then a match has been tied only when the scores are level after the fourth innings has been completed. There have been 56 tied first-class matches, five of which would not have qualified under the current law. The most recent are:

Warwickshire (446-7d & forfeit) v Essex (66-0d & 380)   Birmingham   2003
Worcestershire (262 & 247) v Zimbabweans (334 & 175)   Worcester   2003

BATTING RECORDS
35,000 RUNS IN A CAREER

	Career	*I*	*NO*	*HS*	*Runs*	Avge	*100*
J.B.Hobbs	1905-34	1315	106	316*	**61237**	50.65	197
F.E.Woolley	1906-38	1532	85	305*	**58969**	40.75	145
E.H.Hendren	1907-38	1300	166	301*	**57611**	50.80	170
C.P.Mead	1905-36	1340	185	280*	**55061**	47.67	153
W.G.Grace	1865-1908	1493	105	344	**54896**	39.55	126
W.R.Hammond	1920-51	1005	104	336*	**50551**	56.10	167
H.Sutcliffe	1919-45	1088	123	313	**50138**	51.95	149
G.Boycott	1962-86	1014	162	261*	**48426**	56.83	151
T.W.Graveney	1948-71/72	1223	159	258	**47793**	44.91	122
G.A.Gooch	1973-2000	990	75	333	**44846**	49.01	128
T.W.Hayward	1893-1914	1138	96	315*	**43551**	41.79	104
D.L.Amiss	1960-87	1139	126	262*	**43423**	42.86	102
M.C.Cowdrey	1950-76	1130	134	307	**42719**	42.89	107
A.Sandham	1911-37/38	1000	79	325	**41284**	44.82	107
G.A.Hick	1983/84-2008	871	84	405*	**41112**	52.23	136
L.Hutton	1934-60	814	91	364	**40140**	55.51	129
M.J.K.Smith	1951-75	1091	139	204	**39832**	41.84	69
W.Rhodes	1898-1930	1528	237	267*	**39802**	30.83	58
J.H.Edrich	1956-78	979	104	310*	**39790**	45.47	103
R.E.S.Wyatt	1923-57	1141	157	232	**39405**	40.04	85
D.C.S.Compton	1936-64	839	88	300	**38942**	51.85	123
G.E.Tyldesley	1909-36	961	106	256*	**38874**	45.46	102
J.T.Tyldesley	1895-1923	994	62	295*	**37897**	40.60	86
K.W.R.Fletcher	1962-88	1167	170	228*	**37665**	37.77	63
C.G.Greenidge	1970-92	889	75	273*	**37354**	45.88	92
J.W.Hearne	1909-36	1025	116	285*	**37252**	40.98	96
L.E.G.Ames	1926-51	951	95	295	**37248**	43.51	102
D.Kenyon	1946-67	1159	59	259	**37002**	33.63	74
W.J.Edrich	1934-58	964	92	267*	**36965**	42.39	86
J.M.Parks	1949-76	1227	172	205*	**36673**	34.76	51
M.W.Gatting	1975-98	861	123	258	**36549**	49.52	94
D.Denton	1894-1920	1163	70	221	**36479**	33.37	69
G.H.Hirst	1891-1929	1215	151	341	**36323**	34.13	60
I.V.A.Richards	1971/72-93	796	63	322	**36212**	49.40	114
A.Jones	1957-83	1168	72	204*	**36049**	32.89	56
W.G.Quaife	1894-1928	1203	185	255*	**36012**	35.37	72
R.E.Marshall	1945/46-72	1053	59	228*	**35725**	35.94	68
M.R.Ramprakash	1987-	752	93	301*	**35539**	53.92	114
G.Gunn	1902-32	1061	82	220	**35208**	35.96	62

HIGHEST INDIVIDUAL INNINGS

501*	B.C.Lara	Warwickshire v Durham	Birmingham	1994
499	Hanif Mohammed	Karachi v Bahawalpur	Karachi	1958-59
452*	D.G.Bradman	New South Wales v Queensland	Sydney	1929-30
443*	B.B.Nimbalkar	Maharashtra v Kathiawar	Poona	1948-49
437	W.H.Ponsford	Victoria v Queensland	Melbourne	1927-28
429	W.H.Ponsford	Victoria v Tasmania	Melbourne	1922-23
428	Aftab Baloch	Sind v Baluchistan	Karachi	1973-74
424	A.C.MacLaren	Lancashire v Somerset	Taunton	1895
405*	G.A.Hick	Worcestershire v Somerset	Taunton	1988
400*	B.C.Lara	West Indies v England	St John's	2003-04
394	Naved Latif	Sargodha v Gujranwala	Gujranwala	2000-01
390	S.C.Cook	Lions v Warriors	East London	2009-10
385	B.Sutcliffe	Otago v Canterbury	Christchurch	1952-53
383	C.W.Gregory	New South Wales v Queensland	Brisbane	1906-07
380	M.L.Hayden	Australia v Zimbabwe	Perth	2003-04
377	S.V.Manjrekar	Bombay v Hyderabad	Bombay	1990-91
375	B.C.Lara	West Indies v England	St John's	1993-94
374	D.P.M.D.Jayawardena	Sri Lanka v South Africa	Colombo	2006
369	D.G.Bradman	South Australia v Tasmania	Adelaide	1935-36
366	N.H.Fairbrother	Lancashire v Surrey	The Oval	1990
366	M.V.Sridhar	Hyderabad v Andhra	Secunderabad	1993-94
365*	C.Hill	South Australia v NSW	Adelaide	1900-01
365*	G.St A.Sobers	West Indies v Pakistan	Kingston	1957-58
364	L.Hutton	England v Australia	The Oval	1938
359*	V.M.Merchant	Bombay v Maharashtra	Bombay	1943-44
359	R.B.Simpson	New South Wales v Queensland	Brisbane	1963-64
357*	R.Abel	Surrey v Somerset	The Oval	1899
357	D.G.Bradman	South Australia v Victoria	Melbourne	1935-36
356	B.A.Richards	South Australia v W Australia	Perth	1970-71
355*	G.R.Marsh	W Australia v S Australia	Perth	1989-90
355	B.Sutcliffe	Otago v Auckland	Dunedin	1949-50
353	V.V.S.Laxman	Hyderabad v Karnataka	Bangalore	1999-00
352	W.H.Ponsford	Victoria v New South Wales	Melbourne	1926-27
350	Rashid Israr	Habib Bank v National Bank	Lahore	1976-77

There have been 180 triple hundreds in first-class cricket, W.V.Raman (313) and Arjan Kripal Singh (302*) for Tamil Nadu v Goa at Panjim in 1988-89 providing the only instance of two batsmen scoring 300 in the same innings.

MOST HUNDREDS IN SUCCESSIVE INNINGS

6	C.B.Fry	Sussex and Rest of England	1901
6	D.G.Bradman	South Australia and D.G.Bradman's XI	1938-39
6	M.J.Procter	Rhodesia	1970-71

TWO DOUBLE HUNDREDS IN A MATCH

244	202* A.E.Fagg	Kent v Essex	Colchester	1938

TRIPLE HUNDRED AND HUNDRED IN A MATCH

333	123 G.A.Gooch	England v India	Lord's	1990

DOUBLE HUNDRED AND HUNDRED IN A MATCH MOST TIMES

4	Zaheer Abbas	Gloucestershire	1976-81

TWO HUNDREDS IN A MATCH MOST TIMES

8	Zaheer Abbas	Gloucestershire and PIA	1976-82
8	R.T.Ponting	Tasmania, Australia and Australians	1992-2006
7	W.R.Hammond	Gloucestershire, England and MCC	1927-45

MOST HUNDREDS IN A SEASON

18	D.C.S.Compton	1947	16	J.B.Hobbs	1925

100 HUNDREDS IN A CAREER

	Total		100th Hundred	
	Hundreds	*Inns*	*Season*	*Inns*
J.B.Hobbs	197	1315	1923	821
E.H.Hendren	170	1300	1928-29	740
W.R.Hammond	167	1005	1935	679
C.P.Mead	153	1340	1927	892
G.Boycott	151	1014	1977	645
H.Sutcliffe	149	1088	1932	700
F.E.Woolley	145	1532	1929	1031
G.A.Hick	136	871	1998	574
L.Hutton	129	814	1951	619
G.A.Gooch	128	990	1992-93	820
W.G.Grace	126	1493	1895	1113
D.C.S.Compton	123	839	1952	552
T.W.Graveney	122	1223	1964	940
D.G.Bradman	117	338	1947-48	295
I.V.A.Richards	114	796	1988-89	658
M.R.Ramprakash	114	752	2008	676
Zaheer Abbas	108	768	1982-83	658
A.Sandham	107	1000	1935	871
M.C.Cowdrey	107	1130	1973	1035
T.W.Hayward	104	1138	1913	1076
G.M.Turner	103	792	1982	779
J.H.Edrich	103	979	1977	945
L.E.G.Ames	102	951	1950	915
G.E.Tyldesley	102	961	1934	919
D.L.Amiss	102	1139	1986	1081

MOST 400s: 2 – B.C.Lara, W.H.Ponsford
MOST 300s or more: 6 – D.G.Bradman; 4 – W.R.Hammond, W.H.Ponsford
MOST 200s or more: 37 – D.G.Bradman; 36 – W.R.Hammond; 22 – E.H.Hendren

MOST RUNS IN A MONTH

1294 (avge 92,42)	L.Hutton	Yorkshire	June 1949

MOST RUNS IN A SEASON

Runs			*I*	*NO*	*HS*	*Avge*	*100*	*Season*
3816	D.C.S.Compton	Middlesex	50	8	246	90.85	18	1947
3539	W.J.Edrich	Middlesex	52	8	267*	80.43	12	1947
3518	T.W.Hayward	Surrey	61	8	219	66.37	13	1906

The feat of scoring 3000 runs in a season has been achieved 28 times, the most recent instance being by W.E.Alley (3019) in 1961. The highest aggregate in a season since 1969 is 2755 by S.J.Cook in 1991.

1000 RUNS IN A SEASON MOST TIMES

28   W.G.Grace (Gloucestershire), F.E.Woolley (Kent)

HIGHEST BATTING AVERAGE IN A SEASON

(Qualification: 12 innings)

Avge			*I*	*NO*	*HS*	*Runs*	*100*	*Season*
115.66	D.G.Bradman	Australians	26	5	278	2429	13	1938
104.66	D.R.Martyn	Australians	14	5	176*	942	5	2001
103.54	M.R.Ramprakash	Surrey	24	2	301*	2278	8	2006
102.53	G.Boycott	Yorkshire	20	5	175*	1538	6	1979

Avge			I	NO	HS	Runs	100	Season
102.00	W.A.Johnston	Australians	17	16	28*	102	–	1953
101.70	G.A.Gooch	Essex	30	3	333	2746	12	1990
101.30	M.R.Ramprakash	Surrey	25	5	266*	2026	10	2007
100.12	G.Boycott	Yorkshire	30	5	233	2503	13	1971

FASTEST HUNDRED AGAINST AUTHENTIC BOWLING

35 min	P.G.H.Fender	Surrey v Northamptonshire	Northampton	1920

FASTEST DOUBLE HUNDRED

113 min	R.J.Shastri	Bombay v Baroda	Bombay	1984-85

FASTEST TRIPLE HUNDRED

181 min	D.C.S.Compton	MCC v NE Transvaal	Benoni	1948-49

MOST SIXES IN AN INNINGS

16	A.Symonds	Gloucestershire v Glamorgan	Abergavenny	1995
16	G.R.Napier	Essex v Surrey	Croydon	2011

MOST SIXES IN A MATCH

20	A.Symonds	Gloucestershire v Glamorgan	Abergavenny	1995

MOST SIXES IN A SEASON

80	I.T.Botham	Somerset and England		1985

MOST FOURS IN AN INNINGS

72	B.C.Lara	Warwickshire v Durham	Birmingham	1994

MOST RUNS OFF ONE OVER

36	G.St A.Sobers	Nottinghamshire v Glamorgan	Swansea	1968
36	R.J.Shastri	Bombay v Baroda	Bombay	1984-85

Both batsmen hit for six all six balls of overs bowled by M.A.Nash and Tilak Raj respectively.

MOST RUNS IN A DAY

390*	B.C.Lara	Warwickshire v Durham	Birmingham	1994

There have been 19 instances of a batsman scoring 300 or more runs in a day.

LONGEST INNINGS

1015 min	R.Nayyar (271)	Himachal Pradesh v Jammu & Kashmir	Chamba	1999-00

HIGHEST PARTNERSHIPS FOR EACH WICKET

First Wicket

561	Waheed Mirza/Mansoor Akhtar	Karachi W v Quetta	Karachi	1976-77
555	P.Holmes/H.Sutcliffe	Yorkshire v Essex	Leyton	1932
554	J.T.Brown/J.Tunnicliffe	Yorkshire v Derbys	Chesterfield	1898

Second Wicket

580	Rafatullah Mohmand/Aamer Sajjad	WAPDA v SSGC	Sheikhupura	2009-10
576	S.T.Jayasuriya/R.S.Mahanama	Sri Lanka v India	Colombo	1997-98
480	E.Elgar/R.R.Rossouw	Eagles v Titans	Centurion	2009-10
475	Zahir Alam/L.S.Rajput	Assam v Tripura	Gauhati	1991-92
465*	J.A.Jameson/R.B.Kanhai	Warwickshire v Glos	Birmingham	1974

Third Wicket

624	K.C.Sangakkara/D.P.M.D.Jayawardena	Sri Lanka v South Africa	Colombo	2006
523	M.A.Carberry/N.D.McKenzie	Hampshire v Yorkshire	Southampton	2011
467	A.H.Jones/M.D.Crowe	N Zealand v Sri Lanka	Wellington	1990-91
459	C.J.L.Rogers/M.J.North	W Australia v Victoria	Perth	2006-07
456	Khalid Irtiza/Aslam Ali	United Bank v Multan	Karachi	1975-76
451	Mudassar Nazar/Javed Miandad	Pakistan v India	Hyderabad	1982-83

Fourth Wicket

577	V.S.Hazare/Gul Mahomed	Baroda v Holkar	Baroda	1946-47
574*	C.L.Walcott/F.M.M.Worrell	Barbados v Trinidad	Port-of-Spain	1945-46
502*	F.M.M.Worrell/J.D.C.Goddard	Barbados v Trinidad	Bridgetown	1943-44
470	A.I.Kallicharran/G.W.Humpage	Warwickshire v Lancs	Southport	1982

Fifth Wicket

520*	C.A.Pujara/R.A.Jadeja	Saurashtra v Orissa	Rajkot	2008-09
464*	M.E.Waugh/S.R.Waugh	NSW v W Australia	Perth	1990-91
420	Mohd. Ashraful/Marshall Ayub	Dhaka v Chittagong	Chittagong	2006-07
410*	A.S.Chopra/S.Badrinath	India A v South Africa A	Delhi	2007-08
405	S.G.Barnes/D.G.Bradman	Australia v England	Sydney	1946-47
401	M.B.Loye/D.Ripley	Northants v Glamorgan	Northampton	1998

Sixth Wicket

487*	G.A.Headley/C.C.Passailaigue	Jamaica v Tennyson's	Kingston	1931-32
428	W.W.Armstrong/M.A.Noble	Australians v Sussex	Hove	1902
411	R.M.Poore/E.G.Wynyard	Hampshire v Somerset	Taunton	1899

Seventh Wicket

460	Bhupinder Singh jr/P.Dharmani	Punjab v Delhi	Delhi	1994-95
347	D.St E.Atkinson/C.C.Depeiza	W Indies v Australia	Bridgetown	1954-55
344	K.S.Ranjitsinhji/W.Newham	Sussex v Essex	Leyton	1902

Eighth Wicket

433	V.T.Trumper/A.Sims	Australians v C'bury	Christchurch	1913-14
332	I.J.L.Trott/S.C.J.Broad	England v Pakistan	Lord's	2010
313	Wasim Akram/Saqlain Mushtaq	Pakistan v Zimbabwe	Sheikhupura	1996-97

Ninth Wicket

283	J.Chapman/A.Warren	Derbys v Warwicks	Blackwell	1910
268	J.B.Commins/N.Boje	SA 'A' v Mashonaland	Harare	1994-95
251	J.W.H.T.Douglas/S.N.Hare	Essex v Derbyshire	Leyton	1921

Tenth Wicket

307	A.F.Kippax/J.E.H.Hooker	NSW v Victoria	Melbourne	1928-29
249	C.T.Sarwate/S.N.Banerjee	Indians v Surrey	The Oval	1946
239	Aqil Arshad/Ali Raza	Lahore Whites v Hyderabad	Lahore	2004-05
235	F.E.Woolley/A.Fielder	Kent v Worcs	Stourbridge	1909

BOWLING RECORDS
2000 WICKETS IN A CAREER

	Career	Runs	Wkts	Avge	100w
W.Rhodes	1898-1930	69993	**4187**	16.71	23
A.P.Freeman	1914-36	69577	**3776**	18.42	17
C.W.L.Parker	1903-35	63817	**3278**	19.46	16
J.T.Hearne	1888-1923	54352	**3061**	17.75	15
T.W.J.Goddard	1922-52	59116	**2979**	19.84	16
W.G.Grace	1865-1908	51545	**2876**	17.92	10
A.S.Kennedy	1907-36	61034	**2874**	21.23	15
D.Shackleton	1948-69	53303	**2857**	18.65	20
G.A.R.Lock	1946-70/71	54709	**2844**	19.23	14
F.J.Titmus	1949-82	63313	**2830**	22.37	16
M.W.Tate	1912-37	50571	**2784**	18.16	13+1
G.H.Hirst	1891-1929	51282	**2739**	18.72	15
C.Blythe	1899-1914	42136	**2506**	16.81	14
D.L.Underwood	1963-87	49993	**2465**	20.28	10
W.E.Astill	1906-39	57783	**2431**	23.76	9
J.C.White	1909-37	43759	**2356**	18.57	14
W.E.Hollies	1932-57	48656	**2323**	20.94	14
F.S.Trueman	1949-69	42154	**2304**	18.29	12

	Career	Runs	Wkts	Avge	100w
J.B.Statham	1950-68	36999	**2260**	16.37	13
R.T.D.Perks	1930-55	53771	**2233**	24.07	16
J.Briggs	1879-1900	35431	**2221**	15.95	12
D.J.Shepherd	1950-72	47302	**2218**	21.32	12
E.G.Dennett	1903-26	42571	**2147**	19.82	12
T.Richardson	1892-1905	38794	**2104**	18.43	10
T.E.Bailey	1945-67	48170	**2082**	23.13	9
R.Illingworth	1951-83	42023	**2072**	20.28	10
F.E.Woolley	1906-38	41066	**2068**	19.85	8
N.Gifford	1960-88	48731	**2068**	23.56	4
G.Geary	1912-38	41339	**2063**	20.03	11
D.V.P.Wright	1932-57	49307	**2056**	23.98	10
J.A.Newman	1906-30	51111	**2032**	25.15	9
A.Shaw	1864-97	24580	**2026**+1	12.12	9
S.Haigh	1895-1913	32091	**2012**	15.94	11

ALL TEN WICKETS IN AN INNINGS

This feat has been achieved 81 times in first-class matches (excluding 12-a-side fixtures).
Three Times: A.P.Freeman (1929, 1930, 1931)
Twice: V.E.Walker (1859, 1865); H.Verity (1931, 1932); J.C.Laker (1956)

Instances since 1945:

W.E.Hollies	Warwickshire v Notts	Birmingham	1946
J.M.Sims	East v West	Kingston on Thames	1948
J.K.R.Graveney	Gloucestershire v Derbyshire	Chesterfield	1949
T.E.Bailey	Essex v Lancashire	Clacton	1949
R.Berry	Lancashire v Worcestershire	Blackpool	1953
S.P.Gupte	President's XI v Combined XI	Bombay	1954-55
J.C.Laker	Surrey v Australians	The Oval	1956
K.Smales	Nottinghamshire v Glos	Stroud	1956
G.A.R.Lock	Surrey v Kent	Blackheath	1956
J.C.Laker	England v Australia	Manchester	1956
P.M.Chatterjee	Bengal v Assam	Jorhat	1956-57
J.D.Bannister	Warwicks v Combined Services	Birmingham (M & B)	1959
A.J.G.Pearson	Cambridge U v Leicestershire	Loughborough	1961
N.I.Thomson	Sussex v Warwickshire	Worthing	1964
P.J.Allan	Queensland v Victoria	Melbourne	1965-66
I.J.Brayshaw	Western Australia v Victoria	Perth	1967-68
Shahid Mahmood	Karachi Whites v Khairpur	Karachi	1969-70
E.E.Hemmings	International XI v W Indians	Kingston	1982-83
P.Sunderam	Rajasthan v Vidarbha	Jodhpur	1985-86
S.T.Jefferies	Western Province v OFS	Cape Town	1987-88
Imran Adil	Bahawalpur v Faisalabad	Faisalabad	1989-90
G.P.Wickremasinghe	Sinhalese v Kalutara	Colombo	1991-92
R.L.Johnson	Middlesex v Derbyshire	Derby	1994
Naeem Akhtar	Rawalpindi B v Peshawar	Peshawar	1995-96
A.Kumble	India v Pakistan	Delhi	1998-99
D.S.Mohanty	East Zone v South Zone	Agartala	2000-01
O.D.Gibson	Durham v Hampshire	Chester-le-Street	2007
M.W.Olivier	Warriors v Eagles	Bloemfontein	2007-08
Zulfiqar Babar	Multan v Islamabad	Multan	2009-10

MOST WICKETS IN A MATCH

19	J.C.Laker	England v Australia	Manchester	1956

MOST WICKETS IN A SEASON

Wkts		Season	Matches	Overs	Mdns	Runs	Avge
304	A.P.Freeman	1928	37	1976.1	423	5489	18.05
298	A.P.Freeman	1933	33	2039	651	4549	15.26

The feat of taking 250 wickets in a season has been achieved on 12 occasions, the last instance been by A.P.Freeman in 1933. 200 or more wickets in a season have been taken on 59 occasions, the last being by G.A.R.Lock (212 wickets, average 12.02) in 1957.

The highest aggregates of wickets taken in a season since the reduction of County Championship matches in 1969 are as follows:

Wkts		Season	Matches	Overs	Mdns	Runs	Avge
134	M.D.Marshall	1982	22	822	225	2108	15.73
131	L.R.Gibbs	1971	23	1024.1	295	2475	18.89
125	F.D.Stephenson	1988	22	819.1	196	2289	18.31
121	R.D.Jackman	1980	23	746.2	220	1864	15.40

Since 1969 there have been 50 instances of bowlers taking 100 wickets in a season.

MOST HAT-TRICKS IN A CAREER

7	D.V.P.Wright
6	T.W.J.Goddard, C.W.L.Parker
5	S.Haigh, V.W.C.Jupp, A.E.G.Rhodes, F.A.Tarrant

ALL-ROUND RECORDS
THE 'DOUBLE'

3000 runs and 100 wickets: J.H.Parks (1937)

2000 runs and 200 wickets: G.H.Hirst (1906)

2000 runs and 100 wickets: F.E.Woolley (4), J.W.Hearne (3), W.G.Grace (2), G.H.Hirst (2), W.Rhodes (2), T.E.Bailey, D.E.Davies, G.L.Jessop, V.W.C.Jupp, J.Langridge, F.A.Tarrant, C.L.Townsend, L.F.Townsend

1000 runs and 200 wickets: M.W.Tate (3), A.E.Trott (2), A.S.Kennedy

Most Doubles: 16 – W.Rhodes; 14 – G.H.Hirst; 10 – V.W.C.Jupp

Double in Debut Season: D.B.Close (1949) – aged 18, the youngest to achieve this feat.

The feat of scoring 1000 runs and taking 100 wickets in a season has been achieved on 305 occasions, R.J.Hadlee (1984) and F.D.Stephenson (1988) being the only players to complete the 'double' since the reduction of County Championship matches in 1969.

WICKET-KEEPING RECORDS
1000 DISMISSALS IN A CAREER

	Career	Dismissals	Ct	St
R.W.Taylor	1960-88	1649	1473	176
J.T.Murray	1952-75	1527	1270	257
H.Strudwick	1902-27	1497	1242	255
A.P.E.Knott	1964-85	1344	1211	133
R.C.Russell	1981-2004	1320	1192	128
F.H.Huish	1895-1914	1310	933	377
B.Taylor	1949-73	1294	1083	211
S.J.Rhodes	1981-2004	1263	1139	124
D.Hunter	1889-1909	1253	906	347
H.R.Butt	1890-1912	1228	953	275
J.H.Board	1891-1914/15	1207	852	355
H.Elliott	1920-47	1206	904	302
J.M.Parks	1949-76	1181	1088	93
R.Booth	1951-70	1126	948	178
L.E.G.Ames	1926-51	1121	703	418
D.L.Bairstow	1970-90	1099	961	138

	Career	Dismissals	Ct	St
G.Duckworth	1923-47	**1096**	753	343
H.W.Stephenson	1948-64	**1082**	748	334
J.G.Binks	1955-75	**1071**	895	176
T.G.Evans	1939-69	**1066**	816	250
A.Long	1960-80	**1046**	922	124
G.O.Dawkes	1937-61	**1043**	895	148
R.W.Tolchard	1965-83	**1037**	912	125
W.L.Cornford	1921-47	**1017**	675	342

MOST DISMISSALS IN AN INNINGS

9	(8ct, 1st)	Tahir Rashid	Habib Bank v PACO	Gujranwala	1992-93
9	(7ct, 2st)	W.R.James	Matabeleland v Mashonaland CD	Bulawayo	1995-96
8	(8ct)	A.T.W.Grout	Queensland v W Australia	Brisbane	1959-60
8	(8ct)	D.E.East	Essex v Somerset	Taunton	1985
8	(8ct)	S.A.Marsh	Kent v Middlesex	Lord's	1991
8	(6ct, 2st)	T.J.Zoehrer	Australians v Surrey	The Oval	1993
8	(7ct, 1st)	D.S.Berry	Victoria v South Australia	Melbourne	1996-97
8	(7ct, 1st)	Y.S.S.Mendis	Bloomfield v Kurunegala Youth	Colombo	2000-01
8	(7ct, 1st)	S.Nath	Assam v Tripura (*on debut*)	Gauhati	2001-02
8	(8ct)	J.N.Batty	Surrey v Kent	The Oval	2004
8	(8ct)	Golam Mabud	Sylhet v Dhaka	Dhaka	2005-06
8	(8ct)	D.C.de Boorder	Otago v Wellington	Wellington	2009-10

MOST DISMISSALS IN A MATCH

13	(11ct, 2st)	W.R.James	Matabeleland v Mashonaland CD	Bulawayo	1995-96
12	(8ct, 4st)	E.Pooley	Surrey v Sussex	The Oval	1868
12	(9ct, 3st)	D.Tallon	Queensland v NSW	Sydney	1938-39
12	(9ct, 3st)	H.B.Taber	NSW v South Australia	Adelaide	1968-69
12	(12ct)	P.D.McGlashan	Northern Districts v Central Districts	Whangarei	2009-10
12	(11ct, 1st)	T.L.Tsolekile	Lions v Dolphins	Johannesburg	2010-11
12	(12ct)	Kashif Mahmood	Lahore Shalimar v Abbottabad	Abbottabad	2010-11

MOST DISMISSALS IN A SEASON

128	(79ct, 49st)	L.E.G.Ames			1929

FIELDING RECORDS

750 CATCHES IN A CAREER

1018	F.E.Woolley	1906-38	784	J.G.Langridge	1928-55
887	W.G.Grace	1865-1908	764	W.Rhodes	1898-1930
830	G.A.R.Lock	1946-70/71	758	C.A.Milton	1948-74
819	W.R.Hammond	1920-51	754	E.H.Hendren	1907-38
813	D.B.Close	1949-86			

MOST CATCHES IN AN INNINGS

7	M.J.Stewart	Surrey v Northamptonshire	Northampton	1957
7	A.S.Brown	Gloucestershire v Nottinghamshire	Nottingham	1966
7	R.Clarke	Warwickshire v Lancashire	Liverpool	2011

MOST CATCHES IN A MATCH

10	W.R.Hammond	Gloucestershire v Surrey	Cheltenham	1928
9	R.Clarke	Warwickshire v Lancashire	Liverpool	2011

MOST CATCHES IN A SEASON

78	W.R.Hammond	1928	77	M.J.Stewart	1957

ENGLAND LIMITED-OVERS INTERNATIONALS 2011

AUSTRALIA v ENGLAND

TWENTY20 INTERNATIONALS

Adelaide Oval, 12 January. Toss: Australia. **ENGLAND** won by one wicket. Australia 157-4 (20; S.R.Watson 59). England 158-9 (20; S.R.Watson 4-15). Award: S.R.Watson. England debut: C.R.Woakes.
England became the first side in IT20 history to win eight consecutive games.

Melbourne Cricket Ground, 14 January. Toss: Australia. **AUSTRALIA** won by 4 runs. Australia 147-7 (20; A.J.Finch 53*). England 143-6 (20; M.G.Johnson 3-29). Award: A.J.Finch.

LIMITED-OVERS INTERNATIONALS

Melbourne Cricket Ground, 16 January. Toss: England. **AUSTRALIA** won by six wickets. England 294 (49.4; K.P.Pietersen 78, A.J.Strauss 63). Australia 297-4 (49.1; S.R.Watson 161*). Award: S.R.Watson.

Bellerive Oval, 21 January. Toss: England. **AUSTRALIA** won by 46 runs. Australia 230 (48.2; S.E.Marsh 110, C.T.Tremlett 3-22, A.Shahzad 3-43). England 184 (45; D.E.Bollinger 4-28). Award: S.E.Marsh.

Sydney Cricket Ground, 23 January. Toss: England. **AUSTRALIA** won by four wickets. England 214 (48; I.J.L.Trott 84*, B.Lee 3-27). Australia 215-6 (46; D.J.Hussey 68*, B.J.Haddin 64). Award: B.Lee. England debut: C.R.Woakes.

Adelaide Oval, 26 January. Toss: England. **ENGLAND** won by 21 runs. England 299-8 (50; I.J.L.Trott 102, M.J.Prior 67, D.J.Hussey 4-21, S.P.D.Smith 3-33). Australia 278-7 (50; S.R.Watson 64). Award: I.J.L.Trott.
P.D.Collingwood became the first England batsman to score 5000 runs in LOIs.

Woolloongabba, Brisbane, 30 January. Toss: Australia. **AUSTRALIA** won by 51 runs. Australia 249 (49.3; M.J.Clarke 54, C.R.Woakes 6-45). England 198 (45.3; S.R.Watson 3-25). Award: C.R.Woakes. England debut: S.T.Finn.
C.R.Woakes' figures were the second best LOI bowling analysis for England.
J.M.Anderson (20) and S.T.Finn (35) set a new LOI 10th-wicket partnership record for England of 53 in this match.*

Sydney Cricket Ground, 2 February. Toss: England. **AUSTRALIA** won by two wickets. England 333-6 (50; I.J.L.Trott 137, A.J.Strauss 63). Australia 334-8 (49.2; M.J.Clarke 82, M.G.Johnson 57, S.R.Watson 51). Award: I.J.L.Trott.
J.M.Anderson conceded 91 runs in his spell, the second highest for England in LOIs.

WACA Ground, Perth, 6 February. Toss: Australia. **AUSTRALIA** won by 57 runs. Australia 279-7 (50; A.C.Voges 80*, D.J.Hussey 60, J.M.Anderson 3-48). England 222 (44; M.H.Yardy 60*, M.G.Johnson 3-18, S.W.Tait 3-48). Award: A.C.Voges. Series award: S.R.Watson.

ICC WORLD CUP 2011

See pages 280-281 for details of these matches.

ENGLAND v SRI LANKA

TWENTY20 INTERNATIONAL

County Ground, Bristol, 25 June. Toss: Sri Lanka. **SRI LANKA** won by nine wickets. England 136-9 (20). Sri Lanka 137-1 (17.2; D.P.M.D.Jayawardena 72*). Award: D.P.M.D. Jayawardena. England debuts: J.W.Dernbach, S.R.Patel.

NATWEST SERIES LIMITED-OVERS INTERNATIONALS

The Oval, London, 28 June. Toss: Sri Lanka. **ENGLAND** won by 110 runs (D/L method). England 229-8 (32; C.Kieswetter 61, S.L.Malinga 3-40). Sri Lanka 121 (27; J.M.Anderson 4-18, G.P.Swann 3-18). Award: J.M.Anderson. England debut: J.W.Dernbach.

Headingley, Leeds, 1 July. Toss: England. **SRI LANKA** won by 69 runs. Sri Lanka 309-5 (50; D.P.M.D.Jayawardena 144, K.C.Sangakkara 69). England 240 (45.5; E.J.G.Morgan 52, R.A.S.Lakmal 3-43, H.K.S.R.Kaluhalamulla 3-43). Award: D.P.M.D.Jayawardena.

Lord's, London, 3 July. Toss: England. **SRI LANKA** won by six wickets. England 246-7 (50; A.N.Cook 119). Sri Lanka 249-4 (48.2; L.D.Chandimal 105*, D.P.M.D.Jayawardena 79). Award: L.D.Chandimal.

Trent Bridge, Nottingham, 6 July. Toss: England. **ENGLAND** won by ten wickets (D/L method). Sri Lanka 174 (43.4; K.C.Sangakkara 75, J.M.Anderson 3-24, J.W.Dernbach 3-38). England 171-0 (23.5; A.N.Cook 95*, C.Kieswetter 72*). Award: A.N.Cook.

This was England's third ten-wicket victory in LOIs.

Old Trafford, Manchester, 9 July. Toss: England. **ENGLAND** won by 16 runs. England 268-9 (50; I.J.L.Trott 72, E.J.G.Morgan 57, H.K.S.R.Kaluhalamulla 5-42). Sri Lanka 252 (48.2; A.D.Mathews 62, L.D.Chandimal 54, T.T.Bresnan 3-49). Award: I.J.L.Trott. Series award: A.N.Cook.

ENGLAND v IRELAND

RSA CHALLENGE LIMITED-OVERS INTERNATIONAL

Clontarf Cricket Club, Dublin, 25 August. Toss: Ireland. **ENGLAND** won by 11 runs (D/L method). England 201-8 (42; I.J.L.Trott 69, E.J.G.Morgan 59, J.F.Mooney 3-32). Ireland 117-8 (23; J.W.Dernbach 3-30). Award: E.J.G.Morgan. England debuts: S.G.Borthwick, B.A.Stokes, J.W.A.Taylor.

ENGLAND v INDIA

TWENTY20 INTERNATIONAL

Old Trafford, Manchester, 31 August. Toss: India. **ENGLAND** won by six wickets. India 165 (19.4; A.M.Rahane 61, J.W.Dernbach 4-22). England 169-4 (19.3). Award: J.W.Dernbach. England debuts: J.C.Buttler, A.D.Hales.

NATWEST SERIES LIMITED-OVERS INTERNATIONALS

Riverside Ground, Chester-le-Street, 3 September. Toss: England. **NO RESULT**. India 274-7 (50; P.A.Patel 95, V.Kohli 55). England 27-2 (7.2).

The Rose Bowl, Southampton, 6 September. Toss: England. **ENGLAND** won by seven wickets. India 187-8 (23; A.M.Rahane 54, G.P.Swann 3-33, T.T.Bresnan 3-43). England 188-3 (22.1; A.N.Cook 80*). Award: A.N.Cook.

The Oval, London, 9 September. Toss: England. **ENGLAND** won by three wickets (D/L method). India 234-7 (50; R.A.Jadeja 78, M.S.Dhoni 69, J.M.Anderson 3-48). England 218-7 (41.5/43; C.Kieswetter 51, R.Ashwin 3-40). Award: R.A.Jadeja.

Lord's, London, 11 September. Toss: England. **MATCH TIED** (D/L method). India 280-5 (50; S.K.Raina 84, M.S.Dhoni 78*). England 270-8 (48.5/48.5; R.S.Bopara 96, I.R.Bell 54, R.P.Singh 3-59). Award: R.S.Bopara and S.K.Raina.

Sophia Gardens, Cardiff, 16 September. Toss: England. **ENGLAND** won by six wickets (D/L method). India 304-6 (50; V.Kohli 107, R.Dravid 69, M.S.Dhoni 50*, G.P.Swann 3-34). England 241-4 (32.2/34; I.J.L.Trott 63, A.N.Cook 50). Award: J.M.Bairstow (41* in 21). Series award: M.S.Dhoni. England debut: J.M.Bairstow.

ENGLAND v WEST INDIES

NATWEST TWENTY20 SERIES

The Oval, London, 23 September. Toss: England. **ENGLAND** won by ten wickets. West Indies 125 (19.4; R.S.Bopara 4-10). England 128-0 (15.2; A.D.Hales 62*, C.Kieswetter 58*). Award: R.S.Bopara. England debuts: J.M.Bairstow, S.T.Finn, B.A.Stokes.
This was England's biggest win in IT20s. R.S.Bopara's figures were the best IT20 analysis for England.

The Oval, London, 25 September. Toss: England. **WEST INDIES** won by 25 runs. West Indies 113-5 (20). England 88 (16.4; G.E.Mathurin 3-9). Award: G.E.Mathurin. England debut: S.G.Borthwick.
This was England's lowest score in IT20s.

INDIA v ENGLAND

LIMITED-OVERS INTERNATIONALS

Rajiv Gandhi International Stadium, Hyderabad, 14 October. Toss: India. **INDIA** won by 126 runs. India 300-7 (50; M.S.Dhoni 87*, S.K.Raina 61). England 174 (36.1; A.N.Cook 60, R.A.Jadeja 3-34, R.Ashwin 3-35). Award: M.S.Dhoni.

Feroz Shah Kotla Stadium, Delhi, 17 October. Toss: England. **INDIA** won by eight wickets. England 237 (48.2; R.Vinay Kumar 4-30). India 238-2 (36.4; V.Kohli 112*, G.Gambhir 84*). Award: V.Kohli.

Punjab CA Stadium, Mohali, Chandigarh, 20 October. Toss: England. **INDIA** won by five wickets. England 298-4 (50; I.J.L.Trott 98*, S.R.Patel 70*, K.P.Pietersen 64). India 300-5 (49.2; A.M.Rahane 91, G.Gambhir 58). Award: A.M.Rahane.

Wankhede Stadium, Mumbai, 23 October. Toss: England. **INDIA** won by six wickets. England 220 (46.1; V.R.Aaron 3-24, R.Ashwin 3-38). India 223-4 (40.1; V.Kohli 86*, S.K.Raina 80, S.T.Finn 3-45). Award: S.K.Raina. England debut: S.C.Meaker.

Eden Gardens, Kolkata, 25 October. Toss: England. **INDIA** won by 95 runs. India 271-8 (50; M.S.Dhoni 75*, S.R.Patel 3-57). England 176 (37; C.Kieswetter 63, A.N.Cook 60, R.A.Jadeja 4-33, R.Ashwin 3-28). Award: R.A.Jadeja. Series award: M.S.Dhoni.

TWENTY20 INTERNATIONAL

Eden Gardens, Kolkata, 29 October. Toss: India. **ENGLAND** won by six wickets. India 120-9 (20; S.T.Finn 3-22). England 121-4 (18.4; K.P.Pietersen 53). Award: K.P.Pietersen.

ENGLAND'S RESULTS IN 2011

	P	W	L	T	NR	A
Limited Overs	30	11	16	2	1	–
Twenty20	7	4	3	–	–	–
Overall	37	15	19	2	1	–

500 RUNS IN LIMITED-OVERS INTERNATIONALS IN 2011

	M	I	NO	HS	Runs	Avge	100	50	S/Rate
I.J.L.Trott	29	28	3	137	1315	52.60	2	10	80.03
I.R.Bell	25	24	1	81	612	26.60	–	3	77.86
A.N.Cook	15	15	2	119	600	46.15	1	5	93.16
K.P.Pietersen	19	18	–	78	571	31.72	–	3	89.63
A.J.Strauss	14	14	–	158	513	36.64	1	3	89.37

20 WICKETS IN LIMITED-OVERS INTERNATIONALS IN 2011

	Pl	O	M	R	W	Avge	Best	4wI	Econ
T.T.Bresnan	24	210.2	10	1136	32	35.50	5-48	1	5.40
G.P.Swann	21	192	11	853	31	27.51	3-18	–	4.44
J.M.Anderson	18	156.2	8	873	25	34.92	4-18	1	5.58

ICC WORLD CUP 2011

The tenth ICC World Cup took place in Bangladesh, India and Sri Lanka between 19 February and 2 April.

GROUP A	P	W	L	T	A	Pts	Net RR
Pakistan	6	5	1	–	–	10	+0.76
Sri Lanka	6	4	1	–	1	9	+2.52
Australia	6	4	1	–	1	9	+1.12
New Zealand	6	4	2	–	–	8	+1.14
Zimbabwe	6	2	4	–	–	4	+0.03
Canada	6	1	5	–	–	2	–1.99
Kenya	6	–	6	–	–	0	–3.04

GROUP B	P	W	L	T	A	Pts	Net RR
South Africa	6	5	1	–	–	10	+2.03
India	6	4	1	1	–	9	+0.90
England	6	3	2	1	–	7	+0.07
West Indies	6	3	3	–	–	6	+1.07
Bangladesh	6	3	3	–	–	6	–1.36
Ireland	6	2	4	–	–	4	–0.70
Netherlands	6	–	6	–	–	0	–3.04

Vidarbha CA Stadium, Nagpur, 22 February. Toss: Netherlands. **ENGLAND** won by six wickets. Netherlands 292-6 (50; R.N.ten Doeschate 119). England 296-4 (48.4; A.J.Strauss 88, I.J.L.Trott 62). Award: R.N.ten Doeschate.

M.Chinnaswamy Stadium, Bangalore, 27 February. Toss: India. **MATCH TIED**. India 338 (49.5; S.R.Tendulkar 120, Yuvraj Singh 58, G.Gambhir 51, T.T.Bresnan 5-48). England 338-8 (50; A.J.Strauss 158, I.R.Bell 69, Z.Khan 3-64). Award: A.J.Strauss.

M.Chinnaswamy Stadium, Bangalore, 2 March. Toss: England. **IRELAND** won by three wickets. England 327-8 (50; I.J.L.Trott 92, I.R.Bell 81, K.P.Pietersen 59, J.F.Mooney 4-63). Ireland 329-7 (49.1; K.J.O'Brien 113, G.P.Swann 3-47). Award: K.J.O'Brien.

M.A.Chidambaram Stadium, Chennai, 6 March. Toss: England. **ENGLAND** won by 6 runs. England 171 (45.4; R.S.Bopara 60, I.J.L.Trott 52, Imran Tahir 4-38, R.J.Peterson 3-22). South Africa 165 (47.4; S.C.J.Broad 4-15). Award: R.S. Bopara.

Z.A.Chowdhury Stadium, Chittagong, 11 March. Toss: Bangladesh. **BANGLADESH** won by two wickets. England 225 (49.4; I.J.L.Trott 67, E.J.G.Morgan 63). Bangladesh 227-8 (49; Imrul Kayes 60, A.Shahzad 3-43). Award: Imrul Kayes.

M.A.Chidambaram Stadium, Chennai, 17 March. Toss: England. **ENGLAND** won by 18 runs. England 243 (48.4; A.D.Russell 4-49, D.Bishoo 3-34). West Indies 225 (44.4; J.C.Tredwell 4-48, G.P.Swann 3-36). Award: J.C.Tredwell.

QUARTER-FINALS

Shere Bangla National Stadium, Mirpur, 23 March. Toss: West Indies. **PAKISTAN** won by ten wickets. West Indies 112 (43.3; Shahid Afridi 4-30). Pakistan 113-0 (20.5; Mohammad Hafeez 61*). Award: Mohammad Hafeez.

Sardar Patel Stadium, Ahmedabad, 24 March. Toss: Australia. **INDIA** won by five wickets. Australia 260-6 (50; R.T.Ponting 104, B.J.Haddin 53). India 261-5 (47.4; Yuvraj Singh 57*, S.R.Tendulkar 53, G.Gambhir 50). Award: Yuvraj Singh.

Shere Bangla National Stadium, Mirpur, 25 March. Toss: New Zealand. **NEW ZEALAND** won by 49 runs. New Zealand 221-8 (50; J.D.Ryder 83, M.Morkel 3-46). South Africa 172 (43.2; J.D.P.Oram 4-39, N.L.McCullum 3-24). Award: J.D.P.Oram.

R.Premadasa Stadium, Colombo, 26 March. Toss: England. **SRI LANKA** won by ten wickets. England 229-6 (50; I.J.L.Trott 86, E.J.G.Morgan 50). Sri Lanka 231-0 (39.3; T.M.Dilshan 108*, W.U.Tharanga 102*). Award: T.M.Dilshan.

SEMI-FINALS

R.Premadasa Stadium, Colombo, 29 March. Toss: New Zealand. **SRI LANKA** won by five wickets. New Zealand 217 (48.5; S.B.Styris 57, B.A.W.Mendis 3-35, S.L.Malinga 3-55). Sri Lanka 220-5 (47.5; T.M.Dilshan 73, K.C.Sangakkara 54, T.G.Southee 3-57). Award: K.C.Sangakkara.

Punjab CA Stadium, Mohali, Chandigarh, 30 March. Toss: India. **INDIA** won by 29 runs. India 260-9 (50; S.R.Tendulkar 85, Wahab Riaz 5-46). Pakistan 231 (49.5; Misbah-ul-Haq 56). Award: S.R.Tendulkar.

FINAL

Wankhede Stadium, Mumbai, 2 April. Toss: Sri Lanka. **INDIA** won by six wickets. Sri Lanka 274-6 (50; D.P.M.D.Jayawardena 103*). India 277-4 (48.2; G.Gambhir 97, M.S.Dhoni 91*). Award: M.S.Dhoni.

RECORDS

Match

Highest score	370-4 (50)		India v Bangladesh	Group B	Dhaka
Lowest score	58	(18.5)	Bangladesh v West Indies	Group B	Dhaka
Highest innings	175	V.Sehwag	India v Bangladesh	Group B	Dhaka
Fastest fifty	23 balls	K.A.Pollard	West Indies v Netherlands	Group B	Delhi
Fastest hundred	50 balls	K.J.O'Brien	Ireland v England	Group B	Bangalore
Highest partnership	282	W.U.Tharanga/T.M.Dilshan	Sri Lanka v Zimbabwe	Group A	Pallekele
Best analysis	6-27	K.A.J.Roach	West Indies v Netherlands	Group B	Delhi

Tournament

Man of the Series		Yuvraj Singh	India (362 runs @ 92.50, 15 wkts @ 25.13)
Most runs	500	T.M.Dilshan	Sri Lanka (ave 62.50, strike rate 90.7)
Highest strike rate	150.0	K.A.Pollard	West Indies (180 runs in 120 balls) Qual: 100 runs
Most sixes	14	L.R.P.L.Taylor	New Zealand (324 runs)
Most wickets	21	Shahid Afridi	Pakistan (ave 12.85, economy 3.62)
	21	Z.Khan	India (ave 18.76, economy 4.83)
Most economical	3.14	B.A.W.Mendis	Sri Lanka (134 runs in 42.4 overs) Qual: 30 overs
Most dismissals	14 (10ct, 4st)	K.C.Sangakkara	Sri Lanka
Most catches	8	D.P.M.D.Jayawardena	Sri Lanka

LIMITED-OVERS INTERNATIONALS
CAREER RECORDS

These records, complete to 10 March 2012, include all players registered for county cricket for the 2012 season at the time of going to press, plus those who have appeared in LOI matches for ICC full member countries since 5 October 2010.

ENGLAND – BATTING AND FIELDING

	M	I	NO	HS	Runs	Avge	100	50	Ct/St
K.Ali	14	9	3	39*	93	15.50	–	–	1
T.R.Ambrose	5	5	1	6	10	2.50	–	–	3
J.M.Anderson	154	63	34	20*	199	6.86	–	–	42
J.M.Bairstow	6	5	1	41*	90	22.50	–	–	3
G.J.Batty	10	8	2	17	30	5.00	–	–	4
I.R.Bell	108	104	9	126*	3234	34.04	1	19	35
I.D.Blackwell	34	29	2	82	403	14.92	–	1	8
R.S.Bopara	72	67	12	96	1668	30.32	–	8	23
S.G.Borthwick	2	2	–	15	18	9.00	–	–	–
T.T.Bresnan	58	45	13	80	673	21.03	–	1	15
D.R.Briggs	1	–	–	–	–	–	–	–	–
S.C.J.Broad	87	49	16	45*	393	11.90	–	–	18
J.C.Buttler	1	1	–	0	0	0.00	–	–	–
G.Chapple	1	1	–	14	14	14.00	–	–	–
R.Clarke	20	13	–	39	144	11.07	–	–	11
P.D.Collingwood	197	181	37	120*	5092	35.36	5	26	108
A.N.Cook	45	45	2	137	1781	41.41	4	11	17
R.D.B.Croft	50	36	12	32	345	14.37	–	–	11
S.M.Davies	8	8	–	87	244	30.50	–	1	8
J.L.Denly	9	9	–	67	268	29.77	–	2	5
J.W.Dernbach	14	4	1	5	13	4.33	–	–	3
S.T.Finn	15	8	5	35	62	20.66	–	–	3
J.S.Foster	11	6	3	13	41	13.66	–	–	13/7
P.J.Franks	1	1	–	4	4	4.00	–	–	1
S.J.Harmison	58	25	14	18*	91	8.27	–	–	10
M.J.Hoggard	26	6	2	7	17	4.25	–	–	5
G.O.Jones	49	41	8	80	815	24.69	–	4	68/4
S.P.Jones	8	1	–	1	1	1.00	–	–	–
E.C.Joyce †	17	17	–	107	471	27.70	1	3	6
R.W.T.Key	5	5	–	19	54	10.80	–	–	–
C.Kieswetter	32	30	1	107	861	29.68	1	5	31/8
A.McGrath	14	12	2	52	166	16.60	–	1	4
D.L.Maddy	8	6	–	53	113	18.83	–	1	1
S.I.Mahmood	26	15	4	22*	85	7.72	–	–	4
A.D.Mascarenhas	20	13	2	52	245	22.27	–	1	4
S.C.Meaker	2	2	–	1	2	1.00	–	–	–
E.J.G.Morgan †	52	50	11	110*	1563	40.07	3	10	19
P.Mustard	10	10	–	83	233	23.30	–	1	9/2
G.Onions	4	1	–	1	1	1.00	–	–	–
M.S.Panesar	26	8	3	13	26	5.20	–	–	3
S.R.Patel	25	15	4	70*	340	30.90	–	1	7
K.P.Pietersen	127	116	16	130	4184	41.84	9	23	39
L.E.Plunkett	29	25	10	56	315	21.00	–	1	7
M.J.Prior	68	62	9	87	1282	24.18	–	3	71/8
A.U.Rashid	5	4	1	31*	60	20.00	–	–	2
C.M.W.Read	36	24	7	30*	300	17.64	–	–	41/2
O.A.Shah	71	66	6	107*	1834	30.56	1	12	21
A.Shahzad	11	8	2	9	39	6.50	–	–	4
R.J.Sidebottom	25	18	8	24	133	13.30	–	–	6

	M	I	NO	HS	Runs	Avge	100	50	Ct/St
V.S.Solanki	51	46	5	106	1097	26.75	2	5	16
B.A.Stokes	5	3	–	20	30	10.00	–	–	3
A.J.Strauss	127	126	8	158	4205	35.63	6	27	57
G.P.Swann	67	44	12	34	468	14.62	–	–	25
J.W.A.Taylor	1	1	–	1	1	1.00	–	–	–
J.C.Tredwell	5	3	1	16	27	13.50	–	–	–
C.T.Tremlett	15	11	4	19*	50	7.14	–	–	4
M.E.Trescothick	123	122	6	137	4335	37.37	12	21	49
I.J.L.Trott	44	42	4	137	1836	48.31	3	15	11
J.O.Troughton	6	5	1	20	36	9.00	–	–	1
C.R.Woakes	4	4	2	19*	39	19.50	–	–	1
L.J.Wright	46	35	4	52	701	22.61	–	2	17
M.H.Yardy	28	24	8	60*	326	20.37	–	2	10

ENGLAND – BOWLING

	O	M	R	W	Avge	Best	4wI	R/Over
K.Ali	112.1	4	682	20	34.10	4-45	1	6.08
J.M.Anderson	1275.2	98	6414	208	30.83	5-23	10	5.02
G.J.Batty	73.2	1	366	5	73.20	2-40	–	4.99
I.R.Bell	14.4	0	88	6	14.66	3- 9	–	6.00
I.D.Blackwell	205	8	877	24	36.54	3-26	–	4.27
R.S.Bopara	114.5	7	596	13	45.84	4-38	1	5.19
S.G.Borthwick	9	0	72	0	–	–	–	8.00
T.T.Bresnan	485.5	22	2598	69	37.65	5-48	2	5.34
D.R.Briggs	10	0	39	2	19.50	2-39	–	3.90
S.C.J.Broad	735.2	45	3828	142	26.95	5-23	10	5.20
G.Chapple	4	0	14	0	–	–	–	3.50
R.Clarke	78.1	3	415	11	37.72	2-28	–	5.30
P.D.Collingwood	864.2	14	4294	111	38.68	6-31	4	4.96
R.D.B.Croft	411	25	1743	45	38.73	3-51	–	4.24
J.W.Dernbach	116.4	4	710	20	35.50	4-45	1	6.08
S.T.Finn	142.4	8	670	28	23.92	4-34	2	4.69
P.J.Franks	9	0	48	0	–	–	–	5.33
S.J.Harmison	483.1	29	2481	76	32.64	5-33	3	5.13
M.J.Hoggard	217.4	13	1152	32	36.00	5-49	1	5.29
S.P.Jones	58	9	275	7	39.28	2-43	–	4.74
A.McGrath	38	2	175	4	43.75	1-13	–	4.60
S.I.Mahmood	199.3	7	1169	30	38.96	4-50	1	5.85
A.D.Mascarenhas	137	6	634	13	48.76	3-23	–	4.62
S.C.Meaker	19	1	110	2	55.00	1-45	–	5.78
G.Onions	34	1	185	4	46.25	2-58	–	5.44
M.S.Panesar	218	10	980	24	40.83	3-25	–	4.49
S.R.Patel	150.5	4	839	23	36.47	5-41	1	5.56
K.P.Pietersen	66.4	0	370	7	52.85	2-22	–	5.55
L.E.Plunkett	227.1	7	1321	39	33.87	3-24	–	5.81
A.U.Rashid	34	0	191	3	63.66	1-16	–	5.61
O.A.Shah	32.1	1	184	7	26.28	3-15	–	5.72
A.Shahzad	98	5	490	17	28.82	3-41	–	5.00
R.J.Sidebottom	212.5	12	1039	29	35.82	3-19	–	4.88
V.S.Solanki	18.3	0	105	1	105.00	1-17	–	5.67
A.J.Strauss	1	0	3	0	–	–	–	3.00
G.P.Swann	534	24	2385	92	25.92	5-28	4	4.46
J.C.Tredwell	37	2	200	4	50.00	4-48	1	5.40
C.T.Tremlett	130.4	2	705	15	47.00	4-32	1	5.39
M.E.Trescothick	38.4	0	219	4	54.75	2- 7	–	5.66
I.J.L.Trott	30.3	0	166	2	83.00	2-31	–	5.44

	O	M	R	W	Avge	Best	4wI	R/Over
C.R.Woakes	32.2	1	169	7	24.14	6-45	1	5.22
L.J.Wright	170	2	863	15	57.53	2-34	–	5.07
M.H.Yardy	222	7	1075	21	51.19	3-24	–	4.84

† E.C.Joyce has also made 13 appearances for Ireland and E.J.G.Morgan has also made 23 appearances for Ireland (see below).

AUSTRALIA – BATTING AND FIELDING

	M	I	NO	HS	Runs	Avge	100	50	Ct/St
D.E.Bollinger	39	8	2	30	50	8.33	–	–	12
D.T.Christian	11	11	3	39	191	23.87	–	–	6
M.J.Clarke	212	194	42	130	6953	45.74	7	51	81
P.J.Cummins	3	2	2	11*	17	–	–	–	–
M.J.Di Venuto	9	9	–	89	241	26.77	–	2	1
X.J.Doherty	27	10	6	13*	46	11.50	–	–	13
C.J.Ferguson	30	25	9	71*	663	41.43	–	5	7
P.J.Forrest	7	7	–	104	250	35.71	1	2	4
B.J.Haddin	93	87	7	110	2511	31.38	2	15	127/9
R.J.Harris	21	13	7	21	48	8.00	–	–	6
J.W.Hastings	11	9	4	21*	82	16.40	–	–	2
N.M.Hauritz	58	32	17	53*	336	22.40	–	1	24
M.C.Henriques	2	2	–	12	18	9.00	–	–	–
B.W.Hilfenhaus	20	8	5	16	29	9.66	–	–	9
J.R.Hopes	84	61	8	63*	1326	25.01	–	3	25
D.J.Hussey	50	43	5	111	1379	36.28	1	11	23
M.E.K.Hussey	176	148	44	109*	5088	48.92	3	36	99
P.A.Jaques	6	6	–	94	125	20.83	–	1	3
M.G.Johnson	107	60	20	73*	708	17.70	–	2	24
S.M.Katich	45	42	5	107*	1324	35.78	1	9	13
J.J.Krejza	8	2	1	7	13	13.00	–	–	2
B.Lee	212	102	41	57	1013	16.60	–	2	52
N.M.Lyon	1	1	–	0	0	0.00	–	–	1
C.J.McKay	23	10	2	28	78	9.75	–	–	2
M.R.Marsh	1	1	1	8*	8	–	–	–	1
S.E.Marsh	36	36	1	112	1274	36.40	2	8	8
D.P.Nannes	1	1	1	1	1	1.00	–	–	–
M.J.North	2	2	–	5	6	3.00	–	–	1
T.D.Paine	26	26	1	111	737	29.48	1	5	35/4
J.L.Pattinson	5	2	1	12	12	12.00	–	–	2
R.T.Ponting	375	365	39	164	13704	42.03	30	82	160
P.M.Siddle	17	4	2	9*	21	10.50	–	–	1
S.P.D.Smith	29	19	4	46*	343	22.86	–	–	14
M.A.Starc	7	2	–	17	31	15.50	–	–	1
S.W.Tait	35	7	5	11	25	12.50	–	–	8
A.C.Voges	15	14	5	80*	392	43.55	–	2	2
M.S.Wade	11	11	–	67	341	31.00	–	–	17/2
D.A.Warner	21	21	–	163	716	34.09	2	3	6
S.R.Watson	145	126	24	185*	4307	42.22	6	26	51
C.L.White	87	73	15	105	2037	35.12	2	11	37

AUSTRALIA – BOWLING

	O	M	R	W	Avge	Best	4wI	R/Over
D.E.Bollinger	323.4	28	1482	62	23.90	5-35	5	4.57
D.T.Christian	70.1	2	347	13	26.69	5-31	1	4.94
M.J.Clarke	394.4	7	2006	53	37.84	5-35	2	5.08
P.J.Cummins	23	1	150	5	30.00	3-28	–	6.52

	O	M	R	W	Avge	Best	4wI	R/Over
X.J.Doherty	227.3	4	1030	29	35.51	4-28	2	4.52
R.J.Harris	171.5	13	832	44	18.90	5-19	3	4.84
J.W.Hastings	91	1	410	8	51.25	2-35	–	4.50
N.M.Hauritz	454	12	2152	63	34.15	4-29	2	4.74
M.C.Henriques	15	0	84	1	84.00	1-51	–	5.60
B.W.Hilfenhaus	164.5	13	926	27	34.29	5-33	1	5.61
J.R.Hopes	526.1	32	2384	67	35.58	5-14	1	4.53
D.J.Hussey	103.5	1	544	18	30.22	4-21	2	5.23
M.E.K.Hussey	39	1	227	2	113.50	1-22	–	5.82
M.G.Johnson	872.2	51	4237	168	25.22	6-31	9	4.85
J.J.Krejza	70.5	0	331	7	47.28	2-28	–	4.67
B.Lee	1795.1	132	8512	369	23.06	5-22	23	4.74
N.M.Lyon	8	0	36	0	–	–	–	4.50
C.J.McKay	193.1	15	923	45	20.51	5-28	4	4.77
M.R.Marsh	4	0	19	1	19.00	1-19	–	4.75
D.P.Nannes	7	1	20	1	20.00	1-20	–	2.85
M.J.North	3	0	16	0	–	–	–	5.33
J.L.Pattinson	40	2	227	8	28.37	4-51	1	5.67
R.T.Ponting	25	0	104	3	34.66	1-12	–	4.16
P.M.Siddle	125.1	9	581	15	38.73	3-55	–	4.64
S.P.D.Smith	143.5	0	755	22	34.31	3-33	–	5.24
M.A.Starc	53.4	0	278	9	30.88	4-27	1	5.18
S.W.Tait	281.2	11	1461	62	23.56	4-39	2	5.19
A.C.Voges	25	0	159	1	159.00	1-22	–	6.36
S.R.Watson	873	27	4196	145	28.93	4-36	3	4.80
C.L.White	55.1	2	351	12	29.25	3- 5	–	6.36

SOUTH AFRICA – BATTING AND FIELDING

	M	I	NO	HS	Runs	Avge	100	50	Ct/St
H.M.Amla	57	56	5	140	2881	56.49	9	18	21
D.M.Benkenstein	23	20	3	69	305	17.94	–	1	3
J.Botha	78	50	18	46	609	19.03	–	–	36
M.V.Boucher	290	216	57	147*	4523	28.44	1	25	395/21
M.de Lange	1	–	–	–	–	–	–	–	–
A.B.de Villiers	122	118	21	146	4848	49.97	13	27	94/3
J.P.Duminy	89	82	20	129	2536	40.90	2	15	39
F.du Plessis	21	20	3	72	536	31.52	–	4	10
H.H.Gibbs	248	240	16	175	8094	36.13	21	37	108
A.J.Hall	88	56	13	81	905	21.04	–	3	29
C.W.Henderson	4	–	–	–	–	–	–	–	–
Imran Tahir	5	2	2	1*	1	–	–	–	2
C.A.Ingram	15	13	2	124	388	35.27	2	–	4
J.H.Kallis	316	302	53	139	11469	46.06	17	85	125
C.K.Langeveldt	72	21	10	12	73	6.63	–	–	11
N.D.McKenzie	64	55	10	131*	1688	37.51	2	10	21
D.A.Miller	16	13	4	59	267	29.66	–	2	4
J.A.Morkel	56	41	10	97	760	24.51	–	2	15
M.Morkel	51	18	6	23*	88	7.33	–	–	14
J.L.Ontong	26	15	2	32	184	14.15	–	–	13
W.D.Parnell	22	10	2	49	164	20.50	–	–	7
A.N.Petersen	17	15	1	80	437	31.21	–	4	3
R.J.Peterson	55	25	9	36	258	16.12	–	–	23
V.D.Philander	8	6	3	23	75	25.00	–	–	2
A.G.Prince	49	38	11	89*	940	34.81	–	2	26
J.A.Rudolph	43	37	6	81	1157	37.32	–	7	11

	M	I	NO	HS	Runs	Avge	100	50	Ct/St
G.C.Smith	180	178	10	141	6598	39.27	9	45	97
D.W.Steyn	61	21	6	35	138	9.20	–	–	15
J.Theron	4	1	–	5	5	5.00	–	–	4
L.L.Tsotsobe	31	7	5	4*	14	7.00	–	–	5
M.N.van Wyk	13	13	1	82	331	27.58	–	3	8/1
C.M.Willoughby	3	2	–	0	0	0.00	–	–	–

SOUTH AFRICA – BOWLING

	O	M	R	W	Avge	Best	4wI	R/Over
D.M.Benkenstein	10.5	1	44	4	11.00	3- 5	–	4.06
J.Botha	637.1	13	2916	72	40.50	4-19	1	4.57
M.de Lange	9	1	46	4	11.50	4-46	1	5.11
A.B.de Villiers	2	0	22	0	–	–	–	11.00
J.P.Duminy	198.4	3	1005	25	40.20	3-31	–	5.05
F.du Plessis	20	0	115	1	115.00	1-22	–	5.75
A.J.Hall	556.5	30	2515	95	26.47	5-18	4	4.51
C.W.Henderson	36.1	2	132	7	18.85	4-17	1	3.64
Imran Tahir	39.3	2	150	14	10.71	4-38	2	3.79
J.H.Kallis	1754	77	8446	266	31.75	5-30	4	4.81
C.K.Langeveldt	581.3	29	2962	100	29.62	5-39	3	5.09
N.D.McKenzie	7.4	0	27	0	–	–	–	3.52
J.A.Morkel	329.3	13	1786	47	38.00	4-29	2	5.42
M.Morkel	417.2	19	2013	86	23.40	5-38	7	4.82
J.L.Ontong	89.4	3	396	9	44.00	3-30	–	4.41
W.D.Parnell	181.2	9	1066	33	32.30	5-48	3	5.87
A.N.Petersen	1	0	7	0	–	–	–	7.00
R.J.Peterson	369.3	11	1749	49	35.69	4-12	1	4.73
V.D.Philander	51.5	5	248	7	35.42	4-12	1	4.78
A.G.Prince	2	0	3	0	–	–	–	1.50
J.A.Rudolph	4	0	26	0	–	–	–	6.50
G.C.Smith	171	0	951	18	52.83	3-30	–	5.56
D.W.Steyn	501.4	31	2563	89	28.79	5-50	4	5.10
J.Theron	32.2	0	173	12	14.41	5-44	1	5.35
L.L.Tsotsobe	254.4	21	1163	58	20.05	4-22	4	4.56
C.M.Willoughby	28	2	148	2	74.00	2-39	–	5.28

WEST INDIES – BATTING AND FIELDING

	M	I	NO	HS	Runs	Avge	100	50	Ct/St
A.B.Barath	12	12	1	113	311	28.27	1	1	3
C.S.Baugh	42	30	9	49	418	19.90	–	–	33/9
S.J.Benn	25	16	2	31	109	7.78	–	–	1
D.Bishoo	13	7	2	6*	10	2.00	–	–	2
C.R.Brathwaite	1	1	–	11	11	11.00	–	–	–
D.J.Bravo	117	96	17	112*	1910	24.17	1	5	45
D.M.Bravo	34	31	5	86	856	32.92	–	6	6
S.Chanderpaul	268	251	40	150	8778	41.60	11	59	73
C.D.Collymore	84	35	17	15*	104	5.77	–	–	12
K.A.Edwards	9	9	1	40*	153	19.12	–	–	5
C.H.Gayle	225	220	16	153*	8032	39.37	19	43	98
D.P.Hyatt	9	9	1	39	112	14.00	–	–	1
A.Martin	9	6	5	4*	10	10.00	–	–	3
N.O.Miller	39	24	11	51	252	19.38	–	1	13
J.N.Mohammed	1	1	–	2	2	2.00	–	–	–
S.P.Narine	3	2	1	27*	35	35.00	–	–	1
K.A.Pollard	51	46	1	119	1066	23.68	1	4	20

	M	I	NO	HS	Runs	Avge	100	50	Ct/St
K.O.A.Powell	5	5	–	25	52	10.40	–	–	1
D.Ramdin	89	68	16	96	1067	20.51	–	3	119/5
R.Rampaul	65	28	6	86*	295	13.40	–	1	10
K.A.J.Roach	36	22	10	24*	126	10.50	–	–	4
A.D.Russell	16	13	3	92*	336	33.60	–	2	5
D.J.G.Sammy	70	54	16	58*	720	18.94	–	2	33
M.N.Samuels	125	116	19	108*	2973	30.64	2	22	34
R.R.Sarwan	173	161	31	115*	5644	43.41	4	38	45
L.M.P.Simmons	36	35	3	122	1100	34.37	1	10	14
D.S.Smith	42	40	2	107	1014	26.68	1	5	11
D.C.Thomas	9	7	1	29*	70	11.66	–	–	10/3

WEST INDIES – BOWLING

	O	M	R	W	Avge	Best	4wI	R/Over
S.J.Benn	207.5	13	924	29	31.86	4-18	3	4.44
D.Bishoo	111	3	476	20	23.80	3-34	–	4.28
D.J.Bravo	771.4	29	4055	136	29.81	4-19	4	5.25
S.Chanderpaul	123.2	0	636	14	45.42	3-18	–	5.15
C.D.Collymore	679	45	2924	83	35.22	5-51	2	4.30
C.H.Gayle	1148.1	37	5415	156	34.71	5-46	4	4.71
A.Martin	74	5	296	11	26.90	4-36	1	4.00
N.O.Miller	263.4	14	1219	30	40.63	4-43	1	4.62
S.P.Narine	26	1	121	3	40.33	2-34	–	4.65
K.A.Pollard	238.5	4	1295	37	35.00	3-27	–	5.42
R.Rampaul	452.1	27	2274	77	29.53	5-51	5	5.02
K.A.J.Roach	301.4	10	1489	56	26.58	6-27	3	4.93
A.D.Russell	112.5	6	603	21	28.71	4-35	2	5.34
D.J.G.Sammy	479.5	27	2234	49	45.59	4-26	1	4.65
M.N.Samuels	583.1	13	2786	63	44.22	3-25	–	4.77
R.R.Sarwan	96.5	3	586	16	36.62	3-31	–	6.05
L.M.P.Simmons	15	0	82	1	82.00	1- 3	–	5.46
D.S.Smith	2.5	0	17	0	–	–	–	6.00
D.C.Thomas	1.1	0	11	2	5.50	2-11	–	9.42

NEW ZEALAND – BATTING AND FIELDING

	M	I	NO	HS	Runs	Avge	100	50	Ct/St
A.R.Adams	42	34	10	45	419	17.45	–	–	8
G.W.Aldridge	2	–	–	–	–	–	–	–	–
M.D.Bates	2	1	–	13	13	13.00	–	–	1
H.K.Bennett	12	6	4	4*	7	3.50	–	–	–
D.A.J.Bracewell	5	3	1	8*	9	4.50	–	–	1
D.G.Brownlie	2	2	1	19	21	21.00	–	–	1
C.de Grandhomme	1	1	–	36	36	36.00	–	–	1
G.D.Elliott	37	28	6	115	716	32.54	1	4	6
A.M.Ellis	6	6	1	33	86	17.20	–	–	3
J.E.C.Franklin	94	67	23	98*	1036	23.54	–	3	25
M.J.Guptill	69	58	6	122*	2055	39.51	2	16	20
G.J.Hopkins	25	17	1	45	236	14.75	–	–	27/1
J.M.How	41	37	1	139	1046	29.05	1	7	19
T.W.M.Latham	3	3	1	48	79	39.50	–	–	–
B.B.McCullum	201	173	25	166	4531	30.47	4	22	228/15
N.L.McCullum	33	28	3	65	526	21.04	–	3	11
A.J.McKay	19	10	7	4*	12	4.00	–	–	3
H.J.H.Marshall	66	62	9	101*	1454	27.43	1	12	18
K.D.Mills	135	82	28	54	859	15.90	–	2	34

	M	I	NO	HS	Runs	Avge	100	50	Ct/St
T.S.Nethula	3	1	–	0	0	0.00	–	–	2
R.J.Nicol	9	9	1	146	391	48.87	2	1	4
J.D.P.Oram	155	111	15	101*	2377	24.76	1	13	49
J.S.Patel	39	13	7	34	88	14.66	–	–	12
A.J.Redmond	6	6	–	52	152	25.33	–	1	3
J.D.Ryder	39	33	1	107	1100	34.37	2	6	14
T.G.Southee	55	30	9	32	197	9.38	–	–	8
S.B.Styris	188	161	23	141	4483	32.48	4	28	73
L.R.P.L.Taylor	110	99	14	131*	3185	37.47	5	20	78
D.R.Tuffey	94	52	21	36	295	9.51	–	–	20
D.L.Vettori	272	172	51	83	2105	17.39	–	4	77
B.J.Watling	9	8	–	55	103	12.87	–	1	4
K.S.Williamson	24	22	4	108	633	35.16	2	1	8
L.J.Woodcock	4	2	1	11	14	14.00	–	–	1

NEW ZEALAND – BOWLING

	O	M	R	W	Avge	Best	4wI	R/Over
A.R.Adams	314.1	15	1643	53	31.00	5-22	3	5.22
G.W.Aldridge	19	1	98	1	98.00	1-45	–	5.15
M.D.Bates	14	1	52	2	26.00	1-24	–	3.71
H.K.Bennett	81.2	1	435	20	21.75	4-16	2	5.34
D.A.J.Bracewell	46	6	223	6	37.16	3-55	–	4.84
C.de Grandhomme	1	0	9	0	–	–	–	9.00
G.D.Elliott	95.3	7	464	19	24.42	4-31	1	4.85
A.M.Ellis	35	2	165	3	55.00	1-16	–	4.71
J.E.C.Franklin	580.5	33	2993	74	40.44	5-42	1	5.15
M.J.Guptill	10.5	1	53	2	26.50	2- 7	–	4.89
N.L.McCullum	224.3	3	1064	23	46.26	3-24	–	4.73
A.J.McKay	154.2	7	800	27	29.62	4-53	2	5.18
K.D.Mills	1103.4	101	5189	200	25.94	5-25	8	4.70
T.S.Nethula	30	1	156	4	39.00	2-41	–	5.20
R.J.Nicol	30.3	0	181	9	20.11	4-19	1	5.93
J.D.P.Oram	1112.5	90	4835	168	28.77	5-26	5	4.34
J.S.Patel	300.4	9	1513	42	36.02	3-11	–	5.03
J.D.Ryder	63.5	0	399	11	36.27	3-29	–	6.25
T.G.Southee	447	22	2354	72	32.69	5-33	4	5.26
S.B.Styris	1019	39	4839	137	35.32	6-25	5	4.74
L.R.P.L.Taylor	7	0	35	0	–	–	–	5.00
D.R.Tuffey	722.1	70	3534	110	32.12	4-24	2	4.89
D.L.Vettori	2150.3	90	8880	282	31.48	5- 7	9	4.12
K.S.Williamson	34.2	1	175	4	43.75	2-13	–	5.09
L.J.Woodcock	27.2	0	155	3	51.66	2-58	–	5.67

INDIA – BATTING AND FIELDING

	M	I	NO	HS	Runs	Avge	100	50	Ct/St
V.R.Aaron	4	1	1	6*	6	–	–	–	–
R.Ashwin	32	19	6	38	241	18.53	–	–	5
S.Badrinath	7	6	1	27*	79	15.80	–	–	2
P.P.Chawla	25	12	5	13*	38	5.42	–	–	9
S.Dhawan	5	5	–	51	69	13.80	–	1	1
M.S.Dhoni	203	181	50	183*	6702	51.16	7	45	192/64
R.S.Dravid	340	314	39	153	10768	39.15	12	82	196/14
G.Gambhir	131	127	11	150*	4708	40.58	9	31	34
Harbhajan Singh	227	121	33	49	1166	13.25	–	–	69
R.A.Jadeja	56	39	9	78	856	28.53	–	5	19
M.Kartik	37	14	5	32*	126	14.00	–	–	10

INDIA – BATTING AND FIELDING (continued)

	M	I	NO	HS	Runs	Avge	100	50	Ct/St
Z.Khan	189	95	31	34*	751	11.73	–	–	42
V.Kohli	82	79	11	133*	3233	47.54	9	20	41
P.Kumar	65	33	12	54*	292	13.90	–	1	11
A.Mishra	15	3	1	5*	5	2.50	–	–	2
A.Mithun	5	3	–	24	51	17.00	–	–	1
A.Nehra	117	45	21	24	140	5.83	–	–	17
M.M.Patel	70	27	16	15	74	6.72	–	–	11
P.A.Patel	38	34	3	95	736	23.74	–	4	30/9
I.K.Pathan	112	83	18	83	1468	22.58	–	5	19
Y.K.Pathan	56	41	11	123*	810	27.00	2	3	17
A.M.Rahane	11	11	–	91	340	30.90	–	2	3
S.K.Raina	143	123	23	116*	3432	34.32	3	20	58
W.P.Saha	3	1	–	4	4	4.00	–	–	6
V.Sehwag	235	229	9	219	7812	35.50	15	36	87
I.Sharma	47	16	6	13	47	4.70	–	–	12
R.Sharma	3	1	–	1	1	1.00	–	–	1
R.G.Sharma	77	73	16	114	1889	33.14	2	11	29
R.P.Singh	58	20	10	23	104	10.40	–	–	13
S.Sreesanth	53	21	10	10*	44	4.00	–	–	7
S.R.Tendulkar	460	449	41	200*	18254	44.74	48	95	139
M.K.Tiwary	6	6	1	104*	165	33.00	1	–	3
S.S.Tiwary	3	2	2	37*	49	–	–	–	2
M.Vijay	11	11	–	33	196	17.81	–	–	6
R.Vinay Kumar	21	9	3	18	43	7.16	–	–	3
U.T.Yadav	15	7	7	11*	26	–	–	–	3
Yuvraj Singh	271	249	37	139	7959	37.54	13	49	83

INDIA – BOWLING

	O	M	R	W	Avge	Best	4wI	R/Over
V.R.Aaron	28.1	1	156	6	26.00	3-24	–	5.53
R.Ashwin	284.1	8	1360	46	29.56	3-24	–	4.78
P.P.Chawla	218.4	6	1117	32	34.90	4-23	2	5.10
M.S.Dhoni	2	0	14	1	14.00	1-14	–	7.00
R.S.Dravid	31	1	170	4	42.50	2-43	–	5.48
G.Gambhir	1	0	13	0	–	–	–	13.00
Harbhajan Singh	1989.5	83	8550	255	33.52	5-31	5	4.29
R.A.Jadeja	429.2	16	2127	56	37.98	4-32	2	4.95
M.Kartik	317.5	19	1612	37	43.56	6-27	1	5.07
Z.Khan	1594.5	111	7872	265	29.70	5-42	8	4.93
V.Kohli	45.4	1	266	2	133.00	1-20	–	5.82
P.Kumar	513.2	45	2594	72	36.02	4-31	3	5.05
A.Mishra	127.1	11	575	19	30.26	4-31	1	4.52
A.Mithun	30	1	203	3	67.66	2-32	–	6.76
A.Nehra	939.3	53	4899	155	31.60	6-23	7	5.21
M.M.Patel	525.4	38	2603	86	30.26	4-29	3	4.95
I.K.Pathan	908.4	51	4770	160	29.81	5-27	5	5.24
Y.K.Pathan	243.2	3	1335	33	40.45	3-49	–	5.48
S.K.Raina	150.5	0	762	16	47.62	2-17	–	5.05
V.Sehwag	702	12	3676	93	39.52	4- 6	1	5.23
I.Sharma	358.5	13	2056	64	32.12	4-38	3	5.72
R.Sharma	26.2	0	132	5	26.40	3-43	–	5.01
R.G.Sharma	70.5	2	371	8	46.37	2-27	–	5.23
R.P.Singh	427.3	31	2343	69	33.95	4-35	2	5.48
S.Sreesanth	412.4	16	2508	75	33.44	6-55	3	6.07
S.R.Tendulkar	1340.4	24	6838	154	44.40	5-32	6	5.10
M.K.Tiwary	10	0	69	1	69.00	1-28	–	6.90

	O	M	R	W	Avge	Best	4wI	R/Over
R.Vinay Kumar	155.5	14	870	25	34.80	4-30	1	5.58
U.T.Yadav	120.2	4	727	16	45.43	3-38	–	6.04
Yuvraj Singh	795.2	18	3993	108	36.97	5-31	3	5.02

PAKISTAN – BATTING AND FIELDING

	M	I	NO	HS	Runs	Avge	100	50	Ct/St
Abdul Razzaq	261	225	57	112	5031	29.94	3	23	35
Abdur Rehman	23	17	4	31	92	7.07	–	–	3
Adnan Akmal	5	4	1	27	62	20.66	–	–	3
Ahmed Shehzad	19	19	1	115	477	26.50	2	–	7
Aizaz Cheema	9	4	1	6	15	5.00	–	–	2
Asad Shafiq	28	27	2	78*	766	30.64	–	6	5
Azhar Ali	4	4	–	58	133	33.25	–	1	1
Azhar Mahmood	143	110	26	67	1521	18.10	–	3	37
Fawad Alam	27	25	9	64	603	37.68	–	4	9
Hammad Azam	5	3	1	36	38	19.00	–	–	3
Imran Farhat	50	50	2	107	1493	31.10	1	11	14
Junaid Khan	11	3	2	1*	2	2.00	–	–	1
Kamran Akmal	137	120	14	124	2924	27.58	5	9	136/25
Misbah-ul-Haq	94	83	20	93*	2666	42.31	–	18	47
Mohammad Hafeez	95	95	4	139*	2388	26.24	3	12	31
Mohammad Salman	7	3	1	19*	22	11.00	–	–	8/2
Mohammad Yousuf	288	273	40	141*	9720	41.71	15	64	58
Naved-ul-Hasan	74	51	18	33	524	15.87	–	–	16
Saeed Ajmal	60	37	17	33	175	8.75	–	–	10
Sarfraz Ahmed	15	9	2	24	87	12.42	–	–	15/7
Shahid Afridi	333	309	19	124	6962	24.00	6	33	110
Shoaib Akhtar	158	80	39	43	361	8.80	–	–	20
Shoaib Malik	203	180	21	143	5253	33.03	7	31	70
Sohail Khan	5	1	–	4	4	4.00	–	–	–
Sohail Tanvir	43	26	9	59	268	15.76	–	1	10
Tanvir Ahmed	2	1	–	18	18	18.00	–	–	1
Taufiq Umar	22	22	1	81*	504	24.00	–	3	9
Umar Akmal	58	51	7	102*	1674	38.04	1	13	26/2
Umar Gul	102	49	14	34*	325	9.28	–	–	13
Usman Salahuddin	2	2	–	8	13	6.50	–	–	1
Wahab Riaz	24	16	5	21	88	8.00	–	–	7
Yasir Shah	1	–	–	–	–	–	–	–	–
Younus Khan	237	228	23	144	6747	32.91	6	46	121
Zulqarnain Haider	4	4	2	19*	48	24.00	–	–	1/1

PAKISTAN – BOWLING

	O	M	R	W	Avge	Best	4wI	R/Over
Abdul Razzaq	1808.3	107	8452	268	31.53	6-35	11	4.67
Abdur Rehman	205	11	854	18	47.44	2-20	–	4.16
Ahmed Shehzad	2.3	0	20	0	–	–	–	8.00
Aizaz Cheema	69.2	3	359	15	23.93	4-43	1	5.17
Azhar Mahmood	1040.2	58	4813	123	39.13	6-18	5	4.62
Fawad Alam	60.2	0	332	4	83.00	1- 8	–	5.50
Hammad Azam	18	0	85	1	85.00	1-26	–	4.72
Imran Farhat	19.2	2	110	6	18.33	3-10	–	5.68
Junaid Khan	77.2	4	374	12	31.16	4-12	1	4.83
Misbah-ul-Haq	4	0	30	0	–	–	–	7.50
Mohammad Hafeez	616.5	27	2550	77	33.11	3-17	–	4.13
Mohammad Yousuf	0.2	0	1	1	1.00	1- 0	–	3.00
Naved-ul-Hasan	577.4	25	3221	110	29.28	6-27	7	5.57

	O	M	R	W	Avge	Best	4wI	R/Over
Saeed Ajmal	519.4	25	2155	88	24.48	5-43	4	4.14
Shahid Afridi	2445.1	63	11255	339	33.20	6-38	12	4.60
Shoaib Akhtar	1251.3	93	5953	241	24.70	6-16	10	4.75
Shoaib Malik	1103	34	5019	139	36.10	4-19	1	4.55
Sohail Khan	42.1	1	199	6	33.16	3-30	–	4.71
Sohail Tanvir	343	19	1769	55	32.16	5-48	4	5.15
Tanvir Ahmed	10	0	83	2	41.50	1-38	–	8.30
Taufiq Umar	12	0	85	1	85.00	1-49	–	7.08
Umar Gul	791.1	56	4008	145	27.64	6-42	6	5.06
Wahab Riaz	185.2	9	980	40	24.50	5-46	1	5.28
Yasir Shah	10	0	51	2	25.50	2-51	–	5.10
Younus Khan	43.2	1	260	3	86.66	1- 3	–	6.00

SRI LANKA – BATTING AND FIELDING

	M	I	NO	HS	Runs	Avge	100	50	Ct/St
L.D.Chandimal	33	33	7	111	1070	41.15	2	7	13/1
T.M.Dilshan	235	211	31	160*	6409	35.60	12	26	96/1
R.M.S.Eranga	3	3	1	2	3	1.50	–	–	1
C.R.D.Fernando	146	61	35	20	239	9.19	–	–	27
H.M.R.K.B.Herath	29	11	6	14*	39	7.80	–	–	7
S.T.Jayasuriya	441	429	18	189	13364	32.51	28	68	123
D.P.M.D.Jayawardena	365	343	34	144	10232	33.11	14	63	183
H.K.S.R.Kaluhalamulla	28	15	1	56	239	17.07	–	1	6
S.H.T.Kandamby	38	35	6	93*	870	30.00	–	5	7
C.K.Kapugedera	89	73	7	95	1450	21.96	–	7	28
F.D.M.Karunaratne	2	2	–	60	64	32.00	–	1	–
C.K.B.Kulasekara	4	3	–	19	38	12.66	–	–	1
K.M.D.N.Kulasekara	114	74	25	73	832	16.97	–	2	29
R.A.S.Lakmal	12	5	4	1*	1	1.00	–	–	5
M.F.Maharoof	101	68	17	69*	1019	19.98	–	2	24
S.L.Malinga	115	57	16	56	316	7.70	–	1	16
A.D.Mathews	71	59	15	77*	1447	32.88	–	9	20
B.A.W.Mendis	59	27	13	15*	109	7.78	–	–	8
B.M.A.J.Mendis	19	16	5	48	211	19.18	–	–	4
M.Muralitharan	343	161	63	33*	674	6.87	–	–	128
N.L.T.C.Perera	34	27	5	69*	363	16.50	–	1	14
K.T.G.D.Prasad	12	6	3	31*	63	21.00	–	–	–
S.Prasanna	7	5	1	8*	18	4.50	–	–	1
T.T.Samaraweera	53	42	11	105*	862	27.80	2	–	17
K.C.Sangakkara	315	296	31	138*	10071	38.00	13	66	309/77
S.M.S.M.Senanayake	5	4	2	22*	37	18.50	–	–	2
L.P.C.Silva	75	62	7	107*	1587	28.85	1	13	20
W.U.Tharanga	141	135	7	133	4495	35.11	12	24	25
H.D.R.L.Thirimanne	15	11	–	69	310	28.18	–	3	6
W.P.J.U.C.Vaas	321	219	72	50*	2018	13.72	–	1	59

SRI LANKA – BOWLING

	O	M	R	W	Avge	Best	4wI	R/Over
T.M.Dilshan	637.5	17	3047	67	45.84	4- 4	3	4.77
R.M.S.Eranga	19	0	99	4	24.75	2-38	–	5.21
C.R.D.Fernando	1074.3	53	5612	183	30.66	6-27	3	5.22
H.M.R.K.B.Herath	217.2	7	953	23	41.43	3-28	–	4.38
S.T.Jayasuriya	2458	45	11737	320	36.67	6-29	12	4.77
D.P.M.D.Jayawardena	94.4	1	539	7	77.00	2-56	–	5.69
H.K.S.R.Kaluhalamulla	211.3	5	1008	33	30.54	5-42	1	4.76
S.H.T.Kandamby	29	1	173	2	86.50	2-37	–	5.96

	O	M	R	W	Avge	Best	4wI	R/Over
C.K.Kapugedera	43	0	218	2	109.00	1-24	–	5.06
C.K.B.Kulasekara	13	0	80	0	–	–	–	6.15
K.M.D.N.Kulasekara	891.4	73	4161	122	34.10	4-40	2	4.66
R.A.S.Lakmal	80.5	2	522	13	40.15	3-43	–	6.45
M.F.Maharoof	715.2	48	3439	130	26.45	6-14	6	4.80
S.L.Malinga	944.4	52	4803	185	25.96	6-38	11	5.08
A.D.Mathews	301.4	16	1413	42	33.64	6-20	1	4.68
B.A.W.Mendis	459.2	25	1992	96	20.75	6-13	7	4.33
B.M.A.J.Mendis	105	0	500	14	35.71	3-36	–	4.76
M.Muralitharan	3072.1	195	12066	523	23.07	7-30	25	3.92
N.L.T.C.Perera	222.4	12	1203	48	25.06	5-28	3	5.40
K.T.G.D.Prasad	90.1	3	497	18	27.61	3-17	–	5.51
S.Prasanna	56.3	4	272	8	34.00	3-32	–	4.81
T.T.Samaraweera	117	5	542	11	49.27	3-34	–	4.63
S.M.S.M.Senanayake	45	1	228	4	57.00	2-45	–	5.06
L.P.C.Silva	7	1	33	1	33.00	1-21	–	4.71
H.D.R.L.Thirimanne	4.1	0	25	1	25.00	1-25	–	6.00
W.P.J.U.C.Vaas	2620.1	278	10955	399	27.45	8-19	13	4.18

ZIMBABWE – BATTING AND FIELDING

	M	I	NO	HS	Runs	Avge	100	50	Ct/St
R.W.Chakabva	13	13	1	45	213	17.75	–	–	7
C.J.Chibhabha	60	60	–	73	1247	20.78	–	9	24
E.Chigumbura	139	130	14	79	2786	24.01	–	14	45
C.K.Coventry	37	34	1	194*	821	24.87	1	3	18/1
A.G.Cremer	43	28	9	37	316	16.63	–	–	14
K.M.Dabengwa	37	34	7	45	514	19.03	–	–	12
C.R.Ervine	23	21	3	85	581	32.27	–	4	2
S.M.Ervine	42	34	7	100	698	25.85	1	2	5
M.W.Goodwin	71	70	3	112*	1818	27.13	2	8	20
A.J.Ireland	26	13	5	8*	30	3.75	–	–	2
K.M.Jarvis	16	10	4	13	29	4.83	–	–	4
G.A.Lamb	15	14	3	37	197	17.90	–	–	–
H.Masakadza	115	115	4	178*	3006	27.08	3	18	50
S.W.Masakadza	9	6	2	45*	115	28.75	–	–	6
S.Matsikenyeri	112	109	9	90	2205	22.05	–	13	37
T.M.K.Mawoyo	3	3	–	14	33	11.00	–	–	1
K.O.Meth	11	8	–	53	106	13.25	–	1	1
C.B.Mpofu	62	33	17	6	38	2.37	–	–	10
N.Mushangwe	1	1	–	7	7	7.00	–	–	–
F.Mutizwa	17	15	2	79	403	31.00	–	4	9/2
N.Ncube	1	1	1	0*	0	–	–	–	–
I.A.Nicolson	2	2	–	14	14	7.00	–	–	–
T.Panyangara	25	21	5	16*	94	5.87	–	–	5
R.W.Price	102	59	17	46	406	9.66	–	–	17
V.Sibanda	96	95	2	116	2194	23.59	1	17	34
T.Taibu	149	136	21	107*	3383	29.41	2	22	114/33
B.R.M.Taylor	132	131	13	145*	4112	34.84	6	26	65/18
P.Utseya	139	113	42	68*	1192	16.78	–	3	42
B.V.Vitori	6	2	1	3*	3	3.00	–	–	–
M.N.Waller	24	23	2	99*	468	22.28	–	3	7
S.C.Williams	47	46	7	75	1146	29.38	–	11	17

LOI   **ZIMBABWE – BOWLING**

	O	M	R	W	Avge	Best	4wI	R/Over
C.J.Chihhabha	148	2	1049	20	52.45	2-28	–	7.08
E.Chigumbura	591.2	23	3472	85	40.84	4-28	1	5.87
A.G.Cremer	340.5	14	1601	53	30.20	6-46	3	4.69
K.M.Dabengwa	184.5	2	936	23	40.69	3-15	–	5.06
S.M.Ervine	274.5	10	1561	41	38.07	3-29	–	5.67
T.N.Garwwe	6	0	50	1	50.00	1-50	–	8.33
M.W.Goodwin	41.2	1	210	4	52.50	1-12	–	5.08
A.J.Ireland	221	13	1115	38	29.34	3-41	–	5.04
K.M.Jarvis	127.5	3	804	18	44.66	3-36	–	6.28
G.A.Lamb	107	3	467	12	38.91	3-45	–	4.36
H.Masakadza	191.2	4	1034	29	35.65	3-39	–	5.40
S.W.Masakadza	69.1	2	524	16	32.75	4-46	2	7.57
S.Matsikenyeri	153.2	2	778	16	48.62	2-25	–	5.07
K.O.Meth	67.4	2	419	6	69.83	2-52	–	6.19
C.B.Mpofu	492.4	36	2567	68	37.75	6-52	3	5.21
N.Mushangwe	10	1	50	0	–	–	–	5.00
N.Ncube	8.5	1	69	3	23.00	3-69	–	7.81
I.A.Nicolson	12	0	118	2	59.00	1-44	–	9.83
T.Panyangara	188.3	15	1049	26.	40.34	3-28	–	5.56
R.W.Price	895.4	75	3575	100	35.75	4-22	1	3.99
V.Sibanda	15.3	0	88	2	44.00	1-12	–	5.67
T.Taibu	14	1	61	2	30.50	2-42	–	4.35
B.R.M.Taylor	66	0	406	9	45.11	3-54	–	6.15
P.Utseya	1193.3	57	5103	111	45.97	4-38	2	4.27
B.V.Vitori	55.3	1	305	13	23.46	5-20	2	5.49
M.N.Waller	29	0	178	2	89.00	1-17	–	6.13
S.C.Williams	138.3	2	685	10	68.50	3-23	–	4.94

BANGLADESH – BATTING AND FIELDING

	M	I	NO	HS	Runs	Avge	100	50	Ct/St
Abdur Razzak	129	82	32	35	650	13.00	–	–	27
Alok Kapali	69	66	3	115	1235	19.60	1	5	29
Elias Sunny	2	2	1	1	1	1.00	–	–	–
Farhad Reza	34	31	6	50	412	16.48	–	1	13
Imrul Kayes	48	48	1	101	1315	27.97	1	9	14
Junaid Siddique	54	53	1	100	1196	23.00	1	6	23
Mahmudullah	76	64	19	68*	1374	30.53	–	6	19
Mashrafe Mortaza	118	90	16	51*	1163	15.71	–	1	36
Mohammad Ashraful	169	163	13	109	3397	22.64	3	20	35
Mushfiqur Rahim	104	95	17	101	1987	25.47	1	10	71/30
Naeem Islam	49	41	14	73*	671	24.85	–	2	16
Nasir Hossain	10	8	1	100	254	36.28	1	2	5
Nazmul Hossain	36	21	13	6*	35	4.37	–	–	5
Raqibul Hasan	55	54	7	89	1308	27.82	–	8	18
Rubel Hossain	37	19	11	15*	38	4.75	–	–	7
Shaful Islam	43	23	7	24*	102	6.37	–	–	7
Shahriar Nafees	75	75	5	123*	2201	31.44	4	13	13
Shakib Al Hasan	122	117	19	134*	3398	34.67	5	22	31
Shuvagata Hom	4	3	1	35*	70	35.00	–	–	–
Suhrawadi Shuvo	17	10	3	20*	98	14.00	–	–	9
Tamim Iqbal	109	109	1	154	3115	28.84	3	19	29

LOI   **BANGLADESH – BOWLING**

	O	M	R	W	Avge	Best	4wI	R/Over
Abdur Razzak	1120.3	59	5050	179	28.21	5-29	8	4.50
Alok Kapali	242	12	1255	24	52.29	3-49	–	5.18
Elias Sunny	16	0	82	3	27.33	2-36	–	5.12
Farhad Reza	189.5	12	1017	22	46.22	5-42	1	5.35
Junaid Siddique	2	0	13	0	–	–	–	6.50
Mahmudullah	379.1	8	1954	43	45.44	3- 4	–	5.15
Mashrafe Mortaza	981.5	86	4552	150	30.34	6-26	6	4.63
Mohammad Ashraful	116.1	4	661	18	36.72	3-26	–	5.69
Naeem Islam	276	8	1319	33	39.96	3-32	–	4.77
Nasir Hossain	29.4	0	157	3	52.33	2- 3	–	5.29
Nazmul Hossain	258.5	21	1318	40	32.95	4-40	1	5.09
Rubel Hossain	287.1	10	1573	48	32.77	4-25	4	5.47
Shafiul Islam	299.3	20	1761	50	35.22	4-21	4	5.87
Shakib Al Hasan	1035.2	61	4418	154	28.68	4-16	4	4.26
Shuvagata Hom	2	0	9	0	–	–	–	4.50
Suhrawadi Shuvo	127	7	572	14	40.85	3-14	–	4.50
Tamim Iqbal	1	0	13	0	–	–	–	13.00

ASSOCIATES – BATTING AND FIELDING

	M	I	NO	HS	Runs	Avge	100	50	Ct/St
A.Balbirnie (Ireland)	4	4	–	17	29	7.25	–	–	1
K.J.Coetzer (Scotland)	9	9	1	89*	384	48.00	–	4	6
J.H.Davey (Scotland)	8	8	1	48*	147	21.00	–	–	4
G.H.Dockrell (Ireland)	28	15	8	19	71	10.14	–	–	13
E.C.Joyce (Ireland)	13	13	–	88	397	30.53	–	3	3
A.N.Kervezee (Netherlands)	37	34	2	92	794	24.81	–	3	17
E.J.G.Morgan (Ireland)	23	23	2	115	744	35.42	1	5	9
D.P.Nannes (Netherlands)	1	1	–	1	1	1.00	–	–	–
N.J.O'Brien (Ireland)	49	49	4	72	1198	26.62	–	8	38/7
W.T.S.Porterfield (Ireland)	58	58	3	112*	1745	31.72	5	8	29
W.B.Rankin (Ireland)	37	16	11	7*	35	7.00	–	–	6
P.R.Stirling (Ireland)	36	36	1	177	1418	40.51	4	6	20
R.N.ten Doeschate (Netherlands)	33	32	9	119	1541	67.00	5	9	13
G.C.Wilson (Ireland)	37	36	3	113	952	28.84	1	6	23/7

ASSOCIATES – BOWLING

	O	M	R	W	Avge	Best	4wI	R/Over
K.J.Coetzer	19	1	125	1	125.00	1-35	–	6.57
J.H.Davey	47.2	5	220	13	16.92	5- 9	1	4.64
G.H.Dockrell	221.3	12	932	35	26.62	4-35	1	4.20
A.N.Kervezee	4	0	34	0	–	–	–	8.50
D.P.Nannes	7	1	20	1	20.00	1-20	–	2.85
W.B.Rankin	283.2	19	1391	43	32.34	3-32	–	4.90
P.R.Stirling	153	1	686	18	38.11	4-11	1	4.48
R.N.ten Doeschate	263.2	18	1327	55	24.12	4-31	3	5.03

LIMITED-OVERS INTERNATIONALS RESULTS

1970-71 to 10 March 2012

This chart excludes all matches involving multinational teams.

| | Opponents | Matches | Won | | | | | | | | | | | Tied | NR |
			E	A	SA	WI	NZ	I	P	SL	Z	B	Ass		
England	Australia	113	42	67	–	–	–	–	–	–	–	–	–	2	2
	South Africa	45	19	–	23	–	–	–	–	–	–	–	–	1	2
	West Indies	83	38	–	–	41	–	–	–	–	–	–	–	–	4
	New Zealand	70	29	–	–	–	35	–	–	–	–	–	–	2	4
	India	81	33	–	–	–	–	43	–	–	–	–	–	2	3
	Pakistan	72	42	–	–	–	–	–	28	–	–	–	–	–	2
	Sri Lanka	50	26	–	–	–	–	–	–	24	–	–	–	–	–
	Zimbabwe	30	21	–	–	–	–	–	–	–	8	–	–	–	1
	Bangladesh	15	13	–	–	–	–	–	–	–	–	2	–	–	–
	Associates	17	15	–	–	–	–	–	–	–	–	–	1	–	1
Australia	South Africa	80	–	41	36	–	–	–	–	–	–	–	–	3	–
	West Indies	125	–	63	–	57	–	–	–	–	–	–	–	2	3
	New Zealand	124	–	85	–	–	34	–	–	–	–	–	–	–	5
	India	109	–	64	–	–	–	37	–	–	–	–	–	–	8
	Pakistan	86	–	52	–	–	–	–	30	–	–	–	–	1	3
	Sri Lanka	84	–	53	–	–	–	–	–	28	–	–	–	–	3
	Zimbabwe	28	–	26	–	–	–	–	–	–	1	–	–	–	1
	Bangladesh	19	–	18	–	–	–	–	–	–	–	1	–	–	–
	Associates	16	–	16	–	–	–	–	–	–	–	–	0	–	–
S Africa	West Indies	51	–	–	38	12	–	–	–	–	–	–	–	–	1
	New Zealand	55	–	–	33	–	18	–	–	–	–	–	–	1	4
	India	66	–	–	40	–	–	24	–	–	–	–	–	–	2
	Pakistan	57	–	–	38	–	–	–	18	–	–	–	–	1	–
	Sri Lanka	51	–	–	25	–	–	–	–	24	–	–	–	1	1
	Zimbabwe	32	–	–	29	–	–	–	–	–	2	–	–	–	1
	Bangladesh	14	–	–	13	–	–	–	–	–	–	1	–	–	–
	Associates	19	–	–	19	–	–	–	–	–	–	–	0	–	–
W Indies	New Zealand	51	–	–	–	24	20	–	–	–	–	–	–	–	7
	India	106	–	–	–	57	–	46	–	–	–	–	–	1	2
	Pakistan	120	–	–	–	66	–	–	52	–	–	–	–	2	–
	Sri Lanka	49	–	–	–	26	–	–	–	20	–	–	–	–	3
	Zimbabwe	41	–	–	–	31	–	–	–	–	9	–	–	–	1
	Bangladesh	20	–	–	–	14	–	–	–	–	–	4	–	–	2
	Associates	19	–	–	–	17	–	–	–	–	–	–	1	–	1
N Zealand	India	88	–	–	–	–	37	46	–	–	–	–	–	–	5
	Pakistan	89	–	–	–	–	35	–	51	–	–	–	–	1	2
	Sri Lanka	74	–	–	–	–	35	–	–	34	–	–	–	1	4
	Zimbabwe	35	–	–	–	–	25	–	–	–	8	–	–	1	1
	Bangladesh	21	–	–	–	–	16	–	–	–	–	5	–	–	–
	Associates	13	–	–	–	–	13	–	–	–	–	–	0	–	–
India	Pakistan	120	–	–	–	–	–	47	69	–	–	–	–	–	4
	Sri Lanka	133	–	–	–	–	–	70	–	51	–	–	–	1	11
	Zimbabwe	51	–	–	–	–	–	39	–	–	10	–	–	2	–
	Bangladesh	23	–	–	–	–	–	21	–	–	–	2	–	–	–
	Associates	24	–	–	–	–	–	22	–	–	–	–	2	–	–
Pakistan	Sri Lanka	126	–	–	–	–	–	–	75	47	–	–	–	1	3
	Zimbabwe	44	–	–	–	–	–	–	40	–	2	–	–	1	1
	Bangladesh	29	–	–	–	–	–	–	28	–	–	1	–	–	–
	Associates	22	–	–	–	–	–	–	21	–	–	–	1	–	–
Sri Lanka	Zimbabwe	47	–	–	–	–	–	–	–	39	7	–	–	–	1
	Bangladesh	29	–	–	–	–	–	–	–	27	–	2	–	–	–
	Associates	16	–	–	–	–	–	–	–	15	–	–	1	–	–
Zimbabwe	Bangladesh	56	–	–	–	–	–	–	–	–	26	30	–	–	–
	Associates	43	–	–	–	–	–	–	–	–	34	–	6	1	2
Bangladesh	Associates	32	–	–	–	–	–	–	–	–	–	22	10	–	–
Associates	Associates	134	–	–	–	–	–	–	–	–	–	–	129	–	5
		3247	278	485	294	345	268	395	412	309	107	70	151	26	107

MERIT TABLE OF ALL L-O INTERNATIONALS
1970-71 to 18 February 2011

	Matches	Won	Lost	Tied	No Result	% Won (exc NR)
South Africa	470	294	159	5	12	64.19
Australia	784	485	266	8	25	63.89
Pakistan	765	412	331	6	16	55.00
West Indies	665	345	291	5	24	53.82
India	801	395	365	6	35	51.56
England	576	278	272	7	19	49.91
Sri Lanka	659	309	320	4	26	48.81
New Zealand	620	268	315	5	32	45.57
Bangladesh	258	70	186	–	2	27.34
Zimbabwe	407	107	286	5	9	26.88
Associate Members (v Full*)	221	22	194	1	4	10.13

* Results of games between two Associate Members are excluded from this list; Associate Members have participated in 355 LOIs, 134 LOIs being between Associate Members.

TEAM RECORDS
HIGHEST TOTALS

443-9	(50 overs)	Sri Lanka v Netherlands	Amstelveen	2006
438-9	(49.5 overs)	South Africa v Australia	Johannesburg	2005-06
434-4	(50 overs)	Australia v South Africa	Johannesburg	2005-06
418-5	(50 overs)	South Africa v Zimbabwe	Potchefstroom	2006-07
418-5	(50 overs)	India v West Indies	Indore	2011-12
414-7	(50 overs)	India v Sri Lanka	Rajkot	2009-10
413-5	(50 overs)	India v Bermuda	Port-of-Spain	2006-07
411-8	(50 overs)	Sri Lanka v India	Rajkot	2009-10
402-2	(50 overs)	New Zealand v Ireland	Aberdeen	2008
401-3	(50 overs)	India v South Africa	Gwalior	2009-10
399-6	(50 overs)	South Africa v Zimbabwe	Benoni	2010-11
398-5	(50 overs)	Sri Lanka v Kenya	Kandy	1995-96
397-5	(44 overs)	New Zealand v Zimbabwe	Bulawayo	2005
392-4	(50 overs)	India v New Zealand	Christchurch	2008-09
392-6	(50 overs)	South Africa v Pakistan	Pretoria	2006-07
391-4	(50 overs)	England v Bangladesh	Nottingham	2005
387-5	(50 overs)	India v England	Rajkot	2008-09
385-7	(50 overs)	Pakistan v Bangladesh	Dambulla	2010
377-6	(50 overs)	Australia v South Africa	Basseterre	2006-07
376-2	(50 overs)	India v New Zealand	Hyderabad, India	1999-00
374-4	(50 overs)	India v Hong Kong	Karachi	2008
373-6	(50 overs)	India v Sri Lanka	Taunton	1999
373-8	(50 overs)	New Zealand v Zimbabwe	Napier	2011-12
372-6	(50 overs)	New Zealand v Zimbabwe	Whangarei	2011-12
371-9	(50 overs)	Pakistan v Sri Lanka	Nairobi	1996-97
370-4	(50 overs)	India v Bangladesh	Dhaka	2010-11
368-5	(50 overs)	Australia v Sri Lanka	Sydney	2005-06
365-2	(50 overs)	South Africa v India	Ahmedabad	2009-10
363-3	(50 overs)	South Africa v Zimbabwe	Bulawayo	2001-02
363-5	(50 overs)	New Zealand v Canada	Gros Islet	2006-07
363-5	(50 overs)	India v Sri Lanka	Colombo (RPS)	2008-09
363-7	(55 overs)	England v Pakistan	Nottingham	1992
361-8	(50 overs)	Australia v Bangladesh	Dhaka	2010-11
360-4	(50 overs)	West Indies v Sri Lanka	Karachi	1987-88
359-2	(50 overs)	Australia v India	Johannesburg	2002-03
359-5	(50 overs)	Australia v India	Sydney	2003-04
358-4	(50 overs)	South Africa v Bangladesh	Benoni	2008-09
358-5	(50 overs)	Australia v Netherlands	Basseterre	2006-07
358-6	(50 overs)	New Zealand v Canada	Mumbai	2010-11
357-9	(50 overs)	Sri Lanka v Bangladesh	Lahore	2008
356-4	(50 overs)	South Africa v West Indies	St George's	2006-07
356-9	(50 overs)	India v Pakistan	Vishakhapatnam	2004-05

354-3	(50 overs)	South Africa v Kenya	Cape Town	2001-02
354-6	(50 overs)	South Africa v England	Cape Town	2009-10
354-7	(50 overs)	India v Australia	Nagpur	2009-10
353-3	(40 overs)	South Africa v Netherlands	Basseterre	2006-07
353-5	(50 overs)	India v New Zealand	Hyderabad, India	2003-04
353-6	(50 overs)	Pakistan v England	Karachi	2005-06
351-3	(50 overs)	India v Kenya	Paarl	2001-02
351-4	(50 overs)	Pakistan v South Africa	Durban	2006-07
351-5	(50 overs)	South Africa v Netherlands	Mohali	2010-11
351-6	(50 overs)	South Africa v Zimbabwe	Bloemfontein	2010-11
351-7	(50 overs)	Zimbabwe v Kenya	Mombasa	2008-09
350-4	(50 overs)	Australia v India	Hyderabad, India	2009-10
350-6	(50 overs)	India v Sri Lanka	Nagpur	2005-06
350-9	(49.3 overs)	New Zealand v Australia	Hamilton	2006-07

The highest for Bangladesh is 320-8 (v Zimbabwe, Bulawayo, 2009).

HIGHEST TOTALS BATTING SECOND

WINNING:	438-9	(49.5 overs)	South Africa v Australia	Johannesburg	2005-06
LOSING:	411-8	(50.0 overs)	Sri Lanka v India	Rajkot	2009-10

HIGHEST MATCH AGGREGATES

872-13	(99.5 overs)	South Africa v Australia	Johannesburg	2005-06
825-15	(100 overs)	India v Sri Lanka	Rajkot	2009-10

LARGEST RUNS MARGINS OF VICTORY

290 runs	New Zealand beat Ireland	Aberdeen	2008
272 runs	South Africa beat Zimbabwe	Benoni	2010-11
258 runs	South Africa beat Sri Lanka	Paarl	2011-12
257 runs	India beat Bermuda	Port-of-Spain	2006-07
256 runs	Australia beat Namibia	Potchefstroom	2002-03
256 runs	India beat Hong Kong	Karachi	2008
245 runs	Sri Lanka beat India	Sharjah	2000-01
243 runs	Sri Lanka beat Bermuda	Port-of-Spain	2006-07
234 runs	Sri Lanka beat Pakistan	Lahore	2008-09
233 runs	Pakistan beat Bangladesh	Dhaka	1999-00
232 runs	Australia beat Sri Lanka	Adelaide	1984-85
231 runs	South Africa beat Netherlands	Mohali	2010-11
229 runs	Australia beat Netherlands	Basseterre	2006-07
224 runs	Australia beat Pakistan	Nairobi	2002
221 runs	South Africa beat Netherlands	Basseterre	2006-07
217 runs	Pakistan beat Sri Lanka	Sharjah	2001-02
215 runs	Australia beat New Zealand	St George's	2006-07
215 runs	West Indies beat Netherlands	Delhi	2010-11
212 runs	South Africa beat Zimbabwe	Centurion	2009-10
210 runs	New Zealand beat USA	The Oval	2004
210 runs	Sri Lanka beat Canada	Hambantota	2010-11
209 runs	South Africa beat West Indies	Cape Town	2003-04
208 runs	South Africa beat Kenya	Cape Town	2001-02
208 runs	Australia beat India	Sydney	2003-04
208 runs	West Indies beat Canada	Kingston	2009-10
206 runs	New Zealand beat Australia	Adelaide	1985-86
206 runs	Sri Lanka beat Netherlands	Colombo (RPS)	2002-03
206 runs	South Africa beat Bangladesh	Dhaka	2010-11
205 runs	Pakistan beat Kenya	Hambantota	2010-11
203 runs	Australia beat Scotland	Basseterre	2006-07
202 runs	England beat India	Lord's	1975
202 runs	South Africa beat Kenya	Nairobi	1996-97
202 runs	Zimbabwe beat Kenya	Dhaka	1998-99
202 runs	New Zealand beat Zimbabwe	Napier	2011-12
200 runs	India beat Bangladesh	Dhaka	2002-03
200 runs	New Zealand beat India	Dambulla	2010

LOWEST TOTALS (Excluding reduced innings)

35	(18.0 overs)	Zimbabwe v Sri Lanka	Harare	2003-04
36	(18.4 overs)	Canada v Sri Lanka	Paarl	2002-03
38	(15.4 overs)	Zimbabwe v Sri Lanka	Colombo (SSC)	2001-02
43	(19.5 overs)	Pakistan v West Indies	Cape Town	1992-93
43	(20.1 overs)	Sri Lanka v South Africa	Paarl	2011-12
44	(24.5 overs)	Zimbabwe v Bangladesh	Chittagong	2009-10
45	(40.3 overs)	Canada v England	Manchester	1979
45	(14.0 overs)	Namibia v Australia	Potschefstroom	2002-03
54	(26.3 overs)	India v Sri Lanka	Sharjah	2000-01
54	(23.2 overs)	West Indies v South Africa	Cape Town	2003-04
55	(28.3 overs)	Sri Lanka v West Indies	Sharjah	1986-87
58	(18.5 overs)	Bangladesh v West Indies	Dhaka	2010-11
61	(22.0 overs)	West Indies v Bangladesh	Chittagong	2011-12
63	(25.5 overs)	India v Australia	Sydney	1980-81
64	(35.5 overs)	New Zealand v Pakistan	Sharjah	1985-86
65	(24.0 overs)	USA v Australia	Southampton	2004
65	(24.3 overs)	Zimbabwe v India	Harare	2005
67	(31.0 overs)	Zimbabwe v Sri Lanka	Harare	2008-09
68	(31.3 overs)	Scotland v West Indies	Leicester	1999
69	(28.0 overs)	South Africa v Australia	Sydney	1993-94
69	(22.5 overs)	Zimbabwe v Kenya	Harare	2005-06
69	(23.5 overs)	Kenya v New Zealand	Chennai	2010-11
70	(25.2 overs)	Australia v England	Birmingham	1977
70	(26.3 overs)	Australia v New Zealand	Adelaide	1985-86

The lowest for England is 86 (v A, Manchester, 2001).

LOWEST MATCH AGGREGATES

73-11	(23.2 overs)	Canada (36) v Sri Lanka (37-1)	Paarl	2002-03
75-11	(27.2 overs)	Zimbabwe (35) v Sri Lanka (40-1)	Harare	2003-04
78-11	(20.0 overs)	Zimbabwe (38) v Sri Lanka (40-1)	Colombo (SSC)	2001-02

BATTING RECORDS

HIGHEST INDIVIDUAL INNINGS

219	V.Sehwag	India v West Indies	Indore	2011-12
200*	S.R.Tendulkar	India v South Africa	Gwalior	2009-10
194*	C.K.Coventry	Zimbabwe v Bangladesh	Bulawayo	2009
194	Saeed Anwar	Pakistan v India	Madras	1996-97
189*	I.V.A.Richards	West Indies v England	Manchester	1984
189	S.T.Jayasuriya	Sri Lanka v India	Sharjah	2000-01
188*	G.Kirsten	South Africa v UAE	Rawalpindi	1995-96
186*	S.R.Tendulkar	India v New Zealand	Hyderabad	1999-00
185*	S.R.Watson	Australia v Bangladesh	Dhaka	2010-11
183*	M.S.Dhoni	India v Sri Lanka	Jaipur	2005-06
183	S.C.Ganguly	India v Sri Lanka	Taunton	1999
181*	M.L.Hayden	Australia v New Zealand	Hamilton	2006-07
181	I.V.A.Richards	West Indies v Sri Lanka	Karachi	1987-88
178*	H.Masakadza	Zimbabwe v Kenya	Harare	2009-10
177	P.R.Stirling	Ireland v Canada	Toronto	2010
175*	Kapil Dev	India v Zimbabwe	Tunbridge Wells	1983
175	H.H.Gibbs	South Africa v Australia	Johannesburg	2005-06
175	S.R.Tendulkar	India v Australia	Hyderabad, India	2009-10
175	V.Sehwag	India v Bangladesh	Dhaka	2010-11
173	M.E.Waugh	Australia v West Indies	Melbourne	2000-01
172*	C.B.Wishart	Zimbabwe v Namibia	Harare	2002-03
172	A.C.Gilchrist	Australia v Zimbabwe	Hobart	2003-04
172	L.Vincent	New Zealand v Zimbabwe	Bulawayo	2005
171*	G.M.Turner	New Zealand v East Africa	Birmingham	1975
169*	D.J.Callaghan	South Africa v New Zealand	Pretoria	1994-95
169	B.C.Lara	West Indies v Sri Lanka	Sharjah	1995-96

167*	R.A.Smith	England v Australia	Birmingham	1993
166	B.B.McCullum	New Zealand v Ireland	Aberdeen	2008
164	R.T.Ponting	Australia v South Africa	Johannesburg	2005-06
163*	S.R.Tendulkar	India v New Zealand	Christchurch	2008-09
163	D.A.Warner	Australia v Sri Lanka	Brisbane	2011-12
161*	S.R.Watson	Australia v England	Melbourne	2010-11
161	A.C.Hudson	South Africa v Netherlands	Rawalpindi	1995-96
161	J.A.H.Marshall	New Zealand v Ireland	Aberdeen	2008
160*	T.M.Dilshan	Sri Lanka v India	Hobart	2011-12
160	Imran Nazir	Pakistan v Zimbabwe	Kingston	2006-07
160	T.M.Dilshan	Sri Lanka v India	Rajkot	2009-10
159*	D.Mongia	India v Zimbabwe	Gauhati	2001-02
158	D.I.Gower	England v New Zealand	Brisbane	1982-83
158	M.L.Hayden	Australia v West Indies	North Sound	2006-07
158	A.J.Strauss	England v India	Bangalore	2010-11
157*	X.M.Marshall	West Indies v Canada	King City (NW)	2008
157	S.T.Jayasuriya	Sri Lanka v Netherlands	Amstelveen	2006
156	B.C.Lara	West Indies v Pakistan	Adelaide	2004-05
156	A.Symonds	Australia v New Zealand	Wellington	2005-06
156	H.Masakadza	Zimbabwe v Kenya	Harare	2009-10
154	A.C.Gilchrist	Australia v Sri Lanka	Melbourne	1998-99
154	Tamim Iqbal	Bangladesh v Zimbabwe	Bulawayo	2009
154	A.J.Strauss	England v Bangladesh	Birmingham	2010
153*	I.V.A.Richards	West Indies v Australia	Melbourne	1979-80
153*	M.Azharuddin	India v Zimbabwe	Cuttack	1997-98
153*	S.C.Ganguly	India v New Zealand	Gwalior	1999-00
153*	C.H.Gayle	West Indies v Zimbabwe	Bulawayo	2003-04
153	B.C.Lara	West Indies v Pakistan	Sharjah	1993-94
153	R.S.Dravid	India v New Zealand	Hyderabad	1999-00
153	H.H.Gibbs	South Africa v Bangladesh	Potchefstroom	2002-03
152*	D.L.Haynes	West Indies v India	Georgetown	1988-89
152*	C.H.Gayle	West Indies v South Africa	Johannesburg	2003-04
152	C.H.Gayle	West Indies v Kenya	Nairobi	2001-02
152	S.R.Tendulkar	India v Namibia	Pietermaritzburg	2002-03
152	A.J.Strauss	England v Bangladesh	Nottingham	2005
152	S.T.Jayasuriya	Sri Lanka v England	Leeds	2006
151*	S.T.Jayasuriya	Sri Lanka v India	Bombay	1996-97
151	A.Symonds	Australia v New Zealand	Sydney	2005-06
150*	G.Gambhir	India v Sri Lanka	Kolkata	2009-10
150	S.Chanderpaul	West Indies v South Africa	East London	1998-99
150	G.Gambhir	India v Sri Lanka	Colombo (RPS)	2008-09

HUNDRED ON DEBUT

D.L.Amiss	103	England v Australia	Manchester	1972
D.L.Haynes	148	West Indies v Australia	St John's	1977-78
A.Flower	115*	Zimbabwe v Sri Lanka	New Plymouth	1991-92
Salim Elahi	102*	Pakistan v Sri Lanka	Gujranwala	1995-96
M.J.Guptill	122*	New Zealand v West Indies	Auckland	2008-09
C.A.Ingram	124	South Africa v Zimbabwe	Bloemfontein	2010-11
R.J.Nicol	108*	New Zealand v Zimbabwe	Harare	2011-12

Shahid Afridi scored 102 for P v SL, Nairobi, 1996-97, in his second match having not batted in his first.

Fastest 100	37 balls	Shahid Afridi (102)	P v SL	Nairobi	1996-97
Fastest 50	17 balls	S.T.Jayasuriya (76)	SL v P	Singapore	1995-96

CARRYING BAT THROUGH INNINGS (SIDE ALL OUT)

G.W.Flower	84*	Zimbabwe (205) v England	Sydney	1994-95
Saeed Anwar	103*	Pakistan (219) v Zimbabwe	Harare	1994-95
N.V.Knight	125*	England (246) v Pakistan	Nottingham	1996
R.D.Jacobs	49*	West Indies (110) v Australia	Manchester	1999

D.R.Martyn	116*	Australia (191) v New Zealand	Auckland	1999-00
H.H.Gibbs	59*	South Africa (101†) v Pakistan	Sharjah	1999-00
A.J.Stewart	100*	England (192) v West Indies	Nottingham	2000
Javed Omar	33*	Bangladesh (103) v Zimbabwe	Harare	2000-01

† One batsman retired hurt.

5000 RUNS IN A CAREER

		LOI	I	NO	HS	Runs	Avge	100	50
S.R.Tendulkar	I	460	449	41	200*	**18254**	44.74	48	95
R.T.Ponting	A/ICC	375	365	39	164	**13704**	42.03	30	82
S.T.Jayasuriya	SL/Asia	445	433	18	189	**13430**	32.36	28	68
Inzamam-ul-Haq	P/Asia	378	350	53	137*	**11739**	39.52	10	83
J.H.Kallis	SA/Afr/ICC	321	307	53	139	**11498**	45.26	17	85
S.C.Ganguly	I/Asia	311	300	23	183	**11363**	41.02	22	72
R.S.Dravid	I/Asia/ICC	344	318	40	153	**10889**	39.16	12	83
D.P.M.D.Jayawardena	SL/Asia	370	348	35	144	**10501**	33.54	15	65
B.C.Lara	WI/ICC	299	289	32	169	**10405**	40.48	19	63
K.C.Sangakkara	SL/Asia/ICC	322	303	32	138*	**10330**	38.11	13	69
Mohammad Yousuf	P/Asia	288	272	40	141*	**9720**	41.71	15	64
A.C.Gilchrist	A/ICC	287	279	11	172	**9619**	35.89	16	55
M.Azharuddin	I	334	308	54	153*	**9378**	36.92	7	58
P.A.de Silva	SL	308	296	30	145	**9284**	34.90	11	64
Saeed Anwar	P	247	244	19	194	**8824**	39.21	20	43
S.Chanderpaul	WI	268	251	40	150	**8778**	41.60	11	59
D.L.Haynes	WI	238	237	28	152*	**8648**	41.37	17	57
M.S.Atapattu	SL	268	259	32	132*	**8529**	37.57	11	59
M.E.Waugh	A	244	236	20	173	**8500**	39.35	18	50
H.H.Gibbs	SA	248	240	16	175	**8094**	36.13	21	37
V.Sehwag	I/Asia/ICC	245	239	9	219	**8090**	35.17	15	37
C.H.Gayle	WI/ICC	228	223	16	153*	**8087**	39.06	19	43
Yuvraj Singh	I/Asia	274	252	38	139	**8051**	37.62	13	49
S.P.Fleming	NZ/ICC	280	269	21	134*	**8037**	32.40	8	49
S.R.Waugh	A	325	288	58	120*	**7569**	32.90	3	45
A.Ranatunga	SL	269	255	47	131*	**7456**	35.84	4	49
Javed Miandad	P	233	218	41	119*	**7381**	41.70	8	50
Salim Malik	P	283	256	38	102	**7170**	32.88	5	47
N.J.Astle	NZ	223	217	14	145*	**7090**	34.92	16	41
Shahid Afridi	P/Asia/ICC	338	314	19	124	**6999**	23.72	6	33
M.J.Clarke	A	212	194	42	130	**6953**	45.74	7	51
M.G.Bevan	A	232	196	67	108*	**6912**	53.58	6	46
G.Kirsten	SA	185	185	19	188*	**6798**	40.95	13	45
A.Flower	Z	213	208	16	145	**6786**	35.34	4	55
Younus Khan	P	237	228	23	144	**6747**	32.91	6	46
I.V.A.Richards	WI	187	167	24	189*	**6721**	47.00	11	45
M.S.Dhoni	I/Asia	203	181	50	183*	**6702**	51.16	7	45
G.C.Smith	SA/Afr	181	179	10	141	**6598**	39.04	9	45
G.W.Flower	Z	221	214	18	142*	**6571**	33.52	6	40
Ijaz Ahmed	P	250	232	29	139*	**6564**	32.33	10	37
A.R.Border	A	273	252	39	127*	**6524**	30.62	3	39
T.M.Dilshan	SL	235	211	31	160*	**6409**	35.60	12	26
R.B.Richardson	WI	224	217	30	122	**6248**	33.41	5	44
M.L.Hayden	A/ICC	161	155	15	181*	**6133**	43.80	10	36
D.M.Jones	A	164	161	25	145	**6068**	44.61	7	46
D.C.Boon	A	181	177	16	122	**5964**	37.04	5	37
J.N.Rhodes	SA	245	220	51	121	**5935**	35.11	2	33
Ramiz Raja	P	198	197	15	119*	**5841**	32.09	9	31
C.L.Hooper	WI	227	206	43	113*	**5761**	35.34	7	29
R.R.Sarwan	WI	173	161	31	115*	**5644**	43.41	4	38
W.J.Cronje	SA	188	175	31	112	**5565**	38.64	2	39
A.Jadeja	I	196	179	36	119	**5359**	37.47	6	30
D.R.Martyn	A	208	182	51	144*	**5346**	40.80	5	37

		LOI	I	NO	HS	Runs	Avge	100	50
Shoaib Malik	P	203	180	21	143	**5253**	33.03	7	31
A.D.R.Campbell	Z	188	184	14	131*	**5185**	30.50	7	30
R.S.Mahanama	SL	213	198	23	119*	**5162**	29.49	4	35
C.G.Greenidge	WI	128	127	13	133*	**5134**	45.03	11	31
P.D.Collingwood	E	197	181	37	120*	**5092**	35.36	5	26
M.E.K.Hussey	A	176	148	44	109*	**5088**	48.92	3	36
A.Symonds	A	198	161	33	156	**5088**	39.75	6	30
Abdul Razzaq	P/Asia	265	228	57	112	**5080**	29.70	3	23

The most for Bangladesh 3398 in 117 innings by Shakib Al Hasan.

15 HUNDREDS

		Inns	100	E	A	SA	WI	NZ	I	P	SL	Z	B	Ass
S.R.Tendulkar	I	449	**48**	2	9	5	4	5	–	5	8	5	–	5
R.T.Ponting	A	365*	**30**	5	–	2	2	6	6	1	4	1	1	1
S.T.Jayasuriya	SL	433	**28**	4	2	–	1	5	7	3	–	1	4	1
S.C.Ganguly	I	300	**22**	4	1	3	–	3	–	2	4	3	1	4
H.H.Gibbs	SA	240	**21**	2	3	–	5	2	2	2	1	2	1	1
Saeed Anwar	P	244	**20**	–	1	–	2	4	4	–	7	2	–	–
C.H.Gayle	WI	223	**19**	2	–	3	–	1	4	3	–	2	1	3
B.C.Lara	WI	289	**19**	1	3	3	–	2	–	5	2	1	1	1
M.E.Waugh	A	236	**18**	1	–	2	3	3	3	1	1	3	–	1
D.L.Haynes	WI	237	**17**	2	6	–	–	2	2	4	1	–	–	–
J.H.Kallis	SA	307	**17**	1	1	–	4	3	2	1	3	1	–	1
N.J.Astle	NZ	217	**16**	2	1	1	–	5	2	–	3	–	1	–
A.C.Gilchrist	A	279*	**16**	2	–	2	–	2	1	1	6	1	–	–
V.Sehwag	I	239	**15**	–	–	2	6	–	2	2	–	1	1	–
Mohammad Yousuf	P	273	**15**	–	1	2	1	2	1	2	–	3	3	1
D.P.M.D.Jayawardena	SL	348*	**15**	5	–	1	–	1	2	2	–	–	1	1

* = Includes hundred scored against multi-national side. The most for England is 12 by M.E.Trescothick (in 122 innings), for Zimbabwe 7 by A.D.R.Campbell (184), and for Bangladesh 5 by Shakib Al Hasan (117).

HIGHEST PARTNERSHIP FOR EACH WICKET

1st	286	W.U.Tharanga/S.T.Jayasuriya	Sri Lanka v England	Leeds	2006
2nd	331	S.R.Tendulkar/R.S.Dravid	India v New Zealand	Hyderabad (Ind)	1999-00
3rd	237*	R.S.Dravid/S.R.Tendulkar	India v Kenya	Bristol	1999
4th	275*	M.Azharuddin/A.Jadeja	India v Zimbabwe	Cuttack	1997-98
5th	223	M.Azharuddin/A.Jadeja	India v Sri Lanka	Colombo (RPS)	1997-98
6th	218	D.P.M.D.Jayawardena/M.S.Dhoni	Asia XI v Africa XI	Chennai	2007
7th	130	A.Flower/H.H.Streak	Zimbabwe v England	Harare	2001-02
8th	138*	J.M.Kemp/A.J.Hall	South Africa v India	Cape Town	2006-07
9th	132	A.D.Mathews/S.L.Malinga	Sri Lanka v Australia	Melbourne	2010-11
10th	106*	I.V.A.Richards/M.A.Holding	West Indies v England	Manchester	1984

BOWLING RECORDS
SIX WICKETS IN AN INNINGS

8-19	W.P.J.U.C.Vaas	Sri Lanka v Zimbabwe	Colombo (SSC)	2001-02
7-15	G.D.McGrath	Australia v Namibia	Potschefstroom	2002-03
7-20	A.J.Bichel	Australia v England	Port Elizabeth	2002-03
7-30	M.Muralitharan	Sri Lanka v India	Sharjah	2000-01
7-36	Waqar Younis	Pakistan v England	Leeds	2001
7-37	Aqib Javed	Pakistan v India	Sharjah	1991-92
7-51	W.W.Davis	West Indies v Australia	Leeds	1983
6-12	A.Kumble	India v West Indies	Calcutta	1993-94
6-13	B.A.W.Mendis	Sri Lanka v India	Karachi	2008
6-14	G.J.Gilmour	Australia v England	Leeds	1975
6-14	Imran Khan	Pakistan v India	Sharjah	1984-85
6-14	M.F.Maharoof	Sri Lanka v West Indies	Mumbai	2006-07
6-15	C.E.H.Croft	West Indies v England	Kingstown	1980-81
6-16	Shoaib Akhtar	Pakistan v New Zealand	Karachi	2001-02

6-18	Azhar Mahmood	Pakistan v West Indies	Sharjah	1999-00
6-19	H.K.Olonga	Zimbabwe v England	Cape Town	1999-00
6-19	S.E.Bond	New Zealand v Zimbabwe	Harare	2005
6-20	B.C.Strang	Zimbabwe v Bangladesh	Nairobi	1997-98
6-20	A.D.Mathews	Sri Lanka v India	Colombo (RPS)	2009-10
6-22	F.H.Edwards	West Indies v Zimbabwe	Harare	2003-04
6-22	M.Ntini	South Africa v Australia	Cape Town	2005-06
6-23	A.A.Donald	South Africa v Kenya	Nairobi	1996-97
6-23	A.Nehra	India v England	Durban	2002-03
6-23	S.E.Bond	New Zealand v Australia	Port Elizabeth	2002-03
6-25	S.B.Styris	New Zealand v West Indies	Port-of-Spain	2002
6-25	W.P.J.U.C.Vaas	Sri Lanka v Bangladesh	Pietermaritzburg	2002-03
6-26	Waqar Younis	Pakistan v Sri Lanka	Sharjah	1989-90
6-26	Mashrafe Mortaza	Bangladesh v Kenya	Nairobi	2006
6-27	Naved-ul-Hasan	Pakistan v India	Jamshedpur	2004-05
6-27	C.R.D.Fernando	Sri Lanka v England	Colombo (RPS)	2007-08
6-27	M.Kartik	India v Australia	Mumbai	2007-08
6-27	K.A.J.Roach	West Indies v Netherlands	Delhi	2010-11
6-28	H.K.Olonga	Zimbabwe v Kenya	Bulawayo	2002-03
6-29	B.P.Patterson	West Indies v India	Nagpur	1987-88
6-29	S.T.Jayasuriya	Sri Lanka v England	Moratuwa	1992-93
6-29	B.A.W.Mendis	Sri Lanka v Zimbabwe	Harare	2008-09
6-30	Waqar Younis	Pakistan v New Zealand	Auckland	1993-94
6-31	P.D.Collingwood	England v Bangladesh	Nottingham	2005
6-31	M.G.Johnson	Australia v Sri Lanka	Pallekele	2011
6-35	S.M.Pollock	South Africa v West Indies	East London	1998-99
6-35	Abdul Razzaq	Pakistan v Bangladesh	Dhaka	2001-02
6-38	Shahid Afridi	Pakistan v Australia	Dubai	2009
6-38	S.L.Malinga	Sri Lanka v Kenya	Colombo (RPS)	2010-11
6-39	K.H.MacLeay	Australia v India	Nottingham	1983
6-41	I.V.A.Richards	West Indies v India	Delhi	1989-90
6-42	A.B.Agarkar	India v Australia	Melbourne	2003-04
6-42	Umar Gul	Pakistan v England	The Oval	2010
6-44	Waqar Younis	Pakistan v New Zealand	Sharjah	1996-97
6-45	C.R.Woakes	England v Australia	Brisbane	2010-11
6-46	A.G.Cremer	Zimbabwe v Kenya	Harare	2009-10
6-49	L.Klusener	South Africa v Sri Lanka	Lahore	1997-98
6-50	A.H.Gray	West Indies v Australia	Port-of-Spain	1990-91
6-52	C.B.Mpofu	Zimbabwe v Kenya	Nairobi (Gym)	2008-09
6-55	S.Sreesanth	India v England	Indore	2005-06
6-59	Waqar Younis	Pakistan v Australia	Nottingham	2001
6-59	A.Nehra	India v Sri Lanka	Colombo (RPS)	2005

150 WICKETS IN A CAREER

		LOI	Balls	R	W	Avge	Best	5w	R/Over
M.Muralitharan	SL/Asia/ICC	350	18811	12326	**534**	23.08	7-30	10	3.93
Wasim Akram	P	356	18186	11812	**502**	23.52	5-15	6	3.89
Waqar Younis	P	262	12698	9919	**416**	23.84	7-36	13	4.68
W.P.J.U.C.Vaas	SL/Asia	322	15775	11014	**400**	27.53	8-19	4	4.18
S.M.Pollock	SA/Afr/ICC	303	15712	9631	**393**	24.50	6-35	5	3.67
G.D.McGrath	A/ICC	250	12970	8391	**381**	22.02	7-15	7	3.88
B.Lee	A	212	10771	8512	**369**	23.06	5-22	9	4.74
Shahid Afridi	P/Asia/ICC	338	14742	11315	**341**	33.18	6-38	8	4.60
A.Kumble	I/Asia	271	14496	10412	**337**	30.89	6-12	2	4.30
S.T.Jayasuriya	SL	445	14874	11871	**323**	36.75	6-29	4	4.78
J.Srinath	I	229	11935	8847	**315**	28.08	5-23	3	4.44
S.K.Warne	A/ICC	194	10642	7541	**293**	25.73	5-33	1	4.25
Saqlain Mushtaq	P	169	8770	6275	**288**	21.78	5-20	6	4.29
A.B.Agarkar	I	191	9484	8021	**288**	27.85	6-42	2	5.07
D.L.Vettori	NZ/ICC	272	12903	8880	**282**	31.48	5- 7	2	4.12
Z.Khan	I/Asia	195	9898	8071	**278**	29.03	5-42	1	4.91
A.A.Donald	SA	164	8561	5926	**272**	21.78	6-23	2	4.15
J.H.Kallis	SA/Afr/ICC	321	10636	8558	**270**	31.69	5-30	2	4.82
Abdul Razzaq	P/Asia	265	10941	8564	**269**	31.83	6-35	3	4.69
M.Ntini	SA/ICC	173	8687	6559	**266**	24.65	6-22	4	4.53

		LOI	Balls	R	W	Avge	Best	5w	R/Over
Harbhajan Singh	I/Asia	229	12059	8651	259	33.40	5-31	3	4.30
Kapil Dev	I	225	11202	6945	253	27.45	5-43	1	3.72
Shoaib Akhtar	P/Asia/ICC	163	7764	6169	247	24.97	6-16	4	4.76
H.H.Streak	Z/Afr	189	9468	7129	239	29.82	5-32	1	4.51
D.Gough	E/ICC	159	8470	6209	235	26.42	5-44	2	4.39
C.A.Walsh	WI	205	10822	6918	227	30.47	5- 1	1	3.83
C.E.L.Ambrose	WI	176	9353	5429	225	24.12	5-17	4	3.48
J.M.Anderson	E	154	7652	6414	208	30.83	5-23	1	5.02
C.J.McDermott	A	138	7460	5018	203	24.71	5-44	1	4.03
C.Z.Harris	NZ	250	10667	7613	203	37.50	5-42	1	4.28
C.L.Cairns	NZ/ICC	215	8168	6594	201	32.80	5-42	1	4.84
K.D.Mills	NZ	135	6622	5189	200	25.94	5-25	1	4.70
B.K.V.Prasad	I	161	8129	6332	196	32.30	5-27	1	4.67
S.R.Waugh	A	325	8883	6761	195	34.67	4-33	–	4.56
C.L.Hooper	WI	227	9573	6958	193	36.05	4-34	–	4.36
L.Klusener	SA	171	7336	5751	192	29.95	6-49	6	4.70
C.R.D.Fernando	SL/Asia	147	6507	5648	187	30.20	6-27	1	5.20
S.L.Malinga	SL	115	5668	4803	185	25.96	6-38	5	5.08
Imran Khan	P	175	7461	4844	182	26.61	6-14	1	3.89
Aqib Javed	P	163	8012	5721	182	31.43	7-37	4	4.28
Abdur Razzak	B	129	6723	5050	179	28.21	5-29	3	4.50
N.W.Bracken	A	116	5759	4240	174	24.36	5-47	2	4.41
A.Flintoff	E/ICC	141	5624	4121	168	24.38	5-19	2	4.39
M.G.Johnson	A	107	5234	4237	168	25.22	6-31	3	4.85
J.D.P.Oram	NZ	155	6677	4835	168	28.77	5-26	2	4.34
Mushtaq Ahmed	P	144	7543	5361	161	33.29	5-36	1	4.26
I.K.Pathan	I	112	5452	4770	160	29.81	5-27	1	5.24
R.J.Hadlee	NZ	115	6182	3407	158	21.56	5-25	5	3.31
M.D.Marshall	WI	136	7175	4233	157	26.96	4-18	–	3.54
M.Prabhakar	I	130	6360	4534	157	28.87	5-33	2	4.27
A.Nehra	I/Asia	120	5751	4981	157	31.72	6-23	2	5.19
G.B.Hogg	A	123	5564	4188	156	26.84	5-32	2	4.51
C.H.Gayle	WI/ICC	228	6936	5473	156	35.08	5-46	1	4.73
Shakib Al Hasan	B	122	.6212	4418	154	28.68	4-16	–	4.26
S.R.Tendulkar	I	460	8044	6838	154	44.40	5-32	2	5.10
Mashrafe Mortaza	B/Asia	120	5986	4660	151	30.86	6-26	1	4.67
U.D.U.Chandana	SL	147	6142	4818	151	31.90	5-61	1	4.70

HAT-TRICKS

Jalaluddin	Pakistan v Australia	Hyderabad	1982-83
B.A.Reid	Australia v New Zealand	Sydney	1985-86
C.Sharma	India v New Zealand	Nagpur	1987-88
Wasim Akram	Pakistan v West Indies	Sharjah	1989-90
Wasim Akram	Pakistan v Australia	Sharjah	1989-90
Kapil Dev	India v Sri Lanka	Calcutta	1990-91
Aqib Javed	Pakistan v India	Sharjah	1991-92
D.K.Morrison	New Zealand v India	Napier	1993-94
Waqar Younis	Pakistan v New Zealand	East London	1994-95
Saqlain Mushtaq	Pakistan v Zimbabwe	Peshawar	1996-97
E.A.Brandes	Zimbabwe v England	Harare	1996-97
A.M.Stuart	Australia v Pakistan	Melbourne	1996-97
Saqlain Mushtaq	Pakistan v Zimbabwe	The Oval	1999
W.P.J.U.C.Vaas	Sri Lanka v Zimbabwe	Colombo (SSC)	2001-02
Mohammad Sami	Pakistan v West Indies	Sharjah	2001-02
W.P.J.U.C.Vaas	Sri Lanka v Bangladesh	Pietermaritzburg	2002-03
B.Lee	Australia v Kenya	Durban	2002-03
J.M.Anderson	England v Pakistan	The Oval	2003
S.J.Harmison	England v India	Nottingham	2004
C.K.Langeveldt	South Africa v West Indies	Bridgetown	2004-05
Shahadat Hossain	Bangladesh v Zimbabwe	Harare	2006
J.E.Taylor	West Indies v Australia	Mumbai	2006-07
S.E.Bond	New Zealand v Australia	Hobart	2006-07

S.L.Malinga[2]	Sri Lanka v South Africa	Providence	2006-07
A.Flintoff	England v West Indies	St Lucia	2008-09
M.F.Maharoof	Sri Lanka v India	Dambulla	2010
Abdur Razzak	Bangladesh v Zimbabwe	Dhaka	2010-11
K.A.J.Roach	West Indies v Netherlands	Delhi	2010-11
S.L.Malinga	Sri Lanka v Kenya	Colombo (RPS)	2010-11
S.L.Malinga	Sri Lanka v Australia	Colombo (RPS)	2011
D.T.Christian	Australia v Sri Lanka	Melbourne	2011-12

[1] The first three balls of the match. Took four wickets in opening over (W W W 4 wide W 0).
[2] Four wickets in four balls.

WICKET-KEEPING RECORDS

SIX DISMISSALS IN AN INNINGS

6	(6ct)	A.C.Gilchrist	Australia v South Africa	Cape Town	1999-00
6	(6ct)	A.J.Stewart	England v Zimbabwe	Manchester	2000
6	(5ct/1st)	R.D.Jacobs	West Indies v Sri Lanka	Colombo (RPS)	2001-02
6	(5ct/1st)	A.C.Gilchrist	Australia v England	Sydney	2002-03
6	(6ct)	A.C.Gilchrist	Australia v Namibia	Potchefstroom	2002-03
6	(6ct)	A.C.Gilchrist	Australia v Sri Lanka	Colombo (RPS)	2003-04
6	(6ct)	M.V.Boucher	South Africa v Pakistan	Cape Town	2006-07
6	(5ct/1st)	M.S.Dhoni	India v England	Leeds	2007
6	(6ct)	A.C.Gilchrist	Australia v India	Baroda	2007-08
6	(5ct/1st)	A.C.Gilchrist	Australia v India	Sydney	2007-08
6	(6ct)	M.J.Prior	England v South Africa	Nottingham	2008

100 DISMISSALS IN A CAREER

Total			LOI	Ct	St
472‡	A.C.Gilchrist	Australia/ICC	287	417	55
424	M.V.Boucher	South Africa/Africa	295	402	22
376†‡	K.C.Sangakkara	Sri Lanka/Asia/ICC	322	296	80
287‡	Moin Khan	Pakistan	219	214	73
256	M.S.Dhoni	India/Asia	203	192	64
233	I.A.Healy	Australia	168	194	39
233†‡	B.B.McCullum	New Zealand	201	218	15
220‡	Rashid Latif	Pakistan	166	182	38
206‡	R.S.Kaluwitharana	Sri Lanka	187	131	75
204‡	P.J.L.Dujon	West Indies	169	183	21
189	R.D.Jacobs	West Indies	147	160	29
165	D.J.Richardson	South Africa	122	148	17
165†‡	A.Flower	Zimbabwe	213	133	32
163†‡	A.J.Stewart	England	170	148	15
161	Kamran Akmal	Pakistan	137	136	25
154‡	N.R.Mongia	India	140	110	44
145	T.Taibu	Zimbabwe/Africa	150	112	33
136	B.J.Haddin	Australia	93	127	9
136†‡	A.C.Parore	New Zealand	179	111	25
126	Khaled Masud	Bangladesh	126	91	35
124	D.Ramdin	West Indies	89	119	5
124	R.W.Marsh	Australia	92	120	4
103	Salim Yousuf	Pakistan	86	81	22
101	Mushfiqur Rahim	Bangladesh	104	71	30

† Excluding catches taken in the field. ‡ Excluding matches when not wicket-keeper.

FIELDING RECORDS
FIVE CATCHES IN AN INNINGS

| 5 | J.N.Rhodes | South Africa v West Indies | Bombay (BS) | 1993-94 |

100 CATCHES IN A CAREER

Total			LOI
189	D.P.M.D.Jayawardena	Sri Lanka/Asia	370
160	R.T.Ponting	Australia/ICC	375
156	M.Azharuddin	India	334
139	S.R.Tendulkar	India	460
133	S.P.Fleming	New Zealand/ICC	280
130	M.Muralitharan	Sri Lanka/Asia/ICC	350
127	A.R.Border	Australia	273
125	J.H.Kallis	South Africa/Africa/ICC	321
124	R.S.Dravid	India/Asia/ICC	344
123	S.T.Jayasuriya	Sri Lanka/Asia	445
120	C.L.Hooper	West Indies	227
120	B.C.Lara	West Indies/ICC	299
116	Younus Khan	Pakistan	237
113	Inzamam-ul-Haq	Pakistan/Asia	378
111	S.R.Waugh	Australia	325
110	Shahid Afridi	Pakistan/Asia/ICC	338
109	R.S.Mahanama	Sri Lanka	213
108	P.D.Collingwood	England	197
108	M.E.Waugh	Australia	244
108	H.H.Gibbs	South Africa	248
108	S.M.Pollock	South Africa/Africa/ICC	303
105	J.N.Rhodes	South Africa	245
100	I.V.A.Richards	West Indies	187
100	S.C.Ganguly	India/Asia	311

The most for Zimbabwe is 86 by G.W.Flower (221), and for Bangladesh 36 by Mashrafe Mortaza (118).

ALL-ROUND RECORDS
50 RUNS AND 5 WICKETS IN A MATCH

I.V.A.Richards	119	5-41	West Indies v New Zealand	Dunedin	1986-87
K.Srikkanth	70	5-27	India v New Zealand	Vishakhapatnam	1988-89
M.E.Waugh	57	5-24	Australia v West Indies	Melbourne	1992-93
L.Klusener	54	6-49	South Africa v Sri Lanka	Lahore	1997-98
Abdul Razzaq	70*	5-48	Pakistan v India	Hobart	1999-00
G.A.Hick	80	5-33	England v Zimbabwe	Harare	1999-00
Shahid Afridi	61	5-40	Pakistan v England	Lahore	2000-01
S.C.Ganguly	71*	5-34	India v Zimbabwe	Kanpur	2000-01
S.B.Styris	63*	6-25	New Zealand v West Indies	Port-of-Spain	2002
R.C.Irani	53	5-26	England v India	The Oval	2002
C.H.Gayle	60	5-46	West Indies v Australia	St George's	2002-03
P.D.Collingwood	112*	6-31	England v Bangladesh	Nottingham	2005
S.Dhaniram	79	5-32	Canada v Bermuda	King City (NW)	2008
Yuvraj Singh	50*	5-31	India v Ireland	Bangalore	2010-11
Shahid Afridi	75	5-35	Pakistan v Sri Lanka	Sharjah	2011-12

APPEARANCE RECORDS
250 MATCHES

460	S.R.Tendulkar	India		295	M.V.Boucher	South Africa/Africa
445	S.T.Jayasuriya	Sri Lanka/Asia		288	Mohammad Yousuf	Pakistan/Asia
378	Inzamam-ul-Haq	Pakistan/Asia		287	A.C.Gilchrist	Australia/ICC
375	R.T.Ponting	Australia/ICC		283	Salim Malik	Pakistan
370	D.P.M.D.Jayawardena	Sri Lanka/Asia		280	S.P.Fleming	New Zealand/ICC
356	Wasim Akram	Pakistan		274	Yuvraj Singh	India/Asia
350	M.Muralitharan	Sri Lanka/Asia/ICC		273	A.R.Border	Australia
344	R.S.Dravid	India/Asia/ICC		272	D.L.Vettori	New Zealand/ICC
338	Shahid Afridi	Pakistan/Asia/ICC		271	A.Kumble	India/Asia
334	M.Azharuddin	India		269	A.Ranatunga	Sri Lanka
325	S.R.Waugh	Australia		268	M.S.Atapattu	Sri Lanka
322	K.C.Sangakkara	Sri Lanka/Asia/ICC		268	S.Chanderpaul	West Indies
322	W.P.J.U.C.Vaas	Sri Lanka/Asia/ICC		265	Abdul Razzaq	Pakistan/Asia
321	J.H.Kallis	South Africa/Africa/ICC		262	Waqar Younis	Pakistan
311	S.C.Ganguly	India/Asia		250	C.Z.Harris	New Zealand
308	P.A.de Silva	Sri Lanka		250	Ijaz Ahmed	Pakistan
303	S.M.Pollock	South Africa/Africa/ICC		250	G.D.McGrath	Australia/ICC
299	B.C.Lara	West Indies/ICC				

The most for England is 197 by P.D.Collingwood, for Zimbabwe 221 by G.W.Flower, and for Bangladesh 162 by Mohammad Ashraful.

The most consecutive appearances is 185 by S.R.Tendulkar for India (Apr 1990-Apr 1998).

100 MATCHES AS CAPTAIN

LOI			W	L	T	NR	% Won (exc NR)
230	R.T.Ponting	Australia/ICC	165	51	2	12	75.68
218	S.P.Fleming	New Zealand	98	106	1	13	47.80
193	A.Ranatunga	Sri Lanka	89	95	1	8	48.10
178	A.R.Border	Australia	107	67	1	3	61.14
174	M.Azharuddin	India	90	76	2	6	53.57
150	G.C.Smith	South Africa/Africa	92	51	1	6	63.88
147	S.C.Ganguly	India/Asia	76	66	–	5	53.52
139	Imran Khan	Pakistan	75	59	1	4	55.55
138	W.J.Cronje	South Africa	99	35	1	3	73.33
125	B.C.Lara	West Indies	59	59	–	7	50.42
119	M.S.Dhoni	India	67	41	3	8	60.36
118	S.T.Jayasuriya	Sri Lanka	66	47	2	3	57.39
109	Wasim Akram	Pakistan	66	41	2	–	60.55
108	D.P.M.D.Jayawardena	Sri Lanka	62	40	1	5	60.19
106	S.R.Waugh	Australia	67	35	3	1	63.80
105	I.V.A.Richards	West Indies	67	36	–	2	65.04

The most for England is 62 by A.J.Strauss, for Zimbabwe 86 by A.D.R.Campbell, and for Bangladesh 69 by Habibul Bashar.

100 LOI UMPIRING APPEARANCES

209	R.E.Koertzen	South Africa	09.12.1992	to	09.06.2010
181	S.A.Bucknor	West Indies	18.03.1989	to	29.03.2009
174	D.J.Harper	Australia	14.01.1994	to	19.03.2011
172	D.R.Shepherd	England	09.06.1983	to	12.07.2005
172	S.J.A.Taufel	Australia	13.01.1999	to	28.02.2012
170	B.F.Bowden	New Zealand	23.03.1995	to	26.02.2012
149	Alim Dar	Pakistan	16.02.2000	to	29.02.2012
139	D.B.Hair	Australia	14.12.1991	to	24.08.2008
126	R.B.Tiffin	Zimbabwe	25.10.1992	to	20.02.2012
121	E.A.R.de Silva	Sri Lanka	22.08.1999	to	20.08.2011
112	B.R.Doctrove	West Indies	04.04.1998	to	20.01.2012
107	D.L.Orchard	South Africa	02.12.1994	to	07.12.2003
106	S.J.Davis	Australia	12.12.1992	to	19.02.2012
100	R.S.Dunne	New Zealand	06.02.1989	to	26.02.2002

INTERNATIONAL TWENTY20 RECORDS

MATCH RESULTS

2004-05 to 1 March 2012

	Opponents	Matches	Won												Tied	NR
			E	A	SA	WI	NZ	I	P	SL	Z	B	Ass		
England	Australia	7	3	3	–	–	–	–	–	–	–	–	–	–	1
	South Africa	5	2	–	3	–	–	–	–	–	–	–	–	–	–
	West Indies	7	2	–	–	5	–	–	–	–	–	–	–	–	–
	New Zealand	5	4	–	–	–	1	–	–	–	–	–	–	–	–
	India	4	3	–	–	–	–	1	–	–	–	–	–	–	–
	Pakistan	10	7	–	–	–	–	–	3	–	–	–	–	–	–
	Sri Lanka	3	1	–	–	–	–	–	–	2	–	–	–	–	–
	Zimbabwe	1	1	–	–	–	–	–	–	–	0	–	–	–	–
	Bangladesh	0	0	–	–	–	–	–	–	–	–	0	–	–	–
	Associates	2	0	–	–	–	–	–	–	–	–	–	1	–	1
Australia	South Africa	8	–	4	4	–	–	–	–	–	–	–	–	–	–
	West Indies	5	–	3	–	2	–	–	–	–	–	–	–	–	–
	New Zealand	5	–	4	–	–	0	–	–	–	–	–	–	1	–
	India	6	–	3	–	–	–	3	–	–	–	–	–	–	–
	Pakistan	7	–	3	–	–	–	–	4	–	–	–	–	–	–
	Sri Lanka	6	–	2	–	–	–	–	–	4	–	–	–	–	–
	Zimbabwe	1	–	0	–	–	–	–	–	–	1	–	–	–	–
	Bangladesh	2	–	2	–	–	–	–	–	–	–	0	–	–	–
	Associates	0	–	0	–	–	–	–	–	–	–	–	0	–	–
S Africa	West Indies	6	–	–	5	1	–	–	–	–	–	–	–	–	–
	New Zealand	8	–	–	6	–	2	–	–	–	–	–	–	–	–
	India	5	–	–	1	–	–	4	–	–	–	–	–	–	–
	Pakistan	5	–	–	3	–	–	–	2	–	–	–	–	–	–
	Sri Lanka	5	–	–	3	–	–	–	–	2	–	–	–	–	–
	Zimbabwe	2	–	–	2	–	–	–	–	–	0	–	–	–	–
	Bangladesh	2	–	–	2	–	–	–	–	–	–	0	–	–	–
	Associates	2	–	–	2	–	–	–	–	–	–	–	0	–	–
W Indies	New Zealand	3	–	–	–	0	1	–	–	–	–	–	–	2	–
	India	3	–	–	–	2	–	1	–	–	–	–	–	–	–
	Pakistan	1	–	–	–	1	–	–	0	–	–	–	–	–	–
	Sri Lanka	3	–	–	–	0	–	–	–	3	–	–	–	–	–
	Zimbabwe	1	–	–	–	0	–	–	–	–	1	–	–	–	–
	Bangladesh	3	–	–	–	1	–	–	–	–	–	2	–	–	–
	Associates	1	–	–	–	1	–	–	–	–	–	–	0	–	–
N Zealand	India	3	–	–	–	–	3	0	–	–	–	–	–	–	–
	Pakistan	8	–	–	–	–	3	–	5	–	–	–	–	–	–
	Sri Lanka	9	–	–	–	–	5	–	–	4	–	–	–	–	–
	Zimbabwe	5	–	–	–	–	5	–	–	–	0	–	–	–	–
	Bangladesh	1	–	–	–	–	1	–	–	–	–	0	–	–	–
	Associates	3	–	–	–	–	3	–	–	–	–	–	0	–	–
India	Pakistan	2	–	–	–	–	–	1	0	–	–	–	–	1	–
	Sri Lanka	4	–	–	–	–	–	2	–	2	–	–	–	–	–
	Zimbabwe	2	–	–	–	–	–	2	–	–	0	–	–	–	–
	Bangladesh	1	–	–	–	–	–	1	–	–	–	0	–	–	–
	Associates	1	–	–	–	–	–	–	–	–	–	–	0	–	1
Pakistan	Sri Lanka	7	–	–	–	–	–	–	5	2	–	–	–	–	–
	Zimbabwe	3	–	–	–	–	–	–	3	–	0	–	–	–	–
	Bangladesh	5	–	–	–	–	–	–	5	–	–	0	–	–	–
	Associates	5	–	–	–	–	–	–	5	–	–	–	0	–	–
Sri Lanka	Zimbabwe	2	–	–	–	–	–	–	–	2	0	–	–	–	–
	Bangladesh	1	–	–	–	–	–	–	–	1	–	0	–	–	–
	Associates	3	–	–	–	–	–	–	–	3	–	–	0	–	–
Zimbabwe	Bangladesh	1	–	–	–	–	–	–	–	–	0	1	–	–	–
	Associates	2	–	–	–	–	–	–	–	–	1	–	0	1	–
Bangladesh	Associates	2	–	–	–	–	–	–	–	–	–	1	1	–	–
Associates	Associates	28	–	–	–	–	–	–	–	–	–	–	27	–	1
		229	23	24	28	13	24	17	32	23	3	4	29	5	4

MATCH RESULTS SUMMARY

	Matches	Won	Lost	Tied	NR	Win %
Netherlands	10	6	3	0	1	66.66
South Africa	43	28	15	0	0	65.11
Sri Lanka	38	23	15	0	0	60.52
Pakistan	53	32	20	1	0	60.37
Ireland	20	10	8	0	2	55.55
England	44	23	19	0	2	54.76
India	33	17	14	1	1	53.12
Australia	47	24	21	1	1	52.17
Afghanistan	8	4	4	0	0	50.00
New Zealand	50	24	23	3	0	48.00
West Indies	33	13	18	2	0	39.39
Canada	11	3	7	1	0	27.27
Kenya	15	4	11	0	0	26.66
Bangladesh	18	4	18	0	0	22.22
Scotland	12	2	9	0	1	18.18
Zimbabwe	20	3	16	1	0	15.00
Bermuda	3	0	3	0	0	0.00

INTERNATIONAL TWENTY20 RECORDS
(To 1 March 2012)
TEAM RECORDS
HIGHEST INNINGS TOTALS
† Batting Second

260-6	Sri Lanka v Kenya	Johannesburg	2007-08
241-6	South Africa v England	Centurion	2009-10
221-5	Australia v England	Sydney	2006-07
218-4	India v England	Durban	2007-08
215-5	Sri Lanka v India	Nagpur	2009-10
214-5	Australia v New Zealand	Auckland	2004-05
214-6	New Zealand v Australia	Christchurch	2009-10
214-4†	Australia v New Zealand	Christchurch	2009-10
211-5	South Africa v Scotland	The Oval	2009
211-4†	India v Sri Lanka	Mohali	2009-10
209-3	Australia v South Africa	Brisbane	2005-06
208-8	West Indies v England	The Oval	2007
208-2†	South Africa v West Indies	Johannesburg	2007-08
206-7	Sri Lanka v India	Mohali	2009-10
205-6	West Indies v South Africa	Johannesburg	2007-08
203-5	Pakistan v Bangladesh	Karachi	2007-08
202-6	England v South Africa	Johannesburg	2009-10
202-5†	New Zealand v Zimbabwe	Hamilton	2011-12
201-4	South Africa v Australia	Johannesburg	2005-06
200-6†	England v India	Durban	2007-08
200-2	Zimbabwe v New Zealand	Hamilton	2011-12

The highest total for Bangladesh is 166 (v Zimbabwe, Khulna, 2006-07).

LOWEST COMPLETED INNINGS TOTALS
† Batting Second

67	(17.2)	Kenya v Ireland	Belfast	2008
68	(16.4)	Ireland v West Indies	Providence	2009-10
70		Bermuda v Canada	Belfast	2008
73	(16.5)	Kenya v New Zealand	Durban	2007-08
74	(17.3)	India v Australia	Melbourne	2007-08

				M		I	NO	HS	Avge	50	R/100B
75†	(19.2)	Canada v Zimbabwe		King City (NW)							2008-09
78	(17.3)	Bangladesh v New Zealand		Hamilton							2009-10
79†	(14.3)	Australia v England		Southampton							2005
79-7†		West Indies v Zimbabwe		Port-of-Spain							2009-10
80†	(16.0)	Afghanistan v South Africa		Bridgetown							2009-10
80†	(15.5)	New Zealand v Pakistan		Christchurch							2010-11
81†	(15.4)	Scotland v South Africa		The Oval							2009
81	(17.3)	New Zealand v Sri Lanka		Lauderhill							2010
83†	(15.5)	Bangladesh v Sri Lanka		Johannesburg							2007-08
84	(15.1)	Zimbabwe v New Zealand		Providence							2009-10
85-9†		Bangladesh v Pakistan		Dhaka							2011-12
86†	(15.3)	Netherlands v Ireland		Dubai							2009-10
87†	(16.2)	Sri Lanka v Australia		Bridgetown							2009-10
88†	(19.3)	Kenya v Sri Lanka		Johannesburg							2007-08
88†	(16.4)	England v West Indies		The Oval							2011
89	(18.4)	Pakistan v England		Cardiff							2010

The lowest total for South Africa is 114 (v Australia, Brisbane, 2005-06).

BATTING RECORDS

600 RUNS IN A CAREER

Runs			M	I	NO	HS	Avge	50	R/100B
1352	B.B.McCullum	NZ	47	47	8	116*	34.66	9	131.0
1176	K.P.Pietersen	E	36	36	5	79	37.93	7	141.5
982	G.C.Smith	SA	33	33	2	89*	31.67	5	127.5
953	D.P.M.D.Jayawardena	SL	35	35	5	100	31.76	7	139.3
894	T.M.Dilshan	SL	35	34	6	104*	31.92	6	126.6
883	K.C.Sangakkara	SL	33	32	4	78	31.53	6	119.6
808	D.A.Warner	A	31	31	–	89	26.06	5	142.0
794	J.P.Duminy	SA	35	33	8	96*	31.76	4	126.6
788	M.J.Guptill	NZ	29	27	5	91*	35.81	4	126.4
788	Misbah-ul-Haq	P	39	34	13	87*	37.52	3	110.2
748	Shahid Afridi	P	48	46	3	54*	17.39	1	141.9
733	D.J.Hussey	A	34	32	3	88*	25.27	3	122.1
709	Shoaib Malik	P	39	37	7	57	23.63	2	113.2
704	Kamran Akmal	P	38	33	3	73	23.46	1	124.6
697	G.Gambhir	I	25	24	1	75	30.30	7	121.4
682	Umar Akmal	P	29	28	4	64	28.41	4	119.6
680	A.B.de Villiers	SA	36	35	7	79*	24.28	4	119.9
667	L.R.P.L.Taylor	NZ	39	35	4	63	21.51	3	117.2
632	C.L.White	A	29	28	8	85*	31.60	3	139.5
629	S.T.Jayasuriya	SL	31	30	3	88	23.29	4	129.1
617	C.H.Gayle	WI	20	20	1	117	32.47	6	144.4
601	E.J.G.Morgan	E	21	21	6	85*	40.06	3	135.3

HIGHEST INDIVIDUAL INNINGS

Score	Balls					
117*	51	R.E.Levi	SA v NZ	Hamilton		2011-12
117	57	C.H.Gayle	WI v SA	Johannesburg		2007-08
116*	56	B.B.McCullum	NZ v A	Christchurch		2009-10
104*	57	T.M.Dilshan	SL v A	Pallekele		2011
101	60	S.K.Raina	I v SA	Gros Islet		2009-10
100	64	D.P.M.D.Jayawardena	SL v Z	Providence		2009-10
98*	55	R.T.Ponting	A v NZ	Auckland		2004-05
98*	56	D.P.M.D.Jayawardena	SL v WI	Bridgetown		2009-10
98	66	C.H.Gayle	WI v I	Bridgetown		2009-10

96*	57	T.M.Dilshan	SL v WI	The Oval	2009
96*	54	J.P.Duminy	SA v Z	Kimberley	2010-11
96	56	D.R.Martyn	A v SA	Brisbane	2005-06
94	45	L.E.Bosman	SA v E	Centurion	2009-10
91*	54	M.J.Guptill	NZ v Z	Auckland	2011-12
90*	55	H.H.Gibbs	SA v WI	Johannesburg	2007-08
89*	58	G.C.Smith	SA v A	Johannesburg	2005-06
89*	56	J.M.Kemp	SA v NZ	Durban	2007-08
89	43	D.A.Warner	A v SA	Melbourne	2008-09
88*	44	D.J.Hussey	A v SA	Johannesburg	2008-09
88*	61	H.Patel	C v Ire	Colombo (SSC)	2009-10
88	44	S.T.Jayasuriya	SL v K	Johannesburg	2007-08
88	50	C.H.Gayle	WI v A	The Oval	2009
88	44	G.C.Smith	SA v E	Centurion	2009-10
87*	53	Misbah-ul-Haq	P v B	Karachi	2007-08
86	63	D.P.M.D.Jayawardena	SL v A	Pallekele	2011
85*	46	A.Symonds	A v NZ	Perth	2007-08
85*	45	E.J.G.Morgan	E v SA	Johannesburg	2009-10
85*	49	C.L.White	A v SL	Bridgetown	2009-10

HIGHEST PARTNERSHIP FOR EACH WICKET

1st	170	G.C.Smith/L.E.Bosman	SA v E	Centurion	2009-10
2nd	166	D.P.M.D.Jayawardena/K.C.Sangakkara	SL v WI	Bridgetown	2009-10
3rd	137	M.J.Guptill/K.S.Williamson	NZ v Z	Auckland	2011-12
4th	112*	K.P.Pietersen/E.J.G.Morgan	E v P	Dubai	2009-10
5th	119*	Shoaib Malik/Misbah-ul-Haq	P v A	Johannesburg	2007-08
6th	101*	C.L.White/M.E.K.Hussey	A v SL	Bridgetown	2009-10
7th	91	P.D.Collingwood/M.H.Yardy	E v WI	The Oval	2007
8th	64*	W.D.Parnell/J.Theron	SA v A	Johannesburg	2011-12
9th	44	S.L.Malinga/C.R.D.Fernando	SL v NZ	Auckland	2006-07
10th	31*	Wahab Riaz/Shoaib Akhtar	P v NZ	Auckland	2010-11

BOWLING RECORDS

25 WICKETS IN A CAREER

Wkts			Matches	Overs	Mdns	Runs	Avge	Best	R/Over
56	Shahid Afridi	P	48	180.5	3	1115	19.91	4-11	6.16
55	Umar Gul	P	38	132.4	2	863	15.69	5- 6	6.50
51	Saeed Ajmal	P	37	134.0	1	837	16.41	4-19	6.24
40	B.A.W.Mendis	SL	21	79.0	2	445	11.12	6-16	5.63
40	G.P.Swann	E	29	103.0	2	659	16.47	3-13	6.39
40	S.C.J.Broad	E	33	120.3	–	876	21.90	3-17	7.26
38	S.L.Malinga	SL	31	105.3	–	775	20.39	3-12	7.34
36	M.G.Johnson	A	28	101.2	1	724	20.11	3-15	7.14
35	D.L.Vettori	NZ	28	108.1	1	580	16.57	4-20	5.36
34	N.L.McCullum	NZ	32	84.2	–	548	16.11	4-16	6.49
32	M.Morkel	SA	22	82.5	3	551	17.21	4-17	6.65
32	J.Botha	SA	31	107.2	–	669	20.90	3-16	6.23
30	D.J.G.Sammy	WI	24	73.3	–	460	15.33	5-26	6.25
29	D.W.Steyn	SA	21	78.0	–	531	18.31	4- 9	6.80
29	K.D.Mills	NZ	27	99.4	–	858	29.58	3-37	8.60
28	D.P.Nannes	A/Ne	17	61.0	2	459	16.39	4-18	7.52
28	S.W.Tait	A	19	71.4	2	498	17.78	3-13	6.94
27	T.G.Southee	NZ	23	83.0	1	695	25.74	5-18	8.37
25	Mohammad Hafeez	P	29	75.2	–	518	20.72	4-10	6.87
25	S.E.Bond	NZ	20	77.3	2	543	21.72	3-18	7.00

BEST FIGURES IN AN INNINGS

6-16	B.A.W.Mendis	SL v A	Pallekele	2011
5- 6	Umar Gul	P v NZ	The Oval	2009
5-18	T.G.Southee	NZ v P	Auckland	2010-11
5-19	R.McLaren	SA v WI	North Sound	2009-10
5-20	N.Odhiambo	K v Sc	Nairobi (Gym)	2009-10
5-26	D.J.G.Sammy	WI v Z	Port-of-Spain	2009-10
4- 6	S.J.Benn	WI v Z	Port-of-Spain	2009-10
4- 7	M.R.Gillespie	NZ v K	Durban	2007-08
4- 8	Umar Gul	P v A	Dubai	2009
4- 9	D.W.Steyn	SA v WI	Port Elizabeth	2007-08
4-10	Mohammad Hafeez	P v Z	Harare	2011
4-10	R.S.Bopara	E v WI	The Oval	2011
4-11	Shahid Afridi	P v Ne	Lord's	2009
4-13	R.P.Singh	I v SA	Durban	2007-08
4-13	Umar Gul	P v SL	King City (NW)	2008-09
4-13	W.D.Parnell	SA v WI	The Oval	2009
4-14	Shahid Afridi	P v NZ	Christchurch	2010-11
4-14	S.O.Ngoche	K v Ire	Mombasa	2011-12
4-15	B.A.W.Mendis	SL v Z	King City (NW)	2008-09
4-15	S.R.Watson	A v E	Adelaide	2010-11

HAT-TRICKS

B.Lee	Australia v Bangladesh	Melbourne	2007-08
J.D.P.Oram	New Zealand v Sri Lanka	Colombo (RPS)	2009
T.G.Southee	New Zealand v Pakistan	Auckland	2010-11

WICKET-KEEPING RECORDS

15 DISMISSALS IN A CAREER

Dis			Matches	Ct	St
45	Kamran Akmal	Pakistan	38	17	28
28†	B.B.McCullum	New Zealand	47	21	7
26	K.C.Sangakkara	Sri Lanka	33	15	11
23	D.Ramdin	West Indies	23	21	2
19	M.V.Boucher	South Africa	25	18	1
18	N.E.O'Brien	Ireland	16	10	8
18	M.S.Dhoni	India	30	13	5
17	A.C.Gilchrist	Australia	13	17	–
17	Mushfiqur Rahim	Bangladesh	17	9	8
17†	A.B.de Villiers	South Africa	36	13	4
16	B.J.Haddin	Australia	25	12	4

† *Excluding catches taken in the field.*

MOST DISMISSALS IN AN INNINGS

4 (4 ct)	A.C.Gilchrist	Australia v Zimbabwe	Cape Town	2007-08
4 (4 ct)	M.J.Prior	England v South Africa	Cape Town	2007-08
4 (4 ct)	A.C.Gilchrist	Australia v New Zealand	Perth	2007-08
4 (4 st)	Kamran Akmal	Pakistan v Netherlands	Lord's	2009
4 (3 ct, 1 st)	N.J.O'Brien	Ireland v Sri Lanka	Lord's	2009
4 (4 ct)	M.S.Dhoni	India v Afghanistan	Gros Islet	2009-10
4 (2 ct, 2 st)	A.B.de Villiers	South Africa v West Indies	North Sound	2009-10

MOST STUMPINGS IN AN INNINGS

4	Kamran Akmal	Pakistan v Netherlands	Lord's	2009

FIELDING RECORDS
15 CATCHES IN A CAREER

Total			Matches	Total			Matches
26	L.R.P.L.Taylor	New Zealand	39	16	C.L.White	Australia	29
22	A.B.de Villiers	South Africa	36	16	S.C.J.Broad	England	34
20	D.J.Hussey	Australia	34	16	J.P.Duminy	South Africa	35
18	M.E.K.Hussey	Australia	27	15	Umar Akmal	Pakistan	29
18	D.A.Warner	Australia	31	15	J.Botha	South Africa	31
18	G.C.Smith	South Africa	33	15	J.A.Morkel	South Africa	34
16	S.P.D.Smith	Australia	20	15	Shoaib Malik	Pakistan	39

MOST CATCHES IN AN INNINGS

4	D.J.G.Sammy	West Indies v Ireland	Providence	2009-10

APPEARANCE RECORDS
35 APPEARANCES

48	Shahid Afridi	Pakistan		37	Saeed Ajmal	Pakistan
47	B.B.McCullum	New Zealand		36	A.B.de Villiers	South Africa
39	Misbah-ul-Haq	Pakistan		36	K.P.Pietersen	England
39	Shoaib Malik	Pakistan		35	P.D.Collingwood	England
39	L.R.P.L.Taylor	New Zealand		35	T.M.Dilshan	Sri Lanka
39	Umar Gul	Pakistan		35	J.P.Duminy	South Africa
38	Kamran Akmal	Pakistan		35	D.M.P.D.Jayawardena	Sri Lanka

20 MATCHES AS CAPTAIN

IT20			W	L	T	NR	%age wins
30	P.D.Collingwood	England	17	11	–	2	60.71
29	M.S.Dhoni	India	13	14	1	1	46.42
28	D.L.Vettori	New Zealand	13	13	2	–	46.42
27	G.C.Smith	South Africa	18	9	–	–	66.66
21	K.S.Sangakkara	Sri Lanka	12	9	–	–	57.14
20	W.T.S.Porterfield	Ireland	10	8	–	2	55.55

UNIVERSITY MATCH RESULTS

Played: 166. Wins: Cambridge 58; Oxford 54. Drawn: 54. Abandoned: 1

In 2001, for the very first time, Cambridge hosted the University Match, cricket's oldest surviving first-class fixture, after the ECB's re-organisation of university cricket around six centres of excellence had removed it from Lord's. Dating from 1827 it has, wartime interruptions apart, been played annually since 1838. With the exception of five matches played in the area of Oxford (1829, 1843, 1846, 1848 and 1850), all the previous fixtures had been staged at Lord's. Since 2001 it has been played over four days rather than three.

In 2003, Oxford (with Brookes), Cambridge (with Anglia) and Durham were joined by Loughborough in playing three first-class matches against counties. The other two centres – Cardiff (with UWIC and Glamorgan), and Leeds (with Bradford and Leeds Metropolitan) – also play three counties apiece, but without first-class status.

1827	Drawn	1878	Cambridge	1925	Drawn	1974	Drawn
1829	Oxford	1879	Cambridge	1926	Cambridge	1975	Drawn
1836	Oxford	1880	Cambridge	1927	Cambridge	1976	Oxford
1838	Oxford	1881	Oxford	1928	Drawn	1977	Drawn
1839	Cambridge	1882	Cambridge	1929	Drawn	1978	Drawn
1840	Cambridge	1883	Cambridge	1930	Cambridge	1979	Cambridge
1841	Cambridge	1884	Oxford	1931	Oxford	1980	Drawn
1842	Cambridge	1885	Cambridge	1932	Drawn	1981	Drawn
1843	Cambridge	1886	Oxford	1933	Drawn	1982	Cambridge
1844	Drawn	1887	Oxford	1934	Drawn	1983	Drawn
1845	Cambridge	1888	Drawn	1935	Cambridge	1984	Oxford
1846	Oxford	1889	Cambridge	1936	Cambridge	1985	Drawn
1847	Cambridge	1890	Cambridge	1937	Oxford	1986	Cambridge
1848	Oxford	1891	Cambridge	1938	Drawn	1987	Drawn
1849	Cambridge	1892	Oxford	1939	Oxford	1988	Abandoned
1850	Oxford	1893	Cambridge	1946	Oxford	1989	Drawn
1851	Cambridge	1894	Oxford	1947	Drawn	1990	Drawn
1852	Oxford	1895	Cambridge	1948	Oxford	1991	Drawn
1853	Oxford	1896	Oxford	1949	Cambridge	1992	Cambridge
1854	Oxford	1897	Cambridge	1950	Drawn	1993	Oxford
1855	Oxford	1898	Oxford	1951	Oxford	1994	Drawn
1856	Cambridge	1899	Drawn	1952	Drawn	1995	Oxford
1857	Oxford	1900	Drawn	1953	Cambridge	1996	Drawn
1858	Oxford	1901	Drawn	1954	Drawn	1997	Drawn
1859	Cambridge	1902	Cambridge	1955	Drawn	1998	Cambridge
1860	Cambridge	1903	Oxford	1956	Drawn	1999	Drawn
1861	Cambridge	1904	Drawn	1957	Cambridge	2000	Drawn
1862	Cambridge	1905	Cambridge	1958	Cambridge	2001	Oxford
1863	Oxford	1906	Cambridge	1959	Oxford	2002	Oxford
1864	Oxford	1907	Cambridge	1960	Drawn	2003	Oxford
1865	Oxford	1908	Oxford	1961	Drawn	2004	Oxford
1866	Oxford	1909	Drawn	1962	Drawn	2005	Oxford
1867	Cambridge	1910	Oxford	1963	Drawn	2006	Oxford
1868	Cambridge	1911	Oxford	1964	Drawn	2007	Drawn
1869	Cambridge	1912	Cambridge	1965	Drawn	2008	Drawn
1870	Cambridge	1913	Cambridge	1966	Oxford	2009	Cambridge
1871	Oxford	1914	Oxford	1967	Drawn	2010	Oxford
1872	Oxford	1919	Oxford	1968	Drawn	2011	Cambridge
1873	Oxford	1920	Drawn	1969	Drawn		
1874	Oxford	1921	Cambridge	1970	Drawn		
1875	Oxford	1922	Cambridge	1971	Drawn		
1876	Cambridge	1923	Oxford	1972	Cambridge		
1877	Oxford	1924	Cambridge	1973	Drawn		

CAMBRIDGE UNIVERSITY RECORDS

ALL FIRST-CLASS MATCHES

Highest Total	For 703-9d		v	Sussex	Hove	1890
	V 730-3		by	W Indians	Cambridge	1950
Lowest Total	For 30		by	Yorkshire	Cambridge	1928
	V 32		by	Oxford U	Lord's	1878
Highest Innings	For 254*	K.S.Duleepsinhji	v	Middlesex	Cambridge	1927
	V 304*	E.de C.Weekes	for	W Indians	Cambridge	1950
Highest Partnership						
(2nd wicket)	429*	J.G.Dewes/G.H.G.Doggart	v	Essex	Cambridge	1949
Best Innings Bowling	10-69	S.M.J.Woods	v	Thornton's XI	Cambridge	1890
Best Match Bowling	15-88	S.M.J.Woods	v	Thornton's XI	Cambridge	1890
Most Runs – Season	1581	D.S.Sheppard		(av 79.05)		1952
Most Runs – Career	4310	J.M.Brearley		(av 38.48)		1961-68
Most 100s – Season	7	D.S.Sheppard				1952
Most 100s – Career	14	D.S.Sheppard				1950-52
Most Wkts – Season	80	O.S.Wheatley		(av 17.63)		1958
Most Wkts – Career	208	G.Goonesena		(av 21.82)		1954-57

UNIVERSITY MATCH RECORDS

Highest Total	604		Oxford	2002
Lowest Total	39		Lord's	1858
Highest Innings	211	G.Goonesena	Lord's	1957
Best Innings Bowling	8-44	G.E.Jeffery	Lord's	1873
Best Match Bowling	13-73	A.G.Steel	Lord's	1878

Hat-Tricks: F.C.Cobden (1870), A.G.Steel (1879), P.H.Morton (1880), J.F.Ireland (1911), R.G.H.Lowe (1926)

OXFORD UNIVERSITY RECORDS

ALL FIRST-CLASS MATCHES

Highest Total	For 651		v	Sussex	Hove	1895
	V 679-7d		by	Australians	Oxford	1938
Lowest Total	For 12		v	MCC	Oxford	1877
	V 24		by	MCC	Oxford	1846
Highest Innings	For 281	K.J.Key	v	Middlesex	Chiswick Park	1887
	V 338	W.W.Read	for	Surrey	The Oval	1888
Highest Partnership						
(3rd wicket)	408	S.Oberoi/D.R.Fox	v	Cambridge U	Cambridge	2005
Best Innings Bowling	10-38	S.E.Butler	v	Cambridge U	Lord's	1871
Best Match Bowling	15-65	B.J.T.Bosanquet	v	Sussex	Oxford	1900
Most Runs – Season	1307	Nawab of Pataudi sr		(av 93.35)		1931
Most Runs – Career	3319	N.S.Mitchell-Innes		(av 47.41)		1934-37
Most 100s – Season	6	Nawab of Pataudi sr				1931
	6	M.P.Donnelly				1946
Most 100s – Career	9	A.M.Crawley				1927-30
	9	Nawab of Pataudi sr				1928-31
	9	N.S.Mitchell-Innes				1934-37
	9	M.P.Donnelly				1946-47
Most Wkts – Season	70	I.A.R.Peebles		(av 18.15)		1930
Most Wkts – Career	182	R.H.B.Bettington		(av 19.38)		1920-23

UNIVERSITY MATCH RECORDS

Highest Total	611-5d		Oxford	2010
Lowest Total	32		Lord's	1878
Highest Innings	247	S.Oberoi	Cambridge	2005
Best Innings Bowling	10-38	S.E.Butler	Lord's	1871
Best Match Bowling	15-95	S.E.Butler	Lord's	1871

Match Doubles: P.R.le Couteur (160 and 11-66 in 1910); G.J.Toogood (149 and 10-93 in 1985)

INDIAN PREMIER LEAGUE 2011

The fourth IPL tournament was held in India between 8 April and 28 May.

Team	P	W	L	T	NR	Pts	Net RR
1 Royal Challengers Bangalore (4)	14	9	4	–	1	19	+0.32
2 Chennai Super Kings (3)	14	9	5	–	–	18	+0.44
3 Mumbai Indians (1)	14	9	5	–	–	18	+0.04
4 Kolkata Knight Riders (6)	14	8	6	–	–	16	+0.43
5 Kings XI Punjab (8)	14	7	7	–	–	14	–0.05
6 Rajasthan Royals (7)	14	6	7	–	1	13	–0.69
7 Deccan Chargers (2)	14	6	8	–	–	12	+0.22
8 Kochi Tuskers Kerala (-)	14	6	8	–	–	12	–0.21
9 Pune Warriors (-)	14	4	9	–	1	9	–0.13
10 Delhi Daredevils (5)	14	4	9	–	1	9	–0.44

1st Qualifying Final: At Wankhede Stadium, Mumbai, 24 May (floodlit). Toss: Chennai Super Kings. **CHENNAI SUPER KINGS** won by six wickets. Royal Challengers Bangalore 175-4 (20; V.Kohli 70*). Chennai Super Kings 177-4 (19.4; S.K.Raina 73*). Award: S.K.Raina.

Elimination Final: At Wankhede Stadium, Mumbai, 25 May (floodlit). Toss: Mumbai Indians. **MUMBAI INDIANS** won by four wickets. Kolkata Knight Riders 147-7 (20; R.N.ten Doeschate 70*, M.M.Patel 3-27). Mumbai Indians (19.2; A.C.Blizzard 51). Award: M.M.Patel.

2nd Qualifying Final: At M.A.Chidambaram Stadium, Chennai, 27 May (floodlit). Toss: Mumbai Indians. **ROYAL CHALLENGERS BANGALORE** won by 43 runs. Royal Challengers Bangalore 185-4 (20; C.H.Gayle 89). Mumbai Indians 142-8 (20; D.L.Vettori 3-19). Award: C.H.Gayle.

FINAL: At M.A.Chidambaram Stadium, Chennai, 28 May (floodlit). Toss: Chennai Super Kings. **CHENNAI SUPER KINGS** won by 58 runs. Chennai Super Kings 205-5 (20; M.Vijay 95, M.E.K.Hussey 63). Royal Challengers Bangalore 147-8 (20; R.Ashwin 3-16). Award: M.Vijay. Series award: C.H.Gayle (Royal Challengers Bangalore).

IPL winners:

2008 Rajasthan Royals   2009 Deccan Chargers   2010 Chennai Super Kings

TEAM RECORDS
HIGHEST TOTALS

246-5 (20)	Chennai v Rajasthan	Chennai	2010
240-5 (20)	Chennai v Punjab	Mohali	2008

LOWEST TOTALS

58 (15.1)	Rajasthan v Bangalore	Cape Town	2009
67 (15.2)	Kolkata v Mumbai	Mumbai	2008

LARGEST MARGINS OF VICTORY

140 runs	Kolkata (222-3) v Bangalore (82)	Bangalore	2008
10 wickets	Mumbai (154-7) v Deccan (155-0)	Mumbai	2008
10 wickets	Rajasthan (92) v Bangalore (93-0)	Bangalore	2010
10 wickets	Mumbai (133-5) v Rajasthan (134-0)	Mumbai	2011

Delhi beat Punjab by ten wickets in a reduced game in 2009.

BATTING RECORDS
600 RUNS IN A SEASON

Runs		Year	M	I	NO	HS	Ave	100	50	6s	4s	R/100B
618 S.R.Tendulkar	Mumbai	2010	15	15	2	89*	47.53	–	5	3	86	132.6
616 S.E.Marsh	Punjab	2008	11	11	2	115	68.44	1	5	26	59	139.7
608 C.H.Gayle	Bangalore	2011	12	12	3	107	67.55	2	3	44	56	183.1

HIGHEST SCORES

Score	Balls				
158*	73	B.B.McCullum	Kolkata v Bangalore	Bangalore	2008
127	56	M.Vijay	Chennai v Rajasthan	Chennai	2010
120*	63	P.C.Valthaty	Punjab v Chennai	Mohali	2011
119	56	V.Sehwag	Delhi v Deccan	Hyderabad	2011
117*	53	A.Symonds	Deccan v Rajasthan	Hyderabad	2008

FASTEST HUNDRED

37 balls	Y.K.Pathan (100)	Rajasthan v Mumbai	Mumbai (BS)	2010

MOST SIXES IN AN INNINGS

13	B.B.McCullum	Kolkata v Bangalore	Bangalore	2008
11	S.T.Jayasuriya	Mumbai v Chennai	Mumbai	2008
11	M.Vijay	Chennai v Rajasthan	Chennai	2010

HIGHEST STRIKE RATE IN A SEASON (Qualification: 100 runs or more)

R/100B	Score	Balls			
204.34	188	92	B.B.McCullum	Kolkata	2008

HIGHEST STRIKE RATE IN AN INNINGS (Qualification: 25 runs, 300+ strike rate)

R/100B	Score	Balls			
385.7	27*	7	B.Akhil	Bangalore v Deccan	Hyderabad	2008
346.1	45*	13	K.A.Pollard	Mumbai v Delhi	Mumbai (BS)	2010
316.6	38	12	C.H.Gayle	Bangalore v Kolkata	Bangalore	2011
306.2	49	16	Yuvraj Singh	Punjab v Rajasthan	Mohali	2008

BOWLING RECORDS
MOST WICKETS IN A SEASON

Wkts			Year	P	O	M	Runs	Avge	Best	4w	R/Over
28	S.L.Malinga	Mumbai	2011	16	63.0	2	375	13.39	5-13	1	5.95
23	R.P.Singh	Deccan	2009	16	59.4	1	417	18.13	4-22	1	6.98
22	Sohail Tanvir	Rajasthan	2008	11	41.1	—	266	12.09	6-14	2	6.46
22	M.M.Patel	Mumbai	2011	15	54.2	1	358	16.27	5-21	1	6.58

BEST BOWLING FIGURES IN AN INNINGS

6-14	Sohail Tanvir	Rajasthan v Chennai	Jaipur	2008
5- 5	A.Kumble	Bangalore v Rajasthan	Cape Town	2009
5-12	I.Sharma	Deccan v Kochi	Kochi	2011
5-13	S.L.Malinga	Mumbai v Delhi	Delhi	2011

MOST ECONOMICAL BOWLING ANALYSIS

O	M	R	W				
4	1	6	0	F.H.Edwards	Deccan v Kolkata	Cape Town	2009
4	1	6	1	A.Nehra	Delhi v Punjab	Bloemfontein	2009

MOST EXPENSIVE BOWLING ANALYSIS

O	M	R	W				
4	0	59	1	R.P.Singh	Deccan v Kolkata	Hyderabad	2008
4	0	59	0	S.K.Trivedi	Rajasthan v Punjab	Mohali	2011

NOKIA CHAMPIONS LEAGUE TWENTY20 2011

The third Champions League Twenty20 tournament took place in India between 19 September and 9 October. Thirteen teams took part, having qualified from their domestic Twenty20 competitions: four from India's IPL, two each from Australia, England and South Africa, and one each from New Zealand, Sri Lanka and West Indies. Auckland, Leicestershire and Ruhuna were eliminated in a qualifying round.

GROUP A

Team	P	W	L	T	NR	Pts	Net RR
1 New South Wales	4	3	1	–	–	6	+0.62
2 Mumbai Indians	4	2	1	–	1	5	–0.28
3 Trinidad & Tobago	4	2	2	–	–	4	+0.17
4 Cape Cobras	4	1	2	–	1	3	+0.22
5 Chennai Super Kings	4	1	3	–	–	2	–0.71

GROUP B

Team	P	W	L	T	NR	Pts	Net RR
1 Somerset	4	2	1	–	1	5	–0.55
2 RC Bangalore	4	2	2	–	–	4	+0.32
3 Kolkata Knight Riders	4	2	2	–	–	4	+0.30
4 Warriors	4	2	2	–	–	4	+0.24
5 South Australia	4	1	2	–	1	3	–0.53

1st Semi-Final: At M.Chinnaswamy Stadium, Bangalore, 7 October (floodlit). Toss: Royal Challengers Bangalore. **ROYAL CHALLENGERS BANGALORE** won by six wickets. New South Wales 203-2 (20; D.A.Warner 123*, D.L.R.Smith 62). Royal Challengers Bangalore 204-4 (18.3; C.H.Gayle 92, V.Kohli 84, P.J.Cummins 4-45). Award: V.Kohli.

2nd Semi-Final: At M.A.Chidambaram Stadium, Chennai, 8 October (floodlit). Toss: Mumbai Indians. **MUMBAI INDIANS** won by 10 runs. Mumbai Indians 160-5 (20; A.C.Blizzard 54). Somerset 150-7 (20; C.Kieswetter 62, S.L.Malinga 4-20). Award: S.L.Malinga.

FINAL: At M.A.Chidambaram Stadium, Chennai, 9 October (floodlit). Toss: Mumbai Indians. **MUMBAI INDIANS** won by 31 runs. Mumbai Indians 139 (20; R.R.Bhatkal 3-21). Royal Challengers Bangalore 108 (19.2; Harbhajan Singh 3-20). Award: Harbhajan Singh. Series award: S.L.Malinga.

Champions League Winners: 2009   New South Wales   2010   Chennai Super Kings

TOURNAMENT RECORDS 2009-11

Highest total	215-8		RC Bangalore v S Australia	Bangalore	2011
Lowest total	70		Central Districts v Wayamba	Port Elizabeth	2010
Largest victory	97 runs		Chennai v Wayamba	Centurion	2010
Highest score	135*	D.A.Warner	NSW v Wayamba	Chennai	2011
Most runs overall	535	D.A.Warner (ave 59.44)	New South Wales		2009-11
Most runs in season	328	D.A.Warner (ave 109.33)	New South Wales		2011
Highest partnership	147	D.J.Jacobs/A.G.Prince	Warriors v Central Districts	Port Elizabeth	2010
Best bowling	5-32	S.W.Tait	S Australia v RC Bangalore	Bangalore	2011
Most wickets overall	21	D.J.Bravo (ave 18.57)	T & T, Mumbai, Chennai		2009-11
Most wickets in season	13	R.Ashwin (ave 11.69)	Chennai Super Kings		2010
Most economical	4-0-7-2	H.M.R.K.B.Herath	Wayamba v Central Districts	Port Elizabeth	2010
	4-1-7-2	S.Badree	Trinidad & T v Leics	Hyderabad	2011
Most expensive	4-0-69-0	S.Aravind	RC Bangalore v S Australia	Bangalore	2011

WOMEN'S LIMITED-OVERS RECORDS

1973 to 11 March 2012

RESULTS SUMMARY

	Matches	Won	Lost	Tied	NR	% Won (exc NR)
Bangladesh	1	1	–	–	–	100.00
Australia	251	193	51	1	6	78.77
England	264	148	105	2	9	58.03
India	190	98	87	1	4	52.68
New Zealand	257	128	121	2	6	50.99
Sri Lanka	91	44	44	–	3	50.00
West Indies	95	46	46	1	2	49.46
South Africa	90	40	45	1	4	46.51
Trinidad & Tobago	6	2	4	–	–	33.33
Ireland	120	37	79	–	4	31.89
Pakistan	89	22	65	–	2	25.28
Jamaica	5	1	4	–	–	20.00
Netherlands	101	19	81	–	1	19.00
Denmark	33	6	27	–	–	18.18
International XI	18	3	14	–	1	17.64
Young England	6	1	5	–	–	16.66
Scotland	8	1	7	–	–	12.50
Japan	5	–	5	–	–	0.00

TEAM RECORDS

HIGHEST INNINGS TOTALS

455-5 (50)	New Zealand v Pakistan	Christchurch	1996-97
412-3 (50)	Australia v Denmark	Bombay	1997-98

HIGHEST MATCH AGGREGATES

570-14	New Zealand (263) v Australia (307-4)	Hamilton	2008-09
563-16	England (272) v New Zealand (291-6)	Chennai	2006-07

LARGEST RUNS MARGIN OF VICTORY

408 runs	New Zealand beat Pakistan	Christchurch	1996-97
374 runs	Australia beat Pakistan	Melbourne	1996-97
363 runs	Australia beat Denmark	Bombay	1997-98

LOWEST INNINGS TOTALS

22 (23.4)	Netherlands v West Indies	Deventer	2008
23 (24.1)	Pakistan v Australia	Melbourne	1996-97
24 (21.3)	Scotland v England	Reading	2001

BATTING RECORDS

HIGHEST INDIVIDUAL INNINGS

229*	B.J.Clark	Australia v Denmark	Bombay	1997-98
173*	C.M.Edwards	England v Ireland	Poona	1997-98
168	S.W.Bates	New Zealand v Pakistan	Sydney	2008-09
156*	L.M.Keightley	Australia v Pakistan	Melbourne	1996-97
156*	S.C.Taylor	England v India	Lord's	2006
154*	K.L.Rolton	Australia v Sri Lanka	Christchurch	2000-01
153*	J.Logtenberg	South Africa v Netherlands	Deventer	2007
151	K.L.Rolton	Australia v Ireland	Dublin	2005

2000 RUNS IN A CAREER

Runs		Career	M	I	NO	HS	Avge	100	50
4844	B.J.Clark (A)	1991-2005	118	114	12	229*	47.49	5	30
4814	K.L.Rolton (A)	1995-2009	141	132	32	154*	48.14	8	33
4755	C.M.Edwards (E)	1997-2012	155	145	19	173*	37.73	6	37
4161	M.Raj (I)	1999-2012	132	119	31	114*	47.28	3	33
4101	S.C.Taylor (E)	1998-2011	126	120	18	156*	40.20	8	23
4064	D.A.Hockley (NZ)	1982-2000	118	115	18	117	41.89	4	34
2919	H.M.Tiffen (NZ)	1999-2009	117	111	16	100	30.72	1	18
2844	E.C.Drumm (NZ)	1992-2006	101	94	13	116	35.11	2	19
2806	A.Chopra (I)	1995-2012	124	109	21	100	31.88	1	18
2630	L.M.Keightley (A)	1995-2005	82	78	12	156*	39.84	4	21
2540	L.C.Sthalekar (A)	2001-2012	111	99	21	104*	32.56	2	16
2201	R.J.Rolls (NZ)	1997-2007	104	91	3	114	25.01	2	12
2121	J.A.Brittin (E)	1979-1998	63	59	9	138*	42.42	5	8
2111	S.J.Taylor (E)	2006-2012	66	60	8	129	40.59	4	9
2091	J.Sharma (I)	2002-2008	77	75	7	138*	30.75	2	14
2047	S.Nitschke (A)	2004-2011	80	69	9	113*	34.11	1	14
2035	A.J.Blackwell (A)	2003-2012	87	77	16	106*	33.36	2	14

HIGHEST PARTNERSHIP FOR EACH WICKET

1st	268	S.J.Taylor/C.M.G.Atkins	E v SA	Lord's	2008
2nd	262	H.M.Tiffen/S.W.Bates	NZ v P	Sydney	2008-09
3rd	244	K.L.Rolton/L.C.Sthalekar	A v Ire	Dublin	2005
4th	224*	J.Logtenberg/M.du Preez	SA v Ne	Deventer	2007
5th	188*	S.C.Taylor/J.Cassar	E v SL	Lincoln, NZ	2001-02
6th	139*	S.J.McGlashan/N.J.Browne	NZ v SA	Bowral	2008-09
7th	104*	S.J.Tsukigawa/N.J.Browne	NZ v E	Madras	2006-07
8th	85*	S.L.Clarke/N.J.Shaw	E v Sc	Reading	2001
9th	73	L.R.F.Askew/I.T.Guha	E v NZ	Madras	2006-07
10th	43	A.Sharma/G.Sultana	I v E	Sydney	2008-09

BOWLING RECORDS

SIX WICKETS IN AN INNINGS

7- 4	Sajjida Shah	Pakistan v Japan	Amsterdam	2003
7- 8	J.M.Chamberlain	England v Denmark	Haarlem	1991
7-14	A.Mohammed	West Indies v Pakistan	Dhaka	2011-12
7-24	S.Nitschke	Australia v England	Kidderminster	2005
6-10	J.Lord	New Zealand v India	Auckland	1981-82
6-10	M.Maben	India v Sri Lanka	Kandy	2003-04
6-10	S.Ismail	South Africa v Netherlands	Savar	2011-12
6-20	G.L.Page	New Zealand v Trinidad & T	St Albans	1973
6-31	J.Goswami	India v New Zealand	Southgate	2011
6-32	B.H.McNeill	New Zealand v England	Lincoln, NZ	2007-08

100 WICKETS IN A CAREER

Wkts		Career	M	Overs	Runs	Avge	Best	4wI
180	C.L.Fitzpatrick (A)	1993-2007	109	1002.5	3023	16.79	5-14	11
141	N.David (I)	1995-2008	97	815.2	2305	16.34	5-20	6
138	J.Goswami (I)	2002-2012	117	929.1	2909	21.07	6-31	5
131	L.C.Sthalekar (A)	2001-2012	111	859.0	3208	24.48	5-35	2
102	C.E.Taylor (E)	1988-2005	105	856.4	2443	23.95	4-13	2
101	I.T.Guha (E)	2001-2011	83	627.5	2345	23.21	5-14	4

WICKET-KEEPING AND FIELDING RECORDS

SIX DISMISSALS IN AN INNINGS

6 (4ct, 2st)	S.L.Illingworth	New Zealand v Australia	Beckenham	1993
6 (1ct, 5st)	V.Kalpana	India v Denmark	Slough	1993
6 (2ct, 4st)	Batool Fatima	Pakistan v West Indies	Karachi	2003-04
6 (4ct, 2st)	Batool Fatima	Pakistan v Sri Lanka	Colombo (PSS)	2011

100 DISMISSALS IN A CAREER

Total			Career	LOI	Ct	St
133	R.J.Rolls	New Zealand	1997-2007	104	89	44
114	J.Smit	England	1993-2007	109	69	45

FOUR CATCHES IN AN INNINGS IN THE FIELD

4	Z.J.Goss	Australia v New Zealand	Adelaide	1995-96

40 CATCHES IN THE FIELD IN A CAREER

Total			LOI	Career
45	B.J.Clark	Australia	118	1991-2005
41	L.C.Sthalekar	Australia	111	2001-2012
41	J.Goswani	India	117	2002-2012
41	D.A.Hockley	New Zealand	118	1982-2000

APPEARANCE RECORDS

120 APPEARANCES

155	C.M.Edwards	England	1997-2012
141	K.L.Rolton	Australia	1995-2009
132	M.Raj	India	1999-2012
126	S.C.Taylor	England	1998-2011
124	A.Chopra	India	1995-2012

MOST CONSECUTIVE APPEARANCES

96	M.Raj	India	17.04.2004 to 04.03.2012

100 MATCHES AS CAPTAIN

			Won	Lost	No Result	
101	B.J.Clark	Australia	83	17	1	1994-2005

WOMEN'S INTERNATIONAL TWENTY20 RECORDS

2004 to 17 March 2012

MATCH RESULTS SUMMARY

	Matches	Won	Lost	Tied	NR	Win %
England	48	33	13	1	1	70.21
West Indies	34	23	10	1	–	67.64
Australia	43	23	18	2	–	53.48
New Zealand	47	24	22	1	–	51.06
Ireland	13	6	7	–	–	46.15
India	25	11	14	–	–	44.00
Pakistan	18	6	11	1	–	33.33
Sri Lanka	16	4	11	–	1	26.66
South Africa	21	3	17	–	1	15.00
Netherlands	11	–	10	–	1	0.00

TEAM RECORDS
HIGHEST INNINGS TOTALS

205-1	South Africa v Netherlands	Potchefstroom	2010-11
191-4	West Indies v Netherlands	Potchefstroom	2010-11
186-7	New Zealand v South Africa	Taunton	2007
184-4	West Indies v Ireland	Dublin	2008
180-5	England v South Africa	Taunton	2007
180-5	New Zealand v West Indies	Gros Islet	2010

HIGHEST INNINGS TOTAL BATTING SECOND

165-2	England v Australia	The Oval	2009

LOWEST COMPLETED INNINGS TOTALS

† Batting Second

60† (16.5)	Pakistan v England	Taunton	2009
62 (18.2)	India v Australia	Billericay	2011
65-9	Pakistan v New Zealand	Basseterre	2010
65 (18.5)	Pakistan v West Indies	St Andrew's	2011
69-9†	Netherlands v West Indies	Deventer	2008
69-8†	Sri Lanka v England	Taunton	2009
69 (17.1)	New Zealand v Australia	Sydney	2011-12

The lowest total for England is 96 (v India, Mumbai, 2009-10).

BATTING RECORDS
750 RUNS IN A CAREER

Runs			M	I	NO	HS	Avge	50	R/100B
1214	C.M.Edwards	E	46	45	6	76*	31.12	4	111.3
887	S.W.Bates	NZ	43	43	2	68	21.63	4	101.2
776	S.Nitschke	A	36	35	2	56	23.51	3	105.7
774	S.J.McGlashan	NZ	46	45	3	84	18.42	2	102.5
772	A.L.Watkins	NZ	36	36	3	89*	23.39	3	116.4
762	S.R.Taylor	WI	29	28	6	90	34.63	8	104.1
752	L.J.Poulton	A	37	37	2	61	21.48	2	105.6

HIGHEST INDIVIDUAL INNINGS

Score	Balls				
116*	71	S.A.Fritz	SA v Neth	Potchefstroom	2010-11
112*	45	D.J.S.Dottin	WI v SA	Basseterre	2010
96*	53	K.L.Rolton	A v E	Taunton	2005
90	49	S.R.Taylor	WI v Ire	Dublin	2008

The highest score for England is 76* by C.M.Edwards (v SA, Northampton, 2008) and by S.C.Taylor (v A, The Oval, 2009).

HIGHEST PARTNERSHIP FOR EACH WICKET

1st	170	S.A.Fritz/T.Chetty	SA v Neth	Potchefstroom	2010-11
2nd	118*	S.W.Bates/A.L.Watkins	NZ v A	Taunton	2009
3rd	124	T.Smartt/S.A.C.A.King	WI v Neth	Potchefstroom	2010-11
4th	147*	K.L.Rolton/K.A.Blackwell	A v E	Taunton	2005
5th	118	S.F.Daley/D.J.S.Dottin	WI v SA	Basseterre	2010
6th	68	K.L.Rolton/A.J.Blackwell	A v SA	Taunton	2009
7th	51	S.R.Taylor/M.R.Aguilleira	WI v SL	Cayon	2010
8th	31	S.K.Dolawatte/H.M.D.Rasangika	SL v WI	Cayon	2010
9th	32*	K.J.Martin/M.J.G.Nielsen	NZ v A	Sydney	2011-12
10th	22	H.Kaur/E.Bisht	I v A	Billericay	2011

BOWLING RECORDS

30 WICKETS IN A CAREER

Wkts			Matches	Overs	Mdns	Runs	Avge	Best	R/Over
52	A.Mohammed	WI	32	107.4	1	564	10.84	5-10	5.23
51	L.C.Sthalekar	A	42	158.2	1	949	18.60	4-18	5.99
43	S.Nitschke	A	36	128.0	4	705	16.39	4-21	5.50
39	H.L.Colvin	E	28	106.1	2	568	14.56	3-17	5.35
38	L.A.Marsh	E	41	153.1	2	816	21.47	3-17	5.32
36	D.Hazell	E	28	105.5	–	586	16.27	3-14	5.53
33	N.J.Browne	NZ	34	96.0	2	562	17.03	4-15	5.85
32	E.A.Perry	A	31	103.1	–	631	19.71	4-20	6.11

BEST FIGURES IN AN INNINGS

6-17	A.E.Satterthwaite	NZ v E	Taunton	2007
5-10	A.Mohammed	WI v SA	Cape Town	2009-10
5-11	A.Shrubsole	E v NZ	Wellington	2011-12
5-16	P.Roy	I v P	Taunton	2009
4- 5	S.J.Coyte	A v I	Billericay	2011
4- 9	J.L.Gunn	E v SA	Taunton	2007
4- 9	A.Mohammed	WI v SL	Cayon	2010
4- 9	A.Mohammed	WI v P	St Andrew's	2011

WICKET-KEEPING RECORDS
15 DISMISSALS IN A CAREER

Dis			Matches	Ct	St
29	S.J.Taylor	England	31	10	19
26	R.H.Priest	New Zealand	28	13	13
25	J.M.Fields	Australia	21	13	12
19	S.Naik	India	13	5	14

MOST DISMISSALS IN AN INNINGS

4 (3 ct, 1 st)	J.M.Fields	Australia v New Zealand	Brisbane	2009
4 (1 ct, 3 st)	S.Naik	India v England	Mumbai	2009-10
4 (4 st)	S.A.Campbelle	West Indies v Sri Lanka	Cayon	2010

FIELDING RECORDS
15 CATCHES IN A CAREER

Total			Matches	Total			Matches
32	J.L.Gunn	England	46	17	A.J.Blackwell	Australia	40
22	L.S.Greenway	England	44	16	N.J.Browne	New Zealand	34
20	S.J.McGlashan	New Zealand	46	15	D.J.S.Dottin	West Indies	34

MOST CATCHES IN AN INNINGS

4	L.S.Greenway	England v New Zealand	Chelmsford	2010

APPEARANCE RECORDS
40 APPEARANCES

46	C.M.Edwards	England	42	L.C.Sthalekar	Australia
46	J.L.Gunn	England	41	L.A.Marsh	England
46	S.J.McGlashan	New Zealand	41	A.E.Satterthwaite	New Zealand
44	L.S.Greenway	England	40	A.J.Blackwell	Australia
43	S.W.Bates	New Zealand			

20 MATCHES AS CAPTAIN

IT20			W	L	T	NR	%age wins
44	C.M.Edwards	England	32	10	1	1	74.41
29	M.R.Aguilleira	West Indies	19	9	1	–	65.51
29	A.L.Watkins	New Zealand	19	10	–	–	65.51

MCCA FIXTURES 2012

Sun 22 April   **KNOCK-OUT TROPHY**
St Austell — Cornwall v Oxfordshire (1)
Welwyn Garden City — Hertfordshire v Devon (1)
Shrewsbury — Shropshire v Norfolk (2)
Eastnor — Herefordshire v Cumberland (3)
Gosforth — Northumberland v Cheshire (3)
Henley — Berkshire v Wales MC (4)
Dean Park — Dorset v Buckinghamshire (4)

Sun 29 April   **KNOCK-OUT TROPHY**
Ampthill — Bedfordshire v Hertfordshire (1)
Instow — Devon v Cornwall (1)
Manor Park — Norfolk v Suffolk (2)
Trowbridge — Wiltshire v Shropshire (2)
Leys School — Cambridgeshire v Herefordshire (3)
Penrith — Cumberland v Northumberland (3)
Buckingham — Buckinghamshire v Berkshire (4)
Longton — Staffordshire v Dorset (4)

Sun 6 May   **KNOCK-OUT TROPHY**
Truro — Cornwall v Bedfordshire (1)
Oxford Downs — Oxfordshire v Hertfordshire (1)
Woodhall Spa — Lincolnshire v Norfolk (2)
Ipswich School — Suffolk v Wiltshire (2)
Christleton — Cheshire v Cumberland (3)
Falkland — Berkshire v Staffordshire (4)
Brymbo — Wales MC v Buckinghamshire (4)

Mon 7 May   **KNOCK-OUT TROPHY**
Bovey Tracey — Devon v Bedfordshire (1)
Manor Park — Norfolk v Wiltshire (2)

Sun 13 May   **KNOCK-OUT TROPHY**
Cople — Bedfordshire v Oxfordshire (1)
North Mymms — Hertfordshire v Cornwall (1)
Shifnal — Shropshire v Suffolk (2)
Corsham — Wiltshire v Lincolnshire (2)
Saffron Walden — Cambridgeshire v Cheshire (3)
Brockhampton — Herefordshire v Northumberland (3)
Dean Park — Dorset v Berkshire (4)
Leek — Staffordshire v Wales MC (4)

Mon 21 May   **KNOCK-OUT TROPHY**
Workington — Cumberland v Cambridgeshire (3)

Sun 3-Tue 5 June   **MCCA CHAMPIONSHIP**
Henley — Berkshire v Oxfordshire
March — Cambridgeshire v Buckinghamshire
Dean Park — Dorset v Wiltshire
Bury St Edmunds — Suffolk v Norfolk

Sun 10-Tue 12 June   **MCCA CHAMPIONSHIP**
Barrow — Cumberland v Staffordshire

Exmouth	Devon v Wales MC
Eastnor	Herefordshire v Cornwall
Bishop's Stortford	Hertfordshire v Bedfordshire
Sleaford	Lincolnshire v Northumberland
Bridgnorth	Shropshire v Cheshire

Sun 17 June   **KNOCK-OUT TROPHY Quarter-finals**

Match 1	Winner 1 v Runner-up 3
Match 2	Winner 2 v Runner-up 1
Match 3	Winner 3 v Runner-up 4
Match 4	Winner 4 v Runner-up 2

Sun 24-Tue 26 June   **MCCA CHAMPIONSHIP**

Gerrards Cross	Buckinghamshire v Hertfordshire
St Austell	Cornwall v Devon
Furness	Cumberland v Lincolnshire
Colwall	Herefordshire v Shropshire
Benwell Hill	Northumberland v Staffordshire
Banbury	Oxfordshire v Dorset
Bury St Edmunds	Suffolk v Bedfordshire
Usk	Wales MC v Cheshire
Corsham	Wiltshire v Berkshire

Sun 1 July   **KNOCK-OUT TROPHY Semi-finals**
(Res day 2 July)

Winner Match 3 v Winner Match 1
Winner Match 4 v Winner Match 2

Sun 8-Tue 10 July   **MCCA CHAMPIONSHIP**

Dunstable	Bedfordshire v Northumberland
Falkland	Berkshire v Shropshire
March	Cambridgeshire v Cumberland
Alderley Edge	Cheshire v Dorset
Falmouth	Cornwall v Wiltshire
Sidmouth	Devon v Herefordshire
Long Marston	Hertfordshire v Suffolk
Cleethorpes	Lincolnshire v Norfolk
Challow & Childrey	Oxfordshire v Wales MC
Hem Heath	Staffordshire v Buckinghamshire

Sun 22-Tue 24 July   **MCCA CHAMPIONSHIP**

Bedford Mdn School	Bedfordshire v Cumberland
Finchampstead	Berkshire v Devon
Tring Park	Buckinghamshire v Lincolnshire
Wisbech	Cambridgeshire v Suffolk
Truro	Cornwall v Cheshire
Dean Park	Dorset v Shropshire
Brockhampton	Herefordshire v Oxfordshire
Hertford	Hertfordshire v Northumberland
Manor Park	Norfolk v Staffordshire
Pontardullais	Wales C v Wiltshire

Sun 29-Tue 31 July   **MCCA CHAMPIONSHIP**

| Manor Park | Norfolk v Cambridgeshire |

Sun 5-Tue 7 August   **MCCA CHAMPIONSHIP**

| Slough | Buckinghamshire v Bedfordshire |
| Nantwich | Cheshire v Berkshire |

Exeter	Devon v Dorset
Grantham	Lincolnshire v Cambridgeshire
Manor Park	Norfolk v Hertfordshire
Jesmond	Northumberland v Cumberland
Great & Little Tew	Oxfordshire v Cornwall
Oswestry	Shropshire v Wales MC
Knypersley	Staffordshire v Suffolk
South Wilts CC	Wiltshire v Herefordshire

Sun 19-Tue 21 August	**MCCA CHAMPIONSHIP**
Luton	Bedfordshire v Norfolk
Chester BH	Cheshire v Herefordshire
Sedbergh School	Cumberland v Hertfordshire
Dean Park	Dorset v Berkshire
Jesmond	Northumberland v Buckinghamshire
Whitchurch	Shropshire v Devon
Cannock	Staffordshire v Cambridgeshire
Ipswich School	Suffolk v Lincolnshire
Abergavenny	Wales MC v Cornwall
Devizes	Wiltshire v Oxfordshire

Wed 29 August	**KNOCK-OUT TROPHY Final**
Wormsley	(Res day 30 August)

Sun 9-Wed 12 September	**MCCA CHAMPIONSHIP**
West winners	Championship final

MCCA KNOCK-OUT TROPHY GROUPS

Group 1	*Group 2*	*Group 3*	*Group 4*
Bedfordshire	Lincolnshire	Cambridgeshire	Berkshire
Cornwall	Norfolk	Cheshire	Buckinghamshire
Devon	Shropshire	Cumberland	Dorset
Hertfordshire	Suffolk	Herefordshire	Staffordshire
Oxfordshire	Wiltshire	Northumberland	Wales MC

MCC UNIVERSITIES CHALLENGE

Thu 12 – Fri 13 April	
Usk	Cardiff v Cambridge
Thu 19 – Fri 20 April	
Cambridge	Cambridge v Loughborough
Oxford	Oxford v Leeds/Bradford
Tue 24 – Wed 25 April	
Leeds Weetwood	Leeds/Bradford v Cardiff
Fri 27 – Sat 28 April	
Durham	Durham v Oxford
Thu 3 – Fri 4 May	
Usk	Cardiff v Loughborough
Durham	Durham v Cambridge
Tue 8 – Wed 9 May	
Loughborough	Loughborough v Leeds/Bradford

Thu 10 – Fri 11 May	
Panteg	Cardiff v Durham
Mon 21 –Tue 22 May	
Loughborough	Loughborough v Oxford
Tue 29 – Wed 30 May	
Oxford	Oxford v Cambridge
Wed 6 – Thu 7 June	
Leeds Weetwood	Leeds/Bradford v Durham
Mon 11 – Tue 12 June	
Cambridge	Cambridge v Leeds/Bradford
Loughborough	Loughborough v Durham
Oxford	Oxford v Cardiff
Fri 22 June	
Lord's	MCCU Challenge Final

SECOND XI CHAMPIONSHIP FIXTURES 2012

THREE-DAY MATCHES (* FOUR DAYS)

APRIL

Tue 17	Bristol	Glos v Surrey
Wed 18	Lady Bay	Notts v Lancs
	Hove	Sussex v Somerset
Tue 24	Panteg	Glamorgan v Sussex
	Dene Close	Glos v MCC YC
	Taunton Vale	Somerset v Middx
Wed 25	Chester-le-St	Durham v Notts
	Billericay	Essex v Surrey
	Harrogate	Yorks v Leics

MAY

Tue 1	Lady Bay	Notts v Derbys
Wed 2	Southampton	Hants v Essex
	Uppingham T	Leics v Durham
	Reigate Pr	Surrey v Somerset
	Kidderminster	Worcs v Northants
Wed 9	Belper M'dow	Derbys v Durham
	Bristol CC	Glos v Essex
	High Wycombe	MCC YC v Glamorgan
Tue 15	Southend, GP	Essex v Glamorgan
Wed 16	Crosby	Lancs v Leics
	Campbell Pk	Northants v Derbys
	Arundel	Sussex v Kent
	Barnt Green	Warwicks v Notts
Tue 22	Bristol	Glos v Glamorgan
	Merchant Tay	Middx v Essex
	York	Yorks v Durham
Wed 23	Derby	Derbys v Worcs
	Hinckley	Leics v Warwicks
	Wimbledon	Surrey v Sussex
Tue 29	Manchester	Lancs v Warwicks

JUNE

Tue 5	Shenley	MCC YC v Kent
Wed 6	Halstead	Essex v Sussex
	Stowe S	Northants v Leics
Tue 19	Maidstone	Kent v Hants
	Radlett	MCC YC v Somerset
	Campbell Pk	Northants v Lancs
Wed 20	Kenilworth W	Warwicks v Worcs
Mon 25	Cheam	Surrey v MCC YC
Tue 26	Brandon	Durham v Northants
	B Stortford	Essex v Kent
	Cardiff CC	Glamorgan v Somerset
	Newclose IoW	MCC Univs v Warwicks
	Radlett	Middx v Hants
	Barnsley	Yorks v Worcs

JULY

Mon 2	Durham	MCC Univs v Durham
Tue 3	Denby	Derbys v Yorks

	Southend, GP	Glos v MCC YC
	Panteg	Glamorgan v Hants
	Hove	Sussex v Glos
	Kidderminster	Worcs v Notts
Wed 4	Radlett	Middx v Surrey
Tue 10	Derby	Derbys v Leics
	Kings S, Cant	Kent v Surrey
	Newclose IoW	MCC YC v Sussex
Wed 11	Radlett	Middx v Glos
	Lady Bay	Notts v MCC Univs
	Moseley	Warwicks v Northants
	Worcester RGS	Worcs v Lancs
Tue 17	Coggeshall	Essex v Somerset
	Southampton	Hants v MCC YC
	Lady Bay	Notts v Yorkshire
Wed 18	Cardiff CC	Glamorgan v Kent
	Southport & B	Lancs v Derbys
	Rugby S	Warwicks v Durham
	Worcester RGS	Worcs v MCC Univs
Tue 24	Radlett	MCC YC v Middx
	Northampton	Northants v Yorks
Wed 25	Blackpool	Lancs v MCC Univs
Tue 31	Canterbury	Kent v Middx
	Taunton Vale	Somerset v Glos

AUGUST

Wed 1	Dunstall	Derbys v Warwicks
	Southampton	Hants v Surrey
	Hinckley	Leics v Worcs
	Finedon	Northants v MCC Univs
Tue 7	Southampton	Hants v Glos
	York	MCC Univs v Yorks
	Taunton Vale	Somerset v Kent
	Guildford	Surrey v Glamorgan
Wed 8	Kibworth	Leics v Notts
Tue 14	Swansea	Glamorgan v Middx
	Horsham	Sussex v Hants
Wed 15	S N'berland	Durham v Worcs
	Beckenham	Kent v Glos
	Todmorden	Lancs v Yorks
	Cambridge	MCC Univs v Leics
	Lady Bay	Notts v Northants
Tue 21	Taunton Vale	Somerset v Hants
	Horsham	Sussex v Middx
Wed 22	Middlesbrough	Durham v Lancs
	Cambridge	MCC Univs v Derbys
	Stamford Bdge	Yorks v Warwicks

SEPTEMBER

Tue 4*	tbc	FINAL

SECOND XI TROPHY FIXTURES 2012

ONE DAY

APRIL

Mon 16	Bristol	Glos v Surrey
Tue 17	Welbeck	Notts v Lancs
	Hove	Sussex v Somerset
Mon 23	Panteg	Glamorgan v Sussex
	Dene Close S	Glos v MCC YC
	Taunton Vale	Somerset v Middx
Tue 24	Chester-le-St	Durham v Notts
	Billericay	Essex v Surrey
	Harrogate	Yorks v Leics
Mon 30	Worksop C	Notts v Derbys

MAY

Tue 1	Southampton	Hants v Essex
	Leicester	Leics v Durham
	Reigate P	Surrey v Somerset
	Kidderminster	Worcs v Northants
Tue 8	Belper M'dow	Derbys v Durham
	Bristol CC	Glos v Essex
	High Wycombe	MCC YC v Glamorgan
Mon 14	Southend GP	Essex v Glamorgan
	Northop Hall	Lancs v Unicorns A
Tue 15	Crosby	Lancs v Leics
	Dunstable	Northants v Derbys
	Hove	Sussex v Kent
	C'try/N W'wk	Warwicks v Notts
	Kidderminster	Worcs v Unicorns A
Mon 21	Merchant Tay	Middx v Essex
	Marske	Yorks v Durham
Tue 22	Derby	Derbys v Worcs
	Leicester	Leics v Warwicks
	Wimbledon	Surrey v Sussex
Fri 25	Bristol	Glos v Glamorgan
Mon 28	Manchester	Lancs v Warwicks

JUNE

Mon 4	Shenley	MCC YC v Kent
Tue 5	Halstead	Essex v Sussex
	Stowe S	Northants v Leics
Tue 12	Cheam	Surrey v MCC YC
Mon 18	Maidstone	Kent v Hants
	Radlett	MCC YC v Somerset
	Bedford S	Northants v Lancs
Tue 19	Olton & WW	Warwicks v Worcs
Thu 21	Trent Coll	Notts v Unicorns A
Mon 25	Brandon	Durham v Northants
	B Stortford	Essex v Kent
	Cardiff CC	Glamorgan v Somerset
	Radlett	Middx v Hants
	Pudsey Congs	Yorks v Worcs
Thu 28	Luton, Wardown	Unicorns A v Leics

JULY

Mon 2	Denby	Derbys v Yorks
	Southend, GP	Essex v MCC YC
	Panteg	Glamorgan v Hants
	Hove	Sussex v Glos
	Kidderminster	Worcs v Notts
Wed 4	Wellingboro S	Northants v Unicorns A
Mon 9	Derby	Derbys v Leics
	Kings S, Cant	Kent v Surrey
	Newclose IoW	MCC YC v Sussex
Tue 10	Radlett	Middx v Glos
	Knowle & D	Warwicks v Northants
	Worcester RGS	Worcs v Lancs
Mon 16	Southampton	Hants v MCC YC
	Radlett	Middx v Surrey
	Worksop Coll	Notts v Yorks
Tue 17	Cardiff CC	Glamorgan v Kent
	Westhoughton	Lancs v Derbys
	Birmingham	Warwicks v Durham
Fri 20	Coggeshall	Essex v Somerset
Mon 23	Radlett	MCC YC v Middx
Thu 26	Long Marston	Unicorns A v Derbys
Fri 27	Northampton	Northants v Yorks
	Long Marston	Unicorns A v Warwicks
Mon 30	Taunton Vale	Somerset v Glos
	Stirlands	Sussex v Middx
Tue 31	Dunstall	Derbys v Warwicks
	Southampton	Hants v Surrey
	Leicester	Leics v Worcs

AUGUST

Fri 3	Canterbury	Kent v Middx
Mon 6	Southampton	Hants v Glos
	Taunton Vale	Somerset v Kent
	tbc	Surrey v Glamorgan
Tue 7	Leicester	Leics v Notts
Thu 9	Sheffield Coll	Unicorns A v Durham
Fri 10	Sheffield Coll	Unicorns A v Yorks
Mon 13	Swansea	Glamorgan v Middx
	Horsham	Sussex v Hants
Tue 14	S N'berland	Durham v Worcs
	Beckenham	Kent v Glos
	Todmorden	Lancs v Yorks
	Welbeck	Notts v Northants
Mon 20	Taunton Vale	Somerset v Hants
Tue 21	Middlesbrough	Durham v Lancs
	Leeds W'wood	Yorks v Warwicks
Mon 27	tbc	Semi-Finals

SEPTEMBER

Tue 11	tbc	FINAL

SECOND XI T20 FIXTURES 2012

MAY

				The Oval	Surrey v Sussex
Thu 24	Bristol	MCC YC v Hants	Mon 4	Berkswell	Warwicks v Worcs
Mon 28	Leicester	Leics v Middx	Tue 5	Neston	Lancs v Notts
	Preston Nom	Sussex v Hants	Wed 6	Darlington	Durham v Notts
	B Stortford	Unicorns A v Northants		Ormskirk	Lancs v Yorks
	Ombersley	Worcs v Somerset	Fri 8	Southampton	Hants v Surrey
Tue 29	Derby	Derbys v Durham		Lady Bay	Notts v Yorkshire
	Leicester	Leics v Unicorns A		B Stortford	Unicorns A v Middx
	Purley	Surrey v Kent	Mon 11	Chelmsford	Essex v Leics
	Horsham	Sussex v MCC YC		Cardiff CC	Glamorgan v Somerset
	Kidderminster	Worcs v Glamorgan		Bristol	Glos v Worcs
	Bingley	Yorks v England U19		Shenley	MCC YC v Surrey
Wed 30	Loughborough	England U19 v Durham		Trent Coll	Notts v England U19
	Canterbury	Kent v MCC YC	Tue 12	Glossop	Derbys v Lancs
Thu 31	Cardiff CC	Glamorgan v Glos		Richmond	Middx v Essex
	Oundle S	Northants v Essex		Taunton Vale	Somerset v Glos
	Bingley	Yorks v Derbys		C'try/N W'k	Warwicks v Glamorgan
JUNE			Wed 13	Chester-le-St	Durham v Lancs
Fri 1	Loughborough	England U19 v Derbys		Bristol	Glos v Warwicks
	Chelmsford	Essex v Unicorns A		Maidstone	Kent v Sussex
	Southampton	Hampshire v Kent		Northampton	Northants v Leics
	Uxbridge	Middx v Northants	Fri 15	Arundel	Semi-finals and FINAL
	Taunton Vale	Somerset v Warwicks			

WOMEN'S INTERNATIONAL FIXTURES 2012

Tue 26 June
IT20   Canterbury   England v India

Thu 28 June
IT20   Chelmsford   England v India

Sun 1 July
LOI   Lord's   England v India

Wed 4 July
LOI   Taunton   England v India

Thu 5 July
LOI   Taunton   England v India

Sun 8 July
LOI   Truro   England v India

Wed 11 July
LOI   Wormsley   England v India

Sat 8 September
IT20   Chester-le-St   England v West Indies

Mon 10 September
IT20   Manchester   England v West Indies

Thu 13 September
IT20   Northampton   England v West Indies

Sat 15 September
IT20   Hove   England v West Indies

Sun 16 September
IT20   Arundel   England v West Indies

INTERNATIONAL UNDER-19 CRICKET

Wed 18 July
LOI   Leicester   England v Ireland

Fri 20 July
LOI   Leicester   England v Ireland

PRINCIPAL FIXTURES 2012

CC1   LV= County Championship (1st Div)
CC2   LV= County Championship (2nd Div)
F   Floodlit
FCF   First-Class Friendly
LOI   NatWest Limited-Overs International
40L   Clydesdale Bank 40

T20   Friends Provident t20
IT20   Twenty20 International
[T20]   Other Twenty20 Match
TM   npower Test Match
MCCU   MCC University

Tue 27 – Fri 30 March
FCF   Abu Dhabi   MCC v Lancashire

Sat 31 March – Mon 2 April
FCF   Cambridge   Cambridge MCCU v Essex
FCF   Northwood   Durham MCCU v Middlesex
FCF   Oxford   Oxford MCCU v Glamorgan
       Taunton Vale   Somerset v Cardiff MCCU
       The Oval   Surrey v Leeds/Bradford MCCU

Sun 1 – Tue 3 April
FCF   Nottingham   Notts v Loughborough MCCU

Thu 5 – Sun 8 April
CC1   Nottingham   Notts v Worcs
CC1   Taunton   Somerset v Middlesex
CC1   The Oval   Surrey v Sussex
CC2   Derby   Derbyshire v Northants
CC2   Chelmsford   Essex v Glos
CC2   Leicester   Leics v Glamorgan
CC2   Leeds   Yorkshire v Kent

Fri 6 – Sun 8 April
FCF   Cambridge   Cambridge MCCU v Lancashire
FCF   Chester-le-St   Durham v Durham MCCU
FCF   Southampton   Hampshire v Loughborough MCCU
       Birmingham   Warwicks v Cardiff MCCU

Thu 12 – Sun 15 April
CC1   Chester-le-St   Durham v Notts
CC1   Liverpool   Lancashire v Sussex
CC1   Lord's   Middlesex v Surrey
CC1   Birmingham   Warwicks v Somerset
CC2   Cardiff   Glamorgan v Derbyshire
CC2   Southampton   Hampshire v Glos
CC2   Northampton   Northants v Kent

Fri 13 – Sun 15 April
FCF   Loughborough   Loughborough MCCU v Leics
FCF   Oxford   Oxford MCCU v Derbyshire
       Leeds   Yorkshire v Leeds/Bradford MCCU

Thu 19 – Sun 22 April
CC1   Liverpool   Lancashire v Warwicks
CC1   Lord's   Middlesex v Durham
CC1   Nottingham   Notts v Somerset
CC1   The Oval   Surrey v Worcs
CC2   Derby   Derbyshire v Leics
CC2   Cardiff   Glamorgan v Hampshire
CC2   Canterbury   Kent v Glos
CC2   Leeds   Yorkshire v Essex

Fri 20 – Sun 22 April
FCF   Durham   Durham MCCU v Northants

Thu 26 – Sun 29 April
CC1   Taunton   Somerset v Lancashire
CC1   The Oval   Surrey v Durham
CC1   Hove   Sussex v Warwicks
CC1   Worcester   Worcs v Notts
CC2   Chelmsford   Essex v Northants
CC2   Bristol   Glos v Glamorgan
CC2   Southampton   Hampshire v Leics
CC2   Canterbury   Kent v Yorkshire

Fri 27 – Sun 29 April
       Derby   Derbyshire v Cardiff MCCU

Tue 1 – Thu 3 May
       Leeds, Weetwood   Leeds/Bradford MCCU v Sussex

Wed 2 – Sat 5 May
CC1   Manchester   Lancashire v Notts
CC1   Birmingham   Warwicks v Durham
CC2   Derby   Derbyshire v Glos
CC2   Cardiff   Glamorgan v Essex
CC2   Northampton   Northants v Hampshire
CC2   Scarborough   Yorkshire v Leics

Wed 2 – Fri 4 May
FCF   Oxford   Oxford MCCU v Kent

Thu 3 – Sun 6 May
CC1   Lord's   Middlesex v Worcs

Fri 4 May
40L F   The Oval   Surrey v Somerset

Sat 5 May
FCF   Hove   Sussex v West Indians

Sun 6 May
40L   Bristol   Glos v Netherlands
40L   Manchester   Lancashire v Leics
40L   Edinburgh   Scotland v Surrey
40L   Wormsley   Unicorns v Derbyshire
40L   Birmingham   Warwicks v Northants
40L   Leeds   Yorkshire v Kent

Mon 7 May
40L   Southampton   Hampshire v Glamorgan
40L   Leicester   Leics v Essex
40L   Lord's   Middlesex v Glos
40L   Northampton   Northants v Unicorns
40L   Edinburgh   Scotland v Notts
40L   Worcester   Worcs v Netherlands

Wed 9 – Sat 12 May

CC1	Chester-le-St	Durham v Somerset
CC1	Nottingham	Notts v Middlesex
CC1	Hove	Sussex v Lancashire
CC1	Worcester	Worcs v Surrey
CC2	Chelmsford	Essex v Kent
CC2	Bristol	Glos v Yorkshire
CC2	Southampton	Hampshire v Derbyshire
CC2	Leicester	Leics v Northants

Thu 10 – Sun 13 May

FCF	Northampton	England Lions v West Indians

Sun 13 May

40L	Chester-le-St	Durham v Somerset
40L	Chelmsford	Essex v Worcs
40L	Bristol	Glos v Leics
40L	Uddingston	Scotland v Glamorgan
40L	Hove	Sussex v Unicorns
40L	Birmingham	Warwicks v Derbyshire

Mon 14 May

40L	Voorburg	Netherlands v Middlesex

Wed 16 – Sat 19 May

CC1	The Oval	Surrey v Somerset
CC1	Birmingham	Warwicks v Lancashire
CC1	Worcester	Worcs v Sussex
CC2	Derby	Derbyshire v Glamorgan
CC2	Canterbury	Kent v Northants
CC2	Leicester	Leics v Essex
CC2	Leeds	Yorkshire v Hampshire

Thu 17 – Mon 21 May

TM1	Lord's	ENGLAND v WEST INDIES

Fri 18 – Sun 20 May

FCF	Cambridge	Cambridge MCCU v Glos

Sun 20 May

40L	Canterbury	Kent v Unicorns
40L	Manchester	Lancashire v Essex
40L	Leicester	Leics v Middlesex
40L	Northampton	Northants v Sussex
40L	Uddingston	Scotland v Hampshire
40L	The Oval	Surrey v Durham
40L	Leeds	Yorkshire v Derbyshire

Tue 22 – Fri 25 May

CC1	Taunton	Somerset v Durham

Wed 23 – Sat 26 May

CC1	Liverpool	Lancashire v Middlesex
CC1	The Oval	Surrey v Warwicks
CC2	Chelmsford	Essex v Derbyshire
CC2	Southampton	Hampshire v Glamorgan
CC2	Canterbury	Kent v Leics
CC2	Northampton	Northants v Glos

Thu 24 May

40L F	Hove	Sussex v Yorkshire

Fri 25 – Tue 29 May

TM2	**Nottingham**	**ENGLAND v WEST INDIES**

Fri 25 – Mon 28 May

CC1	Hove	Sussex v Notts

Sun 27 May

40L	Chester-le-St	Durham v Scotland
40L	Northampton	Northants v Warwicks
40L	Taunton	Somerset v Hampshire
40L	Scarborough	Unicorns v Yorkshire
40L	Worcester	Worcs v Middlesex

Mon 28 May

40L	Rotterdam	Netherlands v Lancashire

Tue 29 May – Fri 1 June

CC2	Cardiff	Glamorgan v Leics

Tue 29 May

40L	Rotterdam	Netherlands v Essex

Wed 30 May – Sat 2 June

CC1	Chester-le-St	Durham v Lancashire
CC1	Lord's	Middlesex v Sussex
CC1	Worcester	Worcs v Somerset
CC2	Bristol	Glos v Derbyshire
CC2	Leeds	Yorkshire v Northants

Thu 31 May

40L F	Southampton	Hampshire v Notts

Fri 1 June

40L F	Canterbury	Kent v Warwicks

Sat 2 – Sun 3 June

FCF	Leicester	Leics v West Indians

Sat 2 June

40L	Cardiff	Glamorgan v Surrey

Sun 3 June

40L	Chester-le-St	Durham v Notts
40L	Lord's	Middlesex v Netherlands
40L	The Oval	Surrey v Hampshire
40L	Southend	Unicorns v Sussex
40L	Leeds	Yorkshire v Northants

Mon 4 June

40L	Derby	Derbyshire v Warwicks
40L	Chelmsford	Essex v Glos
40L	Southampton	Hampshire v Scotland
40L	Leicester	Leics v Netherlands
40L	Nottingham	Notts v Somerset

Tue 5 – Fri 8 June

CC1	Chester-le-St	Durham v Warwicks
CC1	Lord's	Middlesex v Somerset
CC2	Leicester	Leics v Derbyshire

Tue 5 June

40L	Manchester	Lancashire v Worcs
40L	The Oval	Surrey v Scotland
40L	Southend	Unicorns v Kent

Wed 6 – Sat 9 June

CC1	Nottingham	Notts v Lancashire
CC1	Horsham	Sussex v Surrey
CC2	Colwyn Bay	Glamorgan v Yorkshire
CC2	Tunbridge W	Kent v Hampshire
CC2	Northampton	Northants v Essex

Thu 7 – Mon 11 June
TM3   Birmingham   **ENGLAND v WEST INDIES**

Fri 8 June
40L   The Hague   Netherlands v Worcs

Sun 10 June
40L   Colwyn Bay   Glamorgan v Durham
40L   Tunbridge W   Kent v Northants
40L   Lord's   Middlesex v Lancashire
40L   Horsham   Sussex v Derbyshire
40L   Worcester   Worcs v Glos

Tue 12 June
T20   Tunbridge W   Kent v Sussex
T20   Leicester   Leics v Notts

Wed 13 June
    Lord's   Middlesex v West Indians
T20   Taunton   Somerset v Warwicks
T20 ^{F} The Oval   Surrey v Essex

Thu 14 June
T20 ^{F} Derby   Derbyshire v Lancashire
T20   Bristol   Glos v Somerset
T20 ^{F} Lord's   Middlesex v Surrey
T20 ^{F} Northampton   Northants v Glamorgan
T20 ^{F} Hove   Sussex v Hampshire

Fri 15 June
T20   Leicester   Leics v Lancashire
T20   Nottingham   Notts v Derbyshire
T20 ^{F} Birmingham   Warwicks v Worcs
T20   Leeds   Yorkshire v Durham

Sat 16 June
LOI   Southampton   **England v West Indies**
    Lord's   Oxford U v Cambridge U

Sun 17 June
T20   Chester-le-St   Durham v Notts
T20   Cardiff   Glamorgan v Warwicks
T20   Beckenham   Kent v Surrey
T20   Lord's   Middlesex v Sussex
T20   Taunton   Somerset v Northants
T20   Worcester   Worcs v Glos
T20   Leeds   Yorkshire v Leics

Mon 18 June
T20 ^{F} Derby   Derbyshire v Yorkshire
T20 ^{F} Southampton   Hampshire v Middlesex

Tue 19 June
LOI   The Oval   **England v West Indies**
T20 ^{F} Birmingham   Warwicks v Northants

Wed 20 June
T20 ^{F} Derby   Derbyshire v Durham
T20 ^{F} Chelmsford   Essex v Kent
T20   Cardiff   Glamorgan v Worcs
T20   Manchester   Lancashire v Leics
T20 ^{F} The Oval   Surrey v Hampshire

Thu 21 June
    Leicester   Leics v Australians
T20 ^{F} Lord's   Middlesex v Essex

T20 ^{F} Birmingham   Warwicks v Somerset

Fri 22 June
LOI   Leeds   **England v West Indies**
T20   Chester-le-St   Durham v Yorkshire
T20 ^{F} Chelmsford   Essex v Surrey
T20   Bristol   Glos v Northants
T20 ^{F} Southampton   Hampshire v Kent
T20 ^{F} Manchester   Lancashire v Notts
T20   Leicester   Leics v Derbyshire
T20   Taunton   Somerset v Glamorgan
T20 ^{F} Hove   Sussex v Middlesex
T20   Worcester   Worcs v Warwicks

Sat 23 June
LOI   Stormont   **Ireland v Australia**
T20 ^{F} Cardiff   Glamorgan v Glos
T20   Northampton   Northants v Worcs

Sun 24 – Wed 27 June
FCF   Oxford   Oxford U v Cambridge U

Sun 24 June
IT20   Nottingham   **England v West Indies**
T20   Canterbury   Kent v Hampshire
T20   Hove   Sussex v Essex
T20   Scarborough   Yorkshire v Notts

Mon 25 June
T20 ^{F} Manchester   Lancashire v Durham

Tue 26 June
F   Chelmsford   Essex v Australians
T20 ^{F} Canterbury   Kent v Middlesex
T20 ^{F} Northampton   Northants v Somerset

Wed 27 June
T20   Chester-le-St   Durham v Derbyshire
T20   Bristol   Glos v Warwicks
T20   Leicester   Leics v Yorkshire
T20   Richmond   Middlesex v Hampshire

Thu 28 June
T20 ^{F} Chelmsford   Essex v Sussex

Fri 29 June
LOI   Lord's   **England v Australia**
T20 ^{F} Derby   Derbyshire v Leics
T20 ^{F} Chelmsford   Essex v Hampshire
T20 ^{F} Northampton   Northants v Warwicks
T20   Nottingham   Notts v Durham
T20 ^{F} Taunton   Somerset v Glos
T20 ^{F} Hove   Sussex v Kent
T20   Worcester   Worcs v Glamorgan
T20   Leeds   Yorkshire v Lancashire

Sat 30 June
T20 ^{F} Cardiff   Glamorgan v Northants
T20   Southampton   Hampshire v Surrey

Sun 1 July
LOI   The Oval   **England v Australia**
T20   Chester-le-St   Durham v Leics
T20   Manchester   Lancashire v Derbyshire
T20   Taunton   Somerset v Worcs

Mon 2 July
T20	Bristol	Glos v Glamorgan

Tue 3 July
T20	Nottingham	Notts v Lancashire
T20 F	The Oval	Surrey v Sussex

Wed 4 July
LOI F	**Birmingham**	**England v Australia**

Thu 5 July
T20 F	Chelmsford	Essex v Middlesex
T20	Bristol	Glos v Worcs
T20 F	Nottingham	Notts v Yorkshire
T20 F	The Oval	Surrey v Kent

Fri 6 July
T20 F	Derby	Derbyshire v Notts
T20	Cardiff	Glamorgan v Somerset
T20 F	Southampton	Hampshire v Sussex
T20 F	Canterbury	Kent v Essex
T20 F	Manchester	Lancashire v Yorkshire
T20	Leicester	Leics v Durham
T20 F	The Oval	Surrey v Middlesex
T20 F	Birmingham	Warwicks v Glos
T20	Worcester	Worcs v Northants

Sat 7 July
LOI	**Chester-le-St**	**England v Australia**

Sun 8 July
T20	Chester-le-St	Durham v Lancashire
T20	Southampton	Hampshire v Essex
T20	Uxbridge	Middlesex v Kent
T20	Northampton	Northants v Glos
T20	Nottingham	Notts v Leics
T20	Hove	Sussex v Surrey
T20	Birmingham	Warwicks v Glamorgan
T20	Worcester	Worcs v Somerset
T20	Leeds	Yorkshire v Derbyshire

Mon 9 – Tue 10 July
FCF	Taunton	Somerset v South Africans

Tue 10 – Fri 13 July
CC1	Worcester	Worcs v Durham

Tue 10 July
LOI F	**Manchester**	**England v Australia**

Wed 11 – Sat 14 July
CC1	Uxbridge	Middlesex v Notts
CC1	Guildford	Surrey v Lancashire
CC2	Cheltenham	Glos v Essex
CC2	Southampton	Hampshire v Yorkshire

Wed 11 July
40L	Amsterdam	Netherlands v Leics
40L F	Birmingham	Warwicks v Sussex

Thu 12 – Sun 15 July
FCF	Birmingham	Warwicks v Sussex

Thu 12 July
40L F	Cardiff	Glamorgan v Somerset

Fri 13 – Sun 15 July
FCF	Canterbury	Kent v South Africans

Fri 13 July
40L F	Northampton	Northants v Derbyshire

Sat 14 – Tue 17 July
CC2	Northampton	Northants v Glamorgan

Sat 14 July
40L	Leicester	Leics v Worcs

Sun 15 July
40L	Chesterfield	Derbyshire v Unicorns
40L	Cheltenham	Glos v Essex
40L	Southampton	Hampshire v Durham
40L	Uxbridge	Middlesex v Leics
40L	Taunton	Somerset v Scotland
40L	Guildford	Surrey v Notts

Mon 16 July
40L F	Canterbury	Kent v Sussex
40L F	Manchester	Lancashire v Middlesex

Tue 17 July
40L	Cheltenham	Glos v Worcs
40L F	Nottingham	Notts v Hampshire

Wed 18 – Sat 21 July
CC1	Manchester	Lancashire v Worcs
CC1	Nottingham	Notts v Surrey
CC1	Taunton	Somerset v Warwicks
CC1	Arundel	Sussex v Durham
CC2	Chesterfield	Derbyshire v Yorkshire
CC2	Cheltenham	Glos v Leics

Wed 18 July
40L F	Chelmsford	Essex v Middlesex

Thu 19 – Mon 23 July
TM1	The Oval	**ENGLAND v SOUTH AFRICA**

Thu 19 – Sun 22 July
CC2	Chelmsford	Essex v Hampshire
CC2	Canterbury	Kent v Glamorgan

Sun 22 July
40L	Chesterfield	Derbyshire v Yorkshire
40L	Cheltenham	Glos v Middlesex
40L	Leicester	Leics v Lancashire
40L	Nottingham	Notts v Scotland
40L	Bath	Somerset v Durham
40L	Arundel	Sussex v Northants
40L	Birmingham	Warwicks v Unicorns

Tue 24 July
T20		Quarter-finals 1 & 2

Wed 25 July
T20		Quarter-finals 3 & 4

Fri 27 – Mon 30 July
CC1	Chester-le-St	Durham v Middlesex
CC1	Nottingham	Notts v Sussex
CC1	Birmingham	Warwicks v Surrey
CC2	Southampton	Hampshire v Kent
CC2	Leicester	Leics v Yorkshire

Fri 27 – Sun 29 July
FCF	Derby	Derbyshire v Australia A

Fri 27 – Sat 28 July
FCF   Worcester   Worcs v South Africans

Fri 27 July
40L   Amsterdam   Netherlands v Glos

Sat 28 July
40L   Taunton   Somerset v Glamorgan

Sun 29 July
40L   Cardiff   Glamorgan v Scotland
40L   Wormsley   Unicorns v Northants
40L   Worcester   Worcs v Essex

Mon 30 July
40L ^{F} Manchester   Lancashire v Glos

Tue 31 July
40L ^{F} Derby   Derbyshire v Kent

Wed 1 – Sat 4 August
CC1   Liverpool   Lancashire v Somerset
CC1   Uxbridge   Middlesex v Warwicks
CC1   Hove   Sussex v Worcs
CC2   Chelmsford   Essex v Leics
CC2   Swansea   Glamorgan v Glos
CC2   Northampton   Northants v Yorkshire

Wed 1 – Fri 3 August
FCF   Chester-le-St   Durham v Australia A

Wed 1 August
40L ^{F} Nottingham   Notts v Surrey

Thu 2 – Mon 6 August
TM2   Leeds   **ENGLAND v SOUTH AFRICA**

Thu 2 – Sun 5 August
CC2   Derby   Derbyshire v Kent

Sun 5 August
40L   Chelmsford   Essex v Leics
40L   Swansea   Glamorgan v Notts
40L   Uxbridge   Middlesex v Worcs
40L   Edinburgh   Scotland v Durham

Mon 6 – Thu 9 August
CC2   Bristol   Glos v Hampshire

Tue 7 – Fri 10 August
CC1   Chester-le-St   Durham v Surrey
CC1   Taunton   Somerset v Notts
FCF   Manchester   England Lions v Australia A

Tue 7 August
40L ^{F} Birmingham   Warwicks v Yorkshire

Wed 8 – Sat 11 August
CC1   Birmingham   Warwicks v Worcs
CC2   Canterbury   Kent v Essex

Wed 8 August
40L ^{F} Derby   Derbyshire v Sussex

Thu 9 August
40L   Northampton   Northants v Yorkshire

Fri 10 – Mon 13 August
CC1   Hove   Sussex v Middlesex
CC2   Northampton   Northants v Leics

Fri 10 – Sat 11 August
FCF   Derby   Derbyshire v South Africans

Fri 10 August
40L ^{F} Cardiff   Glamorgan v Hampshire

Sat 11 August
40L   Chester-le-St   Durham v Surrey

Sun 12 August
LOI   Edinburgh   **Scotland v England**
40L   Chester-le-St   Durham v Glamorgan
40L   Canterbury   Kent v Derbyshire
40L   Manchester   Lancashire v Netherlands
40L   Taunton   Somerset v Notts
40L   Leeds   Yorkshire v Unicorns

Mon 13 August
40L ^{F} Birmingham   Warwicks v Kent

Tue 14 – Fri 17 August
FCF   Birmingham   England Lions v Australia A

Tue 14 August
40L ^{F} Southampton   Hampshire v Somerset

Wed 15 – Sat 18 August
CC1   Nottingham   Notts v Durham
CC1   The Oval   Surrey v Middlesex
CC1   Worcester   Worcs v Lancashire
CC2   Colchester   Essex v Glamorgan
CC2   Bristol   Glos v Kent
CC2   Southampton   Hampshire v Northants
CC2   Leeds   Yorkshire v Derbyshire

Wed 15 August
40L ^{F} Hove   Sussex v Warwicks

Thu 16 – Mon 20 August
TM3   Lord's   **ENGLAND v SOUTH AFRICA**

Sun 19 August
40L   Colchester   Essex v Netherlands
40L   Bristol   Glos v Lancashire
40L   Southampton   Hampshire v Surrey
40L   Northampton   Northants v Kent
40L   Nottingham   Notts v Durham
40L   Edinburgh   Scotland v Somerset
40L   Wormsley   Unicorns v Warwicks
40L   Worcester   Worcs v Leics
40L   Leeds   Yorkshire v Sussex

Tue 21 – Fri 24 August
CC1   Chester-le-St   Durham v Worcs
CC1   Taunton   Somerset v Sussex
CC1   Birmingham   Warwicks v Middlesex
CC2   Leicester   Leics v Hampshire
CC2   Northampton   Northants v Derbyshire

Tue 21 August
40L ^{F} The Oval   Surrey v Glamorgan

Wed 22 August
40L ^{F} Canterbury   Kent v Yorkshire
        Bristol   Glos v South Africans

Thu 23 August
40L ^{F} Chelmsford   Essex v Lancashire

Fri 24 August		
LOI	Cardiff	England v South Africa
Sat 25 August		
T20 F	Cardiff	Semi-finals and FINAL
Mon 27 August		
40L	Derby	Derbyshire v Northants
40L	Chester-le-St	Durham v Hampshire
40L	Leicester	Leics v Glos
40L	Lord's	Middlesex v Essex
40L	Nottingham	Notts v Glamorgan
40L	Taunton	Somerset v Surrey
40L	tbc	Sussex v Kent
40L	Worcester	Worcs v Lancashire
40L	Scarborough	Yorkshire v Warwicks
Tue 28 – Fri 31 August		
CC1	Manchester	Lancashire v Durham
CC1	Taunton	Somerset v Surrey
CC1	Birmingham	Warwicks v Notts
CC1	Worcester	Worcs v Middlesex
CC2	Derby	Derbyshire v Essex
CC2	Cardiff	Glamorgan v Northants
CC2	Leicester	Leics v Kent
CC2	Scarborough	Yorkshire v Glos
Tue 28 August		
LOI F	Southampton	England v South Africa
Fri 31 August		
LOI F	The Oval	England v South Africa
Sat 1 September		
40L	tbc	Semi-finals

Sun 2 September		
LOI	Lord's	England v South Africa
Tue 4 – Fri 7 September		
CC1	Lord's	Middlesex v Lancashire
CC1	The Oval	Surrey v Notts
CC1	Hove	Sussex v Somerset
CC1	Worcester	Worcs v Warwicks
CC2	Bristol	Glos v Northants
CC2	Southampton	Hampshire v Essex
CC2	Canterbury	Kent v Derbyshire
CC2	Leeds	Yorkshire v Glamorgan
Wed 5 September		
LOI F	Nottingham	England v South Africa
Sat 8 September		
IT20	Chester-le-St	England v South Africa
Mon 10 September		
IT20 F	Manchester	England v South Africa
Tue 11 – Fri 15 September		
CC1	Chester-le-St	Durham v Sussex
CC1	Manchester	Lancashire v Surrey
CC1	Nottingham	Notts v Warwicks
CC1	Taunton	Somerset v Worcs
CC2	Derby	Derbyshire v Hampshire
CC2	Chelmsford	Essex v Yorkshire
CC2	Cardiff	Glamorgan v Kent
CC2	Leicester	Leics v Glos
Wed 12 September		
IT20 F	Birmingham	England v South Africa
Sat 15 September		
40L	Lord's	FINAL

TEST MATCH CHAMPIONSHIP SCHEDULE

Months indicate the start of a series. Number of Tests in brackets. All series, especially those involving Pakistan and Zimbabwe, are subject to confirmation.

2012	Apr	West Indies hosts Australia (3)
	May	**England hosts West Indies (3)**
	July	**England hosts South Africa (3)**
	Aug	Zimbabwe hosts Bangladesh (2)
		India hosts New Zealand (3)
	Nov	**India hosts England (4)**
		Australia hosts South Africa (3)
		Sri Lanka hosts New Zealand (2)
		Bangladesh hosts West Indies (2)
	Dec	Australia hosts Sri Lanka (3)
		South Africa hosts New Zealand (2)
		Zimbabwe hosts Pakistan (2)
2013	Jan	South Africa hosts Pakistan (3)
	Feb	**New Zealand hosts England (3)**
		India hosts Australia (4)
		Sri Lanka hosts Bangladesh (2)
	Mar	West Indies hosts Zimbabwe (2)
	Apr	West Indies hosts Sri Lanka (2)
	May	**England hosts New Zealand (2)**

	June	**England hosts Australia (5)**
		West Indies hosts Pakistan (2)
	July	Sri Lanka hosts South Africa (3)
	Oct	Pakistan hosts South Africa (2)
		Zimbabwe hosts Sri Lanka (2)
		Bangladesh hosts New Zealand (2)
	Nov	**Australia hosts England (5)**
		South Africa hosts India (3)
	Dec	New Zealand hosts West Indies (3)
		Pakistan hosts Sri Lanka (3)
2014	Feb	New Zealand hosts India (3)
		South Africa hosts Australia (3)
		Bangladesh hosts Sri Lanka (2)
	May	**England hosts Sri Lanka (2)**
		West Indies hosts New Zealand (2)
	June	**England hosts India (5)**
	July	West Indies hosts Bangladesh (2)
		Zimbabwe hosts South Africa (2)

First published in 2012 by
HEADLINE PUBLISHING GROUP

Cover photographs:
(*Front and spine*) Kevin Pietersen (Surrey and England)
© Anthony Devlin/PA Wire/Press Association
(*Back*) Andrew Strauss (Middlesex and England) holds the ICC trophy to mark
England becoming the top-ranked Test nation, August 2011
© Gareth Copley/Getty Images Sport

3

Cataloguing in Publication Data is available from the British Library

ISBN 978 0 7553 8750 2

Typeset in Times by
Letterpart Limited, Reigate, Surrey

Preface by David Lloyd

Printed and bound in Great Britain by
Clays Ltd St Ives plc

Headline's policy is to use papers that are natural, renewable and
recyclable products and made from wood grown in sustainable forests.
The logging and manufacturing processes are expected to conform
to the environmental regulations of the country of origin.

HEADLINE PUBLISHING GROUP
An Hachette UK Company
338 Euston Road
London NW1 3BH

www.headline.co.uk
www.hachette.co.uk